**The Palaeolithic Societies of Europe**

Palaeolithic societies have been a neglected topic in the discussion of human origins. In this book Clive Gamble challenges the established view that the social life of Europeans over the 500,000 years of the European Palaeolithic must remain a mystery. In the past forty years archaeologists have recovered a wealth of information from sites throughout the continent. Professor Gamble now introduces a new approach to this material. The archaeological evidence from stone tools, hunting and campsites is interrogated for information on the scale of social interaction, and the forms of social life. Taking a pan-European view of the archaeological evidence, he reconstructs ancient human societies, and introduces new perspectives on the unique social experience of human beings.

CLIVE GAMBLE is Professor of Archaeology at the University of Southampton. He is the author of several books, including *The Palaeolithic Settlement of Europe*, published by Cambridge University Press in 1986.

CAMBRIDGE WORLD ARCHAEOLOGY



The Cambridge World Archaeology series is addressed to students and professional archaeologists, and to academics in related disciplines. Each volume presents a survey of the archaeology of a region of the world, providing an up-to-date account of research and integrating recent findings with new concerns of interpretation. While the focus is on a specific region, broader cultural trends are discussed and the implications of regional findings for cross-cultural interpretations considered. The authors also bring anthropological and historical expertise to bear on archaeological problems and show how both new data and changing intellectual trends in archaeology shape inferences about the past.

*Books in the series*

RAYMOND ALLCHIN AND BRIDGET ALLCHIN, *The Rise of Civilization in India and Pakistan* 28550 X
CLIVE GAMBLE, *The Palaeolithic Settlement of Europe* 28764 2
CHARLES HIGHAM, *Archaeology of Mainland South East Asia* 49660 8 HB 56505 7 PB
SARAH MILLEDGE NELSON, *The Archaeology of Korea* 40443 6 HB 40783 4 PB
DAVID PHILLIPSON, *African Archaeology* (second revised edition) 44103 X HB 44658 9 PB
OLIVER DICKINSON, *The Aegean Bronze Age* 24280 0 HB 45664 9 PB
KAREN OLSEN BRUHNS, *Ancient South America* 27761 2
ALISDAIR WHITTLE, *Europe in the Neolithic* 44476 4 HB 44920 0 PB
CHARLES HIGHAM, *The Bronze Age of Southeast Asia* 49660 8 HB 56505 7 PB

CAMBRIDGE WORLD ARCHAEOLOGY

# THE PALAEOLITHIC SOCIETIES OF EUROPE

CLIVE GAMBLE

CAMBRIDGE
UNIVERSITY PRESS

PUBLISHED BY THE PRESS SYNDICATE OF THE UNIVERSITY OF CAMBRIDGE
The Pitt Building, Trumpington Street, Cambridge CB2 1RP, United Kingdom

CAMBRIDGE UNIVERSITY PRESS
The Edinburgh Building, Cambridge CB2 2RU, United Kingdom http://www.cup.cam.ac.uk
40 West 20th Street, New York, NY 10011–4211, USA http://www.cup.org
10 Stamford Road, Oakleigh, Melbourne 3166, Australia



First published 1999

*The Palaeolithic Societies of Europe* succeeds and replaces *The Palaeolithic Settlement of Europe*, published by Cambridge University Press in 1986.

Printed in the United Kingdom at the University Press, Cambridge

Typeset in 10/13pt Trump Medieval in QuarkXPress® [SE]

*A catalogue record for this book is available from the British Library*

*Library of Congress Cataloguing in Publication data*

Gamble, Clive
The Palaeolithic societies of Europe / Clive Gamble.
p. cm. – (Cambridge world archaeology)
"The Palaeolithic societies of Europe succeeds and replaces The Palaeolithic settlement of Europe, published by Cambridge University Press in 1986" – T.p. verso.
Includes bibliographical references (p. 440) and index.
ISBN 0 521 65105 0 (hardback). – ISBN 0 521 24514 1 (paperback)
1. Paleolithic period–Europe. 2. Tools, Prehistoric–Europe.
3. Anthropology, Prehistoric–Europe. 4. Europe–Antiquities.
I. Gamble, Clive. Palaeolithic settlement of Europe. II. Title.
III. Series.
GN772.2.A1G38 1999 98-38087 CIP
936–dc21

ISBN 0 521 65105 0 hardback
ISBN 0 521 65872 1 paperback

For
KIM HAHN and CATHERINE FARIZY

# CONTENTS

# FIGURES

# TABLES

# ACKNOWLEDGEMENTS

Acknowledgement is due to the following for permission to reproduce the following illustrations

1.2 reprinted by permission of Barbara Isaac and Cambridge University Press
1.3, 1.4, 5.15, 6.8 reprinted by permission of Cambridge University Press
2.2 'Communication networks and dispersal patterns in human evolution: a simple simulation model'. J. Steele, *World Archaeology* 26:1994 figure 2 reprinted by permission of Routledge
2.3 'Hunter-gatherer populations and archaeological inference'. J. Yellen and H. Harpending, *World Archaeology* 3:1972 figure 15 reprinted by permission of Routledge
3.2 Wessex Archaeology
3.3 Figure 15 from H. Brody *Maps and dreams* reprinted by permission of Hugh Brody, Douglas and McIntyre and Sheil Land Associates
3.4 Lewis Binford
3.5 and 3.6 'Order without architecture: functional, social and symbolic dimensions in hunter-gatherer settlement organisation', T. Whitelaw, 1994. in *Architecture and order: approaches to social space*, Edited by M. Parker-Pearson and C. Richards, figures 11.4 and 11.6 reprinted by permission of Routledge
3.8 Robert Whallon, *International Monographs in Prehistory*
4.10, 5.24 'La circulation des matières premières au Paléolithique'. J. Féblot-Augustins 1997 figures 22 and 37. Reprinted by permission of Marcel Otte and *ERAUL* volume 75
4.11 *Fairweather Eden* Mike Pitts and Mark Roberts, 1997: figure 38 reprinted by permission of Random House
4.13, 4.20 John Wymer
4.14 photo courtesy of C.S. Fuchs and Hartmut Thieme
4.15 'Middle Pleistocene prehistory in southwestern Europe: the state of our knowledge and ignorance'. P. Villa 1991 figure 2. *Journal of Anthropological Research* 47. Reprinted by permission of Paolo Villa and *Journal of Anthropological Research*
4.18 Antonio Tagliacozzo
4.19 Mauro Cremaschi
4.21, 4.22, 4.24, 4.25, 5.7, 5.25, 6.24 Dietrich Mania

4.3, 5.8, 7.5 Gerhard Bosinski
4.5 'Mosaics, Allelochemics, and Nutrients' by R. Dale Guthrie in *Quarternary Extinctions: A Prehistoric Revolution*, edited by Paul S. Martin and Richard G. Klein. Copyright © 1984 The Arizona Board of Regents. Reprinted by permission of the University of Arizona Press
4.6 Pierre Antoine
5.10, 5.26, 5.27 reprinted by permission of Elsevier Science, Geo Abstracts
5.13, 5.17, 5.23, 5.28, 6.10 Mellars, Paul, *The Neanderthal Legacy*, figures 5.8, 3.9, 5.5, 7.13, and 6.16 Copyright © by Princeton University Press. Reprinted by permission of Princeton University Press
5.18 Nicholas Conard
5.19 Reproduced by permission of the Society for American Archaeology from American Antiquity 152, no1, 1987.
5.20 Erwin Cziesla
5.29, 5.30, 5.31, 5.32 Wil Roebroeks
5.4 reprinted by permission of Jim Rose, *Quaternary Science Reviews*
6.2 reprinted by permission of the Prehistoric Society
6.11, 7.6 *The Human Revolution: behavioural and biological perspectives on the origins of modern humans*. Edited by P. Mellars and C. Stringer, figures 20.3 and 33.1-3 reprinted by permission of Edinburgh University Press
6,12 Les sépultres moustériennes A. Defleur 1993 figure 69. CNRS. Reprinted by permission of CNRS Editions, Paris
6.14, 6.15 Harold Floss
6.18 Anne Scheer
6.20, 7.4, 7.8 Vicky Cabrera-Valdés
6.21 reprinted by permission of the American Anthropological Association
6.23 Susanne Münzel
6.24. 1994 Hommes et bisons du Paléolithique moyen à Mauran (Haute-Garonne). C. Farizy, J. David, and J. Jaubert 1994 figure 128 *Gallia-Préhistoire Supplement* 30. Reprinted by permission of CNRS Editions, Paris
6.6B photo courtesy of Nikolai Praslov
6.9 Hansjürgen Müller-Beck
7.10, 7.14 Bohuslav Klíma
7.15, 7.16 Karel Valoch
7.17 Margherita Mussi
7.18 *Dolní Věstonice II: western slope*. J. Svoboda, Editor. 1991 Fig.6. Reprinted by permission of Marcel Otte and ERAUL volume 54.
7.19 *Dolní Věstonice II*. B. Klíma 1995 Abb 76. Reprinted by permission of Marcel Otte and ERAUL volume 73
7.20 Jiři Svoboda

Whilst every effort had been made to trace the owners of copyright material, in a few instances this has proved impossible and I take this opportunity to offer my apologies to any copyright holders whose rights I may have unwittingly infringed.

# PREFACE

Two conferences were the inspiration for this book. The first, held in Bradford in 1981, examined European social evolution from an archaeological perspective. I gave a paper, a fragment of which is included here in Chapter 1, but did not feel that there was anything to be gained from publishing it since anything prior to the Neolithic looked like a makeweight; a fact borne out by the editor who concentrated his considerable energies on providing additional discussions on every period but the ones dealing with hunters and gatherers. The truth is I had very little to say and I began to wonder why.

The second was the 1986 conference on hunting and gathering societies held in the armchairs of the library of the London School of Economics. My expectations here were higher since the conference pedigree was blue blood. This was the descendant of the first *Man the Hunter* conference in 1968 which gave us the model of the modern hunter gatherer. While invited to present papers the archaeologists were however entirely excluded from the published conference volumes unless they happened to address social issues. Only one did.

While it was often difficult to stay awake in the comfort of the LSE armchairs as experts on the !Kung/Zhu/Ju/'hoansi hotly disputed what to call them and trainspotted unashamedly about which individuals were present at a waterhole on 26 August 1965, I did have one rewarding conversation.

I asked an expert on the Australian Aborigines what he would like to hear from archaeologists? 'How could we make a contribution that would keep anthropologists awake?' I inquired.

He didn't know for sure, 'But something social would be nice', he replied.

'But what do you mean by social?'

'Well, anything with some kinship in it', he stopped. 'Ah, but you archaeologists can't do that, can you?'

There is not much kinship in what follows but there is a good deal about what a social approach means for the study of 500,000 years of one continent's prehistory. As in my previous book *The Palaeolithic settlement of Europe* (1986), I acknowledge the difficulty of defining Europe and employ a nine cell regional model to standardize the problem. Where I depart in this volume is the time range explored. Instead of drawing the discussion to a close at the conventional date of 10,000 BP, I have opted instead to close at 21,000 BP just prior to the last glacial maximum. There are two reasons for this decision. One is the length of this book. To include the late glacial would have made it overlong and unwieldy, and would have restricted the detail which is necessary. Secondly, by moving the cut-off point back in time I rather hope to confuse what is at best an arbitrary division and at worst a convention which prevents the Palaeolithic from being considered as part of later prehistory simply because it took place before the interglacial got underway. Why 500,000 years of prehistory should be frozen out of later syntheses by the weather report seems ludicrous. So, shifting the boundary back in time to a position where it cannot be taken as either arbitrary or indeed significant, but just plain convenient, is not a result of cussedness or exhaustion but is chosen to make a point; social life never stopped in Palaeolithic Europe, it never stood still for the climate and it certainly wasn't invented at some juncture. I plan to give a full treatment to the late glacial in another book.

In the decade which has passed since the publication of *The Palaeolithic settlement of Europe*, there has been a wonderful explosion of major surveys and excavations. The quality and quantity of data necessitated a complete rewrite rather than a second edition. Also my own interests had moved on. I am increasingly disappointed by two models which govern Palaeolithic analysis and which I have characterized to students as the stomach-led and the brain-dead interpretations of the period. The first still dwells on the importance of calories and is fascinated by the abilities of early hominids to kill animals with bits of wood and stone. The other attributes change to a gradual awakening of the hominid grey matter as though they had trouble for many long millennia not only in tying their shoelaces, but also in finding their feet. In effect what both views are saying is that a prime mover can be found to explain the archaeological record. This may be something like the development of co-operative behaviour, a fancy bit of new technology or the appearance of language which confers an advantage and explains new patterns. Arguments using prime movers have never worked in archaeology and they are even less effective in the Palaeolithic. What I have attempted here is to provide a context for generating patterns and in my opinion the only acceptable framework must be social. I will dismay many by championing the individual and presenting an interactional model for the performance of social life. I make no apologies, either for that framework or for the new vocabulary which must accompany it if we are to break away from the theory-laden facts which prevent new analysis. I am also unapologetic because while impressed by the virtuoso skills now evident in the excavation of open and rock-shelter sites from the Palaeolithic, I nonetheless have to ask, what is all this precision in recording artifact coordinates and taphonomy about? What do refitting studies tell us apart from the fact that we can do them and convince grant bodies to fund us? What social archaeologist in the Roman period would bother to invest the same energies in routinely refitting pot sherds on the scale now evident for the Palaeolithic? Have we in fact run out of things to do and questions to ask? I don't think so. What follows is partly an experiment in asking how such precision will allow us to move away from stomach-led and brain-dead explanations and instead direct our analytical ingenuity to the richness of the social data our evidence contains.

Many people have helped me with the ideas and information which follow. The invitation from Wil Roebroeks and Gerhard Bosinski in 1992 to be a co-ordinating member of the European Science Foundation Network on the earliest occupation of Europe provided not only three years of travel, seminars and conferences, but the most rewarding academic environment for the discussion of Palaeolithic matters. The other network co-ordinators, Manuel Santonja, Lars Larsson, Alain Tuffreau, Luis Raposo, Nikolai Praslov and Margherita Mussi, will, I hope, approve of some of the results which I have included here. Our ESF minder, Max Sparreboom, deserves a special thanks for making so many things happen so efficiently.

For field visits, discussions and just plain good times I would like to thank, in no particular order, Thijs van Kolfschoten, John McNabb, John Gowlett, Paul Mellars, Steve Mithen, Nick Ashton, Tjeerd van Andel, Martin Street, Elaine Turner, Sabine Gaudzinski, Paul Pettitt, Leslie Aiello, Mark White, William Davies, Jiři Svoboda, Jehanne Féblot-Augustins, Mark Roberts, Dietrich Mania, Patrick Auguste, John Wymer, Eudald Carbonell, Geoff Bailey, Andrew Lawson, Janusz Kozlowski, Jean-Michel Geneste, Chris Stringer, Alan Turner, Alain Turq, HansJürgen Müller Beck, Elaine Morris, Rob Foley, Nick Conard, Clemens Pasda, Francis Wenban-Smith, Rupert Housley and Geraldo Vega-Toscano. The following all read earlier drafts and gave me valuable comments; Stephen Shennan, Quentin Mackie, Paul Graves-Brown, JD Hill, Wiktor Stoczkowski, Catherine Perlès, Adam Kuper, Vernon Reynolds, Antony Firth, Stephanie Moser, Richard Bradley, Kate Gregory, Nathan Schlanger, Alasdair Whittle, Anne Best, James Steele, Chris Gosden, Wil Roebroeks, Yvonne Marshall and Olga Soffer. As always I have learnt and benefited from the interventions of Lewis Binford with whom there has been something of a race to finish our respective books first!

The research was generously supported by the University of Southampton and by a Special Research Leave Award and travel funds from the British Academy. This allowed me a sabbatical year in 1994/5 and the opportunity to read. I am very grateful to all my colleagues in the Department of Archaeology who shouldered additional administration during this year and to Anthony Sinclair who did my teaching while I was off researching 'monkey men'. Sophie Shennan got the bibliography and index into order and Martin Porr provided valuable bibliographic assistance. Jessica Kuper remained the ever calm and encouraging editor and Janet Hall guided the book through the press. The illustrations were expertly produced by Erica Hemming assisted by Nick Bradford and Peter Hodge. I am very grateful to Mauricio Antón for his cover illustration of the hominids from Sima de los Huesos portrayed in front of their family tree at Atapuerca. The actions and personalities of the 300,000-year-old people we see here created their intimate and effective networks.

Finally, it is a great sadness that Catherine Farizy, who was also part of our ESF family, and Kim Hahn, who helped me so much as a struggling postgrad student, will not be able to give me the benefit of their opinions on what I have written. This book is part of their legacy to Palaeolithic studies and I dedicate it to their memory.

Constitution Hill
Nevis WI
January 1998

CHAPTER 1

# PULLING ASIDE THE PALAEOLITHIC CURTAIN

Society represents a claim, advanced and enacted in order to construct a state of affairs that previously was not.

Eric Wolf
*Inventing society*

## Introduction

The Palaeolithic of Europe is a record of observations and a register of ideas. Using this combination, archaeologists have recognized many patterns in the data and proposed several solutions, at a continental scale, to their recurrence in time and space. These explanations have emphasized the variable biological capacities of early hominids, their adaptations to ecological circumstances and their expression, in the form of stone tools, of persistent regional identities. The transforming powers of human migration, combined with the selective diffusion of cultural elements, have aided both the writing of culture history and the investigation of the same Palaeolithic records as long-term adaptive systems involving continuity and change.

During these examinations of data and the development of analytical concepts the subject of this book, the varied societies of Palaeolithic Europe, has received some attention. But investigating society in the Palaeolithic has never achieved the same research prominence as studies of the subsistence economy, the spatial analysis of settlements, cave art or lithic typology and technology. While great strides forward have been made by archaeologists studying the societies of later prehistory (Hodder 1990a, Renfrew 1973), their insights and approaches have generally only touched upon interpretations of the Upper Palaeolithic (Clark and Lindly 1991, Price and Brown 1985a, Soffer 1987). The half million years of occupation in Europe prior to the Upper Palaeolithic remains peopled by ecological creatures rather than social actors. We have created these half-men, half-beasts, through the unequal juxtaposition of their simple stone technologies against the gigantic forces of Quaternary geology. According to our assessments, they wait patiently for the arrival of modern humans from Africa to put them out of their long servitude to grinding nature.

Gordon Childe was particularly gloomy about the prospects of social reconstruction in this period. Writing in *Social evolution*, he expressed a widespread view:

> The archaeological record is found to be regrettably but not surprisingly deficient in indications of the social organisation or lack of it in lower palaeolithic hordes. From the scraps available no generalizations are permissible. (Childe 1951:85)

Neither was he particularly encouraging about the Upper Palaeolithic and Mesolithic where, even though the record was fuller, it was very one sided.

> It offers a clear picture of nothing more than the economy and material culture adapted to particular environments of ice age Europe and of the northern forest zone in early post glacial times. (*ibid.*)

These Mesolithic folk were also apparently waiting to be replaced, albeit by agriculturalists. Writing thirty years after Childe, Richard Bradley could memorably bemoan that archaeologists still stressed how

> successful farmers have social relations with one another, while hunter-gatherers have ecological relations with hazelnuts. (Bradley 1984:11)

This picture has now begun to change. A degree of self-determination is currently accorded Mesolithic people, while the complexity of their regional archaeological records (Bonsall 1991) is proving a rich source for social reconstruction, as it is in the Upper Palaeolithic.

## The image of the earlier Palaeolithic

Any progress that might be made towards a unified social archaeology generally founders on the rocks of the earlier Palaeolithic. What has happened since Childe's remarks in 1951 is that the Lower and Middle Palaeolithic have now achieved the research status that he gave then to the Upper Palaeolithic and Mesolithic. In the past forty years large-scale, multi-disciplinary projects have recovered a wealth of archaeological and environmental data from sites throughout Europe. Moreover, the development of a continuous Pleistocene chronology based on the deep-sea isotopic record (Imbrie and Imbrie 1979), and science-based dating beyond the period covered by radiocarbon (Aitken 1990), has produced frameworks which encourage interpretation rather than mere description.

These interpretations are frequently presented visually. Many of the projects provide artists' reconstructions of the landscapes these European hominids inhabited (Lumley 1979, Mania and Dietzel 1980). As Moser has argued, these images 'are more than just illustrations which summarize information presented in the text; rather they are reinforcements of . . . theories, and as such constitute arguments in themselves' (1992:833). By presenting the excavated facts as visual summaries, it is also implicit as to how we should interpret them. We see hominids attacking bison in the lake at Bilzingsleben (Mania and Dietzel 1980), living in their tent at Lazaret (Lumley 1969a) or planning, executing and then celebrating the elephant hunt at Torralba/Ambrona (Howell 1965). Through these devices, the unfamiliar deep-past, where the archaeological 'scraps' are indeed meagre when compared to other periods, becomes known and knowable.

These images control our theoretical imaginations rather more than we care to acknowledge (Stoczkowski 1994, Gamble 1992a, Moser 1998, Moser and Gamble 1997, Gifford-Gonzalez 1993). They make us feel comfortable with a natural-history approach to reconstructing the past. The pictures compare with the way geologists created scenes from deep-time during the last century (Rudwick 1976) in order to establish their claims to be able to reconstruct the extinct worlds of the Eocene, the Carboniferous or any geological epoch they chose.

Such reconstructions are valuable in expressing 'natural' relationships between the multifarious strands of data that are routinely collected and analysed on any Palaeolithic site. Nowadays an image of a hominid in a landscape can combine evidence from the analysis of ostracods, mammalian micro- and macrofaunas, herpetofaunas, calcareous nannoplanktons, soil micromorphology, palynology, geology and sedimentology, to name a few of the possibilities now in the Quaternary scientist's armoury. We frequently use these images of the deep-time past, as attendance at any Palaeolithic conference reveals, when it comes to showing what we think all those data mean. Using these images allows us to reach consensus about what regularly took place – hunting, gathering, cooking, eating, child care, tool manufacture, hide scraping, sleeping, burying the dead – and which sexes and age groups were largely responsible (Gifford-Gonzalez 1993, Moser 1989).

But while these images appear to open a window into the Palaeolithic, they also close curtains. The most important curtain they draw across our investigations is the subject of this book, Palaeolithic society. The reason for this is quite straightforward. The Palaeolithic has never been a seed-bed for the discussion of social theory within archaeology. Instead there have been extremely important debates about how the Palaeolithic record was formed and the causes of subsequent variability in lithic and faunal remains (Binford 1973, 1981a, 1981b, Binford and Binford 1966, Bordes and de Sonneville-Bordes 1970, Dibble 1987, Mellars 1996, Mellars 1970, Stiner and Kuhn 1992). Such middle-range theory (Binford 1983a) has been promoted in the fields of taphonomy and the study of site formation processes such that we now have a much clearer idea of what is known and is knowable in the Palaeolithic. New data have been generated, and with them the opportunity to recognize fresh patterns at both a site and a regional scale. However, these patterns have not been explained as the result of social factors. Indeed, the Binfords' critique of the five Mousterian tribes of southwest France (Bordes 1968a, 1972) defined by their different lithic assemblages was a deliberate move away from culture history and social explanation.

While the record of observations has grown enormously, the register of ideas has also kept pace, albeit on a predictable track. The track is indicated by those artists' images which capture the ecological relations between hominids and resources in the landscapes of the Palaeolithic. Elsewhere, these relationships have been usefully expanded through the insights of evolutionary ecology to include discussion of optimality (Bettinger 1991), decision rules (Mithen 1990) or risk avoidance (Torrence 1989) among prehistoric foragers, but the emphasis is firmly on the side of a natural rather than a social prehistory.

Social relationships are not easily portrayed except as symbolic diagrams, but see the cover illustration for this book by M. Antón. Hence an anthropologist will provide a kinship chart rather than a photograph. These charts are an essential aid to their arguments about the structure of social life. For archaeologists, the naturalistic reconstructions of bison hunting at Bilzingsleben are more 'believable', because they are at least refutable through taphonomic enquiry, than the imaginative depiction of the same hominids worshipping the dawn by a lake in eastern Germany 300,000 years ago. An artist's reconstruction of a complex concept such as society would meet similar difficulties, not least because the artist would start without any guidance from scientific convention about how to depict social life in the past. Those geological scenes from deep-time provided a convention for reconstructing the natural landscape to make it accessible. Societies, animal or human, were never shown. Only representative taxa appeared as though in some taxidermist's workshop.

## Palaeolithic oppositions, convictions and solutions

A commitment to a social archaeology has existed for some time in later prehistory (Flannery 1976, Friedman and Rowlands 1977, Redman et al. 1978, Renfrew 1973, Renfrew and Shennan 1982) and from this largely processual and materialist base various alternative social theories have recently been explored (Barrett 1994, Barrett, Bradley and Green 1991, Bradley 1984, Gosden 1994, Hodder 1990a, Moore 1986, Shanks and Tilley 1987a and 1987b, Thomas 1991). In particular, these later works have stressed the archaeological record as text, replete with meanings and inscribed ambiguity, which constitutes a landscape where social actors are involved in deliberate action. The involvement of social agents in the creation of their varied and dynamic social worlds stands in stark contrast to the earlier texts in social archaeology. Here the investigation of the social system and its various regulatory states formed the focus. The social creativity of individuals was crushed by an overbearing system.

The eons of the Palaeolithic when little seems to change, combined with those 'scraps' mentioned by Childe, have never suggested any other interpretation than a natural, or at best a systemic one. But even with the latter it seems that for long periods of time certain key sub-systems, such as religion and craft specialization, were entirely lacking. This makes it even more difficult to argue that change was internally produced by friction between sub-systems and where homeostasis was upset. Dynamic change therefore had to be supplied from outside. This can mean either the replacement of one population by another or the climatic cycles of the Pleistocene forcing changes in subsistence, settlement and associated technologies.

As a result, explanation in the Palaeolithic has stressed oppositions between ancient and modern humans, environment and culture, foraging and agriculture. This approach has established what many archaeologists still see as the truly important purpose of studying earliest prehistory: to discover when and where the foundations of the civilizing process, from which the western world ultimately benefited most, were laid (Gamble 1993a:20–3). For many years the Palaeolithic has been divided from the rest of archaeology by an interpretative curtain founded on these oppositions. For this reason as much as the 'scraps' of data argument, the Palaeolithic has not been part of the later developments in social archaeology, and hence has been largely ignored by post-processualists (but see Hodder 1990a).

Many would regard this neglect as positively beneficial to Palaeolithic studies, and for a long time I would have agreed with them. I have changed my mind not because I am yet convinced by all of the post-processualist agenda, but rather because their attacks have highlighted the poverty of theory in my area of expertise. This poverty touches most on the units of analysis that the Palaeolithic uses and the goals it has set itself. These are explored more fully below and in Chapters 2 and 3. My intention is to tweak that interpretative curtain aside and seek solutions that do not rely upon traditional divisions.

Of course I am not working alone at this project. The tweaking has already begun. The interpretative curtain, which seems to divide an *active* human past involving trade, agriculture, ritual, monuments, towns and power from a *passive* one of adaptation to the conditions of existence, is, in the case of the Mesolithic, already being pulled aside (Bender 1985:21). Neither does there seem to be any problem with drawing it further to include the rich record of the Upper Palaeolithic (Price and Brown 1985a, Soffer 1987). However, while these gains in approaching the past as a continuous stream are not negligible, it does appear that the curtain which separates Us from the Other, Civilized from Uncivilized, now falls across the Middle to Upper, Neanderthal to Modern, transition (Gamble 1991, Stringer and Gamble 1993). All we have apparently done is to shift its position by some 30,000 years.

My contention is that we should scrap this curtain altogether. The deep-time past of the Palaeolithic does not need to be investigated through such oppositions. As long as we maintain these contrasts we can only pursue a divided archaeology, where much of the Palaeolithic will remain remote to the interests of most archaeologists. The study of human origins then becomes nothing more than a story from a faraway land, as remote from people as the epochs of geology.

My solution is to take society as a unifying focus. This may seem a strange choice given the complications of defining, using and interpreting such a concept. I have adopted it due to several convictions explored in a number of previous publications.

Firstly, I can still see no justification why archaeology should have different procedures and standards on either side of an interpretative curtain which divides modern from ancient humanity. There is no reason to switch explanations from predominantly ecological to mainly social just because the nature of the archaeological record changes with the advent of agriculture and sedentism (Barker and Gamble 1985, Gamble 1986a, 1986b, 1986c). Neither is there any reason to change explanations during the Palaeolithic as soon as a more varied record appears with the Upper Palaeolithic. My interest is in the differences among Palaeolithic societies and not the divisions between them. My concern in this book is with analysis rather than definitions.

Secondly, understanding social life in all its different forms should be an archaeological goal since, as anthropologists of the past, we have the data to enlarge and enrich such experience (Gamble 1991a, 1991b, 1993a, 1993b, 1993c). We would be poor anthropologists if we made no contribution to the variety of societies available for systematic study (Gamble and Soffer 1990, Soffer and Gamble 1990, Stringer and Gamble 1993). The investigation of Palaeolithic societies is, in particular, an exploration of alternatives to ethnographic experience. As put by Wobst,

> Archaeologists are the only anthropologists whose data contain information about behavioural variance in all its dimensions: in personnel from single individuals in private to the largest structural poses; in space from the smallest catchment area to the largest continent-wide population matrix, and in time from single events to millennia. (Wobst 1978:307)

Thirdly, the explanation of stasis and change lies at the centre of archaeological enquiry. Social life was the heart which kept the varied systems beating, whether or not change occurred (Gamble 1993a, 1993d, 1995a, 1995b). In most cases the investigation of stasis and change proceeds little beyond opting for a variable in the social system, such as population pressure on resources. Despite a number of telling critiques of such simplistic, asocial, explanations of change and intensification (Bender 1978, 1981, Lourandos 1977, 1985), there remain unreconstructed social evolutionists who trace all human developments to a single cause such as population numbers and environmental constraints (e.g. Johnson and Earle 1987). I will side with the critics of these old-fashioned texts by proposing a different view of the relations between humans and their environments. I will stress the active engagement and mutual involvement of the individual in the construction and negotiation of his/her environment.

Finally, it is time that archaeology claimed its place within the social as well as the historical sciences. To do this we need to set our own comparative agenda, not only to provide reflections on the uses of the past to construct contemporary societies (Gamble 1993b, 1993c), but to provide the prehistoric perspective on those modern interactions (Gamble 1992b). This position is well expressed by Binford:

> we have a chance to understand humankind in a way that no participant, or no social scientist addressing the quick-time events of direct social experience, could ever imagine. To fail to recognise this potential, to fail to grasp a new understanding of humankind from this different perspective – the perspective of the macroforces that con-

dition and modify lifeways in contexts unappreciated by the participants within complex thermodynamic systems – is quite literally to 'abandon our birthright'. (1989a:52)

It can fairly be stated that the social sciences have hardly noticed the absence of prehistoric archaeology, let alone the Palaeolithic, from their syntheses of social life. This situation is unlikely to change unless the case for an historical dimension, and one which involves an understanding of the character of the long-term prehistoric record (Murray 1987), is strongly put. The insights of social theory, and in particular the vocabulary of network analysis, have been adopted in this book in order to effect a translation between the very different evidence for human social action at varied timescales and degrees of resolution. However, I will not be arguing for a palaeosociology of the Palaeolithic any more than for a palaeopsychology or palaeoanthropology of the period. The historical and material basis of archaeology conditions the accounts of past societies and individuals that we produce. There will be no obvious support in such accounts for the claims of one social theory over another that aims to understand individuals and societies in the modern world. The methods and concerns of the present and the past separate these various projects in social analysis.

However, analysing prehistoric societies would ultimately serve little purpose if it only had relevance for archaeologists. Our contribution must therefore be directed towards influencing those future syntheses of social theory. I imagine these syntheses will continue to recognize, in standard post-modern fashion, that industrialization and civilization, while dominant social forms, do not include all human social experience let alone represent its highest achievements. It is here that archaeology has a contribution to make. Synthesis, by the very nature of the process which produces it and the understanding which comes from undertaking it, must continually seek to broaden our experience. Prehistory provides one route for such continuing awareness.

## The narratives of theoretical archaeology

A major factor that has muted our archaeological voice has been the absence of a common structure for discussion and comparison. A reason for this has been Palaeolithic archaeologists' adherence to the scientific method. In its crudest form this subscribes to an objective view of facts as neutral, and a clear belief in a structure that exists 'out there' and which will be revealed through greater analytical precision and yet more facts. For example, Flannery and Marcus have recently expressed their belief in this objectivity as follows:

Whenever science is combined with a social or political agenda – no matter how noble that agenda may be – *it is inevitably science that suffers*. (Flannery and Marcus 1994:441, my emphasis)

On the contrary, I find it difficult to see how a branch of historical science, like Palaeolithic archaeology, *can* be separated from a social or political agenda

(Gamble 1993b, 1993c) if it is to have any value as a form of knowledge. Studying the past, just like studying particle physics, is not a neutral activity undertaken for its own sake by individuals who, while doing it, temporarily suspend their membership of humanity.

Not surprisingly, then, many social theories have had an uncomfortable relationship with the scientific approach to knowledge. The sticking point seems to be the way that knowledge claims are verified and causation established (Clark 1993). Some of these fears lead to an almost entire rejection of the claims of science, as for example in the work of Giddens (1984). This rejection has been picked up by archaeologists who take to task the narrow scientific view which is all too common in archaeological writings. They point out, quite correctly, that it leaves human action out of the equation (Thomas 1991).

However, nearly everyone agrees that the scientific method undoubtedly works as a means to structure the investigation of the world in the physical sciences. Palaeolithic archaeology has made considerable procedural advances by adopting a scientific approach. But, this approach has led, as we shall see, to a rather limited view of what the data can tell us about society. The similarity with my earlier discussion about the restricted range of visual images is striking.

So, by choosing society as my focus I am seeking to expand the present boundaries of Palaeolithic discussion. This does not mean a break with past approaches. In writing this book I have not found it possible, or desirable, to abandon the procedures of the scientific approach in dealing with the question of Palaeolithic societies. I too am concerned with the verification of knowledge claims. Hence there is considerable discussion of ecology and environment in the chapters which follow, not because these provide an objective standard but rather a mutual one for interpreting past human action. What I have attempted to do is to broaden the scope of the scientific method by considering what a common approach between the historical and social sciences might entail. Such a realignment must involve not only the conceptual issues, such as society, which are addressed, but also the manner in which they are expressed. Here, I take my lead from Haraway, who observes in another context – the use of primate studies in contemporary science and society – that facts are only meaningful when contained within stories (1989). However, this approach still needs a caveat for those, like myself, who are interested in how we verify our narratives.

> We should resist the temptation to assume that since stories are stories they are, in some sense, unreal or untrue, for this is to suppose that the only reality or true truth, is one in which we, as living, experiencing beings, can have no part at all. (Ingold 1993:153)

The problem with the Palaeolithic is that currently there are very few stories. Those which exist deal mostly with origins (Conkey and Williams 1991, Knight 1991a, 1991b, Landau 1991) and the inception of change, rather than with the long periods of stasis between these rare moments of excitement. In adopting society as my focus I aim to turn the spotlight on the narrative framework which is needed to examine and explain the data from very long periods of time, the 500,000 years of the European Palaeolithic. It is during this time when our register of ideas, just like the few images in the artist's portfolio, runs low.

A social approach to the Palaeolithic requires, among other things, that as well as recognizing the patterns in the data we can also reproduce them. At the outset it is important to understand that these Palaeolithic societies, however we might eventually define them, are not waiting to be revealed through the simple tabulation of their attributes. The challenge that the Palaeolithic presents, and one reason the interpretative curtain exists, is that the basic assumptions of the elements of social life which underpin so much of social archaeology cannot be taken for granted. Minimally these might concern language, material-based symbolism, reflexive thought, the metaphor of kinship, ritual and the differential exercise of power. From such a potent cocktail we are able to mix many social theories (Turner 1991) without once mentioning subsistence, ecology, natural selection and demography.

## Studies of Palaeolithic society: human social origins

While Childe, in 1951, was pronouncing on the deficiencies of the Lower Palaeolithic record, research had already begun to fashion a model of social organization from those elements just mentioned above. This culminated in one of the great edited syntheses of modern anthropology, *Social life of early man* (Washburn 1961). Among the contributors to this Wenner-Gren symposium were physical anthropologists, palaeontologists, primatologists, psychologists, geneticists, zoologists, geologists and archaeologists.[1]

Although I refer to it as a 'great' synthesis, anyone coming to it cold might be excused for wondering why. The papers seem to be saying very little about social organization and rather more about a timetable of events such as the appearance of cannibalism and the first use of fire (Washburn 1961:viii–ix). There are occasionally conclusions that appear to address a social perspective, even if they seemed to state the obvious:

> All [physical] evidence suggests that the Palaeolithic bands were not territorial units, that they were capable of large migrations, and that sexual relations must have existed between them (Vallois 1961:229)

while developmental pathways were readily inferred:

> In evolutionary perspective a necessary locus and an indispensable condition for a cultural system is an organized system of social action in which social behaviour is patterned by role differentiation . . . A social structure, therefore, can be identified as one of the characteristic features of a protocultural stage in hominid evolution. (Hallowell 1961:240)

However, many of the contributions only seem to engage in speculation about social form and origins based on a minimal ethnography of hunters and gatherers and assertions about how to interpret the archaeological record.

The importance of *Social life of early man* rests on three factors. Firstly, it demonstrated the advantages of a multi-disciplinary approach to human origins. This pattern would be taken up and pursued in early hominid research. The mix of disciplines was heavily towards the natural and physical sciences and it was from their crucibles that the agendas of ancestor research were to be poured.

Secondly, the outstanding paper in the volume was by Washburn and DeVore, 'Social behavior of baboons and early man'. They dealt with troop size, range, diet, population structure, sub-groups and play, mother–child relations, sexual behaviour, economic dependence, dominance, home base, sounds and gestures. This thematic framework has been the standard for subsequent research. Throughout the paper they contrasted the life of baboons with modern foragers, producing a summary table which listed spatial, demographic, affective and behavioural differences for the topics mentioned above. They concluded that 'because of the great behavioural gap between man and his nearest relatives, some reconstruction of [social] behaviour is possible' (Washburn and DeVore 1961:103). This gap presumably indicates extinct transitional stages between the societies of apes and humans.

The third factor is only apparent with hindsight. Washburn and DeVore encouraged Richard Lee to undertake, between 1963 and 1964, his first study of the !Kung San foragers of Botswana (Lee 1979:9–15). This marked the introduction of anthropologists to the multi-disciplinary project of human origins (*ibid.*:9) and led directly to the important *Man the hunter* symposium (Lee and DeVore 1968). This and subsequent comparative volumes on foraging societies (Bicchieri 1972, Burch and Ellanna 1994, Damas 1969, Hunn and Williams 1982, Ingold, Riches and Woodburn 1991, Leacock and Lee 1982, Lee and DeVore 1976, Miracle, Fisher and Brown 1991, Smiley et al. 1980) have provided a rich source for defining the parameters of societies where nothing more was assumed than that they lived in small groups and moved about a lot (Lee and DeVore 1968:11).[2]

### *Characterizing hunters and gatherers*

This description of the nomadic style became the basic model (Mueller-Wille and Dickson 1991:26) for subsequent research into foraging societies. In a comparative synthesis of the papers in *Man the hunter*, Lee and DeVore (*ibid.*:11–12) drew a distinction between elements in the organizational base and the social system (Table 1.1).

As might be expected, this basic model expanded on the views summarized by Washburn and DeVore (1961) in their comparison between foragers and baboons. The emphasis on open systems, alliances, mobility and lack of territory (Lee 1976), while not supported by all the papers in the symposium, did offer an alternative view to the patrilocal, land-holding model of bands promoted by Service (1966, 1971) in his classic statement on social evolution.

Table 1.1. *The nomadic-style model of hunters and gatherers (Lee and DeVore 1968: 11–12).*

*Organizational base*

- open social systems where local groups are commonly associated with a geographical range
- communication between groups takes the form of marriage alliances and visiting. This results in hunting groups consisting of several 'bands' which are part of a larger linguistic and breeding community
- the economic system is based on a core of common features
  - a home base
  - division of labour where the males hunt and the females gather
  - the collected resources are shared

*Social system*

- the prime necessity of mobility restricts personal possessions and material culture. This acts to maintain the egalitarian structure
- food supply keeps the group small, frequently fewer than fifty persons, and population is redistributed between bands, thereby maintaining the effectiveness of units
- intergroup relations through marriage and other means of alliance are the means by which shortfalls in resources are counteracted
- exclusive rights to resources are uncommon
- the environment is the storehouse and food surpluses are rare. This restricts the social use of food resources
- visiting prevents any strong attachment to one area. Conflict within the groups is most commonly resolved by fission

Lee and DeVore's model echoed Lesser's earlier call to adopt, as a working hypothesis,

> the universality of human contact and influence – as a fundamental feature of the socio-historical process; [and] conceive of human societies – prehistoric, primitive or modern – not as closed systems, but as open systems . . . we [should] think of any social aggregate not as isolated, separated by some kind of wall, from others, but as inextricably involved with other aggregates, near and far, in weblike, netlike connections. (Lesser 1961:42)

Ethnographic examples can be found to support both poles of the argument. The reality, as Stanner (Peterson 1986, Stanner 1965) pointed out, is a continuum of differential social access to local groups and the resources they control. This variable association was enshrined in what he termed *estate* (religious core) and *range* (foraging area) relations (Gamble 1986a:33–4). The position of any group on the continuum was strongly influenced by variation in ecological conditions. The closer in size that a group's estate and range become, the more likely it is to find a patrilocal, restricted access system. On the contrary, when resources are poorer, range size will far exceed the area covered by a group's

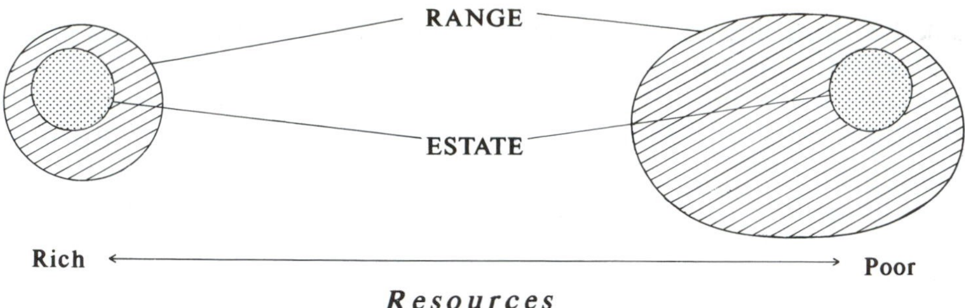


**1.1** The transformation under variable ecological conditions of hunter-gatherer spatial behaviour, as predicted by Stanner (1965).

estate. This generally results in unrestricted access, sharing and an open rather than closed system (Figure 1.1).

Peterson (1986) has shown how this social continuum works for several Australian foraging societies (Table 1.2). Ranged along an ecological gradient[3] of good to poor resources it is possible to see systematic changes in the principles of social integration, association to land and marriage rules. The social principles of inclusion and exclusion which change along this gradient are examined in Chapter 3.

I mention this debate concerning the open or closed nature of foraging groups not only because it relates directly to my main concern, societies, but also because it illustrates a recurrent feature in the way hunters and gatherers are dichotomized (Table 1.3).

Several of these authors do discuss the continuum which Stanner explored so profitably. However, this gloss is often forgotten, and the extremes are used as definitions that structure archaeological analysis and characterize the prehistoric hunter-gatherer way of life (e.g. Johnson and Earle 1987, Keeley 1988).

### *A multi-disciplinary success story*

The polar oppositions in Table 1.3 were introduced from the 1960s when both archaeologists and anthropologists discovered, unlike Childe, that they could investigate the social life of early hominids. The key to this discovery was to adopt a multi-disciplinary approach to the problem of social and biological origins.

This strategy is best exemplified by the success of the Leakeys at Olduvai Gorge, Tanzania, where a cornucopia of fossils and archaeological sites was now dated by scientific techniques (Leakey 1951, Leakey 1971). At the same time they encouraged investigations into chimpanzees, with startling results concerning tool use and group behaviour (Goodall 1986). Key elements in Washburn and DeVore's comparison between baboons and foragers, which had suggested a space for the investigation of social life in the Palaeolithic, could now be investigated for our closest primate relative.

Table 1.2. *Australian social organization along an ecological gradient (after Peterson 1986:Figs. 6:5 and 151–3).*

| Resource gradient | Persons per km$^2$ | Integration | Ties to land | Marriage | Social principle |
|---|---|---|---|---|---|
| Poor | 1:200 (Pintupi) | Generational moieties | Conception | Monogamy | INCLUSIVE |
| Medium | 1:86 (Walpiri, Pitjantjatjara) | Patrilineal generational moieties | Section/ sub-section managers | | |
| Rich | 1:20 (Yolngu) 1:4 (Kurnai) | None | Descent groups | Polygyny | EXCLUSIVE |

Faced with such success, the emphasis, not surprisingly, for such multi-disciplinary research became heavily African (Clark 1976). This research was geared to the *origins* of social life[4] as later expounded in the work of Reynolds (1966), Howell (1965), Isaac (1972, 1978), Leakey and Lewin (1977), Zihlman (1978), Wilson (1980), Tanner (1981), Lovejoy (1981) and Humphrey (1983), and more recently by Parker (1987) Wilson (1988), Foley (1989, 1989), Knight (1991a, 1991b), Maryanski and Turner (1992), Rodseth (et al. 1991), Potts (1993) and Quiatt and Reynolds (1993). Several of these models are reviewed by Richards (1987:206–33) and by Knight (1991a:Chapter 5). A valuable set of feminist critiques is supplied by Fedigan (1986), Conkey (1991) and Sperling (1991).[5]

What emerges from these accounts is that the *social,* in the context of research into human origins, was a way to link disparate, multi-disciplinary data together to form a coherent narrative. It was the paradigm which justified the enterprise, by supporting two different narratives: stories about change and adaptation.

In particular, Glynn Isaac sought to characterize, using the early Pleistocene-age archaeology of East Africa, the nature of these early societies and their developmental trajectories. Hence his discussion of home bases (1978), networks for cultural transmission (1972), and the superstructure of culture (1976) which was placed, in Hallowell's (1961) terms, upon a protocultural base comparable to great-ape organization (Figure 1.2).

### *The worm in the bud*

But all may not be so rosy in the garden of human-origins research. While archaeologists celebrate the achievements of multi-disciplinary research and the products of the scientific method applied to a problem which, only forty years ago, Childe pronounced impossible, we have to ask ourselves what we

Table 1.3. *Some of the dichotomies used in the characterization of hunters and gatherers, past and present.*

| | | | |
|---|---|---|---|
| Local group | *Patrilocal* | *Composite bands* | (Service 1971, Steward 1936) |
| | *Unilocal* | *Bilateral* | (Gardner 1966, Layton 1986) |
| Social organization | *Territorial* | *Non-territorial* | (Lee 1976) |
| | *Tribal level* | *Band level* | (Constandse-Westermann and Newell 1991, Fox 1967) |
| Kinship system | *Complex* | *Elementary* | (Lévi-Strauss 1969) |
| | *e.g. Eskimo* | *e.g. Australian* | (Fox 1967) |
| Network | *Nucleate* | *Anucleate* | (Yellen and Harpending 1972) |
| Interaction pattern | *Closed* | *Open* | (Lee 1976) |
| | *exclusive* | *inclusive* | (Gamble 1993d) |
| | *inegalitarian* | *egalitarian* | (Woodburn 1982) |
| Settlement system | *Collector* | *Forager* | (Binford 1980) |
| | *circulating* | *radiating* | (Marks 1983) |
| Return system | *Delayed* | *Immediate* | (Woodburn 1980) |
| Systemic organization | *Complex* | *Simple* | (Keeley 1988) |
| Knowledge base | *Group opinion* | *Memorate personal experience* | (Gardner 1966) |
| Technological organization | *Curated* | *Expedient* | (Binford 1973, 1979) |
| | *Reliable* | *Maintainable* | (Bleed 1986) |
| Historical position | *'Hot' active* | *'Cold' passive* | (Bender 1985) |
| Social world | *Unencapsulated* | *Encapsulated* | (Woodburn 1991) |
| | *pristine* | *enculturated* | (Service 1971) |
| Evolutionary typology | *Local group: acephalous* | *Family level group: no domestication* | (Johnson and Earle 1987) |

have actually learnt. Not in terms of new archaeological sites, fossil skulls or patterns, but instead in terms of those social origins which the whole multi-disciplinary enterprise was created to investigate.

Latour and Strum (1986) have examined seven accounts of human social origins ranging in age from Hobbes' *Leviathan* (1651) to the sociobiological account of Axelrod and Hamilton (1981). They included one archaeological account, Leakey and Lewin's *Origins* (1977), which differs from all the rest[6] in adhering to a science-based chronology for our social origins and presenting many of these carefully garnered multi-disciplinary facts. However, when they compared *Origins* with Rousseau's *A discourse on the origin of inequality*

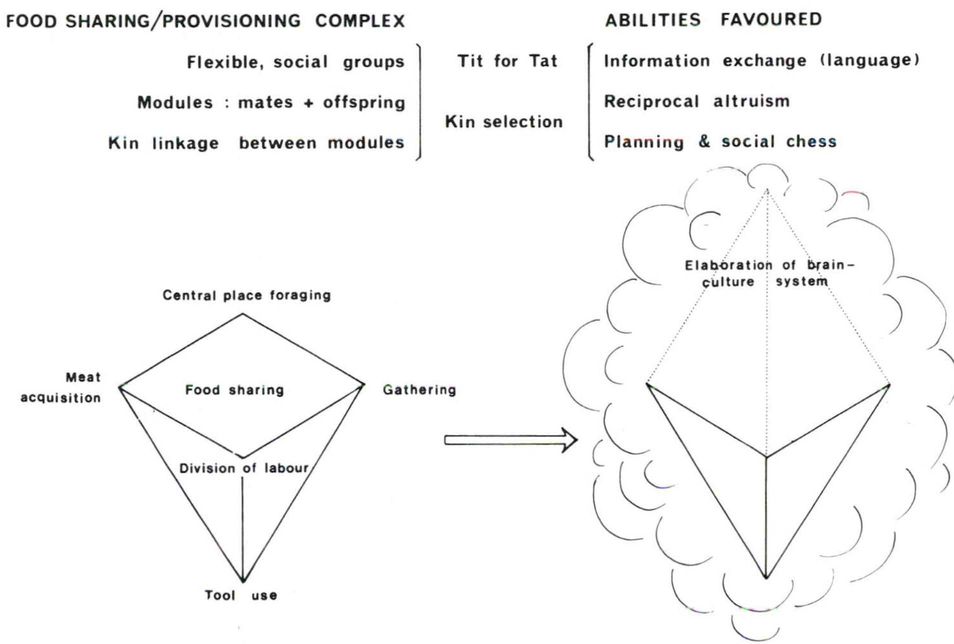


**1.2** The 'food-sharing' or 'central-place foraging' model and its implications for social evolution among early hominids (after Isaac 1989:Fig. 4.14).

(1755), written long before any fossil hominids or Palaeolithic archaeology had been dug up, they found little difference in the structural framework and assumptions. From their brief survey they came to a challenging conclusion:

> We had assumed that the knowledge and introduction of better 'facts' about the origin of socialness would produce better accounts. *Yet this seems not to be the case.* More particularly, there appears to be an inverse law at work in our examples: the more facts exist and are incorporated, the less attention is paid to the coherence of the framework within which those facts are placed. As a result, *the number of facts appears to be almost irrelevant,* since the most coherent accounts in our corpus were those, like Rousseau's, which laid aside all facts, and the least coherent were those with the most facts. (Latour and Strum 1986:185, my emphasis)

Challenging – at least to those who expect that the answer to human social origins will be revealed by joining up the dots. Challenging also to those, like Landau (1991), who regard it as sufficient to point to the repetitive nature of human-origins stories written by archaeologists, without judging their coherence against a wider guild of writers tackling the same subject.

I draw the following conclusions from this cautionary tale of social construction. Facts, as Haraway tells us, are meaningful within stories. We need to balance narrative coherence against the necessary selection of information. We do not need to include everything that has been discovered to produce coherent syntheses, but we do need to pay equal attention to the structure of our narrative. The scientific method needs to recognize the mythic character of accounts of social origins since these are laden with values concerning our present status, roles and rights.

What Latour and Strum are basically reminding us is that we should be explicit about our starting assumptions. There is obviously always scope for tightening logical procedures and considering what exactly it is that makes a scientific account convincing in terms of verifying knowledge claims (Gardin 1980). I also take heart from their critique since although they emphasize the mythic quality of scientific research, they do not dismiss the idea of studying social origins. This is in contrast to the British anthropologist Evans-Pritchard who once declared that such studies were a waste of time; speculations about unanswerable questions (1965).[7] Their insistence on social genealogy, where origins debates are opportunities to negotiate and renegotiate what our society is about, provides a necessary context for justifying the enterprise and one, once again, where science will not suffer by being combined with a noble social or political agenda.

## Studies of Palaeolithic society: the origins of modern foraging societies

The most influential typology of social evolution in the past thirty years identified as its units bands, tribes, chiefs and states (Service 1971). Although most people claim to have outgrown this typology, I suspect that most of them still use it as a mental shorthand (Yoffee and Sherratt 1993). It allows a first approximation whereby an ethnographic or archaeological example can be slotted into an organizational scheme which, by its generality, is expected to tell us more about the subject under scrutiny.

The problem is that while in the broadest sense the divisions have some reality – bands and states *are* different social realities – there is little agreement about the criteria which would classify the conceptually much murkier transitional societies to a particular rung of the typological ladder. Moreover, the inevitable progression implied in the typology, what Johnson and Earle refer to approvingly as an upward spiral (1987:15), is nothing more than a story about the benefits of civilization. While it is a comforting myth about our western social origins, such evolutionism tells us little beyond our belief in progress.

### *Open and closed societies: which came first?*

These problems are well shown with the first category, bands. It took many years for Europeans and North Americans to acknowledge that hunters and gatherers had a social life and for its systematic investigation to begin (Kuper 1988). Once investigation had started, the problem then became one of how to classify such a heterogeneous sample, scattered across the world, exploiting very different resources, and exhibiting a wide range of customs.

Steward (1936, 1955) and Service (1966, 1971) brought some order to this problem by recognizing that many of these bands were the product of contact with the modern world. These were the *composite* bands such as the northern Algonkians and Athabaskans (Service 1971:48–52), whose societies had been destroyed by western contact leaving only a fluid-membership, family-level type of organization (*ibid.*:97). These were seen as remnants of former *patrilocal* bands, which Service defined by exogamy outside the local group and virilocal residence, where on marriage women move to the husband's household or campsite (1971:64). In Lee's phrase, 'the dominant impression one gets from accounts of patrilocal bands is one of semi-isolated, male-centered groups, encapsulated within territories' (Lee 1976:75). These, according to Service, would have been the widespread form of social organization during the Palaeolithic. Ethnographic examples of patrilocal bands included all Australian societies and the central desert Californians.

But this still left a great many bands outside the typological net. For example, the Eskimos and Great Basin Shoshone were regarded as anomalous (Service 1971:83–97) because although affected by European contact they still retained some patrilocal band features. The Bushmen of the Kalahari were, even in the post-*Man the hunter* edition of his work (Service 1971:50), regarded as difficult to classify but certainly not patrilocal in form. Finally, the North West Coast foraging-based societies were on many counts outside the classification of band societies and they were placed in the chiefdom or ranked societies category.

Lee, on the other hand, challenged the widespread nature of patrilocal bands, regarding them as ethnographically rare (1976:76). His model, which traces its origins to Mauss (1906), emphasizes the fission and fusion of groups in which membership is organized bilaterally rather than just through the father's line. The !Kung became the prime example of the 'relatively open, social group with overlapping shared territories [which] seems to be the prevailing form among contemporary hunter-gatherers' (Lee 1976:76). All this suggested a rethink of the status of the composite band. Maybe their form was not entirely due to their near destruction through contact with industrial civilization (Lee 1976:77)?

As we have seen, investigations of our earliest social origins in Africa are mainly interested in the acquisition of the elements of sociality (e.g. technology, territoriality, co-operation, hunting) rather than in identifying social types such as bands. The strategy, as shown by Isaac's influential food-sharing model (1976:Figure 6, 1978), was to add a bit to the primate model of organization and take a bit away from modern hunters (Figure 1.2). The dominant view was that these earliest societies were essentially open, with fluid membership, and were non-territorial. They thus approximate to the descriptions of San groups (Barnard 1992, Lee 1976, Silberbauer 1981). The fluid social structure and immediate-return systems of these modern societies have been put down to their encapsulation by herding and agricultural societies (Woodburn 1991).[8] Hence the suggestion has resurfaced that these societies are in many ways comparable to Service's (1971) assessment of composite bands, as the product of

Table 1.4. *A division of contemporary hunting and gathering societies (Woodburn 1991:35).*

| Encapsulated<br>Immediate return systems | Unencapsulated<br>Delayed return systems |
|---|---|
| **Africa**<br>!Kung<br>Mbuti<br>Hadza | **North America**<br>Inuit societies<br>North West Coast societies |
| **India**<br>Malapantaram<br>Naiken<br>Paliyan | **Australia**<br>Aborigine societies |
| **Malaysia**<br>Batek Negritos | |

enculturation rather than being indicative of earlier widespread social forms (Table 1.4).

An important aspect of the Kalahari research begun by Lee and his colleagues has been to oppose this assessment. They have argued that open network systems should also be regarded as original (Yellen and Harpending 1972:244). The advantage of such systems lay in adjusting population to variation in regional food supplies, using group fission to resolve conflicts by literally 'walking away from the problem' and evening out sex ratios and family sizes between local groups within the bands (Layton 1986, Lee 1979). However, the so-called revisionist critique of hunter-gatherer studies (Schrire 1984, Wilmsen 1989) now strongly supports the notion that the form of these 'open' societies can be traced to the wider economic and social forces that have shaped the recent political history of southern Africa. Individuals, it has been discovered, move between hunting and herding economies with comparative ease and with scant attention to the social niceties of typology.

As a result the pendulum has swung back to consider that those societies, largely unencapsulated by farmers or industrial nations, are in some way more representative of a generalized pre-agricultural social system. In a world consisting exclusively of hunters and gatherers, a higher proportion may have had delayed-return systems (Woodburn 1991:61). Such societies are mostly from the Arctic, the North West Coast of North America and Australia (Table 1.4). Woodburn (1980, 1982) has argued that these societies are characterized by delayed systems of return involving rights over valued assets. These assets take the following forms:

- valuable technical facilities used in production (nets, boats, fish traps)
- processed and stored food usually kept in or near houses

- wild products whose yields have been increased through intensification
- female kin to be bestowed by men in marriage (Woodburn 1991:32)

Australia, the continent of hunters and gatherers, is rather troublesome to Woodburn's suggestions concerning the original form of foraging society. Storage is rare and encapsulation by farmers did not take place until the arrival of Captain Cook. Yet, patrilocally based foraging bands did not exist in the continent (Hiatt 1962). To get round this problem Woodburn proposes that Australian marriage systems were a form of delayed return with the older, initiated men controlling the distribution of women between local groups in a connubium, or marriage universe. 'Australians [are] farmers in disguise who are concerned with farming (and farming out) their women' (Woodburn 1980:108–9).

But by insisting on the system of return, delayed or immediate, as the means to differentiate and characterize foraging societies, Woodburn ignores the importance of space and property as an asset. This is a serious omission since it is the transactions in property, as Layton (1986:30) shows, which shape the long-term processes of hunter-gatherer society and so determine its political structure. In this case property is owned by small descent groups, or clans, numbering from fifteen to fifty individuals (*ibid.*:22). Elsewhere they are referred to as the minimum band (Damas 1972) or local group (Birdsell 1968).

In Australia this property consists of sacred sites over which each clan has exclusive rights. These sites form Stanner's concept of the estate (1965). It is the association of people with the land and their active stewardship of the meanings connected with places that characterizes Australian foraging societies. Such exclusive rights to geographical sites and sacred knowledge are contrasted by Layton (1986:30) with other hunter-gatherers who exercise exclusive rights over territories and the food resources they contain. These rights are also vested in lineages and so form the basis for inegalitarian social structures.

A rather different view is provided by Meillassoux (1973). He argues that the mode of exploitation of the land sets up relations of production that resolve themselves through the physical and social reproduction of society. The relations of production between members of a hunting group do not in his view require continued membership of the group and so do not lead to long-lasting social cohesion. Moreover, where land is the subject rather than the instrument of labour, as is the case with farmers, this results in the rapid depletion of resources and hence the enforced movement of the group from one area to another in search of new food supplies. This makes it difficult, if not impossible, for him to see how hunters develop into farmers without them receiving some extra advantage from the environment.

Property, the spatial use of resources, provides the focus for social action through involvement based on rights and obligations. If we just concentrated on the system of return, the use of resources in time, as Woodburn advocates, we might be tempted into some strange evolutionary arguments. For example, it might be argued that the !Kung would revert to a delayed system, if only they were allowed to by the larger economic and political forces which surround them. Such a view would deny them any active participation in their own history and only requires that they seek some equilibrium in organization. Hunters and gatherers are returned to that passive state where they are acted upon by external forces such as climate or civilization. The members of such societies are barely conceived as active social agents but rather as slaves to nature. The societies they inhabit are 'cold' in terms of the possibilities of self-generated change, relying instead on a push from outside. In this scenario the 'hot' societies emerge as those with agriculture and civilization. They are peopled by 'warm-blooded' participants in the creation of history (Bender 1985:21).

But putting such caricatures aside, this still leaves the problem of how and why such dramatic social change took place. This is clearly Woodburn's concern. He has concluded that

> delayed-return hunter-gatherer systems are, in a sense, pre-adapted for the development of agriculture and pastoralism. They have the organization (the binding ties and the social groups) which should make the development of an economy based on agriculture or pastoralism easy when the techniques become available. (Woodburn 1991:57)

Therefore it was among the now-vanished, unencapsulated, delayed-system societies that such change occurred. In other words their success made them disappear.

Meillassoux also got out of this same problem by pointing to the North West Coast societies, with their reliance on fishing, as the likely seed-bed from which agricultural systems with their rights to tenure and property sprang (1973:201). But like Woodburn, he does not explain why, in these windfall environments, the foraging way of life is still dominant.

### *Simple causes*

These studies point to the difficulties, if not impossibility, of establishing a prototype from ethnography for immediately pre-agricultural societies and then deducing an evolutionary trajectory. This, however, has not stopped Johnson and Earle (1987:18) from presenting the !Kung and the Inuit as examples of two extremes in hunter-gatherer organization representing, respectively, family level and local group organization. Prehistoric foraging societies from Olduvai Gorge to the Middle Palaeolithic of the Dordogne are then fitted to the demographic parameters of the !Kung and the Great Basin Shoshone. Everything that happens in the Upper Palaeolithic was 'impelled by a continued growth in population' (*ibid.*:55). In fact they claim that population growth is the primary determinant of all social change (*ibid.*:3). The intensification precipitated by such growth then produced local group-level societies, such as the coastal Inuit or the interior Nunamiut. Therefore we are left with the view that the open, composite systems are somehow ancestral and that foragers wait passively for change to hit them, in the 'unexpected' guise of population growth, rather than initiating it themselves. This last account of social change is clearly unsatisfactory. The lesson of committing ethnography with a shovel (Wobst 1978) has not yet been fully absorbed into such evolutionist schemes.

## Studies of Palaeolithic society: the origins of Band and complex societies

While anthropologists wrestle with their contradictory typologies, archaeologists have investigated two other concepts whose origin can be traced to such classifications. The first is *Band Society* (with initial capitals) which is regarded by Wobst (1974:v) as the underlying cultural system from which the specific cultural behaviour of particular hunter-gatherer populations emerges. The essential feature of Band Society is group closure and the appearance of boundaries.[9] It relies on the model of demography and ecology put forward by Birdsell (1958, 1953) for Australian dialect tribes which depended for their existence only on 'competence in speech [and] mobility on foot' (1968:232).

The second concept is that of *complex hunter-gatherers* (Ames 1985, Hayden et al. 1985, Marquardt 1985, Shnirelman 1992), a description which increasingly includes several so-called Neolithic farmers (Bender 1985). The impetus for studying complexity among societies which for many years were regarded as nothing more than primitive hordes came, on the one hand, from Service's classification of some hunters as chiefdoms, and on the other from the evolutionary question – where did farmers come from? However, we should be aware that the potential for complexity must be regarded as a property of all modern foraging bands, whichever classification is preferred. The use of the term should not indicate, as Keeley (1988) implies, that these 'complex' hunters rub shoulders with 'simple' foragers.

It is important to keep these concepts of bands, Band Society and complex hunter-gatherers separate. The purpose of reviewing these terms is that, as archaeologists, we can predict with some confidence that Band Society organization is almost certainly necessary to produce material complexity. As a result, the concept of Band Society has been applied to the problem of explaining major change associated with the Upper Palaeolithic (Gilman 1984, Mellars 1973, White 1982).

I shall now discuss each concept in turn.

### *Band Society and alliance*

> The band level of integration is by far the most frequent among known hunters and gatherers and must have been the characteristic, though perhaps not universal, form of social organization during the Palaeolithic era. (Service 1971:47)

But where does this leave the origins of Band Society which Wobst identified as a future major research question in 'culture' change, akin to the physical emergence of humans or the origins of agriculture (1974:vi)?

Table 1.5. *The six postulates of Band Society (Williams 1974).*

- a species divided into social groups which are autonomous with respect to food supply or vital resources will exhibit territoriality
- given that food is shared within the family and that a sexual division of labour, with respect to hunting-gathering acitivities, exists, then territorial groups will tend to be patrilocally based
- social units in hunting-gathering societies are kinship units
- in hunting-gathering society, the kinship unit having maximal autonomy with respect to resources is the lineage band
- the lineage band is exogamic
- optimal band size is the minimal size in which marriage alliances can be maintained with all surrounding bands indefinitely

We must first realize that Band Society is, like Service's definition of the patrilocal band (1971:64), a limited concept, dealing only with the residential and territorial aspects of social organization. Six postulates are recognized (Table 1.5). Williams (1974) examined these through a study of the Birhor from eastern India combined with a computer simulation of the genetic implications of the spatial structures of the marriage networks.

The spatial consequences of these postulates will be explored further in Chapters 2 and 3. Here I will only consider how this model has been used to investigate the origins of the Band Society blueprint, from which the great variety of ethnographically known band societies developed.

Band Society is treated coterminously by Wobst (1976:52) with 'mating networks which are closed to such an extent that the participating local groups derive virtually all of their mates from the same set of personnel'; a view of connubium, or system of marital exchanges, which Fox (1967:176) traces back to Tylor (1881). Within the connubium there is exogamy to establish marital alliances. As a result, 'our Palaeolithic hunting-and-gathering bands . . . exchanged women in order to live at peace with each other' (Fox 1967:176).

The emphasis on the concept of mating network (Wobst 1974) was deliberate, since it supplied an analytical concept comparable to society, culture or population which archaeology lacked but which it needed in order to understand regional-scale processes (Wobst 1976:49). Moreover, these networks could be investigated through the cultural transmission of stylistic elements as personnel moved within the connubium following marriage. The use of the model was comparable to Williams' (1974) study of gene flow, except that artifact styles, rather than alleles, provided the units of measurement.

Closure was the key concept since this defined Band Society organization. Thus network-specific styles, and their ritual underpinning which enforced network loyalty, would be expected. These would be manifest at different spatial scales (Wobst 1977) through the appearance of boundaries. The selection pressure of the mating network was the context for differentiating between dif-

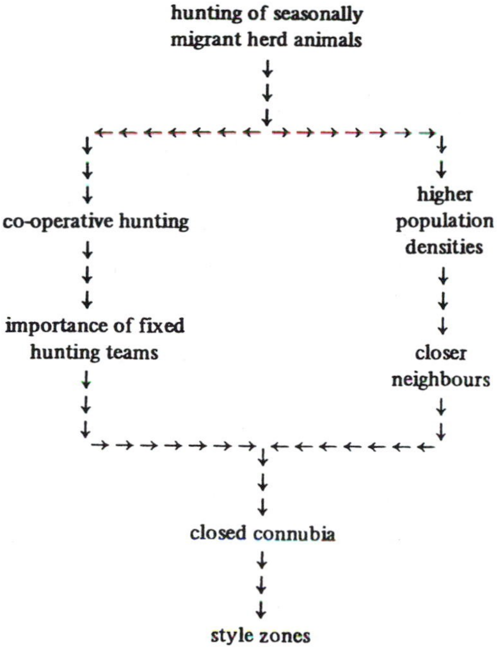


**1.3** The development of closed networks and Upper Palaeolithic style zones according to Wobst (after Gilman 1984:Fig. 2).

ferent levels of information which were needed to maintain it. The messages in such information acts concerned membership and affiliation.

Wobst also demonstrated (1976:55) that mating-system closure produces increased social expense and decreased reproductive success, due to a rise in the costs of social interaction (Chapter 3). This principle, which the Kalahari studies would support (Yellen and Harpending 1972, Lee 1976), establishes the evolutionary trajectory:

> Stylistic elements that may be taken to symbolize boundary processes between ethnic groups and social group affiliation are altogether rare up to the middle of the last glaciation. These considerations indicate that Band Society – and the closed mating system as one of its operational expressions – may not even extend back to early *Homo sapiens*. (Wobst 1976:54)

Using the concept of Band Society, the historical sequence is therefore expected to move from open to closed mating structures, from stating that 'we mate with everyone' to recognizing that 'we mate with members of this band but not that one'.

Gilman (1984:121) has provided a summary (Figure 1.3) of how Band Society might have arisen, especially where co-operation between members of local groups had become advantageous (Wobst 1976:55). This co-operation might have been a response to the existence of herd animals that were worth co-operating to hunt. But, rather than tying such developments to specific ecological

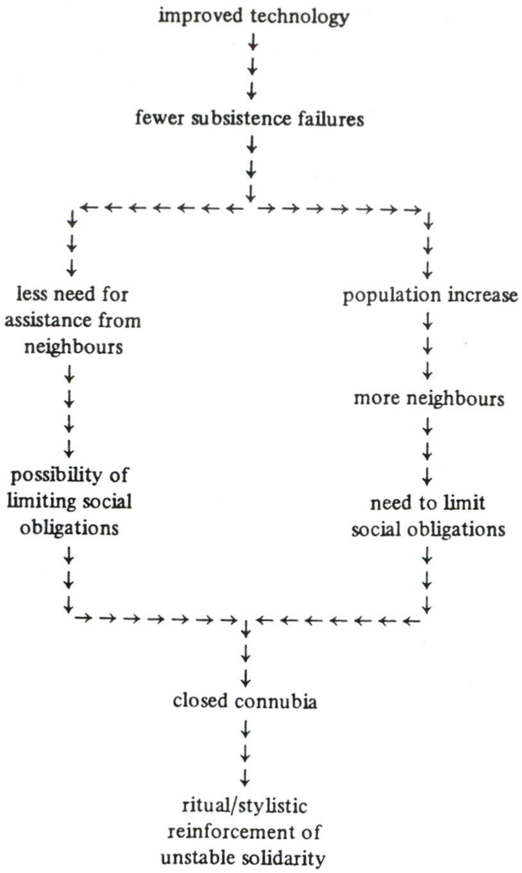


**1.4** The relation between technological improvements and social change during the Upper Palaeolithic revolution (after Gilman 1984:Fig. 3).

settings, Gilman prefers to focus on the general social relations of production (Figure 1.4) using the alliance theory of kinship structures (Barnard 1992, Fox 1967, Kuper 1988, Lévi-Strauss 1969) to account for the recruitment of labour. As a result he highlights a major weakness of Wobst's Band Society model, which equates the social with the demographic. The mating network, although an important component in social organization, is *not* a society, except perhaps from an ultra-reductionist, sociobiological viewpoint. Indeed, primatologists following Wrangham's (1980) lead, which identified female-bonded social organization as the key to understanding social behaviour (Foley and Lee 1989), clearly distinguish between the mating system and social organization (Quiatt and Reynolds 1993:51–2).

However, there is a weakness in Gilman's model of Band Society. In his alliance theory Lévi-Strauss attached paramount importance to exogamic marriage as the means by which integration of groups into a larger whole was achieved (1969:480). His interpretation took as axiomatic that kinship organized, according to rules, the long-term exchange relations between groups.

But marriage is only one form of alliance and groups are not necessarily the only or logical units of society (Chapter 2). Other forms of alliance not based on kinship involve individuals negotiating partnerships, friendships, gangs and cliques based on age and sex. Alliances can be defined through affective, material and symbolic ties; pots and partners, songs and feasts, love and aggression (Chapter 2).

The variable structure of alliances, defined as an achieved social status based to a large extent upon negotiation (Guemple 1972:56), has been explored elsewhere for prehistoric foragers (Gamble 1982).

> These negotiable alliances provide a means by which the viability of individuals and local groups is achieved within a regional framework. A network of such alliances defines an often diverse set of social relationships where circulation and exchange of persons and goods establishes and maintains ties of variable commitment and duration. (Gamble 1986a:54)

The alliance network, negotiated by individuals, rather than the mating network with its emphasis on groups, provides a more comprehensive, larger unit for the analysis of Palaeolithic society. The boundaries to the alliance network may be closed as well as open (Gamble 1991b). The spatial scale of such open alliance systems may be much greater than those of the connubium, thereby fulfilling both Wobst's (1976) and Bender's (1978) call for analytical units which are bigger than the on-the-ground group, since local variation is in part conditioned by regional and inter-regional processes of adaptation (Gamble 1986a:54–62). Band Society is one way of expressing the network of social alliances which are involved in the analysis of Palaeolithic society.[10]

### *Complex foragers*

> All societies at the band level of integration are foragers of wild food. Not all wild-food foragers are at the band level, however. Along the Northwest coast of North America were large populations of maritime peoples whose environment was so remarkably bountiful that they lived in complex communities at the level of chiefdoms . . . The Palaeolithic era thus may well have had some such forms of society in addition to bands. (Service 1971:47)

The past twenty years has not borne out Wobst's (1974:vi) prediction that Band Society would become a major issue in the study of culture change. The interest instead has been in the issue of how cultural complexity emerged (Koyama and Thomas 1982, Price and Brown 1985a). Archaeologists have pursued those chiefs among the bands (King 1978, Mueller-Wille and Dickson 1991).

The Price and Brown volume *Prehistoric hunters and gatherers: the emergence of cultural complexity* (1985a) is instructive in the way the problem is framed. Complexity, which refers to that which is composed of many interrelated parts (Price and Brown 1985b:7), became a major factor in social life from

35,000 BP, the onset of the European Upper Palaeolithic, as shown by several papers in their volume (Conkey 1985, Mellars 1985, Soffer 1985a). Wide geographical coverage points to the potential of all societies after the social revolution of the Upper Palaeolithic to become complex. Whether this implies that they were always surrounded by simple societies is not clear. It is more likely, as Bender (1981) has put it, that there were always, in the long term, and at a continental scale, shifting geographical centres of power and complexity.

These centres of complexity are recognized in the archaeological record through a checklist. The items are

- population density
- maximum settlement size
- permanent shelter
- permanent ceremonial grounds
- art styles
- differences in burials due to grave wealth, location and the energy investment in grave preparation (Brown and Price 1985:437).

It could be argued that since a large number of hunting and gathering societies have some of these items, and all have art styles, then they are all complex and hence the classification is redundant. This, I believe, is indeed the case, and in Chapter 2 I will develop the argument that being complex can be assumed; not only for the Upper Palaeolithic but for all the societies prior to this social revolution. What matters is leading complicated social lives. Hence Brown and Price's conclusion that 'the potential for social and cultural complexity resides in hunter-gatherer economies' (1985:436) is correct only if complexity is defined in terms of items on their checklist. I would rephrase it to state that economic and cultural complexity resides in hunter-gatherer social life. It is here that the mobilization of resources and the involvement of actors in the production of the material world are structured through their own negotiations.

On the positive side, and just as Constandse-Westermann and Newell are trying to prolong its life, Brown and Price (1985:436) finally bury the use of the band as a unit in an evolutionary typology. As archaeologists, their concern is with culture change and complexity where

> we intend to spotlight the variety of adaptations that characterize prehistoric hunter-gatherers as well as to delineate some of the primary features of societal complexity. (Price and Brown 1985c:xiii)

They identify three themes: the intensification of food procurement; the origins of sedentary communities; and the emergence of social inequality and hierarchical organization. They provide a clear orientation to investigate these topics:

> We deal not only with the origins of such phenomena but also with relationships; that is, how such aspects of human adaptation as settlement, population, subsistence, exchange, conflict, and technology may be involved in the elaboration of society. (*ibid.*)

Being social therefore emerges as part of their adaptive explanation (Price and Brown 1985c:Fig. 1.1). The appearance of complex social life will, it is argued, be tied to particular historical and economic circumstances and these will explain the variable cultural forms, both chronologically and geographically, that it takes.

There is another way to look at this adaptive approach where the social forms part of the explanation. I have already discussed Layton's (1986) view that it is involvement with and transactions in property which shape the long-term processes in hunter-gatherer society. He argues that social complexity will vary, in terms of inequality, if expressed through either subsistence goods or immaterial knowledge involving ritual (*ibid.*:30). This would contrast the North West Coast and Arctic societies with those from Australia or the Kalahari. Variation in complex behaviour is not therefore necessarily adaptive but rather an emergent property of the way society is structured, a point explored in Chapter 2.

### Culture and two narratives

If studying the evolution of society in the Palaeolithic is proving difficult, why not settle instead for the development of culture? By culture archaeologists usually mean the system of rules and symbols which provide the extrasomatic means of adaptation that humans have at their disposal. These are highly varied and as a result we have many different cultures. What has concerned anthropologists, however, is that beneath such myriad forms lies a set of simple universal social principles. Their task is to strip away culture to reveal this underlying structure and then reassemble the parts to see how it was transformed. An appropriate analogy would be between an organism's genotype (social structure) and phenotype (cultural expression). The former provides us with a nose, skin and two legs. The latter expresses this basic structure in terms of how big, what colour and how long they are.[11]

Culture is also set up as an opposition to Nature. The familiar argument is that we have culture, animals do not. The possession of culture is therefore taken as our defining quality. It is what makes our adaptation extrasomatic since it exists outside us and is part of our social life as humans. It takes the form not only of ritual, custom and technology but also of skill, knowledge and information.

The problem however with accepting this nature:culture juxtaposition is that once again it drops that interpretative curtain across the Palaeolithic (Gamble 1991a). The task then becomes one of determining when we became cultural (i.e. not natural) beings, what new capacities, for example language, this entailed, and whether the pace of change involved either a pre- or a protocultural stage. The concept of culture is therefore unhelpful to the study of the Palaeolithic unless the main aim is to examine our own definitions. The problem, which has been pointed out many times in anthropology, is that culture cannot be used to explain culture.

The current trend among primatologists and biologists is to adopt a continuum approach to the study of human and non-human primate societies. In this view culture is the means by which the social processing of information, vital to survival, is structured (Quiatt and Reynolds 1993:179). Culture regulates social knowledge and interaction. It can change and can be transmitted. The information it channels is subject to selection pressure. This selection is why we find patterns in the Palaeolithic record, and also why we can find explanations for them. Culture can be adaptive and exaptive, fit by reason of its form rather than designed by history for some purpose (Gamble 1993a:5, Gould 1991, Gould and Vrba 1982). It is hence patterned but with an unpredictable trajectory.

But culture is not just information. It is a means of expressing social principles that concern the lives of individuals but it has no life of its own and cannot be used as an explanation of the patterns we find in our data. Culture is not something which was developed during human evolution but springs from the active engagement of people in the business of living and interacting. In that sense it represents a continuum between animals and humans, early and modern hominids, ourselves and our ancestors. Culture varies between species and through time because individuals call selectively on different resources to sustain relationships and promote social projects (Chapter 2).

### *The worm becomes a serpent then a symbolic gesture*

Two examples will point to the strengths and weaknesses of a cultural approach to human social origins. They are two narratives with different perspectives on the problem but with a shared concern to use the Palaeolithic record to structure their story.

In a challenging account, Knight (1991a, 1991b) has argued that the evolution of society depended upon the loss of female power. Culture in his thesis is an expression of solidarity. Female culture was based on a collective sex strike made possible through concealed ovulation and menstrual synchrony tied to the signal rhythms of lunar cycles. In this way groups were formed from collective action the purpose of which, Knight argues, was to motivate their menfolk to organize hunting. On their successful return, meat was then exchanged for sex. The cultural link was between the blood of the women and the blood of the animals. The female sex strike constituted the first taboo and set the scene for the use of blood as a powerful agent in cultural life. The basis of symbolic behaviour with its substitute signs and referred meanings was therefore established.

Here then was the pre- or incipient cultural state. The revolution in the Upper Palaeolithic which overturned this ancient pattern and made us fully cultural beings is put down to ecological decline:

> as the game herds diminished, as female-inspired collective hunting increasingly proved unreliable, and as it became more and more advisable for people to disperse, women's solidarity would have begun to break down. (Knight 1991b:35)

Women lost their power over men because the animals betrayed them. The ice ages took their toll on animal numbers, the success of hunters dwindled and the women paid the price. The cultural state of female power based on common ritual and collective action collapsed, but not before it set up the trajectory for the world as we know it (*ibid*.:37). Out of this cultural past the notion that blood symbolized female sexual solidarity survived. Raiding the rituals and mythologies of the world, Knight (1991a) has made the case that male initiation and myths concerning the stealing of power are resonances from the time that women lost their power. This cultural exaptation is shown in the elaborate dragon and serpent myths found in many of the world's mythologies. These legends are bound up with themes of fire, blood, birth and rebirth, marriage and threats to marriage, masculine sexual potency and the origins of male ritual power (Knight 1991b:44). By appropriating the symbolism which formerly marked female power, the dragon-slaying Upper Palaeolithic men seized the cultural basis for their own collective, group power.

Such a bold narrative, even though it is so heavily dependent upon environmental and sociobiological determinism to make its vision of culture work, almost deserves to succeed. While I disagree with it in both essence and detail, I nonetheless acknowledge that it is a compelling account which studies of Palaeolithic society need, if only to show us that this is not what we want.

Contrast this with my second narrative example, André Leroi-Gourhan's *Le geste et la parole*, originally published in 1964–5 and largely ignored outside France until translated into English in 1993 as *Gesture and speech*. Leroi-Gourhan is best known to archaeologists for his study of Palaeolithic cave art (1968) and his pioneering studies of area excavations as at Arcy sur Cure (1961, 1964) and Pincevent (Leroi-Gourhan and Brézillon 1966, Leroi-Gourhan and Brézillon 1972). *Gesture and speech* is something else entirely, representing an approach to the evolution of society and the study of human action that is breathtaking in its audacity.

The argument he presents is complex and I will return to it many times in the chapters which follow. Although he rarely acknowledges it, he owed most to Mauss' (1936) study *Les techniques du corps* (the techniques of the body), where it was established that techniques are first and foremost social productions (Lemmonier 1993:3). By uniting technical and social processes, Leroi-Gourhan proposed a single approach to the study of the Palaeolithic. He achieved this without once discussing culture as a concept. No longer, therefore, do we have to bemoan the lack of social data, as Childe did, because this period seems so impoverished in relevant materials compared to those which followed. Instead, as Leroi-Gourhan shows, we can fuse these concerns and study the long-term trajectory of social change by studying the evolution of techniques. Moreover, this fusion does away with the distinction between style and function in artifact analysis (White 1993a:xviii). Society does not just reside in the former as rules about identity and ethnicity but as social representations literally embodied in the acts of manufacture, use and discard.

Here then is a very different vision of social archaeology and an understanding of culture. It is based on a concern with biology, form and growth. It deals with the body as a source of value and the importance of rhythms which link the varied operational sequences (*chaînes opératoires*) that produce forms and traditions of doing, what archaeologists would usually call cultures.

In Leroi-Gourhan's view of human evolution we have today arrived at the place where the individual is now outdated. What matters is the species as the infrastructure of humankind (1993:253). This point has been reached because of the continuing externalization of human memory. As we go through time, so new ways have developed to store cultural memories outside our bodies. The result has been to change the way human societies were organized by changing the structure of action.

> We are again and again available for new forms of action, our memory transferred to books, our strength multiplied in the ox, our fist improved in the hammer. (Leroi-Gourhan 1993:246)

Culture in the form of a network of symbols has come to replace the body as the source of those rhythms which structure action. Organizing time and space in this manner represents the evolutionary penchant of our species. The appearance of advanced technology and robots is the culmination of the process since the prospect is opened up of the artificial which can now socially reproduce itself. Confidence for the future depends instead on 'the view that the individual is infinitely socializable' (1993:407) and that the individual's relationship with society can, as it always has in our past, be rethought.

Here is a narrative which, while it has a quaint faith in progressive change, nonetheless does deserve to succeed. Why? After all Leroi-Gourhan also has a revolution, coinciding with the appearance of the graphic arts in the Upper Palaeolithic, to account for the trajectory whereby memory has become increasingly externalized. Such graphism established new rhythmic systems and involved signs and words. A new language of forms was created, new gestures and operational sequences (White 1993a:xix).

It should prevail as an approach not because it gives us another grail – the origin of graphism – to pursue, but more importantly because it reunites the Palaeolithic with the rest of archaeology and history as a social project. In so doing, it regards the long-term evolution of our species as part of the ongoing investigation into our social behaviour as we rethink our relationship with society.

## Summary

There have been two uses of a social focus in Palaeolithic studies. The first, associated with the study of human origins in Africa, has used the social as a means to underwrite the multi-disciplinary effort. Human social origins have provided a deductive goal and a research paradigm towards which, and by which, the observations from anatomists, geologists, archaeologists and a host of other specialists can be directed. Defining the proto-cultural platform from which we sprang has been a major aim.

The second use has been directed towards the other end of the Palaeolithic timescale. Here the interest has been in the development of Band Society or the emergence of complex society as a component of modern humans. Here the social *is* the explanation rather than the research paradigm. Hence we have social (Stringer and Gamble 1993) and cultural (Knight 1991a, 1991b) revolutions which drove the changes seen in the broader human revolution (Mellars and Stringer 1989). This is regarded as necessary in order adequately to explain the record of the Upper Palaeolithic revolution (Gilman 1984:123), which is different because it is marked by the appearance of style and the definition of time–space cultures. Symbolism and style are the basis for Conkey's (1978:78) complex social geography which appears late in human evolution during the Upper Palaeolithic. The origin of this brave new world is believed, understandably, to require primarily a social rather than a cultural materialist explanation (Bender 1978:218).

I have not set out in this chapter to choose between the various explanations. Rather I am interested in the conceptualization of the problem as Latour and Strum (1986) have insisted upon. In the accounts so far discussed it might also be claimed that there is very little which is truly social. We have descriptions of the partial properties of a system, be these mating networks (Williams 1974, Wobst 1974, 1976) or technological systems (Gilman 1984). The study of the origin of Band Society, which ignores a wider view of its alliance networks, is therefore a study of group rather than individual dynamics and the prehistory of a particular type of institution. This institution exists in the present in two main forms (Service 1971, Woodburn 1991) which can be arranged in ancestral order. The social is the explanation since it is the explanation which determines the order – did open systems lead to closed, or vice versa?

Through its focus on social origins at either end of the Palaeolithic, this chapter has also highlighted how the period in between has received very little attention. What studies there have been have made little impact (e.g. Schmidt 1936). This period between the dispersal of *Homo erectus* from sub-Saharan Africa and the Upper Palaeolithic revolution is usually only described in ecological and subsistence terms. The data from Europe are well suited to examining change and stasis during half a million years, and maybe more, when the continent was peopled. But we can only explore the social life of these hominids in the middle if we have a more developed sense of what we mean by the social and society than that regularly used by Palaeolithic archaeologists.

CHAPTER 2

# THE INDIVIDUAL, SOCIETY AND NETWORKS

Men make their own history, but they do not make it just as they please, they do not make it under circumstances chosen by themselves, but under circumstances directly encountered, given and transmitted from the past

Karl Marx, 1869

## Groups and individuals[1]

Social archaeology has concentrated on the study of groups and institutions. These are variously classified in terms of cultures, traditions, systems, sub-systems and civilizations. They most famously follow the evolutionary procession of band, tribe, chief and state (Service 1971). This approach to the study of social institutions in prehistory has been successful for a very simple reason: archaeologists already know what they are going to find. Those chiefdoms and states, and their systems and sub-systems, are already defined before the digging begins. Discoveries of shrines and longhouses, rich burials and exotic raw materials, wall paintings and monumental sculpture can then be accommodated within existing classifications. The classic technique has been a checklist against which archaeological discoveries are compared (Gamble 1986b). Nor does a one hundred per cent match have to be achieved. Prehistoric cultures, like modern societies, are polythetic entities when it comes to their cultural makeup (Clarke 1968).

The individual has not been considered in these schemes. According to Clark, only the cumulative results of group activities are preserved because the actions of individuals are beyond the resolution of the Palaeolithic record (1992a:107). Mithen has effectively countered this view:

> A good explanation in archaeology requires explicit reference to individual people going about their day to day business. They need to be explicitly attributed with knowledge of the world, a capacity to plan and make decisions, an ability to respond creatively and intelligently to the challenges of their social and physical environment. (Mithen 1993a:396)

He further argues that the social archaeology of the 1970s and 1980s, with its emphasis on group adaptation, swamped prehistoric people with huge impersonal, mechanistic forces such as 'group selection' and 'population pressure'.[2]

The absence of the individual from the Palaeolithic, and from prehistory generally, can be seen as a casualty of the 'primitive society' model (Kuper 1988) with its emphasis on pre-existing institutions into which people are born and so rendered powerless.

There is agreement with this approach from another theoretical quarter. Shanks and Tilley's argument, derived from structuration theory, states that

> the individual cannot be screened out of archaeological analysis. The individual is to be conceived as knowledgeable and active and yet at the same time positioned in relation to social structures and strategies, a trace within a structured social field. This means that social relations cannot be reduced to interacting creative individuals. (Shanks and Tilley 1987a:210)

This issue of micro and macro scale, the individual and the group, has never been adequately addressed in the discussion of Palaeolithic society. Such discussion needs to take place in the context of different ways to understand society. On the one hand we have to avoid introducing individuals as analytical units which are simply ciphers, thereby replacing one abstract with another (Wolf 1988:760), and on the other we cannot ignore the very obvious constraints on individual action which are set by wider social structures.

The first, a bottom-up approach, takes the individual as the starting point. The second, or top-down approach, sees the group as dominant. In the former model the individual plays an active role in *performing* society and its structures into existence. In the latter, society *precedes* and shapes the individual through the power of its institutions. These opposed models are discussed below. In order to illustrate how the study of Palaeolithic society would benefit by shifting its focus to the bottom-up model I will draw on the similarities in approach that are currently offered by the study of primate societies and structuration theory. This leads to an examination of network analysis which provides a formal but flexible structure for bridging the micro and macro scale. Because of the emphasis which network studies place on the individual, they are appropriate for a bottom-up approach to social analysis. Particular attention is paid to the resources and rules in these networks and which produce demographic patterns.

## Two approaches to society

The ethologist Robert Hinde (1976, 1987) has described the difference between two models of society. The distinction is fundamental but, as Hinde comments, not mutually exclusive. In the top-down approach

> human social structures can be viewed as the product of enduring relationships, organisations and institutions which constrain individual behaviour; or as the outcome of the behaviour of individuals who create the social world about them. The former structural view involves a high degree of abstraction from the real-life data, but provides a procedure for viewing societies as unities of interdependent parts and processes according to principles of wide validity (Hinde 1976:14)

while the bottom-up approach

> starts from the individual, seeking for statements about the manner in which he manages his relationships, and attempting to map the relationships in which he is involved. (*ibid.*)

This differentiation also involves two sometimes opposed anthropological views of culture (Ingold 1994). The cognitivist approach is primarily an exercise in classification involving mental representations of social structures where the stability of culture is achieved through linguistic transmission. By contrast, the phenomenological approach stresses the active engagement of people with their environment. The rhythms and gestures of the body during the performance of social life, the habitual actions of living (Leroi-Gourhan 1993:231–2), mean that social memory is passed on in non-textual, non-linguistic ways (Connerton 1989:72). These distinctions are explored more fully in Chapter 3.

### *Society as architecture, a top-down approach*

In the structural, top-down approach, society is like a building, constructed at some point in the past, used by present inhabitants but rarely altered. It is, if you like, a community theatre peopled by groups where individuals are only recognized by their institutional roles such as chief, big man or priest-king. This has been the dominant model used by social archaeologists (Redman et al. 1978). They knew what they were going to find in terms of social categories because they had a model that society *precedes* its members. In other words individuals are born into an existing social framework. They enter into relationships which have already been determined by those groups to which they are admitted by reason of birth. These relationships are coded in culture. Consequently the study of social evolution emphasizes the points of transition as well as the maintenance of institutions.

The view that groups are paramount and underpin the structures of society is derived from social anthropology. Among 'primitive societies', where formal institutions were often difficult to define, the most important institution for the anthropologist was the kinship group. This could also be broken down into constituent institutions such as the clan, moiety, lineage, locus and family. These institutions produced solidarity which permitted social life through the operation of a collectivity of action, a widely held view most closely associated with Durkheim (Ingold 1986a:227–30, Kuper 1988:118–20).

The model appears to make good sense. Obviously a baby requires a long period of parenting. It is introduced during childhood to the institutions of society and grows into the norms and beliefs of group life. It is adapted, designed by its history, to the group. The problem for social analysis is that the individual becomes a demiurge, skilfully serving the will of the institution. Creativity is largely denied.

*Society as an improvised script: a bottom-up approach*

Hinde's (1976) second model of society stresses the individual rather than the group. In contrast to the view that society precedes is one where it is *performed*. Instead of being entered as a pre-existing structure, society is created through the actions of individual actors.

Society in these terms is produced by interaction between individuals and creates overlapping fields of social relationships (Grönhaug 1978:120). Social structure is an abstraction derived ultimately from these interactions (Hinde 1987). Society emerges from the many networks which are constructed by individuals rather than containing them.

With this perspective the insights of social theory become relevant since one of its goals is to combine the investigations about human behaviour from both micro-scale and macro-scale processes (Turner 1991:632). This combines the individual and the institution. The scale varies from a fleeting moment when individuals meet in the street to the long-term persistence of moral codes and international institutions.

If individuals negotiate society then the networks of alliances they produce will not just be based on ties of kin or marriage. In addition there will be a wealth of partnerships involving relationships based on fictive kinship, trade, ceremony and friendship and enacted during visits, rituals, feasts and conversations. Ethnographic examples of this creativity are plentiful among foragers.

> Kinship in Zhu [!Kung] society, rather than being a static straitjacket, is a dynamic keyboard on which individuals play variations on a theme of options. It is . . . *up to the individual to create and manage an effective social network.* (Wilmsen 1989:180, my emphasis)

A Zhu regional band is a node within a kinship field wherein persons negotiate their relationships to a wider polity (*ibid.*:117). An excellent example of such choices is provided by Wiessner's (1982) detailed study of hxaro trading partnerships among the !Kung. These are primarily formed between relatives but wind between camps with the result that very large networks of people become linked. Interaction and choice are important in the construction of the system. Among many foragers, fictive kinship, where a limited number of names are used so that strangers can be included in ego's network, are also common solutions to the negotiator's aim of constructing a network (Lee 1979).

In his study of the Hill Pandaram in southern India, Morris concludes that they 'create their social life as they go along' (Morris 1982:150). Each generation negotiates its own social system which is based on dyadic bonds of affection, in other words interaction between two individuals.

In a very different environmental setting the involvement of individuals in creating their social lives comes across clearly in Guemple's account of the Inuit of Belcher Island:

> the kinship system is not an ascribed status system at all but a *negotiable* one . . . it is also a system which rests upon a social metaphysic which implies that *social*

*relatedness is a matter to be worked out by the participants in social encounter*, and that the major criteria to be used are first, that people must actively participate in the system to be counted as kinsmen in a meaningful way, and second, that those who enter the field of *face-to-face relations* must be treated as kinsmen whether genealogical connexions exist to support the claim or not. (Guemple 1972:75, my emphasis)[3]

Kinship, as Wilson observes (1988:36), is not an institution in the way that it has normally been used to define primitive society. Instead it is a reservoir of potential but vague connections which can form a social focus when required. Bahuchet's study of the Zaire Pygmies provides just such an example of rules and choice. The rule is for patrilocal and virilocal residence (1992:247). However, he found many examples where the son-in-law broke the rule by staying in his wife's camp rather than moving with her to his own. As a result, choice, based on interaction and preference, made the residence pattern bi- rather than unilocal as expected (*ibid*.:219).[4]

## Primate societies

Studying the societies of monkeys and apes presents comparable difficulties to the study of Palaeolithic societies. Primatologists can observe behaviour but they still have to infer social life. They have no self-declared structure, in the form of kinship or preferentially expressed social relationships, with which to reconstruct primate society. They have no insight into the intentions of their subjects, only observations concerning actions and, by studying sequences, the opportunity to predict action in future situations. Palaeolithic archaeologists can only study the static residues of past action. From these we infer behaviour and social life.

This being the case, it is interesting to observe the resolution of two conceptual issues in current studies of primate societies. These concern the units of analysis and the characterization of society. Firstly, Quiatt and Reynolds (1993:52) state that in studies of non-human primate social behaviour the individual animal is necessarily the unit of observation and most likely the unit of analysis as well. Secondly, the concept of primate society has undergone its own transformation, paralleling the demise of 'primitive society' as documented by Kuper (1988).

Strum and Latour (1987), Cheyney and Seyfarth (1990) and Rowell (1991) have shown how the study of non-human primate social life now depends not so much on new techniques but on a change in the concept of society. This has involved moving away from the architectural metaphor based around group behaviour and towards a performance model where negotiation through interaction plays a central role as individuals pursue their social agendas. Kummer's (1968) study of baboons and in particular Hinde's (1976, 1987) model of social structure have been particularly important. As summed up by Strum and Latour,

Table 2.1. *A simple model of society (after Hinde 1976).*

> If we grant that *baboons are not entering into a stable structure* but rather negotiating what that structure will be, and monitoring and pushing all other such negotiations, the variety of baboon society and its ill fit to a simple structure can be seen to be a result of the 'performative' question. (Strum and Latour 1987:78)

Such an approach had previously been conceptualized by Hinde as three tiers of interactions, relationships, and surface, or social, structure (Table 2.1).

The model integrates micro- and macro-level processes and recognizes constraints passing between each of the levels. Face-to-face interactions between individuals are identified as the basic elements of social structure, while relationships are defined as a succession of interactions between two individuals (Hinde 1976:3). Relationships emerge from simple rules of interaction where sociality is an emergent property derived from the interactions between individuals (Foley and Lee 1996). Group structure, the highest level in Hinde's scheme, can be described in terms of the nature, quality and patterning of the relationships by which it is constituted (Hinde 1976:3).

The primates being studied are recognized as individuals with multiple relationships. As Rowell points out (1991:258), it is the compromises between these varied relationships which lead to the structure of the group. Thus the different personalities of individuals, which are obvious to any primate watcher (and not just primates, most animals), are incorporated into the model (Asquith 1996). This allows a more fluid view of society to emerge, one based less on hard-wired structure – a biological/genetic model of society – and more on the highly variable behaviour used in the negotiation of social life. Social structure in non-human primates therefore emerges as those aspects of the content, quality, and patterning of social relationships that show regularities across individuals and between social groups (Cheney and Seyfarth 1990).

Hinde also stresses the temporal element in his model of society. Interactions only last for a limited time-span while relationships have to be remembered, picked up, reinforced. In short, the patterning of relationships in time has to be understood by the animals (Hinde 1976:7) and this also applies to the macro-scale, surface structure. In their study of the small-bodied East African vervet monkeys (*Cercopithecus aethiops*), Cheyney and Seyfarth make this critical point:

> what defines a relationship is not simply the behaviours themselves (grooming, hugging, fighting etc.) but also the temporal relations among behaviours and the way each activity is carried out. (1990:176)

In their study of vervet interaction these relationships are density dependent and defined through offers of assistance. The way that interactions lead to alliances and the number of these which can be managed and maintained provide a measure of vervet social skills. Alliance occurs 'whenever two individuals are involved in an aggressive interaction and a third, previously uninvolved animal intervenes to aid one of them in attack or defense' (Cheney and Seyfarth 1990:27). Vervet society is based around a core of females, and alliances are formed more commonly among female kin than with unrelated animals. As a general rule intergroup alliances in non-human primates appear to be based on propinquity (Cheney and Seyfarth 1990:299).

## Agency, structure and the individual

There are many models of social theory (Turner 1991) but few, if any, have been concerned with the Palaeolithic. From this vast array I have selected aspects of structuration theory (Giddens 1984) to illustrate the convergence that exists in methods and questions with the study of primate societies. Archaeologists have already applied structuration theory to later prehistory and to the archaeology of modern humans (Barrett 1994, Gosden 1994, Shanks and Tilley 1987a and 1987b). However, because of its core principles Giddens' model is equally appropriate for the exploration of Palaeolithic society. On the one hand he insists on the importance of time and space for understanding social action, and on the other he deals in a unitary way with problems of scale from the individual to the integration of systems.

Giddens' theory of structuration refers to the 'structuring of social relations across time and space, in virtue of the duality of structure' (1984:376).[5] What he means by the duality of structure is that it is *not* something which exists out there, external to the individual. Rather, structure is contained in action itself, and action involves agency, the act of doing (*ibid*.:10).

Agency leads us back to the individual. It applies to Moderns, Neanderthals and *Homo heidelbergensis* since it is the capacity for action which is important in social life. Such potential contradicts a pre-ordained structure, the top-down approach, where a code which already exists determines how people act. The critical distinction, as Godelier has remarked, is that 'contrary to the other social animals, human beings do not content themselves with living together, they produce society for living' (quoted in Bahuchet 1992:253).

Giddens' notion of *duality*, which rolls structure and agency up together (1984:162), is in marked contrast to Durkheim's *dualism* where social structure is separated from, and therefore exists outside, the individual. Social structure for Durkheim was just a negative constraint inhibiting the free initiative of individuals. This pre-existing constraint produced coherent and consistent social action through group solidarity and collective participation in 'society'.

Instead, a key point in Giddens' theory is that structure is both constraining *and* enabling. He constantly points to the duality of most social concepts but

Table 2.2. *A hierarchy of interaction (after Goffman 1963:18).*

| | | |
|---|---|---|
| Social occasion | – | Bounded by time and space. Named locales, architecture, equipment and objects are often involved |
| Situation | – | The full spatial environment which begins when mutual monitoring between individuals ends |
| Gatherings | – | Are located within the boundaries of situations and involve two or more individuals in one another's immediate presence (=co-presence) |

how in much of social theory only one element has been stressed. The discussion of power is a prime example. Usually it is seen only as an authoritative force, signalling the existence of conflict (Giddens 1984:257). But that is only one face of power since, as Firth put it, 'social structure does not merely impose limits on freedom of action; it offers positive advantages to the individual who conforms to its principles' (1951:56). This conformity is a dialogue which starts in childhood between the individual and the social organism (Leroi-Gourhan 1993:228). The duality of structure stems from the fundamental opposition of two elements, *resources* and *rules*. It is from these that the forms of social life are fashioned. Life is not constraint free, as Marx famously pointed out in the passage which opened this chapter, but neither is it just dominated by prescriptive rules that determine the norms of behaviour through a pre-existing structure.

Giddens provides the example of language (1984:170). We do not choose our native language. We learn it and the system of rules which undoubtedly constrain thought and guide action. However, learning language also enables the individual to expand those same cognitive and practical capacities and so become an active, creative being. Rather than being simply adapted to speak, the possession of language makes the individual exapted, fit by reason of its form (Gamble 1993a, Gould 1991, Gould and Vrba 1982), to explore, negotiate, create and perform society. Society stems from this duality and not from the dualism which separates individuals from society in the group-structure model.

Appreciation of this point depends upon a further linkage of concepts, those of social and system integration (Giddens 1984:142). Social integration is what people do together. It covers the many and varied interactions that take place, face to face, in what is termed co-presence (Goffman 1959, 1963). At this micro scale of human action Goffman (1963:17) pointed out that co-presence combines the richness of information flow with the ease of feedback between individuals. As a result this type of interaction has immense structuring significance for the study of relationships, which he expressed as a simple hierarchy (Table 2.2).

System integration is concerned with how the patterns of social integration are extended *in absentia* (see below).

The scales of social and system integration vary from the chance encounters between individuals to the long-term persistence of moral practices and international organisations. They range in time from the fifteen minutes it took to knap a Palaeolithic handaxe to the duration of the Solutrean over 3,000 years. The spatial scales of interaction encompass the debris at the feet of the knapper and the distribution of distinctive projectile points across France, Spain and beyond of the Solutrean world. What marked the difference between Palaeolithic societies was, as we shall see below, the *resources* – emotional, material and symbolic – which were brought to these interactions, and the *rules* – limits to network size and organization – which emerged from them, and with which relationships were fashioned.

## Central questions in social evolution

The conceptual approaches to primate and human social life briefly discussed above provide a very useful framework and vocabulary of terms for conceptualizing society. I have selected them not because of intellectual fashion but instead because they deal with key issues in refocusing the study of Palaeolithic society away from a top-down group approach where, as we saw in Chapter 1, it has been languishing. The common issues in both approaches deal with the individual as an active social actor; the importance of performance in the creation of social life by such actors; and the importance of personal interaction as the context for the negotiation of social life.

However, frameworks and vocabularies need questions which are relevant. I can identify two major areas where primate and structuration studies of social life touch on the long-term evolutionary questions which must be contained in Palaeolithic data. These questions are, in simple terms,

- what happens, socially, when you leave a gathering?

and

- how did social life get so complicated?

### *The release from proximity*

As soon as we move away from co-presence we encounter one of the principal questions of social theory, which asks

> how the limitations of individual 'presence' are transcended by the 'stretching' of social relations across time and space. (Giddens 1984:35)

The question is, quite literally, how can you be in two places at the same time? If society is performed into being during face-to-face interaction, when attention is at its highest, then how can a similar intensity be extended after your interaction partner has gone? Furthermore, how is it possible to conduct a similar relationship with people you have never met and yet make your presence felt?

Such a question has an obvious historical dimension. Moreover, it is highly pertinent to the Palaeolithic where the media and mechanisms for this stretching appear at first glance to be both rudimentary *and* developing.

This same question has also been identified independently by primatologists. Rodseth (et al. 1991:240) emphasize the importance of uncoupling relationships from spatial proximity in human rather than ape societies. They term this very aptly the 'release from proximity'. Quiatt and Reynolds (1993:141) discuss a similar problem in terms of social cognition, where 'going beyond' the information available is a hallmark of humans. Constructing social life through personal interaction is very obviously part of our primate heritage. Going beyond that and having equally intense relationships with artifacts like sports cars or pets (especially when no one else is looking) and the occasional 'love-affair' with a complex and unimaginable-in-detail entity like Greece or the Italian Quattrocento is something that we do and which, I am willing to bet, *Ardipithecus ramidus* almost five million years ago did not do. When people went beyond the rules of social life set by the immediate resources of their own bodies, voices and actions, is truly one of the Palaeolithic's big questions.

### *Complex and complicated societies*

The second question addresses the issue of performance. Here Strum and Latour have drawn a useful distinction between human and non-human primate *performed* societies. They recognize non-human primate society as socially complex and human society as socially complicated. For example,

> baboons live in complex societies and have complex sociality. When they construct and repair their social order, they do so only with limited resources, their bodies, their social skills and whatever social strategies they can construct. (Strum and Latour 1987:790)

Baboons need social skills in order to enroll others in the actor's definition of what society is (Strum and Latour 1987:795), hence the performance nature of the bonds in society. The body becomes an instrument for expressing and interpreting social value (Leroi-Gourhan 1993:Chapter 11). As a result, a baboon is best described as a *competent member* in a social context, which is

> a social actor having difficulty negotiating one factor at a time, constantly subject to the interference of others with similar problems. (Strum and Latour 1987:790)

The consequence is a limit to the degree of social stability since this can only be achieved as a function of interaction intensity and the frequency by which relationships, such as alliances in aggressive contexts, are produced.

The human alternative introduces complication into social life. 'Something is complicated', Strum and Latour argue, 'when it is made of a succession of simple operations' (1987:791). They regard this as essential to producing greater stability. As well as the body and social skills, humans also use materials and, most importantly, symbols to enforce or reinforce a particular view of 'what society is'. This has the effect of making social tasks less complex.

These elements are essential to answer Giddens' central question about how social structure exists *in absentia*, how it is stretched beyond the limits of co-presence. Simplification, by using symbols centred on people and objects, allows a variety of factors to be held constant in any social context. As a result the variable demands of social life can be sequentially negotiated one at a time (Strum and Latour 1987:792–3).[6] The *skilled practitioner* in a complicated society is therefore a specialist. She/he has the resources to effect time–space distanciation, that stretching of social life beyond the practical limits set on co-presence interaction by time, the body and space.

## Networks and their components

The bottom-up approach that I am advocating for the study of social life in the Palaeolithic requires a framework which can express interactions in time and space. Without such a methodology the questions raised above will remain unanswered. While structuration theory and primate studies provide a means of conceptualizing the problem, neither is particularly interested, as archaeologists must be, in the role of objects, either as the means to investigate social life or in their contribution as to how it is structured.

I have found that network analysis provides such a framework to formalize social concepts based on interaction and negotiation by individuals. Network analysis specifically counters the group-centred approach to anthropological and sociological analysis (Barnes 1972, Bott 1957, Maryanski 1993, Milardo 1992, Mitchell 1974, Turner and Maryanski 1991, Wellman and Berkowitz 1988). It is important to stress, however, that it is a form of analysis rather than a theory of social action (Boissevain 1979:392, Mitchell 1974:282).

In a network analysis individuals are creative, mobile nodes who form ties of variable commitment, content and duration. An individual's networks are constantly changing but remain the minimum level at which social relations can be investigated (Douglas 1973:89). The networks form a set of weblike contacts which have been described elsewhere as overlapping social fields (Grönhaug 1978, Lesser 1961, Paine 1967). Society ultimately becomes a network of networks (Boissevain 1979:392), a continuum as indicated in Table 2.3.

The following components of networks can be identified and need to be examined briefly before turning to resources and rules.

### *The ties that bind*

Individuals are knowledgeable social actors and the ties they create through interaction both bind and bond. The relationships which individuals construct (Table 2.1) are patterned by different forms of tie. Two in particular are impor-

Table 2.3. *A network model of society (after Boissevain 1968).*

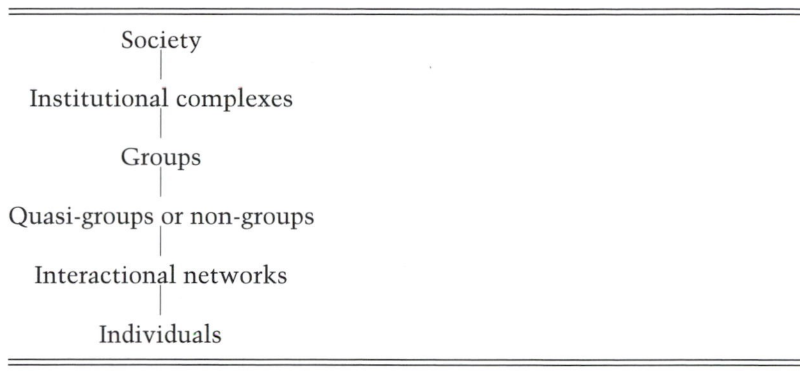


tant. Multiplex ties comprise several strands to a relationship forged between two individuals, for example a sister or close friend. They are multiplex because they are based on history and a variety of activities and contexts for performance. The ties might include affinal, economic, affective and social strands. The weave of the strands makes it likely that such ties will endure. By contrast, uniplex ties characteristically involve a single-capacity link in a relationship. Examples would include the social relationship with the greengrocer or bus-driver. The quality of the tie does not necessarily depend on the frequency of interaction. You may see your sister once a year at Christmas and the bus-driver every day on your way to work.

### *Density and connectivity*

Networks can be quantified to some extent through the density and connectivity of social ties which arise from interaction and ensuing relationships (Milroy 1987). The density of network ties examines the extent to which ties that could possibly exist among individuals do in fact exist.[7] A high-density network often implies highly standardized values conditioning individual behaviour, while low density is often correlated with strong individualism (Boissevain 1974, Turner and Maryanski 1991).

Centrality is a measure of accessibility. It is largely a function of the size and structure of the network and is generally higher where density is lower. The more central an individual the better able he/she is to bring about communication.

Transitivity of ties refers to the degree to which there is a transfer of a relation between non-interacting individuals. If A knows B and B knows C, then in a transitive tie A also knows C. High transitivity will result in high-density networks since the links which potentially exist are being fully exploited by talking through friends of friends. Transitive ties also measure the reachability of a network. This is defined as the number of links needed to reach a complete stranger and be introduced to them via a network of friends and acquaintances. The figure is surprisingly small. In populations ranging from 300,000 people to 200 million, only 3–5 links are needed to reach some randomly selected person, via an individual's multiplex network ties, and arrange for a personal introduction (Boissevain 1974, Jacobson 1978). These limited degrees of separation are an example of transitivity and clustering of ties where an individual can act as a broker (Turner and Maryanski 1991).

The properties of network structure have been examined graphically for their properties of density and connectivity (Figure 2.1). Information is one way of measuring the output from different arrangements. For example, Argyle (1969:309) discusses the structure of the network in terms of problem solving. Using five persons arranged in circle-, chain-, Y- and wheel-shaped networks, he reports Leavitt's work which studied how the different structures affected communication and hence problem solving. The circle was the slowest, made most mistakes and needed the most messages. The Y pattern made the fewest errors. Kapferer (1973) reports that the low-density wheel was the most efficient network for solving problems based on sharing information. This was followed by all-channel high-density and finally the circle.

Table 2.4 quantifies the properties of different spatial networks (Figure 2.1). Attention is paid to the extent and structure of the links that define them. The table illustrates some of the consequences for high- and low-density networks and the degree of centrality enjoyed by some nodes in some networks. One outcome of such measures is to show how the different structure of networks can influence the form of interaction particularly through the costs which depend on location (e.g. Mandryk 1993, Wobst 1976). The consequences of operating in either a low- or high-density network then become apparent. For example, Steele (1994) has simulated patterns of dispersal using network ties in three different lattice structures (Figure 2.2). This allows him to observe how traits are culturally transmitted between nodes in these networks. The density of ties determines how easy it is for a new trait to be adopted. He found that the weaker ties in his Poisson network and the lower connectivity in his Low Density network resulted in new adaptive traits spreading through the system faster. On the contrary, the very high density pattern of ties in his Tribal network produced its own internal resistance to the spread of new traits, thus underscoring how such structures can enforce behavioural norms.

### *The effect of age on network structure*

Network diagrams (Figure 2.3) with their ties and nodes are a useful descriptive device to express either the movement of individuals down their time–space paths (Carlstein 1982) or the flow of information and objects (Isaac 1972, Yellen and Harpending 1972). Networks persist because individuals routinely travel the same tracks as they create their social lives. But networks also change as the individual grows older and achieves different positions within them. A good

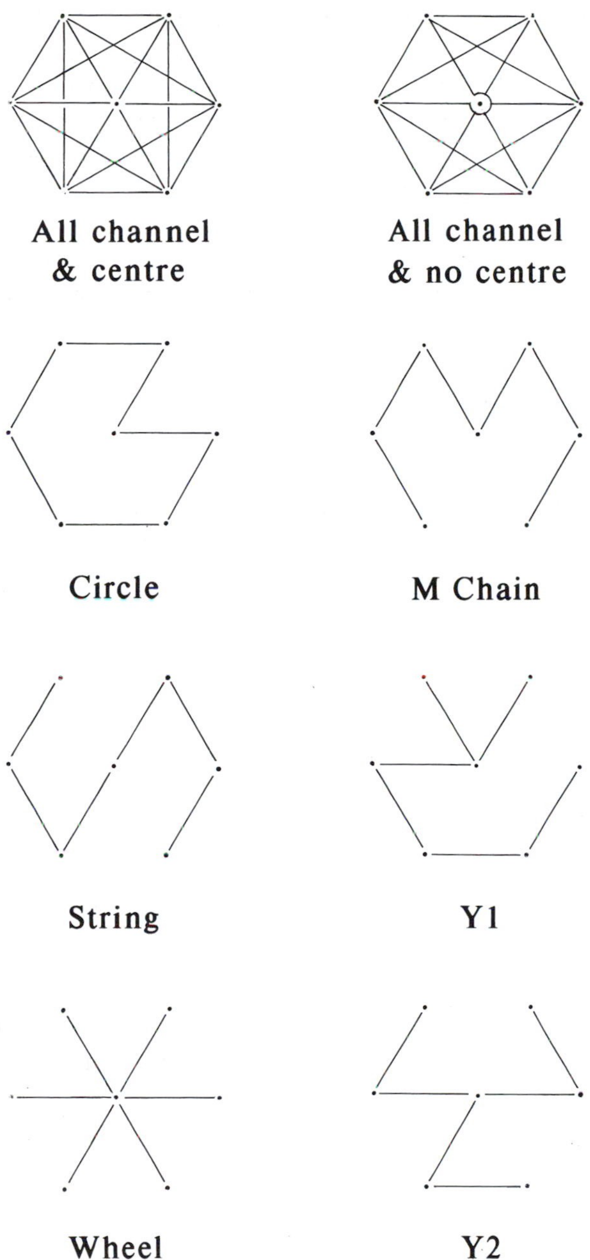


**2.1** Alternative network patterns using seven nodes and their information/resource flows (see Table 2.4).

Table 2.4. *Examples of variation in network structure. Density is calculated according to Boissevain's formula (1974).*

| | Density | Ties and connectivity | | | Number of ends | Number of ties in network |
|---|---|---|---|---|---|---|
| | | Centre to edge | End to centre | Edge to edge | | |
| All channel (*high density no centre*) | 87 | 0 | 0 | 1 | 0 | 18 |
| All channel (*high density centre*) | 80 | 1 | 0 | 1–2 | 0 | 15 |
| Circle | 33.3 | 0 | 0 | 1–6 | 0 | 7 |
| M chain | 27 | 1–2 | 3 | 1–4 | 2 | 6 |
| String | 33.3 | 1–5 | 6 | 1–4 | 1 | 6 |
| Y1 | 20 | 1–3 | 1–4 | 1–2 | 3 | 6 |
| Y2 | 20 | 1 | 2 | 1–2 | 3 | 6 |
| Wheel (*low density*) | 0 | 0 | 1 | 2 | 6 | 6 |

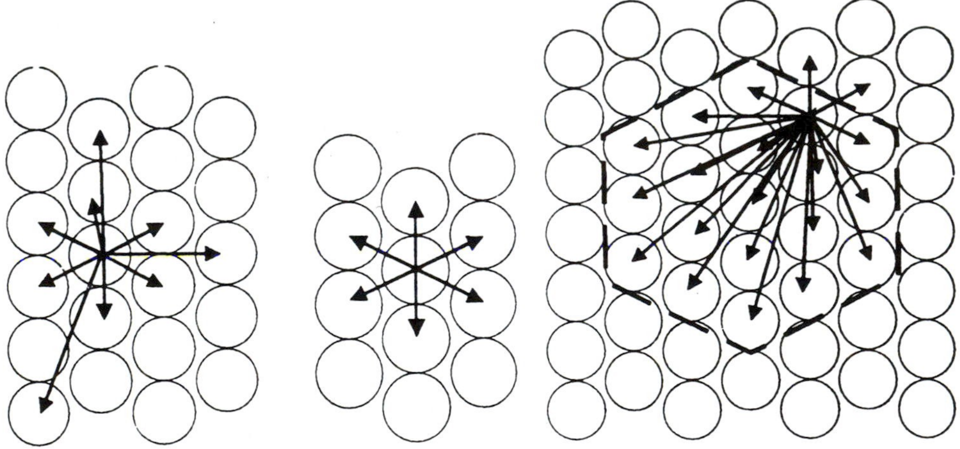

**2.2** Three model networks used in simulations of communication and dispersal patterns. From left to right, the Poisson network, the Low Density network and the Tribal network (after Steele 1994:Fig. 2).

example is provided by Wiessner (1982) where the number of negotiated hxaro exchange partners among the !Kung changes with age and commitments (Table 2.5).

It is not surprising that the greatest expansion of the hxaro networks occurs when the San are looking for spouses for their children (*ibid*.:74).

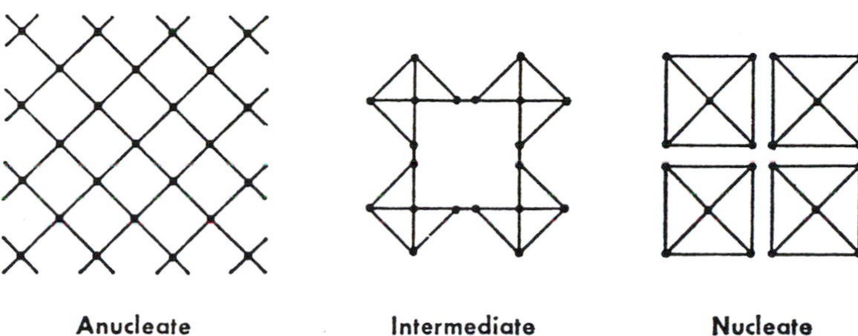


**2.3** The links and information flows between nodes which could be individuals or groups in open and closed networks (after Yellen and Harpending 1972:Fig. 15).

This example points to some of the basic structuring of networks by age. Obviously within this category individuals will build very different networks which, as defined through the frequency of interaction, will vary in intensity and duration. The standard deviations in Table 2.5 indicate such variation.

*Sexual division of labour and network structure*

Howell (1988) comments on network differences between sexes among the !Kung. The women have shorter generation times, twenty-eight years as compared to thirty-five years for the men (*ibid.* 1988:70–1). !Kung women obtain their social connections through marriage at a considerably younger age than their brothers and therefore their connectedness scores 'peak early'. Men are therefore much less likely to outlive their connections.

An example of the importance of the division of labour on network structure is provided by Maryanski and Ishii-Kuntz's (1991) study of role segregation among non-human primates. The study is based on Bott's (Bott 1957, Kapferer 1973) research into urban networks where she concluded that the density of interaction in family networks, measured by the number of ties and their emotional content, can explain the degree to which the roles of the sexes are segregated. Maryanski and Ishii-Kuntz measured the strength of ties between the sexes in non-human primates on a scale ranging from absent to strong. Their table (2.6) reveals that network density is closely related to the pattern of dispersal. Close-knit (high-density) female networks prevail when males disperse, and vice versa. When both sexes leave home then low density networks for both males and females prevail (Maryanski and Ishii-Kuntz 1991:417).

Maryanski and Ishii-Kuntz find support, irrespective of the reproductive arrangement in non-human primates, for Bott's main hypothesis, namely 'the greater the density of the network of at least one sex, the greater the level of role segregation' and, conversely, 'the less dense the network, the greater the degree of convergence in male–female roles' (Maryanski and Ishii-Kuntz 1991:417).[8] When the male and female dispersal patterns in Table 2.6 are

Table 2.5. *Hxaro partners by age category (from Wiessner 1982:table 3.1).*

| Age category | Number of San interviewed | Mean number of hxaro partners per person | |
|---|---|---|---|
| | | x | s.d. |
| Adolescents | 6 | 10 | 4 |
| Marriageable young adults | 4 | 16 | 5 |
| Adults with small children | 27 | 13 | 7 |
| Adults with mature children | 14 | 24 | 8 |
| Old partially dependent adults | 8 | 12 | 6 |

Table 2.6. *The density of network ties between the sexes in non-human primates and its relation to role segregation (from Maryanski and Ishii-Kuntz 1991:Table 1).*

| Roles | Dispersal at puberty | Network density pattern | | Species |
|---|---|---|---|---|
| | | Male | Female | |
| Highly segregated | Male | Low | High | Patas monkey |
| | Male | Low | High | Geladas |
| | Female | High | Low | Hamadryas baboons |
| | Female | Medium | Low | Common chimpanzee |
| Medium segregated | Male | Low | High | Common baboons |
| Medium segregated | Male & female | Low | Low | Gorilla |
| Joint | Male & female | Low | Low | Gibbons |

*Notes:*
Role segregation between mating partners was measured with respect to (a) leisure time spent together, (b) male involvement in child care, (c) shared maintenance activities, (d) dominance.

compared with Steele's simulations (1994:Figure 2.2), we see that male hamadryas baboons have a Poisson-type network, based on dispersal with low density and some transitivity. The females on the other hand would have a Tribal-style network based on very high, frequent interaction among all the co-resident females.

Finally, Table 2.7 compares the common chimpanzee (*Pan troglodytes*) with the smaller bonobo (*Pan paniscus*) and reveals very different sex-structured networks (see also Foley and Lee 1996, Foley and Lee 1989). The implication from two such closely related species, with very similar sexual dimorphism as measured by weight, is that social structure is derived as much from history as from

Table 2.7. *Variation in network density in two very similar species as measured genetically and by sexual dimorphism (Parish 1996).*

| Common chimp | Bonobo |
|---|---|
| Females disperse | Females disperse |
| Females solitary with infants [low-density networks] | Females form alliances [high-density networks] |
| Multi-male alliances [high-density networks] | Males solitary [low-density networks] |
| Females 84% of the size by weight of males | Females 82.5% of the size by weight of males |

the genes. So long as it does not affect reproductive success either pattern of sex-based alliance is possible. But while this makes it difficult to specify the ancestral hominid pattern for even more similar species – such as *Homo heidelbergensis*, *Homo neanderthalensis* and *Homo sapiens* – the implications for network density remain constant.

**Resources and network structure**

Now that we have examined some of the components which make up networks we can turn to the resources which generate particular structures. Turner and Maryanski (1991:550) have discussed the content of networks in terms of three interlinked resources: emotional, symbolic and material. These are available for the negotiation of the social ties between individuals. Table 2.8 presents a model of how individuals use the resources at their disposal for the purposes of constructing society through a framework of personal and global networks.

The emotional resources are those which create the high-density affective ties among close kin and friends. They depend upon face-to-face contact and frequent reaffirmation. It is from their intensity that the individual derives security. The constraint on the size of the intimate network is that the number of people with whom ego can interact at this intensity in order to achieve that psychological state is limited. The embodiment of interaction, which makes this network so distinctive, limits the relationships which emerge through performance to no more than a small intimate circle. Grooming time, whatever it involves, is a constraint for all primate intimate networks (Cheney and Seyfarth 1990, Dunbar 1992a).

Material resources can be illustrated by the exchange of marriage partners. For example, Sahlins' (1972:194–5) distinction between generalized and balanced reciprocity recognizes that the latter applies to alliance generated through marriage. On the contrary, generalized reciprocity has no counter-

Table 2.8. *Changes in resources and the content of interactions and networks.*

| | *RESOURCES* | | | |
|---|---|---|---|---|
| | Emotional (Milardo 1992, Boissevain 1968, 1974) | Material/exchange (Sahlins 1972, Valeri 1992) | Symbolic/stylistic (Wobst 1977) | |
| *NETWORKS* | | | | |
| INTIMATE (5) | •••• Significant others | Generalized ••• Household | • Immediate household | PERSONAL NETWORK |
| EFFECTIVE (20) | ••• Colleagues, friends | Generalized ♀♀♀ Lineage/village sector | •• Friends, relatives | |
| EXTENDED (100–400) | •• Friends of friends | Balanced •♀ Tribal sector | ••• Target group socially distant | |
| GLOBAL (2500) | • Neutral or antagonistic | Negative • Intertribal sector | • Non-target group socially very distant | |

*Notes:*
Filled circles indicate the relative use of each resource. The size of each network is indicated in parentheses. The networks are described in Table 2.9.

obligation 'stipulated by time quantity, or quality: the expectation of reciprocity is indefinite' (*ibid.*:194). This distinction is seen here as the difference between intimate/effective and extended networks relative to an individual.

The different relationships in these networks redefine the material resources used to author them. Hence the same materials can change from being gifts to becoming commodities between an individual's effective and extended network (Gregory 1982). As described by Valeri (1992:15), the transition from 'buying' to 'gift-giving' coincides with the creation of relatedness (Figure 2.4). As indicated in Table 2.8, material resources are more important in both the intimate and effective networks. But they will be very different in kind. Voluntary sharing of food, equipment and raw materials may be common in the former network. The latter will be dominated by the exchange of marriage partners and the ritual consumption of food in social situations. Finally, negative reciprocity – the attempt to get something for nothing – defines dealings with the 'other' in the global network where social distance is so great that people are strangers. The affirmation of alliance through exchange allows an individual to overcome otherness by bringing selected persons into his or her personal network.

Table 2.9. *A hierarchy of ego-based networks.*

**Intimate network** has a high investment of genetic and emotional resources. It provides the individual with ontological security that the natural and social worlds are as they appear to be (Giddens 1984). A high level of face-to-face interaction is involved.

**Effective network** deals with the logistics of daily life. These people are instrumental for ego in his/her pursuit of reproductive, economic, political and social ends. Material resources are an important means of creating bonds.

**Extended network** contains friends of friends who are known to ego and could be brought into the effective network if required. Symbolic resources, organized through style and material culture, are important when negotiating this network.

These three networks can be described as the **Personal network** which will vary in scale and content of the social ties from individual to individual. The varieties of negotiated alliance bond individuals within the personal network.

**Global network** is defined by 'otherness'. It contains total strangers or at best casual acquaintances. They can be reached, but in terms of alliance, built on interaction, remain neutral to ego. This is because they are either never encountered (as in small-scale foraging societies) or because there are limits to the numbers of people which although encountered (as in a football crowd or on the underground) can be interacted with and are not therefore the subject of further sustained negotiation. A feature of urban rather than foraging societies, the means used to cope with such co-presence would be an example of Goffman's unfocused interaction (1963).

The symbolic resources are, in human societies, expressed through material culture. The information content of such expressions has traditionally been analysed through the concept of style. Wobst (1977) pointed out that if information contributed to survival then it would be under selection. Hence stylistic behaviour follows rules and these can be assessed in terms of the target population which was receiving the message (Figure 2.5). If people in such a group were the subject of frequent, even daily contacts (friends and colleagues), then coding and sending information stylistically was unnecessary. In her analysis of a restricted code governing such frequent interaction, Douglas (1973) concludes that it is expressed in a poverty of ritual and symbolic/stylistic resources. She makes the point that

> The condition for a restricted code to emerge is that the members of a group should know one another so well that they share a common backcloth of assumptions which never need to be made explicit. (1973:78)

Restricted code thrives upon face-to-face contact, embodied performances and frequent interaction. The strong affective ties using emotional resources are therefore negatively correlated (Table 2.8) with the presence of symbolically organized resources expressed stylistically. Symbolic resources are dedicated to the effective and especially to extended networks.

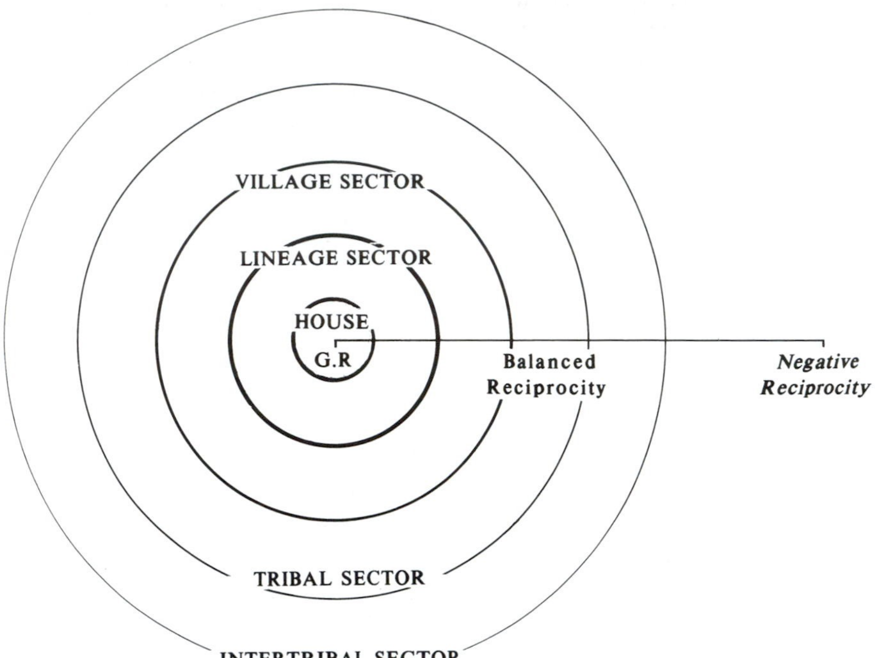


**2.4** Reciprocity and kinship sectors, where the latter represent a hierarchy of integration with changing relationships expressed through exchange and gift giving. GR = Generalized reciprocity (after Sahlins 1972:Fig. 5.1).

It is not my intention in classifying these networks and the resources that define them to start a search for their archaeological correlates. My aim is to provide a conceptual framework that expresses the selective pressure that all the networks in which an individual participates exert on negotiation, affiliation and reciprocity. In short, the sum of the networks affects decisions in all aspects of an individual's life. The social ties which form the networks both bind and bond.

## Rules to explain the size of networks

Two rules are important in limiting the size of networks:

- temporal, especially where affective behaviour involves grooming and language,

and

- cognitive, where our capacity to handle information is seen as crucial

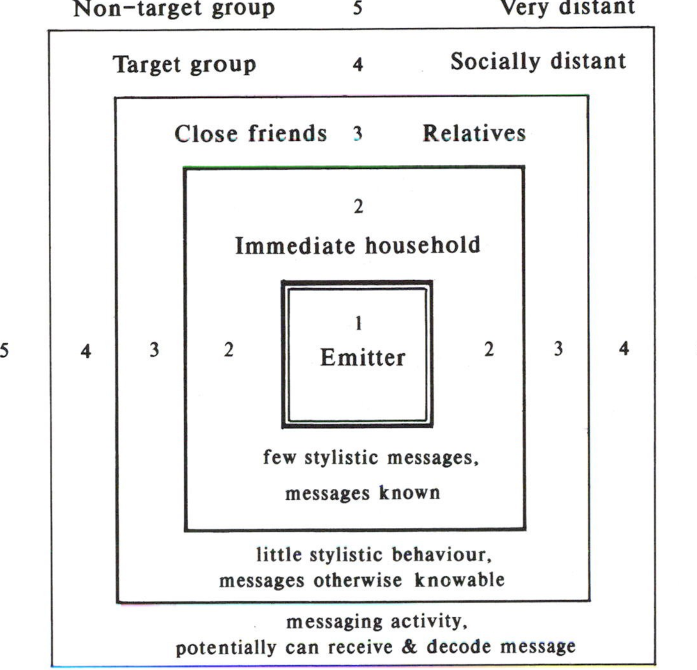


**2.5** The target groups of stylistic messages also form a hierarchy of integration which has implications for the design and display of visual culture (after Wobst 1977:Fig. 1).

### *Networks and time*

Dunbar (1992a) has raised the important issue of time as a resource in negotiation.

> Even if a [primate] species has the cognitive capacity to manage all the relationships involved in large groups, there may be circumstances under which the animals simply do not have the time to devote to servicing those relationships through social grooming. Relationships that are not serviced in this way will cease to function effectively; as a result, the group will tend to disperse and the population will settle at a new lower equilibrium size. (Dunbar 1993:687)

Cheyney and Seyfarth's (1990) study of vervet monkeys differentiated grooming between individuals at intervals of 5–10, 10–15, 15–20, 20–25 and more than 25 minutes. Dunbar (1992a) has shown how the amount of time per day spent grooming increases with group size. As the latter increases so pressures mount on individuals to form coalitions to counter harassment by other members of the group. In the vervet example these coalitions are small although total group size is large. In my terminology the vervet coalitions are comparable to the intimate and effective networks (Table 2.8). This is where alliances are negotiated in the context of cohesive group living.

Table 2.10. *Selected predictions for average group size, and for home range diameters for group sizes in the range 25–300, from Steele (1996:Tables 8.7 and 8.8).*

| | Average group size | Home range diameters (km) | |
|---|---|---|---|
| | Predicted from group size/ total brain and body weight | Primate model | Carnivore model |
| *H. habilis* s.s | 91.3 | 3.0–8.5 | 26.2–78.0 |
| *H. rudolfensis* | 74.7 | 3.6–10.4 | 32.4–96.2 |
| *H. erectus* | 107.6 | 3.7–10.6 | 32.9–97.9 |
| Neanderthal early a.m. | 308.7 | 3.6–10.5 | 32.6–96.8 |
| *H. sapiens* | 312.1 | 3.8–11.0 | 34.4–102.2 |

Among baboons the amount of time spent socializing varies between seven and twenty per cent of their annual time budgets. This variation has not led to appreciable differences in the social organization of these different populations as shown for example in mean group size. Dunbar concludes (1992a:42) that the major constraint is the amount of time that a baboon has to spend feeding.

Devoting about 20 per cent of the day (2.4 hours in 12 hours of daylight) to social grooming seems to be an absolute upper limit for non-human primates (Dunbar 1993:688). Even with high grooming rates group sizes are small, ranging between 30 and 40 individuals (*ibid.*:Figure 3). A human group size of 150 would, according to Dunbar's regression equation, need a massive 42 per cent of the total time budget to be devoted to grooming.

This would only be a constraint if permanent group stability was the goal of social grooming. Humans with their fission–fusion system which changes group size and membership can lessen the problem by reducing the size of co-resident groups. Alternatively, Dunbar argues, humans can use language as a grooming substitute. In the vocal grooming hypothesis, developed with Aiello (and Dunbar 1993), a relationship is claimed between group size and the size of the neocortex (Dunbar 1992b, 1993, 1996). The neocortex, quite literally the grey matter, is the 'thinking part' of the brain (Dunbar 1992b:473) and its expansion in the past two million years is why we now have such large brains.

Steele (1996) has extended this analysis and estimated hominid average group size (Table 2.10). He achieves this by comparing known primate group size with brain and body size. Moreover, by using body mass for the same comparative sample (Grant, Chapman and Richardson 1992) it is also possible to calculate hominid home range size according to either a primate or carnivore model (Table 2.10). The figures show a consistent pattern for all the later species of *Homo* and the archaeological evidence for these ranges is presented in Chapter 3.

Aiello and Dunbar argue that language provided a more efficient method of servicing the interactions which produce stable relationships within these larger groups (1993). It is a 'cheap' form of social grooming because several people can be 'groomed' in the course of a single conversation, thereby saving time. Moreover, information can be quickly exchanged about people not present. Time does not have to be spent observing others. What is minimally required is a concept of a relationship so that social information can be exchanged. Finally, Dunbar is insistent that

> The limit imposed by neocortical processing capacity applies only to the *number* of individuals with whom a stable interpersonal relationship can be maintained. This in no sense commits us to any particular way of structuring those groups (e.g., via kinship). (Dunbar 1993:692)

### *Networks, information exchange and the mind*

Time is very important in limiting the size of the intimate and effective networks. It appears that cognitive rules govern extended and global networks. The explanation for repeated demographic sizes (see below) relates to the capacity of the individual to process and store information (Bernard and Killworth 1973, Johnson 1982, 1978, Kosse 1990, Williams 1981).

But what is an item of information? I would define it as whatever is required to act as a knowledgeable agent in those interactions and encounters of social life. As an act of communication the relevant information will relate to other individuals and their interrelationships. What has to be exchanged, transmitted and remembered as information is the differential use of the emotional, symbolic and material resources which combined produce the rounded characters with which we interact.

The cognitive view of memory divides the process of remembering into short-term memory and long-term memory. Simon (1974) has identified the transfer of information from the short-term memory to the long-term memory, and its fixation there, as the key problem in understanding problem solving. The short-term memory is very limited. Experimental tests have shown that only some seven items, and perhaps as few as four, can be held in it. From there it takes about five to ten seconds to fix information in the long-term memory (Simon 1981:75). The 'magic number' of seven (Miller 1956) can be interpreted as a psychological restriction (Bernard and Killworth 1973) on our capacity to remember and integrate information.

Since the short-term memory has a limit on what it can hold, the solution to expanding memory has been to combine, or chunk, the information (Miller 1956, Simon 1981, 1974).[9] The term chunk, as introduced by Miller (1956), is deliberately vague but helps us to make the important distinction between the continuous stream of information (for example phonemes, words or sounds) and a chunk of that flow which is identified with either a particular psychological or social significance (Simon 1974:482).

Using the concept of an *information source*, which varies in scale from the individual to larger population units, Johnson (1978) has analysed the costs of integrating increasing numbers of such units, with five to seven such units representing a threshold in how information exchange is achieved. For example, the model of forager territories predicts that each local group should have six neighbours as this optimizes the geographical packing by reducing contact distances in a hexagonal lattice. When the number of actual boundaries are measured, as shown for example in Tindale's maps of aboriginal Australia (1974), the values are close to but less than the expected six contiguous neighbours. Johnson puts this down to the lack of hierarchy in hunter-gatherer society which, if available, would overcome the problem of integrating such information sources.

Elsewhere this has been discussed as a problem of scalar stress (Johnson 1982) which recognizes that the problem is not the number of people which need to be integrated, but rather the number of chunks or information sources. An example from the study of small-group dynamics helps to make the point at the level of individual interaction. Argyle (1969:231) showed that as the number of people in problem-solving groups of three to eight people increased, so the pattern of interaction changed dramatically. While individuals never, as we would expect, contribute equally to the group, it is only when size increases to five that a hierarchy of interaction occurs with one person emerging as a 'leader' in the sense of dominating the conversation. At the same time the other members' contributions decline dramatically and become much more equal. The structure of such a gathering is therefore both created by the individuals and influenced by the relationship which different numbers produce. It is an example of integrating information sources through the emergence of an integrating mechanism – in this case a leader.

The organizational problem of increasing scale, Johnson argues (1982:394), is a problem of communication stress where integration due to our own cognitive abilities breaks down unless Miller's magic number of five to seven chunks is preserved. Therefore, as long as the numbers of people can be reclassified from streets to towns to cities to nations, or from families to lineages to tribes, and the hierarchies or spans of control introduced to integrate such units, then the total number of people in the system can keep on growing. The psychological restriction of seven units which Bernard and Killworth (1973) identify as the control on group and sub-group size provides a sociometric example of this same principle.

According to Johnson (1982:392), increasing difficulties in communication arise because the 'potential exchange of information in group decision making should be a function of maximum potential group interaction'. Maximum interaction is where every group member interacts with every other group member on a face-to-face basis. This seems a very long-winded and time-consuming way to reach a decision. It is unlikely to guarantee either a reduction in conflict, because information is now equally shared, or better decisions, because information will need to be constantly updated. The solution is to

Table 2.11. *!Kung group organization in terms of organizational chunks (from Johnson 1982:Table 21.3).*

| Group | Organizational chunks | Units per group Range | Mean | Mean group population |
|---|---|---|---|---|
| Dry season camp | Extended family | 3–4 | 3.5 | 40.00 |
| Rainy season camp | Nuclear family | 2–6 | 3.08 | 14.83 |
| Extended family | Nuclear family | 1–5 | 3.00 | 11.43 |
| Nuclear family | Adult | 2–3 | 2.10 | 3.43 |
| Social unit | Adult | 1–3 | 1.86 | 2.96 |

provide spokespeople and reorganize the number of units by chunking (Williams 1981:248).

Johnson (1982) provides an example of chunking which produces an amended organizational structure. The data come from Yellen's (1977) study of !Kung campsites, where the numbers of people varied from a mean of eleven to one of forty for the larger camps (Table 2.11). However, Johnson's analysis shows that the number of chunks remained constant at around three units per camp. What happens therefore is that larger aggregations of people are integrated by people camping not as nuclear families, as they do in the smaller camps, but as larger extended families.

By increasing (chunking) the size of the units the communication stress that would be expected from an increase in numbers is compensated for, and aggregation can proceed without necessitating a formal hierarchy to achieve integration.

These limits are explained by Kosse as the cognitive load which individuals can carry when running a face-to-face network. This maximal unit is set by Kosse as $500 \pm 100$ people (Kosse 1990:291). However, we have already seen through a network approach that although we may know the names of 500 people, we do not know all the relationships between them (see below, Colson 1978). Knowledge of relationships decreases through the personal network from the intimate to the extended zones. As knowledge based on face-to-face, regular contact declines, so this is replaced by the increased use of symbolic/stylistic signalling.

### The demographic size of networks

These resources and rules can now be put into context by examining the demographic size of the four networks defined in Tables 2.8 and 2.9. Since networks using all three resources are common to all human societies, we can use data based on network analysis in contemporary industrial, urban societies, supplemented by observations in traditional rural communities.

*Personal Networks*

*Intimate*

In a cross-cultural study of western societies Milardo (1992:Table 1) discovered that the number of people interacting at the highest intensity with ego ranged on average from three to seven persons, with an overall mean of five. These were people whom respondents categorized as important, those significant others. Intensity is measured by the frequency of contact usually involving face-to-face contact. In Milardo's sample only 50 per cent of the people in these networks were immediate kin, a point emphasized in a study of a Toronto neighbourhood community (Wellman, Carrington and Hall 1988). This is perhaps surprising given the argument of kin selection (Quiatt and Reynolds 1993) and where we expect greater cohesion between related individuals to protect and promote their genetic resources. Rather, the important feature of the intimate network is its stability and persistence rather than the genetic capital it represents. This unit, which Williams (1981:249) calls a household, does form a network for economic, social and political calculations in all societies. The high costs of creating the network, for example through parenting, care giving and the demands of buddy-friendships, are only repaid if the social bonds so created stand the test of time. The intimate network is above all a security network, providing an individual with unspoken and unquestioning support. This assurance contributes to the confidence and trust that the natural and social worlds are as they appear to be to the individual (Giddens 1984:375). The ties are therefore multiplex and high density. Multiplex ties comprise several strands to a relationship forged between two individuals, for example a brother/sister or close friend. They are multiplex because they are based on history and a variety of contexts for their performance. They are high density because the number of ties which could possibly exist between two individuals do in fact exist (Boissevain 1974, Milroy 1987, Turner and Maryanski 1991).

*Effective*

These are the people who provide the individual with material and emotional assistance during the routines of daily life. Milardo (1992 :Table 2) found that the average size of this network (which he called the exchange network) was twenty persons and that kin members dropped to 40 per cent of the named network (see also Cubitt 1973). The range of average network size in his eight samples was from 10.05 to 22.8 people. Milardo noted considerable variation. If 95 per cent confidence limits are placed around the means of the samples then most individuals will, he suggests, have effective networks ranging from six to thirty-four members.

A classic example of the effective network can be found in Thrasher's (1927) study of Chicago neighbourhood adolescent male gangs. In a sample of 895 gangs, 90 per cent had fewer than 50 members while 60 per cent ranged in size from 6 to 20 members. Thrasher explained the dominant gang size, or clique, by the necessities of maintaining face-to-face relationships. This interactional basis set limits on gang size where what was said by one member of the group could be heard by everyone. Fission took place when common experience, maintained by a high intensity of interaction and performance, broke down (Hare 1976:215).

The effective network is less permanent and stable than the smaller intimate network. The ties between individuals are both multiplex as well as uniplex or single stranded. These multiplex ties are well illustrated by Damas' (1972:24–5) discussion of sharing practices among the Copper Eskimo. Their system of *piqatigiit* recognizes fourteen major divisions of the ringed seal which are shared out among that number of partners. The successful hunter will on other occasions receive a designated portion when one of his other partners makes a kill.

Colson (1978) has shown among the Gwembe of Zambia how reasonably permanent coalitions of lineage mates usually ranged from ten to twelve persons. Interactions with the dead were also part of these effective networks and for that reason between eight and fifteen ancestral shades, who might intervene in human affairs, were generally considered sufficient for each individual. When combined, this would produce an effective network for the Gwembe of between eighteen and twenty-seven people. Among the !Kung, Howell (1988) has estimated that the combination of their demographic probabilities and kinship rules results in some sixteen relatives per person.

*Extended*

This is the network of acquaintances and friends-of-friends. The ties that ego has with people in this network will vary in terms of whether they are currently active or passive. It will include people where interaction is a card at Christmas as well as those who are met at the workplace or the local shops on a regular basis. Most of the network ties will be uniplex rather than multiplex. The difference would be your interaction with a service provider, such as a shop assistant, as compared with a close friend or relative.

In particular the strength of transitive ties will be significant in shaping the network. These ties measure the degree to which there is a transfer of a relationship between non-interacting individuals (Milroy 1987, Turner and Maryanski 1991). The effective and extended networks are therefore distinctive. Milardo (1992) discovered only a 25 per cent overlap in membership between the extended and effective networks. Temporary coalitions may also be produced from within the extended network, for example the fifteen-strong work parties recruited among the Gwembe (Colson 1978), but these are short lived and dependent upon context. Such coalitions could also include people from the effective network.

The size of the extended network is more difficult to estimate. The basis of acquaintanceship and the category friends-of-friends is often vague and difficult to define for the purposes of quantitative assessment. Milardo (1992:455) cites Gurevich's study of 27 volunteers who recorded everyone with whom they interacted over a 100-day period. The average was 400 people but the range was from 72 to over 1,000. Barth (1978:175) records a similar experiment over a 14-day period where he interacted with 109 different people and his younger colleague in the same period with 175. Boissevain (1968) calculated his extended network to be 300 persons which is a figure that Colson (1978) suggests for an individual in the Gwembe District.

Bernard and Killworth (1973) have examined the structure of groups and sub-groups in terms of the matrix of interactions between individuals. They conclude that a psychological restriction exists on the number of people or units which can be integrated. They conclude with the hypothesis that 'any group of more than at most 140 elements must form its own sub-groups, and in so doing produce its own formalised hierarchy to deal with this' (Bernard and Killworth 1973:184). A link between a recurrent network size of 150 supported by bonds created through language has been identified by Dunbar (1993:686). Larger extended networks can be built by clustering ties as well as by using transitive ties to overcome the psychological restrictions that lead to problems of integration and interaction.

These estimates, while not entirely satisfactory for determining the size of extended networks, do point to three conclusions. Firstly there is tremendous variation in the size of networks between individuals (Killworth, Bernard and McCarty 1984, 1990). This confirms the utility of network models rather than group-based studies of society, since variation at the level of the individual must be expected in the past and was the material for selective change. Secondly, as Milardo comments, this tremendous variation emphasizes the remarkable influence that the tiny intimate network of five persons has on an individual's decisions, security and network building in comparison to

> the sheer number of people contacted in the routine business of daily living and the breadth of opportunities they present or deny in terms of opportunities for social comparison, companionship and access to scarce resources. (Milardo 1992:455)

Finally, we must conclude that only a finite number of ties can be effectively forged. New ties can only be made by surrendering some and replacing them with others (Wellman, Carrington and Hall 1988). Hence the effective and extended networks will see a good deal of interchange and much less stability in composition than the intimate network (Boissevain 1968:547).

In summary, a figure of between 100 and 400 people represents the best approximation we currently have of a person's extended network. When added to that person's intimate and effective networks, the complete personal network is of the order of 130 to 430, with an upper limit of possibly 1,000 people.

### *Global Network*

While the three subdivisions of the personal network have finite sizes, the global network, since it deals with the social category of 'otherness', is potentially unbounded. More specifically, it represents opportunities for new ties to be brought into the personal network. Some investigation of how individuals in western societies operate networks at this scale has been undertaken to assess the extent of reachability and hence recruitment (Killworth, Bernard and McCarty 1984) and as we saw earlier, experiments show that only three to five links are needed to arrange for a personal introduction with someone selected at random (Boissevain 1974, Jacobson 1978). These limited degrees of separation are an example of transitivity and clustering of ties.

But what of global network size at low population densities? Kosse (1990:278) has identified a threshold of 2,500 which she regards as the upper limit on the area-level adaptation (Hill 1978). This is supported by Wiessner's estimate of 2,000 people in the !Kung hxaro trading system (1982) and by the mean figure of 2,815 people in Constandse-Westermann and Newell's survey of Band-level linguistic families (1991, Newell and Constandse-Westermann 1986). At these densities the likelihood of encountering anyone from the wider population, apart from indirectly through trading partnerships, was remote until modern communications appeared. Interestingly, Bernard and Killworth's sociometric study (1973:183) produced a figure of 2,460 as the maximum group size which has some stability without a formalized hierarchy governing interaction.

Beyond this unit, as in Alaska,

> There are many stories of small groups of men hunting deep in the hinterlands suddenly (and accidentally) encountering each other and having some very tense moments. First, they would try to identify themselves to one another's satisfaction. Failing that, the result varied depending on the relative numbers and condition of the people involved. If the groups appeared to be of equal strength, the tendency was for both sides to withdraw, thenceforth to avoid each other. If one group was obviously stronger, violence of some sort often followed. (Burch 1975:25)

The lone seal-hunter, who went adrift on sea ice and could not identify himself to the villagers where he washed up, was usually beaten to death (Burch 1975). In this way the limits to social interaction were primarily defined through a principle of exclusion which had to be negotiated away (Mauss 1967:79).

For those of us living in industrial societies our personal and global networks might appear unbounded thanks to unprecedented opportunities for travel and communication. But it is a relative concept. Even with jumbo jets, mobile phones and the Internet we cannot construct, even if we wanted to, personal networks with all six billion people on the planet. Neither can an individual among the Gwembe Tonga of Zambia build a personal network with everyone in a neighbourhood of only 600 people (Colson 1978). Neither is it likely that they would do so if the Internet and mobile phones were freely available. As Colson discovered, the Gwembe may give the impression that the 600-strong neighbourhood was bound up in a single network with a high rate of interaction. For example, everyone was known by name by everyone else. But,

> closer inspection of the evidence suggests that in fact they restricted intensive interaction to a small fraction of those available to them, and handled contacts with the rest as though they were members of the crowd or by a superficial courtesy which permitted them to meet and pass on without further involvement. *Such courtesy required recognition of an encounter rather than assignment of persons to roles or their treatment as complete persons.* (Colson 1978:153, my emphasis)

This example underscores the resource of time in forming relationships through interaction. The problem is not so much remembering people as having time to service the relationships with the appropriate resources (Table 2.8). This dichotomy is nicely described by Colson as 'people shock' (1978:155), experienced by her, and many anthropologists, working in communities which, by western urban standards, are tiny but which are overpowering to us in a way that the millions of people in New York are not. The answer is that the Gwembe have a similar way of coping with a crowd as we do. Their equivalent of staring straight ahead, talking if you have to about the weather and apologizing (if you are British) when someone steps on your foot, is contained in a comparable ritualized greeting ceremony (see Chapter 3).

The important point is that knowledge of names may be one thing but the ability to negotiate relationships through interaction is something else entirely. We can remember a lot of names but negotiate comparatively few relationships, because of time constraints, at the level of the intimate and effective networks. We are limited by the resources which define these two networks from including more than a certain number of people within them. If these networks are to function by supplying us, as individuals, with ontological security, defined as the

> confidence or trust that the natural and social worlds are as they appear to be, including the basic existential parameters of self and social identity (Giddens 1984:375)

then time has to be devoted to them since they require considerable expenditure of emotional resources.

What humans have developed, Colson argues, is unrelated to the size of our global network within which we make our way. It is our ability to *exclude* so that the intensity of interaction with those in our personal network is held constant. This exclusion is directed by the rules governing interaction and the different resources which are available. Out of such interaction emerge individuals who appear as rounded characters, capable of engaging our sympathies and making demands which must be met (Colson 1978:151), for example through generalized and balanced reciprocity and the mutual exchange of visual information (Table 2.8).

### Rules in action: hunter and gatherer magic numbers

These network sizes of 5 (intimate), 20 (effective) and 100–400 (extended) are familiar in demographic studies of hunter-gatherers. Here they have entered the literature as Birdsell's 'magic numbers' (1958, 1968, 1976). These consist of

- nuclear families of 5 persons
- a local group/minimum band of 25 with ranges of 20–70 people normally associated with a named locality (Peterson 1986, Stanner 1965, Williams 1981:240, Wobst 1974:170)
- an effective breeding unit or connubium with ranges of between 150–200 people, and where population numbers were of sufficient size to cope with any stochastic fluctuations in sex ratios, mortality and fertility (Howell and Lehotay 1978, Williams 1974, Wobst 1974)
- the much-disputed dialect tribe, or maximum band, of 500 and with a wide range (Burch 1975, Constandse-Westermann and Newell 1991, Dixon 1976, Tindale 1974).

The point about these 'magic numbers' is that they have become the demographic institutions of Palaeolithic hunter-gatherer society. They provide a good example of the one-way, top-down approach to the study of society which I have been arguing needs revising. The demographic patterns exist but do not have to be interpreted as proof for a group based model of society.

I contend that recasting these groups as networks, constructed by and centred on the individual, as many anthropologists advocate (Bahuchet 1992:247, Carrithers 1990, Guemple 1972:75, Morris 1982:150, Wiessner 1982, Wilmsen 1989:180), rather than on the institution of the kin group and the breeding population, provides a more flexible approach to key issues such as cultural transmission (Steele 1994) and the formation of society. The approach also facilitates cross-species comparison in social behaviour and network ties (Maryanski and Ishii-Kuntz 1991, Maryanski 1996) where the relationships defined by emotional, material and symbolic resources differentiate the extent of network elaboration.

## Summary

While Giddens may point out that '"Society" has a useful double meaning . . . signifying a bounded system, and social association in general' (Giddens 1984: xxvi), he also reminds us that in practice these boundaries are rarely specifiable and that it is the variety and cross-cutting of social systems which is important. This is one reason why I have used a network approach to help define what we mean by social life in the Palaeolithic. However, the problem is knowing where to start. One route is to proceed from the top down. This route supposes that society exists as a structure. It is often presented through architectural metaphors of construction and edifice. Once assembled, these societies are then lived in, with people entering and exiting the building but having little impact upon its design. A second route begins with the interactions between individuals which is the scale at which social life takes place irrespective of the size of that society or its material complexity. In a bottom-up approach these actors then negotiate with each other and in so doing perform society into existence. Obviously the key point is persistence. How do any performances last longer than those fleeting moments? How do they leave a trace which is then built into higher-level relationships and the persistence of social forms? The answer can be found in the dual nature of structure where action both enables and constrains (Giddens 1984, Hinde 1976). Structure and interaction are a two-way process. It is involvement with the world through social life, and the compromises/constraints this activity holds, which makes the performative view preferable to the structural model that society somehow precedes us. Society does not make us or vervet monkeys into social beings. First and foremost we are all social actors whose involvement with the world makes society the rich, individual experience, that it is for all of us. It is only when the anthropologist visits the !Kung, or the primatologist the chimps at Gombe, or the archaeologist the ice age Dordogne, or the sociologist the neighbourhood gangs of Chicago, that we feel the need to compare structures beyond the involvement of people, and animals, in the immediacy of social life.

I have proposed in this chapter that the way to carry these arguments into the Palaeolithic, which traditionally has resisted the individual as an object of analysis and where the rarity of social data is usually bemoaned (Chapter 1), is to examine the rules and resources which organize interaction. This bottom-up approach identified the recurrent sizes of an individual's networks as dependent upon temporal and cognitive constraints. These vary between individuals but produce predictable outcomes in terms of the content of the ties which are negotiated and the sizes of the resource-based networks. Now that I have examined the patterning in human interaction, we can proceed to examine a framework for the study of social life in the Palaeolithic.

CHAPTER 3

# A PALAEOLITHIC FRAMEWORK: LOCALES, RHYTHMS AND REGIONS

Why do I go into such detail?
Because the charged atmosphere made every little thing stand out as a performance, a movement distinct and vastly important. It was one of those hypersensitive moments when all your automatic movements, however long established, however habitual, become separate acts of will. You take nothing for granted, absolutely nothing at all.

Raymond Chandler
*The Long Good-Bye*

I will argue in this chapter that investigating Palaeolithic society, rather than Palaeolithic settlement, involves two levels of analysis, *locales* and *regions*, which are linked by the rhythms of social technology. The strong spatial emphasis reflects the contexts of interaction and the construction of social networks by individuals. These two spatial scales provide the methodological piers in the bridge which has to be built between Palaeolithic data and the individuals and societies which produced them. They are spanned by a series of closely linked concepts, which I refer to jointly as *rhythms*. These actions, fundamental to the concept of agency, are of course invisible to the Palaeolithic archaeologist. They consisted of operational sequences, movements along well trodden paths and attention paid to others. Rhythms provide us with the conceptual link between the dynamics of past action and the inert residues of those actions. They have to be inferred from the artifacts left behind. They link the action to the region, the individual to a wider social structure and ourselves to the past.

In this chapter, locales are discussed in terms of the archaeology of *encounters, gatherings, social occasions* and *places* (Gamble 1998). The regional scale is supplemented by two further concepts: the *landscape of habit* and the *social landscape* (Gamble 1993d, 1995b, 1996a). The discussion of *rhythms* draws heavily on the insights of Leroi-Gourhan ((1966)1993) as well as on recent discussions of temporality and landscape (Gosden 1989, 1994, Head, Gosden and White 1994, Ingold 1993, Pickering 1994).

The purpose of introducing these concepts is to provide the missing vocabulary for the investigation of social life, including change and stasis, during the European Palaeolithic (Chapters 4–7).

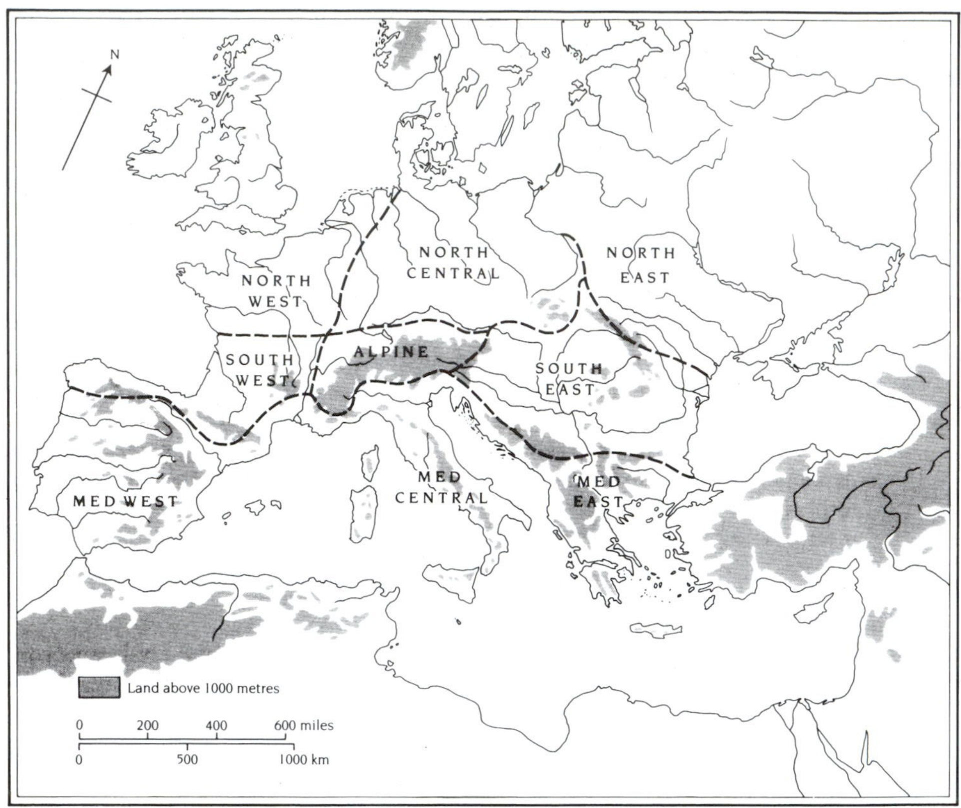


**3.1** A regional model of Europe for the investigation of long-term survival strategies by mobile populations (after Gamble 1986a:Fig. 3.1).

## Palaeolithic settlement reviewed

This framework builds on an earlier approach where I identified three behavoural domains – spatial, demographic and social – for analysing the Palaeolithic record (Gamble 1986a). There I drew up a simple regional model with nine divisions (Figure 3.1) to observe variation in behaviour that could be predicted from the ecological structure of resources. At a continental scale this variation in settlement can be related to latitude, longitude and relief. These unchanging factors controlled continentality, growing season and hence the productivity of resources within Europe. This was irrespective of the prevailing climatic conditions, glacial or interglacial.

Using this simple model it can be shown that at any one time Palaeolithic settlement varied across the nine regions of the continent, not in terms of artifact types, but rather in the density and frequency of occupation. There were also changes during the Palaeolithic whose behavioural significance could be traced not just through the appearance of art, new projectile points or knapping strategies but instead in terms of enhanced settlement histories at a regional scale. The comparative yardstick in the model was provided by ecology and selection on adaptive behaviour. This selection was viewed against the repetitive climatic changes which began 775,000 years ago with the first of the eight interglacial/glacial cycles of the Middle Pleistocene.

This may sound like a form of ecological determinism. However, I also argued (Gamble 1986a:61) that as far as settlement behaviour was concerned social relations were dominant over ecological relations (Ingold 1981). The latter might determine many of the patterns of long-term land use and site occupation but we should not expect them to account for all the variation in the Palaeolithic record. This was easy to assert since the nine regions were obviously large enough to encompass most social systems. But demonstrating the dominance of social relations was more difficult. The case studies which could show this concentrated on the Upper Palaeolithic where interregional contacts and exchanges could be demonstrated (*ibid.*:Chapter 8). The periods prior to 40,000 years ago seemed dominated by ecological rather than social relationships (Chapter 1 this volume). In retrospect this conclusion was unsurprising given that I took a group-centred approach to the social units which inhabited the nine regions. Moreover, my bridging argument between the statics of the evidence and the dynamics of past behaviour was largely based on ecological priorities.

The present approach still takes account of the regional scale and the model (Figure 3.1) will be used in later chapters where the data are examined. However, I have expanded the approach to use locales and regions as a framework for a detailed analysis of Palaeolithic societies but now with those rhythms, the generators of social life, acting as the bridge. I have also chosen these levels to counter the observation that many discussions of adaptation tend to be overspecific. We need to achieve, as Gould has pointed out (1994:28), the right level of abstraction that the data will support. On the one hand we do not want to treat archaeology as an exercise in working towards definitions, and on the other we must not leave the theory stranded from the data for want of a methodological bridge. It is with this narrative requirement in mind that the three analytical levels – locales, rhythms and regions – have been identified.

## A framework for studying Palaeolithic society

In previous chapters I repositioned the study of Palaeolithic society to focus on the individual, the creation of networks and the role of performance in social life. This approach means that social archaeology no longer begins with the richer record of the Upper Palaeolithic but instead extends throughout the hominid record, from five million years ago to the present day. Instead of the central question being the origins of band society with its implications of group closure, style and ethnicity (Gilman 1984, Williams 1974), we are required to explain the 'release from proximity', where social relations came to be

Table 3.1. *A framework for studying Palaeolithic society.*

| LOCALES | *RHYTHMS* | REGIONS |
|---|---|---|
| Encounters<br>Gatherings | *Chaîne opératoire* | Landscape of habit |
| | *Taskscape* | |
| Social occasions<br>Place | *Paths & tracks* | Social landscape |
| INDIVIDUALS | ⟵⟶ | NETWORKS |

stretched across time and space, and the related question of social complication (Chapter 2).

In order to address these questions we need to bridge the various scales of analysis; the brief moments of interaction and five million years of complex social life; the locale where a gathering took place and the wider regions where social lives were independently performed; the individuals and the collective surface structures which they both created and which defined their actions. The focus that personal and global networks provide for the study of Palaeolithic society now requires a spatial and temporal framework (Table 3.1).

With this framework in place analysis can begin by treating the Palaeolithic as an interpretative exercise where we 'tack', rather like a yacht (Figure 3.2), between data and theory (Wylie 1993:23–4). In order to construct and confirm arguments we move from the precision of mint-fresh artifacts, so-called flagship sites, to the coarse palimpsest of heavily rolled stone tools, dredgers by comparison, found in river terraces (Gamble 1996b). Reconstructing behaviour involves tacking from the patches, whether fine or coarse structured, to the scatters of which they are a part. The point of such methodological manoeuvres is to contrast the scale of past behaviour as preserved in the archaeological record. As we shall see in later chapters, we *can* recover fifteen-minute episodes that took place half a million years ago and we also recover assemblages averaged across 70,000-year chunks of time. The tacking works because we can recognize through the structure of the record exactly what temporal resolution is attainable. Archaeology commonly relies on this method of making arguments, and the Palaeolithic is no exception, even though its spans of time are larger.

## Locales

### *The spatial arrangement of interaction*

Locales, rather than sites, are where interaction took place and is preserved. They take a number of forms. The starting point is the individual and her/his movement through their environment. This involves ambulatory perception

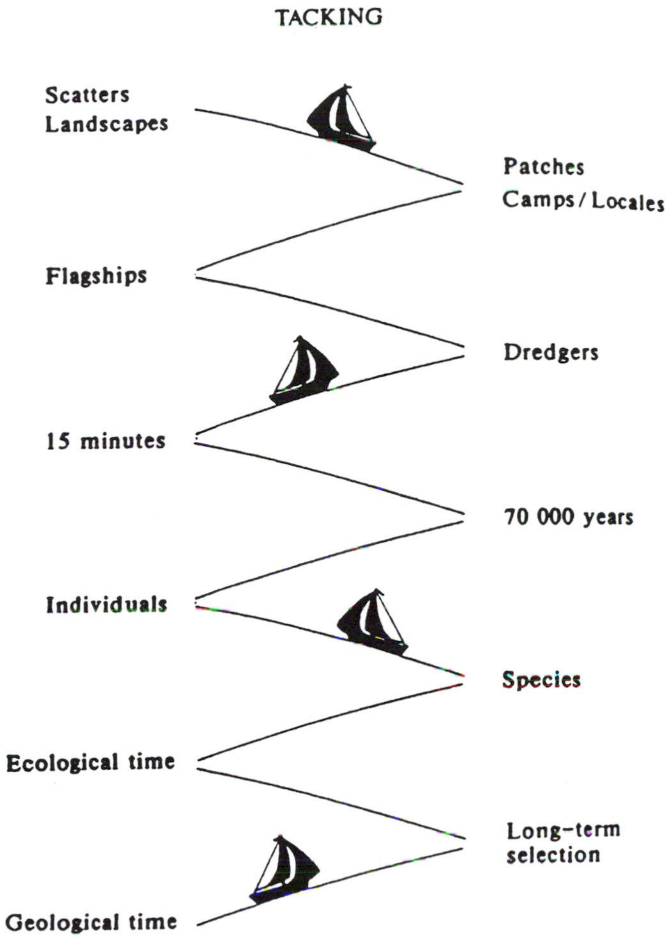

**3.2** 'Tacking' as a strategy to interpret the different scales and resolutions of data in the Palaeolithic (after Gamble 1996b:Fig. 7.1).

(Gibson 1979) along paths and tracks. From this starting point we can begin to build a model of interaction. As individuals move so they perceive the affordances, or use values, along the track they walk. Where their path intersects with another we can describe a locale or node where such perceptual interaction takes place. The *encounter* may involve an animal running across the hunter's path or another person coming into view. These encounters will also involve plants and raw materials such as timber or stone. These consequences of ambulatory perception can be illustrated by the example of a hunter's trapline (Figure 3.3 and Ingold 1986). Both the encounter pattern of foragers and the intercept pattern of collectors (Binford 1980) can be described in these terms.

The affordance of the encounter will lead to decisions about immediate and future action – eat the plant food, kill and carry the reindeer, make the spear,

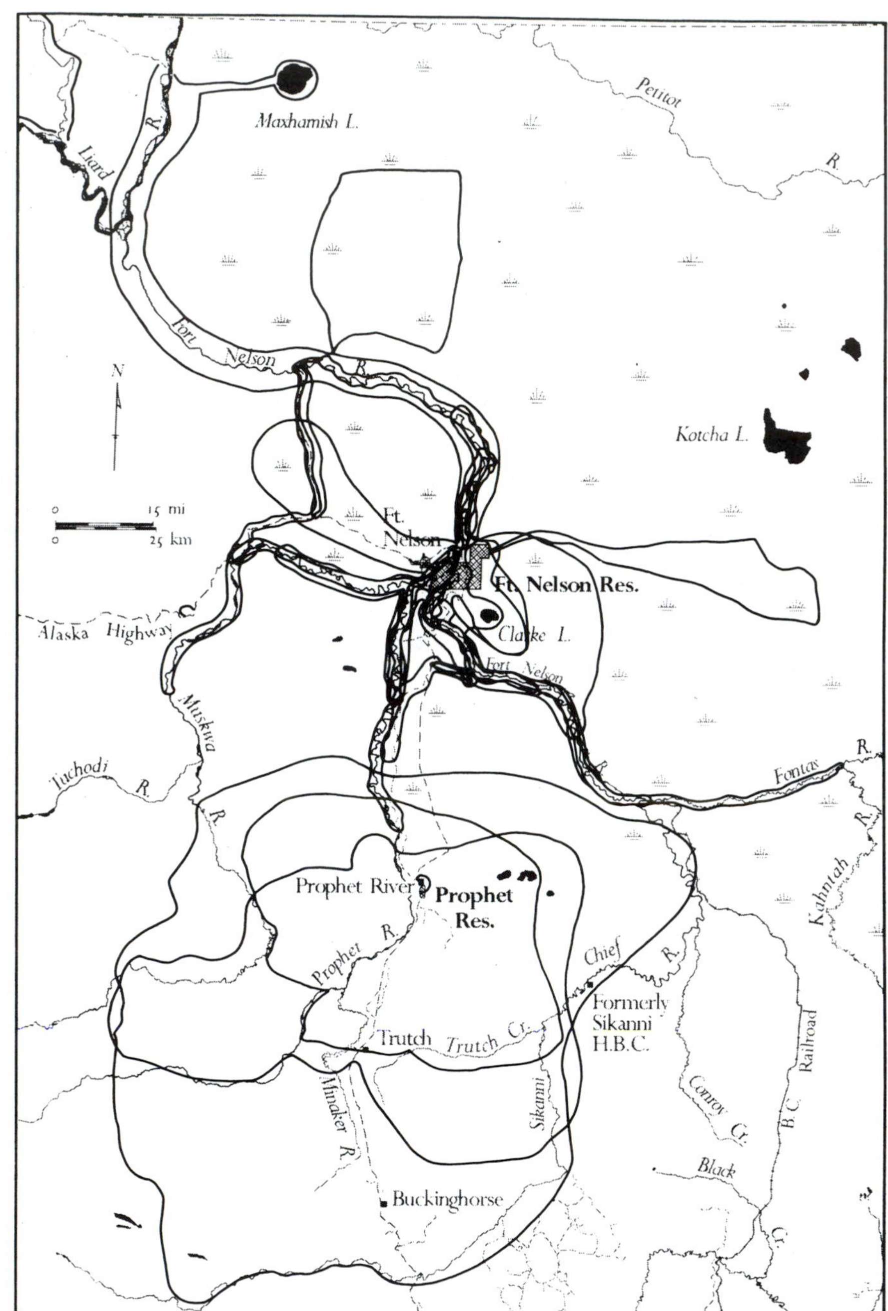


**3.3** Paths and tracks drawn and used by hunters based in the Fort Nelson and Prophet River reserves in the Canadian sub-Arctic. Prophet River people drew wide circles to show hunting that is done without a sense of limitation by terrain. Such areas are criss-crossed by individual paths. By contrast the Fort Nelson tracks follow a few wooded valleys and are limited by difficult muskeg country to the north (after Brody 1981:Fig. 15).

pick up the stone, greet the network partner, flee the stranger, remember and recount the information to others in your network. Encounters are information 'sound-bites' about the environmental track along which the hominid is travelling. They do not result in a residue that will survive.

*Gatherings* are enduring locales. They endure because of the quality and quantities of the residues left behind. These will accrue from either a single or multiple visits. Encounters happened all the time. Gatherings are the encounters which have survived. In both contexts the individual provides information which is either sent or exuded. This may literally be *embodied* in the form of words, frowns, gestures, blows etc. and can only be transmitted when the body is present. But such information can also be *disembodied* in the form of art, sculpture, letters, photos, tracks, artifacts etc. Here the individual has done something which traps and holds information through the affordances of cultural objects to extend co-presence no matter how far apart the parties are. It is such intensity which extends intimate and effective networks *in absentia* (Chapter 2), produces societies of immense individual variety and which also structures the archaeological record.

The actions which occurred at gatherings may have been solitary, for example when a hunter killed a reindeer, or they may have involved two or more actors building a hut, enacting a ceremony or butchering a woolly rhino. We do not have to specify interaction between people to infer a gathering which, adapting Goffman's (1963) terminology (Table 2.2), can imply either face to face interaction or its symbolic substitute. The only criterion is that a residue from that interaction is left behind.

Gatherings use portable resources such as food, stone and bodies. These materials form part of the performance between individuals as they negotiate social ties. They structure the interaction and, coincidentally, determine the spatial structure of the archaeological record. For example, the hearth preserves the gathering in the patterning of the residues which build up around it as interaction takes place. These patterns remain robust enough to survive a range of taphonomic processes (Stapert 1992, Whallon 1984).

A gathering identifies an individual's capacity for involvement and is, at this micro scale of analysis, a fleeting, or at best a short-lived, event. Context is generated from such associations, so that Goffman could declare that the proper study of interaction was not 'men and their moments. Rather moments and their men' (1967:3). In his example juries, banquets and race meetings are all moments. These are the structures which constrain the interaction rituals that take place between the gatherings of people at these events.

The size of the human body and its sensory faculties impose environmental limits on the spatial scale of interaction at the level of the gathering. Two people engaged in face-to-face interaction need, at a minimum, to be able to see and hear each other. These minimum conditions are only met by reasonably close spatial proximity. Dunbar (1993:690–1) has presented evidence which shows that human conservational group sizes are limited to about four people

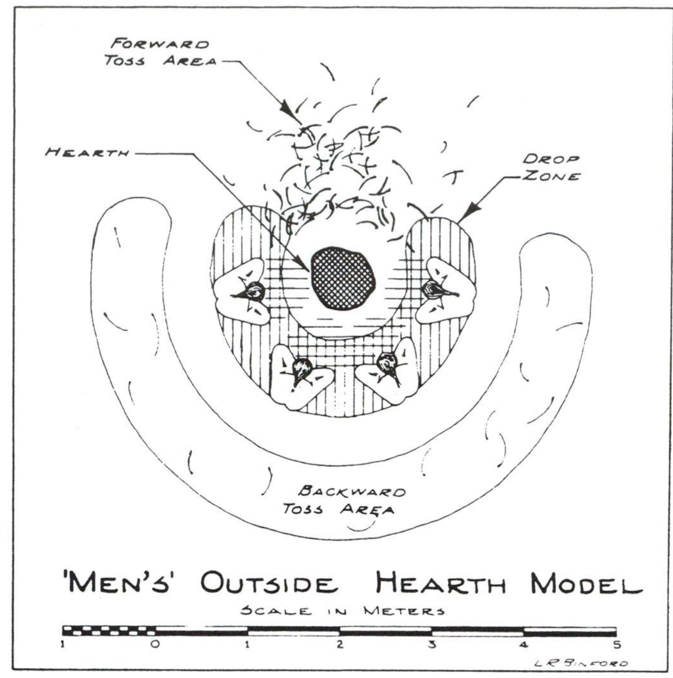


**3.4** Spatial patterns produced around hearths. Based on observations at the Mask Site in Anaktuvak Pass, Alaska (after Binford 1983a:Fig. 89).

(one speaker plus three listeners). As people join a gathering so cliques form within it, effectively splitting the group into conversational units of similar size. Clique formation occurs in multiples of four and can be readily seen among groups in refectories, pubs, theatre foyers, at wedding receptions etc. Two is company, three's a crowd, and four it seems is time to start another conversation (see Dunbar 1993:Fig. 4). One reason for these limits is the rate at which speech attenuates with the distance between speaker and hearer under normal ambient noise levels. Dunbar (1993) cites evidence that 1.7 m, nose to nose, forms the upper limit for comfortable conversation between dyads. Allowing a shoulder to shoulder spacing of half a metre permits five people to form a conversational ring (Figure 3.4). At this point the addition of other people into the ring is likely to result in a new conversation clique being formed.

An ethnoarchaeological example of such a conversation ring is provided by Binford's (1978a) study of a Nunamiut hunting stand. This was known as the Mask Site on account of the craft activities undertaken there. Activities such as sleeping, card playing, target practice and game watching were also observed in the three day study. When seated around hearths the dominant activities were eating and conversation (Binford 1983b[1978]:Table 21.6). Some mask making and card playing also took place in the horseshoe-shaped seating

Table 3.2. *Four seating measurements around the hearths at the Mask Site (Binford 1983b:[1978] 303).*

| Number of men in horseshoe circle | Mean distance of left kneecap to ember edge of fire | Mean distance between left and right knees of adjacent men |
|---|---|---|
| 3 and 4 | 62 ± 6.8 cm | 33 ± 4 cm |
| 5 | 71 ± 8.2 cm | 24 ± 3 cm |

pattern around the hearth. Conversation groups were rarely more than four or five people. This activity produced the dimensions shown in Table 3.2.

Since the hearths were between 50 and 75 cm in diameter (*ibid.*:Figure 21.3), men seated on opposite sides of the fire would be 190 to 217 cm apart when five were in the group and 174 to 199 cm when four were seated. The figures are very comparable to those quoted by Dunbar for standing gatherings. The Mask Site figures suggest that with five people face-to-face interaction will become more difficult. No data are available on whether the larger group size of five resulted in conversational cliques forming but I would suspect this was the case.

Binford does provide information on the spatial scatters that resulted from throwing away food items, packaging and the wood shavings from mask making. The residues are size sorted. Small items were discarded in a drop zone where the men were sitting. Larger items were thrown either through the fire (if no one was sitting there!) or over the shoulder. The drop zone forms a ring some 50 to 100 cm from the edge of the fire. The toss zone lies some 2.25 to 2.75 m from that same edge (Figure 3.4).

But, so long as the size of the body, rather than the performances in which it was involved, is the means to interpret our spatial information from caves and open locales (Binford 1983a) then, as Whitelaw (1994) has argued, such studies remain mechanical and descriptive. The hearth should also be the focus for further interpretation of the social use of space as indicated in Figure 3.5 (see also Wilson 1988:36).

However, we cannot simply identify patterns as manifesting a particular cultural meaning (Whitelaw 1994:229). This is a general problem when investigating the symbolic organization of space in the Palaeolithic record. The human body and its faculties may set conditions on communication but the content of the interactions which such acts service is not implicit in the spatial patterns they produce.

Without material culture there can be, from an archaeological perspective, no symbolic partitioning of space. The Palaeolithic record contains no evidence for interactions which took place in the equivalent of the street or across a crowded room. Residues must be generated and we have, as in this instance of middle-range theory, to understand what generates such patterns. The function of the Mask Site, it emerges, was not to watch for game as we might suppose,

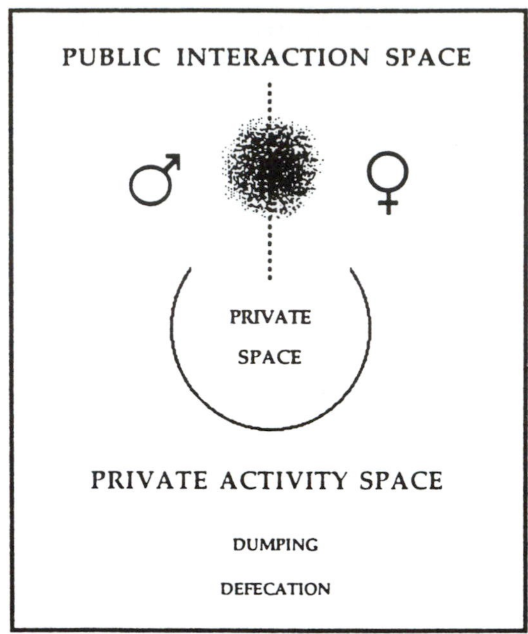


**3.5** A model of !Kung San hearth-side spatial organization (after Whitelaw 1994:Fig. 11.4).

but rather to engage in pursuits which reduced boredom, such as playing cards (Binford 1983b[1978]: 291). In other words to interact. The lonelier pursuits of mask making and watching for game took place when the gathering was small (*ibid.*:Figs. 21.1 and 21.12), the opportunities for interaction reduced and so less noise was made which might break the craftsman's concentration. The social context, as Binford points out (*ibid.*:315), may not change, but the pattern of interaction certainly does. It changes in expected ways as a function of gathering size related to the spatial arrangement of fires at the Mask Site locale. Gathering size and material structures such as hearths both act as uniformitarian anchors to the past.

Materials associated with gatherings are therefore best regarded as an extension of the social actor, a gesture as described by Leroi-Gourhan (1993), where gesture is synonymous with material action (White 1993a). The use-value, or affordance, in social transactions of portable resources, which includes tools, is therefore closely linked to their association with the body as it performed those social ties.

At gatherings, relationships will be negotiated through interaction using the appropriate resources (Table 2.8). The locales where this occurs are contexts for performance organized either by competent members, who bring only the resources of the body to such interactions, or by skilled practitioners who carry additional externalized resources to structure the gathering.

*Social occasions, places and the importance of attention*

I draw a further distinction between gatherings and *social occasions* (Table 3.1). The latter involve a context for performance which is established by objects disembodied from the actor. The social occasion commonly involves architecture as well as non-portable objects (Table 2.2).

However, a built environment is not necessary for a social occasion to happen. It can occur at a named locale invested with associations and meanings. In order to avoid confusion I refer to such social occasions as *place* (Table 3.1), which has been defined by Ingold as deriving its special character from

> the experiences it affords to those who spend time there – to the sights, sounds and indeed smells that constitute its specific ambience. And these, in turn, depend on the kinds of activities in which its inhabitants engage. (Ingold 1993:155)

That classic Palaeolithic site type, the cave, provides an example of place. Here is an affordance which provides shelter for humans and other animals. It may contain the spent resources of hyena bone lairs, the pellets from owls with their rodent remains, or the carcasses of bears which died during hibernation. A cave may also contain the stone tools, bodies, hearths, art and food remains of humans. The constraints of size, aspect, head height and floor surface, while not symbolically created as is the case with architecture, will nonetheless structure behaviour (Gorecki 1991, Nicholson and Cane 1991). The spatial pattern of interaction and the relationships it produces have to accommodate the cave's structure. As Parkington and Mills (1991) show in their comparative study of open windbreak camps and cave sites occupied by San people in southern Africa, the use of the latter must have been fundamentally different because of the arena they defined for social performance. The caves allowed privacy where no constant communal monitoring of herding or sharing was possible. But at the same time those close arm's-length relationships, so characteristic of interaction in the windbreak camps, were impossible.

The limestone cliffs at Les Eyzies in the Dordogne were and remain such a place for social occasions. Under their overhangs hunters moved throughout the Palaeolithic. While waiting for game to cross at the fords along the Vézère they made stone tools and later engraved antler, bone and the rocks themselves. These were places with associations based upon the rhythms of encounters, seasons, hunting, growing up, sleeping and eating around hearths and under rock abris. These rhythms established an hourly, daily, annual and generational pace. They produced forms of doing and adapting which recurred and persisted through repeated gatherings and social occasions over many millennia. We investigate them in our gatherings and social occasions of the excavation, laboratory, conference and publication which move to other social rhythms. The creation of form and pattern is what makes the deep past accessible to our inquiry. It depends, as an act of investigation, upon those associations being social.

These various locales – gatherings, social occasions and places – raise the important issue of *attention*. Wilson (1988:4) has shown how visual attention in such gatherings is of prime importance to humans, and to non-human primates. This is because attention contributes to our ontological security which occurs when the natural and social worlds are as they appear to be (Chapter 2).[1]

Locales are above all where social life is performed, where attention occurs. Moreover we do not have to specify these micro-scale contexts, such as gatherings, through structures which precede the individual. Neither, at a macro scale, do we need to hold to a notion that society precedes its actors. What is important about locales are the resources which these actors bring to them – their bodies and material objects – and how they are replicated in time and space.

What is important is the persistence of gatherings and social occasions, their recurrence in time and space. Are they attached to particular locales or are they moveable feasts around the landscape? How often do they occur: weekly, yearly or every generation? Do the resources used in making social ties have to be used in different ways? And what mechanisms exist for such persistence arising from nothing more than the interaction of persons with limited embodied and disembodied means of communication? These are all relevant to the wider question discussed in the previous chapter of how people, equipped with these social skills and information, use them to 'go beyond' (Quiatt and Reynolds 1993:141) the context of the gathering and the social occasion.

This is where the network as a unit of analysis proves important. It is the mechanism to answer the questions above since networks bond and bind individuals together. They provide a pretext as much as a context for co-presence to occur. As Goffman puts it, through interaction analysis

> We look within an act for the involvement it seems to express; we look to the involvement for the regulations by which it is bound; and we look to these regulations as a sign of what is owed to the gathering and its social occasion as realities in their own right. (Goffman 1963:247)

### *Sharing, co-operation and social structure*

At a wider scale of analysis Whitelaw (1991, 1989, 1994) has argued that variations in the layout of camps and the numbers of people living in them can be directly related to variations in the social relations of production within such groups. The data come from 1,762 different social occasions in 800 communities and 124 different hunter-gatherer cultures (Whitelaw 1991:141). Within this sample camp layout is studied by measuring the distances between shelters and houses and the patterns they take – for example circular or linear (Figure 3.6). Here we see that occupation density (the number of people per hectare) falls dramatically as the population size of the camp increases.

The degree to which co-operation and sharing act as a means to cope with the risk of dietary failure goes some way, in Whitelaw's analysis, to explaining the degree of clustering and interaction distance on camp sites. This produces three

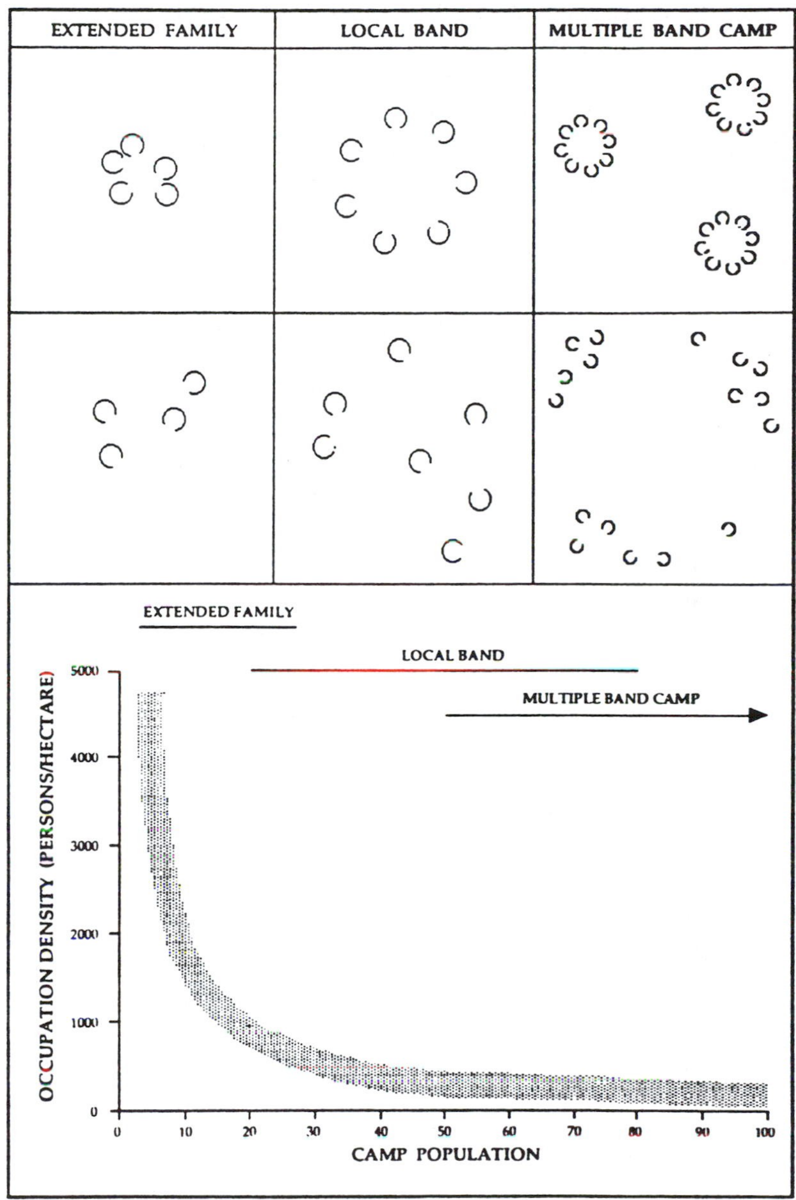


**3.6** General model of hunter-gatherer social organization, community layout and occupation density (after Whitelaw 1994:Fig. 11.6).

different solutions from the global sample of settlements (Figure 3.7). Firstly, in the Arctic and Australian arid zones where households are generally self-sufficient, campsites cover large areas with households widely spaced. Secondly, in the tropical rainforests, co-operation is often the best strategy for reducing risk. Hence the small, high-density Efe Pygmy camps in Zaire where many hands are needed to hold the nets in order to catch the dispersed, small

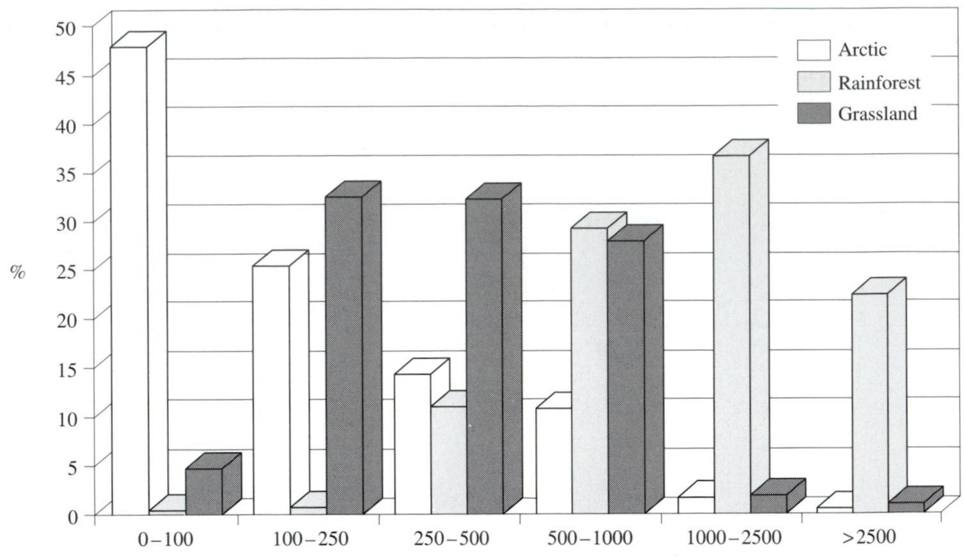


**3.7** Variation in hunter-gatherer campsites in three major habitats. High-density camps generally indicate co-operation between individuals and households whereas low density points to household independence (from Whitelaw 1989).

forest fauna (Fisher and Strickland 1991). Finally, it is in the savannahs and grasslands that the greatest range of camping arrangements is found. These range from low- to high-density camps, reflecting the mosaic structure of these habitats and the variable degree to which co-operation and sharing reduce risk. These elements of social structure are therefore mapped out in the spatial arrangement of people on campsites (Whitelaw 1991).

At a more detailed scale, Binford (1991) has examined Nunamiut campsites. He concluded that their camping patterns were structured by the organization of the workforce and consumers (*ibid.*:128) rather than by kinship. In summer security is lowest as the caribou are lean and prey densities low. Consequently

> alliances, emotional ties, and kin obligations all take a back seat to the fielding of as many hunting parties as possible with as many combinations of partners going to as many different places as possible. (*ibid.*:126)

These flexible parties are drawn from the large populations living on spring and summer camps. Households are interdependent at this time since the best chance of hunting success is for young males to form hunting teams and search for mountain sheep and small herds of caribou. But this co-operation, in contrast to Whitelaw's model, does not lead to small high-density campsites with households camping close together. Instead, on summer sites the campers are further apart (mean distance between tents 69.7 m) than at any other time of the year (Figure 3.8). In terms of spacing between tents everyone seems to be independent and indeed they are in terms of consuming the food once caught.

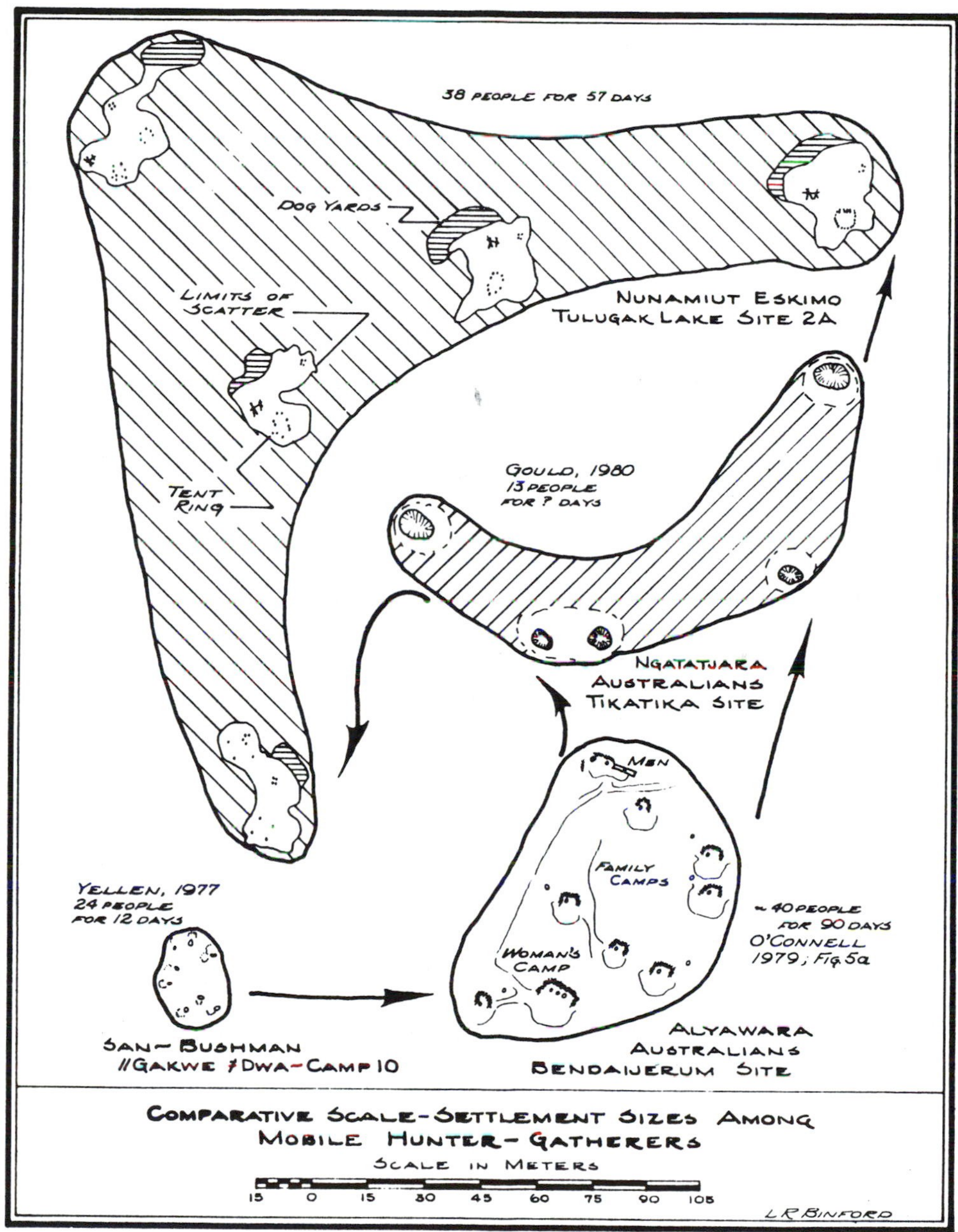


**3.8** Hunter-gatherer camp sites in different ecological settings (after Binford 1991:Fig. 19).

According to Binford it is not kinship but the separation between the organization of work and consumption that is preserved in spatial layout. In the winter and fall all campers are closer together (mean distance between tents 26.2–29.9 m) even though this is a time when people are living off stored food obtained during the fall migrations and household independence is therefore greatest.

However, although he comes to a different conclusion his main point is very similar to Whitelaw's in that social structure, defined here as the relationships based on variable levels of interaction, is preserved in spatial patterning.[2]

*Attaching and detaching rituals*

The challenge now is to unfreeze the performance of social life through interaction at locales as different archaeologically as the Lower Palaeolithic gathering of Bilzingsleben with its lake, trees, stone and bone anvils (Mania 1990) (Chapter 4) and Upper Palaeolithic Dolní Věstonice, where a social occasion was based on a built environment of huts, graves, ovens and middens (Svoboda 1991) (Chapter 7).

One way to approach this question is by considering attaching and detaching rituals of people to gatherings as well as to social occasions and places. For Goffman (1959, 1963), such structured interaction has its own rituals of engagement, glance, touch, speech patterns and disengagement. Indeed, the whole basis of social conduct could be described as a set of rules for guiding an individual in his/her attachment to and detachment from social gatherings (Goffman 1963:246).

Attaching and detaching rituals represent intense interactions for any highly social mammal, as the non-linguistic greeting ceremonies among chimpanzees and elephants testify (Moss 1988, Reynolds 1966). Sometimes they can even put the standing ovation for the leader at a political party conference to shame:

> The two subgroups of the family will run together, rumbling, trumpeting, and screaming, raise their heads, click their tusks together, entwine their trunks, flap their ears, spin around and back into each other, urinate and defecate, and generally show great excitement. A greeting such as this will sometimes last for as long as ten minutes. I believe that the greeting ceremony maintains and reinforces the bonds among the family members. (Moss 1988:128)

It is by such attaching, or greeting, rituals that an elephant defines its society as a network of negotiated relationships (Moss 1988:125). The elephant family unit of eight animals, and bond group of twenty, bears some similarity to our intimate and effective networks (Chapter 2). This is presumably because of the similar nature of the resources which are used to define relationships within each of these resource networks (Table 2.8).

## Rhythms and social technology

The rituals of attaching and detaching ourselves from gatherings and social occasions are two examples of social performance. It is the rhythms of the body – walking, treading, digesting, sleeping, making – which produce a temporality in human action uniting social and technical behaviour.

> Rhythms are the creators of space and time, *at least for the individual*. Space and time do not enter lived experience until they are materialised within a rhythmic frame. Rhythms are also the creators of forms. (Leroi-Gourhan 1993:309, my emphasis)

Table 3.3. *The grounding of social structure in individual agency. The scheme recognizes a permeable boundary between the two forms of consciousness (Giddens 1984:7).*

| | |
|---|---|
| Discursive consciousness<br>\| | *What actors are able to say about social conditions, especially the conditions of their own actions* |
| Practical consciousness | *What actors already know or believe about social conditions but cannot express discursively. This includes habit and routine* |
| - - - - - - - - - - - - - - - - - -<br>Unconscious motives | |

*Forms of consciousness*

Many of these rhythms can be described as habitual actions where, as Gosden has pointed out (1994:188), we can act in complex ways because much of what we do occurs without giving it much thought. Elsewhere Giddens (1984) has described this as practical consciousness and has drawn the distinction between this and a discursive or problem-solving consciousness (Table 3.3).

The difference had previously been particularly well put by Leroi-Gourhan:

> Most of the sequences we perform between waking and going to bed require only slight conscious intervention; they take place, not in a state of automatism where consciousness would be nil, but in a psychological twilight from which the individual is aroused only by some unforeseen occurrence. In the gestures we perform when washing and dressing or eating our meals or writing, the return to full consciousness is exceptional but it is decisive, and that is why I prefer to speak of 'mechanical operational sequences' rather than of automatic, unconscious, or instinctive ones. (1993:231–2)

This passage produces a striking paradox for archaeologists investigating why brains got bigger during human evolution. Why did selection favour growth in such an energetically expensive organ if all that it seems to do is carry out increasingly routine tasks? But the paradox probably stems from approaching consciousness with the model of cartesian dualism which separates mind and body. Instead, if we unite mind and body, as in the philosophies of Heidegger and Husserl, then we do not need to infer the world but rather we start with it, in it, of it (Magee 1987:261). This means that we do not have to construct a map or model of the world in order to interpret, organize and understand it. Practical know-how is transparent. It does not even pass through our discursive consciousness. Dreyfus describes the process as follows:

> A driver has the same experience shifting from first to second gear. He does a lot of fancy footwork with the clutch, but he may, at the same time, be absorbed in a deep philosophical conversation. *His coping need not enter consciousness.* (in Magee 1987:260, my emphasis)

It is only when something goes wrong, the gear won't engage, the door knob sticks, the pan boils over, that the actor reverts to traditional type by *noticing*.

She/he then becomes a problem-solving, rational animal as involvement with the world moves from practical to discursive consciousness.[3] As Leroi-Gourhan put it, 'mechanical operational sequences [practical consciousness] form the basis of individual behaviour; they are our essential element of survival' (1993:232).

*Archaeological detectives*

This unification of action, the involvement of individuals *in*, rather than detached and separate *from* the world, is directly addressed by the concept of rhythms and practical consciousness. Such agency, the act of doing, is also basic to the bottom-up model of society which I favoured in Chapter 2. The issue is fundamental to developing the study of Palaeolithic society. However, it can become tortuous and frequently impenetrable if left to the words of Heidegger. While I would recommend Gosden's summary and interpretation (1994), let me try putting the distinction another way.

Archaeology is often likened to the trade of the detective and in particular to Sherlock Holmes. The ability to deduce a person's life history from a frayed collar or a muddy boot has always appealed to our discipline. It is a fine example of cartesian dualism, the application of thought to the world. By contrast, I opened this chapter with a passage from another detective, Philip Marlowe. In this situation he was well aware that his discursive consciousness had temporarily taken over from his practical routines. A man in your living room with a smoking gun puts a whole new light on making a cup of coffee. For Holmes deduction is normal. With Marlowe, who generally goes with the flow of life, it is the other way around. He is in the world and surrounded by it rather than, like Holmes, waiting for cases to come to him for solution in his Baker Street rooms.

*Chaîne opératoire*

Rhythms and forms are integral to Leroi-Gourhan's concept of the chaîne opératoire or operational sequence which fuses social and technical activity (Boëda 1988, Boëda, Geneste and Meignen 1990, Coudret et al. 1994, Dobres and Hoffman 1994, Edmonds 1990, Julien 1992, Karlin and Julien 1994, 1986, Lemmonier 1990, Pigeot 1990, Schlanger 1996, White 1993b, 1993c).

At a basic, technical level, the chaîne opératoire

> takes the form of an ordered train of actions, gestures, instruments or even agents leading the transformation of a given material towards the manufacture of a product, through major steps that are more or less predictable. (Karlin and Julien 1994:164)

Unfortunately, the chaîne opératoire has become synonymous with 'lithic reduction sequence' and applied mostly to the production of stone tools (Hodder 1990b:157). But the concept of an operational sequence is, however, much broader than this common usage. I believe Schlanger is closer to the spirit of the concept when he describes the chaîne opératoire as examining 'the interplay between fixed and flexible' (1994:144).

What exactly does he mean? Material action, or gesture, is in part determined by physical laws. Therefore it is to some extent fixed. Stone and wood have different properties which determine not only what can be made but how it can be made. But material action is also flexible. There are choices to be made concerning the what and how of any technical process. The flexibility of these choices stems from social and cultural contexts, the gatherings and social occasions with actors engaged in the performance of society. Consequently, the fixed properties in any operational sequence do not in themselves make the technical act less social, cultural or indeed human. As White points out (1993a:xviii), the concept of operational sequences removes the dichotomy between style, expressing social identity, and function, which has exercised American archaeologists for over thirty years of sometimes heated debate. Leroi-Gourhan's essential point was therefore that technical acts are at the same time social acts (Schlanger 1990:23).

This use of the chaîne opératoire does not underestimate the importance of the disagreements where

> the identification, location and deciphering of technological choices correspond to a series of crucial questions regarding how, and in what respect, technologies are a mediation (as well as a compromise) between inescapable universal physical laws and the unbounded inventiveness of cultures (Lemmonier 1993:10)

but instead stresses that they will never be resolved so long as the division between function and style is related to two different behavioural domains rather than to one, the social.

This social fusion occurs because many operational sequences are needed to ensure material survival. These come from the rhythms of collective tradition as ways of doing and acting. But far from imposing rigid conditions on the form of objects such operational sequences vary considerably in terms of local and individual output (Leroi-Gourhan 1993:253). Here lies the flexibility with the chaîne opératoire defined as socialized action applied to matter (Lemmonier 1980:1, Schlanger 1994:145). The chaîne opératoire is more than just a suite of muscle memories about how to do things without thinking about them. It is the acts themselves and the linkages they provide across time and space which matter.

Graves (1994:440) has pointed out that Leroi-Gourhan did not, however, fully integrate the social. He insisted on a collective view of society as well as stressing the human capacity to achieve a cartesian separation between both our internal and external environments (Leroi-Gourhan 1993:235). This was particularly apparent in one key area, our faculty for symbolic projection. This was the means by which the collective was maintained and by which, through the exteriorization of memory, human development was channelled. He defined symbolism as that property of the human brain that consists in maintaining a *distance* between lived experience and the organism that serves as its medium. (Leroi-Gourhan 1993:234–5, my emphasis)

As a result, the individual gradually disappears into the collective world with each technical advance that places more of our operational sequences outside the body – figurative art, writing, print, film, electronic communication and digital storage. Leroi-Gourhan does not explain why these changes occurred except as an implied progressive tendency which involves a move from natural to artificial rhythms; from the corporeal rhythms of the forager to the symbolic rhythms of the city dweller.

So, while Leroi-Gourhan provides many insights about the structure of action and foreshadowed developments in social theory,[4] it is not difficult to see why the chaîne opératoire has been used to analyse lithic reduction rather than social action.

*Artifacts in gatherings*

This raises the interesting question of how we characterize the use of artifacts in gatherings. If such performances are regarded as symbolic, because they are based upon a concept of relationships, then it would follow that the objects incorporated into such interaction must also be symbolic. They are literally charged with the body as a source of social power and performance. Technology is not just about making stone axes to chop down trees. The gestures which are used to make the axe and then use it embody social representations, or ideas, which are part of wider symbolic systems (Lemmonier 1993:3).

As an embodied gesture the cup, spear, costume or paintbrush have symbolic power as thought in action. When the artifact was being made, handled and transported it took on the properties of the person as a social actor. This is another reason why we need to reject in the Palaeolithic the distinction between an artifact's function and its style (Sackett 1982). The latter is generally recognized as that part of the artifact which communicates about social identity and values, something which is added after the business of function has been sorted out. Looking at the same artifact from the perspective of material action, the gesture, makes us consider the social aspects of techniques as ways of doing which have their own repeated forms, movements and rhythms. Technology plays an active role, rather than the passive voice of style alone, in the stasis and change of social life as individuals interact and perform society through the construction of networks.

However, it could equally be argued that those social representations embodied in technology are the result of habitual routines and therefore not symbolic. This was discussed above in terms of the symbolic change which accrues to objects used in gatherings and social occasions. For example, what happens when the tool is put down and the gesture broken? Once separated from the body as a reference for action and power, how can it remain a symbolic extension of action? Freed from its direct association the handaxe would cease to be a gesture and would become just another pebble on the beach. As Schlanger has indicated, Leroi-Gourhan's seminal idea was that the real existence of the tool is when it is in action, when it is animated by gestures (Schlanger 1990:20). I would therefore argue for a narrow definition of symbolic behaviour. I would reserve it for interaction between people which takes place *away* from the co-presence found in gatherings. In this sense artifacts are ambiguous not because we have traditionally wrestled with their contradictory voices of style and function but rather

> by their sheer physicality and inanimacy [artifacts] are intrinsically thing-like, but in their incorporation into the nexus of social relations they are also personified. (Ingold 1994:335)

We can form intimate relations with objects because we can also stretch social relations beyond the gathering. When artifacts become people we have achieved that release from proximity which is our primate social heritage.

### *Paths and tracks*

The chaîne opératoire also leads us between locales via paths and tracks (Boëda, Geneste and Meignen 1990, 1991, Geneste 1988a, 1988b). Mobile foragers are concerned with intersection points where they either cross those of their prey or encounter a plant resource. The locales and paths, rather than the surface-area territories which surround them, are the important elements in the foragers' socially constructed landscapes.

This applies to highly forested habitats, where in northern boreal forests traplines form the track through otherwise unexplored territory (Brody 1981: map 12, Nelson 1973), and in tropical rainforests where Bahuchet describes the territory of the Mbuti of Zaire as 'characterised by narrow paths, which connect several successive hunting camps' (Bahuchet 1992:214). Among these African rainforest foragers the path is synonymous with the home range or territory. A similar pattern of habitual tracks is reported by Politis (1996) for the Nukak foragers of Colombian Amazonia.

Paths are also important in open landscapes such as central Australia, where, for example,

> An estate, for practical purposes of life, might amount only to places on a track, or a set of tracks, between exiguous waters in a wasteland. (Stanner 1965:2)

The image that foragers have of the world is linked to an itinerary (Leroi-Gourhan 1993:326), not to a concentric surface area as proposed by site catchment analysis (Vita-Finzi and Higgs 1970). Furthermore, the image that any individual has of the world is of a similar track. This is due to our ambulatory mode of perception (Gibson 1979). Paths and tracks link individuals to each other and so to the wider landscape and region.

*The taskscape*

A further rhythm is needed to broaden the concept of operational sequences and linear movements which are all too frequently linked to acquiring raw materials and making stone tools. This is supplied by Ingold's (1993:157) notion of the *taskscape* which is built on activities which carry forward the processes of social life. The taskscape is an array of related activities just as, in his terms, a landscape is an array of related features (*ibid*.:158). It is a mutual environment which surrounds an individual, moves with that person and so provides affordances for action (Gibson 1979).

The value of the concept lies in its stress upon the continuous character of the activities in which an individual is engaged. Ingold makes the obvious, but important point, that activity produces sound (1993:162). We see our environment as we walk through it and we perceive its affordances. However, we only know that those affordances are being used when we hear the sound of stone being knapped, deer screaming as they are killed, children playing with the echoes in caves, or feet stamping rhythmically in a dance. In this sense actions 'speak' louder than words. Our eyes alert us to possibilities and our ears confirm the social character of action. We relate to the taskscape through skills such as walking, listening, watching, making and doing. These are skills which have to be learnt and that learning takes place in the context of social life.

Just as a landscape is continuous so is the taskscape. The landscape is what we see and the taskscape is what we hear (*ibid*.:163). In both cases activities cannot be chopped up into little segments and analysed bit by bit.

The taskscape therefore has its own intrinsic temporality based on the rhythms of action (Ingold 1993:157). The network of movements produces forms which are interpreted by the senses. These may be movements associated with a technique such as making a bow or butchering an animal or they may move to the rhythms of face-to-face gatherings and social occasions. Moreover,

> The temporality of the taskscape is social . . . not because society provides an external frame against which particular tasks find independent measure, but because people, in the performance of their tasks, *also attend to one another*. (Ingold 1993:159–60, my emphasis)

People notice each other through observing movement and hearing sounds of activity. Such attention provides the reference among individuals for patterned and sequenced forms of behaviour. This point has been emphasized by Wilson:

> The seeing, perception, and understanding of others occurs most immediately within a framework or context of a social arrangement by means of which individuals most effectively prove their survival and well-being. Attention operates within this framework at the same time as it serves to support the structure. (Wilson 1988:15)

The taskscape is therefore close in concept to Leroi-Gourhan's chaîne opératoire where

> human beings are only human to the extent that they are in the midst of others and clothed in symbols that give purpose to their existence . . . The human act *par excellence* is perhaps not so much the creation of tools as . . . the creation of a human time and space. (Leroi-Gourhan 1993:313)

The taskscape adds to these collective insights into how temporality is constructed by rhythms which re-engage rather than distance individuals in the social world of human action (Gosden 1994:188). While this occurs in locales it is also conditioned by action and operational sequences at our next analytical level: the region.

## Regions

### *Landscapes of habit*

The wider region, traversed by the individual and all those with whom he or she interacts, forms a spatial network of intersecting paths. To express this pattern I have previously developed the concept of a local hominid network (Gamble 1993d, 1995b, 1996a, 1998) which identifies a common structure in the space–time behaviour of foragers, past and present. It encompasses both subsistence and social behaviour. The network contains other hominids, non-hominid competitors and resources. It is centred on the individual and the decisions he or she must make. In this sense it is the wider spatial network for the negotiation and reproduction of social life that occurs at locales.

However, to avoid confusion with other uses in this book of the term network, I have renamed this concept the landscape of habit, as described by Gosden (1994:182). This change of term emphasizes how the everyday routines which are performed at locales also have a temporal sequence that structures the contexts of interaction. This continuous process involves interactions between individuals where negotiation is achieved through display, gesticulation, grooming, language, performance, sign and symbol. In other words the routinization of life, described as that

> habitual, taken for granted character of the vast bulk of the activities of day-to-day social life; the prevalence of familiar styles and forms of conduct. (Giddens 1984:376)

### *Scale of the landscape of habit*

From earliest prehistory the form of hominid societies is expected to be variable. For this reason attention focuses here on the networks which supported this social variety. These component networks are likewise variable in the use of space and resources. However, the latter can be investigated for qualitative and quantitative changes in the flows and use of materials, particularly lithics. These items define the networks which contributed to the negotiation of society at particular times and places.

Elsewhere (Gamble 1993d, 1996a) I have discussed the dimensions of this spatial concept using data on raw-material transfers. Recent studies from

Table 3.4. *Proportions of raw materials present and utilized on Middle Palaeolithic sites in southwest France (Geneste 1988a, 1988b). The same relationships hold for Upper Palaeolithic material and in many different regions (see footnote for references).*

| Km radius from site | % of stone on site | % utilized, made into tools |
|---|---|---|
| 'Local'=within 5 km | 55–98 | 1–5 |
| Region=5–20 km | 2–20 | 1–20 |
| 'Distant'=30–80 km | <5 | 74–100 |

different continents and time periods have produced consistent results,[5] which concern both the distances over which materials were regularly transported and the effect this has on the quantity and morphology of stone implements in archaeological sites.

The dimensions are summarized in Table 3.4 by referring to Geneste's important study of Middle Palaeolithic material from southwest France (1988a, 1988b, 1989).

These studies of raw materials have led to the following general principle concerning the use of raw material by foragers: *distant raw materials are represented by the later stages of the reduction sequence* (Gamble 1993d:36). Using Geneste's summary (Table 3.4) we see that *distant* refers to materials transferred over 30–80 km. From a larger worldwide sample the raw-material data indicate a common scale for the landscape of habit with a radius of 40 km and an upper limit of 100 km (Gamble 1993d:42). Within this radius we can refer to all activities as *local* in terms of their social and organizational implications. The raw-material principle is the result of mobile hominids optimizing an aspect of their provisioning strategies. It expresses a simple relation between mobility and the distance separating resources. It is an example of an operational sequence embedded and embodied in a network of movements. These establish a rhythm to this aspect of material action which is repeated as a recognizable form at a regional spatial scale. It is the counterpart of the chaînes opératoires found in the manufacture of stone tools (see above, and Boëda 1988, 1990, Lemmonier 1993, Schlanger 1990) at the spatial scale of the gathering and social occasion.

*Exploration and the landscape of habit*

The landscape of habit is part of our hominid ancestry. We can trace it archaeologically through raw-material transfers which represent the rhythms that resulted in paths and tracks (see above). What these transfers record, however, are individuals constructing their own landscapes of habit through the routines of social life. The transfer of raw materials is embedded in social activities.

An ethnographic example of the scale and variety of such habitual activities

Table 3.5. *Reasons for Aka visits and the average distances travelled (Hewlett, van de Koppel and Cavalli-Sforza 1986:Table 4.5).*

| | | |
|---|---|---|
| Family visits | average distance | 47.6 km |
| Hunting | average distance | 22.8 km |
| Dancing, ceremonies | average distance | 17.6 km |
| Work for villagers | average distance | 66.4 km |

is provided by Hewlett et al.'s (1986) study of visiting among the Aka pygmies. They found, by asking individuals about their knowledge of the area, that visits among the Aka ranged from 1 to 175 km, with 96 per cent being less than 100 km and half of all visits less than 50 km (Table 3.5).

They calculated a half-range, the median of the distances from place of residence to places visited at least once, for individual travel. They then called this the exploration range, 'where subsistence activities take place, a spouse is encountered, and other aspects of geographical as well as social knowledge are acquired and transmitted' (Hewlett, van de Koppel and Cavalli-Sforza 1986:65). Men had a larger exploration range of 58 km compared to 32 km for women. The combined average was 35 km.

Among the Aka, population density also influenced these distances. Between the regions of Bagandou (high density at 0.031 persons per km$^2$) and Ndele (low density at 0.017 persons per km$^2$), Hewlett (et al. 1986) show that in the former 77 per cent of Aka men and 83 per cent of Aka women live after marriage within 25 km of where they were born. In Ndele this distance accounts for only 44 and 22 per cent respectively. Here 72 per cent of men and 77 per cent of women live up to 75 km from their birthplace.

This study of individual ranges, albeit in a tropical rainforest setting, provides some support for the dimensions of a landscape of habit. A further, theoretical example of the activities which result in the transfer of materials is Wobst's group based study of marriage systems among foragers (1976). These systems consisted of between 175–475 people and estimates of their spatial extent at different densities are given in Table 3.6.

Wobst's figures suggest a maximum of some 300 km. He predicts that this figure marks a threshold for mating-network size beyond which the costs of interaction to maintain a closed system involving ritual, exchange and food sharing would become prohibitive.

What emerges from this review of actual and modelled spatial relations is that individuals' exploration ranges, and even the distances they move at marriage, are unlikely to exceed 300 km, and while necessarily variable, are probably mostly under 80 km as indicated by the nearest-neighbour distances (Table 3.6) and supported by the data on raw material transfers (Table 3.4). Among the high-density population of Bagandou the average exploratory range for adult

Table 3.6. *Mating network area and the distance relationships between population density and intra-mating density in a hexagonal lattice with nineteen local groups.*

| Population density (persons/km$^2$) | Area km$^2$ | Diameter km | NN km | Distance between most distant local groups, km | Distance between central and most distant groups, km |
|---|---|---|---|---|---|
| 0.005 | 95,000 | 382 | 76 | 303 | 151 |
| 0.008 | 59,375 | 302 | 60 | 240 | 120 |
| 0.01 | 47,500 | 270 | 54 | 214 | 107 |
| 0.02 | 23,750 | 191 | 38 | 152 | 76 |
| 0.05 | 9,500 | 120 | 24 | 96 | 48 |

*Note:*
NN=nearest neighbour (from Wobst 1976:tables 1 and 2).

males is 27.5 km (Hewlett, van de Koppel and Cavalli-Sforza 1986). These are the scales at which the intimate and effective networks are played out. These dimensions can also include the extended network. But this is also the strand in the personal network which may exhibit the greatest spatial extent, reflecting the mobility of individuals.[6]

It is probable that these exploration distances have a great antiquity. They point to the repeated scale of the landscape of habit which is common to all hominids. In this respect Steele's estimates of home-range size based on brain size and body mass provide an independent check. The upper limit for a carnivore scale model for most hominids indicates home ranges between 32 and 102 km in diameter (Table 2.10). The landscape of habit constructed around an individual's intimate and effective networks is therefore an integral part of hominid heritage.

### *Social landscape*

The social landscape is distinguished as a spatial concept by the scale which negotiations achieve. It is the spatial outcome of individuals developing their extended network and the appearance of the global network (Tables 2.8 and 2.9). In Tindale's apt phrase for aboriginal Australia, these networks deal with 'tracks, travel, trespass and trade' (1974:75). Their development redefined the personal network and the way in which resources were used within it during interaction and negotiation. The social landscape also produces that surface structure of the group, which is a convenient shorthand for the summation of intersecting networks, based on the individual and represented by a variety of geographical scales. The term group has the advantage of focusing attention on how cultural forms persist in time and space, how they seem to have a 'life' beyond the individual and his or her networks. One further aspect of the group

Table 3.7. *Models of human and primate societies compared with a structure for the evolution of Palaeolithic society. While there is no strict equivalence between the terms in these three schemes the relative positions are indicated in order to clarify the archaeological structure.*

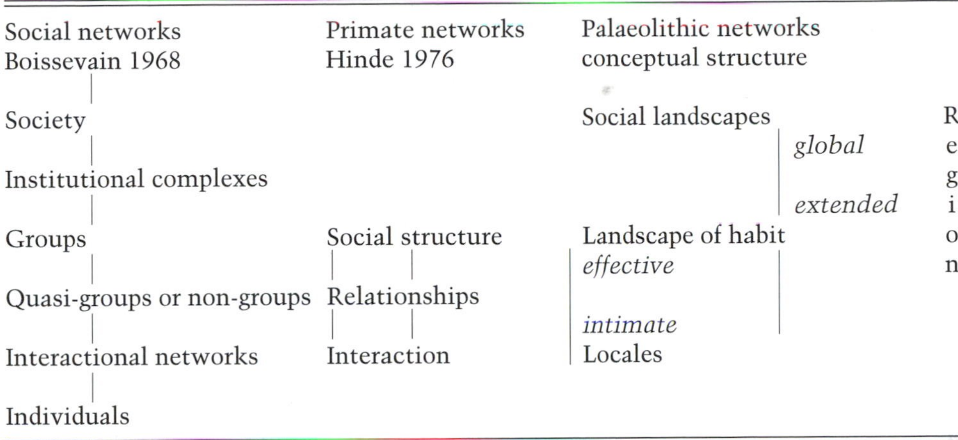

| Social networks Boissevain 1968 | Primate networks Hinde 1976 | Palaeolithic networks conceptual structure | | |
|---|---|---|---|---|
| Society | | Social landscapes | | Region |
| | | | *global* | |
| Institutional complexes | | | | |
| | | | *extended* | |
| Groups | Social structure | Landscape of habit | | |
| | | *effective* | | |
| Quasi-groups or non-groups | Relationships | | | |
| | | *intimate* | | |
| Interactional networks | Interaction | Locales | | |
| Individuals | | | | |

concept is that it is defined by the 'other', discussed in Chapter 2, through the global network.

Just as the group transcends the individual so the social landscape encompasses a number of landscapes of habit. It does not replace them but rather redefines them. In the same way, participation in global networks did not replace an individual's intimate and effective networks which were part of our primate heritage. The bottom-up approach advocated earlier is preserved, with groups an unintended consequence of the interactions of individuals but nonetheless influencing the form of those interactions.

*Social structure and change in the Palaeolithic*

These spatial relationships are summarized in Table 3.7 and placed within the wider framework derived from studies of human and primate societies. The scheme is not meant to imply that Palaeolithic society only existed when a social landscape can be claimed. Rather it is the case that without a social landscape we have a different form of society.

The landscape of habit represents a social structure in Hinde's (1976) sense since it has a full personal network based on intimate, effective and extended ties. It is therefore a regional concept.

The linkages between locales and regions in Table 3.7 indicate how this network structure developed and I will be examining the evidence for this in the chapters which follow. There were always rhythms which linked the locale to the region. What changed during the Palaeolithic was the character and extent of the regional scale. It is my contention that the extended network was the key to this change because it led to the possibility of individuals negotiating their global networks. The material requirements of extended networks (Table 2.8) within a social landscape rather than a landscape of habit led to the restructuring of resources and the elaboration of culture to carry the novel social representations.

*The development of inclusive social systems*

The social landscape therefore achieves the distanciation, or stretching, of social systems across space–time. It is through the social landscape that the actions of individuals achieve that release from proximity (Chapter 2) and where extended and global networks are explored at social and spatial removes, as indicated in Table 3.7.

What makes the social landscape different is that these negotiations are fixed, not just by interaction, but by the *possibility* of interaction regardless of whether it takes place or not. These are societies of distant relatives and comparative strangers. The hominid environment is therefore truly extended beyond either a foraging or a subsistence scale. It transcends habitual action and the pattern of life routines contained in the landscape of habit. Most importantly the social landscape sees a shift from social life being complex to becoming complicated in the sense discussed in Chapter 2. In essence this replaced 'a complexity of shifting, often fuzzy and continuous behaviours, relationships and meanings with a complicated array of simple, symbolic, clear-cut items' (Strum and Latour 1987:791). The distinction is well made by Rowell (1991:260):

> By use of symbols and material resources [complicated societies] can separate social problems into a series of simpler tasks, and this allows each individual to handle a greater elaboration of social arrangements.

Moreover, alongside social elaboration we also find both syn- and diachronic variety as the mechanism of negotiation leads to exaptive social outcomes. Among the social problems Rowell refers to are those which arise from infrequent encounters and the ability of individuals to recognize a network of acquaintances (1991:266).

But how can a population-wide system be maintained without the sort of complex and frequent interactions to negotiate its structure? This is certainly a limiting factor for the landscape of habit where social life was characterized as local and exclusive. The solution is that in addition to exclusive systems, the social landscape entertains the possibility of including others in an extended network (Gamble 1993d). As a result, a social landscape that incorporates several landscapes of habit, and which is associated with a complicated system of negotiation, will be regional, as well as local. It will also be either *inclusive* or *exclusive* in terms of boundary maintenance. An important element in achieving these outcomes is the use of objects in the 'performing' of social structure and hence their contribution to the exercise of individual power at a distance (Gosden 1994). This leads to the crucial point made by Strum and Latour (1987:796) that with the creation of symbolic and material bonds the actors now *appear* to be entering a pre-existing social structure rather than creating it. This impression has led to the confusion, discussed in Chapter 2, over the proper way to characterize Palaeolithic society.

*Objects and places as people*

As individuals move along tracks between gatherings and social occasions so they construct the social landscape as they also constructed the landscape of habit. Objects also move along these tracks. In the landscape of habit they moved with people, carried as raw material or tools as a portable and attached affordance. Their transfer is embedded in other activities such as hunting, visiting and the rituals of attaching and detaching from gatherings and social occasions. McBryde's study of the extensive exchange systems in Central Australia makes this point:

> The [distribution] system is embedded not in the economic or subsistence regimes of the societies concerned, but in their social and ceremonial life in which material goods and exchange play substantial roles. The meanings of the goods and the significance of their source location are explained and maintained over time by the stories that also map the symbolic and geographical world of these long distance transactions. (McBryde in press)

The difference with the social landscape is that in a very real sense objects now become people. As artifacts and manuports are transferred between individuals they express relationships which refer to wider social structures. Through exchange these objects supply a social affordance since this practice incorporates the social acts of collecting materials and manufacturing items. As a result the gestures involved in exchange are comparable to the gesture which made the artifact or collected the manuport because both of them are based on operational sequences. In this way material action incorporates social representations from the wider community, the group as defined above. The use of objects in the 'performing' of social structure and the construction of the social landscape produces time–space distanciation (Giddens 1984). Social systems are stretched due to the mechanisms of system integration, the means by which they are extended *in absentia* (Chapter 2).

*Symbolism, culture and the social landscape*

This stretching is usually put down to the emergence of symbolism. As Leroi-Gourhan put it, but without telling us why the shift took place,

> symbolic 'domestication' allowed the human to pass from the rhythmicity of seasons to the rhythmicity regulated and packaged within a network of symbols. (Leroi-Gourhan 1993:315)

According to this view, culture came to organize our lives through its collective representations. It became our unique means of adaptation (White 1959:3) and during human evolution the individual became increasingly submerged within the group (Leroi-Gourhan 1993:253).

The problem with this familiar explanation, that sees symbolism, usually associated with language, as the final ingredient in the mixture which made us human, is that it starts to look suspiciously like culture explaining culture. This is no explanation at all.

My answer to such a circular argument is the social landscape, which is the sum total of individual networks. Since individuals are active agents, responsive to, but also creating rhythms, movements and forms they never surrender to this collectivity of symbols, this tyranny of culture. The social systems they inherit are also those they can change. These social actors are both constrained and enabled by their bodies, which allow mobility, negotiation and the extension of social ties through networks which involve different resources (Chapter 2). They are spatial as well as temporal beings rather than simply programmed participants in culture.

In this respect the social landscape consists of making tracks between individuals as well as between places. These people in turn become named 'places' in the sense that they form a social network – their associations and movements providing the meanings of their own, and other individuals', environment. Moreover, the association of people with physical places is the basis for generating social contexts for action. These are variously constituted by the numbers and kinds of people in the network who visit and interact.[7] It is through the knowledge of these paths and places, either for sacred or for secular purposes, that the social landscape is constructed and the movement along paths between places conceptualized. These places are effectively people in the landscape because they are incorporated into networks. They are, to put it simply, personified.

*The scale of the social landscape and the creation of symbols*

There are no upper limits to the spatial dimensions of the social landscape. The American flag still stands on the Moon and Voyager II heads out of the galaxy. It is not so much where hominids have been but where they can potentially go. This potential has not however been a characteristic of all hominids during prehistory and the limiting factor reverts to their different negotiation of social life (Gamble 1993d).

The change in scale with the social landscape is significant. Ingold (1993:162–3) sets the limits of the taskscape as coterminous with the limits of the auditory world. It is therefore local and mutual to individuals as they engage in activities. The landscape of habit as shown above has an upper limit of 80–100 km. Among recent foragers this potential for spatial extension in a social landscape can readily be assessed by the movement of resources.[8] An ethnographic review by Féblot-Augustins and Perlès (1992) of stone and other transported materials indicates distances well beyond the upper limit of 100 km of the landscape of habit. Transfer of materials over 600 to 3,000 km among hunters and gatherers can be readily documented.

A classic example of such extended networks among recent foragers is provided by the Australian axe trade (McBryde 1978, 1988, in press 1993). In her study McBryde found that stone from the greenstone quarries of Victoria was being moved as much as 800 km and on average 228 km from the Mt William source. While such stone might be regarded as utilitarian and necessary for the manufacture of stone hatchets it is clear from McBryde's work that we have now moved beyond the landscape of habit and into a domain of social value where the objects are items for negotiation and affiliation to extended networks.

The same transformation can be traced with prestige goods, those gewgaws of social life, such as beads, jewellery and ornaments, as well as raw materials such as ochre, grinding stones and obsidians. By travelling far an object does seem to be automatically transformed from being mundane to being special (Gould 1980:142–3). The same transformation also happens to the travellers and the knowledge of exotic places they bring back (Helms 1988). But as Féblot-Augustins and Perlès point out (1992:13), we do not know exactly where this occurs. There is no magic distance beyond which an axe always ceases to be an axe and becomes a prestige good; where it is no longer just an affordance to chop down a tree but becomes a symbol of distant persons who *in absentia* now determine the performance of social relationships. It could be 5 km or 500 km. What needs to be understood are the social contexts which require the transformation in value from local to distant, from object to symbol (Gamble 1993d:37). Understanding these contexts must be based on the role of objects in the negotiation of networks.

With the social landscape inclusive systems can also be negotiated, and where openness and individual mobility are common. Here prestige goods serve a further function of allowing tolerated trespass onto others' territories in times of shortage. Hill sums this up well when she points out that in Australia the focus on lexicon as opposed to phonological differentiation of languages

> cannot be predicted by the dialect tribe model, but appear[s] to result from interpenetration into the properties of local systems by area systems of adaptation. (Hill 1978:18)

The variety of Australian social systems shows, at a continental scale, the two poles of social structure, inclusive/exclusive. These negotiated outcomes can in part be understood, as Peterson (1986) argues for Australia, by different ecological circumstances setting the conditions of existence and determining integration, ties to land and marriage customs (Table 1.2).

At these levels of analysis the mode of transfer (exchange, visiting, partnership, kin-based etc.) is of less importance than demonstrating the existence of the extended social landscape where the tracks which define it are now longer, and more varied, than those associated with the ambulatory preception of any individual. What can be said is that local dispersal, those tracks associated with the habits and routines of the landscape of habit, is no longer the only mechanism to explain the generation of spatial patterning in material culture.

### Summary

Social life in the Palaeolithic involved hominids in the continuous and different construction of their surrounding environment. To investigate this proposition I have set out a conceptual scheme using the spatial scales of locales and regions. These are linked by rhythms, illustrated here by the paths and tracks which Palaeolithic hominids trod, the operational sequences by which they made their tools and the taskscapes where they attended to one another.

I have further defined locales for archaeological purposes by the unfamiliar terms, encounter, gathering and social occasion/place. They will serve as a basis for analysis in the chapters which follow. I have used these terms rather than the more familiar campsites, home bases, satellite camps, or Binford's (1980) distinctions between residential camp, location, caches and field stations. The reason is quite simple. These terms are very useful for investigating settlement. They have been used widely as a set of definitions toward which archaeological analysis aspires. I have used them myself on many occasions. But they are so closely associated with the dichotomous approach to the study of foragers (Table 1.3) that they have become theory laden. We do not need to abandon them but rather to restrict their use to the analytical approaches that they best serve.

The point about a fresh vocabulary is its declaration that a new agenda is being explored: in this case a study of Palaeolithic society rather than Palaeolithic settlement. As we have seen at some length in the previous chapters, this shift will only succeed if we change our concepts about society and adjust our terms and methods accordingly.

In this respect the work of Leroi-Gourhan (1993) is important in stressing the social nature of technical acts. This may be flint knapping which occurs at a locale, or collecting and transporting the raw material from one locale to another. These operational sequences (the chaîne opératoire) are social productions which evolve their rhythms and form as the body engages in material action (*le geste*). With this perspective a social archaeology is not therefore confined to the stylistic elaboration of projectile points or the architecture of institutions believed to represent social information. Instead, a social approach involves all aspects of mobility, production, consumption and discard. Repetition and persistence of material action in time and space produce the well-known entity of the archaeological culture. These entities are the results of individuals repeating the technical gestures they learned rather than the collective mind of a group producing a pattern of culture to be followed.

At the regional scale two further concepts are proposed: the landscape of habit and the social landscape. The distinction between these two concepts includes complex and complicated societies and the role of practical and discursive consciousness in deriving structure from agency (Table 3.3). The landscape of habit represents a social structure following Hinde's discussion of primate society (1976). Within this structure individuals build their own networks but their extended networks are only weakly developed and the global network is nonexistent. The social principle is one of exclusion alone. The spatial dimensions of the landscape of habit can be determined from the distribution of raw materials in the archaeological record. These supply a record of movements; an example of rhythms and operational sequences as individuals engaged in the activity of social living.

I propose that the social landscape was an historical development from this common hominid heritage. Individuals extended the spatial and social scale of their action and interaction. This was aided by the use of material resources as social objects. Symbolic resources were the key to change. The web of networks was enlarged and additional resources were required to service them. This led to new operational sequences and the elaborated use of technical processes as social representations. The social landscape could therefore contain both exclusive and inclusive social systems. As a result the group emerges as a property of the density, scale and interactive intensity of individuals' networks. There may not be more people in the system but instead many different ties that both enable and constrain social activity. Strangers were never absolute in the social landscape but instead formed a relative social category defined by the response on encounter. This was in contrast to the landscape of habit where absolute strangers could potentially exist. The difference lay in the stretching of social relationships across time and space. The limits to action set by co-presence were therefore removed and the potential for society to grow in numbers and geographical area became almost unlimited.

The historical development between a landscape of habit and a social landscape cannot be put down to a single factor such as enhanced memory, language, discursive consciousness or technology. Neither was it a gradual trend where the externalization of memory through symbols was progressively increased. In Palaeolithic Europe it was both a process of long-term innovation and contingent upon the replacement of population. It is to the issues of stasis and change that these concepts and models of Palaeolithic society have been directed and, so constructed, I will now turn to the narrative of the data to test my proposals.

CHAPTER 4

# THE FIRST EUROPEAN SOCIETIES 500,000–300,000 YEARS AGO

Notre monde européen, et surtout sa partie occidentale, est un cul-de-sac vers lequel les vagues humaines, arrivées de l'est ou de sud sous les impulsions inconnues, sont venues mêler et superposer leurs sédiments

Abbé Henri Breuil, 1912

## Defining Palaeolithic Europe

The geographical boundaries of Palaeolithic Europe were flexible. In the north, successive ice sheets changed the habitable area of the continent, while in the west the continental shelf was drowned and exposed under the alternating climatic rhythms of interglacial to glacial. In the south it seems most probable that the Straits of Gibraltar were always open during the Pleistocene ice ages although islands in the central Mediterranean must have served as stepping-stones from Africa during times of low sea level.

But the east provides the weakest set of geographical boundaries for Pleistocene Europe. The steppes of the Ukraine and Russia, the Caspian and Black Sea, and the upland plateaux and mountains of Turkey, the Caucasus and the Near East provide no obvious absolute barrier either to settlement by or to subsequent contact with other populations in the Old World. Instead, the lack of boundaries emphasizes the peninsular nature of Europe which the Abbé Breuil once described as a cul-de-sac, into which several waves of humans and animal species had been washed (Breuil 1912).

The difficulties of defining the size and shape of Palaeolithic Europe may seem unimportant. After all, defining Europe today faces similar problems (Graves-Brown, Jones and Gamble 1995), and the suggestion that modern political and cultural boundaries should somehow be significant in the Pleistocene is obviously nonsensical. However, there is a serious point to the exercise. Identifying the geographical scale at which we should investigate Palaeolithic societies is important from an evolutionary perspective. We need to ask if the selective pressures for change and variation in hominid behaviour operated at the scale of this Asian and African peninsula, or were they part of a long-term set of environmental changes enacted over a much larger landmass? The regional model based on latitude, longitude and relief (Figure 3.1) is sufficient for examining variation in Palaeolithic behaviour within central and western Europe (Gamble 1986a), but it may be inappropriate for unravelling the long-term processes involved in hominid evolution. This possibility emerges when we start to ask an historical question – such as when did hominids first colonize Europe? – and to examine what light the answer throws on their social networks.

## Chronology, climates and habitats

There are several aspects of Pleistocene chronology which need to be considered in any discussion of the arrival of hominids in Europe. The first large-scale glaciation, and hence the commencement of the Pleistocene period, is now dated to 2.3 Myr BP (Zagwijn 1992). This was a period of strong cooling which can be traced both in the terrestrial pollen records and as a signal in the deep-sea core isotopic record (Ruddiman and Raymo 1988). Such a timescale adds an additional 700,000 years to the traditional length of the Pleistocene, where the boundary with the Pliocene is fixed at 1.6–1.8 Myr BP (Aguirre and Pasini 1985).[1]

The cooling at 2.3 Myr BP marks the start of a long-term climatic trend. This was partly the result of changes in the earth's orbit, spin and tilt (Goudie 1977, Imbrie and Imbrie 1979) as well as the cumulative effects of mountain building, particularly the Himalayas and the Tibetan plateau, which affected global weather patterns (Ruddiman and Raymo 1988). When combined, these two forces produced a recurrent pattern of global climate which, in Europe, alternated between temperate – interglacial – phases with greater forest and woodland vegetation, and cooler – glacial – episodes with open vegetation and low sea levels. On occasion this resulted in the advance of northern ice sheets over Scandinavia and Britain as well as smaller southern ice caps in the Pyrenees, Alps, Carpathians, Balkan and Caucasus mountains. Quaternary research has shown however that within these broad categories of interglacial and glacial there were many varied conditions which were magnified in particular parts of the continent. These will be discussed, where relevant, in the following chapters.

### *Changes in the duration and amplitude of climatic cycles*

Although cooling and deforestation in the Netherlands can be demonstrated at 2.3 Myr BP (de Jong 1988), the early cycles have a very weak signal in the deep-sea cores. This is measured in terms of the magnitude between the glacial lows and interglacial highs of temperature, vegetation, sea levels and ice extent. Zagwijn (1992:figure 2) has estimated, on the basis of the Netherlands pollen record, that July temperatures fluctuated between an average of 10°C to 20°C during the period 2.3–1.5 Myr BP. After this time the range increases, with averages now fluctuating between 5°C and 20°C, which would have had major repercussions for plant growth and the structure of vegetation communities. One result is seen in the Netherlands Bavel interglacial at 1 Myr BP. This is the first time that a pollen profile shows any stratigraphic succession

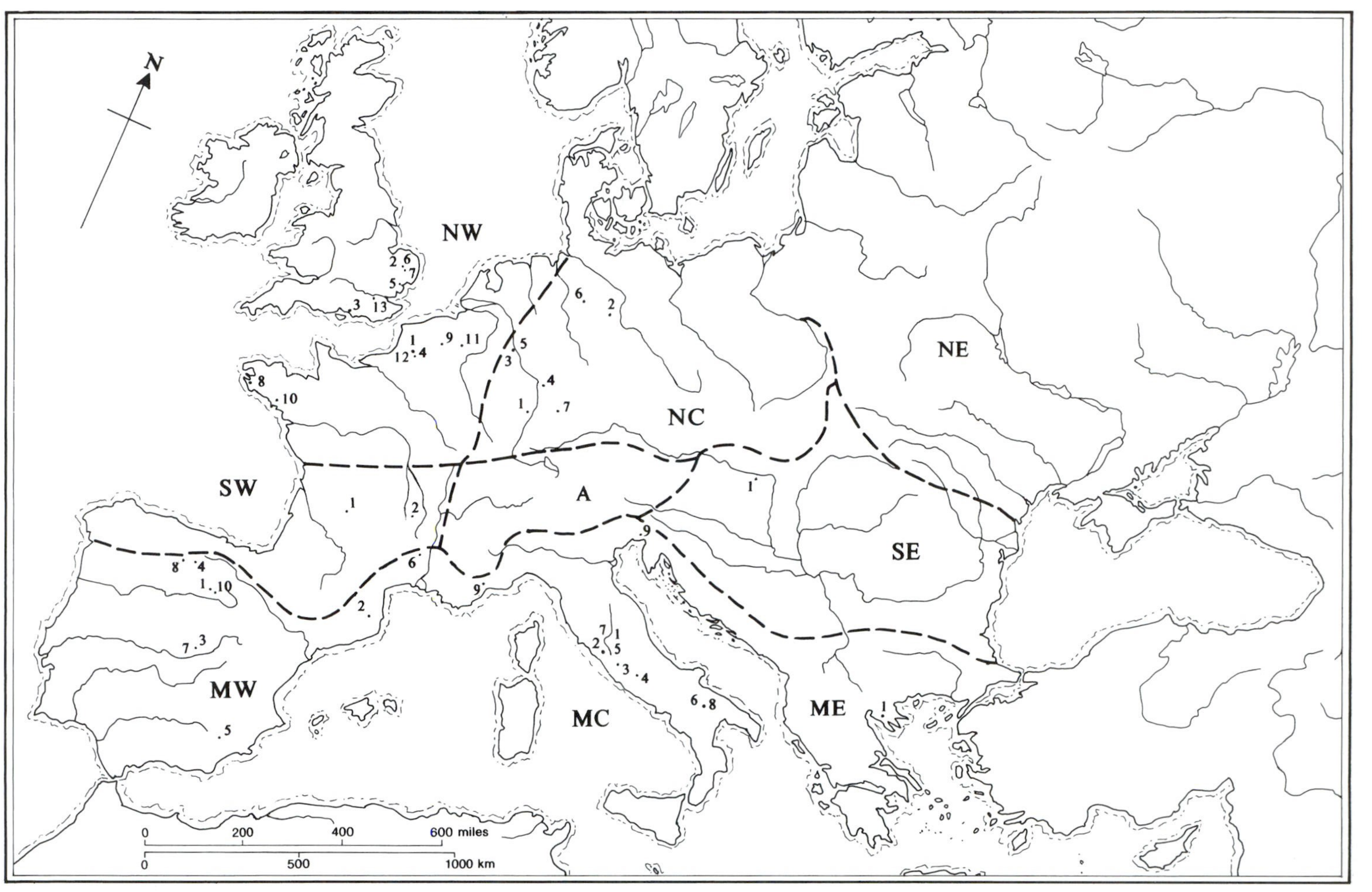
N
NW
NE
NC
SW
A
SE
MW
MC
ME
0 200 400 600 miles
0 500 1000 km

**4.1** Principal locales discussed in this chapter and referred to in Tables 4.3 and 4.19.

KEY: by region

| | NW | NC | SW | SE |
|---|---|---|---|---|
| 1 | Abbeville | Achenheim | Barbas | Vértesszöllös |
| 2 | Barnham | Bilzingsleben | Soleihac | |
| 3 | Boxgrove | Kärlich | | |
| 4 | Cagny | Mauer | | |
| 5 | Clacton | Miesenheim | | |
| 6 | High Lodge | Schöningen | | |
| 7 | Hoxne | Steinheim | | |
| 8 | Menez-Drégan | | | |
| 9 | Pa d'la L'iau | | | |
| 10 | Saint-Colomban | | | |
| 11 | Sprimont | | | |
| 12 | St Acheul | | | |
| 13 | Swanscombe | | | |
| | MW | MC | ME | |
| 1 | Ambrona | Casal de' Pazzi | Petralona | |
| 2 | Arago | Castel di Guido | | |
| 3 | Aridos | Fontana Ranuccio | | |
| 4 | Atapuerca | Isernia | | |
| 5 | Cúllar de Baza | La Polledrara | | |
| 6 | Orgnac | Notarchirico | | |
| 7 | Pinedo | Torre in Pietra | | |
| 8 | San Quirce | Venosa-Loreto | | |
| 9 | Terra Amata | Visogliano | | |
| 10 | Torralba | | | |

in the immigration, spread and subsequent decline of forest elements in northern Europe (de Jong 1988). Previously the interglacial pollen diagrams show that climate had little effect on the composition of forests, which possibly indicates that in the cooler phases plant refuge areas were much closer so that recolonization during the interglacials was extremely rapid. Moreover, Zagwijn (1992:587) has pointed out that these early interglacials had different soil conditions which limited the spread of acidiphilous elements such as *Abies* (silver fir) or *Picea* (spruce) which are key elements in recognizing forest succession.

After 1 Myr BP the trend to cooler climates and greater differences between succeeding glacials and interglacials is much clearer. In terms of establishing a Pleistocene chronology for this trend, a very significant palaeomagnetic event occurs at $775 \pm 10$ Kyr BP with the switch to normal from reversed magnetic polarity (Bassinot et al. 1994). This abrupt transition can be measured in igneous rocks, such as basalts, which can also be dated by isotope decay methods such as Potassium/Argon (K/Ar) (Aitken 1990). This worldwide marker distinguishes the Matuyama from the Brunhes chron and is recognized as the boundary between the Lower and the Middle Pleistocene.[2]

This palaeomagnetic chronology can also be applied to the sediments in the deep sea cores. These cores consist of muds and oozes which are continually being deposited on the ocean floor. They also contain, in stratigraphic order, the microscopic marine organisms which once lived at the surface. The calcium carbonate skeletons of these microscopic foraminifera absorbed the oxygen isotopes in the ocean at the time they were alive. Since the core produces a stratigraphic column, these organisms can be used to measure changes through time in the ratio of two important oxygen isotopes, $^{16}O$ and $^{18}O$ (Figure 4.2). Such isotopic changes reflect the size of the oceans at the time these foraminifera were alive. If the oceans were large, as they were during an interglacial, then they contain a larger amount of $^{16}O$. When they become smaller, because the moisture which once fell on the oceans is now locked up in the ice caps, they have greater amounts of the 'heavier' oxygen isotope $^{18}O$ since the lighter one, $^{16}O$, has been evaporated.

The outcome is that through the shape of the curves we can see the global changes in Pleistocene climate. These are set out in Table 4.1 which shows that the length of cycles more than doubled in the Brunhes chron after 0.775 Myr BP as well as becoming more variable.

A visual inspection of the Oxygen Isotope Stage (OIS) curve (Figure 4.2) also shows that the amplitude (the difference between the values for the interglacial and glacial stages of any one cycle) becomes more marked through time. One way to illustrate this trend is to compare the number of cycles in each chron which are equal to or greater than the two best-studied stages in the last interglacial/glacial cycle (Table 4.2). The last interglacial (OIS 5e) lasted for 10,000 years (Chapter 5) and is marked by isotope values which indicate very high sea levels as the result of more extensive melting of the polar ice caps

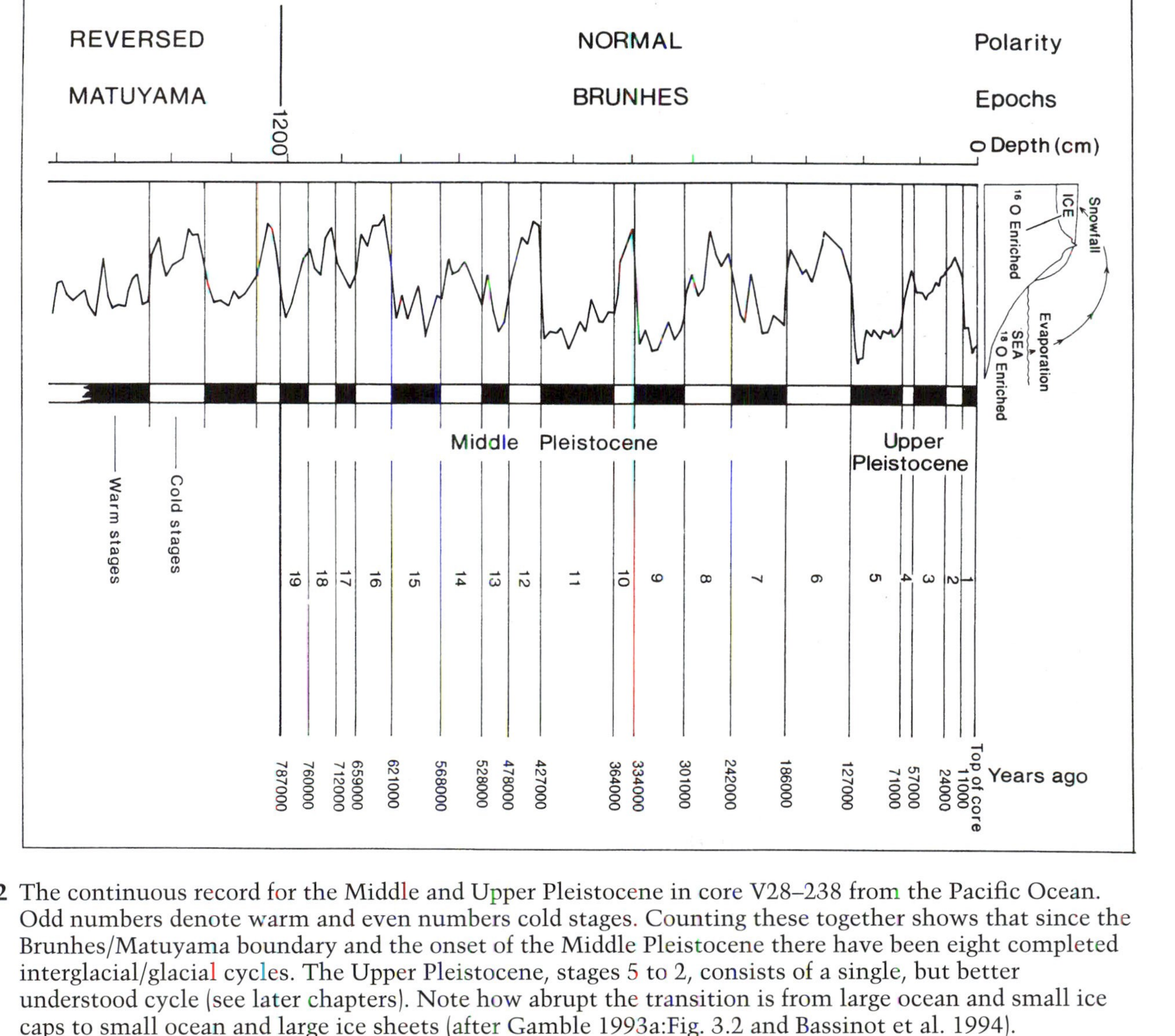


**4.2** The continuous record for the Middle and Upper Pleistocene in core V28–238 from the Pacific Ocean. Odd numbers denote warm and even numbers cold stages. Counting these together shows that since the Brunhes/Matuyama boundary and the onset of the Middle Pleistocene there have been eight completed interglacial/glacial cycles. The Upper Pleistocene, stages 5 to 2, consists of a single, but better understood cycle (see later chapters). Note how abrupt the transition is from large ocean and small ice caps to small ocean and large ice sheets (after Gamble 1993a:Fig. 3.2 and Bassinot et al. 1994).

Table 4.1. *A comparison of the climatic cycles in the Brunhes and Matuyama chrons (Gamble 1995c:table 2).*

| | |
|---|---|
| **Brunhes Chron** | **0.012–0.775 Myr** |
| Starts at OIS | 19 |
| Number of interglacial/glacial cycles | 8 |
| Length of cycles | |
| mean Kyr | 96.88 |
| range Kyr | 115–75 |
| sd | 13.31 |
| **Matuyama Chron** | **0.775–1.636 Myr*** |
| Starts at OIS | 63 |
| Number of interglacial/glacial cycles | 22 |
| Length of cycles | |
| mean Kyr | 40.91 |
| range Kyr | 45–38 |
| sd | 2.01 |

*Notes:*
* The Matuyama chron lasted from 0.775–2.47 Myr BP. The data shown here are from the period after the Olduvai magnetic reversal (Bassinot et al. 1994, Ruddiman, Raymo and McIntyre 1986:table 3). OIS: Oxygen Isotope Stage.

Table 4.2. *A comparison of the amplitude of climatic cycles in the Brunhes and Matuyama chrons as measured against the isotope values (Figure 4.2) for the last interglacial (OIS 5e) and last glacial maximum (OIS 2).*

| Chron | Number of cycles | High sea levels & forests % of cycles ≥ last interglacial (OIS 5e) | Low sea levels & forests % of cycles ≥ last glacial maximum (OIS 2) |
|---|---|---|---|
| Brunhes 0.012–0.775 Myr | 8 | 25 | 75 |
| Matuyama 0.775–1.63 Myr | 22 | 23 | 32 |

(Shackleton 1987). The last glacial maximum, 18,000–20,000 years ago, was not, as Figure 4.2 shows, the greatest reduction in ocean volume, but it was still a significant glaciation.

These data indicate that the two chrons had similar proportions of high sea-level interglacials but that the proportion of major glaciations increased dramatically in the Brunhes. It is against this background of longer and more varied, in terms of amplitude, climatic cycles that we must view the colonization of Europe. Furthermore, the long-term trend was towards longer periods of cooler, more open continental conditions.

*The major glaciation OIS 12, 427–478 Kyr BP*

The task facing Pleistocene geologists after the publication in 1973 of a continuous deep-sea core chronology (Shackleton and Opdyke 1973) has been to assign their discontinuous terrestrial evidence to this global framework. The existing four-stage schemes of northern and Alpine Europe now had to be matched to the eight interglacial/glacial cycles of the Middle and Upper Pleistocene contained within the Brunhes palaeomagnetic chron (Figure 4.2), not to mention to the twenty-two cycles in the preceding Matuyama chron (Table 4.1). The solution has not yet been determined to the satisfaction of all Pleistocene stratigraphers.

However, Quaternary geologists have always recognized that during the Pleistocene there was one glacial episode which had more impact than any of the others.[3] In Northern Europe the most southerly extension of moraines from the Scandinavian ice sheets could be attributed to the Elster glaciation in the Netherlands and Northern Germany, the Oka glaciation in Russia, while in England it was the Anglian ice advance.[4] As far as general agreement is ever forthcoming among Pleistocene stratigraphers, this major glaciation in the middle Pleistocene is widely correlated to OIS 12, dated between 427–478 Kyr BP (Sibrava 1986:chart 1).[5]

If OIS 12, the Anglian–Elsterian–Oka, forms a hinge in the Pleistocene, for reasons to be explained shortly, then the working solution that matches up the terrestrial evidence of the middle Pleistocene with the deep-sea pattern of climatic cycles involves four glacial/interglacial complexes. The first of these, the Cromerian, predates OIS 12 (Table 4.3; Figure 4.2) and consists of four interglacials and three glaciations (C. Turner 1996). The complex starts before the Brunhes/Matuyama boundary, possibly in OIS 21 or 23. Cromer IV, the last interglacial in the cycle, can be correlated with OIS 13.[6]

The second complex, the Holsteinian, comes after OIS 12 and includes OIS 11–9. Currently there is some controversy over dating OIS 9- and OIS 11-age sites (Bowen et al. 1989), probably because the intervening cold period OIS 10 is so short, only 30 Kyr (Figure 4.2). This brevity no doubt reduced the faunal and floral differences between OIS 11 and 9 which in turn would contribute to problems of correlation as similar marker species are found in both warm periods. Furthermore, both interglacial peaks have very marked $^{16}$O values, indicating high sea levels only matched elsewhere by the last interglacial, OIS 5e (Shackleton 1987). These extreme events appear to correlate with the appearance of *Abies* (silver fir) in northern Europe where today it is only found in the Alps (Zagwijn 1992:figure 10).[7] The implication is that these were interglacials with a more pronounced oceanic climate (*ibid*.: 590).[8]

The main archaeological sites for these two complexes as well as the major glaciation are shown in Table 4.3.

Table 4.3. *Cromer and Holstein chronology with major archaeological and palaeontological locales. (hominid fossils in italic)*

| OIS | Kyr BP | NW | NC | SW | SE | MW | MC | ME |
|---|---|---|---|---|---|---|---|---|
| 9–11 | 301<br>HOLSTEIN | Barnham<br>Cagny l'Epinette<br>Cagny la Garenne<br>Cagny-Cimetière<br>Clacton<br>Hoxne<br>Menez-Drégan 1<br>Saint-Colomban<br>Sprimont<br>*Swanscombe* | Achenheim<br>*Bilzingsleben*<br>Kärlich H<br>Schöningen 12<br>Schöningen 13<br>*Steinheim* | Barbas 7 | | Ambrona<br>Arago A–C<br>Cúllar de Baza I<br>*Orgnac III*<br>Pinedo<br>*Sima de los Huesos*<br>Terra Amata<br>Torralba | Torre in Pietra m | *Petralona* |
| 12 | 427–478<br>ANGLIAN / ELSTER / OKA | Boxgrove<br>Cagny la Garenne<br>Cagny-Cimetière<br>Pa d'la L'iau<br>St Acheul-Rue de Cagny | | | | *Arago D–G* | | |
| 13+ | CROMER | Abbeville–Carpentier<br>*Boxgrove*<br>High Lodge<br>Sprimont | Kärlich G<br>*Mauer*<br>Miesenheim I | Soleihac | *Vértesszöllös* | Arago H–L<br>*Atapuerca TD6*<br>Atapuerca TD3–TD5 | *Ceprano*<br>*Fontana Ranuccio*<br>Isernia<br>La Polledrara<br>*Notarchirico*<br>Venosa–Loreto | |

The third complex, the Saalian, covers two major glaciations, OIS 8 and OIS 6, with one weaker interglacial, OIS 7, that is divided into three substages (Ninkovitch and Shackleton 1975). This complex is discussed in Chapter 5. The fourth complex, the last interglacial/glacial cycle, OIS 5e–2, is examined in detail in Chapters 6 and 7.

The importance of OIS 12 as a hinge is based not just on the relative size of the Anglian–Elsterian–Oka glaciations but, more importantly, on bio-stratigraphic correlations. Here changes in large- and small-mammal faunas can be traced far beyond the immediate glacial geology of northern Europe.

One of the most important aspects of this bio-stratigraphy is now based upon the evolution of the rodents. These small mammals have several advantages for the bio-stratigrapher since they existed in a wide range of European biotopes and were unaffected by human or large-carnivore predation. They also have higher rates of evolution (Stuart 1982, Sutcliffe and Kowalski 1976). In a series of studies, van Kolfschoten (Koenigswald and Kolfschoten 1996, 1993, Roebroeks and Kolfschoten 1995) has studied the chronological implications of the evolution during the early and middle Pleistocene of the water vole from *Mimomys* to *Arvicola* forms. This evolution can be seen very clearly in the loss of roots in the molars (Figure 4.3), as well as in subsequent changes in the thickness of the enamel between various sub-species of the later form, *Arvicola*. On stratigraphic evidence the *Mimomys/Arvicola* transition occurred sometime after 550 Kyr BP and in most parts of Europe *before* OIS 13, the Cromer IV interglacial.[9] The transition is marked by an increased number of water voles having rootless molars. For example, at the Italian site of Isernia (Coltorti et al. 1982) 20 per cent of the molars still show indications of root formation, but remain rootless (Roebroeks and Kolfschoten 1994:495).[10] At Atapuerca (Figure 4.4) the '*Mimomys* extinction' occurs in TD 6 (Carbonell and Rodriguez 1994:300). This level was originally placed well above the Brunhes/Matuyama boundary which early studies placed in TD 3, and was correlated to OIS 13 (*ibid.*:Figure 8, Carbonell et al. 1995:456 and Table 1). But further analysis of the sediments (Carbonell et al. 1995, Parés and Pérez-González 1995) has led to a revision of the palaeomagnetic stratigraphy with claims that the earliest artifacts and human remains are almost double the previous ages (compare Carbonell and Rodriguez 1994 with Carbonell et al. 1995). One unresolved problem with this new scheme lies in the bio-stratigraphical data where special pleading is needed to accommodate the new dates for Atapuerca within the European sequence of vole evolution (Koenigswald and Kolfschoten 1996).

The large mammals are generally less sensitive chronological indicators. This is because of their slower evolutionary rates, environmental tolerances and patterns of recolonization. However, when examined together it is possible to see the importance of OIS 12 in marking a change in the structure of this community and particularly the balance between carnivores and herbivores.

This change is shown in Table 4.4 in terms of the number of major taxa in each of Cordy's (1992) four biozones that come before and after OIS 12.[11]

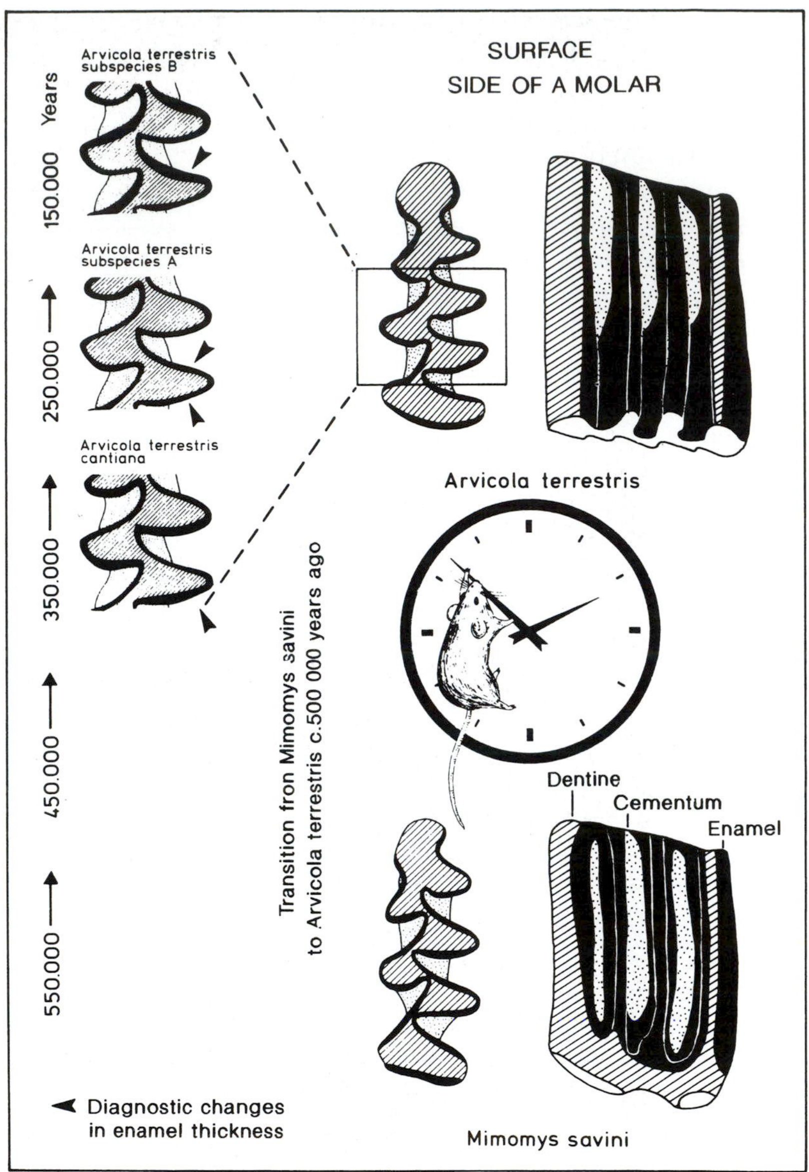


**4.3** The vole clock, which uses the evolution of *Mimomys* to *Arvicola* and then the subsequent changes in *Arvicola* as a bio-stratigraphic dating tool. Note the loss of roots in the molars (after Van Kolfschoten in Bosinski 1992a:Abb. 6).

Of particular interest is the decline in the number of large carnivore species, particularly hyena and the large cats which included the sabre- (*Homotherium*) and dirk- (*Megantereon*) toothed tigers and the giant short-faced hyena, *Pachycrocuta brevirostris* (A. Turner 1990, 1992).

There are also important changes in the structure of the herbivore community

**4.4** A view of Gran Dolina as exposed in the former railway cutting at Atapuerca, Spain, MW region. Level TD6 is below the lowest figure on the scaffolding (photo by the author).

after OIS 12. The longer, cooler cycles are now dominated by the mammoth/woolly rhino (*Mammuthus/Coelodonta*) fauna (Khalke 1994) that links it to the wider faunal province of western Asia, Siberia and Beringia. This biotope has been aptly described by Guthrie as the mammoth steppe (1990, 1984),

Table 4.4. *Faunal changes in the European Pleistocene. The figures shown are the average number of species for each of the major taxa in the four biozones (Cordy 1992). This shows, for example, that the number of rhino species doubles in the biozones after 478 Kyr BP (after Gamble 1995c).*

| | Biozones I–IV OIS 26–13 | Biozones V–VIII OIS 12–2 |
|---|---|---|
| Mammoths | 1.25 | 1.25 |
| Rhinos | 1 | 2 |
| Horses | 1.75–2 | 1.5–1.75 |
| Bos | 1.75–2 | 2.75 |
| Ovibos | 1.5–2 | 1 |
| Ovicaprids | 1.25 | 2–2.25 |
| Antelope | 0 | 1.25 |
| Cervus | 6.25–7.75 | 5.5–6.75 |
| Canis | 1–1.25 | 1.25 |
| Vulpes/Alopex | 1.25 | 1.5–1.75 |
| Cuon | 1.75–2 | 1 |
| Ursus | 1.5–1.75 | 2 |
| Hyena | 2–2.75 | 1.25 |
| Large cats | 2.5–3 | 1 |

which was highly productive, supporting a diverse community whose characteristic element was the grazing woolly mammoth (*Mammuthus primigenius*).[12]

This trend can be traced through the growing importance of reindeer (*Rangifer tarandus*) which appears in OIS 12 (Cordy 1992, Khalke 1994:80). By OIS 8 it is possible at locales such as Ariendorf (Kolfschoten and Turner 1996, E. Turner 1990, 1991) in Germany to identify the appearance of a classic glacial fauna, dominated by arctic elements, which now include the collared lemming *Dicrostonyx torquatus*.

The impact of OIS 12 on the landscapes of northern Europe was particularly dramatic. In central and eastern Europe the glacial phases after OIS 12 are marked by increased loess deposition as sediments were exposed for wind erosion by the sluggish meltwater streams that flowed out from the ice sheets. The same landscapes were also subjected to intense periglacial activity with frost wedges, cryoturbation and mass wasting of sediments downslope. The ice sheets of OIS 12 also changed drainage patterns by pushing south the major rivers such as the Thames (Bridgland 1994) and Rhine (Gibbard 1988). This impact can also be seen in the low sea-level phases when a major river appeared in the English Channel and the extension of those rivers in France and England which fed it (Allen and Gibbard 1994, Antoine 1990).

*Responses by flora and fauna to the climatic cycles*

During glacial phases plant species became locally extinct in northern Europe. It was not the case that vegetation zones were depressed south but instead plant taxa, and especially tree species, survived in localized refugia in southern/Mediterranean Europe. Indeed it is only in southern Europe that continuous pollen sequences exist (Tzedakis and Bennett 1995). It was from these southern refuges that recolonization took place in succeeding warmer phases. The history of recolonization explains why each interglacial in northern Europe possesses an individual character (de Jong 1988) while at the same time following a broadly similar succession for forest regeneration.

Animals were also part of these southerly refuges (Kolfschoten 1992). During the warm phases when the forests returned to the European peninsula, key animals such as the mammoth and reindeer became extinct and recolonization came later from the huge continental steppes to the east. The location of the European large-mammal refugia no doubt varied from glacial period to glacial period. The timing and mixing of elements from the steppe and the forest produced what in modern animal community terms are very strange associations of animals,[13] but which can be understood in terms of the generalist feeders which such productive environmental structures favour (Geist 1978, Guthrie 1984).

This long-term pattern, of successive colonizations by new species and recolonization from refuges by older community members, favoured those areas of northern Europe which were in close proximity to the topographically diverse refuge areas to the south (Tzedakis 1993). In such areas recolonization distances would be short and forest regeneration rapid. The reduced effects of seasonality in the west of the continent, due to the oceanic effect, would also have produced more tightly packed vegetation mosaics. By contrast in the east, outside the distribution of middle Pleistocene hominids, distances between the plains and the sheltered refuge areas were much larger. Seasonality, as measured by intra-annual variation in temperature, would also be much greater. Biotopes in the west would therefore be more ecologically resilient because they were less prone to crashes in animal numbers. The main factor reducing such seasonality is the oceanic effect.

*The structure of the mammoth steppe*

The mammoth steppe (Guthrie 1990, 1982, 1984, Khalke 1994:abb. 13) which develops after OIS 12 expands the boundaries of Palaeolithic Europe from Breuil's cul-de-sac to include Alaska as part of the palaeocontinent of Beringia. The mammoth steppe was an ecologically complex, medium- to high-latitude suite of vegetation mosaics that produced a diverse fauna of grazing generalists. These mosaics depended primarily upon the length of the growing seasons and these varied between regions and particularly, as might be expected using latitude, longitude and relief as a guide to relative productivity, on a north–south transect (Guthrie 1990:263ff). The main ecological feature of its

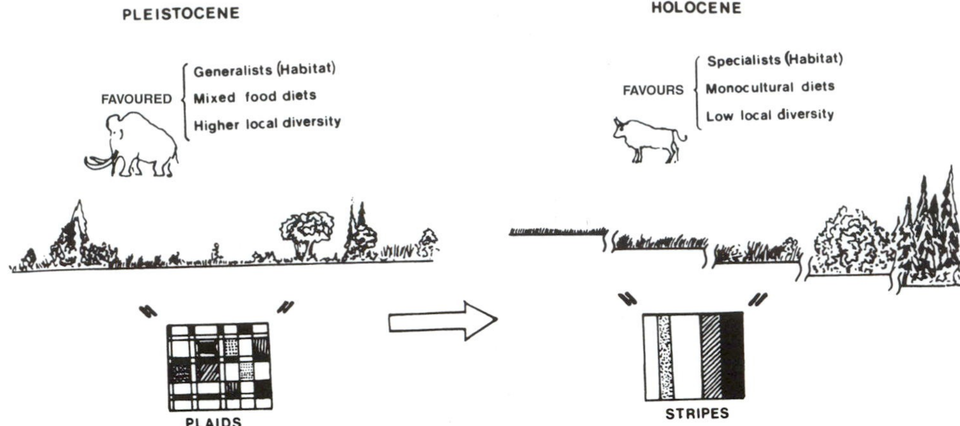


**4.5** Plaids and stripes: two ecological structures during the Pleistocene and Holocene. The productivity of the mosiac environments with plaid structure is reflected in the high species diversity which includes megafauna such as mammoth (after Guthrie 1984:Fig. 13.1).

plant communities was the mosaic of conditions that, using Guthrie's terms (1984), produced a structure whose 'fabric' is compared to the weave in a plaid, rather than a striped, textile (Figure 4.5). These mosaics would contribute to the ecological resilience of the mammoth steppe where disruption through fire or overgrazing is quickly repaired, especially where recolonization distances were short.

The interglacial/glacial cycles altered the patch size of the vegetation mosaics, and although it is not possible at present to quantify by how much, we can assume that the extent of the oceanic effect had a controlling influence (Auguste 1995, Gamble 1995c, Koenigswald 1992). However, the alternating environments in any one interglacial/glacial cycle did not produce a 'striped' and then a 'plaid' community. Instead we are dealing with two forms of mosaic – forest and steppe – two plaids with different plant and animal communities.

*Normal environments for recovery of archaeological evidence*

The major environments from which archaeological material dating to the period 500–300 Kyr BP has been recovered are consistent between the eight occupied regions (see Villa 1991:193–6). The evidence comes predominantly from lakeside and riverine settings as in the Venosa basin in Italy (Mussi 1992, 1995), the major catchments of the Iberian peninsula (Raposo and Santonja 1995, Santonja 1992, Santonja and Villa 1990), the unglaciated areas of England and northern France (Antoine 1990, Antoine and Tuffreau 1993, Roberts et al. 1995, Roe 1981, Tuffreau and Antoine 1995, Wymer 1968) and the Neuwied basin in Germany (Bosinski 1992a, Bosinski 1995a, E. Turner 1990).

As an example, occupation at Cagny la Garenne at Amiens in the 27-m

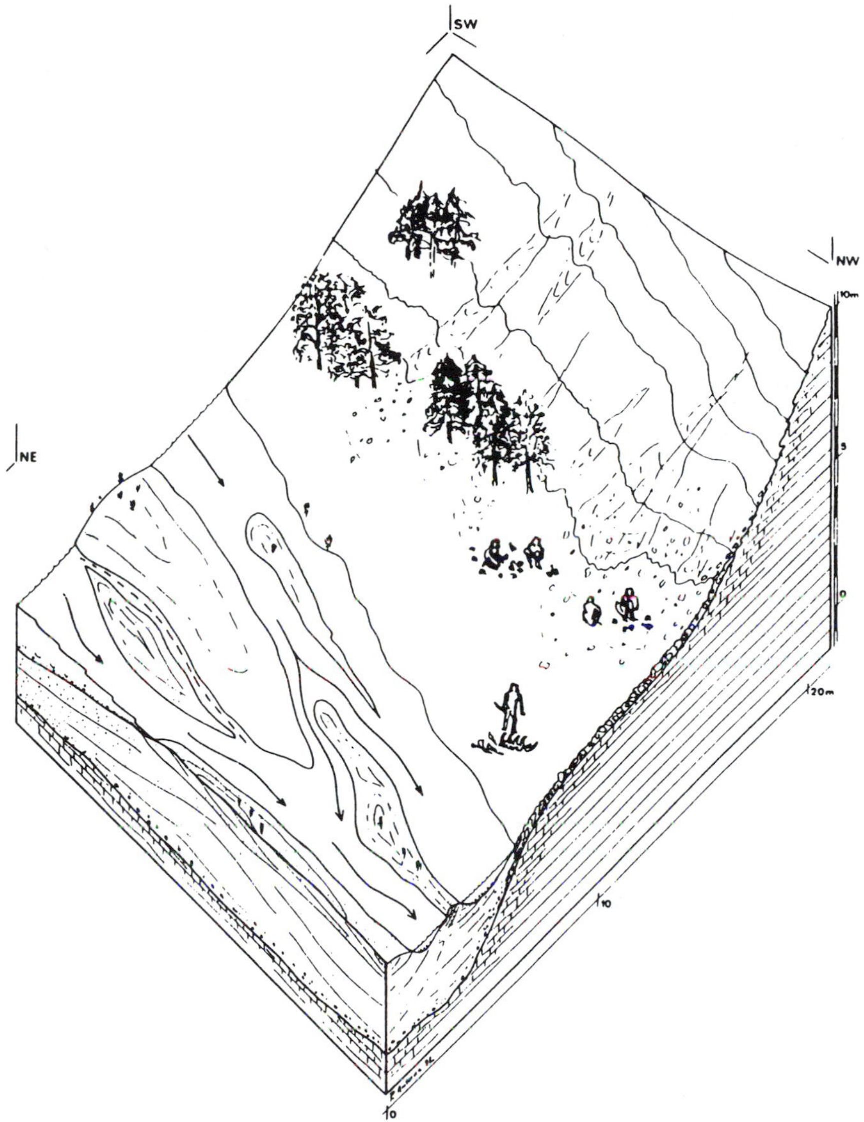


**4.6** A reconstruction of the Cagny la Garenne locale, France, NW region (after Antoine and Tuffreau 1993:Fig. 4).

terrace of the Somme starts in OIS 12. Hominids were attracted to a small protected area, c. 12 m wide, in front of the chalk talus which formed the south bank of the river (Figure 4.6). Water and stone materials, combined with shelter beside the talus from the prevailing wind, singled it out as a preferred location (Antoine and Tuffreau 1993:246) which was returned to on several occasions.[14]

Archaeological materials have been found in primary context covered by low-energy fluvial and lacustrine sediments. Such localities as Miesenheim I (Bosinski, Kolfschoten and Turner 1988, 1989, E. Turner 1990, 1991),

Notarchirico (Belli et al. 1991, Cassoli et al. 1993) and Hoxne (Singer, Gladfelter and Wymer 1993) are remarkable examples of preservation and provide a snapshot of the remote past. Such site integrity can also be found in the travertine springs of the north-central region at Bilzingsleben (Mania 1991a) and Stuttgart (Reiff 1986), and in the southeast region at Vértesszöllös (Kretzoi and Dobosi 1990). These springs fed small lakes and in the case of Stuttgart formed a travertine terrace of the Neckar.

In one instance a substantial landscape has been preserved. This occurs in southern England along the line of the 43-m Sussex raised beach. This can be traced for almost 30 km (ApSimon, Gamble and Shackley 1977, Roberts, Gamble and Bridgland 1995, Woodcock 1981).[15] Incorporated in the marine sediments which lie in front of this feature are a number of important findspots of which Boxgrove and Slindon are the best known. Terra Amata in the Mediterranean west region (Lumley 1969b, 1975) is less well preserved (Villa 1982) but still important evidence for beach occupation.

However, these are the flagship sites (Gamble 1996b). The vast majority of locales associated with rivers, lakes, springs and marine sediments are in secondary, derived contexts. Indeed describing such material as 'sites' is very misleading. At best they are findspots with differing numbers of items which were gathered from a number of old land-surfaces, at different times and from a range of distances.

In northern and southern regions the land surfaces onto which artifacts were dropped have in many instances moved downslope due either to later periglacial or to stream action. Once deposited in the valley bottoms (aggradation) the material was then incorporated into fluvial sand and gravel terraces as the rivers cut down (degraded) their bed. As a result many of the stone tools show different degrees of rolling and the association between, say, fauna and artifacts is lost. In the Mediterranean regions, periglacial action was much reduced but stone artifacts were still swept into the river systems when vegetation cover was reduced in arid phases. In all eight regions the hominid habit of camping on river banks and gravel bars in amongst braided river channels did not ensure their archaeological records a generally well-preserved future (Figure 4.7).

Good preservation does not just depend on activities being covered by fine-grained, low-energy fluvial sediments. Material buried by wind-blown loess deposits, as in the Somme valley (Antoine 1990) and at Kärlich in western Germany (Bosinski et al. 1986), can also preserve in-situ material.

Cave occupation is comparatively rare for this period due to later scouring and the removal of deposits. However, the Caune de l'Arago at Tautavel (Lebel 1992, Lumley 1979), Orgnac III (Combier 1967) and the Grotte Vaufrey levels XII and XI (Rigaud 1988a) in France, and Atapuerca in Spain (Bermúdez 1995, Carbonell and Rodriguez 1994) do contain long sequences of material. Arago and Atapuerca (Sima de los Huesos and TD 6) have produced large collections of human remains (Arsuaga, Bermúdez de Castro and Carbonell 1997, Arsuaga

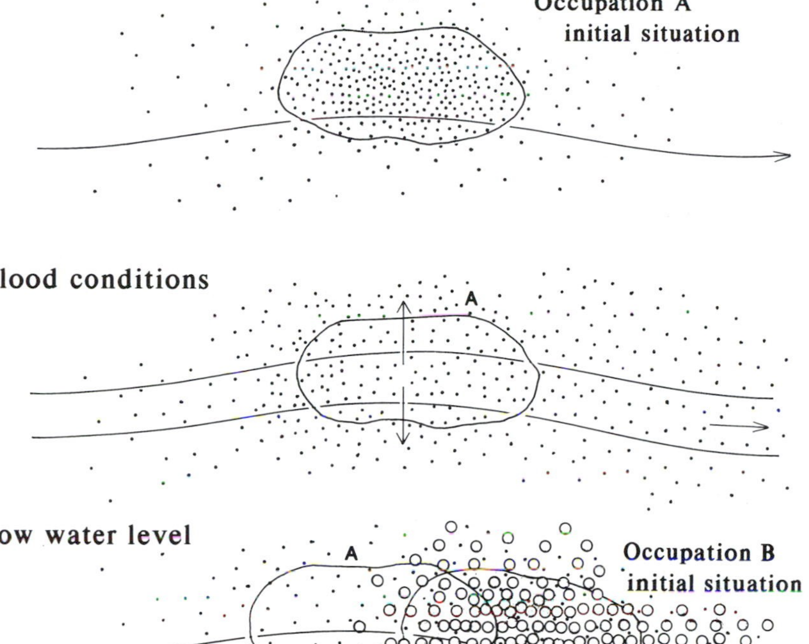


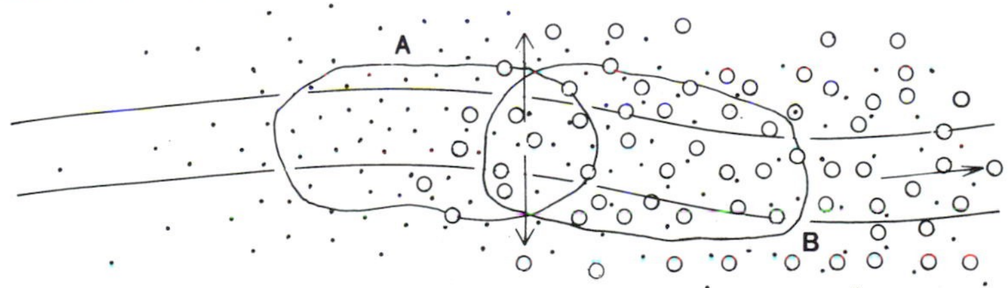


**4.7** A model of how successive Lower Palaeolithic gatherings at streamside locales become mixed into palimpsests (after Santonja 1991–2:Fig. 4).

et al. 1993, Bermúdez de Castro et al. 1997, Carbonell et al. 1995, Lumley and Lumley 1979, Lumley 1976).

*Long and short chronologies for the initial occupation of Europe*

There are currently two views on the earliest occupation of Europe. The case for a long chronology can be found in the edited volumes by Peretto (1992), Bonifay and Vandermeersch (1991) and Gibert (1992) and in a comprehensive review by Bosinski (1992b) and Carbonell (et al. 1996). They claim Europe was

Table 4.5. *Selected sites in the long chronology (from Bonifay and Vandermeersch 1991:319). Sites have been grouped according to 0.5-Myr blocks as presented by these authors. Most of those sites which date to the 0.5–1-Myr BP chronological block (e.g. Vallonnet, Prezletice and Kärlich A) are placed at its beginning, in the Jaramillo palaeomagnetic reversal at c. 0.9 Myr BP.*

| Site | Country | Age Myr | Artifacts | Hominid remains |
|---|---|---|---|---|
| Duero valley | Spain | 1–1.5 | Pebble tools | |
| Cueva Victoria | Spain | 1–1.5 | Pebble tools | ? |
| Venta Micena | Spain | 1–1.5 | Manuports | ? |
| Orce | Spain | 0.5–1 | Flakes | |
| Atapuerca TD 6 | Spain | >0.78 | Pebble tools | Yes |
| Chillac | France | >1.5 | Pebble tools | |
| Soleihac | France | 0.5–1 | Pebble tools/structure? | |
| Escale | France | 0.5–1 | Fire, flakes | |
| Vallonnet | France | 0.5–1 | Pebble tools | |
| Monte Poggiolo | Italy | 1–1.5 | Pebble tools | |
| Belleroche | Belgium | 0.5–1 | Pebble tools | |
| Kärlich A | Germany | 0.5–1 | Pebble tools | |
| Stránská Skála | Czech Republic | 1–1.5 | Pebble tools | |
| Beroun | Czech Republic | >1.5 | Pebble tools | |
| Prezletice | Czech Republic | 0.5–1 | Pebble tools | ? |
| Korolevo | Russia | 1–1.5 | Pebble tools | |

occupied prior to the Brunhes/Matuyama boundary at 775 Kyr BP and in some cases in excess of 1.5 Myr BP. The sites which are commonly used to support the long chronology are shown in Table 4.5. If the lower Pleistocene dates recently proposed for Atapuerca TD 6 (Bermúdez de Castro et al. 1997, Carbonell et al. 1995) are accepted, as seems likely, then this would be the only long chronology site with unquestioned hominid remains.

Other locales such as Caune de l'Arago, Mauer, Isernia and Abbeville, which supporters of the long chronology often refer to, have been omitted from Table 4.5. In some cases they are substantial archaeological sites which, as we shall see, can be more precisely dated to the time block 0–0.5 Myr BP. In other cases they have uncontested hominid remains, unlike those in Table 4.5 where, for example, the Prezletice human molar has been reidentified as a bear (Fridrich 1989:29) and the 'hominid' skull from Venta Micena as a horse (Moyà-Solà and Köhler 1997, Palmqvist 1997).

All of the sites in Table 4.5 fall within the European cul-de-sac. Some support for accepting their great ages comes from a further series of finds outside this area but nonetheless in close geographical proximity (Bosinski 1992b). These are listed in Table 4.6.[16]

The short chronology has been most forcefully put by Farizy (1993), Raynal,

Table 4.6. *Some early sites surrounding 'Europe'.*

| Site | Country | Age Myr | Artifacts | Hominid remains | |
|---|---|---|---|---|---|
| Ubeidiyah | Israel | 1–1.5 | Pebble tools Flakes | | Bar Yosef (1980) |
| Yiron gravel | Israel | >2.4 | Flakes, cores | | Ronen (1991) |
| Dmanisi | Georgia | 1.6–1.8? | Pebble tools Flakes | Mandible | Dzaparidze et al. (1989) |
| Achalkalaki | Georgia | 0.7 | A single flake | | Loubine and Bosinksi (1995) |
| Riwat | Pakistan | 2 | Pebble tool | | Dennell et al. (1994) |
| Pabbi hills | Pakistan | 1–2 | Pebble tools Flakes | | Dennell et al. (1994) |
| Kuldara | Russia | 0.8–1 | Flakes | | Ranov (1991) |
| Casablanca | Morocco | 0.9 | Pebble tools Flakes | | Raynal et al. (1995a) |

Magoga and Bindon (1995), Roebroeks and Kolfschoten (1994) and Roebroeks and Kolfschoten (1995), following a review of the artifactual and dating evidence for many of the sites in Table 4.5.[17] They found that much of the dating evidence for these sites is still open to question and that in many cases the claims for stone artifacts are doubtful. However, the subsequent redating of Atapuerca has led to a modification of their original timetable (Dennell and Roebroeks 1996).

We should not be surprised that disagreement still exists over the artifactual status of some stones. Rocks fracture naturally and their edges can be modified by trampling and cryoturbation in sediments to mimic hominid retouch. These are known as geofacts. Volcanic activity also produces very convincing tephrofacts (Raynal, Magoga, and Bindon 1995).[18]

Moreover, it is often possible to find convincing flakes, pebble tools and even cores within most gravel deposits where 99.99 per cent of the material will be unmodified. It depends on how long you are prepared to keep looking. This fact was appreciated in the eolith (literally, dawn stones) debate that preoccupied British Palaeolithic archaeologists in the first half of this century. Eolith supporters claimed Pliocene age artifacts from the Cromer forest bed of East Anglia. These have now all been discounted as the products of 'accidental concussion' (Warren 1914:449), for example when waves smash pebbles on the beach, producing geofactual flakes and pebble tools.[19] The key point for the unwary collector was clearly set out by Hazzledine Warren, the most prominent eolith debunker:

What is important . . . is the fact that such phenomena as the flaking of flints and occasional bulbs and also edge-knapping are produced by causes entirely apart from direct human effort. The likeness between the flaking produced by Nature and that produced by human agencies is sufficient to shift any burden of proof upon those who maintain the human origin of the stones; and *this must not be done by a careful selection of picked specimens, but by a survey of the whole group.* (Warren 1920:250, my emphasis)

The same criteria when applied to the sites in Table 4.5 produce comparable doubts about the criteria of selection. Although, as Roebroeks has pointed out (1996), the eolith debate is largely forgotten, it does furnish us with a very considerable body of negative evidence with which to assess claims for very early artifacts. As a result of the controversy collections were picked over in some detail and only then rejected as evidence for hominid activity. Early Pleistocene and Pliocene deposits were regularly visited by collectors not only in England but also on the continent. The result was the eventual dismissal of the few claims for early tools.

What changed this picture were the discoveries in East Africa, primarily at Olduvai Gorge (Leakey 1971), and the development of absolute dating. At Bed I in Olduvai pebble tools and flakes, together with fossil remains of *Homo habilis* and *Australopithecus boisei*, were dated by Potassium Argon isotope decay techniques to 1.8–2 Myr BP. Roebroeks shows (1996) how this new timescale affected the claims and chronological estimates for similar pebble tools and flakes in Europe. Absolute early dates for tools and fossil skulls in one part of the world acted in another like setting a speed limit on the motorway. It encouraged the growth of extravagant claims in Europe so that this continent could catch up in the early-'man' race. With hindsight we can now see that the artifacts were not artifacts, and even if they were their dating lacked the precision achieved at Olduvai and elsewhere in East Africa, thanks to the presence of regular volcanic horizons.

This critical approach to origins research should also be applied by the appropriate regional specialists to the sites in Table 4.6 although in most of these cases it is the age, rather than the authenticity of the stone tools or fossil remains, which is in question. This was also the case at the genuine artifact site of Isernia la Pineta in Italy (Cremaschi and Peretto 1988, Palma di Cesnola 1996, Peretto 1991, Peretto, Terzani and Cremaschi 1983). Palaeomagnetic measurements and absolute dates placed this site below the Brunhes/Matuyama boundary and hence earlier than 775 Kyr BP (Coltorti et al. 1982). However, and as we have already seen, the presence of *Arvicola terrestris cantiana* indicates, on bio-stratigraphic grounds, a much later date during the *Mimomys* to *Arvicola* transition between OIS 15 and 13 (Koenigswald and Kolfschoten 1996).

The case for the short chronology, which I also support, rests on the earliest undisputed evidence for human occupation around the Cromer IV interglacial. If this is accepted as OIS 13, which lasted from 528–478 Kyr BP, it will include finds from Kärlich G, the primary context locale of Miesenheim I and the *Homo*

Table 4.7. *Changes in the European Palaeolithic record before and after 500 Kyr BP (after Roebroeks and Kolfschoten 1994:table 1).*

| Before 500,000 years ago | After 500,000 years ago |
|---|---|
| Very small artifact collections selected from a natural pebble background; few or no stone refits, suggesting natural fracture | Large collections of artifacts; excavated knapping floors with refitted stone nodules, indicating human manufacture |
| 'Geofacts' found in coarse matrix, disturbed secondary contexts | Artifacts found in fine grained matrix, primary context locales |
| Contested 'primitive'-looking assemblages of flakes and pebble tools | Uncontested Acheulean (biface) and non-Acheulean stone industries |
| No human remains | Human remains common |

*heidelbergensis* mandible from Mauer, all of which are associated with *Arvicola terrestris cantiana* (Kolfschoten and Turner 1996, Roebroeks and Kolfschoten 1994:497, E. Turner 1990). As Dennell and Roebroeks (1996) have argued, the older dates for Atapuerca and possibly Fuente Nueva 3 in the Orce basin (Roe 1995) suggest that the northern rim of the Mediterranean may have been occupied at an earlier date than Europe north of the Pyrenees and Alps. The earliest age of 800 Kyr BP for well-stratified stone-tool assemblages at Casablanca is also comparable to that proposed for the Iberian sites (Raynal et al. 1995).

*The changing archaeological record after 500 Kyr BP*

Even if you choose not to accept the short chronology, with its rejection as geofactual of such 'classic' early sites as the Vallonnet cave,[20] the ballpark date of 500 Kyr BP for the earliest occupation still represents a sharp division in the Palaeolithic record. Supporters of the long chronology will need to explain this away (Table 4.7).

An example of the change in the record after 500 Kyr BP is provided by the primary-context locale of Boxgrove in southern England (Roberts, Gamble and Bridgland 1995, Roberts, Stringer and Parfitt 1994). Occupation took place (Figure 4.8) during OIS 13 as shown by the presence of species which in England became extinct after OIS 12, the Anglian glaciation. These include *Stephanorhinus hundsheimensis* and *Ursus deningeri*. The Boxgrove water voles are *Arvicola terrestris cantiana*. There are no absolute dates for the sequence, which spans an entire interglacial as well as the commencement of the succeeding glacial phase.[21]

During the interglacial, the Boxgrove landscape was dominated by a collapsing chalk sea-cliff and a changing coastal geography. Over time the path of the sea into a large embayment became blocked, thereby creating a large salt-water, tidally fed lagoon. This was filled by the Slindon silts which preserve in

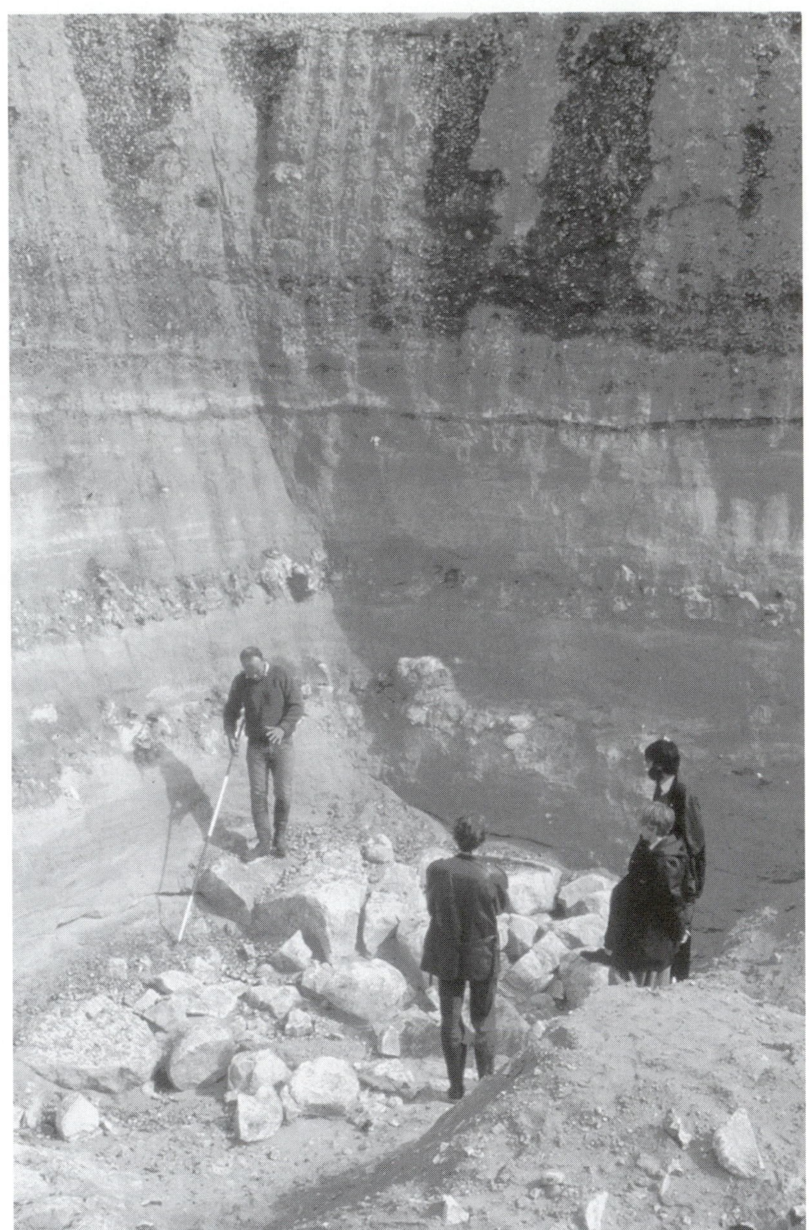

**4.8** Interglacial sediments of OIS 13 age, 500 Kyr BP, at Boxgrove, England, NW region. The people are standing on chalk blocks from a collapsed sea cliff over which sands and then silts accumulated. At the top of the section are thick deposits of soliflucted gravels from the neighbouring hills which mark the return to cold conditions in OIS 12 (photo by the author).

fine-grained detail the activities of the hominids who used this extensive, flat landscape.

Excavations in front of the cliff have found several discrete areas of flint knapping and animal butchery. Flint was grubbed from the collapsed cliff, tested for quality, and then carried two or three hundred metres out onto the silts before being knapped and used (Figure 4.9). There are very few formal flake tools. Several of the knapping episodes produced bifaces and these were mostly ovate, limandes and cordate in form (Bordes 1961a). A biface took between ten and fifteen minutes to make, less if the roughing-out part of the reduction sequence was undertaken at the cliff (Bergman et al. 1990). In some cases small tranchet flakes can be refitted back to the ovates. These were the last stage in the reduction and may have been removed after the biface had been used for cutting as revealed by use-wear analysis (*ibid.*:figure 11). However most of the bifaces were thrown away without further modification, soon after use as butchering tools on the animal carcasses which were scattered across the exposed tidal mudflats. Refitting the biface reduction scatters emphasizes the integrity of the locale and its primary context. The lithic material lies where the users dropped it. In December 1993, a robustly built tibia was found which is attributed to *Homo* cf *heidelbergensis* (Roberts et al. 1994) and dated with the rest of the archaeology to c. 500 Kyr BP in OIS 13. Two lower teeth from another individual have since been found.

Boxgrove is a locale of exceptional preservational quality but others, e.g. Miesenheim I and Bilzingsleben (Germany), the lower loams at Swanscombe, the Hoxne lake shore and Clacton (England), also have good preservation in the period after 500 Kyr BP. The peat deposits at Schöningen in eastern Germany preserve both fauna and wooden artifacts, including 2.5-m-long spears (Thieme 1997, Thieme and Maier 1995). At Cagny la Garenne and Cagny Cimetière (northern France) preservation is also good in a number of different climatic settings. The combined pollen and geological evidence points to occupation beginning in OIS 12 and continuing into OIS 11 (Antoine and Tuffreau 1993:246).

None of the sites in Table 4.5, allowing for the redating of Isernia, has this combination of evidence. At Venta Micena in Andalucia there is a very rich animal fauna with sabre tooth cats (*Homotherium*) and the giant hyena (*P. brevirostris*). The fauna has several similarities to that from the early Pleistocene-age site of Dmanisi where a robust hominid mandible classified as *Homo erectus* (Gabunia and Vekua 1995) was found directly beneath a skull of *Megantereon* (Dzaparidze et al. 1989) and could be as old as 1.6–1.8 Myr BP. However, the skull fragments which have been published as hominid specimens from Venta Micena (Gibert 1992) have been reidentified as a horse skull (Moyà-Solà and Köhler 1997, Palmqvist 1997). The lithic specimens at Venta Micena are not artifacts and on inspection are difficult to accept even as manuports.[22] Elsewhere in the Orce region there are good artifacts at Fuente Nueva (Roe 1995) and the results of current excavations are now awaited to establish

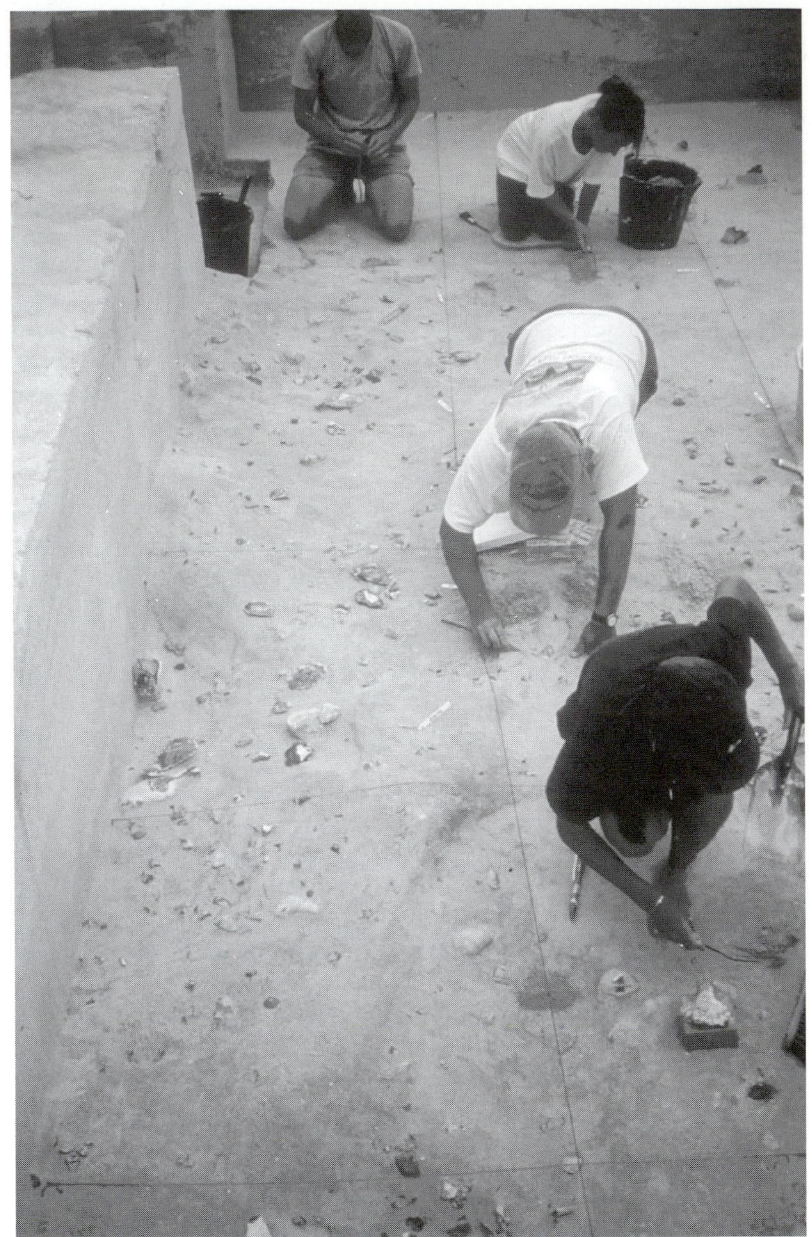

**4.9** Excavating bifaces, knapping waste and animal bones, several with cut-marks, at Boxgrove, England, NW region (photo by the author).

their position within the Pleistocene succession in this old lake basin (Raposo and Santonja 1995, Santonja 1992:56–9).

*Opening the gates of Europe*

Getting the age of the first occupation of Europe correct is obviously a goal in itself; but it is not the only, or indeed the most important objective. I side with the short chronology simply because I can see little reason why the archaeological record should change so dramatically after 500 Kyr BP unless it coincides with the appearance of hominids in the continent. It might be argued that preservation just happened to get better at this time. This is a very weak counter. For example, the very good preservation on well-dated early Pleistocene palaeontological sites such as Untermassfeld in eastern Germany (Roebroeks and Kolfschoten 1994:500) or West Runton in eastern England (Stuart 1996) shows that this is not the case.

However, accepting the short chronology does raise some problems for interpretation. Why did hominids stand at 'the gates of Europe' in Morocco, Georgia and Israel from at least one million years ago and, if the lower dates at Dmanisi are accepted, from as much as 1.6–1.8 Myr BP (Bosinski 1992b)? We are back to the problem that there appear to be no obvious barriers to settlement from the east and yet, if we accept the short chronology, we must ask hominids to kick their heels for either a half or one million years before colonizing Europe.

One solution, put forward by A. Turner (1992), is that the barrier consisted of a large carnivore guild.[23] The balance of this guild, as Turner argues, was maintained between the flesh-eating carnivores – the sabre- and dirk-toothed cats – and the carcass destroyers – principally the hyenas. Although the members of the guild changed between 1.5–1 Myr BP this produced no appreciable advantage to a potential hominid colonist (Turner 1992:121). But at 500 Kyr BP (Table 4.4) there was a dramatic decline in both the giant hyenas (*Pachycrocuta brevirostris* and *Pachycrocuta perrieri*) and the giant cats (*Homotherium latidens* and *Megantereon cultridens*). Turner argues that although many smaller carnivores remained after 500 Kyr BP the change in carcass destroyers and flesh eaters opened up, for the first time, a significant niche for hominid scavenging. He concludes that 500 Kyr BP

> will probably be the time at which an increasing density of more permanent hominid occupation will be seen to have occurred. Before that time, occupation is likely to have been much more sporadic, at least back as far as 1.5 Myr. (1992:122)

This is an attractive argument to explain the meagre archaeological record used to support a long chronology. However, we are not dealing so much with a change in the number of findspots after 500 Kyr BP (Table 4.3), but rather with a complete transformation of the archaeological record (Table 4.7) which in my opinion can only be explained by the fact that it is at this time that occupation first took place.[24]

Turner's model certainly provides a solution to that long wait at the 'Gates of Europe'. The demise of the big cats and giant hyenas at 500 Kyr BP marks a significant shift towards Europe being dominated by Asian/Beringian rather than African/Asian faunal communities. It also coincides with the shift to greater duration and amplitude in the glacial/interglacial cycles (Gamble 1995c:table 1); this culminated in the emergence of the mammoth/woolly rhino communities on the steppes which eventually stretched from the Pyrenees to Alaska (Khalke 1994). Intriguingly, Turner also points to the different composition of the carnivore guild around the north Mediterranean rim and particularly in Iberia (1992:122). In contrast to northern Europe this zone had major carcass producers rather than carcass destroyers. He believes a case can be made on palaeoecological grounds for earlier occupation in some, if not all, of the Mediterranean regions.

*Explaining late colonization as a social constraint*

I have argued (Gamble 1995c) that European colonization occurred as part of climatic and biotope changes that took place in long-term evolutionary time and at a continental scale. The combination of southern plant and animal refugia, faunal migrations from the east, the variable westerly oceanic effect and, at a regional scale, the existence of mosaic landscapes were the necessary conditions for permanent colonization, whether achieved in a single or, as seems most probable, a series of colonizing events. The colonization of the European peninsula took place during a long-term trend that led to an increase in faunal diversity (Table 4.4) and most probably augmented productivity, as expressed by animal biomass.

The short chronology points to one important conclusion for this colonization – it involved all but the northeast region (Figure 3.1). This finding suggests that any one region of Europe could only be colonized if it was colonized at the same time as most of the others. The implication is that to sustain population at a continental scale, and so cross the threshold of archaeological visibility, it was a necessary condition that large areas had to be occupied. Only then would a demographic balance be assured within the continent rather than continually relying on further immigration to counter local extinctions.

The limitations to this continental scale of colonization were precisely those which stalled the hominids at the eastern gates of Europe – extreme seasonality in the plains environment of large parts of the northwest, north-central and southeast regions. In terms of hominid behaviour this seasonality could only be overcome through greater annual mobility and the fissioning of population.[25] These necessary distances and separation of population in the more widely spaced plant and faunal 'plaid' mosaics of the plains could not be supported by the mechanisms available to middle Pleistocene social systems (Gamble 1993a, 1993d, Stringer and Gamble 1993:figure 82). As a result, population in the Caucasus, Middle East and North Africa did not expand into Europe even though very similar topographic conditions which concentrated resources existed in central Italy (Mussi 1995). Only with alterations to the seasonality regimes in central and western Europe, which coincided with changes that were detrimental to the large carnivores, did a match emerge between the scale of the hominids' social systems and the spatial structure of resources in the environment which permitted colonization.[26]

Examining the issue of colonization at a continental and world scale (Gamble 1993a, 1993e) is one reason why the debate between a long and a short chronology is important. However, to be meaningful, such a debate should now be based on the premise that the colonizing capabilities of these hominids was not limited solely by environmental conditions but rather by their own organizational responses to the structure of such environments. They were social beings, assisted by culturally transmitted behaviour to expand their ranges. They were not simply dancing to the rhythms of the Pleistocene.

## Rhythms and social technology

We have now seen where the evidence for the earliest European hominids is normally recovered and the opportunities these contexts provide for discussing issues of colonization, change and adaptation. But how do we go further and investigate their skills, not just in survival but in creating distinctive and different societies? How do we investigate the all-important rhythms of human action (Table 3.1)?

Lithics provide the key to these questions not just because they survive but because they vary. They preserve different orders of temporality in their acquisition, manufacture and discard. They bridge spatial scales from the knapping scatter to the region where raw material was obtained. Perlès (1992:224) has summarized the task for studies of such lithic variability by reminding us that they are not exclusively typological but simultaneously conceptual, technical and economic. In brief we are dealing with a social technology. We can now examine the evidence according to the rhythms of action which link the region to the locale, the individual to the cultural tradition, decisions to selection pressure and the gesture to the raw material (Table 3.1). The three rhythms involve analysing

- raw-material acquisition and transfer to illustrate paths and tracks
- the technology and tool production covered by the chaîne opératoire
- the skills involved in creating the environment surrounding the hominid, the taskscape.

### *Paths and tracks: raw-material acquisition and transfers*

The evidence from all these locales for the use of raw materials is predominantly local. Lebel's (1992, Svoboda 1987, L. Wilson 1988) study of the Caune de l'Arago in southern France provides a good example. His study dealt with four levels (D, E, F and G) which are correlated with OIS 12, the Anglian–Elster–Oka glaciation of northern Europe. The two largest collections

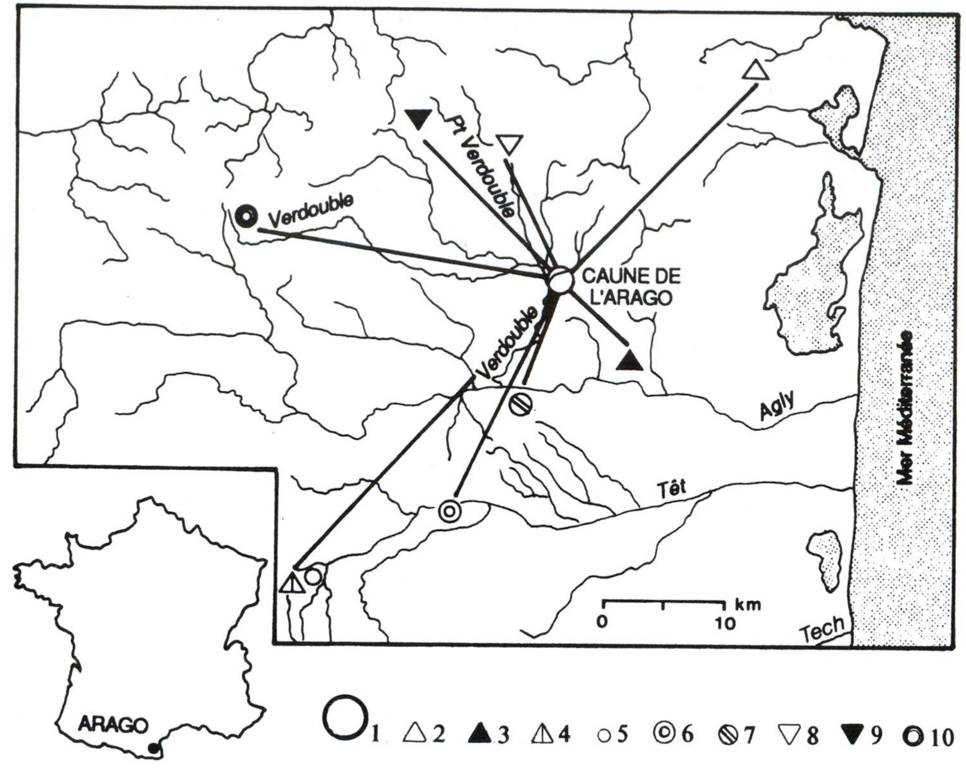


**4.10** Raw-material transfers at Caune de l'Arago, France, MW region (after Lebel 1992).

KEY:

1 Limestones, sandstone, quartz, quartzites
2 Flint, chalcedony (Roquefort-des-Corbières)
3 Jurassic flint (La Joliette)
4 Brown jasper (Vinça)
5 Bluish quartz (Vinça)
6 Quartzite (Millas)
7 Pegmatite, albite, quartz crystal, gneiss (l'Agly)
8 Chalcedony, quartzite (Segure)
9 Chert (Col de Couisse)
10 Quartz and bluish quartzite (Soulatge)

came from levels F and G and number 118,000 lithic pieces which utilized 99 different types of rock (Wilson 1988:377). These could be grouped into eight major types of which the flints, quartzites/quartz and limestones are the most important.

Lebel's analysis confirms the Geneste principle (Chapter 3:Table 3.4), that the majority of lithic materials (80 per cent) came from within 5 km of the cave (1992:63). The furthest distance was 35 km (Figure 4.10). The amount of cortex, the outer surface of the original nodule, is greater among the local rocks such as the quartzites and limestones and almost nonexistent with the flints which came from 7 to 30 km away. The fine-grained materials are represented only by the later stages of the chaîne opératoire (Lebel 1992). In other words the full sequence of reduction from nodule to core–flake–retouched piece is not present.

The data are fairly sparse on the movement of materials but a recent review by Féblot-Augustins (1997) indicates a similar pattern of local procurement within the southwest region. In other regions the data are much poorer but do not contradict the pattern. For all Europe a sample of ninety-four raw material transfers from thirty-three sites/layers produced only fifteen which were greater than 30 km. The largest distance was 80 km from the site of Labastide d'Anjou in France (Féblot-Augustins 1997:inventories 15–18). The average distance for the furthest transfer in each site/level was 28 km.

All the indications are therefore that local materials were used. An example of this is provided by the distribution of quartzite and other non-flint artifacts in southern England (MacRae 1988). These are only found as artifacts in the gravel deposits of the Bunter areas where quartzite occurs locally. The flint-bearing areas of southern England have no quartzite artifacts (*ibid.*:figure 1). Local quartzite was also commonly used in the Rheinland where, for example at Kärlich, a quartzite biface was found (Bosinski 1992a:Abb. 17).

The transfer of materials beyond the 80–100-km threshold, noted in Chapter 3 as significant, is not found during this period. Finally there is no evidence from any region for the transfer of marine molluscs, fossil shells, ochre, ivory or any other raw material which can be provenanced.

### *Chaîne opératoire: technology and tool production*

There is now general agreement that the technology of this period is neither as complicated, in terms of units of culture history, as once thought nor indicative of evolutionary stages in hominid culture. The change in thinking can be illustrated with the British sequence. Although its concerns may be parochial in one sense, questioning long-established local cultural groupings, it nonetheless serves to illustrate the sea-change which approaches to lithic analysis have recently undergone.[27]

For many years it was thought that in the northwest region two parallel phyla, or traditions of flint working, existed – the Clactonian and Acheulean (Gamble 1986a:141ff). These represented a flake/core/chopping-tool industry that was contrasted with a biface (handaxe)/flake/core industry. The discussion has always centred on the relation between these two cultural entities. Were they industrial variants related to function; did their differences express some sort of ethnic affiliation; or the impact of environment on patterns of cultural transmission (Mithen 1994); or were they a reaction to immediate circumstances that invoked either an expedient (Clactonian) or a curated (Acheulean) response?[28] However, following recent excavations at the OIS 11 site of Barnham (Ashton et al. 1994) and at the older OIS 13 site of High Lodge (Ashton

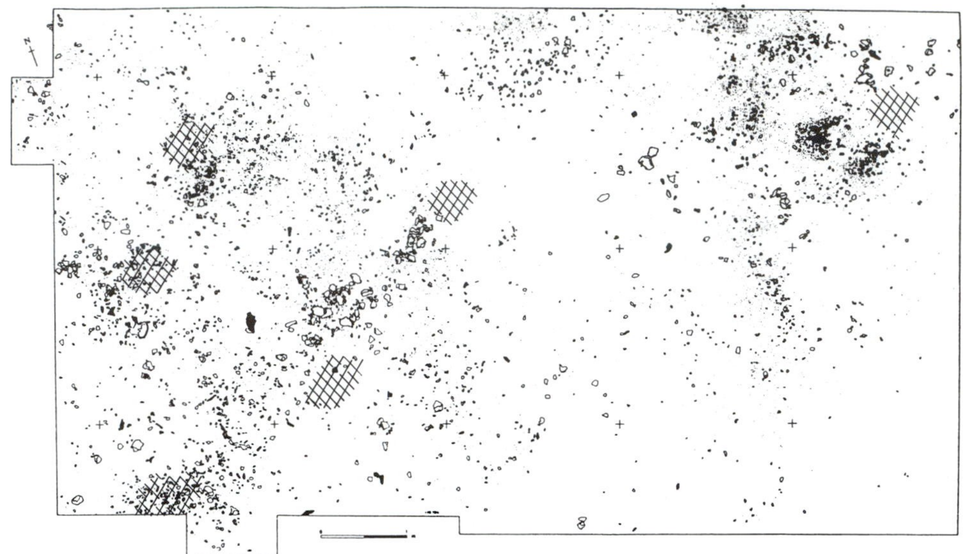

**4.11** The distribution of flint artifacts (white or stippled) and animal bones (black) from Geological Test Pit (GTP) 17 at Boxgrove, England, NW region. Most of the bones probably come from a single horse skeleton. The cross-hatching indicates the position of six flint blocks carried to the carcass and from which flakes were knapped (after Pitts and Roberts 1997:Fig. 38). If bifaces were made then they were dropped outside the area covered by this trench.

and McNabb 1992), we can now see that the Clactonian can no longer be regarded as a typological, technological and hence cultural entity distinct from the wider Acheulean tradition. At Barnham, extensive excavation has shown that in the same time horizon both traditions exist but are related to different small micro-habitats in this riverine locale. A key factor appears to be the availability of good raw material as well as its position in the landscape. Rather than being bound by cultural preference, the decision to follow an Acheulean or a Clactonian reduction sequence was bound up in the immediate context of deploying stone to assist behaviour (see below).

What we see instead at a locale like Barnham is a continuous process where the so-called Clactonian technique that smashes nodules on anvils, so producing irregular, but highly serviceable flakes, is but one part of a longer sequence of gestures by which bifaces were also produced.

This same pattern is well illustrated at Boxgrove in area GTP 17 (Pitts and Roberts 1997). At least six large blocks of flint were brought a few hundred metres from the collapsed sea-cliff to a horse carcass (Figure 4.11). They were then flaked to produce large, irregular flakes for use in butchering this animal. If this had been the only excavated part of the locale then no doubt Boxgrove would have been classified as Clactonian. However, on the same contemporary horizon, but in other parts of this half-million year old landscape, there is abundant evidence for the manufacture of ovate-shaped bifaces.

These same ovates also come as a surprise to conventional typological thinking which once placed artifacts in a chronological scheme that went from crude to finely made implements. The ovates should, by such reckoning, come towards the end of such a scheme. But here at Boxgrove, dated to 500 Kyr BP, they come at the beginning. Furthermore, at High Lodge, the non-biface industry is dominated by flakes which are made into end and side scrapers using semi-invasive, semi-scalar and non-stepped retouch. Such retouch was once thought to be the hallmark of later, Middle Palaeolithic traditions. However, the artifact bearing sediments at High Lodge can conclusively be shown to have been subsequently transported as a block in the base of the OIS 12, Anglian, ice sheet (Ashton et al. 1992). They are therefore the same age as the Boxgrove material.[29]

*The processes of façonnage and débitage*

But where do we go from here? Sorting out a local difficulty in flint technology is always satisfying but how does it advance our investigation of Palaeolithic society? One answer is to broaden our understanding of technology and typology by using the concept of the chaîne opératoire (see Chapter 3). The advantages of employing this procedure are twofold. Firstly it stems from the notion that technical acts are social acts. Secondly it explicitly aims to link the scales of archaeological analysis from the artifact to the landscape, the locale to the region (Table 3.1). The emphasis is on the processes of manufacture and consumption as well as those of acquisition and transportation.

Indeed this stress on process, the rhythms of action and the gestures they embody, is a necessary antidote to the significance usually attached to the importance of artifact form. According to the latter the image of the implement sat in the mind of the Palaeolithic knapper guiding his/her actions. Such mental templates allow archaeologists to talk of pre-determined shapes and forms among lithic artifacts. The mental template also underpins the notion of Palaeolithic cultures. The shapes of handaxes and side scrapers follow traditional patterns of culture. These patterns are translated into artifact forms by a mental blueprint which in these days of computer analogies of the mind might be described as hard-wired cognitive structures.

Davidson and Noble have aptly referred to this approach as the 'fallacy of the finished artefact' (1993:365). They point out that we cannot assume that the final shape of a stone tool was the intended shape. If this is the case then neither can we infer from these same objects the chain of manufacture nor its implications for the cognitive skills and problem-solving abilities of hominids. Instead, as Schlanger (1996) has argued, we must follow the gestures in such reduction strategies flake by flake. When this is done it reveals that there was no separation between doing and thinking in the act of knapping stone.

But while it is necessary to redress the balance in lithic studies by emphasizing process as well as form, we still need some general direction for such studies. This is supplied by Boëda's (et al. 1990) applications of the chaîne opératoire based on two principles of manufacture. These are *façonnage*, where the final object, such as a biface (Figure 4.12), is revealed within the block of raw material in a progressive manner, rather like a sculptor carving a statue: and *débitage*[30] where, using a range of methods, the volume of the raw material is sub-divided. Débitage produces many different forms and volumes by processes which are standardized, recurrent or lineal according to circumstance (*ibid.*:45). These two different approaches have been used to characterize, respectively, the Lower Palaeolithic with bifaces, and the Middle Palaeolithic with flakes.

Boëda (et al. 1990) distinguish two further families of chaîne opératoire based on the manner in which the volume of a block of lithic material is conceived. This can either be as a tool (Fr. *outil*) or as a blank (Fr. *support*) which may later be retouched into a tool. For example a biface can either be made on a blank or reduced down from a nodule. The former is an example of débitage, the latter of façonnage.[31]

With these distinctions the chaînes shown in Table 4.8 can be recognized.

The notion of recurrent or repeated forms is particularly important for the chaîne opératoire since it establishes that the knappers were not aiming to produce a single artifact from a single block of raw material.[32] Therefore the artifact is not the representation of an isolated idea, a construct in the mind of the knapper. Rather they interacted with the raw material in a creative manner and not as demiurges driven by a pre-existing mental template. Their creativity was of course constrained by the material and the traditions which structured and informed the suite of gestures involved in knapping. Therefore the artifact is not the physical representation of an idea shared by all, but instead a social skill negotiated through gestures and inscribed in the bodily movements and rhythms which we call knapping.

This approach has recently been clarified by White and Pettitt (1995), who make an important distinction between the manufacturing principles of façonnage and débitage. The former is a reducing process where the methods are organized in relation to a *secant plane*. They define this conceptual plane as dissecting a solid such as a nodule of flint (*ibid.*). Since volume is distributed around this plane, it follows that reducing the mass of the raw material in relation to it will necessarily involve removing material from above and below it (see Figure 5.17). Adding the notion of the secant plane to that of façonnage allows us to unify our technological conception of how biface and levallois technologies (Chapter 5) were similarly organized.

White and Pettitt (1995:29–30) also extend the three dimensional division of material through débitage by describing it further as a *migrating plane technology*. To return to the local difficulty of the British Clactonian we can now see, by using the chaîne opératoire, that in terms of technological organization this represents the process of débitage, although secant plane technology linked to

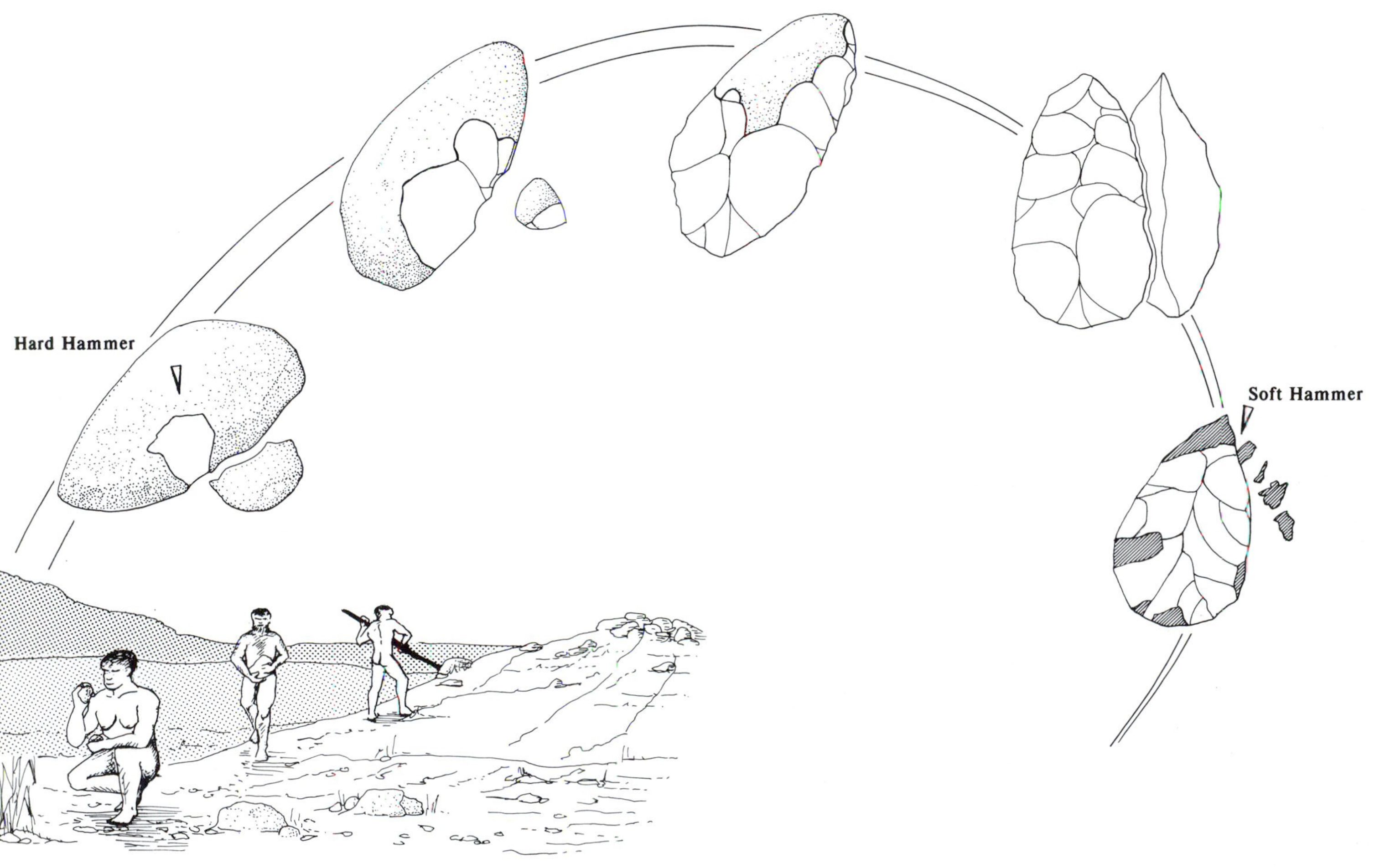


**4.12** Chaîne opératoire for biface façonnage (after Lhomme and Maury 1990).

Table 4.8. *The major chaînes opératoires in the Lower and Middle Palaeolithic (Boëda, Geneste and Meignen 1990).*

| | | |
|---|---|---|
| Bifacial chaîne opératoire | | |
| bifaces knapped as tools | | (façonnage) |
| bifaces made on blanks | | (débitage) |
| Trifacial chaîne opératoire | | |
| trifacially knapped cores and edge trimming flakes | | (débordant) |
| Levallois chaîne opératoire | | |
| linear | – preferential flake | |
| recurrent | – unipolar | |
| | – bipolar | |
| | – rotating | (centripètes) |

Table 4.9. *The outcomes for major lithic technologies of different manufacturing principles (based on a provisional scheme kindly supplied by P. Pettitt). It should be emphasized that this scheme does not aim to classify end-products.*

| | Plane | |
|---|---|---|
| | Secant | Migrating |
| Façonnage | Biface production | Pebble tool production of choppers |
| Débitage | Levallois technology<br>Prismatic technology<br>Disc-core (centripetal) technology | Globular core technology<br>Pebble tool production of cores |

façonnage was obviously practised, as the occasional finds of handaxes in such assemblages demonstrate (McNabb and Ashton 1993).

A simple division of the major lithic technologies can now be proposed (Table 4.9) which unites different traditions, as with the levallois and prismatic, which until recently were held to represent the Middle and Upper Palaeolithic respectively.

An appreciation of the expertise associated with these different techniques is provided by Steele's (et al. 1995) video analysis of the motor skills involved in experimentally knapping a biface and Clactonian core/chopper. Viewed as finished artifacts, both would be examples of façonnage but employing different techniques organized around two distinctive conceptual planes (Table 4.9). The former took 301 strikes and 24 minutes, the latter 78 strikes and 6 minutes. Most importantly, the frame-by-frame analysis assessed the different cognitive load by measuring the position of the arm/elbow wielding the hammer and the preparation time between each strike. A very good correlation existed between the length of preparation time (1–3 seconds) and the motor complexity of the following knapping gesture (*ibid.*:253). The more complicated the gesture the greater the preparation time. This was particularly marked when a soft, antler hammer replaced a hammerstone for the last 188 strikes in making the biface. While the experiment was designed to test notions of linguistic capabilities manifested in artifact manufacture, it also shows how motor and cognitive skills are not working to produce a final, pre-determined shape. Instead the process of manufacture by façonnage or by débitage is literally 'in hand' (Schlanger 1996:248). The outcome is a seamless construction between the mental and gestural activities of the knapper on the one hand and on the other hand with the material being knapped.

The fallacy of the finished artifact has for many years prevented us from seeing the essential unity of Palaeolithic technology. However, we can see that the interpretative challenge now facing studies of early Palaeolithic technology revolves, as White and Pettitt argue (1995:31), around two questions:

- the variation between systems based on façonnage and débitage
- variation within façonnage to discover why bifaces only occur in some assemblages and, when they do, why they vary in form.

Their answer is to stress the situational character of early Palaeolithic technology. The quality and availability of raw material, site function and other immediate circumstances are thus critical in determining the material output and not some pre-existing mental blueprint. Consequently, 'shape does not form a template but is rather the rhythmic repetition of an adaptable technological repertoire' (White and Pettitt 1995:32).

Raw-material availability has been examined in detail by White (1995) as one reason for the variety of technological solutions. Following Roe's (1964) metrical demonstration that the British Lower Palaeolithic biface industries consisted of two major groupings, composed of pointed (e.g. Stoke Newington) and ovate forms (e.g. Hoxne Lower industry), White has examined the raw materials in such assemblages (Figure 4.13). His findings are that pointed forms correlate with the use of river gravel flint which is generally of poorer flaking quality. It is difficult if not impossible to make ovate bifaces using such material. The ovate industries are invariably found in close proximity, as at Slindon Park or Boxgrove, to a source of large sized nodules often in primary geological context.

Swanscombe (Table 4.10) provides an example of how the changing availability of raw material influenced biface shape (see also Callow 1986a and 1986b, Villa 1991). The pointed bifaces from the upper middle gravels were made on material derived from the layer below and now incorporated into a river beach. Above this level, in the upper loams, ovate bifaces were common at a time when the gravels had been covered by up to a metre of sand (Bridgland 1994). White suggests (1995:13) that with the loss of an immediate raw-mate-

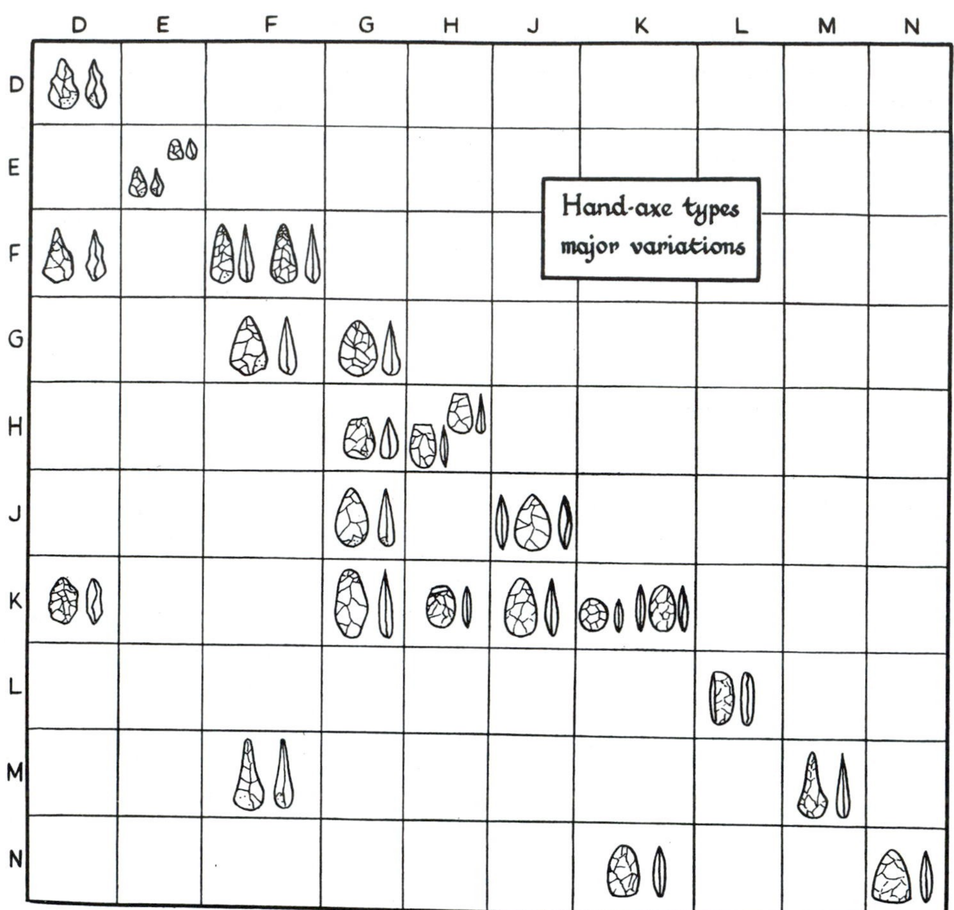


**4.13** A matrix of biface shapes (after Wymer 1968:Fig. 27).
KEY:
D Pointed; more than 10 cm in length, irregular cutting edges, rapidly made
E Pointed; 10 cm or less in length, and rapidly made
F Pointed; well made with thin edges and heavy butt
G Sub-cordate
H Cleaver
J Cordate
K Ovate
L Segmental chopping tool
M Ficron
N Flat-butted cordate

rial source, higher quality raw material was carried in from a short distance away.[33]

White concludes that the preferred biface was an ovate with the implication that maximizing the circumferential edge was the knapper's goal. Such a view runs counter to the notion that these hominids intended bifaces to look the way

Table 4.10. *The Swanscombe sequence, OIS 11.*

| Depositional environment | Unit | Industry | Biface form |
|---|---|---|---|
| Land-derived sediments | Upper gravel | Acheulean | |
| | Upper loam | Acheulean | Ovate |
| Aggrading stream deposits | Upper middle gravel | Acheulean* | Pointed |
| | Lower middle gravel | | |
| Overbank deposits | Lower loam | Clactonian | |
| Aggrading river deposits | Lower gravel | Clactonian | |

*Note:*
* =hominid skull horizon.

they do (Wynn 1993a:302). However, White's study also shows that their preferred procurement strategy was to use an immediate, rather than the best, source for raw material even if a short distance was involved. It seems they were quite prepared to settle for a pointed biface. Finally, we must remember that Swanscombe also has two levels with 'Clactonian' flakes and cores (Conway, McNabb and Ashton 1996). The two depositional environments, gravel and loam (Table 4.10), combined with the evidence from Boxgrove and Barnham, indicate that these limited chaînes occur with both pointed and ovate biface forms. Flake and biface traditions therefore emerge as different outcomes to immediate conditions. The extent to which such outcomes were planned beyond the perception of an immediate affordance appears on this evidence to be limited.

*Organic artifacts*

Lithics dominate the record of social technology during this period. However, some important examples of organic artifacts are also known which shed further light on the chaîne opératoire. In particular, the evidence for the use of organic raw materials now includes a remarkable set of worked wooden spears from Schöningen in eastern Germany (Thieme 1997, Thieme and Maier 1995). At site 12 one of these artifacts even has a very probable hafting splice, presumably for a stone tool. At site 13 a complete short thrusting spear, 78 cm in length and pointed at both ends was found. Longer throwing spears, 2.5 m in length, have also been excavated from the peats (Figure 4.14). Three of these are made from felled spruce trees (Thieme 1997:809) with the tips worked from the hard dense wood at the base of the tree. Effort and, according to some, anticipation (Dennell 1997) have gone into their manufacture. But too much emphasis on such evidence of forward planning could merely repeat the finished-artifact fallacy in wood rather than stone (Davidson and Noble 1993). The fact that the Schöningen examples seem to have been lost or discarded when still apparently serviceable strikes a chord with the appearance of many of the stone bifaces.

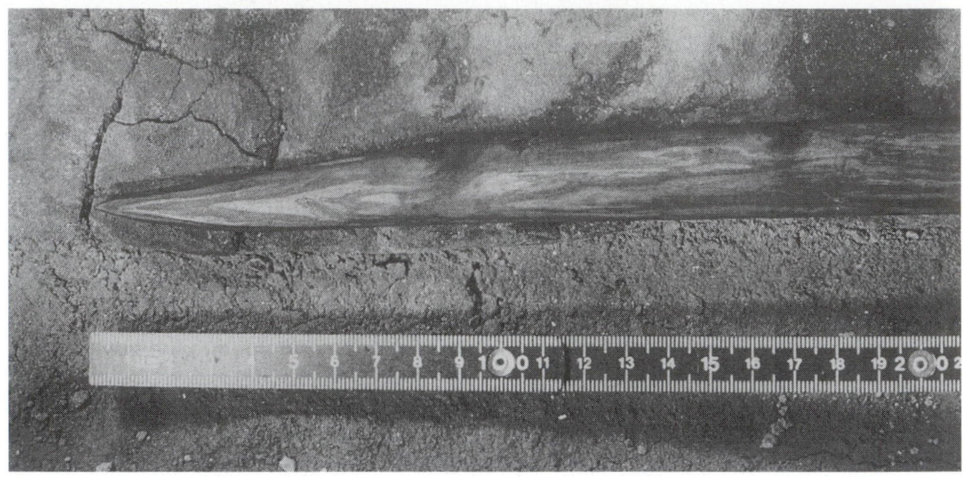

**4.14** Throwing spear II from Schöningen, Germany, NC region. Made from spruce (*Picea*), the total length of this spear is 2.30 m and it was found near a horse pelvis. The tip is shown in detail (after Thieme 1997:Fig. 5).

Could it be that all items of technology were only carried infrequently and only over short distances? Such behaviour runs counter to the notion that implement curation reflects the degree of energy investment (Binford 1973, 1977). This suggests a wider role for such components of a social technology than just killing horses.

Other wooden objects are known such as the broken Clacton spear point (Oakley et al. 1977) and various wooden pieces from Torralba (Freeman and Butzer 1966) and Bilzingsleben (Mania 1990). All of these would be examples of façonnage technology.

Bone tools are also widely accepted and include flakes struck on anvils from elephant and rhino long bones also from Bilzingsleben (Mania 1990) and Isernia (Anconetani et al. 1995), Fontana Ranuccio (Segre and Ascenzi 1984:Fig. 3.2) and La Polledrara in Italy (Anzidei and Huyzendveld 1992). Villa (1991) has drawn attention to these bone tools from Italy and in particular the pointed bone biface from Castel di Guido (Figure 4.15). The use of these organic materials points to local affordances being taken and being worked by both façonnage and débitage.

*Tool maintenance*

There is little evidence for this aspect of social technology. Tranchet flake removals from the tips of many of the Boxgrove bifaces (Roberts 1986) point to

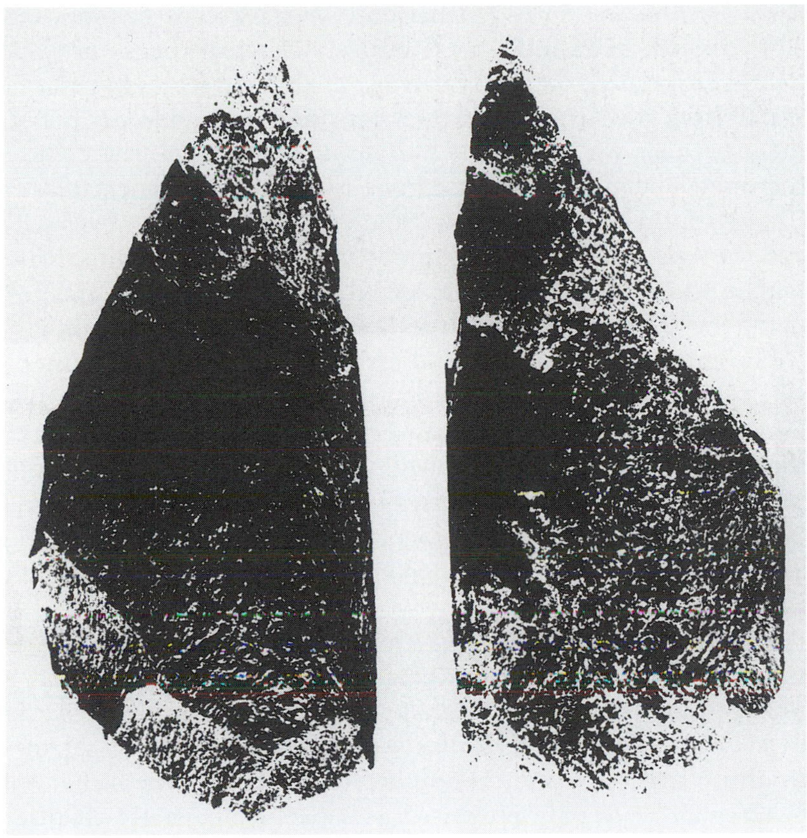

**4.15** A biface on elephant bone from Castel di Guido, Italy MC region. Length = 18.7 cm (after Villa 1991:Fig. 2).

more than one phase in the use of such implements. But refitting indicates that such reuse was local and presumably part of a continuous activity. In other words the artifact was not put down and picked up hours or even days later and then knapped again to remove the small 're-sharpening' flake. With the emphasis in this period upon façonnage rather than débitage (Boëda, Geneste and Meignen 1990) the recycling, reuse and modification of implements seen in later periods (e.g. Dibble 1987) is not to be expected. This same, immediate, approach to technology was applied to organic artifacts. As we have seen above, these are currently few in number and little elaborated.

### *Taskscape: skills and the surrounding environment*

The taskscape is an array of related activities which carry forward the processes of social life (Chapter 3). These activities can be seen as skills which are continuous rather than divided up into discrete functions such as hunting, flint knapping or butchery. They are continuous activities because social life which creates these skills, and is also created by them, is also uninterrupted in its daily rhythms and flows. Furthermore, the taskscape surrounds the individual. This concept owes much to Gibson's ecological theory of visual perception (1979). He pointed out that in terms of what we see, organisms cannot be separated from their environment. A person is surrounded by his or her environment because we see that it literally touches them, the environment *is* the hominid. Therefore to mention one is to suppose the existence of the other. Thus a mutual environment surrounds an individual, moves with that person and provides affordances for action. It is only our brains which have been taught, through such common analytical concepts as the mental template, to make the distinction between an organism and its environment.

The taskscape for this period can be illustrated by discussing two sets of skills; *generic*, or transferable, and *specific* skills. These would be transmitted between individuals as the learned routines of social life and survival. They are therefore constantly under selection and always with the individual. These skills summarize the capabilities of hominids to change in ways that can be directly measured in the archaeological record. Two examples dealing with adaptation to local ecology and food procurement will be used here to illustrate skills in the taskscape.

One way to do this is to return to the Clactonian, where it was suggested above that the term needs abolishing (Conway, McNabb and Ashton 1996, McNabb and Ashton 1993). Paradoxically, getting rid of the Clactonian in order to see Lower Palaeolithic flint working as a dynamic set of routines and rhythms makes it more complex than before when the Acheulean and Clactonian were only presented as separate but static traditions. With the chaîne opératoire we now have the methodological tools and a conceptual model for moving the debate onto the productive pastures of hominid involvement with their taskscapes. For example, were these taskscape skills merely those of tool assisted hominids (Binford 1989b) or are we dealing with more sophisticated capabilities comparable in many respects to modern humans (Thieme 1997)?

To examine the point I will compare two Lower Palaeolithic taskscapes of comparable date but from very different latitudes. The two locales are Olduvai Gorge (Leakey and Roe 1994), lying on the equator, and Swanscombe at 51°N in southern England (Conway, McNabb and Ashton 1996). This provides plenty of opportunity for variation in behaviour to be linked in a foraging lifestyle to ecological production (Kelly 1995). Moreover, the youngest levels at Olduvai, the Masek Beds, are approximately the same Middle Pleistocene age as Swanscombe, equivalent to Oxygen Isotope Stage 11, some 400,000 years ago.

The overriding conclusion from this comparison is how similar the archaeology looks (Figure 4.16). The FLK excavation in the Masek Beds uncovered a stream channel which contained a hominid mandible (OH 23) and 2,465 stone artifacts, of which 193 were tools, from an area of approximately 38 m$^2$ (Leakey and Roe 1994:Fig. 6.2). The scatter of bones and stone tools reveals no special

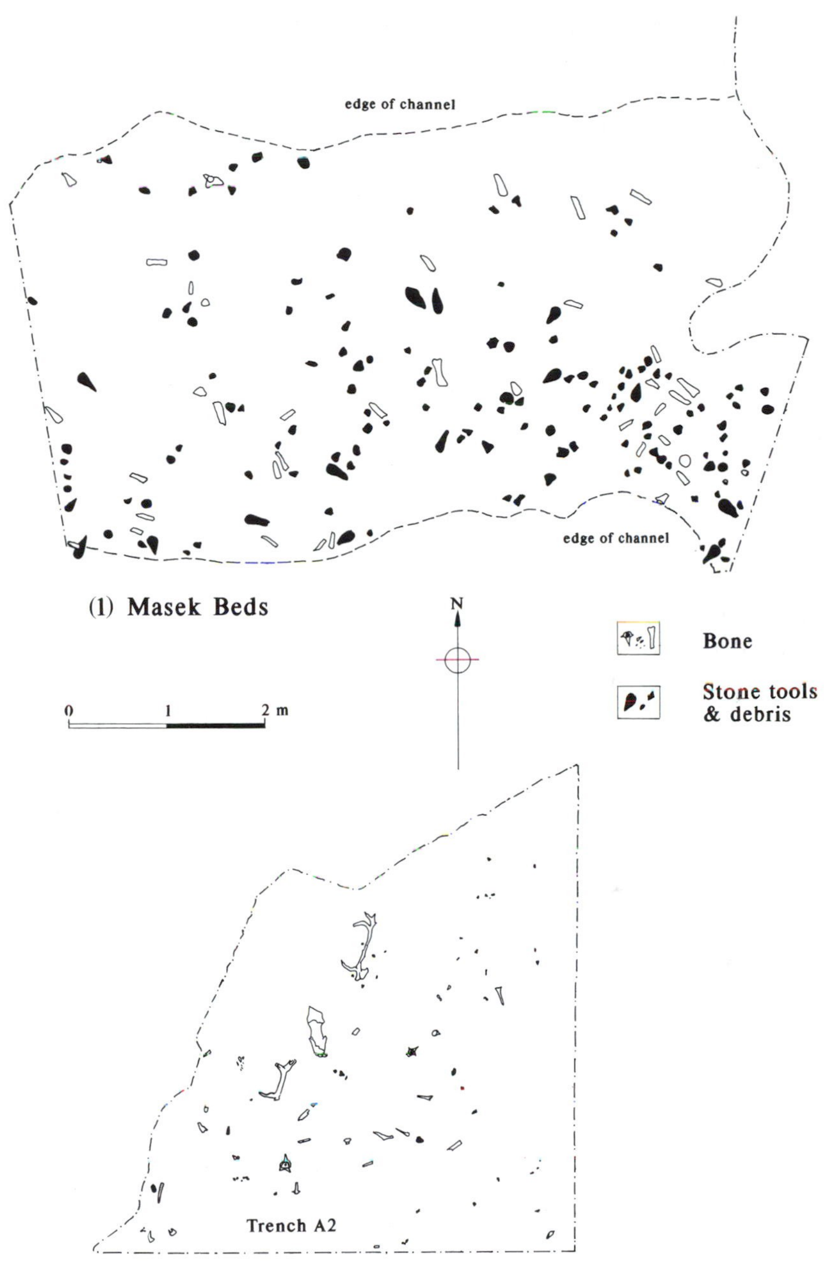


**4.16** A comparison of well-preserved, low-density 'living floors' at Olduvai, FLK site in the Masek Beds, and Swanscombe, Lower Loam. Both locales are linked to fluvial activity and contain stone tools, faunal remains but no distinctive spatial patterning. A similar low-density situation can be seen in Figures 4.11, 4.20, 5.7, 5.30 and 5.34 and the higher density version in Figures 4.18, 4.19, 4.22 and 4.24 (after Leakey and Roe 1994:Fig. 6.2, Waechter 1969).

patterning which might be attributable to hominids. The FLK site produced sixteen mammalian taxa (*ibid.*:table 7.2).

At 51° of latitude to the north, the site of Swanscombe also has evidence of human occupation associated with stream channels and banks. According to the excavator the lower loams produced some 375 stone artifacts from 200 $m^2$, while from the lower gravels 104 artifacts came from 62.5 $m^2$ (Waechter, Newcomer and Conway 1970). Twenty-eight mammalian taxa have been identified from the lower gravel and lower loams as well as a hominid skull from the upper middle gravels (Table 4.10).

However, despite good preservation and the opportunity to find differences in the archaeological record which might relate to the effects of latitude on ecological productivity, the overwhelming impression from the two locations is one of similarity. The wide range of mammal species points to the richness of the grasslands surrounding both sites even though they are separated by 50° of latitude. The northern grasslands were possibly even richer in animal biomass, as revealed by species diversity, than their tropical counterparts. But even so, the Swanscombe hominids would have been faced with the severe limiting factor, even during an interglacial, of how to make a living during the long winters in this northern locality. But this selection pressure is not obviously reflected either in technology or in camp-site evidence.

Instead it is the absence at both locales of hearths, post holes (which could have been preserved, like the animal footprints, in the Swanscombe loams) or indeed any structured activity, other than flint knapping or carcass butchery, which is striking (Figure 4.16). How different, in terms of technology, settlement systems and camp-site organization, would a similar latitudinal transect be among modern foraging peoples (Kelly 1995).

I interpret such similarity in the archaeology from Olduvai and Swanscombe as evidence for generic, or transferable, skills applied to different ecological conditions. If generic skills characterized these early hominids then I would expect that the ability of hominids to maintain occupation would vary in the two very different environments. Population would ebb and flow into and out of the northern environments, as represented by Swanscombe, and this process will provide the strongest archaeological signature of variation in behaviour at a regional scale. A different skills model with hominids solving problems through culturally transmitted means would predict the development of specific skills along that same transect. Storage techniques, for example, might be developed to cope with the long northern winters, but evidence for these is lacking.

The taskscape surrounding these hominids was therefore one of immediate attention and co-presence. Their diet also reflects this pattern. In their expensive tissue hypothesis, Aiello and Wheeler (1995) have examined the consequences for human evolution which stem from the observation that our brains account for less than 2 per cent of our body weight but use more than 20 per cent of our energy intake. Furthermore, that energy intake needs to be higher quality foods such as animal protein. Their model sees the enlargement of the brain occurring at the expense of the size of the stomach. Novel behaviours to compensate for the reduced processing power of the gut would be selected for. Among these cooking meat, the equivalent of an external digestive system (Aiello and Wheeler 1995), would be particularly advantageous.

Moreover, in terms of landscape use such a dietary change would in turn entail a shift from a primate to a carnivore pattern of range behaviour. As a result larger territories would be covered (Steele 1996:Table 8.8). There would also be social costs associated with this new scale of land use, with longer periods of separation. Traditional patterns of maintaining social alliances through constant, or at best very frequent, time-consuming interaction involving mechanisms such as social grooming would also have to change.

What pressures selected for such significant change? Larger brains, it has been suggested, were selected for in order to manage social life. This social intellect hypothesis (Byrne and Whiten 1988, Humphrey 1976) is preferred here over models that either technology (Oakley 1949) or diet (for review see Byrne 1995:chapter 14, Milton 1988) primarily selected for large brains. Instead, larger brains provided opportunities for enhanced communication, with vocal grooming now complementing other aspects of social grooming. The result, as Dunbar (Aiello and Dunbar 1993, 1996) has proposed, is that stable networks, larger than other primates can sustain, were possible even without a fully symbolic language.

The expensive tissue hypothesis therefore predicts finds such as the Schöningen spears which provide efficient means of killing animals for a large-brained hominid colonizing northern latitudes. This is supported by the raw-material transfer data which indicate carnivore- rather than primate-size ranges (Gamble and Steele 1998) with distances of 28 km for the furthest transferred stones common. The figure for Lower Palaeolithic Africa is, by comparison, only 14.6 km (Féblot-Augustins 1997:Inventaire 4–13). This does not mean that animals were neither killed nor eaten in East Africa. Rather the doubling of the maximum transfer distances is an indication of the effect of latitude on resources which affect land use and home range size. As noted above, spatial variation of this order would be expected over 50° of latitude among modern hunters and gatherers (Kelly 1995).

These raw-material transfer data therefore point to the generic rather than specific character of the technical skills that fashioned the Schöningen spears and the Boxgrove bifaces. We have ovate bifaces at FLK in the Masek beds and we have ovates 6,800 km to the north at Boxgrove. I suggest that only preservation prevents us from finding well-made wooden spears in East Africa. I conclude that the social skills along this transect were also generic and small in spatial scale.

## Regions

### *Landscapes of habit*

I would further argue that these social skills were firmly based on the use of emotional and material resources in a hominids' intimate and effective network (Table 2.8). This scale is supported by evidence both from the transfer of raw materials and from the reduction of nodules down to flakes, cores and bifaces that the temporality of action was short term. The rhythms were set at most by the activities of a few days. The majority of the distances involved (maximum 80 km, most less than 30 km) and the response to immediate needs indicate an even shorter rhythm, possibly of a day.

The paths and tracks which individuals made around these landscapes – for example along the Sussex raised beach (ApSimon, Gamble and Shackley 1977, Woodcock 1981), around the small lakes fed by karst springs of the Wippertal (Mania and Dietzel 1980) or along the riverbanks of the Somme (Antoine and Tuffreau 1993) and Aniene rivers (Anzidei and Huyzendveld 1992, Mussi 1995) – were set by the varied rhythms of mutual responses to the environment.

Preservation can be exceptional in these settings, pointing the way towards a future ethnography for these early hominids (Conard 1994) and the study of the individual. At a wider regional scale this resolution is blurred by periglacial and fluvial action which has sorted, reworked and accumulated archaeological material. This has resulted in time-averaged collections (Stern 1993) where the blocks of time involved may be between 50–100 Kyr as determined by the Pleistocene cycles (Table 4.1). But these data provide an important insight into the regional use of landscapes. For example, if we compare the recent survey of Palaeolithic materials in the riverine deposits of southern England (Wymer 1996) with a study of the Duero catchment (Santonja 1991–2) we can see that material clusters in some sections of the rivers (Figure 4.17). Santonja provides estimates of artifact numbers for the southwest corner of the Duero catchment (Table 4.11).

It is of course an inference that this patchy distribution points to areas which were more frequently utilized within these time-averaged palimpsests. We need to know more about the history of modern land use, the role of artifact collectors and the geological circumstances of accumulation. These factors have been studied by Hosfield (1996) for a part of the English rivers data. His analysis of the artifacts in the Solent river, and in particular in the urban centres of Southampton and Fareham, does allow some of the factors of discovery to be ascertained through a study of the Palaeolithic as industrial archaeology. His conclusion is that with these factors removed we can still see differences in the density and distribution of Acheulean material in these larger landscapes, differences which relate to hominid behaviour. This suggests that the non-industrial, and largely non-urban, Duero catchment in Spain can be interpreted in a similar fashion to that proposed some years ago by Wymer (1968:fig. 109). He

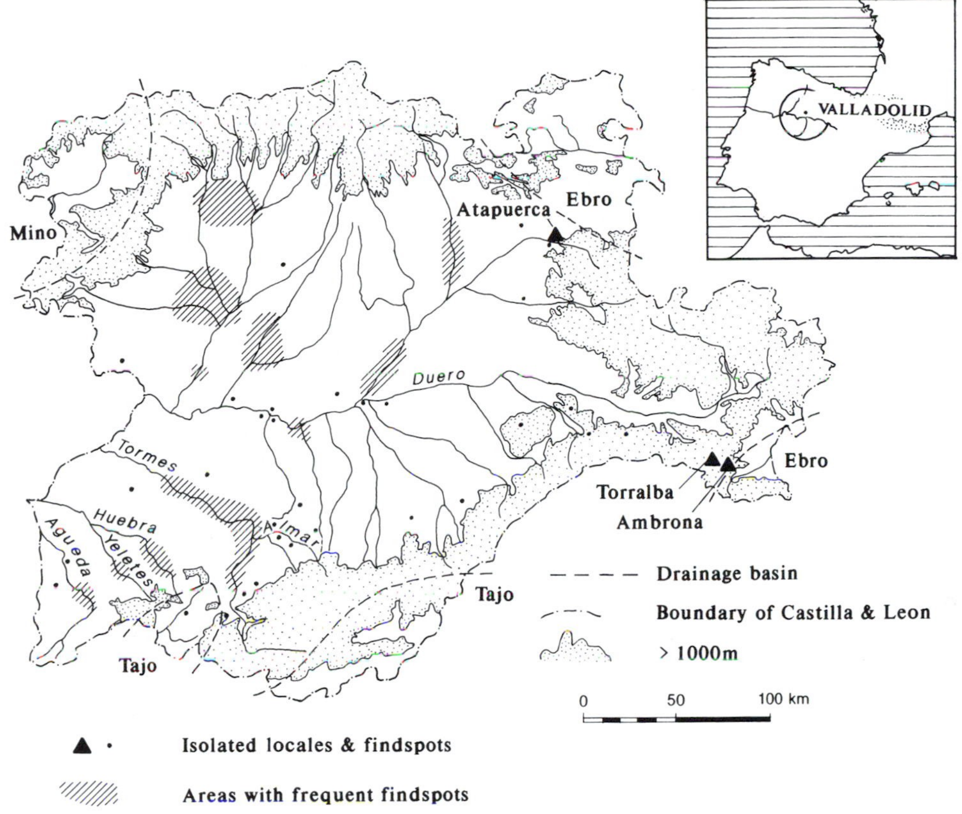


**4.17** The distribution of Lower Palaeolithic findspots and major locales in the Duero basin, Spain, MW region (after Santonja 1991–2:Fig. 2).

pointed out that the major concentrations in England were along the Ouse, Thames and Solent. After the OIS 12 Anglian diversion of the Thames these were the three major rivers, and their productivity acted as an attractor for hominids. The higher density of bifaces and flakes which have been recovered from their gravels therefore reflects the frequency with which the paths in the landscapes of habit crossed them.

These landscapes of habit combined the multiple taskscapes of individuals, ready for and replete with activity. They are reflected archaeologically by actions which used for the most part only the immediate affordances of the environment – stone, wood, bone. These cumulative actions can build up into a deeply buried, off-site signature of hominid activity that varies across the region in terms of patches. The 'sites' which we see such as Miesenheim I or Bilzingsleben are just exceptional pockets of preservation within these regional patches which are a signature of long-term, habitual land use. This is one reason why I prefer the term locale. In the landscapes of habit during this period we would expect individuals to behave towards each other at encounters in the

Table 4.11. *The southwest Duero catchment and Acheulean findspots (Santonja 1991–2).*

| River valley | Findspots | Estimate of artifacts collected |
|---|---|---|
| Agueda | 8 | 520 |
| Yeltes | 7 | 920 |
| Huebra | 7 | 890 |
| Tormes | 27 | 1,820 |
| Almar | 3 | 30 |
| Alagon | 1 | 10 |

same, immediate, mutual way. Social life was a continual journey of discovery along familiar paths set by necessary routines but subject to capricious alteration. The moods of the weather, prey and rivers would be matched by the moods of the individuals encountered, and with whom a social resolution had to be negotiated. The resources which structured these interactions were primarily emotional and material and from these emerged the repeated demographic and technological character of the intimate and effective networks.

### *Social landscapes*

Consequently there is no evidence for a social landscape which I defined in Chapter 3 as the means by which distanciation, that stretching of social relations beyond the present and the here-and-now, was achieved with symbolic resources. The absence of such social networks would have had repercussions on the ability of these hominids to colonize the more seasonal, northern, environments of Europe since this could only be achieved by fragmenting the group to cope with shortages and feeding opportunities. Without the symbolic means to augment co-presence there would have been considerable difficulties in maintaining social life at such scales through bonds based just on affective and effective means (Table 2.8).

## Locales

We can now examine further the skills which can be reconstructed from locales where evidence for technology, and by implication social action, has been recovered. As with the taskscape, one question which needs asking is to what extent were the skills apparent at one locale transferable to other locales in different regions of Europe? Were these skills specific to particular animals, landscapes and the structure of local resources, or could they be applied anywhere? I will approach these questions by comparing the locales as gatherings since these provided the context for the performance and transmission of skills.

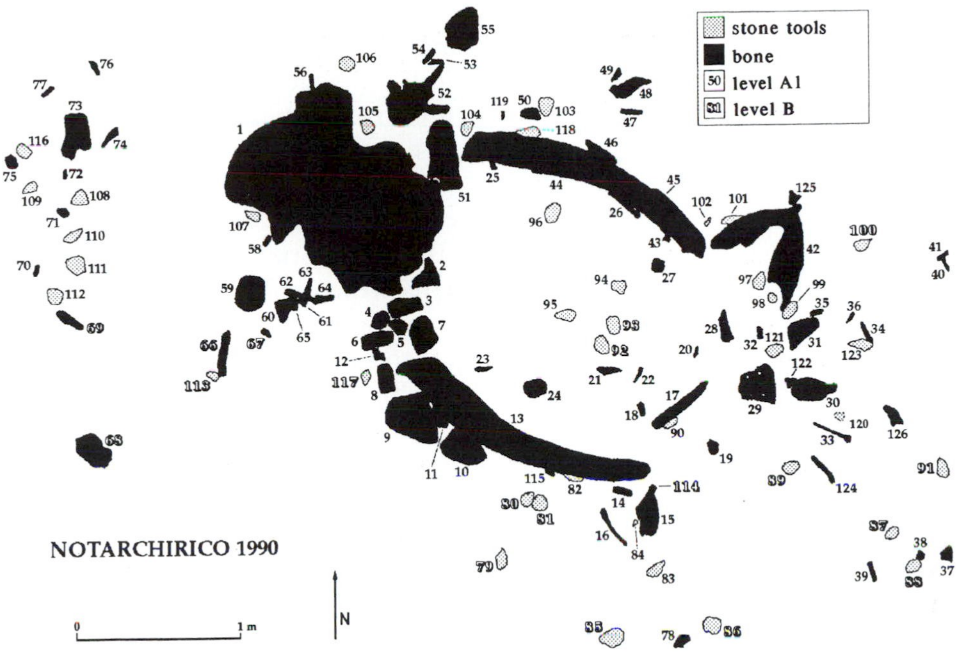


**4.18** The elephant area at Notarchirico, Italy, MC region. The skull is number 1 and the mandible is number 42 (after Cassoli et al. 1993:Fig. 2).

### *Riverside gatherings with megafauna*

The most common gatherings we have in the archaeology of this period involve the association of artifacts and animals. Factors of preservation and recovery often, but by no means always, result in the association being with large animals. The Italian data illustrate this circumstance very well.

At Notarchirico in the Venosa basin (Belli et al. 1991, Cassoli et al. 1993, Mussi 1992), excavations have uncovered in a 24-m$^2$ area, on a gravel lake beach, the upturned skull and mandible of an adult elephant (*Elephas antiquus*).[34] The tusks are still in place and the mandible has only moved a short distance (Figure 4.18). Altogether eighty-five bones and forty-one stone artifacts were found. Besides the remains of elephant were a few bones of red deer and possibly the extinct fallow deer (*Dama clactoniana*). The artifacts range from limestone choppers to a few pointed bifaces (Cassoli et al. 1993:fig. 4) made in flint as well as smaller denticulates and scrapers.

With hindsight we can see that the excavation area was too small to recover all of the skeleton. Butchering big animals takes up a lot of space, as O'Connell (et al. 1992) discovered in their ethnoarchaeological study of the Hadza of Tanzania. They found that the size of the animal carcass accounted for 75 per cent of the variation in the size of the area over which it was butchered (*ibid.*:330). The largest animal they observed being butchered was a giraffe (750 kg) which involved three separate areas. The diameter of the three butchery sites ranged from 32m to 68m with a mean of 51 m. The total area over which parts of one of the giraffes were moved during the butchery process was estimated as 750 $m^2$ (*ibid.*:340), double the intensively studied area of 355 $m^2$ at Bilzingsleben, where rhino and mammoth are both well represented, and thirty times that at Notarchirico.[35]

However some further points need to be borne in mind before applying such ethnoarchaeological observations. Firstly, the Hadza study shows that the dismemberment of the big animals was a socially structured activity with age and sex determining the formation of work parties, the placement of hearths and the transport of parts of the carcass. None of this organization can be assumed for the large-animal butchery event at Notarchirico. It has to be demonstrated. Secondly, within the large butchery field the various segments of the Hadza giraffe were dealt with by the task groups in much smaller areas ranging from c. 3 to 7.5 m in diameter (O'Connell, Hawkes and Blurton-Jones 1992:Figure 3). This would be a comparable spatial scale for the Notarchirico skull and mandible and well within the areas excavated at Bilzingsleben.

Of course, at Notarchirico much rests on demonstrating an association between the artifacts and the skull. Cut marks are not preserved although impact fractures are (Cassoli pers. comm.). The excavators pay considerable attention to the fluvial mechanics of the sediments and conclude that the association is not the result of a hydraulic jumble (Isaac 1989:143) but does reflect the human use of the trunk and head (Cassoli et al. 1993). This does not of course establish whether the animal was killed or scavenged.

These associations are less clear at other elephant locales such as Kärlich Seeufer in Germany (Bosinski 1995a, Gaudzinski et al. 1996), Aridos (Santonja 1992, Santonja et al. 1980) and Torralba (Santonja 1992, Shipman and J. Rose 1983) in Spain.[36] The stream sorting and rolling of the elephant bones at Torralba makes it difficult to assess the strength of the association between humans and these large resources. Both here and at Kärlich Seeufer the association of preserved wood and stone tools may be a natural one (Gaudzinski et al. 1996).[37] At Aridos the higher energy stream deposits have resulted in the collection of artifacts and smaller bones behind the tusks and skull. In Italy the locale of La Polledrara di Cecanibbio, northwest of Rome, has produced a rich palimpsest of stone artifacts and faunal remains, in particular elephants and aurochs, *Bos primigenius* (Anzidei and Huyzendveld 1992, Arnoldus-Huyzendveld and Anzidei 1993).[38] The large bones and tusks also acted as barriers in the stream and account for the dense accumulations of material. Elsewhere in the excavated area there were the remains of at least two elephants and a wolf preserved in situ, in fine-grained low-energy sediments. Five thousand animal bones and 350 stone tools made on small-sized local raw material and showing rudimentary reduction (choppers, denticulates and scrapers) have been recovered (Mussi 1992, 1995). Both here and at Isernia la Pineta and Fontana Ranuccio, there is evidence for flaking bone into artifacts

Table 4.12. *The quantity of material from section I, cut 3a at Isernia (Giusberti, Ferrari and Peretto 1991).*

| | N. | Density per m$^2$ |
|---|---|---|
| Travertine blocks | 1,256 | 8 |
| Pebbles and slabs | 292 | 2 |
| Flint artifacts | 137 | 1 |
| Bone | 722 | 5 |

(Giusberti, Ferrari and Peretto 1991, Segre and Ascenzi 1984, Villa 1991:fig. 3). Experimental work has also shown the intentional fracturing of bison bones at Isernia for marrow extraction, while at Castel di Guido (Figure 4.15), close to La Polledrara, several bone bifaces have been found (Anzidei and Huyzendveld 1992:146, Villa 1991).

These Italian locales provide a very detailed picture of complex fluvial processes. These are not derived sites in the sense of the fluvio-glacial gravels containing heavily rolled bifaces and flakes from England and northern France (Antoine 1990, Bridgland 1994, Wymer 1996). However the Italian evidence, as discussed by Cassoli (et al. 1993) and Anzidei and Huyzendveld (1992, see also Mussi 1995), points to a range of depositional environments ranging from low to high energy which have consequently produced a variety of associations between stones and bones.

The interpretative problems posed by these locales are well illustrated at Isernia (Cremaschi and Peretto 1988, Peretto, Terzani and Cremaschi 1983). In Settore I t.3a, 130 m$^2$ have been excavated, revealing that deposition of bones, stone artifacts, cobbles and travertine blocks took place on an unconsolidated mud flat interspersed with gravel bars. The accumulation of material (Table 4.12; Figure 4.19) was then covered by high-energy fluviatile deposits.

The fauna is dominated by bison with several well-preserved skulls. No cut marks have been observed although intentional fracturing of bone can be demonstrated. The stone artifacts are small in size and irregular in terms of fracture and retouch (Peretto 1991). Flakes, denticulates and simple scrapers characterize the numerically small assemblage. As at Bilzingsleben (Mania 1991a), the mass of bones and travertine blocks in such 'paved areas' are interpreted as consolidation and used as evidence for shelters and a living floor (Cremaschi and Peretto 1988, Peretto, Terzani and Cremaschi 1983:fig. 27). Such claims are difficult to support given the strong evidence for fluvial activity in this section of the locale.

*Cave gatherings*

The information from caves and abris is very sparse. The details from the rich, multilevel locale of Caune de l'Arago, Tautavel, will be important for assessing hominid food-management strategies but is currently only published in

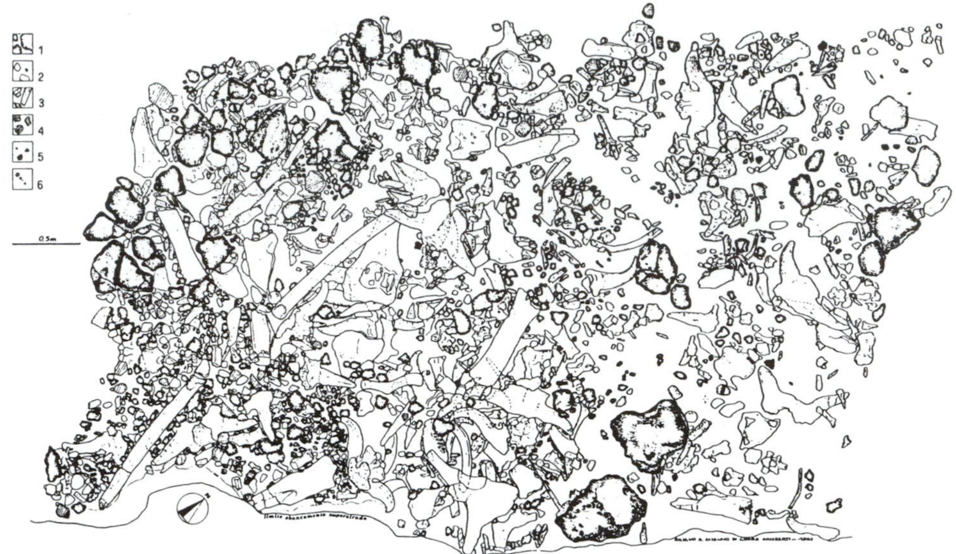

**4.19** Plan of Isernia la Pineta level t.3a. in the higher excavation level, Italy, MC region (after Cremaschi and Peretto 1988:Fig. 18).
KEY:
1 Travertine
2 Pebbles
3 Bone remains
4 Limestone tools
5 Flint tools
6 Traces of colouration

preliminary form (Table 4.13). The animal faunas are particularly rich (Jourdan and Moigne 1981) and document major changes in species between an interglacial (OIS 13) and glacial stage (OIS 12). The low numbers of carnivores suggest that at various times deer, horse and mouflon were the main prey species.[39] H. and M-A. de Lumley (1979) report on forty-four hominid specimens coming from at least fifteen individuals mostly from sol G equivalent to OIS 12. Here 40 per cent of the sample came from children, with one fifty-year-old female and the rest of the adults less than twenty-five years old.

Elsewhere at Atapuerca the archaeological material mostly comes from sink holes and fissures in the galeria (TG) and dolina (TD) sections. Recent finds in the Aurora stratum in TD6 have produced thirty-six hominid fragments associated with technologically simple stone tools (Bermúdez de Castro et al. 1997, Carbonell et al. 1995). Also at Atapuerca but in the Sima de los Huesos (pit of the bones), part of a deep underground cave system, excavation has so far produced the remains of at least 32 individuals (Table 4.14) from a sample of over 1,000 excavated specimens (Arsuaga, Bermúdez de Castro and Carbonell 1997, Arsuaga et al. 1993, Bermúdez de Castro 1995). Such a large sample provides a rare opportunity to examine the structure of a Middle Pleistocene population.

Table 4.13. *The large mammal fauna from Caune de l'Arago (Jourdan and Moigne 1981).*

| OIS<br>LAYER | | 13<br>KL<br>% | 13<br>HIJ<br>% | 12<br>DEFG<br>% | 12<br>SOL G<br>% | 12<br>F2<br>% | 12<br>F1<br>% | 12<br>E<br>% |
|---|---|---|---|---|---|---|---|---|
| **Carnivores** | | | | | | | | |
| *Canis etruscus* | (Etruscan wolf) | | 10 | 3 | 2 | 4 | 4.3 | 5 |
| *Cuon priscus* | (dhole) | | | 1.1 | 1.5 | | 0.8 | |
| *Vulpes praeglacialis* | (extinct fox) | | | 0.5 | 0.5 | 4 | | |
| *Vulpes sp.* | (fox) | | | 0.5 | | | 0.8 | 5 |
| *Ursus deningeri* | (Deninger's bear) | | 7.5 | 2.5 | 3.5 | | 1.7 | |
| *Felis sylvestris* | (wild cat) | | 5 | 0.2 | 0.5 | | | |
| *Felis lynx* | (lynx) | + | | 0.5 | 0.5 | | 0.8 | |
| *Panthera pardus* | (leopard) | | | 0.5 | | | 0.8 | 5 |
| *Panthera spelaea* | (cave lion) | | | 1.1 | 1 | | 0.8 | 5 |
| ***% of carnivores*** | | | ***22.5*** | ***9.9*** | ***9.5*** | ***8*** | ***10*** | ***20*** |
| **Herbivores** | | | | | | | | |
| Woodland and forest | | | | | | | | |
| *Cervus elaphus acoronatus* | (crownless deer) | | 27.5 | 12.4 | 14 | 4 | 12.1 | 5 |
| *Cervus elaphoides* | (medium size deer) | | 17.5 | | | | | |
| *Praemegaceros* | (giant deer) | | 7.5 | | | | | |
| *Dicerorhinus mercki* | (Merck's rhino) | | 5 | 1.4 | 2.5 | | | |
| *Bos or Bison* | (Bos or bison) | | | 4.4 | 4.5 | 4 | 4.3 | 5 |
| % | | | ***57.5*** | ***18.2*** | ***21*** | ***8*** | ***16.4*** | ***10*** |
| Steppe | | | | | | | | |
| *Equus mosbachensis* | (Mosbach horse) | + | 5 | 21.4 | 30.5 | 8 | 10.4 | 14 |
| *Dicerorhinus hemitoechus* | (steppe rhino) | | 2.5 | 3.2 | 5 | 4 | 0.1 | |
| *Praeovibos priscus* | (extinct musk-ox) | | | 5.2 | 5.5 | 12 | 3.5 | 5 |
| *Rangifer tarandus* | (reindeer) | + | 2.5 | 2.2 | 2 | | 3.5 | |
| % | | | ***10*** | ***32*** | ***43*** | ***24*** | ***17.5*** | ***19*** |
| Mountain | | | | | | | | |
| *Ovis ammon antiqua* | (extinct mouflon) | | 2.5 | 31.3 | 18 | 48 | 49.5 | 38 |
| *Hemitragus bosali* | (thar) | | 7.5 | 7.4 | 7.5 | 12 | 4.3 | 9 |
| *Rupicapra rupicapra* | (chamois) | | | 0.2 | | | 0.8 | |
| *Marmota marmota* | (marmot) | | | 0.5 | 0.5 | | | 5 |
| % | | | ***10*** | ***39.4*** | ***26*** | ***60*** | ***54.6*** | ***52*** |
| **MNI** | | 7 | 40 | 364 | 199 | 25 | 115 | 21 |

*Notes:*
MNI = Minimum Number of Individuals, + = present in very small numbers.

Table 4.14. *Palaeodemography of the Sima de los Huesos hominid sample (Bermúdez de Castro and Nicolás 1997:Table 3).*

| Years | Male | Female | Unidentified | % |
|---|---|---|---|---|
| 0–5 | | | 1 | 3 |
| 6–10 | | | 2 | 6 |
| 11–15 | 2 | 1 | 5 | 25 |
| 16–20 | 1 | 5 | 3 | 28 |
| 21–25 | 2 | 1 | 1 | 13 |
| 26–30 | 3 | 2 | 1 | 19 |
| >30 | | 1 | 1 | 6 |
| **MNI** | **32** | | | |

Eighteen of the individuals could be sexed; ten were female and eight male. The maximum age of any individual was estimated by Bermúdez de Castro (1995) as thirty-five years. The fossil population had an age profile, marked, unlike Tautavel, by very few infants and young children.

There are no artifacts in the Pit of the Bones and the only other remains come from bear. Opinion is still divided over the explanation of this deposit (Santonja 1992:50). Either a single catastrophe killed an entire group, or corpses were intentionally placed in the cave system over a longer period of time. These were later washed into the Sima de los Huesos. Carnivore gnawing is present on some of the bones (Andrews and Fernandez Jalvo 1997).

*Travertine gatherings*

Vértesszöllös in Hungary (Kretzoi and Dobosi 1990) is a travertine locale from the southeast region. Its dating is still debated because the absolute ages for the travertine are considered too young for the fauna. This contains *Arvicola terrestris cantiana*, suggesting an age of about 350 Kyr BP and therefore comparable to the Holsteinian age for the travertine locale of Bilzingsleben, north-central region.[40]

There are three main areas of archaeological interest within the Vértesszöllös travertine quarry. Site I is interpreted as a settlement area. It consists of a dense scatter of highly fragmented bones interspersed with stone tools. The fauna is dominated (48 per cent) by the large extinct horse (*Equus mosbachensis*) with all the deer (fallow, red and giant) making up 27 per cent of the total. Bear is present (6.3 per cent), although all other carnivores are rare. *Stephanorhinus etruscus* (Etruscan rhino), the dominant taxon at Bilzingsleben, accounts for only 5 per cent of the sample.

Site II, located in another part of the quarry, presents a big contrast and has been interpreted as a carnivore den.

The deposition of bones in Site II began in a closed fissure which later became

Table 4.15. *Vértesszöllös. Comparison of the fauna between Sites I and II (Kretzoi and Dobosi 1990:532).*

| | % | |
|---|---|---|
| | Site I | Site II |
| Carnivores | 1 | 27 |
| Omnivores including bear | 6 | 69 |
| Herbivores | 93 | 4 |
| **Number of specimens** | **1,916** | **1,135** |

an open trench. Apart from bear which hibernated there, the two carnivores are the extinct wolf *Canis mosbachensis* (13 per cent), and the extinct lion *Leo gombaszögensis* (14 per cent). Both species occur in very small numbers at Site I (Table 4.15).

About 60 m$^2$ was excavated at Site I between 1963 and 1968. The animal bone was highly fragmented and scattered everywhere, as the large-scale site plans in Kretzoi and Dobosi (1990) indicate. Much of the bone is reported as burnt, and in his excavation notes Vértes wrote (Kretzoi and Dobosi 1990:532) that there were heavily burnt patches indicating fireplaces but that no charcoal was found in these fireplaces. The similarities with Bilzingsleben (see below) continue with the discovery, in 1965, of the remains of two individuals. Vértesszöllös I is a seven-year-old child and the four teeth came from the excavation. The second hominid, an occipital bone of a young adult male, was found after dynamite blasting in a travertine block about 8 m from Site I.

The stone tools were studied by Vértes (Kretzoi and Dobosi 1990, Kretzoi and Vértes 1965, Svoboda 1987). The collection has very many small-sized pebble tools and flakes. Local raw materials dominate.

Finally, in level 3 Site III at Vértesszöllös, preserved animal footprints were discovered in an area of 40 m$^2$. This was a muddy zone used as a wallow by rhino, bear, bison and deer. No horse hoofprints were found even though its bones were common in Site I.

Vértesszöllös reminds us of the types of landscape and evidence with which we are dealing. All three sites in the quarry are of similar, but not contemporary, age. However, they provide very different pictures of what was happening in the immediate vicinity of the spring. Sites II and III have no good associated human evidence. But this does not mean that Site I was entirely the outcome of hominid gatherings.

*In-situ foreshore, lake shore and riverbank gatherings*

Boxgrove is a well-preserved locale from this period. The archaeological evidence consists of knapping episodes and their association with animal carcasses. One in particular deserves mention: the butchery at site GTP 17 of a horse which started as a complete carcass (Figure 4.11). The hominids brought six large flint nodules to this resource and flaked the artifacts they required in situ (Pitts and Roberts 1997). As already mentioned, these were flakes, rather than the bifaces found in other parts of the landscape, resulting from the reduction of large flint blocks. Other butchered animals in the Boxgrove landscape are rhino and red deer. The scatter of bones is at a low density and there is a lack of any other features – for example, pits, post holes and hearths. In this respect the settlement evidence at this locale points to gatherings rather than social occasions where elaboration by hominids of their immediate environment would be expected.

The lakeside locale of Hoxne in eastern England (Singer et al. 1993) has produced similar evidence. The shoreline, as at Bilzingsleben (see below), provided a good area for preservation. The animal bones and pointed bifaces were being discarded in a few inches of water. This would explain the lack of post holes and other signs of structures. However, at Hoxne there are twelve clusters of stones in level C associated with the lower, ovate biface, industry (Figure 4.20). These are about one metre in diameter and contain a few broken bones, flecks of charcoal and occasional artifacts. Wymer has described them as resembling the contents of an emptied sack (1985:171–3). In the upper, flake industry of Bed 5 he found a collection of dispersed flints, possibly dumped, he suggested, to create a firmer base in the soft flood silt (*ibid.*:173).[41]

Finally, at Miesenheim I in Germany, E. Turner (1989, 1990) has examined the taphonomy of this Cromer IV interglacial site, comparable in age to Boxgrove (Bosinski 1995a, Bosinski, Kolfschoten and Turner 1988). There are one hundred flint artifacts at the locale and a number of partial skeletons particularly of two large bovids, four horses, six red deer and at least nine roe deer, six adults and three juveniles. Over 100 $m^2$ has been excavated (E. Turner 1989:530). Stone artifacts are therefore rare although near to the animal skeletons is a 5-$m^2$ patch of pebbles which Bosinski (1995a:114) regards as adequate proof for human involvement as they tried to consolidate the marshy sediments of the riverbank. However, Turner reminds us that while such an association would, a few years ago, have been sufficient to argue for hominid intervention, it is no longer adequate. Most importantly, there is no evidence for cut marks on the bones or for deliberate bone breakage for marrow extraction. Of course, animals can be butchered with very little evidence for cut marks and in particular small animals, such as roe deer, show much lower proportions of cut marks (Binford 1981b, von den Driesch and Boessneck 1975). Eight per cent of the bone was gnawed at Miesenheim I and the bones of one of the large bovids were widely dispersed and are interpreted as the remains of a wolf kill. Turner concludes that Miesenheim, for all its in-situ preservation, was at most a short-stay locale used by hominids working stone. They may also have scavenged the carcasses but the evidence is inconclusive.

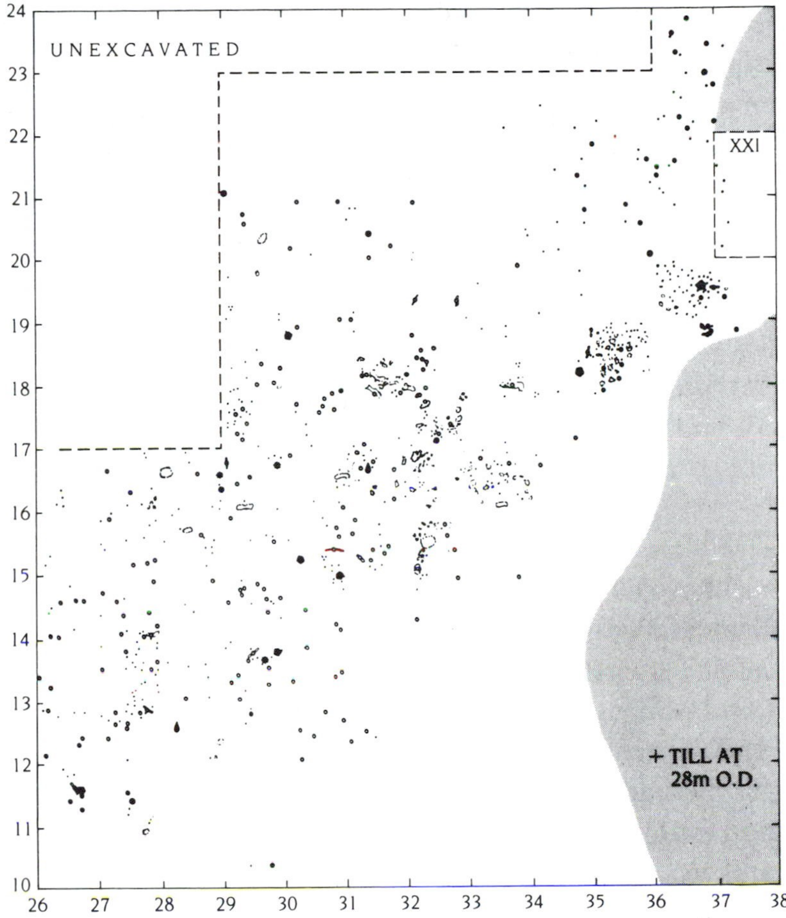


**4.20** Excavations along the lake shoreline at Hoxne, England, NW region. Preservation was particularly good in this exposure of the Lower Industry, stratum C, at the locale. But even so this detailed plot of animal bone (open symbols) and stone material (shaded and dots) points to the limited evidence for patterning at such locales. Note the lack of fireplaces (after Wymer 1985:Fig. 58). Grid co-ordinates are at metre intervals.

### Locales: Bilzingsleben, a case study

These patterns in the preservation and use of locales can now be investigated through a more detailed case study.

The Bilzingsleben locale in eastern Germany lies in the Wipper valley, a tributary of the Saale river which in its turn is a tributary of the Elbe. The locale was preserved by a travertine spring which first covered the archaeological evidence with sand and lake carbonates (Seekalk) and finally sealed it with a hard travertine crust (Figure 4.21). Quarrying the travertine for building stone revealed the locale and twenty years of excavation by Dietrich Mania

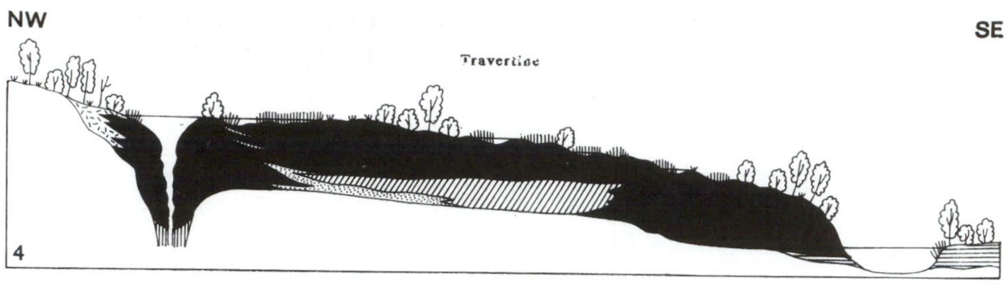


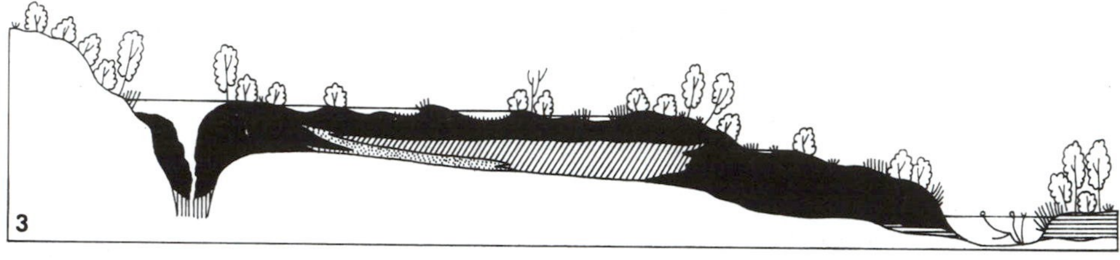


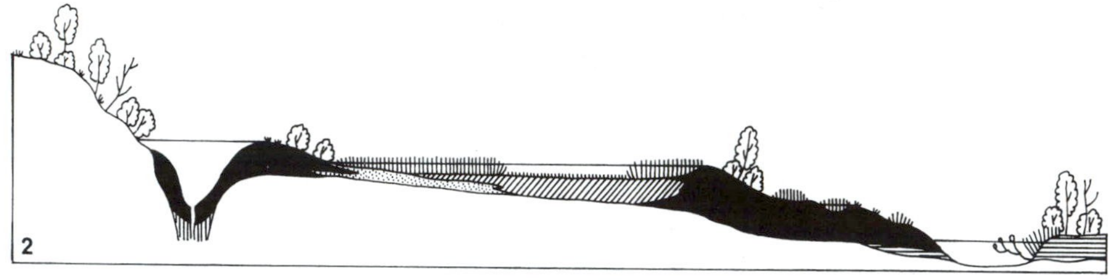


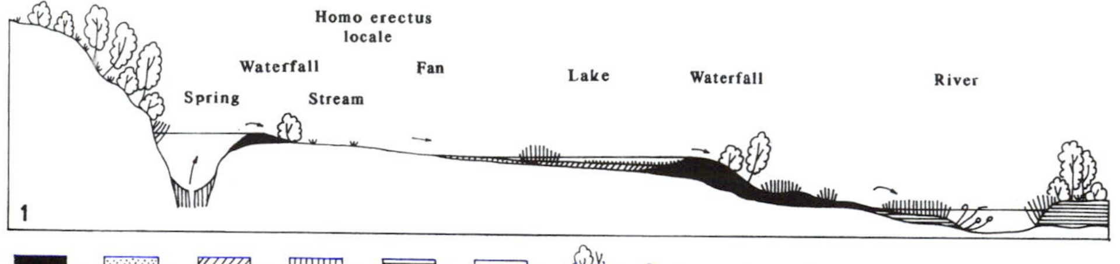

**4.21** The geological development of the Bilzingsleben locale, Germany, NC region (after Mania 1995:Fig. 4).
KEY:
1 Travertine
2 Travertine sand
3 Lacustrine limestone
4 Redeposited debris in the spring
5 Stream muds
6 Scree deposit
7 Trees
8 Shrubs
9 Grasses
10 Sedges
11 Reeds
12 Aquatic plants

have produced one of the most detailed accounts we have of a Holsteinian interglacial locale (Fischer et al. 1991, Mai et al. 1983, Mania 1990, Mania and Dietzel 1980, Mania, Toepfer and Vlcek 1980, Mania and Weber 1986).

*Chronology and environment*

There are three interglacials preserved in the Bilzingsleben deposits and it is the second which contains the archaeological horizon. Absolute dates by Schwarcz (et al. 1988, Mania 1995: 90) using 230Th–234U and ESR place the Bilzingsleben II interglacial between 350–320 Kyr and 414–280 Kyr BP, which confirms its position in the Holsteinian complex, but does not resolve the question of whether it is OIS 11 or OIS 9.

The environmental evidence is particularly rich. Mediterranean and south-east-European snails, including the water snail *Theodoxus serratiliniformis*, indicate warm conditions as do remains of giant beaver (*Trogontherium cuvieri*), which is found in other Holstein complex locales in northern Europe, and the straight-tusked elephant (*Palaeoloxodon antiquus*). Leaves and wood fragments are preserved as they are at many travertine sites. From these macrofossils a rich oak-mixed forest can be reconstructed. The woods around the locale also contained southern exotics such as juniper (*Juniperus sabina*) and wild grape (*Vitis sylvestris*) as well as many shrub-trees including box (*Buxus sempervirens*), *Pyracantha*, *Celtis* and *Syringia* (Mania 1995). These fringed the lake with denser stands of trees on the bank above the spring (Figure 4.21).

The molluscan fauna contains ninety species of which one third are woodland indicators. However, the molluscs are dominated numerically by open-terrain taxa which Mania interprets as evidence for a local environment of broken, rather than closed, woodlands; a form of forest steppe (1995). Taken together the floral and faunal remains indicate a relatively warm and dry climate with an annual average temperature of $+10°$–$+11°$ C with estimated January and July averages of $-0.5°$–$+3°$C and $+20°$–$+25°$C respectively (Mania 1995).

*Hominid remains*

The locale has also produced, between 1972 and 1989, the fossil remains of at least three individuals.[42] These consist of skull fragments and isolated teeth (Table 4.16). No postcranial remains have yet been found.

Hominids 1 and 2 were adults and were originally classified by Vlček (1978) as *Homo erectus* although others believe they should be classified as *Homo heidelbergensis*, the generic name for the earliest Europeans (Roberts, Stringer and Parfitt 1994).[43] The single specimen of Hominid 3 is a lower milk molar and hence comes from a juvenile.

*The excavated surface*

Altogether some 600 m$^2$ has been excavated (Mania 1986, 1991a), although interpretation has concentrated upon an area of 355 m$^2$. The locale is divided

Table 4.16. *The hominid remains from Bilzingsleben (Mania 1991a:22–3).*

| | Number of skull fragments | Number of teeth and tooth fragments |
|---|---|---|
| Hominid 1 | 6 | 1 |
| Hominid 2 | 4 | 5 |
| Hominid 3 | | 1 |

into two main areas clearly demarcated by the edge of a former small lake. At the time of hominid occupation this lake had been filled by a fan deposit (Schwemmfächerfazies) at the mouth of the spring welling up from the limestone below. This fan was criss-crossed by rivulets draining into what remained of a small lake. Consequently it contains a large amount of redeposited material including the remains of Hominid 1. The site is traversed by a series of minor geological faults (Spalten) that occurred after the hominid occupation.

The second major area in the excavation consists of a largely dry land deposit made up of sands (Üferfazies). It is described as a small shore terrace at the edge of a shallow lake (Mania 1995:91) and was close to the outflow of the spring. Finds here are not regarded as redeposited but in primary context (Mania 1991a:17). They include the remains of Hominid 2 as well as the reconstruction of a campsite with three shelters (Figure 4.22).

*Large animal fauna*

Animal bones are found in both the fan and shore deposits. There are almost no carnivore bones, except bear. Neither is there any indication of their presence through gnawing marks. Among 256 bones identified to species (Mania 1991a:table 3) the most common are rhino (27 per cent), beaver (14 per cent), red deer (13 per cent), elephant (12 per cent) and bear (11 per cent). This small collection comes from the excavated area of 355 $m^2$.

From the larger, 600-$m^2$ area, 627 elephant teeth and bones were identified and a further 1,578 unidentifiable bone and tooth fragments recovered (Mania 1991a:table 4). All skeletal parts are present but the assemblage is dominated by head and tooth elements. One hundred and eighteen of these teeth can be aged (Guenther 1991) and show that up to 65 per cent of the animals were less than fourteen years old. Among this age cohort most of the animals were aged between two and six years old (47 per cent) with very young calves, less than two years in age, accounting for a further 30 per cent of the young cohort (Figure 4.23).

While the elephant teeth point to the predominance of young animals, the bones tell a different story. The feet as well as shoulder blades, ribs and vertebrae come from older animals. Mania (1991a) comments further on the degree of fragmentation. There are forty-eight bones identified to humerus, radius,

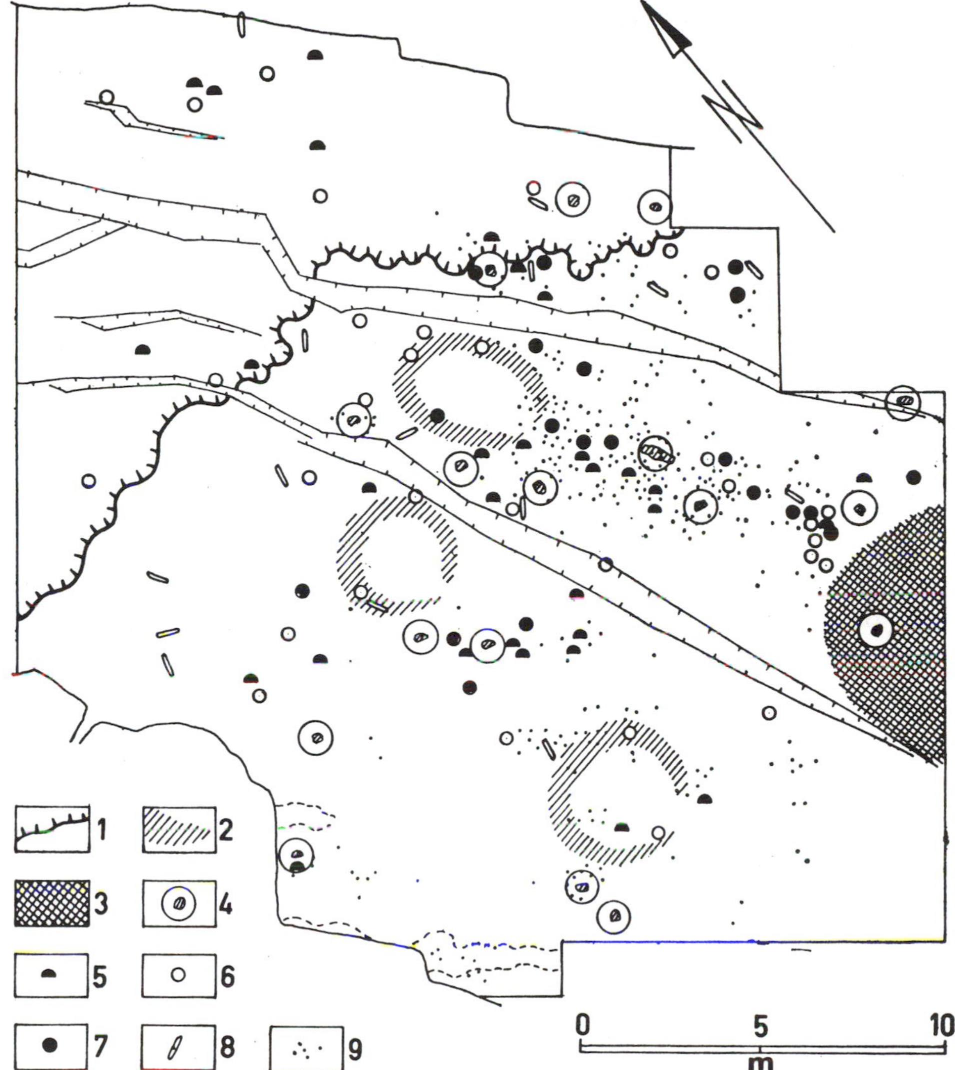


**4.22** A reconstruction of the Bilzingsleben 'campsite' based on the distribution of artifacts, Germany, NC region (after Mania 1991a:Fig. 2).
KEY:
1 Lake edge
2 Dwelling structures
3 Central, paved zone
4 Anvils
5–9 Bone tools and modified bones

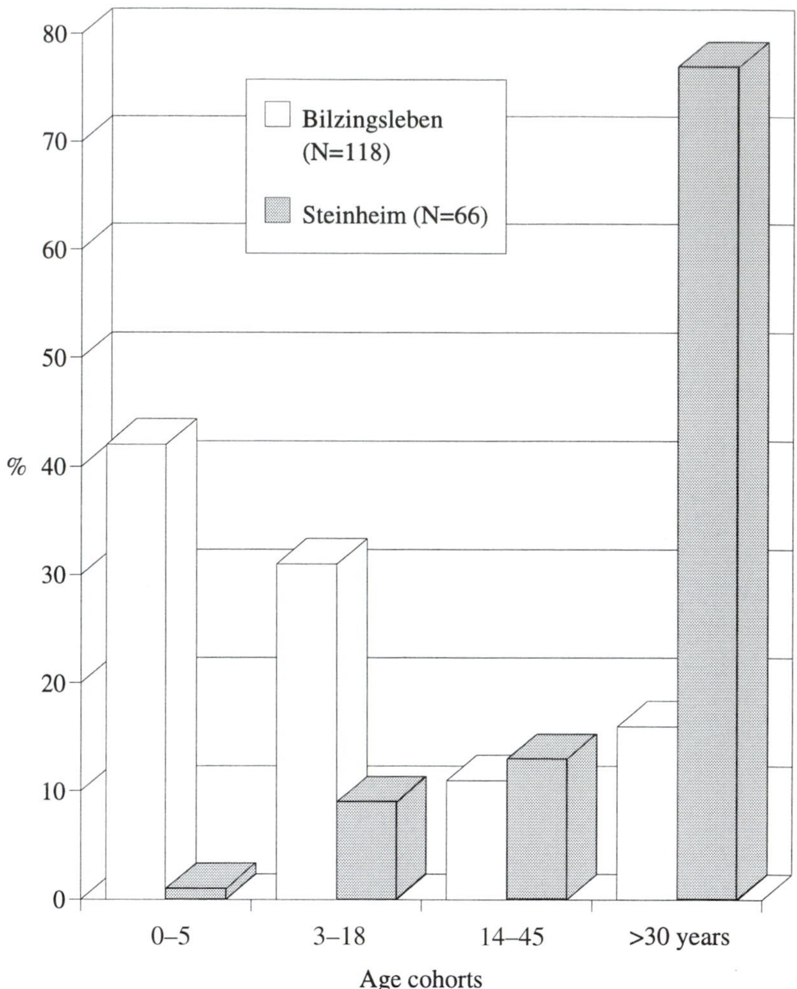


**4.23** The age profile of elephants (*Palaeoloxodon antiquus*) at Bilzingsleben and Steinheim, Germany, NC region. The Bilzingsleben profile, where preservation and recovery were good, displays a catastrophic mortality profile (see Figure 5.28A). At Steinheim the preponderance of older animals possibly points to selective recovery. Neither age profile is necessarily indicative of human hunting; compare with Figure 5.22 for prime-age profile resulting from hunting (after Guenther 1991).

femur and tibia. Of these, eleven are almost complete specimens. However, there are a further 665 bone splinters and 252 flakes from long bones. Mania has also identified a further 119 intentionally modified bones. He explains the discrepancies in representation as the result of the Bilzingsleben hominids selecting the long, thick-walled and dense bones of elephant as raw material for the production of bone flakes and other artifacts.

Table 4.17. *The activity zones at Bilzingsleben (Mania 1986, 1991a).*

| Activity zone | Human fossil remains | Anvils | Burnt stone charcoal | % of items <10 cm | Antlers per $m^2$ | Interpretation |
|---|---|---|---|---|---|---|
| I and Ia | Yes | | | 88 | 0.34 | Garbage dump |
| II | | Yes | | 55 | 0.5 | Shore activities |
| III | ? | | Yes | | 0.14 | Shelters |
| IV | Yes | Yes | | 70 | 0.14 | Workshop |
| V | Yes | Yes | | 83 | | Central paved area |
| VI | | | | | | Stone alignment |

By comparison, the rhino remains are interpreted as the result of specialized hunting (*ibid.*:21). Fifty per cent of the remains come from young animals and the bones were not used as raw material. Only selected parts of the rhino were brought back to the campsite. This was also the case with bison and horse. It is only with red deer and smaller species that more complete skeletons are found.

*Activity areas, shelters and objects*

The excavated areas at Bilzingsleben have been divided in terms of their contents into six activity zones (Table 4.17; Figure 4.22).

Three semi-circular structures have been identified in the shore deposits (Figure 4.22). These are defined by larger blocks of travertine and animal bones which are thought to have acted as weights to secure a windbreak structure (Mania 1990:83). From the plans published in Mania (1986, 1990:Abb. 58, 59 and 62) I have constructed Table 4.18 which describes the materials associated with these shelters.

The table shows that we are dealing with a relatively low density of large-sized elements but that a considerable variety of evidence is present in each shelter area. The low density is also indicated by the identified bones which occur in the more intensively studied area of 355 $m^2$ at a frequency of 0.7 specimens per $m^2$.

One aspect which is currently not available is the extent to which refitting between either bones or stone tools was possible. Nor is it possible to determine from these plans the relationship between large- (>10 cm) and small- (<10 cm) sized objects. In other words the data cannot be assessed from the point of view of seeing what was selected by the excavators in order to define the oval and circular shapes of these shelters. The refitting would also be essential, as Villa (1976–7) showed in her study of the material from the fossil beach site of Terra Amata (Lumley 1969b, 1975:761–70) and where several similar-shaped oval scatters of large bones and stones had been reconstructed as a large covered

Table 4.18. *The contents of the three Bilzingsleben structures (Mai et al. 1983, Mania 1986, 1990, 1991a).*

| Shelters | Source Mania 1990 | Shape | Diameter max. metres | Area $m^2$ | Hominid remains | Bones/ teeth | Bone tools | Engraved bones | Antler tools | Wooden artifacts | Elephant tusks | Stone blocks and slabs | Stone anvils | Burnt stone | Small/large hammerstones | Pits | Hominid charcoal |
|---|---|---|---|---|---|---|---|---|---|---|---|---|---|---|---|---|---|
| 1 | Abb. 58 | Oval | 4.5×3 | 13.5 | 0 | 95 | 4 | 1 | 3 | 2 | 0 | 76 | 3 | 39 | 21 | 0 | + |
| 2 | Abb. 59 | Circular | 3.5 | 10 | 0 | 64 | 7 | 1 | 4 | 1 | 1 | 70 | 3 | 7 | 26 | 0 | + |
| 3 | Abb. 62 | Circular | 5 | 20 | 1 | 152 | 14 | 0 | 2 | 49 | 1 | 97 | 3 | 16 | 19 | 2 | + |

shelter measuring 8 m × 4 m with internal fireplaces (Lumley 1975:figure 4). However, Villa demonstrated by refitting 232 groups of flints that 40 per cent came from different stratigraphic units with an average vertical displacement of 20 cm. Her findings challenged the view that the Terra Amata evidence was in situ and therefore amenable to the reconstruction of successive 'living floors' each with its temporary shelter.

Bilzingsleben is also said to be in situ and this may well be the case. However, the intense fragmentation of bone (Table 4.17) in most zones of the locale suggests that we also need the supporting evidence from refitting lithic groups to establish the degree of site integrity.

In Mania's reconstruction each shelter is associated with a patch of burning and a working area which usually contains large elephant bones and a stone anvil, sometimes made from a travertine block. In addition there is zone V (Figure 4.24), described as a central paved area where stone slabs and pebbles have been pressed into the surface of soft sediments. The area, partially excavated in 1986, measures some 3–4 m$^2$.[44] The slabs in this 'pavement' are of mixed origin, coming from an older travertine deposit some 200 m away. Local Muschelkalk, quartzite, crystalline and flint material were also used. Two skull fragments, both from hominid 2, were found in the deposit. These frontal and parietal pieces could be refitted and were 3.3 m apart. In the middle of the 'paved' area is a well preserved bison skull with horn cores lying in front of a large quartzite block. This is interpreted as an anvil because of the microscopic bone chips still sticking to its surface. However there were no hammerstones or bone splinters found around it (Mania 1991a:23). Activity zone VI, a 5-m line of medium-sized pebbles, leads into the 'paved area' from the southwest (Mania 1991a:23).

The stone industry, like the stone 'pavement', is also made on diverse but locally available raw materials. There are large pebble tools and hammer stones made on quartzite and Muschelkalk (Mania 1978:Abb. 10). An early study of 2,486 pieces showed that 93 per cent were made of flint, obtained from less than 10 km distant (Weber 1986), and that of these 87 per cent were <1 cm in length. Retouched pieces accounted for 12.5 per cent of the stone assemblage and these were between 1 and 6 cm in length. The forms include knives and backed knives (Keilmesser), scrapers, handaxe shaped points, Tayac and Quinson points (see Brézillon 1968, Denénath and Dibble 1994, Hahn 1991) as well as denticulates and notches (Mania 1995).[45]

As already mentioned, some bones, especially those of elephant, appear to have been intentionally flaked, while among the wooden pieces rod, hook and spade-like forms are described although they show little standardization.

Finally, one of the best-known aspects of Bilzingsleben are the 'engraved' bones. Four such objects are described by Mania (1990). These are inscribed with rhythmic marks and are all on large mammal bone, mostly elephant. On both sides of a flat elephant foot bone are a series of fine lines scored by a stone artifact which Mania regards as symbolic, geometrical markings (Figure 4.25).

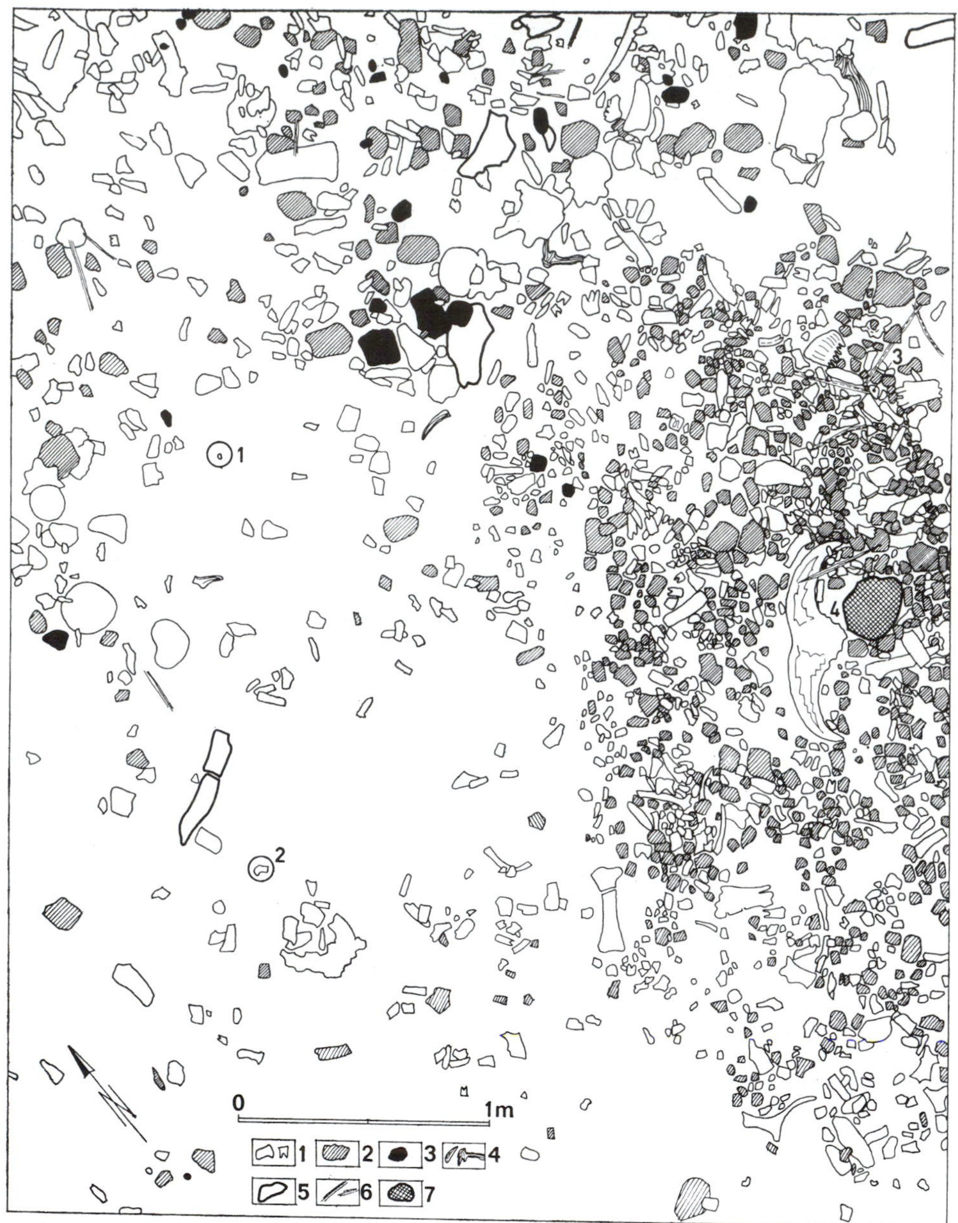


**4.24** The central paved area at Bilzingsleben, Germany, NC region, following the 1986 excavations (after Mania 1991a:Fig. 5).
KEY:
1 Bones and teeth
2 Stone slabs and pebbles
3 Pebble tools
4 Antlers and antler tools
5 Bone tools
6 Wood remains
7 Anvil
1, 2 and 3 are hominid remains while 4 is a bison skull adjacent to the quartzite anvil.

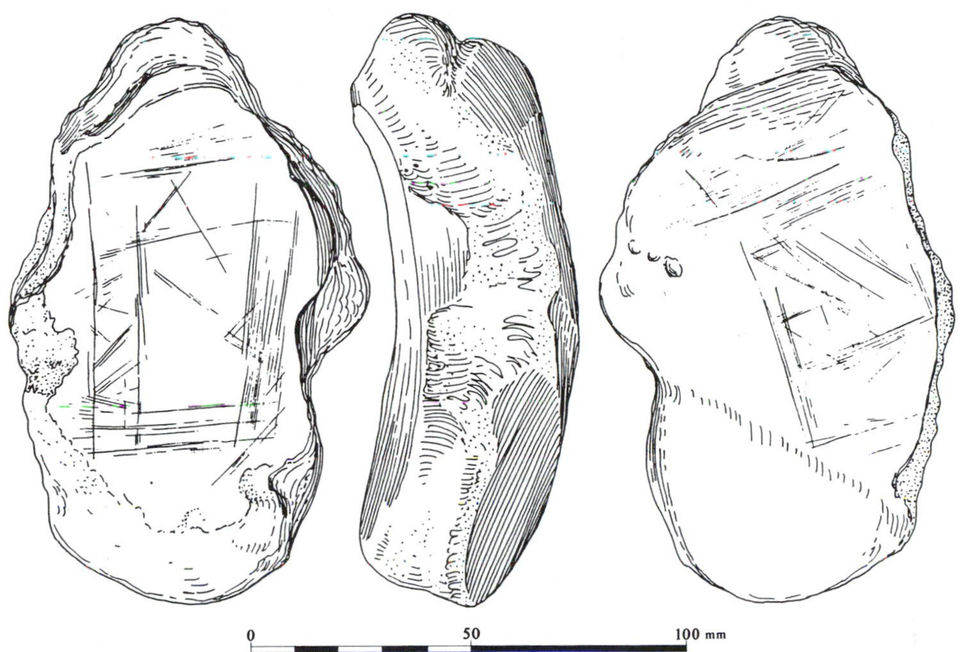


**4.25** An elephant foot bone with cut marks from Bilzingsleben, Germany, NC region (after Mania 1990:Abb. 232).

## *Social information in the early Palaeolithic*

The reconstruction of Bilzingsleben favoured by Mania represents an extreme case of the evidence for institutions which a social analysis is generally thought to require. These include shelters, an organized campsite, stone and bone anvils, wooden and bone artifacts as well as an abundant stone technology, fireplaces, symbolically engraved bones, specialist rhino hunting, human fossil remains and a comparative rarity of bone-modifying carnivores such as hyena, lion and wolf.

If correctly identified, the locale would be a rich interpretative source for the type of social archaeology that I reviewed in Chapter 1. The shelters would represent the frequent visits of social groups to the same locale, while their contents and workplaces, not to mention the central paved area, would preserve the ritual, economic and social institutions of the group. Indeed, from this evidence it might seem that there were only technological and environmental differences between Bilzingsleben and locales 350 Kyr later (Chapter 7) where similar reconstructions of campsites have been made for *H. sapiens* in the Upper Palaeolithic.

What follows is not a critique of the Bilzingsleben interpretation just because it flatly contradicts any social change during the European Palaeolithic. My interpretation is based instead on the fact that, as we have seen in this chapter, the locale is unique and therefore difficult to assess. I offer my alternative interpretation while discussing more generally the social character of the earliest hominids in Europe using the terminology discussed in Chapters 2 and 3.

*Encounters*

As with all social life, the hominids in the period 500–300 Kyr BP had many encounters which produced no archaeological trace. However, the hallmark of these 200,000 years is that the variety of encounters was itself limited. Evidence for encounters with resources rather than with other people dominates a superficial reading of the archaeological record. These encounters involved intercepting animals, both dead and alive, as well as extracting raw materials and utilizing fixed shelter in the form of caves and abris. At this time we are dealing with a taskscape of sounds and activity which demand attention, rather than a social landscape that extended co-presence through the use of symbols and the infusion of meaning into places, through either the construction of architecture or the transformation of objects into social artifacts.

But how could a hominid still be social and yet be so limited? Mithen (1996) provides an answer by suggesting that the cognitive domains of these early hominids were still firmly partitioned. Look at his proposition this way. A tree is a tree. It affords shade, firewood, materials for spears, escape from hyenas, leaves for bedding and a territory to hunt for small animals such as squirrels. But at this stage of hominid evolution a tree is not transferred into another cognitive realm where it has social values of endurance, dependability and within which spirits are thought to dwell. In the same way animals, when encountered, are affordances for food and a source of other raw materials – hides, bones, sinews. Most importantly, the hunter does not take on the property of the animal. The animal does not become the symbol for aggression, or the token by which networks and the stable groupings which emerge from them are identified, the image of the clan or group. In short, there is no transference between these different cognitive domains which results in the kaleidoscope of human culture as we know it. If, and it seems highly improbable, Hominid 1 at Bilzingsleben thought she or he was a rhino, because that is what they encountered most, they kept the information to themselves. They never used it as a means to structure and augment social bonds by appealing to a wider cultural principle that would have been self-evident to those in the network. Their mutual environment was not personified.

*Gatherings*

This conclusion may seem extreme, so let me now investigate the archaeological evidence for gatherings to support my reading of the evidence that only limited social resources were brought to bear on encounters, irrespective of what or whom was encountered. The crucial point is that we are investigating a social life which was complex rather than complicated (Chapter 2). It was also one, as indicated in the earlier discussion of the landscape of habit and social landscape, where individuals were primarily focused on supporting their intimate and effective networks and invested their limited resources accordingly.

The earlier review of gatherings in the early Palaeolithic pointed to the problems of interpreting the associations between bones and stones. It also suggested that more complex structures including shelters and fireplaces have not yet been found, even in primary context sites.[46] The evidence is overwhelmingly of the immediate use of resources, be they stone, animal or wood. The only feature that a number of excavators comment on is the possible use of stone and bone to consolidate damp, soft ground (Hoxne, Miesenheim I, Isernia, Bilzingsleben).

In Table 4.19 and Figure 4.26 the densities of lithic finds from excavated locales of Holstein and Cromer age are plotted. The scatter plot shows that most excavated areas are under 300 $m^2$ (mean=225, but with a very large standard deviation of 298). Two conclusions can be drawn. Firstly locales which have to some extent been created by fluvial action (Ambrona, Casal de Pazzi and Swanscombe upper middle gravels and Isernia) produce both low- and high-density outcomes. Secondly, the locales with in-situ evidence, e.g. Boxgrove area A and Cagny l'Epinette, have been excavated intensively over much smaller areas but do not produce very large quantities of lithics. It is only when excavations are very small, as at San Quirce II (Santonja 1992), that densities jump dramatically to 448 lithics per $m^2$ from an excavated area of only 5.5 $m^2$. When density of lithics is plotted against area excavated, this pattern of low-quantity, low-density lithics on primary-context sites can be clearly seen. The archaeological signature for this period throughout Europe is therefore of low-density use of locales as reflected by the deposition of lithics. Bilzingsleben falls within the higher values in Table 4.19 but is not significantly different from other locales.

*Bilzingsleben; a rings and sectors approach*

This wider picture of early Palaeolithic locales suggests another look at Bilzingsleben and its apparent evidence for social occasions based on the reconstructions of three dwellings and their associated workplaces and hearths (Mania and Weber 1986).

I have done this by applying Stapert's ring and sector model (1992) to the central, circular-shaped dwelling (Mania 1990:Abb 59).[47] This is separated from the northern dwelling by a small geological fault (Figure 4.22). In his spatial analysis of the structures the excavator has always removed this natural feature and joined the surface back together (compare Abb. 3 with Abb. 4 in Mania and Weber 1986).

Stapert based his analytical method on the ethnographically observed drop and toss zones (Binford 1978a) which have been discussed in Chapter 3. His method is centred on the patterns which radiate out from a feature, usually a hearth, or within a structure, normally a tent. The rings measure the amount of material dropped within 50-cm bands. The sectors, ranging from two to six depending on the number of finds, measure the dispersion of materials.

Table 4.19. *Lithic density data for Cromerian- and Holstein-age open locales (Anzidei and Gioia 1992, Anzidei and Huyzendveld 1992, Ashton et al. 1994, Bergman et al. 1990, Cassoli et al. 1993, Freeman 1975, Howell 1966, Mussi 1995, Oakley and Leakey 1937, Peretto, Terzani and Cremaschi 1983, Piperno and Biddittu 1978, Santonja 1992, Santonja, Lopez-Martinez and Perez-Gonzalez 1980, Singer et al. 1973, Thieme and Maier 1995, Tuffreau et al. 1986, Turner 1989, Waechter, Newcomer and Conway 1970, Weber 1986, Wymer 1968).*

| Site | Layer | Region | Age | $m^2$ excavated | Total stone | Density per $m^2$ |
|---|---|---|---|---|---|---|
| Clacton | Marl layer 3 | NW | Holstein | 375 | 136 | 0.4 |
| La Polledrara | | MC | Holstein | 350 | 250 | 0.7 |
| Castel di Guido | | MC | Holstein | 350 | 300 | 0.9 |
| Ambrona | Lower | MW | Holstein | 1,047 | 1,020 | 1.0 |
| Miesenheim | I | NC | Cromer | 100 | 100 | 1.0 |
| Casal de' Pazzi | | MC | Holstein | 1,200 | 1,700 | 1.4 |
| Swanscombe | LG layer 7e | NW | Holstein | 62.5 | 104 | 1.7 |
| Notarchirico | Elephant site | MC | Cromer | 24 | 41 | 1.7 |
| Schöningen 13 | | NC | Holstein | 95 | 170 | 1.8 |
| Swanscombe | LL all series | NW | Holstein | 200 | 375 | 1.9 |
| Torre in Pietra | m | MC | Holstein | 200 | 378 | 1.9 |
| Torralba | B4a | MW | Holstein | 300 | 761 | 2.5 |
| Clacton | Gravel layer 4 | NW | Holstein | 375 | 1,088 | 2.9 |
| Clacton | Gravel layer 3 | NW | Holstein | 25 | 76 | 3.0 |
| Clacton | | NW | Holstein | 47.7 | 190 | 4.0 |
| Aridos | 2 | MW | Holstein | 7.5 | 34 | 4.5 |
| Aridos | 1 | MW | Holstein | 30 | 333 | 11.1 |
| Boxgrove | Area A | NW | Cromer | 84 | 1,029 | 12.3 |
| Cagny-L'Épinette | I-J | NW | Holstein | 44 | 720 | 16.4 |
| Bilzingsleben | Üferzone | NC | Holstein | 230 | 4,965 | 21.6 |
| Swanscombe | UMG layer E | NW | Holstein | 346 | 8,638 | 25.0 |
| San Quirce | S.I.1 | MW | Holstein | 24 | 759 | 31.6 |
| Bilzingsleben | All areas | NC | Holstein | 355 | 11,385 | 32.1 |
| Isernia | Sett. I t.3a | MC | Cromer | 130 | 5,000 | 38.5 |
| Bilzingsleben | Schwemmfächer | NC | Holstein | 125 | 6,420 | 51.4 |
| Barnham | Area I | NW | Holstein | 40 | 2,500 | 62.5 |
| Isernia | Sett. II t.3a | MC | Cromer | 68 | 4,589 | 67.5 |
| San Quirce | S.II | MW | Holstein | 5.5 | 2,464 | 448.0 |

Using this technique, Stapert has set out to examine the claims for tents and shelters at Palaeolithic locales. His analysis discovered either unimodal or bimodal distributions of material among the settlement plans. However, in his opinion none of the patterns which produced unimodal distributions has any evidence of traces for huts or tents (1992:196). The bimodal distributions do relate to such structures, with the second peak coinciding with the tent wall which acts as a barrier.

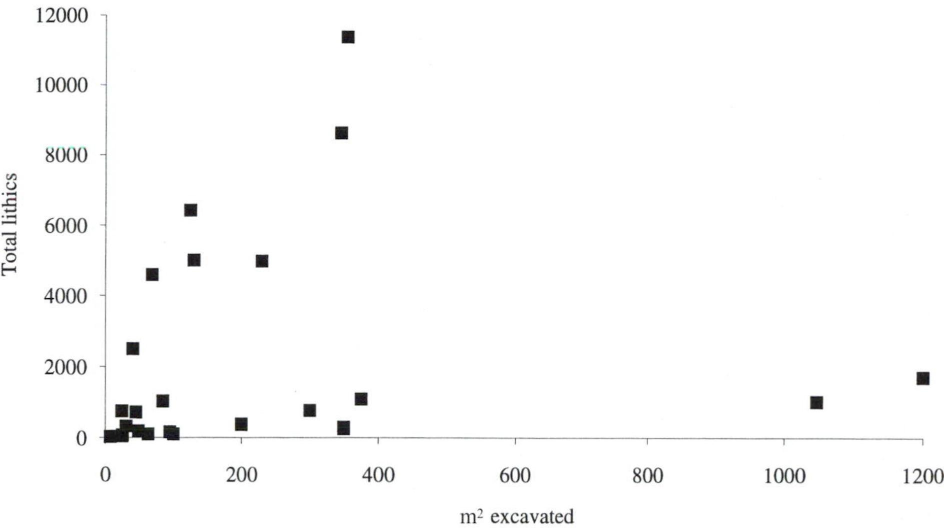


**4.26** Excavated density data of artifacts from Cromer and Holstein open locales; see Table 4.19.

Stapert's ring and sector model therefore provides us with a spatial model which can be used to assess the probability of shelters. Demonstrating their existence would be important in interpreting Bilzingsleben as a social occasion (Table 3.1) rather than just a series of gatherings.

In my analysis of the circular Bilzingsleben shelter (Figure 4.27), I drew the rings from a central position within the feature. The 184 objects that could be counted in Figure 4.27 display a unimodal tendency with the peak occurring between 1.5 and 2 m from the notional centre of the shelter (Figure 4.28). When subdivided into a north and south sector the pattern is still unimodal apart from a second peak beyond 2.5 m in the southern sector where the workplace is located. The location of a single peak at 2 m fits the expected pattern from an open-air distribution (see Chapter 3). It coincides with the edge of a drop zone around a hearth and does not necessarily require the existence of a structure to explain its form.

But we have seen repeatedly in this chapter that hearths and fireplaces do not exist in this period. So what can account for the circular, 'tent-like' patterning? Stapert has analysed a similar, low-density scatter of 183 artifacts (1992:202 and Fig. 17) from the Middle Palaeolithic locale of Rheindahlen where a structure has also been claimed (Thieme 1983, 1990). A simple ring and sector analysis revealed a unimodal pattern. Stapert concluded that Rheindahlen was created in the open air and that the empty space was probably a tree (*ibid.*:203). While he acknowledges that his idea cannot be proven, it certainly provides a more economical explanation than the construction of a hut from the same scatter.

Could this also be the case at Bilzingsleben? Certainly the environmental

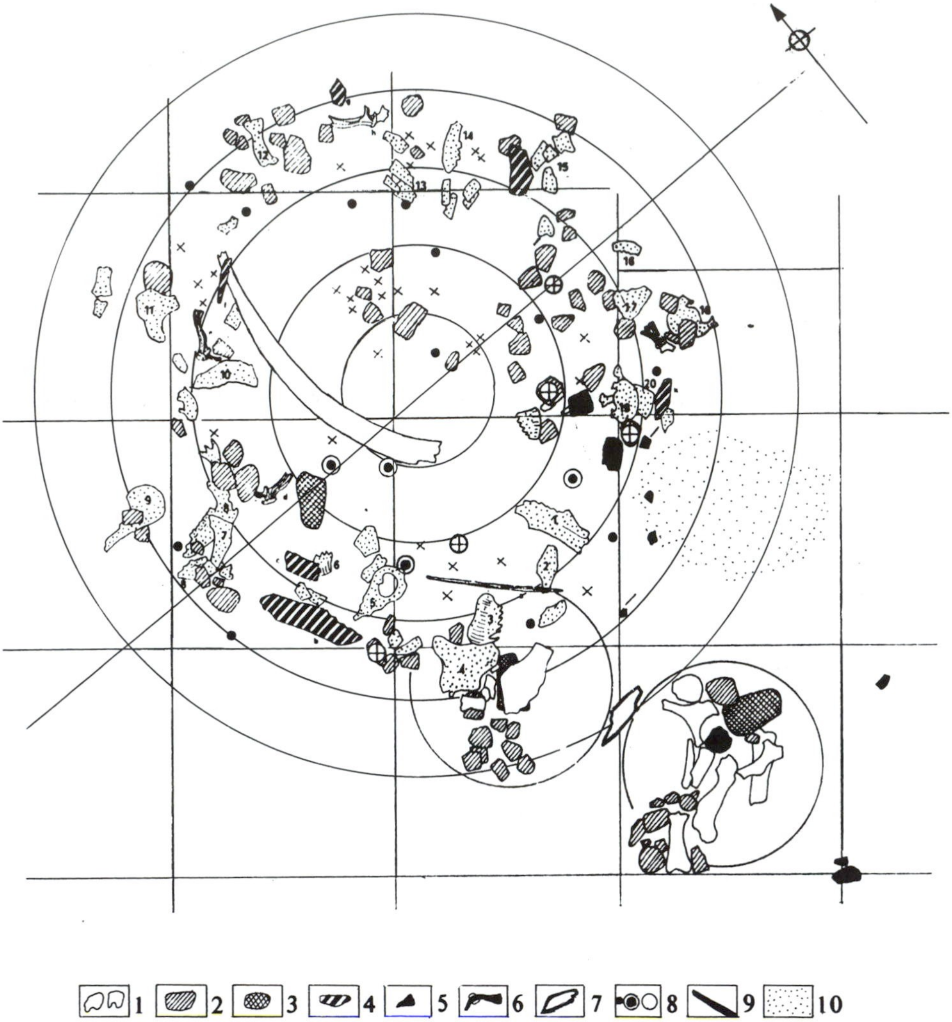

**4.27** Ring and sector analysis for shelter 2 at Bilzingsleben, Germany, NC region (data from Mania 1990:Abb. 59).

KEY:

1 Bones and teeth
2 Stone blocks and slabs
3 Stone anvils
4 Bone tools
5 Stones with evidence for burning
6 Antler tools
7 Bone artifact with engraving
8 Small, larger hammerstones, pebble tool
9 Stick-like wooden artifact
10 Charcoal

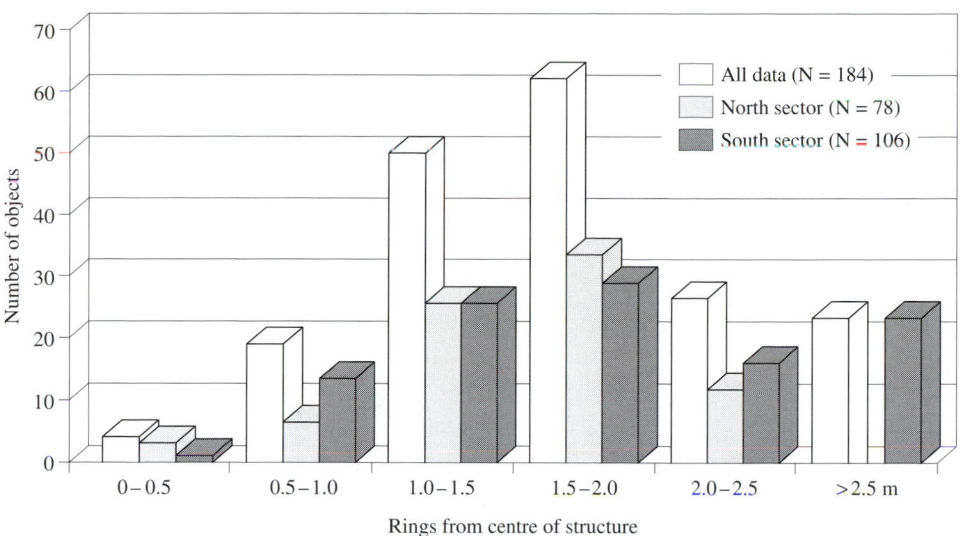


**4.28** Distribution of material in the sectors at Bilzingsleben, Germany, NC region (data from Mania 1990:Abb. 59).

evidence supports it. The preserved leaves and the presence of beaver and macaque monkey (*Macacca sylvana*) are good indicators of trees in the immediate environment. The wood remains (Mania 1991a:Tab. 4) are dominated by alder (*Alnus*) which today regularly reaches 20 m in height with a trunk 60 cm in diameter. Even thickets of box (*Buxus*) reach heights of 10 m with trunks 25 cm in diameter.

To speculate further, but perhaps less ingeniously than Mania's original interpretation, the numerous wood remains in the third structure (Table 4.18), which also has a large charcoal scatter, resulted from a fallen tree being burnt on the spot by the hominids. The fact that the openings of the 'dwellings' all face south could reflect, for example, either prevailing winds during storms or the direction in which trees were felled by the beavers at the locale.

Like Stapert I cannot prove this scenario but offer it as an alternative to discussing the social life of the earliest occupants of Europe. This option suggests to me that we might gain a great deal by reversing the way we approach the social analysis of these locales. If our goal is to find shelters in order to use them as a summary of social life in the early Palaeolithic, then I have no doubt that we have the analytical ingenuity and imagination to find them (e.g. Bosinski 1983, Lumley 1969a, 1969b). The problem, as discussed in earlier chapters, is that if the paraphernalia of social occasions, *our* social occasions, such as hearths, huts and burials, is the only means by which we recognize social life, then we either have to discover them at a locale such as Bilzingsleben or admit that people at that time had no society and move to a more promising part of the Palaeolithic record. The balance is between sustainable interpretations of the archaeological record and the exploration of alternatives.

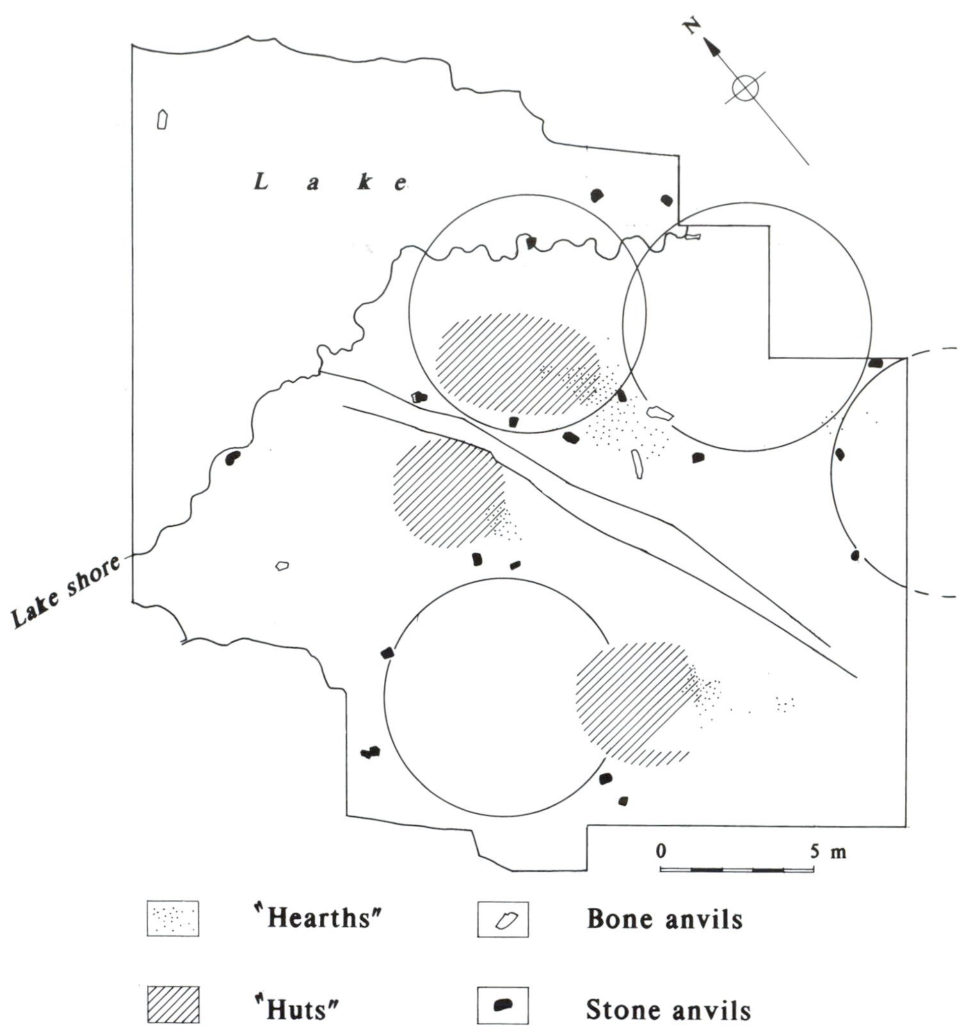


**4.29** An interpretation of the Bilzingsleben locale as a series of gatherings rather than as a campsite with huts and hearths. The distribution of anvils has been used to identify interaction areas of c. 4 m radius. These identify performance spaces where individuals interacted with each other and the resources of the locale (based on data in Mania 1990:Abb. 83, 1991:Fig. 1).

So, rather than start with the shelters, I will begin instead with the very interesting stone and bone anvils that have been brought in and positioned in relation to some affordance at this locale. Since these must have been carried in, and left behind, by individuals, they provide a starting point for a reanalysis of the gatherings at Bilzingsleben.

When these anvils are plotted (Figure 4.29), they form three rings with a diameter of approximately 8 m each. The two northern examples closest to the lake edge overlap, and one surrounds the tree/shelter. To the south the two remaining trees/shelters lie outside the rings defined by the anvils. A fourth ring is possibly indicated in the paved area with the bison skull.

What follows is a speculative scenario of the use of space at such a locale as defined by anvils as objects used in gatherings. This approach not only applies to Bilzingsleben but could be extended to other locales such as Boxgrove, Miesenheim I, Hoxne, Arago, Terra Amata and Vértesszöllös. I offer it to provoke discussion about the form which social analyses of this period might take if we remain sceptical, as many do, that our present reconstructions of shelters and our understanding of artifact and ecofact associations remain poor.

### *Bilzingsleben as performance*

The focus of social life was not the organized social occasion, centred on hearth or hut, but rather the opportunity, intercepted, encountered and available for subsequent negotiation.

The woods around the spring and lake proved advantageous as a locale over many years and visits. Hominid paths and animal tracks criss-crossed the lake shore and the small streams which flowed across the lake fan and which drained into the river.

Ecologically the affordances of the locale were varied, concentrated and reliable. The comparative absence of carnivore interest was an extra advantage, and indeed the locale was ignored by them even though large bones of megafauna were lying around long after the hominids had moved on and more had accumulated before they returned. This security resulted in larger gatherings and longer stays, although the exact durations are unknown.

The important social act, the attaching ritual, was setting up the anvil. This was how individuals were attached to the gathering, to other people and to the locale. Carrying the anvil a few metres or a few hundred signified the commencement of structured activity, the start of rhythmic gesture and, for the archaeologist, the possibility of patterns which might survive. The gathering now began as a result of a material action that produced spatial and temporal consequences for social interaction. Sitting beneath the trees or beside their charred remains once they had fallen and been burnt, these were the places for transmitting skills, breaking bones on the anvils, knapping stones, stripping flesh, sharing, eating, rhythmically striking bones to form patterns and occasionally producing ordered cut-marks on their surfaces.

Individuals carried their own blocks. Individuals invested the locale with social meaning by sitting or standing and facing each other in relation to these blocks. Attention was fixed, action could commence.

Such co-presence over a distance of 8 m (Figure 4.29) also fostered the use of the space, so enclosed, for performances that involved the rhythms of manufacture as bones and stones were smashed and fashioned. At the same time, individuals would be returning to the locale, introducing food, bones, stones, wood, fire, shells and plants as well as sounds, smells and the opportunities to touch and groom, into these small, loosely defined spaces of attention and co-presence. As they returned to such places they performed the bonds that bound them into wider social networks. These performances emphasized the transient nature of the gathering and its lack of continuing structure beyond the immediate presence of those at the locale. All ages and sexes were present at the locale and the remains of three individuals survive. Children, emulating adults, carried in stones and surrounded a bison skull. Stimulated by the rhythms of manufacture and processing, they built their own path of stones leading to the area being trampled over by the others. They were learning the consequences of participation in their social world. But while creative, what they created had no lasting effect once co-presence was broken and once this locale was left. This was a locale where gatherings produced their own complex dramas.

It would be easier to say that the evidence for social activity at Bilzingsleben is extremely limited. I conclude however that the social richness of this locale is such that we have hardly begun its exploration. If we are searching for groups as examples of Palaeolithic society, then we will constantly be thwarted in this aim by the record from the Middle Pleistocene. We will be disappointed because we will not be able to identify the material works that are the surviving traces of the corporate institutions and group structures which are needed in such a model of society. However, if we approach the same record as the fine-grained signature of individuals negotiating what those networks and structures were to be, then the possibility is presented for further analysis. This signature has of course been confused by later visits, trampling by other animals and the ravages on the archaeological record brought about by falling trees, building travertine and geological faults. But the social study of any archaeological record faces similar procedural hurdles.

### Summary

Understanding the archaeology of the early Palaeolithic requires a tacking strategy between different scales of analysis and different levels of preservation and resolution (Chapter 3). We can tack from the coarse, regional scale which consists of the background data to the fine-grained, primary-context material. Archaeologically we are comparing dredgers with flagships in terms of integrity and resolution (Gamble 1996b). The numerous flakes and bifaces preserved in the English rivers, the Somme terraces or the Duero basin are examples of the dredgers. These establish an extensive regional presence for these early hominids. Although many of the findspots are from derived, fluvial contexts, they contribute to a broader picture of landscape use, raw material transfer and artifact diversity. The flagship sites would include Miesenheim I, Notarchirico and Bilzingsleben. Analytically we can tack from the dredgers, those time-averaged collections of 50–100-Kyr duration (Table 4.1), to the flagships where it took fifteen minutes to find a good piece of flint in the Boxgrove cliff, test it, carry it onto the tidal flats and finish knapping it into a biface.

Both types of data are needed to assess the social capabilities of these early hominids. When considered together, we can conclude that social life in this period was routinized. Hominids led complex social lives with only minimal extension of co-presence beyond the gathering. The archaeological record throughout the eight occupied regions of Europe is very comparable. Where primary-context locales exist we see a picture of low densities of stone and bone artifacts. Raw material is immediate or obtained within 30 km and usually less. In some cases there seems a good correlation between artifact shape and the quality of raw material. Symmetry among bifaces or on the rare engraved bones springs from the rhythms of encounters and gatherings where attention and co-presence are a feature of display and performance.

This accords with the investment of individuals in the construction of intimate and effective networks. Bonding and binding relied heavily on affective resources which demand time and co-presence. We should not be surprised that the archaeological record is deficient in direct evidence for these critical social activities. But the record is very clear about the bonds in the effective network. The use of resources does not point to any collective action based on symbolic resources. Individuals may gather at the carcass of an elephant or beside a drowned herd of bison. They may have killed these animals as the result of co-ordinated labour, although the evidence is clearer on this point after 300 Kyr BP. I would not be surprised if they did, since all mammals are social and some, like lions, hyenas and chimpanzees, are known to hunt co-operatively. This is presumably because they too can turn the resources in their equivalent of a hominid's intimate, and to a lesser extent effective network, into just such a social expression. The difference with hominids is that at their gatherings the process of consumption becomes the focus for negotiation. As a result effective networks were intense and circumscribed. Extended networks hardly figured because there simply was not time to service them.

The outcome of this differential network development was most strongly felt in the colonizing abilities of middle Pleistocene hominids. With the accent on the intimate/effective network as the co-operative and social unit there would have been strong selection by environmental forces against range extension. Competition from the large carnivore guild has been put forward as an example (A. Turner 1992), but more generally the structure of resources prior to 500 Kyr BP could not support the necessary intensity of interaction between well-defined but separate regional populations to allow permanent continental expansion. This raises the question, to be examined in the next chapter, of the pattern of population ebb and flow in the occupied regions of middle Pleistocene Europe.

CHAPTER 5

# NEANDERTHAL SOCIETIES 300,000 TO 60,000 YEARS AGO

Yet land there is about Europa's scene
Away to south, where, though the frosts be keen,
Can well clad hardy life, to cold inured,
Of ample means of living be assured . . .
Here too the mammoth, in his hairy hide,
If cold should prove no greater can abide.
So here rhinoceroses, 'woolly' dressed,
May for a time their further flight arrest.
And Man indeed will not forsake a land,
Where prey – his food and clothing – is at hand

Henry Knipe, 1905
*From Nebula to Man*

## The diversity of Neanderthal life

There are three questions to ask about Neanderthal societies: what environments could they cope with; did their societies differ across the continent; and was their social life based on spoken language?

The archaeological record of their quarter of a million years is particularly rich. Many more sites are known than in the previous two hundred thousand years. Preservation in open locales continues, on occasion, to be good and there are more occupied cave sites whose sediments package archaeological remains. This circumstance assists a narrative approach to the analysis and interpretation of stone tools as shown for example by François Bordes in *A tale of two caves* (1972).

Several absolute dating techniques now cover this period, while the fossil evidence sees the appearance of *Homo neanderthalensis*, the regional descendant of *Homo heidelbergensis*.[1] Neanderthals, with their distinctive skulls and limb proportions, are only found in Europe and restricted parts of the Near East (Stringer and Gamble 1993:figure 1). They first appear between 300–250 Kyr BP. They are often regarded as the hominids of the Middle Palaeolithic and makers of Mousterian industries.

These last two stereotypes have both been recently challenged; firstly, by absolute dates of >90 Kyr BP for anatomically modern humans from Qafzeh cave in Israel (Valladas et al. 1988), who were found with Mousterian artifacts. Secondly, similar ages now exist for blade technologies of Upper Palaeolithic form from northern Europe (Conard 1992, Révillion and Tuffreau 1994a). While no hominid fossils have yet been found with these blade assemblages it is currently assumed, in the absence of any *Homo sapiens* fossils older than 35 Kyr BP from anywhere in Europe, that they were made by Neanderthals.

These challenges to the traditional picture have broadened the question of Neanderthal diversity which is here approached through the three questions which opened this chapter. In this chapter I will explore these aspects further with a social perspective; but first, the framework.

## Chronology, climates and habitats

One of the great advances in the study of this segment of the Palaeolithic has been the advent of absolute dates. Thermoluminescence (TL) dating of burnt flints and sediments, Electron Spin Resonance (ESR) dating of animal teeth and Uranium series dating of cave stalagmites and travertine spring deposits has, in the past fifteen years, revolutionized the chronologies of this period (Aitken 1990). The theoretical lower limits of these techniques extend back into the early Pleistocene. However, most dating scientists set the current lowest age estimates of these techniques as no more than 300 Kyr BP. Even within this conservative range some of the dates have to be treated with caution. For example, the sequence at Swanscombe dated on bio-stratigraphical evidence to OIS 11 (362–423 Kyr BP) has two TL dates of 202 ± 15.2 for the Upper Loam and 228.8 ± 23.3 for the Lower Loam (Bridgland 1985, 1994:figure 4.12). These dates suggest an OIS 7 age but this cannot be supported on either geological or faunal grounds (Bowen et al. 1989, Bridgland 1994, Currant 1989). However, while the dates must be dismissed, their internal consistency does at least point to the rapid accumulation during a single temperate stage of the Swanscombe sediments.[2] It is these problems of resolving stratigraphic correlations with the small number of absolute age determinations, and the uncertainties surrounding some of the techniques, that currently set the lower limits for TL and ESR well within their potential dating range.[3]

But even for well-dated locales within the past 300 Kyr care still needs to be taken. The Netherlands site of Maastricht-Belvédère (Roebroeks 1988) has a TL date on burnt flint of 250 ± 20 Kyr BP (Huxtable 1993) which places it in OIS 7. The artifacts lie in the climatic optimum of this interglacial as revealed by the associated molluscs which, in Subunit IVC, have been dated by ESR to 220 ± 40 Kyr BP. But these molluscs belong in an oceanic climate and are therefore at odds with the expectation of a more continental climate during a comparatively low sea-level interglacial such as OIS 7 (Zagwijn 1992). Kolfschoten (et al. 1993:89) are happy to leave the site in OIS 7 as the current 'best fit', while not entirely confident about the match between stratigraphic, bioclimatic and absolute methods of dating.

The same uncertainty surrounds the eastern German travertine locales of Burgtonna, Weimar and Taubach. Environmental evidence indicates an OIS 5e age (Table 5.1) and yet the absolute dates (Table 5.2) are consistently younger.

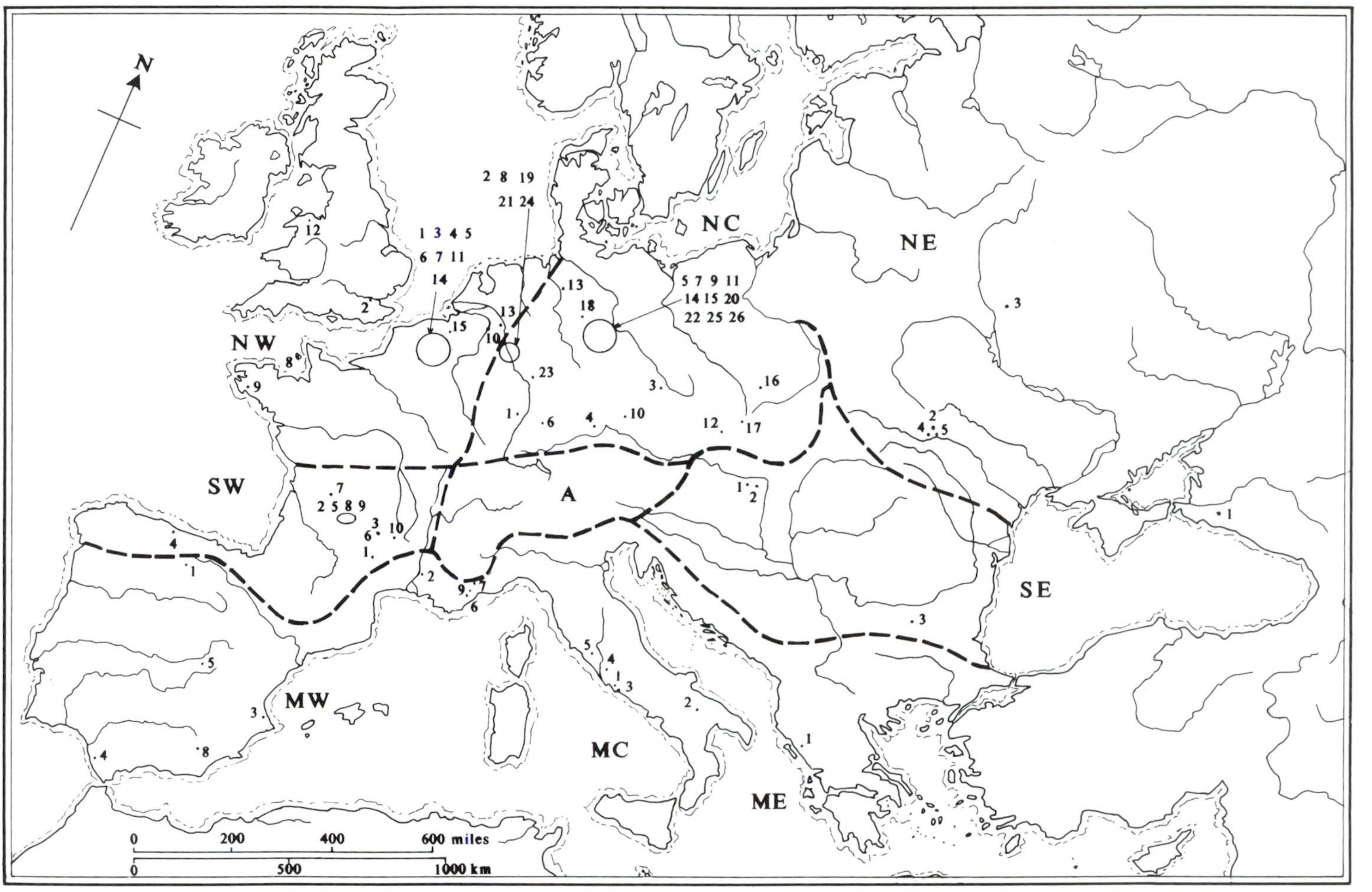

N
NW
SW
NC
NE
A
SE
MW
MC
ME
0 200 400 600 miles
0 500 1000 km

**5.1** Principal locales discussed in this chapter and referred to in Tables 5.1, 5.2, 5.12 and 5.18.

KEY: by region

| | NW | NC | NE | SW | SE | MW | MC | ME |
|---|---|---|---|---|---|---|---|---|
| 1 | Atelier Commont | Achenheim | Il'skaya | Abri des Canalettes | Érd | Atapuerca | Guattari | Asprochaliko |
| 2 | Bakers Hole | Ariendorf | Ketrosy | Combe Grenal | Tata | Bérigoule | Monticchio | |
| 3 | Bapaume | Becov | Khotylevo | Coudoulous | Temnata | Cova de Bolomor | Moscerini | |
| 4 | Beauvais | Bockstein | Korman | El Castilló | | El Aculadero | Saccopastore | |
| 5 | Biache St. Vaast | Burgtonna | Molodova | Grotte Vaufrey | | El Pinar | Torre in Pietra | |
| 6 | Gouzeaucourt | Cannstatt | | La Borde | | Lazaret | | |
| 7 | Hermies | Ehringsdorf | | La Chaise | | Pié Lombard | | |
| 8 | La Cotte | Eifel volcanoes | | La Micoque | | Solana di Zamborino | | |
| 9 | Le Mont Dol | Gröbern | | Pech de l'Azé | | Terra Amata | | |
| 10 | Maastricht-Belvédère | Hunas | | Rescoundudou | | | | |
| 11 | Mesvin IV | Königsaue | | | | | | |
| 12 | Pontnewydd | Kulna | | | | | | |
| 13 | Rheindahlen | Lehringen | | | | | | |
| 14 | Riencourt | Markkleeberg | | | | | | |
| 15 | Seclin | Neumark-Nord | | | | | | |
| 16 | | Piekary | | | | | | |
| 17 | | Předmostí | | | | | | |
| 18 | | Salzgitter-Lebenstedt | | | | | | |
| 19 | | Schweinskopf | | | | | | |
| 20 | | Taubach | | | | | | |
| 21 | | Tönchesberg | | | | | | |
| 22 | | Veltheim | | | | | | |
| 23 | | Wallertheim | | | | | | |
| 24 | | Wannen | | | | | | |
| 25 | | Weimar | | | | | | |
| 26 | | Zwochau | | | | | | |

Table 5.1. *Saalian, Eemian and early Weichselian chronology with major archaeological and palaeontological locales.*

| OIS | Kyr BP | | NW | NC | NE | SW | SE | MW | MC | ME |
|---|---|---|---|---|---|---|---|---|---|---|
| 4<br>PLENIGLACIAL | 58<br>71 | | Beauvais<br>Reincourt C & B | Kulna 9–7a<br>*Salzgitter*<br>Tönchesberg IB | Il'skaya II/2–3 | Combe Grenal 49 | Temnata TD1 6 | Pié Lombard | | |
| 5a<br>Odderade | 85 | E<br>A<br>R<br>L<br>Y | | Ariendorf 3<br>Königsaue | | Abri des Canalettes/2<br>Grotte Vaufrey II<br>Pech de l'Azé II/4 | | | Guattari 4 & 5<br>Moscerini 25 & 26 | |
| 5b | 95 | | Le Mont Dol | | Il'skaya I<br>Ketrosy<br>Korman IV<br>Molodova I/4–8<br>Molodova V/IIb–12 | Grotte Vaufrey III<br>El Castilló 23 | | El Pinar | | |
| 5c<br>Brørup | 105 | G<br>L<br>A<br>C | Reincourt CA<br>Seclin | Bockstein IIIa<br>Kulna 11<br>Wallertheim D–F | | La Chaise 7<br>Pech de l'Azé II/3<br>*Rescoundudou C1* | Temnata TD1 7 | | Moscerini 38 & 39 | Asprochaliko |
| 5d | 118 | I<br>A<br>L | | Tönchesberg 2B<br>Wallertheim C | | | | El Pinar | | |
| 5e | 128 | E<br>E<br>M<br>I<br>A<br>N | | Burgtonna<br>Gröbern<br>Lehringen<br>Neumark-Nord<br>*Taubach*<br>Veltheim<br>Wallertheim A & B<br>Weimar | Il'skaya II/7<br>Khotylevo I | Grotte Vaufrey IV<br>La Chaise 11 | Tata | Cova de Bolomor II<br>Atapuerca TG | | |
| 6 | 186 | S<br>A | *Biache St. Vaast IIA*<br>*La Cotte A & B, 3–6*<br>Rheindahlen W & B3 | Achenheim sol 74<br>Ariendorf 2<br>Becov I<br>Kulna 14<br>Piekary II<br>Předmostí<br>Schweinskopf<br>Tönchesberg 1A & 2A<br>Wannen | | Coudoulous I level 4<br>Grotte Vaufrey VII–VIII<br>La Borde<br>La Micoque N/M<br>Pech de l'Azé II/6–9<br>Rescoundudou E3, E2 | | Cova de Bolomor XIII<br>*Lazaret* | | |

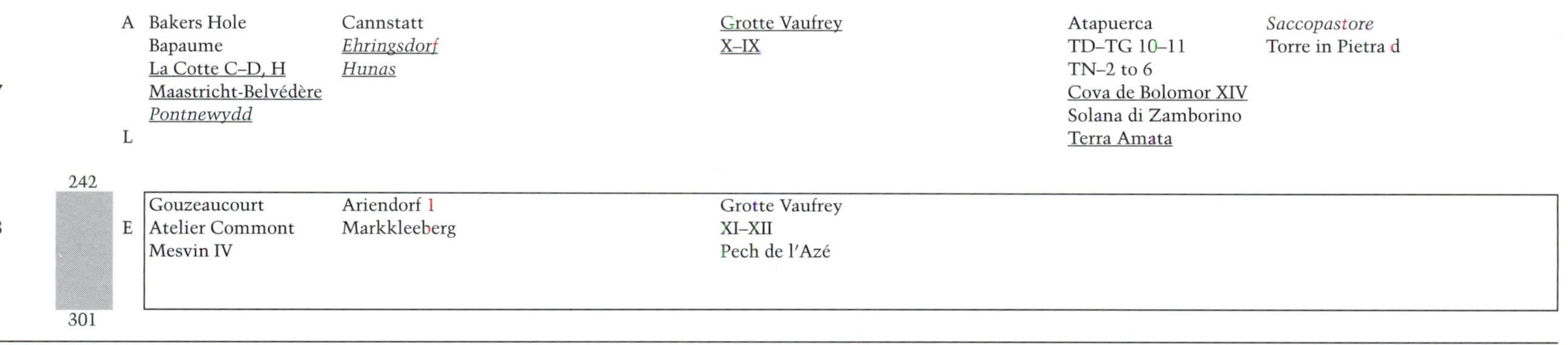

| | | | | | | | |
|---|---|---|---|---|---|---|---|
| | | A | Bakers Hole | Cannstatt | Grotte Vaufrey | Atapuerca | *Saccopastore* |
| | | | Bapaume | *Ehringsdorf* | X–IX | TD–TG 10–11 | Torre in Pietra d |
| | | | La Cotte C–D, H | *Hunas* | | TN–2 to 6 | |
| 7 | | | Maastricht-Belvédère | | | Cova de Bolomor XIV | |
| | | | *Pontnewydd* | | | Solana di Zamborino | |
| | | L | | | | Terra Amata | |
| | 242 | | | | | | |
| | | | Gouzeaucourt | Ariendorf 1 | Grotte Vaufrey | | |
| 8 | | E | Atelier Commont | Markkleeberg | XI–XII | | |
| | | | Mesvin IV | | Pech de l'Azé | | |
| | 301 | | | | | | |

key: hominid fossils in italic; absolute dates underlined.

Table 5.2. *Absolute dates in the Saalian, Eemian and early Weichselian, 242–60 Kyr BP. Selected locales from the Middle East have been included for comparative purposes. Caution needs to be used when interpreting these dates since there are many contradictions between bio-stratigraphical evidence and absolute age determinations. For example the locales of Burgtonna, Taubach and Weimar are placed in OIS 5e on bio-stratigraphic evidence (Table 5.1) although their absolute dates fall within 5d (Stringer and Gamble 1993: appendix with additions, stage boundaries after Bassinot et al. 1994).*

| Locale | Layer | Region | | Dating method | Hominids | Archaeology | Kyr bp | ± |
|---|---|---|---|---|---|---|---|---|
| **STAGE 3/4 BOUNDARY 58 Kyr BP** | | | | | | | | |
| Kebara | Units XII–VI, 38 dates | Middle East | | TL | Neanderthal | Mousterian | ≈60 | |
| Kebara | Units Xi–Xii | Middle East | | ESR | Neanderthal | Mousterian | 60 | 6 |
| Pech de L'Azé II | Layer 3 | Europe | SW | ESR | | Mousterian | *60–72* | |
| Combe Grenal | Level 55 | Europe | SW | TL | | Mousterian (Typical) | 61 | 7 |
| Combe Grenal | Level 50 | Europe | SW | TL | | Mousterian (Typical) | 62 | 7 |
| Brugas | Level 4 | Europe | SW | TL | | Mousterian (Quina) | 63 | 5.8 |
| Kebara | Units Xi–Xii | Middle East | | ESR | Neanderthal | Mousterian | 64 | 6 |
| Temnata | Layer 6 | Europe | SE | TL | | Middle Palaeolithic | 67 | 11 |
| Combe Grenal | Level 49 | Europe | SW | TL | | Mousterian (Typical) | 68 | 7 |
| Douara | IIIB | Middle East | | Fission Track | | Mousterian | 70 | |
| Abri Pié-Lombard | | Europe | MW | TL | | Mousterian (Typical) | 70 | 7.7 |
| La Chaise | Level 7 (Bourgeois Delaunay) | Europe | SW | U series | Neanderthal | Middle Palaeolithic | 71 | 6 |
| Guattari | Stratum 4 | Europe | MC | ESR | | Mousterian (Pontinian) | 71 | 27 |
| **STAGE 4/5a BOUNDARY 71 Kyr BP** | ***Odderade*** | | | | | | | |
| Pech de l'Azé II | Layer 4 | Europe | SW | ESR | | Mousterian | *71–87* | |
| Abri des Canalettes | Level 2 | Europe | SW | TL | | Mousterian (Typical) | 73.5 | 6 |
| Moscerini | Strata group 3, stratum 26 | Europe | MC | ESR | | Mousterian (Pontinian) | 74 | |
| Grotte Vaufrey | Level II | Europe | SW | U series | | Middle Palaeolithic | 74 | 18 |
| Douara | IVB | Middle East | | Fission Track | | Mousterian | 75 | |
| El Kowm | Oumm 4 | Middle East | | U series | | Yabrudian–Mousterian | 76 | 16 |
| Guattari | Stratum 5 | Europe | MC | ESR | | Mousterian (Pontinian) | 77.5 | 9.5 |
| Abri Laborde | Layers 29–32 | Europe | SW | TL | | Mousterian (Ferrassie) | 78.5 | 7.5 |
| Moscerini | Strata group 3, stratum 25 | Europe | ME | ESR | | Mousterian (Pontinian) | 79 | |
| Skhul | Layer B | Middle East | | ESR | Early Modern | Middle Palaeolithic | 81 | 15 |
| **STAGE 5a/b BOUNDARY 85 Kyr BP** | | | | | | | | |
| Zobiste | Lowest level | Europe | NC | TL | | Middle Palaeolithic | 85.5 | 8.5 |
| Tabun | Layer B | Middle East | | ESR | | Mousterian | *86–103* | |

| | | | | | | | | |
|---|---|---|---|---|---|---|---|---|
| Coudoulous II | Plancher 4–5 | Europe | SW | U/Th | | Mousterian | *87.8–135.6* | |
| El Castillo | Level 23 flowstone | Europe | SW | U series | | Lower/Middle Palaeolithic | 89 | 1 |
| La Chaise | Level 7 (Bourgeois Delaunay) | Europe | SW | U series | Neanderthal | Middle Palaeolithic | 89.5 | 5 |
| Seclin | D4 | Europe | NW | TL | | Middle Palaeolithic blades | 91 | 11 |
| Grotte Vaufrey | Level III | Europe | SW | U series | | Middle Palaeolithic | 91 | 51 |
| Qafzeh | Layers XXIII–XVII | Middle East | | TL | Early Modern | Mousterian | 92 | 5 |
| La Chaise | Upper stalagmite (Abri Suard) | Europe | SW | U series | Neanderthal | Middle Palaeolithic | 94 | 22 |
| Seclin | D7 | Europe | NW | TL | | Middle Palaeolithic blades | 95 | 10 |
| Zuttiyeh | 76ZU 1 | Middle East | | U series | | Yabrudian–Mousterian | 95 | 10 |
| **STAGE 5b/c BOUNDARY 95 Kyr BP** | ***Brørup*** | | | | | | | |
| Moscerini | Strata group 4, stratum 39 | Europe | MC | ESR | | Mousterian (Pontinian) | 96 | |
| Zuttiyeh | 76ZU 6 | Middle East | | U series | | Yabrudian-Mousterian | 97 | 13 |
| Zobiste | Lowest level | Europe | NC | TL | | Middle Palaeolithic | 97.5 | 7 |
| Tata | | Europe | SE | U series | | Middle Palaeolithic | 98 | 8 |
| Asprochaliko | Layer 18 | Europe | ME | TL | | Mousterian | 98.5 | 12 |
| El Kowm | Tell 6 | Middle East | | U series | | Yabrudian | 99 | 16 |
| Tata | | Europe | SE | U series | | Middle Palaeolithic | 101 | 10 |
| Qafzeh | Layers XV-XXI | Middle East | | ESR | Early Modern | Middle Palaeolithic | 100 | 10 |
| Moscerini | Strata group 4, stratum 38 | Europe | ME | ESR | | Mousterian (Pontinian) | 101 | |
| Burgtonna | | Europe | NC | U series | | Taubachian | 101 | |
| La Chaise | Upper stalagmite (Abri Suard) | Europe | SW | U series | Neanderthal | Middle Palaeolithic | 101 | 7 |
| La Chaise | Level 7 (Bourgeois Delaunay) | Europe | SW | U series | Neanderthal | Middle Palaeolithic | 101 | 12 |
| Skhul | Layer B | Middle East | | ESR | Early Modern | Middle Palaeolithic | 101 | 12 |
| Tabun | Layer C | Middle East | | ESR | Neanderthal | Mousterian | *102–109* | |
| Ehringsdorf | | Europe | NC | U series | ? Early Neanderthal | Middle Palaeolithic | *102–244* | |
| Pech de l'Azé II | Level 3 | Europe | SW | U series | | Mousterian | 103 | 27 |
| Burgtonna | | Europe | NC | U series | | Taubachian | 104 | |
| Hummal Well, El Kowm | Level 6b | Middle East | | TL | | Mousterian | 104 | 9 |
| Combe Grenal | Layer 60 | Europe | SW | TL | | Acheulean | 105 | 14 |
| Combe Grenal | 60 | Europe | SW | TL | | Acheulean | 105 | 14 |
| Temnata | Layer 7 | Europe | SE | TL | | Middle Palaeolithic | 105 | 35 |
| **STAGE 5c/d BOUNDARY 105 Kyr BP** | | | | | | | | |
| Moscerini | Strata group 3, stratum 33 | Europe | ME | ESR | | Mousterian (Pontinian) | 106 | |
| Abri Pié-Lombard | | Europe | MW | TL | | Mousterian (Typical) | 108.4 | 9.8 |
| Taubach | | Europe | NC | U series | | Taubachian | 110 | |
| Burgtonna | | Europe | NC | U series | | Taubachian | 111 | |
| La Chaise | Level 11 upper (B. Delaunay) | Europe | SW | U series | Neanderthal | Middle Palaeolithic | 112 | 5 |
| Combe Grenal | Layer 60 | Europe | SW | TL | | Acheulean | 113 | 13 |
| La Chaise | Level 7 (Bourgeois Delaunay) | Europe | SW | U series | Neanderthal | Middle Palaeolithic | 114 | 7 |
| Weimar | | Europe | NC | U series | | Taubachian | 115 | |

Table 5.2 (*cont.*)

| Locale | Layer | Region | | Dating method | Hominids | Archaeology | Kyr bp | ± |
|---|---|---|---|---|---|---|---|---|
| Rescoundudou | Lower stalagmitic floor | Europe | SW | U/Th | | Mousterian | *115–123* | |
| Taubach | | Europe | NC | U series | | Taubachian | 116 | |
| La Chaise | Level 11 upper (B. Delaunay) | Europe | SW | U series | Neanderthal | Middle Palaeolithic | 117 | 8 |
| **STAGE 5d/5e BOUNDARY 118 Kyr BP** | ***Eem*** | | | | | | | |
| Weimar | | Europe | NC | U series | | Taubachian | 118 | |
| Skhul | Level B | Middle East | | TL | Early Modern | Mousterian | 119 | 18 |
| Grotte Vaufrey | Level IV | Europe | SW | TL | | Mousterian | 123 | 20 |
| Qafzeh | | Middle East | | ESR | Early Modern | Middle Palaeolithic | 120 | 8 |
| Cova de Bolomor | Level II | Europe | MW | TL | | Middle Palaeolithic | 121 | 18 |
| Tabun | Layer D | Middle East | | ESR | | Mousterian | *122–166* | |
| La Chaise | Level 11 upper (B. Delaunay) | Europe | SW | U series | Neanderthal | Middle Palaeolithic | 123 | 17 |
| La Chaise | Level 51 (Abri Suard) | Europe | SW | TL | Neanderthal | Middle Palaeolithic | 126 | 15 |
| **STAGE 5e/6 BOUNDARY 128 Kyr BP** | | | | | | | | |
| Sclayn Cave | Layer 5b | Europe | NW | TL | | Middle Palaeolithic | 130 | 20 |
| Pech de l'Azé II | Layer 6–9 | Europe | SW | ESR | | Acheulean | *130–162* | |
| El Kowm | Oumm 3 | Middle East | | U series | | Yabrudian | 139 | 16 |
| Grotte Vaufrey | Level VIII | Europe | SW | U series | | Middle Palaeolithic | 142 | 130-68 |
| La Chaise | Level 11 (Bourgeois Delaunay) | Europe | SW | U series | Neanderthal | Middle Palaeolithic | 146 | 16 |
| Zuttiyeh | 76ZU 4 | Middle East | | U series | *Late H. heidelbergensis* | Pre-Yabrudian | 148 | 6 |
| Ehringsdorf | | Europe | NC | U series | ? Early Neanderthal | Middle Palaeolithic | *150–250* | |
| La Chaise | Level 11 lower (B. Delaunay) | Europe | SW | U series | ? Early Neanderthal | Middle Palaeolithic | 151 | 15 |
| Tabun | Layer Eb | Middle East | | ESR | | Mousterian | *151–168* | |
| Weimar | | Europe | NC | U series | | Taubachian | 151 | |
| Cova de Bolomor | Level XIII | Europe | MW | TL | | Middle Palaeolithic | 152 | 23 |
| Tabun | Layer Ea | Middle East | | ESR | | Mousterian | *154–188* | |
| El Kowm | Humm 2 | Middle East | | U series | | Yabrudian | 156 | 16 |
| Grotte Vaufrey | Level VII | Europe | SW | U series | | Middle Palaeolithic | 158 | 10 |
| Hummal Well, El Kowm | Level Ib | Middle East | | TL | | Yabrudian | 160 | 22 |
| Zuttiyeh | 76ZU 1a | Middle East | | U series | *Late H. heidelbergensis* | Pre-Yabrudian | 164 | 21 |
| Rheindahlen | Fleckenlehm | Europe | NW | TL | | Middle Palaeolithic | 167 | 15 |
| Biache-Saint-Vaast | IIA | Europe | NW | TL | ? Early Neanderthal | Middle Palaeolithic | 175 | 13 |
| Tabun | Layer Ec | Middle East | | ESR | | Mousterian | *176–199* | |
| Tabun | Layer Ed | Middle East | | ESR | | Mousterian | *182–213* | |
| Vértesszöllös | | Europe | SE | U series | *? H. heidelbergensis* | Pebble tools, microlithic | 185 | 25 |

| | | | | | | | | |
|---|---|---|---|---|---|---|---|---|
| **STAGE 6/7 BOUNDARY 186 Kyr BP** | | | | | | | | |
| Pontnewydd Cave | | Europe | NW | TL | ? Early Neanderthal | Acheulean | 200 | 25 |
| Grotte Vaufrey | Level IX | Europe | SW | U series | | Middle Palaeolithic | 208 | 8 |
| Maastricht-Belvédère | Unit IV | Europe | NW | ESR | | Middle Palaeolithic | 220 | 40 |
| Bad Cannstatt | | Europe | NC | U series | | Pebble tools, microlithic | 225 | |
| Cova de Bolomor | Level XIV a & b, breccia | Europe | MW | TL | | Above Middle Palaeolithic | 225 | 34 |
| Ehringsdorf | | Europe | NC | U series | ? Early Neanderthal | Middle Palaeolithic | 230 | |
| Terra Amata | | Europe | MW | TL | | Middle Palaeolithic | 230 | 40 |
| Cova de Bolomor | Level XIV a & b, breccia | Europe | MW | TL | | Above Middle Palaeolithic | 233 | 35 |
| La Cotte | Layers C–D | Europe | NW | TL | | Middle Palaeolithic | 238 | 35 |
| Arago | | Europe | MW | TL | *H. heidelbergensis* | Middle Palaeolithic | 240 | 74 |
| El Kowm | Oumm 5 | Middle East | | U series | | Pre-Yabrudian | 245 | 16 |
| Grotte Vaufrey | Level X | Europe | SW | U series | | Middle Palaeolithic | 246 | 76 |
| Maastricht-Belvédère | Unit IV | Europe | NW | TL | | Middle Palaeolithic | 250 | 20 |
| Hunas | P1 | Europe | NC | Th/U | *H. heidelbergensis* | Middle Palaeolithic above | 260 | 40–60 |
| **STAGE 7/8 BOUNDARY 242 Kyr BP** | | | | | | | | |

So, while absolute dates for this period are very welcome, we should not conclude that all those listed in Table 5.2 are unproblematic. Neither should we regard these as precise dates, as we might with C14, but rather as age estimates. This caution will be important when it comes to discussing the habitat preferences of Neanderthals.

For these reasons I prefer the broad chronological framework outlined in Chapter 4. Our period spans the Saalian (OIS 8–6) and more than half of the last interglacial/glacial cycle (OIS 5e/5d–4). This includes three cool/glacial phases (OIS 8, 6 and 5d–4) and two interglacials (OIS 7 and 5e). The deep sea core V19–30 (Figure 5.2) charts the general course of global climate during the period.

*Comparing the cool periods*

The details of the two Saalian cool periods with low ocean volume (OIS 8 and OIS 6) are still only known in outline. The earlier stage sees an increase in arctic mammal species, especially lemming (*Dicrostonyx*) and reindeer. It is from this stage that the mammoth steppe (Guthrie 1990) and the *Mammuthus/Coelodonta* faunal complex (Khalke 1994) dominate vegetation and animal communities. Moreover, as we saw in Chapter 4, this distinctive biotic province extends to take in much of northern Asia.

The later Saalian cool period, OIS 6, has been compared to the last glaciation by analysing the dust in the Vostok ice core drilled into the East Antarctica ice cap. Increases in dust point to colder conditions producing larger deserts in the southern hemisphere and hence more intense winds and erosion. Jouzel et al. (1993:411) use this core to show that the OIS 6 cold stage lasted from 200–140 Kyr BP. This was a much longer period of cold than the last glaciation maximum. Temperatures were more uniformly cold during the period, while the extent of the Saale/Riss moraines indicates a very major glaciation even though ice-core data from Greenland suggest that OIS 6 was in fact less cold and less variable than the last glaciation (Dansgaard et al. 1993). Van Andel and Tzedakis (van Andel 1996, van Andel and Tzedakis 1996) have provided a reconstruction of conditions at the height of glaciation in OIS 6 (Figure 5.3). Extensive cold steppes existed in southern and Mediterranean Europe, while the corridor between the Alpine and Scandinavian ice caps saw a mixture of tundra and steppe elements. This was made up of grasses, sagebrush, chenopods and sedges. No modern analogue exists. A feature of both OIS 8 and OIS 6 is the very rapid return to full ocean conditions at the end of these cold stages, as can be seen in Figure 5.2.

The last glacial period (OIS 5d–2) is known in much more detail. This is known as the Devensian/Weichselian/Valdai in northern Europe and the Würm in the Alps and southern Europe.

Until recently it has been the practice to reconstruct the vegetation history of this period by piecing together cores from northern Europe. However, long continuous sequences spanning both this and earlier periods now exist in Greece (Tzedakis 1993, 1995) and Italy (Watts, Allen and Huntley 1996). The

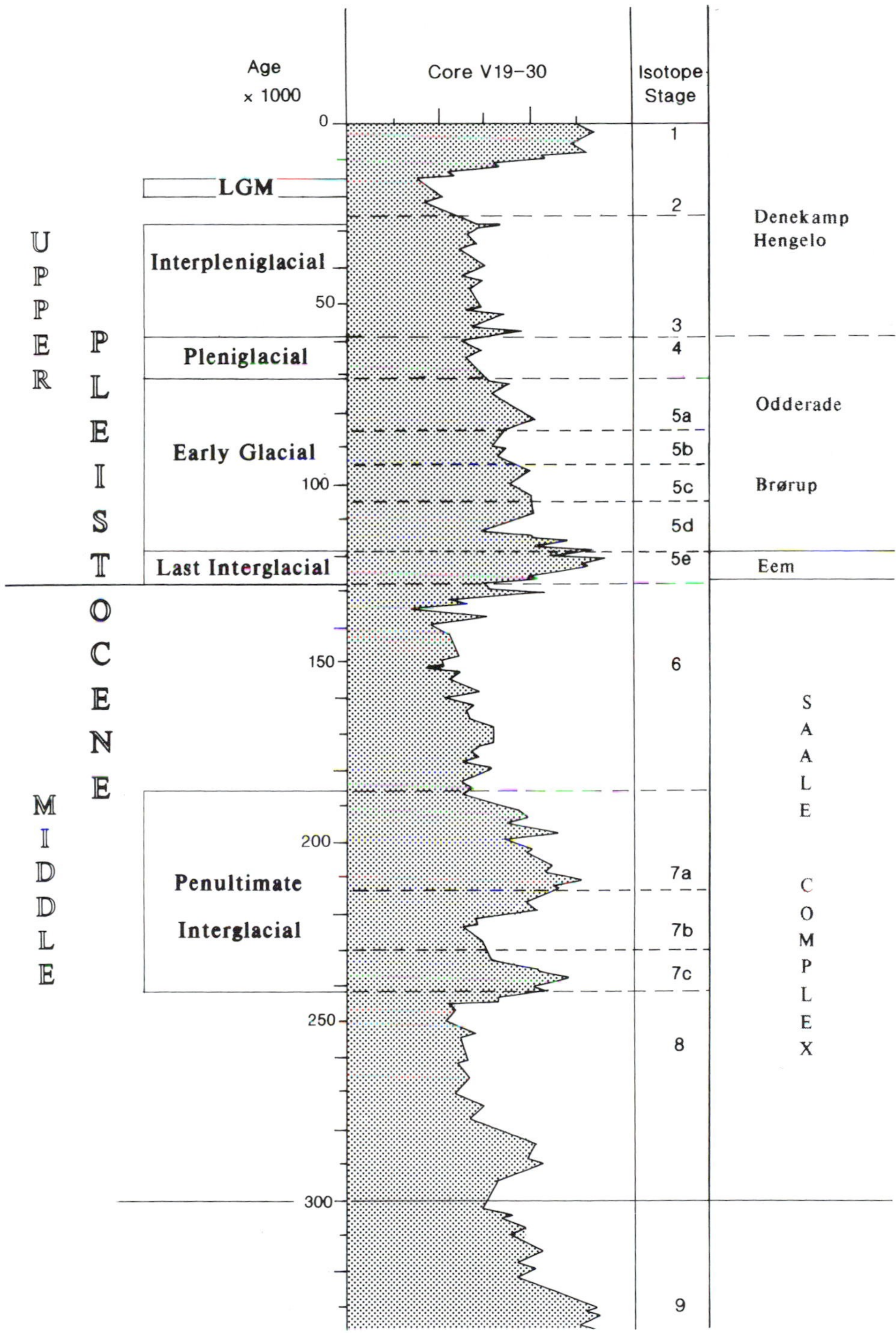


**5.2** Changes in ice cap (unshaded) to sea level (shaded) volumes as indicated by oxygen isotope values in deep-sea core V19-30 during the past 300 Kyr. LGM = Last glacial maximum (after van Kolfschoten et al. 1993:Fig. 7; Bassinot et al. 1994).

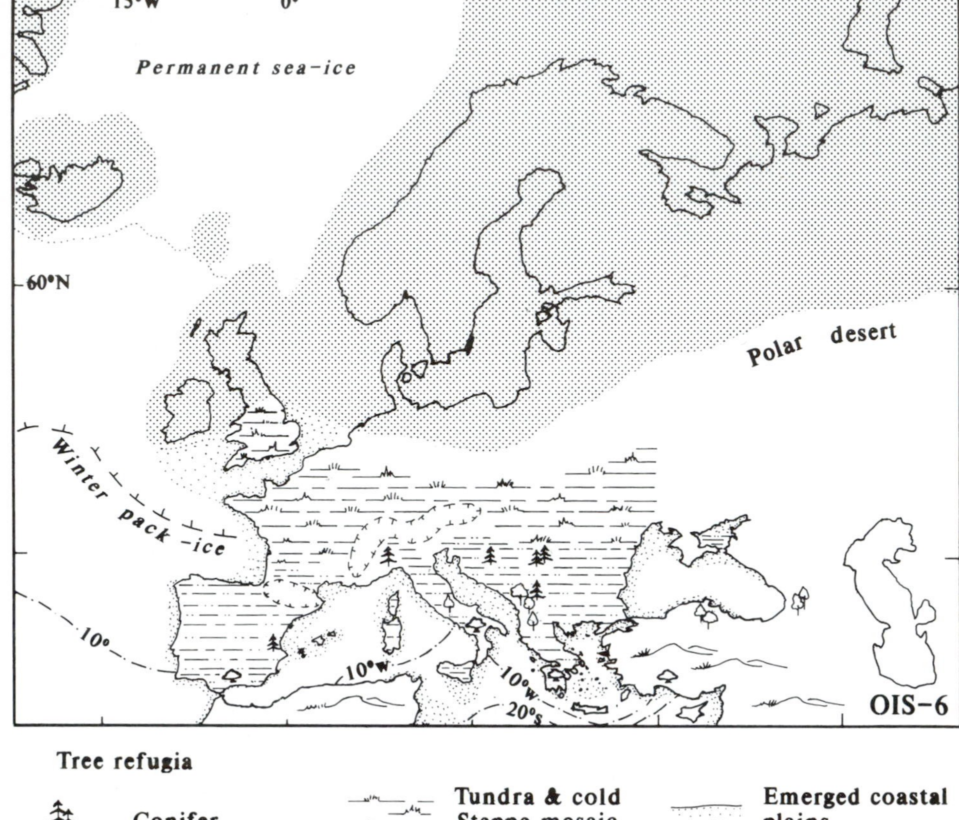


**5.3** European habitats during OIS 6, the penultimate glacial period, at 150 Kyr BP (after van Andel and Tzedakis 1996:Fig. 6).

detailed study of Lago Grande di Monticchio at an elevation of 656 m in southern Italy has so far been examined in detail from OIS 5a to the present. Dating is particularly precise due to annual laminations which can be counted in the core. These provide an absolute timescale back to 76.3 Kyr BP.

The Monticchio core reveals for this time period a very variable record of tree, shrub and vine pollen to herb pollen (Figure 5.4). Open, colder conditions as indicated by herb pollen are more common from 36–14 Kyr BP than from 75–50 Kyr BP. This supports estimates of ice cap to ocean sizes (Figure 5.2) which point to OIS 4 being considerably less than the last glacial maximum in OIS 2. Further details of this core are discussed in Chapter 6.

Such detail from an area outside the immediate influence of glaciation pro-

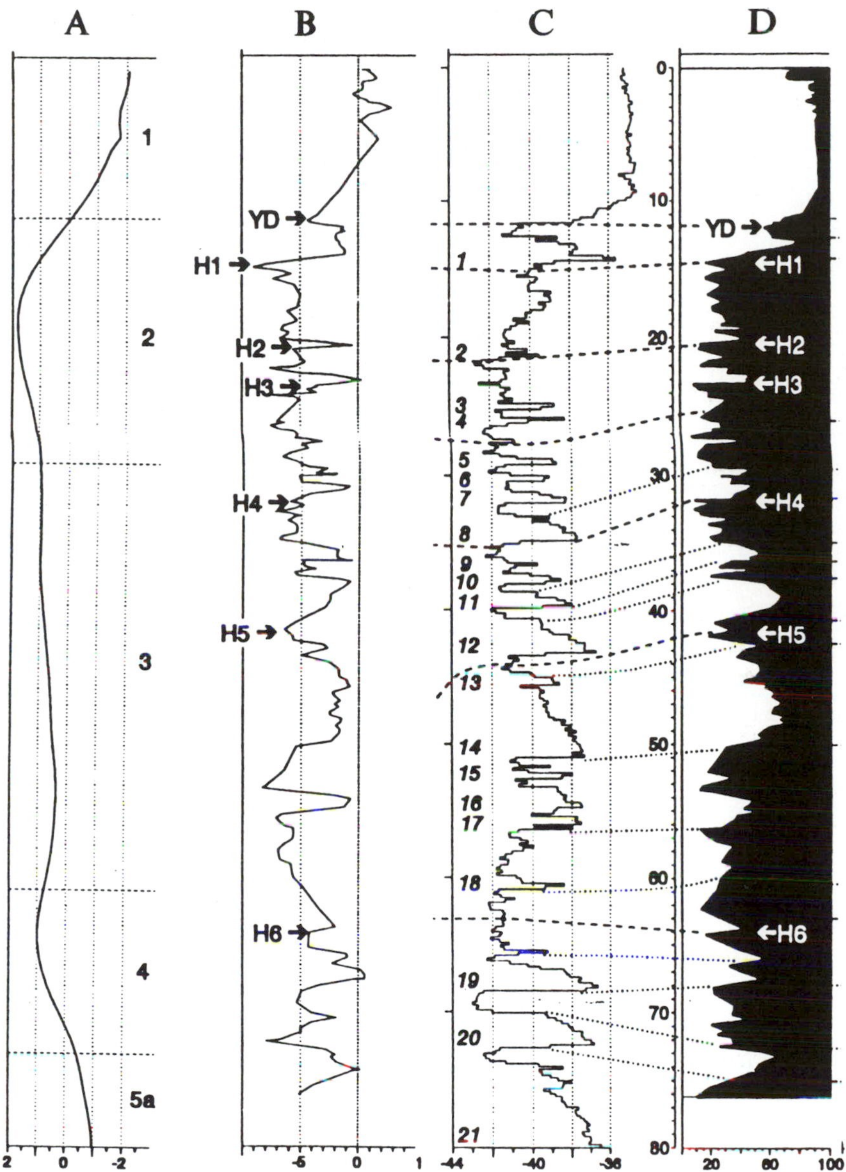


**5.4** Selected data from the Monticchio pollen core, Italy, MC region, compared with the Greenland Ice Core Project. The absolute timescale, in Kyr BP, is shown against column D (after Watts et al. 1996:Fig. 5).

KEY:

A SPECMAP Ocean:Ice volume

B Mean temperature of coldest month from Monticchio pollen

C GRIP ice core. Numbers are interstadial events

D Cumulative pollen %s. White = tree, shrub and vine; black = herb

YD = Younger Dryas

H1–H6 Heinrich events caused by iceberg discharge

Table 5.3. *Correlation of interstadial sub-stages of the early glacial (Behre 1989:Fig. 8).*

| Netherlands | Germany | Denmark | Poland | France | Greece | OIS |
|---|---|---|---|---|---|---|
| | Odderade | | Rudunki | St Germain II | Elevtheroupolis | 5a |
| Brørup<br>Amersfoort | Brørup | Brørup | Amersfoort | St Germain I | Drama<br>Doxaton | 5c |
| Eemian | Eemian | Eemian | Eemian | Eemian | Eemian | 5e |

vides a necessary perspective for the better-known northern profiles. Behre (1989:fig. 7) has provided a detailed reconstruction from pollen sites in northern and central Europe. It is now clear that there are some seven temperate interstadials between the last interglacial (Eemian=OIS 5e) and the maximum of the last glaciation in OIS 2. Two of these, Amersfoort/Brørup and Odderade, occur prior to 60 Kyr BP and are shown in Figure 5.2.[4]

The last glacial period is subdivided into a number of phases, of which early glacial, pleniglacial, interpleniglacial, last glacial maximum and late glacial are the most common. These terms are applied differently by Quaternary scientists and correlation to the deep-sea record is still not universally agreed.

*Early glacial (118–71 Kyr BP)*

The early glacial spans sub-stages 5d–5a. The very short but large-ice-volume OIS 5d and 5b are separated by the longer forested/temperate interstadials of OIS 5c and OIS 5a.[5] These isotope peaks indicating higher ocean volume can now be matched to a number of pollen profiles in north, southern and Mediterranean Europe. The local stage names are given in Table 5.3.

These early glacial interstadials are very clear in the Grande Pile pollen profile from the Voges mountains in France (Guiot et al. 1989, Woillard 1978) and in the Lake Ioannina core 249 from northwestern Greece (Tzedakis 1993, 1995). In the northern pollen diagrams they appear as a two-phase – birch followed by pine – succession.[6] Guiot (et al. 1989) have proposed that 5c and 5a were interglacials rather than interstadials, and that conditions are very similar today in terms of temperature. This may be the case but the brief, extreme changes in ice volume, and presumably in temperature, in OIS 5d and OIS 5b are such that the immigration of deciduous forest elements was very restricted. This vegetation pattern confirms their interstadial rather than interglacial character as judged from a northern perspective.[7]

One reason for this lack of deciduous taxa in northern pollen profiles may be the extent in the severe cold phases, 5d and 5b, of continuous permafrost into western Europe. These 10-Kyr high-ice-volume sub-stages (Tables 5.1 and 5.2) severely disrupted the reimmigration patterns of plant taxa in the shorter temperate sub-stages OIS 5c and OIS 5a.

The section at Königsaue in eastern Germany (Mania 1991b, Mania and Toepfer 1973) illustrates this rapid climatic succession. Here the 25-m section consists of sands and gravels interstratified with peat horizons. From this section it is possible to reconstruct the climatic history of the area as shown by the expansion and contraction of a small lake, the Aschersleben See (Figure 6.4). The last interglacial is identified in level $Ia_1$ where rich organic silts complement the peat horizons. Above this there are seven interstadial/peat horizons and lake transgressions before the glacial maximum in stage VI of the sequence. Fossil ice wedge casts, indicative of permafrost conditions, are found between these interstadial horizons.

At Königsaue the three archaeological horizons occur in stage Ib. This was orginally attributed to the Brørup interstadial but now that the importance of the earlier Amersfoort has been downgraded (Behre 1989) would seem instead to be of Odderade age. This would be equivalent to OIS 5a if the Brørup is equivalent to OIS 5c (Table 5.3) and stage $Ia_2$ in the Königsaue profile. AMS and conventional C14 determinations (Table 5.2 and Figure 6.4) must be regarded as minimum ages and do not necessarily reflect the age of the locale, which should be between 71–85 Kyr BP.

Frenzel (1973:figure 100) provided a general picture of vegetation during an Early glacial interstadial. His reconstruction follows a zonal distribution for major vegetation units with tree cover thinning towards the east. Spruce, pine, birch and fir forest dominates in western and central Europe, while in central and southeastern Europe the more continental conditions resulted in steppe with stands of pine–spruce–birch. The Iberian peninsula had spruce–fir forests in the north with the addition of warmer, deciduous elements. The central meseta was a grass steppe, while in the south and extending into the centre of the peninsula were oak forests with pines. Oak (*Quercus*) remains an important element in the Ioannina 249 core in northern Greece during the Pleniglacial (Tzedakis 1993:Fig. 3). Indeed, it is interesting to note at this 470-m-altitude lake basin, surrounded by a major mountain chain, that arboreal pollen is found during all the open vegetation periods in this 430-Kyr-long vegetation record (*ibid.*:438). This finding points to the presence of long-term refugia for trees and other plant taxa in Mediterranean Europe, a point now supported by the Monticchio evidence (Watts, Allen and Huntley 1996).

*Pleniglacial (71–58 kyr BP)*

The Early Glacial is followed by the Pleniglacial, or full glacial, which corresponds to OIS 4. In the Königsaue profile this is marked by an increase in ice wedge formation and permafrost activity generally. In northern Europe sporadic permafrost now stretches to the Atlantic seaboard. The Pleniglacial has no significant interstadials. It is characterized in the deep-sea cores by higher ice volumes, and hence lower sea levels. However no major continental glaciation took place. The Pleniglacial is therefore a longer, sustained cool period with very little or no tree cover in northern Europe. In character it was prob-

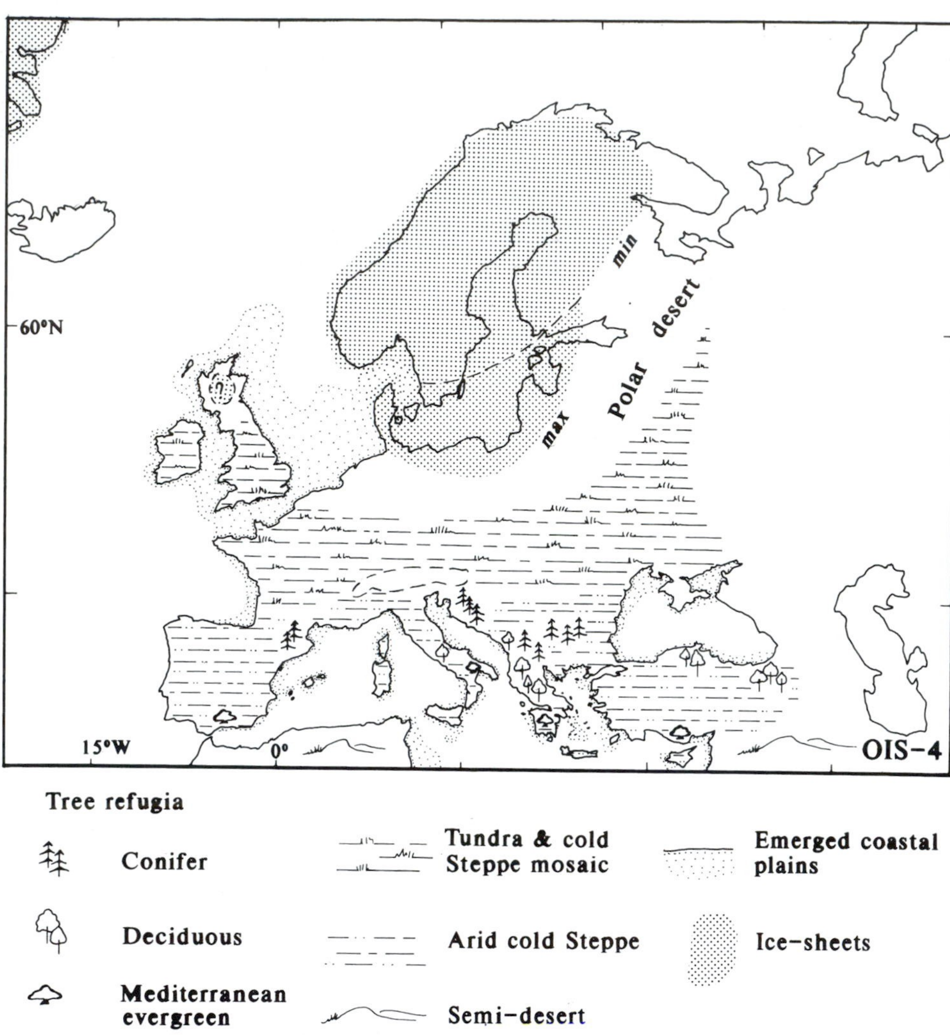


**5.5** European habitats during OIS 4, the pleniglacial, at 65 Kyr BP (after van Andel and Tzedakis 1996:Fig. 13).

ably comparable to sub-stages 5b and 5d, although it represents a more extreme version in terms of vegetation changes and in particular the diminution of trees in the Mediterranean (Watts, Allen and Huntley 1996). In northern Europe the pollen records of OIS 4 are often blank due to the types of vegetation and arctic-style peat formation where pollen production is so low that no record has been preserved (Zagwijn 1992). A reconstruction of the zonal pattern of OIS 4 vegetation (van Andel and Tzedakis 1996) points to more mixed steppe/tundra than was found in the larger OIS 6 glaciation (Figure 5.5). By comparison with the succeeding Interpleniglacial environments (Chapter 6) these northern Pleniglacial habitats were poor, while in southern and Mediterranean regions

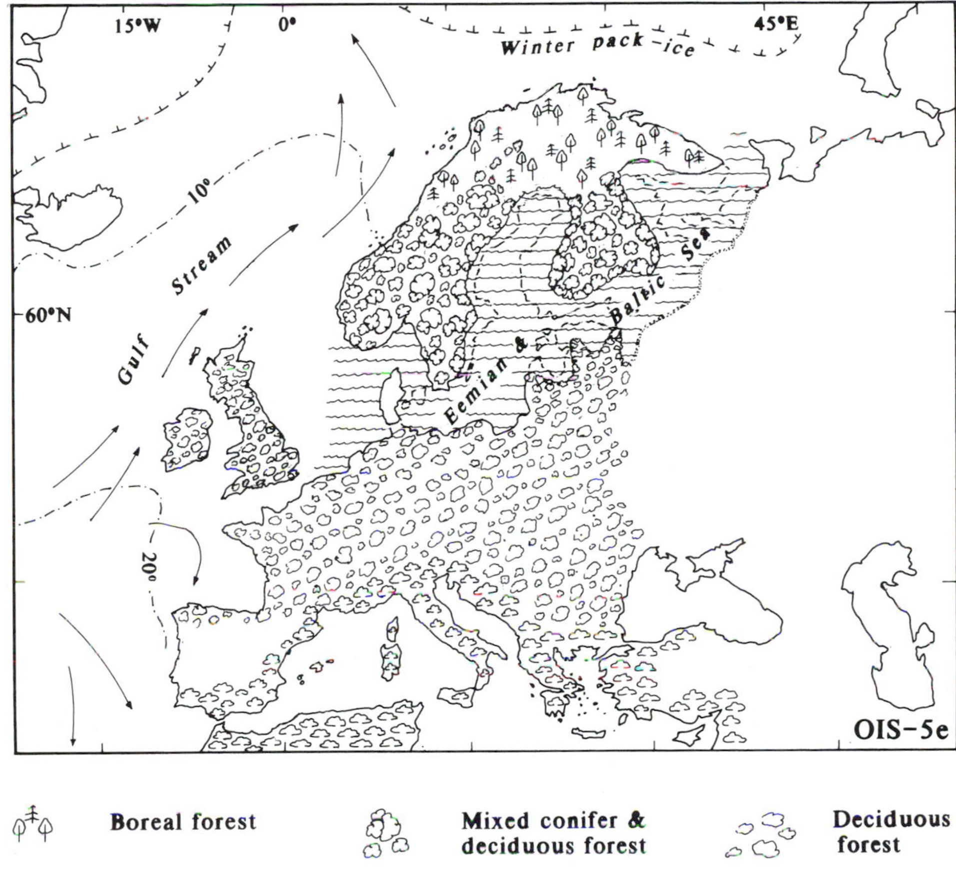


**5.6** European habitats during OIS 5e, the last interglacial period, at 120–125 Kyr BP. Note the island status of Scandinavia (after van Andel and Tzedakis 1996:Fig. 9).

productive steppe conditions flourished alongside forest refugia (Suc and Zagwijn 1983).

It is to be expected that as OIS 6 and OIS 8 come to be better understood internal divisions comparable to the Early Glacial and Pleniglacial of the last cycle will be discovered. Moreover, they may also have their own individual markers, as at the OIS 5a/4 boundary with the eruption of Toba in the Indian ocean which led, some believe, to a volcanic winter which hastened the onset of the Pleniglacial (Ramaswamy 1992). Events such as these may explain some of the contradictions to Pleistocene climate as predicted by Milankovitch's theory of orbital forcing (Imbrie and Imbrie 1979).

The upshot is that we must recognize these Early Glacial and Pleniglacial periods as a mosaic, not only in terms of the distribution of plant taxa within

Europe, but also from the perspective of their short duration, c. 10 Kyr, and internal changes. While OIS 6 appears to have been cooler for longer, it is also possibly the case that the maximum extension of the Saale/Riss ice sheets was comparatively short lived within this 60-Kyr period.

*Comparing the warm periods*

Internal differentiation has now been established for the two interglacial periods OIS 7 and OIS 5e. The former is a low-sea-level interglacial, while the latter is one of the highest in the middle Pleistocene (Shackleton 1987). For example, Van Andel and Tzedakis's (1996) reconstruction of OIS 5e is dominated by the Eemian and Baltic Sea. This isolates Scandinavia, and provides a long and highly productive northern coastline (Figure 5.6), while the greater oceanic effect of the very high sea levels results in the northern extension of silver fir (*Abies*) well beyond its normal range.

*The penultimate interglacial (242–186 Kyr BP)*

OIS 7 has been divided into three parts, with sub-stage 7b identified as a short ice age (Andrews 1983) commencing about 230 Kyr BP and lasting for 10–15 Kyr. Values for ice volumes appear to have been equivalent to the Pleniglacial, OIS 4, rather than to OIS 5d or OIS 5b in the Early Glacial. At present it is not possible to determine the climatic differences between sub-stages OIS 7a and OIS 7c.

The end of the OIS 7b Pleniglacial has been accurately dated by the single-grain 40Ar/39Ar technique (Van den Boggard et al. 1989). This has been applied to the east Eifel volcanic field in the Rhineland and in particular to Ariendorf site 8. The technique is applied to dating the Hüttenberg (H) tephra that is found in the transition between a loess and a palaeosol therefore pointing to a transition from cold to temperate conditions. Tephrochronology indicates that this transition took place at $215 \pm 4$ Kyr BP (*ibid.*:Fig. 4).

Assigning archaeological sites to these three sub-stages is proving difficult. Most sites are simply interglacial in character with floral and faunal remains very reminiscent of the earlier travertine site at Bilzingsleben. But what is surprising is that for such an isotopically 'weak' interglacial (Shackleton 1987) the faunal and floral evidence is either equivalent to, or greater than, temperatures and tolerances in both the present and the last interglacial which have a very 'strong' isotopic signature.

For example, at the lakeside site of Neumark-Nord in eastern Germany the vegetation was dominated by oak, hazel, hornbeam, yew, lime, box and holly. Pond tortoise (*Emys orbicularis*), regarded as a good indicator of full interglacial conditions (Mania 1991b, Mania et al. 1990), is also present, which is one reason why some would prefer to see this site as OIS 5e (Vandenberghe, Roebroeks and Kolfschoten 1993). But pond tortoise has also been found at another OIS 7 locale, Maastricht-Belvédère (Kolfschoten and Roebroeks 1985). If its eggs are to hatch it requires a mean July temperature of 17–18°C, combined with a considerable amount of sunshine with few damp, cloudy or rainy days. These temperatures are in excess of today's (Stuart 1982). The travertines at Stuttgart-Bad Cannstatt (Reiff 1986) also contain this taxon along with leaves and fruits of box (*Buxus sempervirens*) and other oak-mixed forest elements. These tree taxa are also present in the lower travertine at Ehringsdorf (Steiner and Wagenbreth 1971). Remains of macaque monkeys (*Macaca* sp), indicative of forested conditions, have been found in the oceanic interglacials OIS 11 and OIS 9 in northern sites such as Bilzingsleben and Swanscombe. But this species is also found in the more continental interglacial of OIS 7 at Hunas, a collapsed cave in Bavaria, where an upper molar of *Macaca* cf *florentina* occurs in levels above a stalagmite floor with a Thorium/Uranium date of 260 Kyr (Carls et al. 1988, Groiss, Kaulich and Reisch 1995). Currant (1989) lists macaque in English faunas which may be of similar age to Hunas.

## The last interglacial, Eemian (128–118 Kyr BP)

Just how complicated the final analysis of OIS 7 might become is shown by recent work on the Eemian or last interglacial, OIS 5e. This interglacial lasted for some 10–15 Kyr. It can be studied in high resolution through the $^{18}O$ ratio in ice cores drilled in Greenland. Two studies are available. One by Greenland Ice-Core Project (GRIP) members (1993) analysed the Summit core and divides OIS 5e into five further sub-stages. This shows that, far from being stable, the Eemian was marked by high-frequency oscillations in ice volume. One event at the end of OIS 5e1 lasted only an estimated seventy years but saw the oxygen isotope values plunge to mid-glacial levels (*ibid*.:206). These findings are confirmed by Dansgaard et al.'s (1993) study of the same core, where they calculate that OIS 5e2 and OIS 5e4 lasted 2 and 6 Kyr respectively. These periods were as cool as 5a and 5c in the Early Glacial. Taken as a whole, OIS 5e seems less stable climatically than OIS 7 (*ibid*.:220). White (1993:186) has commented how these data demonstrate that changes within interglacials of up to 10°C are possible in twenty years or even within a decade.[8]

What all this tells us is that interglacial climates fluctuated with rapid internal shifts of temperature. These changes happened within the lifetime of individuals. Hominid adaptation to several millennia of constant climate, sea level and presumably plant cover is looking less and less likely as a scenario for the period 300–60 Kyr BP.

Such rapid shifts as indicated by the deep-sea and ice cores have still to be assimilated into interpretations of plant and animal distributions. Currently it seems that the response time is so slow to these quick-time oscillations in the oceans and ice caps that there is comparatively little change at the sort of timescales suggested by the GRIP members. Moreover, it will take some time to match the interglacial sites in Table 5.1 with such a fine-scale chronology. At the present time it is possible to see in England, for example, that the presence of *Hippopotamus amphibius* correlates exclusively with OIS 5e and has been absolutely dated as such in Victoria Cave (Gascoyne, Currant and Lord 1981). But when this species arrived and how long it stayed are now important unanswered questions in the light of the new subdivisions of OIS 5e.

*Normal environments for recovery of archaeological evidence*
The excavation of cave and open locales shows that all nine regions (Figure 3.1) were occupied during this period. Four major environments for the preservation of archaeological locales need to be considered: fluvial, lacustrine, loess and caves.

*Fluvial and colluvial environments*
Locales in river deposits can be found in all nine regions. They display a comparable range of preservation discussed in the equivalent section in Chapter 4. There are flagship sites with excellent preservation such as Maastricht-Belvédère in the Netherlands and Salzgitter-Lebenstedt in northern Germany, as well as many collections in derived contexts from all the major river basins such as the Thames (Bridgland 1994, Gibbard 1988, Wymer 1968, Wymer 1996), Duero (Santonja 1991–2) and Aniene (Mussi 1992, 1995).

However, the evidence from the northeast sector of the regional model is interesting because this was the first time that it was settled. The evidence is best known from the river valleys of western Russia, Moldavia and the Ukraine. These fluvial settings include locales such as Ketrosy (Praslov 1981), Korman IV (Goretsky and Tseitlin 1977), Molodova I (Goretsky and Ivanova 1982) and Molodova V (Chernysh 1961, Ivanova and Chernysh 1965, Ivanova and Tseitlin 1987) along the narrow canyon-like section of the middle Dnestr (see also Boriskovsky 1984, Soffer 1989). Hoffecker (1987) has reviewed the geological setting of the Dnestr archaeological locales which lie above the alluvial deposits of the second terrace. The locales usually occur in reworked loess or loam deposits, probably colluvial in origin. They are interspersed with palaeosoils of variable thickness.

Sites of last interglacial age are unknown (Hoffecker 1987:270). Instead, Middle Palaeolithic occupation on the Dnestr terraces at Korman IV occurs in soils which developed during the late Early Glacial and Pleniglacial. However, in the same stretch of the Dnestr at Molodova I and V, Pleniglacial occupation is found in gleyed horizons which show only slight evidence of soil formation.

On the Desna river the important archaeological locale of Khotylevo I (Zavernyaev 1978) has a Middle Palaeolithic assemblage associated with a freshwater mollusc *Unio pictorum*, which is characteristic of the last interglacial in the region. It occurs here at the base of the second terrace. But reindeer is also present (Hoffecker 1987: 272) and there is no palaeosoil, so that the assemblage may be Early Glacial in date and therefore comparable in age to the Dnestr locales.[9]

In the northern foothills of the Caucasus are the locales of Il'skaya I and II located on a tributary of the Kuban' river (Hoffecker, Baryshnikov and Potapova

1991). The archaeological horizons are also in colluvial deposits overlying a low river terrace. The lowest palaeosoil at Il'skaya I is tentatively correlated to the Early Glacial, while the middle palaeosoil is either a later part of this same stage or else should be dated to OIS 3 (*ibid.*: 117).[10]

The fine-grained, calcareous, colluvial deposits interspersed with palaeosoils have led to excellent preservation of fauna in the Dnestr, Middle Desna and Il'skaya locales. These locales have a long history of being examined for spatial information (Chernysh 1961).

*Lake and spring environments*

The travertine spring site of Tata in Hungary, in the southeast region, has been dated by Th/U to c. 100 Kyr BP (Schwarcz and Skoflek 1982, Svoboda 1989, Svoboda 1994b, Vertes 1964), which makes it comparable in age to the Ganovce, Bojnice, Weimar, Taubach, Burgtonna and Ehringsdorf upper travertine sites in the north central region (Svoboda, Lozek and Vlček 1996). Preservation of macro botanical material – leaves, wood, fruit – as well as animal faunas is particularly good. Steiner and Wagenbreth (1971:Abb. 9) reconstruct the older OIS 7 lower travertine Ehringsdorf landscape as a wooded environment bordering a marshy, reed sump that was criss-crossed by sluggish karst-fed streams. Bars of older travertine provided easy access into the middle of the area.

Lake environments continue to be important in all regions. The deposits in the tectonically active Gadix-Baja basin (Santonja and Villa 1990, Vega Toscano 1989) cover an oval area of 100 by 60 km. Preservation at the margin of these old lake sediments is good, as shown by Solana del Zamborino (Botella, Vera and Porta 1976), dated to the Saalian complex.

Due to modern mineral extraction it has been possible to study some of the lakes in eastern Germany, north-central region, often on a large scale. These include Lehringen (Thieme and Veil 1985), Gröbern (Erfurt and Mania 1990, Heussner and Weber 1990) and Königsaue (Mania and Toepfer 1973).

The largest study in this part of the north central region has been undertaken at Neumark-Nord (Mania et al. 1990) located in the Geisel valley near Halle. Open-cast mining using huge grab-lines to extract brown coal has also stripped off the overlying Saalian-age deposits. Mania (1991b, et al. 1990) argues for an OIS 7 date for the two well-preserved lake shorelines that occur in levels 4 and 6 although as we have seen above many others prefer a 5e age. These shorelines are interstratified within a sandy, coarse detritus mud, level 5. A fine mud, level 8, also contains material. Salvage work undertaken since 1985 has recovered finds of animal skeletons and stone tools (Table 5.4) over an area of currently c. 4 hectares (Mania 1991b:Abb. 8).

In levels 5 and 8 the excavators found twenty-five partial or complete fallow deer skeletons. These were not associated with artifacts and show no signs of either butchery or carnivore gnawing. The animals probably drowned in the lake and were rapidly incorporated into the sediments before disarticulation

Table 5.4. *Recovery of faunal and lithic material at Neumark-Nord (Mania et al. 1990:Tab. 2–4, Tab. 9–11).*

| | Level | Stone tools | Animal skeletons |
|---|---|---|---|
| Fine-detritus mud | 8 | A few | 6 fallow deer skeletons |
| Upper shore | 6 | 654 | Butchered animal bone, forest rhino butchery locale |
| Sandy, coarse-detritus mud | 5 | A few | 19 fallow deer skeletons, a female aurochs, a giant deer |
| Lower shore | 4 | 250 | Butchered animal bone, aurochs butchery locale (Figure 5.7) |

| | Flakes with edge damage from use | Unmodified flakes | Cores, artifacts and hammerstones | Total chipped stone |
|---|---|---|---|---|
| Upper shore line | 105 | 336 | 213 | 654 |
| Lower shore line | 30 | 94 | 126 | 250 |

could take place. By contrast, in the shoreline deposits, levels 4 and 6, the remains of fallow, red and giant deer are fragmentary (Mania et al. 1990:Tab. 1, Tab. 5). Artifacts are not particularly abundant in these deposits (Table 5.4).

Only a few artifacts were found at the lower shoreline locale where a sub-adult aurochs (*Bos primigenius*) skeleton was, according to Mania, dismembered. The remains lie on the contact between the coarse muds in the lake and the sands of the shore. Four stumps of 20–30-cm-thick trees lined the shore along with other larger pieces of tree trunks and a broken stone anvil.

The remains of this near-complete aurochs carcass were found in two clusters about 3 m apart (Figure 5.7). The head, neck and most of the vertebrae were present. Among the limbs only the pelvis, left scapula and radius and right metacarpal and femur were missing as well as some of the ribs. Gnawing, probably by a wolf, can be seen on some of the transverse processes of the vertebrae (Mania et al. 1990:43). No cut marks are visible on the bones (Mania et al. 1990). Four retouched lithic pieces and several unmodified flakes were found in amongst the bones and a further nine strewn around the anvil.

The case for a direct association between the bones and the stones is very plausible, but still open to some doubt since elsewhere at Neumark-Nord a similar low density of stone artifacts was found in an identical lakeside shore setting but without an animal carcass (Mania et al. 1990:Abb. 23). It is possible that the hominid gathering may instead have been associated with the trees and their varied affordances and that the deposition of the aurochs carcass was another, unrelated event. This interpretation is also possible with other less-complete carcasses at Neumark-Nord such as a forest rhino, *Dicerorhinus*

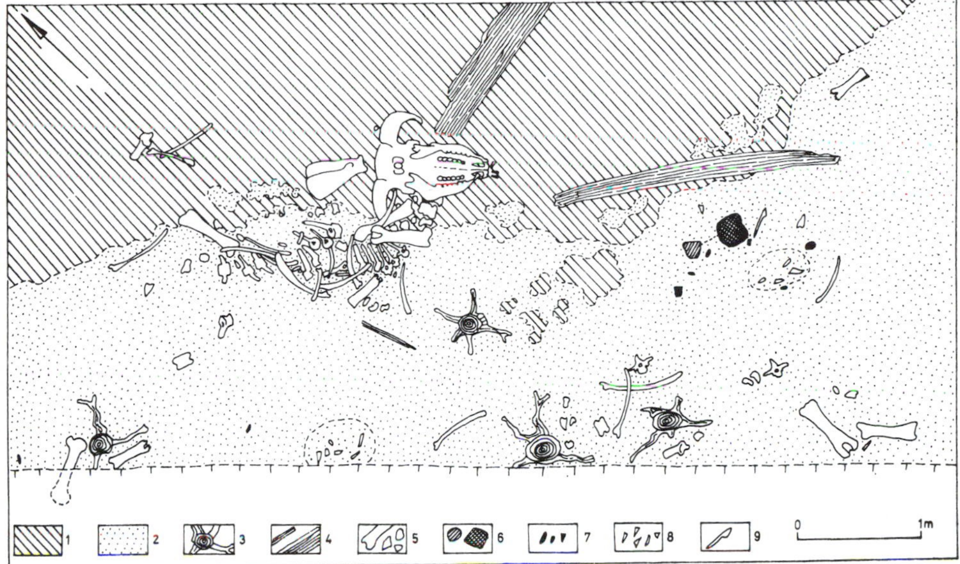


**5.7** A partial aurochs (*Bos primigenius*) skeleton found on the lower shoreline at Neumark-Nord, Germany, NC region (after Mania 1991b: Abb.11).
KEY:
1 Sandy, coarse lake muds
2 Beach sand
3 Tree stumps
4 Branches
5 Aurochs bones
6 Anvil of crystalline rock with refitted piece
7 Flint artifacts
8 Bone splinters
9 Tusk fragments

*kirchbergensis* (Mania et al. 1990:45–7, Abb. 19) from the upper shoreline. There are no reported traces either of animal gnawing or of cut marks. One flint flake was found a metre away from the skull.

*Loess sediments and crater fills*

A number of locales are preserved in wind-blown loess deposits. These include site J at Maastricht-Belvédère (Roebroeks 1988), the upper part of the Biache-St-Vaast sequence (Tuffreau 1988) as well as Rheindahlen (Bosinski 1966) and Czechoslovakian sites in the north-central region such as Bohunice and Předmostí (Svoboda, Lozek and Vlček 1996).

When, as at Beauvais 'La Justice', in the northwest region, these aeolian sediments contain a significant calcareous component, good bone preservation is possible. The fauna at this locale is dominated by reindeer with woolly rhino, mammoth, horse and bison. A Pleniglacial age is most probable (Locht et al.

1994).[11] Seclin, in the same region, is also regarded as a loess site (Tuffreau et al. 1994). The artifacts in levels D4 and D7 are dated to the Brørup interstadial, OIS 5c (Table 5.1). Moreover, the pollen profile in layer D7, with its forest maximum, dominated 60–97 per cent by conifers, also points to an interstadial phase. Micromorphological work on the clay component of the sediments sets the older D7 occupation in a humid prairie environment which enjoyed relatively temperate conditions (Tuffreau et al. 1994:30). A reduction in tree cover led to conditions becoming more steppic in level D4. Animal bone is not preserved.

A series of loess sites which span the entire Saalian complex and continue through to the Pleniglacial have been thoroughly investigated in the east Eifel volcanic field, north-central region (Bosinski et al. 1986). The cones of these extinct volcanoes formed natural traps for loess and protected it from subsequent erosion.

Occupation occurs within the loess at Kärlich Jb, Schweinskopf and Wannen and within palaeosoils at Tönchesberg and Hummerich (Figure 5.8). At the non-volcano site of Ariendorf (E. Turner 1991) the major occupations 1 and 2 occur in loesses dated respectively to OIS 8 and OIS 6.

The Tönchesberg volcano erupted in 202 ± 14 Kyr BP at the beginning of the penultimate glacial period, OIS 6 (Conard 1992:15). Small occupations at Tö1A and Tö2A occur in loesses dating respectively to the the middle and end of this stage.

The main archaeological horizon, Tö2B, occurs in dark colluvial humic sediments that developed on a loess in which the artifacts already lay. It was formed during a period with a sparsely forested grass landscape. Animal bone is poorly preserved due both to heavy weathering and to decalcification of the sediments. Open-landscape taxa including horse, steppe ass, aurochs and rhino (*Dicerorhinus hemitoechus*) have been identified as well as fallow deer. On stratigraphic and TL dating grounds the loess probably just postdates the Eemian interglacial, and Conard argues for an OIS 5d date at about 115 Kyr BP (*ibid.*:23). Loess sedimentation needs very specific environmental conditions and these might not have been present during the shorter OIS 5e4 and 5e2 cold episodes within the interglacial sub-stage.

The later, small occupation of Tö2D occurs in a loess deposit that could either be within the Early Glacial or instead in the Pleniglacial. Tö1B, also in loess, is stratigraphically comparable to a horizon dated by TL to 66 ± 6 Kyr BP (*ibid.*:24).

The east Eifel volcanoes provide the only data on settlement in that local region during this period. What advantages existed for hominids within these small, steep-sided craters is still not altogether clear, although the presence of animal bones associated with stone artifacts in all of them shows that resources were not lacking.

*Caves and abris*

Perhaps the use of these volcanoes should be viewed in the same way as caves: comparatively small, protected pockets for sedimentation, within a wider environment that was otherwise potentially destructive for archaeological materials of this age.

For example, at Pontnewydd Cave (Green 1984) in north Wales, northwest region, the OIS 7 deposits were sludged into the cave by periglacial activity during OIS 6. Later in this glacial stage, and again in OIS 2, an ice sheet must have completely covered the cave, but did not scour out its deposits, which contained volcanic rock bifaces and levallois flakes, animal bones and fourteen hominid remains representing at least four individuals and possibly as many as seven, of which five are juveniles (Aldhouse-Green 1995).

While Pontnewydd is an extreme example of how fragile evidence can survive, this period generally sees a great rise in the number of caves and abris (rock shelters) which now preserve archaeological materials (Bosinski 1967, Gabori 1976, Laville, Rigaud and Sackett 1980, Mussi 1992, Svoboda, Lozek and Vlček 1996). Not surprisingly, these are concentrated in the limestone regions of Europe including the Crimea and the Caucasus (Boriskovsky 1984, Ljubin and Bosinski 1995). In the north central region there are long, detailed stratigraphic sequences at Kulna (Valoch 1988), Sesselsfelsgrotte (Weißmüller 1995) and the Bockstein (Wetzel and Bosinski 1969). There are also numerically rich collections from the northwest and north-central regions, as at the coastal cave locale of La Cotte on Jersey in the English Channel Islands (Callow and Cornford 1986). But the frequency of such large collections is much less than in the southwest region where there are long stratigraphic sequences often with many artifact levels.

The classic area for cave and abri archaeology at this time is southwest France. The flagship sites are represented by the Grotte Vaufrey (Rigaud 1988a), La Micoque (Laville, Rigaud and Sackett 1980), Pech de l'Azé II and Combe Grenal (Bordes 1972) as well as the La Chaise complex and the La Quina rock shelter in the Charente region (Debenath 1976, 1992). These well-known locales have recently been supplemented by the sink-hole (Fr. *aven*) sites of Coudoulous (Jaubert, Brugal and Quinif 1993) and La Borde (Jaubert et al. 1990) in the Lot region. Both sites have excellent faunal preservation and are dominated by bison, 98 per cent of all animal bones preserved at Coudoulous, and aurochs, 93 per cent at La Borde.

Also in the southwest region is El Castilló cave in Cantabrian Spain (Bischoff, Garcia and Straus 1992, Cabrera-Valdes 1984, Straus 1992). Here four composite levels with artifacts underlie the stalagmitic flowstone in level 23 dated by TL to 89 ± 11 Kyr BP. Above this floor are three levels with Mousterian artifacts (Figure 5.9). The numbers of artifacts in these seven levels are not enormous, although Cabrera (1984) found during her research that many from the earlier excavations of Breuil and Obermaier had been lost. It is rather the number of stratigraphic levels with collections of c. 100 retouched tools, the minimum

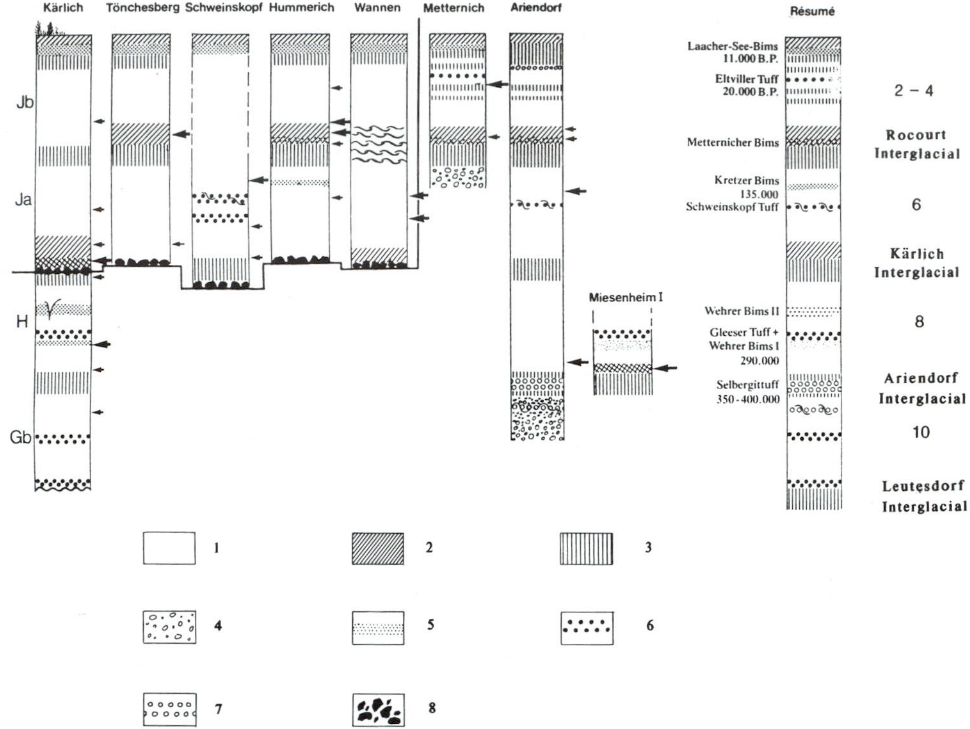


**5.8** The location and stratigraphy of the major volcano sites in the east Eifel region of western Germany, near Neuwied, NC region (after Bosinski et al. 1986:Abb. 4 and 5)
Key:
Locales map
27 Laacher See
49 Tönchesberg
51 Hummerich
52 Wannen
53 Schweinskopf
58 Kärlich
Ideal stratigraphic profiles
1 Loess
2 Humus
3 Soil horizon
4 Gravels
5 Pumice (Bims)
6 Basalt volcanic tuff
7 Selbergit volcanic tuff
8 Basalt lava
The small arrows indicate isolated artifact finds and the large arrows major archaeological levels.

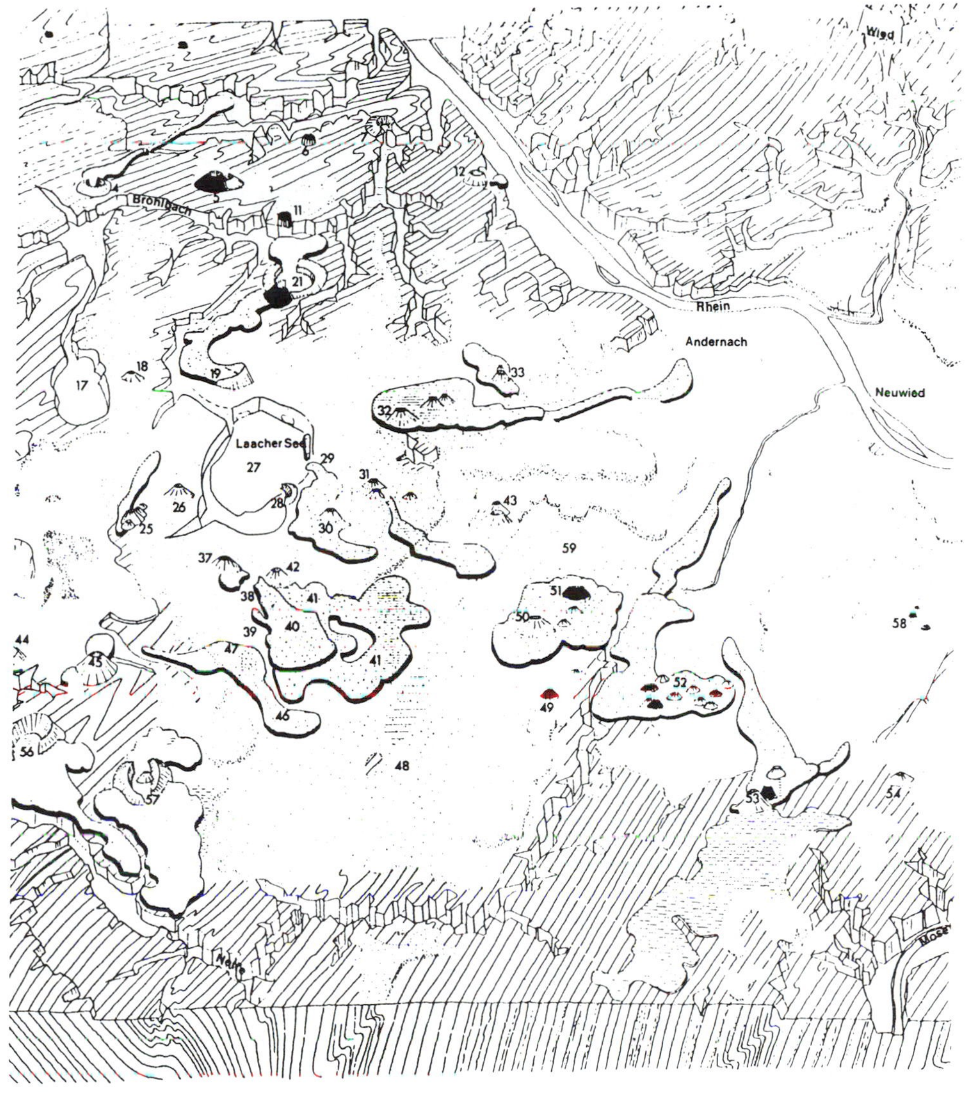


5.8 (*cont*)

usually regarded as necessary to undertake a typological analysis (de Sonneville-Bordes 1974–5:17), that differentiates caves in these regions from those in the north. Multilevel sites are also common in the Mediterranean regions, as in the Spanish Cova de Bolomor (Peris, Calatayud and Valle 1997, Peris, Calatayud and Valle 1994), the Italian caves of Riparo Tagliente (Mussi 1992), Grotta Fosselone and Grotta Moscerini (Caloi et al. 1988) and at Asprochaliko in northwest Greece (Bailey, Papaconstantinou and Sturdy 1992).

Quantifying these aspects of the Palaeolithic record is not easy because the information is unstandardized. Further information on the cubic area that had

**5.9** Excavations in the Mousterian levels of El Castilló cave, Spain, SW region. The long sequences at this locale provided important evidence for the timing and character of the transition from the Middle to the Upper Palaeolithic (photo by the author).

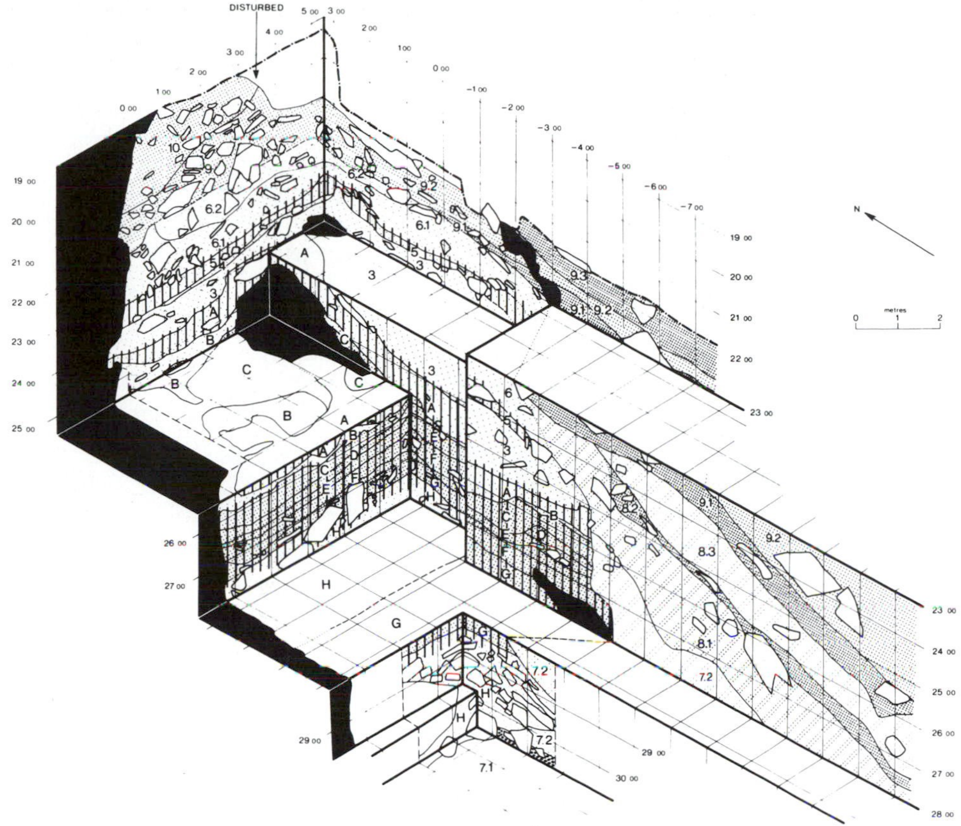


**5.10** An isometric section through the Saalian- and Weichselian-age deposits of La Cotte, Jersey, NW region, indicating the volume of deposits which were removed from the north ravine to produce the artifact assemblages; see Table 5.6 (after Callow 1986c:6.4).

to be excavated in order to recover these quantities of artifacts is almost never forthcoming. Therefore it is impossible to compare artifact densities. However, having visited many excavated cave sites throughout Europe my impression is that in the north whole caves were regularly emptied, as at Nietoperzowa (Figure 5.11) (Chmielewski 1961), Kents Cavern (Campbell and Sampson 1971), the Hohlenstein-Stadel (Beck in preparation, Gamble 1979, 1995d) and Ciemna (Svoboda 1994b). This can result in very large excavated areas indeed for comparatively few artifacts. But at some northern flagship sites the large areas dug, for example 3,000 m$^3$ at Kulna (Valoch 1988), and at La Cotte (Figure 5.10), the excavators were rewarded with large artifact collections (Table 5.6 below).

Total, or near-total clearance is less common in the southern and Mediterranean caves. Considerable areas remain to be excavated (see Figure 5.9). The survival of substantial deposits in these caves and shelters is possibly due to earlier excavators recovering enough lithics for typological analysis,

**5.11** The interior of the Nietoperzowa Cave, Jerzmanovice, Poland, NC region. Before excavations started earlier this century the deposits filled the cave almost to its roof. The small artifact collections, see Table 6.10, came from a very large volume of excavated deposit (photo by the author).

usually the main object for digging, and so halting their investigations (Gamble 1986a:357–9). The target of one hundred retouched artifacts was not so speedily achieved in the northern sites with the result that excavations tended to be larger in an attempt to increase the artifact return.

Although quantified evidence is not readily available I would suggest that, in general terms, the three factors shown in Figure 5.12 guided the scale of cave excavations. If this relation holds, then it further suggests that the archaeological evidence from caves varies in predictable ways across the continent and may reflect differing intensities in the long-term use of the northern and of the southern/Mediterranean regions.

## Rhythms and social technology

The approach, as set out in Chapter 4, is to examine the three rhythms which link the varied scales of analysis in our investigation of Palaeolithic society. These rhythms will concentrate on the first question, posed at the beginning of this chapter, about Neanderthal societies – what environments could they cope with? This will explore their skills in social living if we follow the proposition that technical acts are also social acts (Chapter 3). Once again, stone tools provide the bulk of the evidence for investigating the question. I will examine the evidence for changes in scale through the paths and tracks across landscapes and among the gestures of production and maintenance. The material and social

**NORTH**

**Small collections & few assemblages in each excavated section**

**Large excavations**

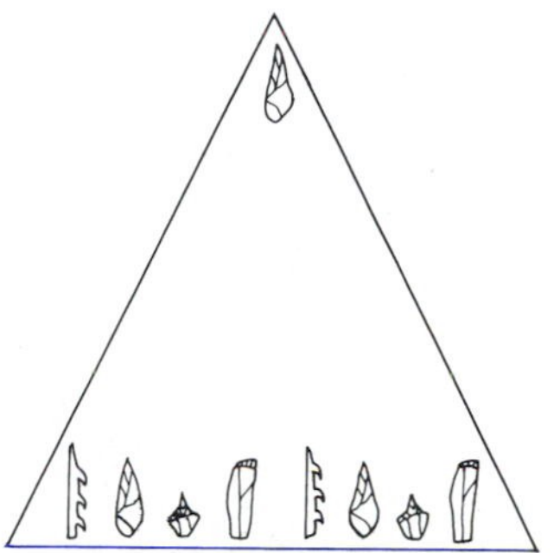

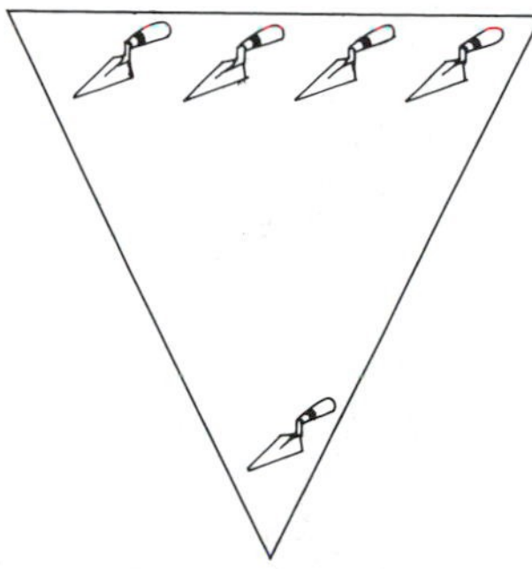

**Large collections & many assemblages in each excavated section**

**Small excavations**

**SOUTH**

**5.12** Different excavation strategies in the northern and southern provinces of Europe. These result from the density of artifacts in cave deposits. When typological analysis of flint artifacts is the main goal of excavation then this relationship is apparent. A change in aims, for example the recovery of spatial information, could lead to a reversal of this pattern (see Gamble 1986a:Fig. 8.8).

skills of Neanderthals can then be put into a broader context by considering their taskscapes, those surrounding environments they constructed for living in with their varied skills, but which in turn constrained and selected their actions.

*Paths and tracks: raw-material acquisition and transfers*

Did Neanderthal tracks and paths across the regions of Pleistocene Europe vary due to the combination of latitude, longitude and relief and the impact such constants had on the distribution and abundance of resources (Figure 3.1)?

The evidence from all locales is that the use of raw materials remains predominantly local (as defined in Chapter 3). Geneste's (1988b) study of the Grotte Vaufrey in southwest France and Callow's (1986a and 1986b) examination of raw-material use at La Cotte in the northwest region provide examples of the general pattern.

At Grotte Vaufrey nine different flint sources were recognized among the raw materials in the eleven levels in the cave (Figure 5.13). Quartz and miscellaneous provided two further categories.

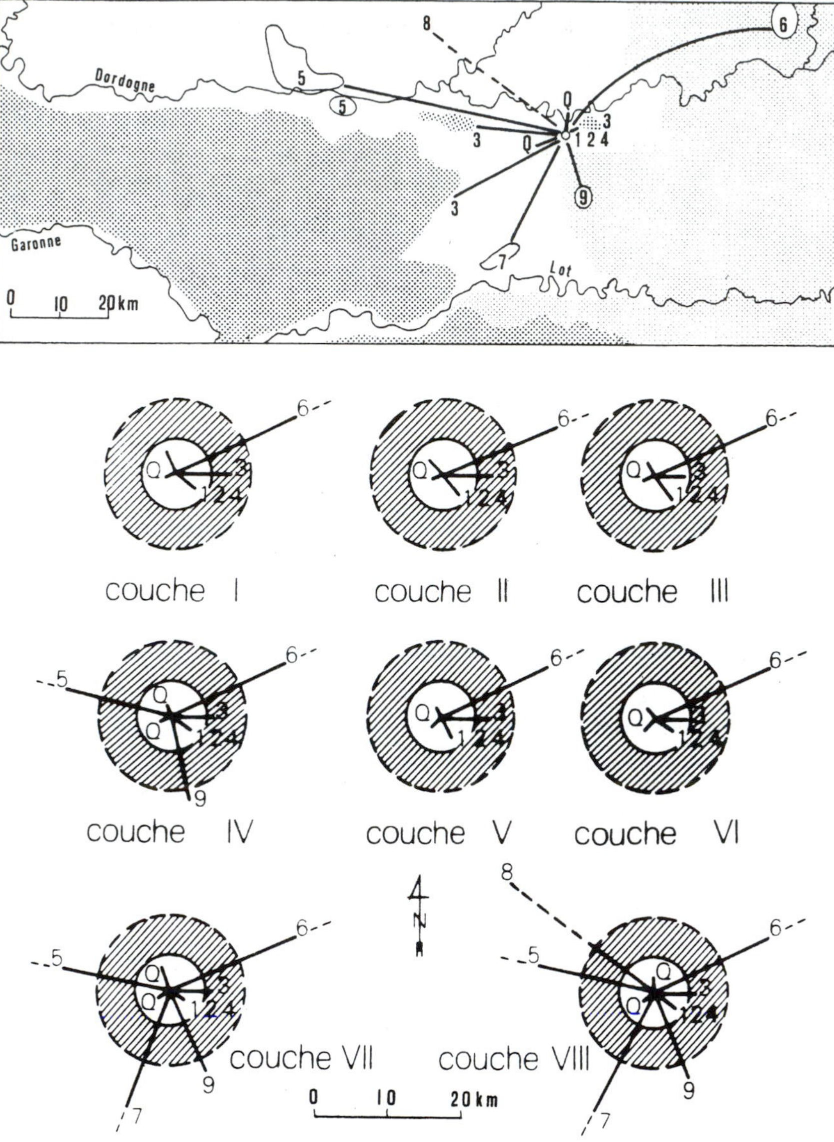


**5.13** Raw-material sources exploited in eight of the levels of the Grotte Vaufrey, France, SW region (after Geneste 1988b, Mellars 1996:Fig. 5.8).

The largest number of artifacts come from level VIII (Table 5.5). The raw materials are dominated by sources 1 and 2, 48 and 42 per cent respectively. This is repeated in all other levels. The distant sources 5–9 (Figure 5.13), up to 80 km from the cave, never individually account for more than 2 per cent of the raw material. They are invariably retouched pieces (Geneste 1988b).

At La Cotte, a coastal cave on the island of Jersey, Callow (1986a) has plotted

Table 5.5. *Aspects of raw material use at Grotte Vaufrey (Geneste 1988b:Fig. 2).*

| Level | Number of raw-material sources | Number >10 km | Artifact sample | Dominant raw material % | Maximum distance km |
|---|---|---|---|---|---|
| I | 4 | 0 | 112 | 60 | 6 |
| II | 7 | 1 | 531 | 49 | 30 |
| III | 4 | 1 | 100 | 71 | 30 |
| IV | 9 | 3 | 461 | 41 | 70 |
| V | 7 | 1 | 121 | 50 | 30 |
| VI | 6 | 1 | 190 | 42 | 55 |
| VII | 9 | 4 | 558 | 39 | 80 |
| VIII | 9 | 5 | 2,075 | 48 | 60 |
| IX | 4 | 0 | 36 | 72 | 6 |
| X | 5 | 0 | 84 | 52.5 | 6 |
| XI | 4 | 0 | 97 | 49 | 6 |

Table 5.6. *Raw materials at La Cotte (Callow 1986b:Tables 24.1, 24.2, Hivernel 1986:Table 27.1).*

| | Retouched artifacts | Retouched fragments | Cores | Unretouched flakes, chips and chunks |
|---|---|---|---|---|
| Flint | 8,953 | 6,904 | 1,495 | 49,214 |
| % | *13* | *10* | *3* | *74* |
| Stone | 489 | 677 | 69 | 6,332 |
| % | *6* | *9* | *1* | *84* |
| Quartz | 904 | 0 | 296 | 10,729 |
| % | *8* | *0* | *2* | *90* |

the changes by number and weight between the three main raw-material types, flint, quartz and other hard rock stones, for example igneous material. There is no flint on the island and the nearest outcrop is now submerged c. 20 km north of the site, and requires a fall of sea level of 25 m before it can be exploited (*ibid.*:205). Other flint-bearing sources are 40 km away. The cortex surviving on many of the implements shows however that beach pebbles rather than nodular flint was being used. As sea levels changed so different flint sources seem to have been used but, as Callow argues, these were always close to the cave, probably within 3 km. Some indication of this proximity, using Geneste's model based on his Aquitaine studies, can be gleaned from the proportions of knapping flakes to retouched pieces for flint and stone (Table 5.6).

Table 5.7. *Raw-material transfer distances during the Lower and Middle Palaeolithic (data from Féblot-Augustins 1997:Figures 24, 28, 30 and 31).*

| | % <20 km | % 20–80 km | % >80 km | N |
|---|---|---|---|---|
| Lower Palaeolithic | 75 | 24 | 1 | 76 |
| Early Middle Palaeolithic | 65 | 31 | 4 | 80 |
| Late Middle Palaeolithic | | | | |
| Western Europe | 83 | 16 | 1 | 322 |
| Central Europe | 48 | 33 | 19 | 100 |

The overwhelming proportions of this category lead us to expect that sources within 10 km were predominantly utilized.

In her inventory of 578 raw-material transfers in the period OIS 7 to 4, Féblot-Augustins (1993, 1997) found that very few exceeded 80 km and most were less than Geneste's threshold distance of 20 km (Table 5.7).

One of the largest distances has been found in central Europe at the Moravian cave of Kulna (Valoch 1988). Here, in level 11, 12 pieces out of 1,713 analysed (0.7 per cent) were Jurassic flints from Krakow in southern Poland, 230 km to the northeast. Interestingly since these contradict the Geneste principle regarding distance (Chapter 3), they were introduced to the site as blanks and rough cores (Féblot-Augustins 1993:table 4) rather than as retouched pieces. This is also the case at the Schweinskopf in the east Eifel volcano field, where the largest distance for a transfer is 120 km (Floss 1994). However, 96 per cent of all the stone at this locale comes from less than 4 km away (Féblot-Augustins 1997:inventaire 20).

The data show that raw-material transfers are considerably longer in the north-central than in the southwest region. This finding had already been demonstrated by Roebroeks (et al. 1988:figure 4) and can be seen in more detail in Féblot-Augustins's synthesis (1993:figures 3 and 5) and the detailed work of Floss on raw materials in the Middle Rhine (1994). These greater distances (Table 5.7 and Figure 5.14) can be interpreted as larger foraging tracks resulting from increased continentality and the separation of resources within the plaid mosaic (see further discussion in Chapter 6).

The effect of environmental pressure on hominid range size can also be seen between the Würm I (Early Glacial) and Würm II (mostly Pleniglacial) raw-material transfers in southwest France. The increase in both the absolute and average distances over which raw-material transfers occurred coincides with the shift towards more open, colder climatic conditions which, in Aquitaine, sees a shift from red deer to reindeer in many faunas from the caves and rock shelters (Bordes and Prat 1965, Delpech 1976, Dennell 1983).

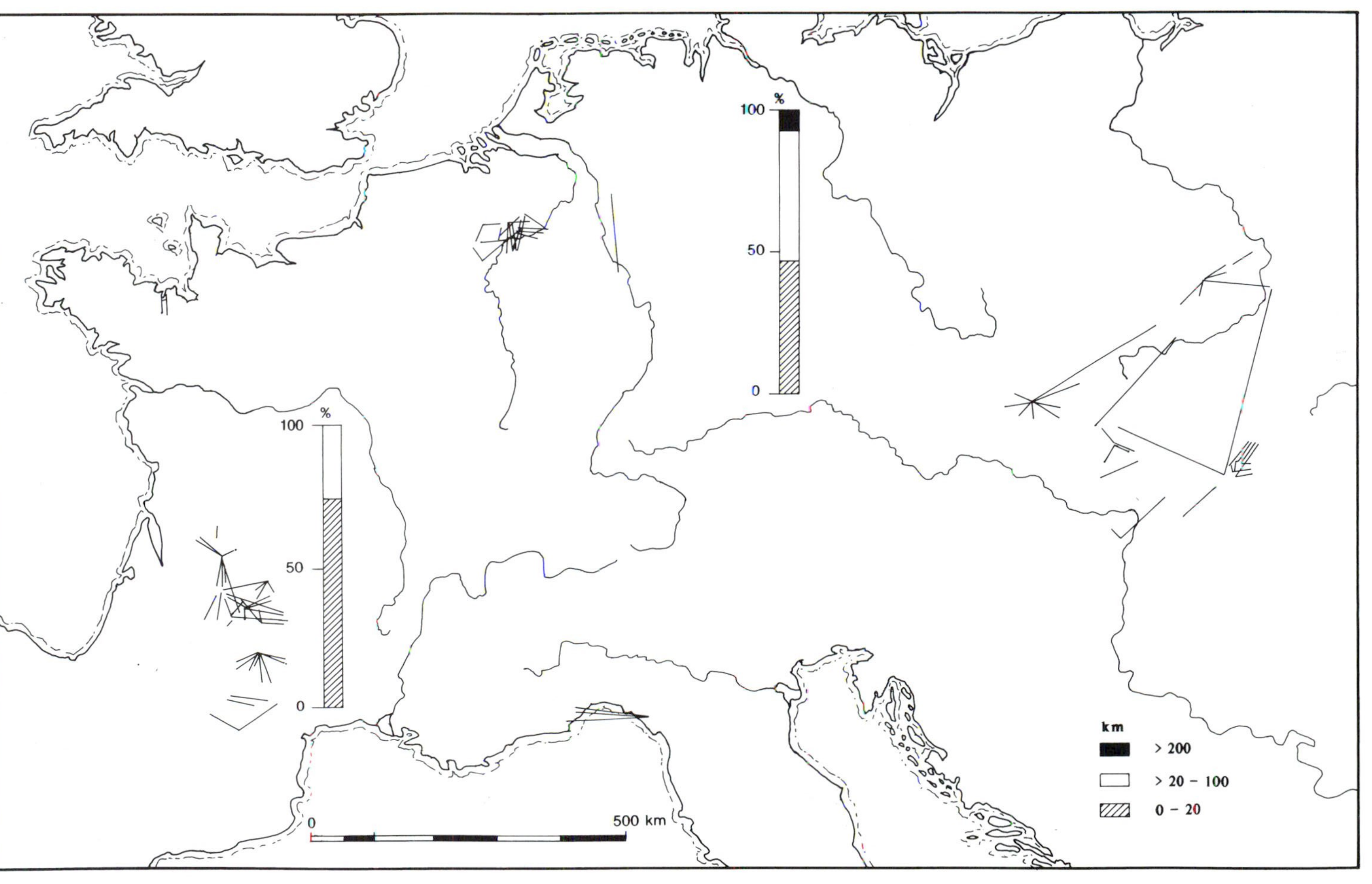


**5.14** The effect of continentality on lithic raw-material transfers in the late Middle Palaeolithic. The distances are plotted for the SW and NC regions. The bar graphs show the frequency of transfers in those two regions in relation to distance (after Féblot-Augustins 1993:Fig. 8, 1997).

Apart from small amounts of ochre found at Maastricht-Belvédère (Roebroeks 1988:39), there is no evidence for the transfer of raw materials other than stone. The hematite is thought to have been picked up locally in the Maas valley.[12]

It is also possible to identify during this period workshop/quarries where coarser-grained local raw materials were worked at source. In Germany there are extensive quartzite 'factories' at Reutersruh (Luttropp and Bosinski 1971), Lenderscheid, Troisdorf and Ratingen (Bosinski 1994). The very large artifact collections at Markkleeberg may represent a similar use of large flint sources (Baumann et al. 1983, Grahmann 1955). In northern France the quarry workshops of Etouvies, Ault-Onival and Saoul-en-Amienois (Roebroeks and Tuffreau 1994) appear to be comparable to the German workshops as does Khotylevo I (Zavernyaev 1978) in the northeastern region. In Mediterranean France the undated Mousterian 'village' of Canjuers may be another example where chipped stone on a natural outcrop covers several hectares (Lumley 1969c:231). All of these quarry/workshop sites are difficult to date but are believed to be of Saalian to end-of-Pleniglacial age. Markkleeberg is placed in OIS 8 (Mania 1995).

### *Chaîne opératoire: technology and tool production*

There are important developments in lithic technology during this period. In traditional terms these involve the preparation and predetermination of the shape of flakes and blades prior to their detachment from the core. This resulted in levallois and blade core reduction techniques. What is surprising to conventional schemes is the dating of soft hammer, prismatic blades to at least 100 Kyr BP when such techniques were once regarded as exclusively Upper Palaeolithic, i.e. post-40 Kyr BP. This further stresses the unity of early Palaeolithic technology, where the major trend is towards the elaboration of systems of débitage rather than façonnage using secant plane technology (Table 4.9, White and Pettitt 1995:33).

### *Typology and assemblage variation*

The variable use of levallois technique (Bordes 1968a, 1972, 1980), the variety of forms produced by edge retouching flakes, whatever technique was used to strike them from a nodule (Bordes 1961b), and now the widespread use of blades[13] in the Middle Palaeolithic (Révillion and Tuffreau 1994a), has greatly expanded the notion of variability between lithic assemblages. But the period still lacks those distinctive type fossils which characterize, by time and place, many of the assemblages in the Upper Palaeolithic. Instead, the biface and flake assemblages that we examined in the previous chapter have now been overlaid with a complexity of techniques and a corresponding gamut of explanations. In particular the role of raw material has been examined (Barton 1988, Dibble 1987, Dibble and Rolland 1992, 1990, 1991, Geneste 1988a, Rolland and Dibble 1990, Tavoso 1984, Turq 1992b) and chaîne opératoire models have been applied to the material (Boëda 1988, Boëda, Geneste and Meignen 1990, Geneste 1988b, Schlanger 1990, 1996, Turq 1989). The original Bordes/Binford debate over the explanation of variability in Mousterian assemblages (Binford 1972, 1973, 1983a, Binford and Binford 1966, 1969, Bordes 1972, 1973, Bordes and de Sonneville-Bordes 1970, Guichard 1976, Mellars 1969, 1970, Rolland 1981) is authoritatively presented and discussed by Mellars (1996). The debate, as Mellars also shows, has now been extended to consider more elaborate settlement systems and patterns of mobility which affect the differential deposition of artifact types and the employment of distinctive knapping techniques (Kuhn 1991, 1992, 1995). At the same time, Bordes' view that five Neanderthal tribes made five different lithic assemblages (Table 5.8) has been elaborated to consider alternative explanations. For example, Turq concludes (1989, 1992b:80) in his study of the Quina Mousterian that it is not a culture, in Bordes' sense.

Instead it can be explained by a combination of time-economizing procedures, the availability of good, local raw material and the performance of specialized, but unknown, activities. Variability is also explained by patterns of cultural transmission and aspects of cognition (Mithen 1993b, 1996). Finally, a chronological framework has been established for some of the variants (Mellars 1996, Turq 1992b:77) although there are no obvious linear trajectories of assemblage change and development, but rather, as Bordes described it, an *évolution buisonnante* (1950).

*The bordian analysis*

Bordes introduced a systematic approach to the classification and analysis of lithic assemblages with his justly celebrated type list (Bordes 1953, 1961a, 1981, Bordes and Bourgon 1951). His landmark analyses treated the flake and the biface components separately. Among the flakes some sixty-three types are recognized. In addition there are a further twenty-one types of biface (Gamble 1986a:Appendix 3). Scrapers (type list numbers 9–29) and points (numbers 3–7) are particularly important for classifying assemblages. Notched and denticulate pieces are also very common in assemblages (numbers 42 and 43), although they lack the formal attributes of careful retouch.

Two counts of flakes are made in a bordian analysis. The *real* count includes all unretouched levallois flakes, numbers 1–3 in the type list, even though they carry no secondary retouch. The *essential* count leaves these out, along with the slightly retouched category, numbers 46–50. The proportions of the various flake tools in excavated assemblages are presented by means of a cumulative percentage curve. Five repeated profiles were produced from all the many assemblages studied (Gamble 1986a:figure 4.5). A number of technical indices are also calculated. These deal with the incidence of levallois working (IL), the prevalence of blades (ILam), as well as a series of typological indices that compared, for example, all the side scrapers (IR). All of these calculations and their analytical application are described by Bordes (1972).

The Bordian method, developed during the 1950s and 1960s, is still the main

Table 5.8. *The major assemblage variants in the Mousterian of southwest France (Bordes 1953, 1972, 1981).*

| | ASSEMBLAGE VARIANT | Levallois Index IL % | Side scraper Index IR % | Quina Index IQ % | Biface Index IB % | Upper Palaeolithic types Group III % | Denticulates Group IV % |
|---|---|---|---|---|---|---|---|
| | *Charentian* | | | | | | |
| 1 | Quina subtype | <10 | 50–80 | 14–30 | Absent/rare | | Low |
| 2 | Ferrassie subtype | 14–30 | 50–80 | 6–14 | Absent/rare | | Low |
| 3 | *Typical* | Very variable | >50 | 0–3 | Absent/rare | | Moderate |
| 4 | *Denticulate* | Very variable | 4–20 | 0 | Low | | 60 |
| 5 | *Mousterian of Acheulean Tradition (MTA)* | | | | | | |
| | subtype A | Very variable | 25–45 | Very low | 8–40 | Seldom >4 | Common |
| | subtype B | Very common | 4–20 | Very low | Absent/rare | Strong | 60 |

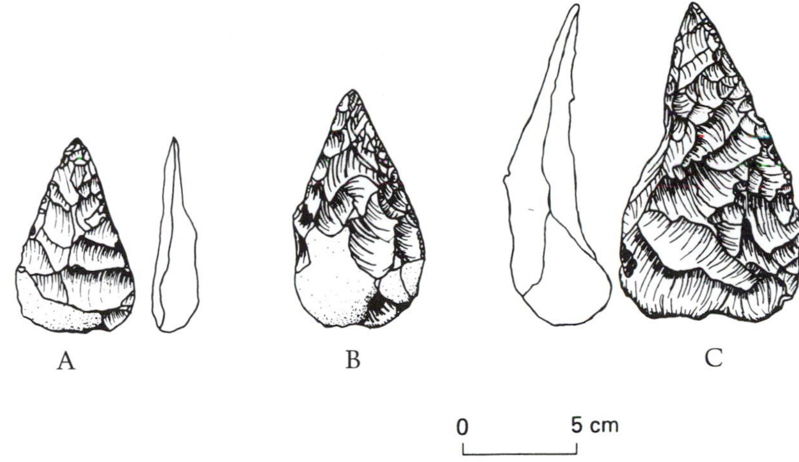


**5.15** Micoquian bifaces from the last glacial (after Gamble 1986a:Fig. 5.1).
Key:
A La Micoque level 6 (SW region)
B&C Bocksteinschmiede level IIIa (NC region)

method by which French archaeologists, and many others in Europe, compare their material. It is by no means the only system being used and should be compared with Bosinski (1967) and Gabori (1976), who concentrate more upon type fossils to classify the smaller Middle Palaeolithic assemblages from central and eastern Europe, and Carbonell (et al. 1995) and Weißmüller (1995) who seek to provide a unified system for all lithic analysis. Descriptions of artifact types can be found in Brézillon (1968) and Hahn (1991).

*Biface industries*

Bifaces continue to be made throughout the period both by façonnage and by débitage. They vary enormously in size and shape. For example the OIS 7 gravel site of Stanton Harcourt in England has produced very large pointed handaxes, one almost 27 cm in length, although this is exceptional (Bridgland 1994: Figure 2.17). The pointed, late Acheulean bifaces from Salzgitter-Lebenstedt (Tode 1982), now dated to the Pleniglacial, are large in size and are an example of bifaces knapped as tools. On the other hand the pointed micoquian handaxe/biface can be small, for example the asymmetrical bifaces (Figure 5.15) from level IIIa in the Bockstein cave in southern Germany (Wetzel and Bosinski 1969). Many of these smaller micoquian bifaces are made on supports as shown by the example in Figure 5.15 from La Micoque.

Not everything belongs to the pointed tradition of biface production. In England and France there are ovates from this period (Roe 1981:table 14), some with a distinctive twist in their profile as at the Atelier Commont, a non-levallois assemblage, in the Somme valley (Antoine 1990).

*The Micoquian*

The Bockstein assemblage is regarded as a variant within the Micoquian tradition that links assemblages throughout the northern province in Belgium, Germany, Poland, the Czech and Slovakian Republics and western Russia including the Crimea and Caucasus (Bosinski 1967, Gabori 1976, Mania and Toepfer 1973, Svoboda 1994a, Ulrix-Closset 1975, Valoch 1988).

In many instances the bifaces from these assemblages are aptly described as knives, as in the term 'Bocksteinmesser' that was used by Wetzel (1958) to describe the curved, bifacially worked pieces he was excavating from that site. The pradniks, often with their distinctive tranchet 're-sharpening' flake, are also regarded as a variant of these bifacial knives. Pradnik bifaces are widespread in the European Middle Palaeolithic.

*Levallois reduction sequences*

Particular attention has been directed to the levallois technique[14] and its characterization as a chaîne opératoire. In one of his last papers, Bordes (1980) summarized his views on the technique. He stressed that the central idea is determining the shape of the flake/blade by careful preparation before the flake is detached (Fig. 5.16). This might involve preparing the striking platform, but not necessarily. Neither does it mean that only one such flake was detached. In an experiment Bradley (1977), who worked closely with Bordes, knapped twenty tabular blocks of flint measuring 4 cm thick by 15 cm in diameter. He set a limit of 6 cm as the critical threshold for the production of a levallois flake. Once the size dropped below this value he abandoned the core and started on the next nodule. He produced on average 4.35 levallois flakes (range 3–8) per core. At the same time an average of 102 other flakes, many of them useful blanks for retouching into scrapers, were also produced. The secant plane technology as applied to the reduction of the core provides an example of façonnage. This emphasizes the importance of the knapping gestures in the early stages of the chaîne opératoire (Table 5.9 below) in setting up the possibilities for later, varied débitage.

This approach to nodule reduction has been termed the recurrent method by Boëda (1988, 1994), who has made a detailed study of the material from the late OIS 7/early OIS 6-age assemblage at Biache St. Vaast level IIA. He summarizes the technique as follows:

> Le concept levallois réside essentiellement dans la conception volumétrique du nucléus à laquelle seront adjoints les critères techniques de prédétermination (convexités latérales et distales), mais aussi dans les plans de fracturation des enlèvements prédéterminés (2a, 2b) qui sont toujours parallèles au plan d'intersection des deux surfaces. La capacité de production d'enlèvements prédéterminés (3) est limitée au volume compris entre la surface de préparation levallois et le plan d'intersection. (1988:188, the numbers refer to Figure 5.17)

The graphic description (Figure 5.17) of secant plane technology (White and Pettitt 1995) neatly demonstrates why levallois can be described as débitage

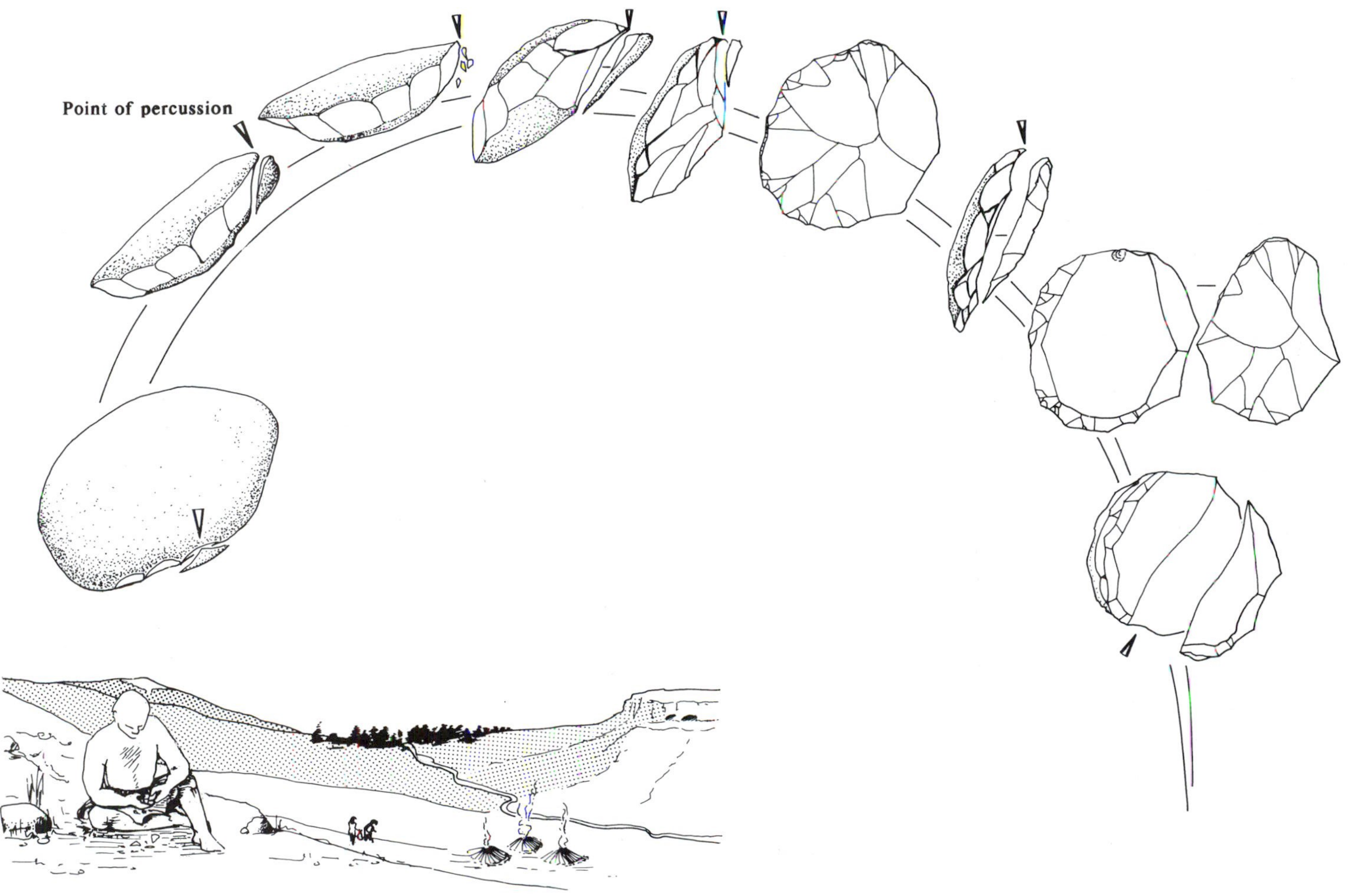


**5.16** A chaîne opératoire for levallois débitage (after Lhomme and Maury 1990)

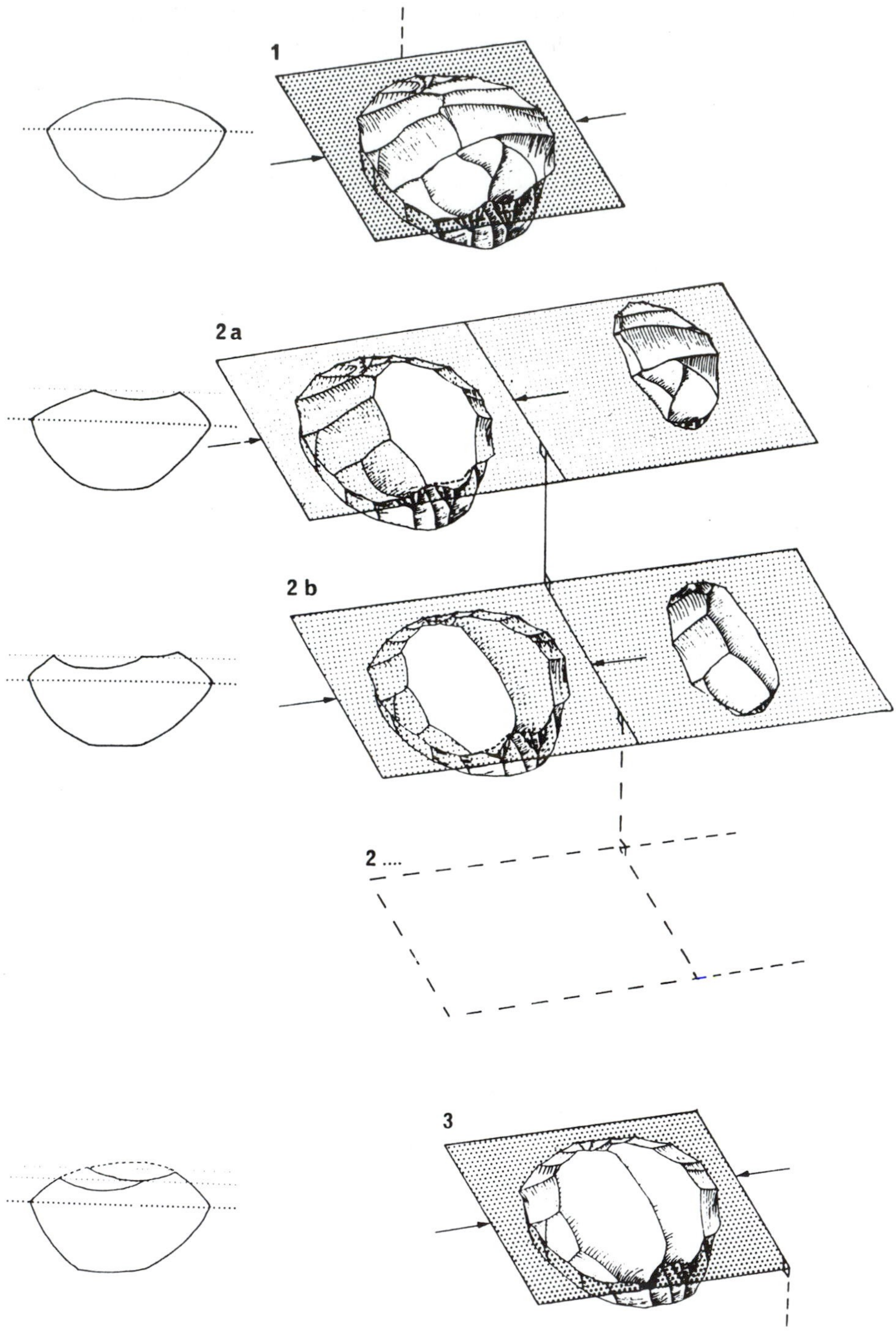


**5.17** Secant plane technology as illustrated by Boëda's 'recurrent unipolar' levallois technique. The upper face of the core is prepared to produce two immediately successive, overlapping levallois flakes. For description of phases see text (after Boëda 1988:Fig. 18.2).

technology (Table 4.9). Boëda's aim is to understand lithic collections on the basis of the dynamic of technology, comparable to Leroi-Gourhan's gesture and material action (Chapter 3), rather than what he sees as the static approach of Bordes which is based on classifying the form of the finished object (Boëda 1988:211). Consequently the levallois concept, as explained above, leads to many manifestations (Table 4.8). For example, at Biache IIA the nodules were worked as bipolar or unipolar cores. But what is important, as Boëda stresses, is that at an assemblage level we see deliberate choices being made. The levallois technique is inscribed, he writes, in a tradition.

> Les connaissances mises en jeu témoignent d'un acquis transmis de génération en génération. Ces connaissances correspondent à une option parmi un ensemble de possibles. (Boëda 1988:213)

The selection of gesture is therefore not solely determined by the quality or shape of the raw material but by the knowledge, acquired culturally, that informs and structures the gestures of the knapper. The ability of the Biache knappers to produce blanks (supports) that almost exactly fitted the future shape of the tool unites in this instance the links in the chain of material action. In Boëda's analysis this shows very clearly that the products of knapping are not just adaptive responses but rather are enshrined in traditions of cultural techniques. This involves rhythms and gestures and the material action of the body. Rather than learning the artifact's shape and then working to achieve it, the knappers master the actions of making. In that sense the levallois technique is not one of pre-determining flake size and shape as so often claimed. Instead it is a technique which disciplines the body to perform a routine sequence of gestures which happen to make what we call levallois flakes.

Here is a rich field for the future examination of cultural transmission and learning (Shennan 1996). But what is currently lacking are the more general applications of such analyses. Will we find, for example, in all lithic assemblages, whether levallois or not, that the range of choices is limited? If so, are we perhaps dealing with a restricted number of ways in which cultural transmission worked among Neanderthals? Most intriguingly, were the different techniques they used possibly associated with different places, gatherings and social occasions, providing us with that link between social life, negotiation and material action?

Alas, it is not currently possible to say. But certainly deconstructing the levallois, and recognizing it as a series of techniques which can be studied, rather than just a set of finished products, opens up an interesting line with which to study the individual through the most durable of Palaeolithic materials.

*How important was raw material?*

For many years there has been speculation about the decision of Palaeolithic knappers to employ the levallois technique. The availability of large, high-quality raw material as at Bakers Hole in the Ebbsfleet Valley, a tributary of the Lower Thames (Bridgland 1994), is often cited as an example (Roe 1981). But at the same time, and Bordes as a good flint-knapper was always quick to point this out, the levallois technique also used quartzites and other materials which we regard as inferior to flint. The workshop/quarry of Reutersruh in the north-central region (Luttropp and Bosinski 1971) is one such instance and the volcanic rocks used at Pontnewydd cave, Wales, another (Aldhouse-Green 1995).

The wider role of raw material in the chaîne opératoire has been studied by Geneste (1985, 1988a, 1988b) at the Grotte Vaufrey in southwest France. His analysis combines further experimental work on flint knapping and adds, through the sourcing of raw material in the landscape, a regional scale to the chaîne opératoire. There are twenty-seven technological categories in his chaîne opératoire for stone tools, of which the last three are flake size categories (Table 5.9).

The remaining twenty-four are grouped into four phases which have been identified in a chaîne opératoire that is intended to produce predetermined flakes according to the levallois concept (Geneste 1988b:443).

Phase 0 Selection of raw material
Phase 1 Initial shaping of the block in order to enable the production of flakes
Phase 2 The production of débitage. This is the longest phase and accounts for eighteen of the twenty-four categories.
Three subdivisions are recognized (Table 5.9)
Phase 3 A completion stage and the addition of retouch

In level VIII at Grotte Vaufrey 2,075 stone artifacts were excavated from a surface of 85 m$^2$. Of these, 673 were analysed through the chaîne opératoire and included 520 broken (Fr. *bruts*) and 183 retouched pieces. The total inventory used nine of the twelve raw-material categories and nearly all the technological categories were present. The presence of complete chaînes opératoires rather than segments which might indicate the transport of blanks and retouched tools was also confirmed by refitting. For example, core K14–363 was a local flint. When knapped it formed a discrete cluster, 2.5 m in extent and with a vertical displacement of 50 cm.[15] What needs to be stressed here is how this analysis departs from the bordian description of technology and typology. In his typological analysis of the material Rigaud (1988a) classifies level VIII as typical mousterian rich in side scrapers and with a high levallois index. However, it is the link to a wider region through the emphasis laid on raw materials and the conception of technology as a sequence, rather than as just the end product of flake or retouched artifact, which marks the major difference in Geneste's study of the same material. As a result, typological/technological comparisons between assemblages, which gave us the important Bordes/Binford debate over the nature of variability in lithic collections, now

Table 5.9. *The products of the levallois chaîne opératoire (Geneste 1988b).*

| Category | Technological description | Phase | | |
|---|---|---|---|---|
| 0 | Block of raw material | 0 | ACQUISITION | |
| 1 | Cortical flake (>50%) | | | |
| 2 | Residual cortical flake (<50%) | 1 | SHAPING | FAÇONNAGE · Secant plane technology · DEBITAGE · Migrating plane technology |
| 3 | Naturally backed knife | | | |
| 4 | Flake, ordinary points, and resharpening flakes | | | |
| 5 | Blade | | | |
| 6 | Atypical levallois detachment | | | |
| 7 | Levallois flake | 2a | PRODUCTION | |
| 8 | Levallois blade-like detachment | | | D |
| 9 | Levallois point | | | |
| 10 | Pseudo-levallois point | | | E |
| 11 | Disc core | | | |
| 12 | Other core types | | | B |
| 13 | Levallois point and flake core | | | |
| 14 | Levallois blade core | 2b | OF | I |
| 15 | Trimming flake (débordant) | | | |
| 16 | Crested fake/blade | | | T |
| 17 | Core fragment | | | |
| 18 | Kombewa flake core | | | A |
| 19 | Truncated and thinning flake | 2c | BLANKS | |
| 20 | Kombewa flake | | (SUPPORTS) | G |
| 21 | Indeterminable flake fragment without cortex | | | |
| 22 | Biface retouch flake | | TRANSFORMATION | E |
| 23 | Retouching or resharpening (ravivage) flake | | OF BLANKS | |
| 24 | Debris >29 mm without cortex | 3 | RESIDUE | |
| 25 | Debris <30 mm with or without cortex | | AND | |
| 26 | Small flake, complete or fragmentary, <30 mm | | VARIOUS | |

Table 5.10. *The chaîne opératoire as applied to the Quina Mousterian (Turq 1992b:77).*

Quina Mousterian chaîne opératoire:

- Introduction of raw material to the site in the form of previously tested blocks.
- The removal of one or two primary 'trial' flakes from the nodule. This can be either uni- or bipolar removals.
- The production of cortically backed knives. Any 'waste' elements produced at this stage are accidental. They include *outrepasse* removals and so-called 'Siret' fractures.
- The remainder of the nodule, either its centre or one of its extremities, is transformed into a core through the preparation of several striking platforms, or by the limited removal of cortex.
- The production of *supports* through débitage. These include naturally backed knives, Clactonian flakes and asymmetrical flakes. Undifferentiated flakes as well as fragments may also be produced.
- In the final stages of flaking, some cores, either on flakes or from nodules, may be further modified into tools.
- The majority of the *supports* (flakes) are transformed by retouch into tools and include denticulates, scrapers and notches.

operate at a more dynamic level of choice, selection and mobility. This can be related not to the actions of groups masquerading as assemblages, but instead to individual action. The latter is observed through refitting studies and raw-material transfers. The individual is therefore inscribed within those systems of cultural transmission which result in local styles of manufacture. The flexibility of choice within such traditions is demonstrated by the selection of blanks for retouching into side scrapers and the less formal notches and denticulates. In five of the eight Middle Palaeolithic levels at Grotte Vaufrey, the side scrapers are usually made on levallois blanks. It is difficult, as Boëda has commented (1988:213), to see such patterns purely in terms of functional responses.

*The Quina mousterian: a non-levallois case*

Contrast these findings with the Quina variant (Table 5.8), which mostly dates to the Pleniglacial OIS 4 (Mellars 1996:188, 353, Turq 1992b:77). It is dominated by transverse side scrapers and typically has a levallois index of less than 10 per cent.

Turq (1992b:77) stresses that the distinctive aspect of the chaîne opératoire for this late Mousterian variant rests on the observation that a range of clearly predetermined products (*supports* and *outils*) could be produced by a series of comparatively simple but alternative knapping methods. The Quina Mousterian is an example of the elaboration of débitage; the hallmark of Middle Palaeolithic variability and where raw material is divided in a variety of ways using both secant and migrating plane technology. The reduction sequence is summarized in Table 5.10.

The flexible Quina approach to produce *supports* for retouching into scrapers is very different to the constraints of biface manufacture through façonnage (Chapter 4) or even their production through recurrent levallois sequences using débitage (see above). This is in spite of the fact that both sequences may have employed secant plane technology (White and Pettitt 1995). The low incidence of levallois in Quina as opposed to other scraper-dominated assemblages (Table 5.8) emphasizes the choices that were available to make either blade or flake *supports*.

However, there is patterning to be seen. Turq (1992a and 1992b) has made a detailed study of this variant and points out that very few examples of Quina Mousterian are found outside cave and rock shelters. The provisioning territories are very small, between 5 and 10 km from these locales (Turq 1990:417), emphasizing the use of local raw materials. Quina artifacts are not transported around the landscape, unlike those made in other assemblages with the levallois technique (Geneste 1989). This contrasts with the Mousterian of Acheulean Tradition in OIS 3, where raw-material territories have a larger radius of between 15 and 20 km (see Chapter 6).

Turq's findings are therefore at variance with the predictions from Rolland and Dibble's model of assemblage variation and raw material (Table 5.11) that Quina assemblages will be made on distant raw materials.

This contradiction identifies a problem with Dibble and Rolland's model. This concerns their local : distant division and how they have applied it to their goal – understanding Mousterian variability. The problem is that they have qualitatively determined these two distance categories in order to account for the patterning they wish to explain. As a result, their continuous reduction model is a description of what they know to be variable, rather than a model which might generally help to explain variation in behaviour, and for which the Mousterian data are an obvious test case. However, without any sense of scale or distance in their model we are only left with qualitative descriptions of local and exotic distances, which can be manipulated to fit the patterning, expressed in Table 5.11, rather than testing it. As Turq shows, once some distances are added then the power of the Rolland–Dibble model to explain assemblage variability declines. For example, Quina assemblages are made on local rather than distant flint.

### When does the levallois appear?

Is it possible to date the appearance of the levallois technique? On the basis of the Lower Thames terraces, Bridgland (1994:26) proposes that the technique first appears widely in OIS 8, in the uppermost levels of the Corbet's Tey and the basal unit of the Mucking formations. The technique is rare in sites of the same age in the middle terrace of the Somme (Tuffreau 1982:146) as at the Atelier Commont in Rue de Cagny where the sables roux are now dated to OIS 8 (Antoine 1990). However, at the older Cagny la Garenne, OIS 11 and 12, there is a form of levallois working that is associated with the production of bifaces.

Table 5.11. *The anticipated effect of distance to good raw material on the composition of Middle Palaeolithic stone tool assemblages (after Dibble and Rolland 1992, Rolland and Dibble 1990).*

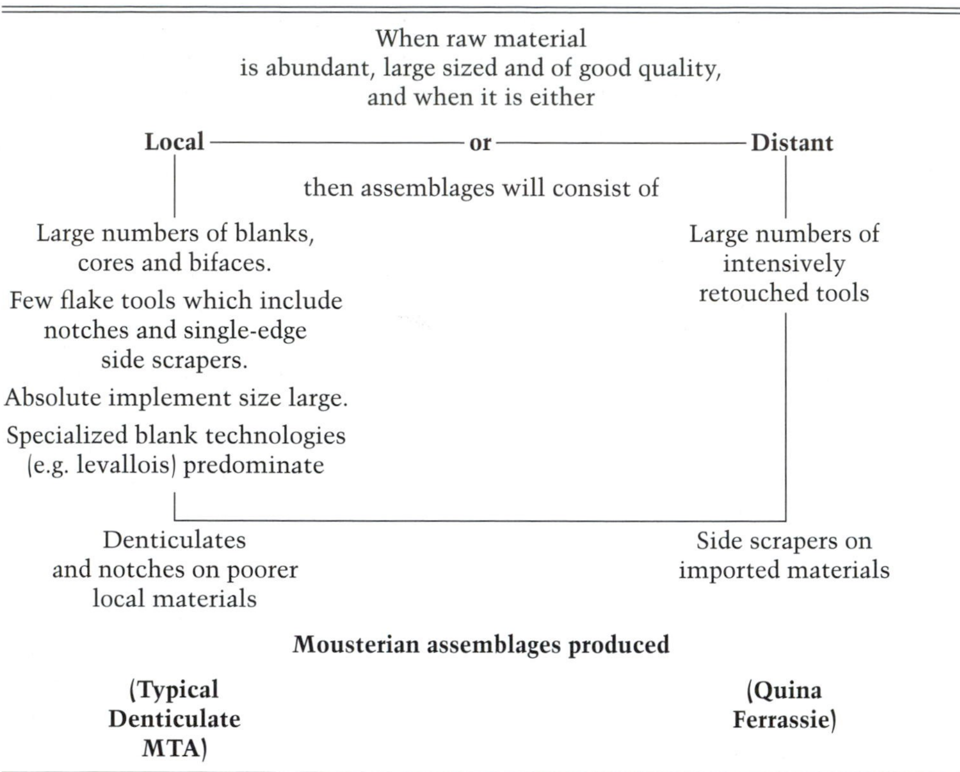
When raw material
is abundant, large sized and of good quality,
and when it is either
Local
or
Distant
then assemblages will consist of
Large numbers of blanks, cores and bifaces.
Few flake tools which include notches and single-edge side scrapers.
Absolute implement size large.
Specialized blank technologies (e.g. levallois) predominate
Large numbers of intensively retouched tools
Denticulates and notches on poorer local materials
Side scrapers on imported materials
Mousterian assemblages produced
(Typical Denticulate MTA)
(Quina Ferrassie)

Tuffreau and Antoine (1995) regard the morphology of the bifaces as comparable to that of levallois cores[16] especially when they break during knapping. They conclude that a clear conceptual link exists between the production of bifaces and the presence of levallois flaking methods. Façonnage and secant plane technology (Chapter 4) may well be the route by which the levallois technique emerged. If this is the case then White and Pettitt (1995:33) are correct in identifying the appearance of levallois as the only major technological innovation in the period 500–200 Kyr BP and therefore as justifying a division between a Lower and a Middle Palaeolithic.

The dating is still vague but it is possible that the widespread use of levallois, as we have seen at Biache St. Vaast and Grotte Vaufrey, may first appear in the Saalian complex, after 300 Kyr BP. If so, then the availability of suitable raw material may not be a relevant factor in its development. It is more likely that selection for novel technology came with changes in patterns of mobility. Geneste's (1989:83) study of raw materials in Aquitaine shows that the most mobile elements of any Mousterian technology, as judged by the use of distant raw materials, involve levallois elements. The transportation of levallois flakes assisted hominids in adapting to less predictable environmental conditions by promoting flexibility. White and Pettitt suggest (1995:34) that bifaces were also transported short distances but proved less flexible in meeting contingencies. While the wider importance of levallois has often been seen as indicative of linguistic capabilities, based on assumptions about the pre-planned intentions of the knappers (Noble and Davidson 1996:200–1), it now seems more fruitful to examine the technique in terms of the tactics of individual mobility (Kuhn 1995).

*Levallois and non-levallois flake assemblages*

A brief glance at the Middle Palaeolithic literature reveals a large number of local names to describe flake-based assemblages. These far exceed Bordes' five tribes centred upon southwest France. I have mentioned the Micoquian since it is a widespread type. In the north-central region the Taubachian (Schafer 1981, Svoboda 1989, 1994a, 1994b), an unstandardized flake industry, has widespread currency. These are reviewed in Gamble (1986a:chapter 5). The question of assemblage variation in the Middle Palaeolithic has now to be seen as the outcome of façonnage and débitage and the application of secant- and migrating-plane technologies (Table 4.9).

*Laminar industries*

One instance of secant-plane technologies requires further discussion. The dating of the northern early blade industries, referred to by Conard (1992:88) as the Middle Palaeolithic Blade Group, is well understood (Figure 5.18). Typically they occur in the Early Glacial as at Crayford (Cook 1986), Seclin (Révillion and Tuffreau 1994c), Wallertheim (Conard et al. 1995a, 1995b) and Tönchesberg (Conard 1992), and extend into the Pleniglacial at Riencourt-les-Bapaume (Tuffreau 1993). Currently, seven sites cluster in the northwest and north-central regions (Révillion and Tuffreau 1994b). There is also a strong blade component in some northeast region sites, principally Molodova V, and several sites, for example Kabazi, in the western Crimea (Cabaj and Sitlivyl 1994).

The point about the northwest and north-central sites is the dual reduction sequence. On the one hand blanks in these assemblages were produced using levallois, and on the other through non-levallois techniques closely resembling Upper Palaeolithic reduction sequences (Révillion and Tuffreau 1994:12). But what makes this blade production very different from the Upper Palaeolithic are the very small numbers of blanks which are then retouched to standard types. It is, if you like, an Upper Palaeolithic technology that lacks Upper Palaeolithic types. Moreover, as the papers in Révillion and Tuffreau (1994a) show, the blade technique is often a small component of the assemblages. At Vinneuf the assemblage is characterized by its bifaces and micoquian-style implements, including pradniks, rather than by the small amounts of blades

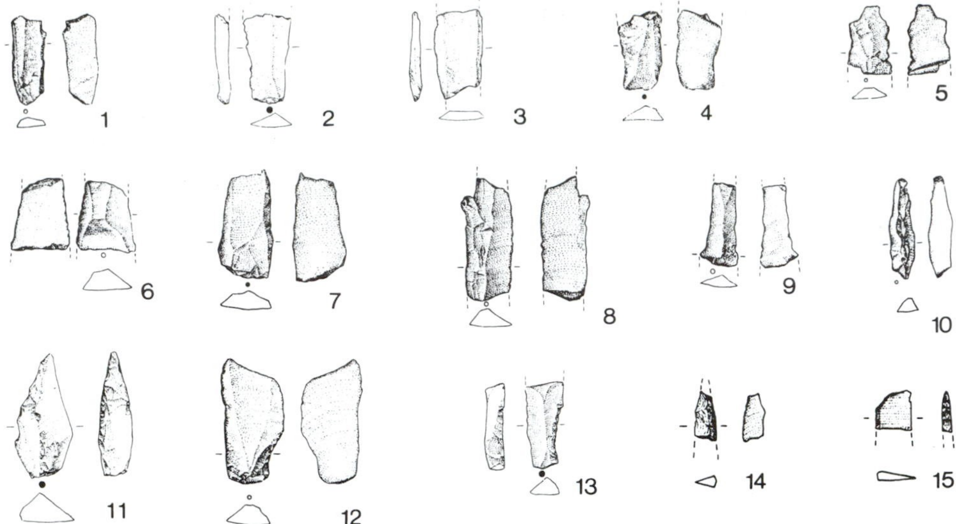


**5.18** Middle Palaeolithic blades from Tönchesberg, western Germany, NC region. The raw material is gray tertiary quartzite and several of the pieces are broken (after Conard 1992:Fig. 43 scale 2:3).
Key:
1–9 Unretouched blades and bladelets
10 Crested blade
11 & 14 Backed point, point tip
12, 13 & 15 Backed blade and bladelets

(Gouédo 1994). This is also the case at Riencourt-les-Bapaume (Tuffreau 1993) where in level CA the phase 3 artifacts in the chaîne opératoire (Table 5.9) are dominated by side scrapers, burins and denticulates (Ameloot-van der Heijden 1994:table 1). The number of retouched pieces is small, n=118, and apart from the burins no Upper Palaeolithic types were produced. At Tönchesberg 2B (Conard 1992) the raw material, unlike at the French sites, is predominantly quartzite. Its flaking properties limit the length of blanks, which it might be thought would favour the production of flakes, yet blades were systematically knapped although only rarely retouched into tools.

Elsewhere in southern France the Abri du Maras in the Ardèche (Moncel 1994) has a strong blade component, but this is part of a levallois reduction sequence. Indeed, blades were often produced, as Geneste (1988b) and Boëda (1988) have shown. What is interesting about this northern group is the extreme elongation of blade blanks. At Rocourt (Otte 1994) the cores are truly prismatic, hence an Upper Palaeolithic technique was employed.

*Organic artifacts*

The evidence for non-lithic technology is limited. There are claims for antler artifacts fractured in a consistent way at Hunas (Groiss, Kaulich and Reisch 1995), although Conard (1992) has shown that similar fracture patterns at

Tönchesberg resulted from pressure by the overlying sediments. However, at Salzgitter-Lebenstedt an unshed reindeer antler has been chopped with a stone tool to create a pick-like implement (Tode 1982:Abb. 123).

The Lehringen yew spear (Thieme and Veil 1985), like the Salzgitter antler pick, was a product of façonnage and a short chaîne opératoire. Preliminary accounts of the older Schöningen spears (Thieme 1997, Thieme and Maier 1995) indicate that they were manufactured in similar ways.

Various, isolated 'symbolic' objects and scratchings on bones have been much discussed (Marshack 1990) but with little agreement as to their function or significance (Chase and Dibble 1987, Davidson and Noble 1989:127, Noble and Davidson 1996). A recent detailed study using microscopy has concluded that most of the oft-cited engraved and pierced pieces are entirely natural (D'Errico and Villa 1997). Among this heterogeneous collection the polished mammoth lamellar from Tata in the southeast region (Marshack 1990:figure 17.11) has attracted the most attention, largely, I suspect, because it is unique.

*Tool maintenance and the big puzzle*

Mobility and the degree to which artifacts are recycled in a curated technology have been examined as a way to understand variation in lithic collections (Binford 1973, 1977, Conard and Adler 1997, Kuhn 1995, Torrence 1983, 1989).

Binford's model proposes two main strategies for hunter-gatherers who are either residentially mobile foragers, or logistically organized collectors (1980). The foragers will replace artifacts when exhausted, while the collectors will replace based on the probability of failure (Kuhn 1989:42). In the latter system individual implements will in fact show less evidence for renewal, resharpening or repair, because they are replaced at a much earlier stage in their life cycle so as to minimize failure (Kuhn 1989:43). Consequently evidence for reuse, as Kuhn points out, does not provide a measure of the extent to which artifacts were maintained or curated, but instead reflects the pattern of mobility and land use.

The Quina Mousterian variant (Turq 1989, 1992b) provides an example. It has the greatest number of retouched implements and uses high-grade, local raw material. For Dibble (1987), the transverse Quina scraper is the final chapter in the life of a retouched tool (Figure 5.19). His expectation (Table 5.11) is that such resharpening conserved valuable imported raw materials, but as we have seen this variant is usually made on local stone (Turq 1992b).

So, before concluding that high resharpening rates indicate a forager approach to artifact replacement we need to consider the combination of factors which affected the frequency of artifact retouch (Kuhn 1995:159). These involved keeping raw materials on hand, which was conditioned by the nature and/or duration of the activities being undertaken. Relevant to any outcome would be the costs involved in obtaining workable stone and whether or not the inventory of tools was transported. Such considerations are important since they

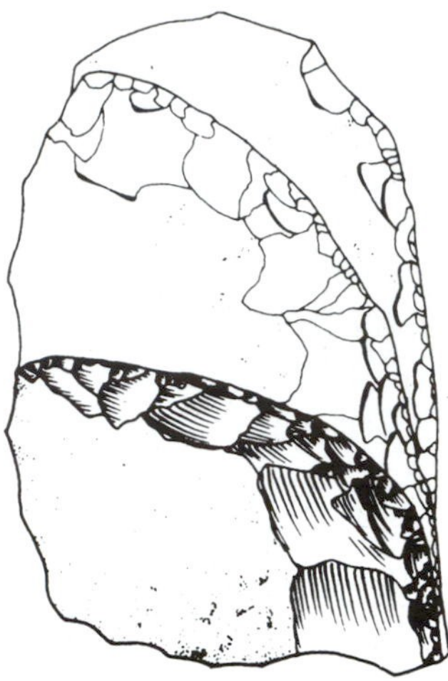

**5.19** The biography of a stone tool (i). Reduction changes the form of the implement from a single-edged to a transverse side scraper (after Dibble 1987).

require a chaîne opératoire that encompasses scales and gestures as divergent as those producing tiny retouching flake as well as hominids moving along the paths of their landscape.

One major strand in this unified approach has been the recent widespread interest in artifact refitting. These studies are aptly named, and well reviewed, in the publication *The Big Puzzle* (Cziesla et al. 1990) and by Cziesla's thorough study of refitting practices and rates (1987).[17] He makes the important distinction (Cziesla 1990:9) that there are three kinds of refit which need to be studied (Figure 5.20). The German terms are not easily translated by a single English word (Cziesla 1987:105).

- Refitting of production sequences (*Aufeinanderpassungen*) This is the reconstruction of the chaîne opératoire/core reduction sequence (e.g. Figure 5.31). This is the most common form of refitting as at Maastricht-Belvédère, Grotte Vaufrey and Biache St. Vaast.
- Refitting broken artifacts (*Aneinanderpassungen*) which may include non-intentional breakages (e.g. Figure 5.18). In the Middle Palaeolithic there are no examples of refitting broken artifacts between distant locales, but several examples of such refittings between and within knapping clusters do occur (Cziesla et al. 1990).
- Refitting artifact modifications (*Anpassungen*), such as resharpenings, to the artifact from which they were removed. These would include tranchet flakes and burin spalls. The numerous (n=2,195) specialized long sharpening flakes at La Cotte (Cornford 1986:Fig. 29.1) are an example, even though only one could be refitted to its implement (*ibid*.: Fig. 29.3).

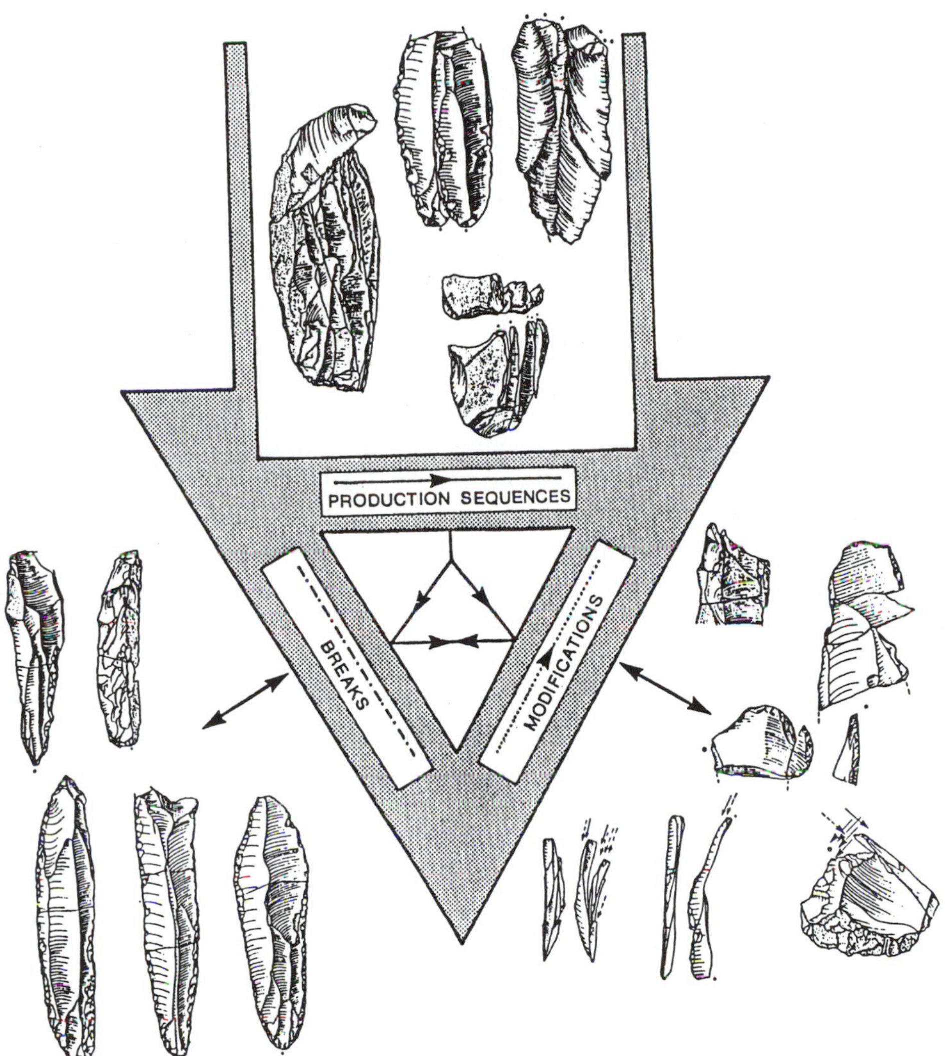


**5.20** The biography of a stone tool (ii). A model of dynamic artifact processes as revealed by refitting (after Cziesla 1990:Fig. 6).

It is still early days for refitting studies and, as we shall see in Chapters 6 and 7, most studies have been undertaken in the later periods. But already some interesting results are emerging. For example, refitting the laminar-based technology at Wallertheim D allowed the reconstruction of a complex retooling event in what appears to be a logistically organized system involving forward planning (Conard and Adler 1997). Roebroeks (et al. 1993:78) have suggested that locales with a high density of lithics and abundant refitting may reflect tool maintenance activities such as core preparation, blank production and their retouching into implements. At such locales we would expect production sequences and modification refits to predominate. Artifactually poor locales with few refittings may relate to specific activities, and here refits of broken artifacts should be more common with some modifications such as resharpenings. This may mark a differentiation of space from earlier locales such as Boxgrove where all three refitting patterns are found (Bergman et al. 1990).

### *Taskscape: skills and the surrounding environment*

How far were these changes in the transfer of raw materials and the organization of technology matched by the skills associated with the use of the environment? In particular, did these innovations result in the colonization of new areas and a wider array of habitats? These are questions for the taskscape where people attend to each other while going about their business. The role of the taskscape concept is to counter the view that the external ecosystem was the dominant force to which Palaeolithic societies had to adapt. By contrast, the taskscape surrounds us and moves with us. While the concept acknowledges the importance of environmental selection on behaviour, it avoids portraying social life as a separate activity (Gamble 1986a:figure 2.1).

#### *At home in the taskscape*

It is during this period that the first movement onto the plains of Russia and the Ukraine took place. The NE region (Figure 3.1) is settled late and the available evidence, admittedly poorly dated, points to its first colonization during the Eemian rather than during the earlier Saalian complex (Hoffecker 1987).[18]

Soffer (1989:724, 1994) has made the case that preferred conditions for Neanderthal people even during the last interglacial/glacial cycle were in those areas of greatest topographic variety. She contrasts the settlement records of the Dnestr and the Middle Desna. The former river runs through broken topography which results in a complex and diversified mix of biotic resources (Soffer 1989). These would represent a comparatively dense 'plaid' in the mammoth steppe mosaic. On the contrary the Middle Desna, represented by the important open-air locale of Khotylevo I (Zavernyaev 1978), where levallois technique and bifacial points are common, is in a flatter, lower-altitude situation. This would be a setting where the mosaic might take on a more zonal, or 'striped', character (Guthrie 1984).

Soffer interprets the environmental contrasts and the archaeological evidence to indicate a more continuous human presence in some parts of the western Russian and Ukrainian plains, and a more sporadic discontinuous presence in others such as the Middle Desna (Soffer 1989:figure 34.5). She develops the following hypothesis:

> since the Russian Plain repeatedly underwent increases in hyperzonality and concomitant decreases in resource diversity during various stadial periods of the early and middle Valdai [Würm/Weichsel], the repeated environmental degradation made resources on

the plain proper far more unpredictable than in the Dnestr–Prut region and in the Crimea. (Soffer 1989:724)

The broken topography of the Crimea (Boriskovsky 1984, Klein 1965), as well as the Caucasus (Baryshnikov and Hoffecker 1994, Liubin 1989), would, according to Soffer's model, also have an impact on the continuity of settlement by concentrating resources which on the plains to the north would be dispersed. Praslov (pers. comm.) has also suggested that settlement was earlier in the Urals which form the eastern boundary to the Russian plain. There were however altitudinal limits to such settlement. Baryshnikov and Hoffecker (in press:11) have found that occupation above 1,000 m in the Caucasus generally dates to after 60 Kyr BP (Chapter 7). However, recent investigations in north Ossetia at Weasel Cave have uncovered a well-stratified 24-m deep sequence of Mousterian occupations that could extend into the Middle Pleistocene. The cave lies at 1,125 m on the edge of a broad plateau (Hidjrati 1995:Fig. 2).

The Russian and Ukrainian evidence supports a model of population ebb and flow at a regional scale. This is not unexpected and seems to have been a feature in all the northern regions (Gamble 1983a, 1986a, Müller-Beck 1988). In England it has often been remarked that the Middle Palaeolithic, so abundantly represented at a varied topographic setting such as La Cotte (Callow and Cornford 1986), is very difficult to find in the less diverse landscapes of the unglaciated parts of southern England (Roe 1981). Moreover, there is the absence of human occupation during OIS 5e in England, although *Hippopotamus* was present in this sub-stage as far north as Yorkshire (Gamble 1986a, Stuart 1982).

In the north-central region the settlement evidence for the Pleniglacial in Germany as opposed to the Early Glacial and Eemian is much sparser. The dating is still not precise enough and OIS 4, the Pleniglacial, may have witnessed, as Auguste has argued for northern France (1995), a reduction in population, rather than total abandonment. This reduction could be measured either by the numbers of permanent residents in the region, or by the frequency with which people used the North European Plain. It is difficult to determine between the two scenarios.

*Optimum habitats*

I have previously argued (Gamble 1984, 1986a, 1986c) that the absence from England of hominids during the climatic optimum of the Eemian (OIS 5e) is a pointer to the structure of the environments they preferred. The mature deciduous forests in the western, and hence most oceanic, part of northern Europe would have resulted in lower densities for prey such as red and roe deer. Larger animals such as aurochs and forest bison would have similarly occurred at lower population numbers and been more dispersed through such a forest landscape. Aggregations into huge herds would have been rare. The numbers and herding patterns of the megafauna, the straight-tusked elephants and forest rhinos, were also affected by the general structure of resources. The effect of the forest was to reduce the predictability and biomass of the mosaics to a point where the expectation for hominids of encountering an animal resource, either dead or alive, declined to a threshold where dietary requirements could not be met without some form of intensification of effort.[19]

I have suggested that we look to changes in the organization of hominid behaviour, particularly social life (Gamble 1993a, Whallon 1989), as the factor which led to an intensification of effort in acquiring resources. But this intensification also had unexpected consequences that resulted both in new colonization and in different settlement histories within previously occupied regions.

*Living in forests*

An alternative viewpoint has been argued by Roebroeks (et al. 1992), Auguste (1995) and Conard (1992). They ignore the global picture of colonization and concentrate instead on the European evidence. This is a mistake as it leads them to conclude that Saalian-age hominids could live anywhere and do anything. Blessed with such powers, their 'decision' to remain in a restricted part of the old world makes them, according to this assessment, even more unusual than they are normally portrayed, since they apparently resisted evolutionary pressure to expand their range.

Roebroeks (et al. 1992) are correct to point out that at the same time that England was inhabited by hippos rather than hominids, people were living around the travertine springs of Weimar or trying to retrieve an elephant which they had, rather carelessly from a retrieval point of view, speared in a lake at Lehringen (Thieme and Veil 1985). But they have also forgotten a simple fact of European climate. In today's interglacial climate the July isotherms are distributed zonally, but in January they follow a meridional pattern. The 0°C isotherm differentiates between today's oceanic and continental provinces (Lockwood 1974:fig. 9.2) which is effectively the boundary between the northwest and north-central province (Figure 3.1). The position of this boundary will be pushed and pulled east and west depending upon the strength of the oceanic effect. During the high sea level interglacials OIS 5e, 9 and 11 (Shackleton 1987) it will therefore move east. During the low sea level interglacials OIS 13 and 7, as well as sub-stages 5c and 5a, it will move west.

The effect of such movement is difficult to predict but there are two areas where a considerable impact must have been felt. In the first place the limiting factor throughout the Pleistocene – interglacial, early glacial, pleniglacial, full glacial – must have been the availability of resources in winter. The movement of the 0°C January isotherm would have affected the length of the winters, reducing resources during the critical survival period. The way to solve the longer periods of environmental hibernation would have been through systematic food storage for which there is no evidence, such as pits, during this period. But secondly, and more importantly, would have been the impact of the isotherm positions on the structure of the mosaic environments. Rather than dense forests the effect of continentality would have been to create mosaic structures and break up the uniform, zonal, production of mature climax forest. This may help Vandenberghe (et al. 1993) out of their local difficulty of explaining why the optimum phase at Maastricht-Belvédère fits better into the climatic conditions of OIS 5e than into OIS 7 where the TL and ESR dates would place it.

Concentrating attention on these three interglacials, OIS 11, 9 and 5e, which account for only 8 per cent of the Middle and Upper Pleistocene, does however raise the question of how we assess hominid habitat preferences with these data. On the one hand we have the environmental vocabulary of climax forest, while on the other we have the ecological descriptions of mosaic habitats with stripes and plaids. The two do not mix easily. It is rare to see a pollen diagram turned into an ecological assessment of plant productivity. Instead we are treated to zonal maps of the continent at specific moments such as the Eemian (Roebroeks, Conard and Kolfschoten 1992:fig. 3, van Andel 1996), where any site north of the Alps must have been buried by trees (Figure 5.6).

Until these problems of identifying how the ecological structures varied are addressed, we can do little to resolve this argument to anyone's satisfaction (Gamble 1992c). I would suggest however that what we might discover, and what the evidence will currently bear as an interpretation, is that these Saalian hominids had skills which could be readily transferred from one environment and resource setting to another, but that these were still limited by social factors as expressed through gesture and material transfers on a routine and often immediate basis.

Hence I still expect to find archaeological evidence for the ebb and flow of population within these larger mosaic environments. But it may be that the scale at which we can presently investigate the data means that we can only see such shifts in the demographic distribution between the north, south and Mediterranean provinces. This would also include a west-to-east basis, as demonstrated to most people's satisfaction by the late colonization of the Russian and Ukrainian Plains.

*Living with the carnivore guild*

These broad environmental patterns are important since it is within these that individuals created their taskscapes. Furthermore, these surrounding environments also exerted selection pressure on action and performance. In order to carry this argument forward let me turn to another body of evidence, the geographical distribution of carnivores, to help characterize some of these selection factors in the taskscapes of Neanderthals.

The presence of carnivore activity is sometimes seen as a negative feature of the archaeological record because of their destructive powers. However, their presence provides an opportunity to understand the selection pressures upon hominid behaviour in contrasted ecological settings (Binford 1981b, Gamble 1983b, 1984, 1995e). In particular, we can consider the question of the hominid

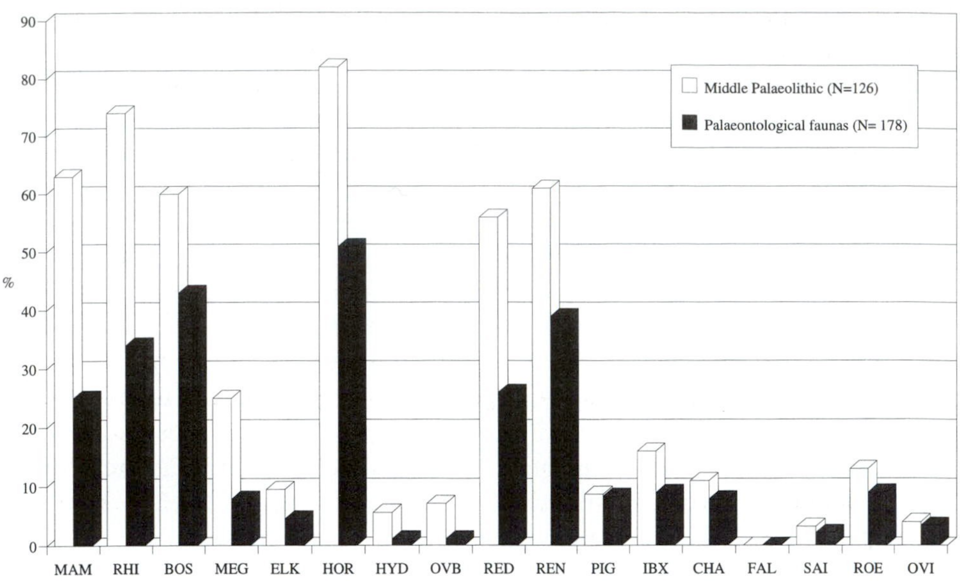


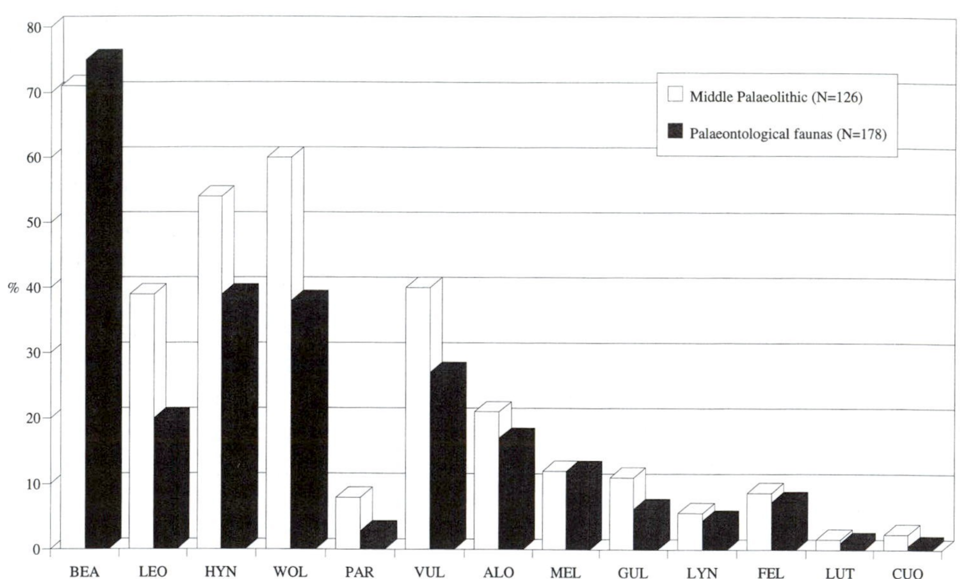


**5.21** A comparison of the frequency with which herbivore (A) and carnivore (B) species occur in faunal assemblages from caves in the NC region. The histograms contrast assemblages where Middle Palaeolithic artifacts are present (c. 100–40 Kyr BP) with palaeontological collections where they are not (c. 100–10Kyr). Human activity corresponds to richer resources as measured by the frequency with which taxa occur (after Gamble 1995e:Figs. 2, 5, 8 and 9).

niche within the carnivore guild of the Middle Palaeolithic. To do this we need to examine wider distributions and frequencies of taxa.

Elsewhere (Gamble 1995e) I have argued that our data, coarse as it is, can provide us at a regional scale with a measure of community richness. Figure 5.21 shows the frequency with which the large mammals occur in 126 faunal assemblages dated to the Middle Palaeolithic in the north-central region of Europe (Figure 3.1). Judging by the frequency with which lion, hyena and wolf are present in the faunas, we will have widespread carnivore involvement in the creation and modification of these faunas. While these figures are simply presence/absence data, they nonetheless remind us just how rich and diverse animal communities were in northern Europe. In these 126 assemblages there are on average 5 herbivore and 3.4 large carnivore species. It is instructive to compare these figures with 178 faunal assemblages that are not associated with any obvious human activity in the form of lithics (Figure 5.21). The average number of herbivores declines to 2.72. The carnivores display a smaller decline to 2.5 species per palaeontological assemblage.

These samples, scattered across a wide geographical area and through c. 70 Kyr, OIS 5d–4, are obviously coarse data. But what they suggest is that we are monitoring relative resource richness. Within their taskscapes the hominids are competing with the major carnivores in areas of the highest prey biomass. These areas are tightly focused rather than widely distributed through the landscape, a key component of the environmental mosaic. This in turn suggests an environment which would select for specific skills in the social act of subsistence.

Stiner has suggested (1993) that evolutionary success lay with that member of the carnivore guild who responded to selection pressure by increasing its take of prime-aged resources. Hominids are most likely to have met this pressure by changing their social technology, one facet of which would have been the way they used their taskscapes. All members of the carnivore guild had specialized food-getting skills which could be transferred from one habitat to another. However, only the Neanderthals had the opportunity to externalize and extend such skills through material acts which required longer chains of action and time–space distanciation (Chapter 2). Let us now briefly examine the evidence for this move to specialized, prime-aged hunting as an example of the skills which created the taskscapes of the Middle Palaeolithic.

**5.21** (*cont.*)
Key:
Herbivores
MAM = woolly mammoth, RHI = woolly rhino, BOS = aurochs or bison, MEG = *Megaceros*, ELK = *Alces*, HOR = horse, HYD = steppe ass, OVB = musk ox, RED = red deer, REN = reindeer, PIG = wild pig, IBX = *Capra*, CHA = *Rupicapra*, FAL = *Dama*, SAI = saiga, ROE = *Capreolus*, OVI = *Ovis*.
Carnivores
BEA = bear, LEO = lion, HYN = hyena, WOL = wolf, PAR = leopard, VUL = fox, ALO = arctic fox, MEL = badger, GUL = wolverine, LYN = lynx, FEL = wild cat, LUT = otter, CUO = dhole.

*Specializing in animals: an example of emerging specific skills*

It is noticeable that during the Saalian period the character of bone assemblages changes (Mellars 1996). The uncertainty over the association between animal bones and human activity diminishes markedly. There are three main types of occurrence we need to consider (see Gaudzinski 1995 for full discussion).

- open locales and fissure sites where faunal remains are abundant, often well preserved and characterized by low species diversity and high dominance by one taxon (Table 5.12)
- open locales, such as Neumark-Nord (Mania et al. 1990), where a single animal is more closely associated with stone artifacts (discussed above)
- palimpsest sites, typically caves, where there is a variable amount of carnivore and human activity (discussed below, section Locales).

The evidence for direct human intervention in the form of either cut marks or intentional bone fracture with distinctive impact scars is very common. Moreover, the large bone collections from open locales allow the reconstruction of age profiles for the prey species. When this is combined with observations on anatomical-part representation and evidence of carnivore damage through gnawing, it is possible to examine aspects of how hominids managed these resources, particularly from the point of view of mobility and transport (Stiner 1994). These changes also raise the issue of the transference of these food-management skills to different species and in contrasted resource settings. At issue is the extent of their knowledge in this vital area and its transmission between individuals.

*Hunting and scavenging as different levels of skill*

We now have a definition of hunting that depends less on the ability to kill animals and more on the planning and organization of people and technology in time and space (Gamble 1993a:117–23). The degree of anticipation, or planning depth, can be shown by aspects of behaviour involving curation, storage and the use of facilities (Binford 1980, 1989b, Kelly 1983, Torrence 1983, 1989). These skills are often regarded as specialized in that increases in planning depth require ever greater amounts of knowledge about the behaviour of particular prey. This escalation of knowledge either adds to security (Binford 1991) or reduces risk (Torrence 1983) and is manifest in the design and tactical disposition of technology (see discussion above of Kuhn 1989). This knowledge reduces search time, because the hunter knows where to go, and technology assures a higher success rate and so lowers time spent in pursuit.

Scavenging on the other hand is mostly seen as a searching strategy with low investment in technology (Gamble 1987) and, in Binford's (1980) terms, mapping onto resources akin to foraging for plants. The density and availability of resources is what matters.

It has, however, been apparent for some time that these terms are unhelpful when posed as behavioural opposites to characterize past hominid adaptations

Table 5.12. *Specialized animal faunas of Saalian/Eemian and early Weichselian age (Auguste 1992, Gabori-Csank 1968, Gaudzinski 1992, 1995, Hoffecker, Baryshnikov and Potapova 1991, Jaubert et al. 1990, Patou-Mathis 1993, Conard 1995, Delpech 1988, Gamble 1995d, Jaubert 1994, Klein and Cruz-Uribe 1994, Kleinschmidt 1953).*

| Site | Layer | Archaeology | Region | OIS age | No. of IDs | No. of carnivore species/bones | No. of herbivore species/bones | Dominant species | % of identified bones | MNI |
|---|---|---|---|---|---|---|---|---|---|---|
| Coudoulous I | 4 | Mousterian | SW | 6 | | | | Bison | 98 | 94 |
| La Borde | | Mousterian | SW | 6 | 440 | 1/10 | 4/430 | Aurochs | 93 | |
| Il'skaya | | Mousterian | NE | 5d–4 | 1,446 | 5/35 | 7/1,411 | Bison | 92 | 51 |
| El Castilló | 19–22 | Mousterian | SW | 4 | 1,222 | 0/0 | 3/1,222 | Horse | 91 | 60 |
| Erd | | Mousterian | SE | 4 | 14,862 | 9/13,699 | 12/1,163 | Bear | 89 | c.480 |
| Wallertheim | E | Mousterian | NC | 5c | >190 | 2/? | 2/? | Bovid | c.85 | |
| Wallertheim | F | Mousterian | NC | 5c | >467 | 2/? | 4/? | Horse | c.78 | |
| Wallertheim | B1 | Mousterian | NC | 5d | 1,131 | 3/3 | 5/1,128 | Bison | 76 | 52 |
| Grotte Vaufrey | VIII | Mousterian | SW | 6 | 1,009 | 6/109* | 5/894 | Red deer | 74 | |
| Salzgitter-Lebenstedt | | Upper Acheulean | NC | 5d–4 | | 1/? | 5/? | Reindeer | 72 | c.80 |
| Wallertheim | All | Mousterian | NC | 5d | 2,436 | 3/86 | 7/2,350 | Bison | 67 | |
| Stadel | VIII | Mousterian | NC | 5 | 1,608 | 11/1,200 | 9/468 | Horse | 56 | |
| Abri des Canalettes | 3 | Mousterian | SW | 5a | 1,222 | 7/38 | 9/1,184 | Red deer | 53 | 19 |
| Biache St. Vaast | II base | Mousterian | NW | 7–6 | 435 | 2/92 | 8/343 | Bovid | 48 | 8 |
| Abri des Canalettes | 2 | Mousterian | SW | 5a | 382 | 2/6 | 9/376 | Red deer | 47 | 11 |
| El Castilló | 24–26 | Acheulean | SW | 6? | 579 | 2/150 | 7/429 | Red deer | 36 | 33 |

*Note:*
* does not include bear. MNI = Minimum number of individuals

(Brugal and Jaubert 1991). They are both part of a system of transferable skills with the difference being the time necessary to learn them. The forager searching for carcasses may also be searching for animals to kill. The resource, dead or alive, is the affordance along that search track. When encountered, the next decision is to exploit it, or not, and this will depend upon a wide array of factors inherent in that gathering. There may be lions on the kill, or the deer may take off at speed and elude the hunter.

The difference in skill between a dedicated hunter and a full-time scavenger, if such categories exist, is a spatial one. Where in the landscape are the live resources habitually found? And if they are missing, which is the next locale to visit on the track? Binford's (1980) distinction between the pin-pointed resources of the collector, and the generalized distributions of resources used by the forager, makes the distinction neatly since it does not imply an evolutionary trajectory, but merely an organizational response to differing regional circumstances.

*Hunters of prime-aged animals at open locales*

In a recent review Stiner has reminded us that 'virtually all foragers will make seasonal or local (i.e. short term) adjustments to food availability' (Stiner 1992:447), and if these involve concentrating upon a particular taxon then specialization is automatically produced.

Specialization, in this narrow sense, was very clearly a property of Neanderthal food-management strategies (Auguste 1993:table 1, Chase 1989, 1995, Gaudzinski 1992, Mellars 1996). However, as Stiner has also argued (1994), the evolution of the hominid niche within the guild of large Pleistocene carnivores was as an intercept hunter of prime-aged prey. Only lion among the other large carnivores takes prime condition animals (*ibid*.:table 11.3). Hyena and wolf mostly kill the young and the old (Stiner 1994).

There is growing evidence that Neanderthals not only concentrated upon particular taxa (Table 5.12) but that they also regularly took prime-aged prey. Gaudzinski (1995, 1992) has shown this with a comparison of three sites, Wallertheim B1, La Borde (Jaubert et al. 1990) and Il'skaya (Hoffecker, Baryshnikov and Potapova 1991). At Wallertheim she was able to show that the remains of horse, the second most abundant species, were not present as a result of human activity. The old-animal age profile and the lack of human modification on the *Equus* bones point to other agencies such as lions or wolves (Gaudzinski 1995:62). This important finding must make us cautious in interpreting faunal asemblages where such detailed taphonomic studies have not been undertaken.

As Table 5.12 shows, there are also a further number of locales with large faunal collections where one taxon dominates. At the open locale of Erd in the southeast region, the abundant cave-bear remains are probably the remains of a hibernation den since many neonate cubs were identified. The dominant herbivore taxon was horse which accounts for 44 per cent of all non-bear bones.

Table 5.13. *Proportions of butchered bone from Biache St. Vaast (Auguste 1992:Table 2), Taubach (Bratlund pers. comm.) and Grotte Lazaret (Valensi 1991).*

| | Number of identified specimens | % of specimens with butchery information |
|---|---|---|
| *Biache* | | |
| Aurochs | 9,771 | 31 |
| Bear | 7,013 | 35 |
| Rhino | 3,151 | 19 |
| *Taubach* | | |
| Bear | 1,557 | 19 |
| Rhino | 1,224 | 8 |
| *Lazaret* | | |
| Red deer | 2,855 | 9 |

However, at Taubach (Bratlund pers. comm.) and Biache (Auguste 1988), not only is bear common, but there are significant numbers of cut marks and intentional fracturing of its bones (Table 5.13). The Erd fauna should also be examined for such evidence.

The proportions of butchered bone at Biache (Table 5.13) appear high. However, at Grotte Lazaret, Valensi (1991) regards the proportion of red deer butchered bone as low (Table 5.13). But all of these figures are high when we compare them with the absence of cut marks at some older locales with well-preserved fauna, such as Miesenheim I, which I reviewed in the previous chapter. What needs to be resolved in future comparisons is whether the higher incidence of hominid butchery also coincides with prime-aged profiles for particular, well-represented taxa at selected locales.

At La Borde, aurochs (*Bos primigenius*) comprise 93 per cent of the assemblage which numbers 440 identified remains and contains only 4 other species.[20] A minimum number (MNI) of forty individuals is represented by the aurochs teeth. Size criteria point to a concentration on females among the adult classes. The age of the animals (Figure 5.22) indicates a prime-dominated mortality pattern (Stiner 1994:figure 10.2) which, as Gaudzinski shows, is also the case at Wallertheim B1 and Il'skaya (Gaudzinski 1992, 1995).[21] She notes that at these locales carnivore activity was very low. There is no carnivore gnawing at Biache (Auguste 1992:61) and over 90 per cent of the aurochs (n=9771) are prime-aged adults (*ibid.*:Fig. 4).

At all these locales, repeated gatherings by hominids focusing on one or two prey animals and selected age/sex classes have produced a prime-aged assemblage.

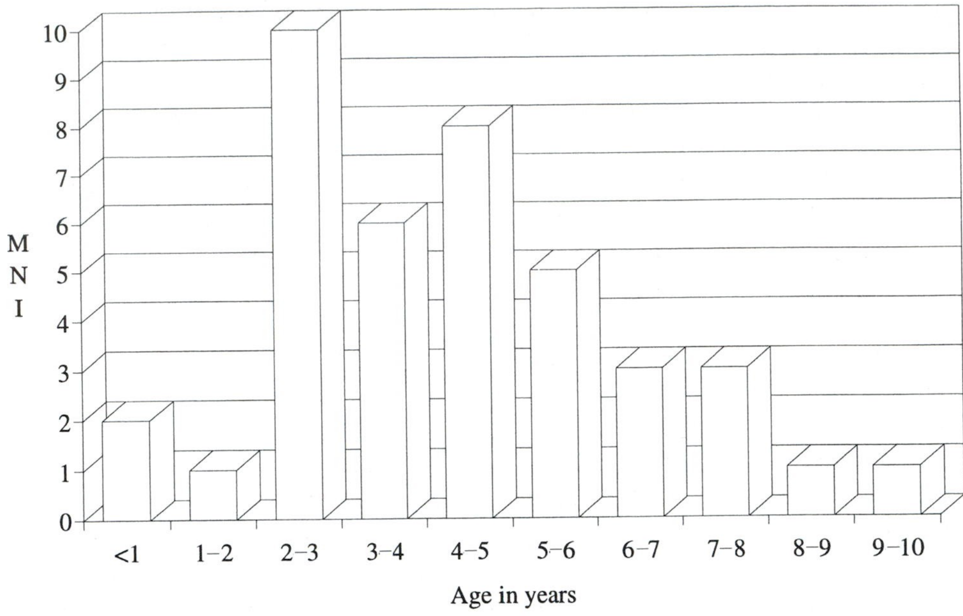


**5.22** The mortality profile of prime-aged aurochs (*Bos primigenius*) from La Borde, France, SW region (after Jaubert et al. 1990:Fig. 46).
KEY:
MNI = Minimum Number of Individuals

*Neanderthal skills*

We now have an answer to our first question – what environments could Neanderthals cope with? This has been answered by examining the changed rhythms in this period of movement, making and acquiring resources. Attention has been placed on the physical nature of the surrounding environment and the selective pressures for amended and novel forms of action which this brought to bear as hominids created their taskscapes. As a result we can see that the range of habitats within the nine regions (Figure 3.1) has indeed increased beyond what might be expected due to factors such as younger sites and better preservation. We shall see below in the section on locales if this increase also included specific social skills. However, we can note here from the section on social technology that Neanderthals appear to have become prime-age hunters *without* developing an external system of symbols that either were inscribed on the landscape, to form a context for a social occasion, or involved objects at gatherings.

This conclusion does not mean that prime-age hunting lacked a social dimension. In fact the action of being social was embodied in the gestures and negotiations which were needed to meet the elementary conditions of existence worked out in the taskscape. But food-management strategies, like raw-material provisioning, were not just economic activities where behaviour was constrained by costs and benefits, supply and demand. Neither were they simply a series of technical acts related only to the function of satisfying and avoiding hunger.

In comparison with the first Europeans (Chapter 4), the rhythms of Neanderthal life lengthened and multiplied the chaînes opératoires (Geneste 1990, 1991), increased the distance over which materials were transferred and, as the faunal evidence shows, built alternative ways to manage food resources. Hence, the picture which now emerges of Middle Palaeolithic diet and niche is one of varied response as skills were transferred and elaborated to circumstances, rather than simple predictable strategies.

The transferable skill was still *being* social. It was not tool making, ambush hunting, planning depth or specific knowledge of the seasons and resources. The skill was based on engagement with, rather than analysis of, the world in which an individual lived. These skills were transferred to the exploitation of different species (Table 5.12) and different climates, habitats and regions within Middle Palaeolithic Europe and beyond to the wider Neanderthal world (Stringer and Gamble 1993:figure 1). We will examine below whether they led to specific skills and hence highly variable societies (Regions) as well as the formation of social occasions and places (Locales).

## Regions

Neanderthal societies, like Neanderthal subsistence, are usually expected to follow a standard pattern with little variation beyond adaptation to ecological conditions. Regional patterns in flint working and typology may be seen as culturally determined – for example, the Quina versus the Denticulate Mousterians competing for the rock shelters of the Perigord (Bordes 1973) – but the implication is that beneath such surface features societies were very similar. We will now examine this question of variation using the network model (Table 2.8) applied at a regional scale.

### *Landscapes of habit*

The transfer of skills, which made Neanderthals so successful in their long-term occupation of a diverse continent, was achieved by individuals negotiating their effective networks more intensively. It stemmed from their use of the appropriate resources of emotion and materials, as expressed through gesture embedded in temporal rhythms. These rhythms flowed from attention to others who were part of the mutual environment, the taskscape, which surrounded and moved with each individual. This intensification can be identified through the diversity of rhythms which were now available for structuring action. The evidence from social technology points to complex patterns not only of making and maintaining artifacts within contemporary episodes (Conard and Adler 1997) but also in the acquisition of materials – stone and animal – involving a wider circuit of movement and relationships (Féblot-Augustins 1997, Floss 1994, Kuhn 1995).

Some of the measures of variation, notably raw-material transfers, can in part be explained by ecology (see above). Yet beyond this, regional patterns in the use of material resources (Table 2.8) clearly exist, which indicate that Neanderthal societies did vary across Europe. Féblot-Augustins (1993:239) has described the pattern of transfers as star-shaped in the SW region and predominantly linear in her sample from the NC region. The latter is particularly linear in northeastern Hungary where distances of 100 km are concerned (Féblot-Augustins 1997:Figure 56). She also notes that the few examples of distances greater than 100 km traverse the Carpathian watersheds, while those below this threshold are always within a circumscribed geographical unit (Féblot-Augustins 1993:240, Kozlowski 1994). Féblot-Augustins argues for north–south movements of Neanderthal populations who are apparently sticking to similar, rather than moving to exploit complementary, habitats such as plains and uplands (1993:249). However it is also the case that most of these large distances fall in the period 60–40 Kyr, and this will be discussed further in Chapter 6.

Geneste provides a more detailed assessment of the Aquitaine, star-shaped patterns (Figure 5.23). Based on data from the Grotte Vaufrey level VIII he reconstructs a procurement territory around the cave of 3,000 km$^2$ (1988b:464). His conclusion about the palimpsest of visits and activities represented in the sample from level VIII illustrates the character of the Neanderthal landscape of habit:

> L'hypothèse d'un seul groupe revenant régulièrement ne nous semble pas particulièrement s'adapter à un nomadisme spontané tel que nous le concevons pour ces populations paléolithiques anciennes. Les vestiges lithiques de la couche VIII peuvent témoigner d'occupations fugaces dans le temps et dans l'espace laissés par de petits groupes humains en quête de subsistance, pour lesquels l'approvisionnement de matières premières ne semblait pas être le souci majeur au vu de leur extrême maîtrise des techniques de débitage, de l'existence délibérée des artisans en matière de choix des supports et de leur facilité à abandonner dans cette cavité des produits débités et leur équipement. (1988b:464)

Kuhn's study (1995, 1991, 1992) of Mousterian assemblages from a number of Italian caves can also be used to shed light on my concept of the landscape of habit. His analysis showed that these also involved short-distance transfers where the availability of raw material, and its suitability, is reflected in the degree to which cores were exploited or thrown away when serviceable flakes could still be detached. Kuhn makes the useful heuristic distinction between provisioning people and provisioning places with implements and raw materials (Kuhn 1992:191). His expectation is that the frequency of residential moves, and the availability of good raw materials, will determine the extent to which tools are carried and cores exploited rather than the intensity of retouch on implements (1991).

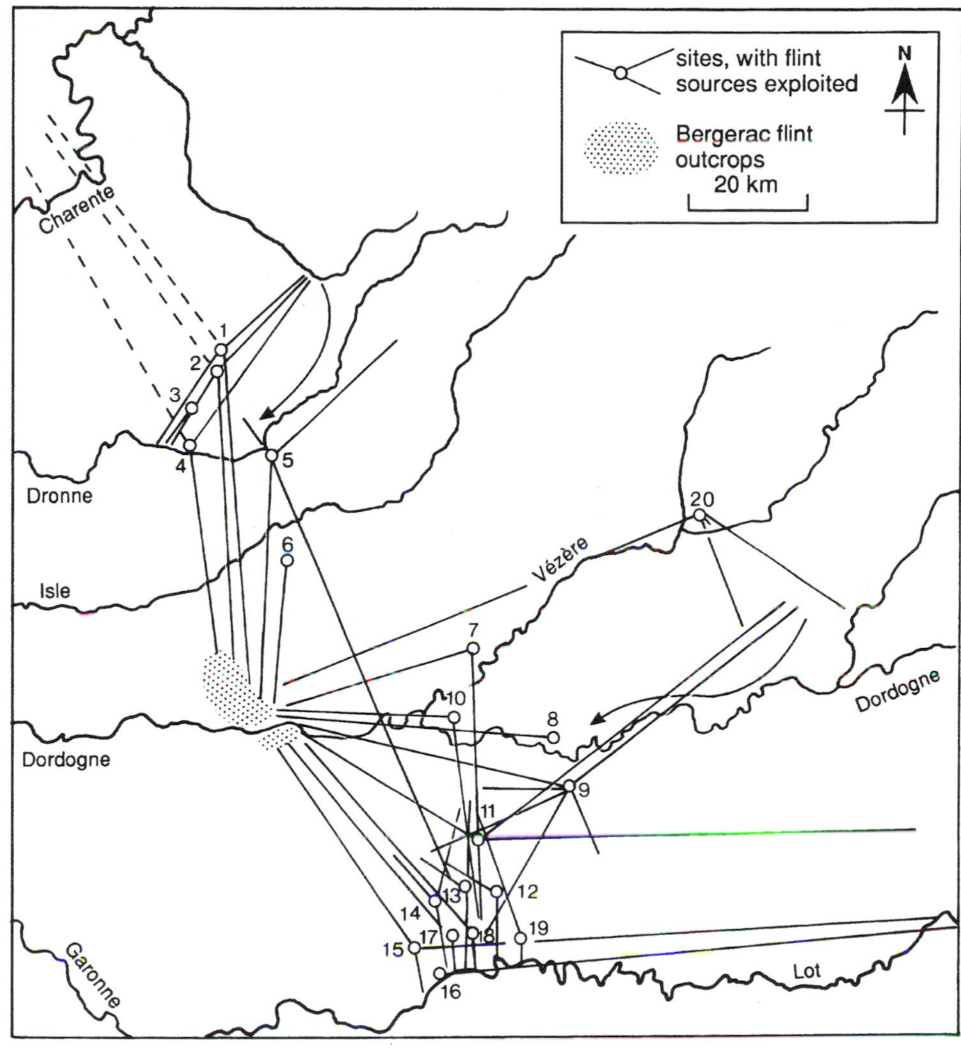


**5.23** The pattern of raw-material transfers in Aquitaine, France, SW region (after Geneste 1989, Mellars 1996:Fig. 5.5).
KEY:

| | |
|---|---|
| 1 Sandougne | 14 La Burlade |
| 2 Abri Brouillaud | 15 Plateau Cabrol |
| 3 Le Roc | 16 Moulin de Milieu |
| 4 Fonseigner | 17 Las Pélénos |
| 5 Les Festons | 18 Les Ardailloux |
| 6 Coursac | 19 La Grave |
| 7 Le Moustier | 20 La Chapelle-aux-Saints |
| 8 Le Dau | |
| 9 Grotte Vaufrey | |
| 10 Roc de Marsal | |
| 11 La Plane | |
| 12 La Lizonne | |
| 13 Ségala | |

Within this long period of time there are also changes. Geneste (1990) identifies the Eemian as an important watershed. Before this local materials dominate and few implements are carried. After the last interglacial there is some spatial extension based, he argues, on a greater anticipation of needs. Raw materials now came from further away and correspond to evidence for larger subsistence territories generally. However, I would agree with Kuhn's conclusion:

> data from Europe . . . clearly suggest that Neanderthals . . . regularly carried tools as a hedge against unforeseen, generalized needs. Evidence for more complex, long-term strategies such as the provisioning of occupations with cores or raw materials is elusive. (Kuhn 1992:206)

I support this dynamic view of how Neanderthals used their landscape. Geneste identifies that all-important, but rarely stated, connection between the spatial scales in the chaîne opératoire where the gestures involved in procurement and production are intimately linked as the body moves within its surrounding environment. Neanderthal technology was expressed, as a social act, in more complex chaînes and through elaborated gestures such as the recurrent levallois technique. Raw materials were drawn from more sources and from further afield. Consequently the act of making artifacts reflected the wider networks which constituted a Neanderthal society through the actions of individuals in gatherings at particular locales. In this respect the pattern noted by Geneste (1989:83), that levallois débitage is commonly on those raw materials which have been transferred furthest, is of considerable interest. The widespread appearance of levallois during the Saalian points to different and more extensive patterns of personal mobility than in the earlier Cromer and Holstein periods (Chapter 4).

But even so, the dimensions of the Neanderthal landscape of habit, and the length of their chaînes opératoires that we can reconstruct from either procurement or production sequences, are small. A good example of this is provided by the study of the modes of lithic exploitation (Table 5.14) in the early Middle Palaeolithic of Europe (Figure 5.24).

These modes illustrate the effect of distance on chaînes opératoires. Notice how only the products of mode 8, blanks and tools with no primary waste or nodules, are found above 11 km from source. Many of these mode 8 elements will be levallois products.

Within the regional scale represented here by the landscape of habit and measured by raw-material transfers, the effective networks of individuals structure the degree to which social life was extended. I therefore conclude that life was still very local and usually immediate. This is borne out by the scale of activity (Figure 5.23) as well as by the immediacy of the taskscape evidence from such gatherings as Gröbern (see below). The dimensions of the landscape of habit, as discussed in Chapter 3, were rarely exceeded (Figure 5.14), as indicated by the lack of materials, other than stone, which were transferred over any distance.

Table 5.14. *The eight modes of lithic exploitation (Féblot-Augustins 1997:24–5 and Table 1).*

| | Quantitative | | |
|---|---|---|---|
| Qualitative | Unmodified stock | Impoverished stock | Enriched stock |
| Complete chaîne opératoire | Mode 1<br>all phases of artifact manufacture | Mode 2<br>all phases of artifact manufacture but no blanks and tools | Mode 3<br>all phases of artifact manufacture with an excess of blanks and tools |
| Chaîne opératoire slightly incomplete | Mode 4<br>roughing out, preparation and primary flaking | | |
| Chaîne opératoire mostly incomplete | Mode 5<br>waste from blank production, blanks present | Mode 6<br>waste from blank production, but no blanks | Mode 7<br>waste from blank production with an excess of blanks and tools |
| Chaîne opératoire represented only by intentional products of débitage | Mode 8<br>no production, presence of blanks and tools only | | |

*Social landscape*

Nor can I see additional evidence to argue for a more elaborate social landscape than we encountered for the earlier period (Chapter 4). Certainly there are a few instances of longer raw-material transfers, but the signs of extension beyond the routinization of behaviour are lacking. Familiar gestures carried forward the bulk of their lives within a landscape of habitual action. There are no signs that some of that routinization was now being externalized through symbols and the inscription of place and landscape and so adding to the surrounding environment through which they moved and created and which created them. Their extended networks remained largely unnegotiated and undeveloped. The wider ramifications of social life were carried by the resources available to the effective network (Table 2.8). The degree to which these resources were used differentially in the production of Neanderthal society strongly suggests that our second question – did Neanderthal societies vary across Europe? – must be answered positively, thereby suggesting a hitherto unexpected complexity in their social lives.

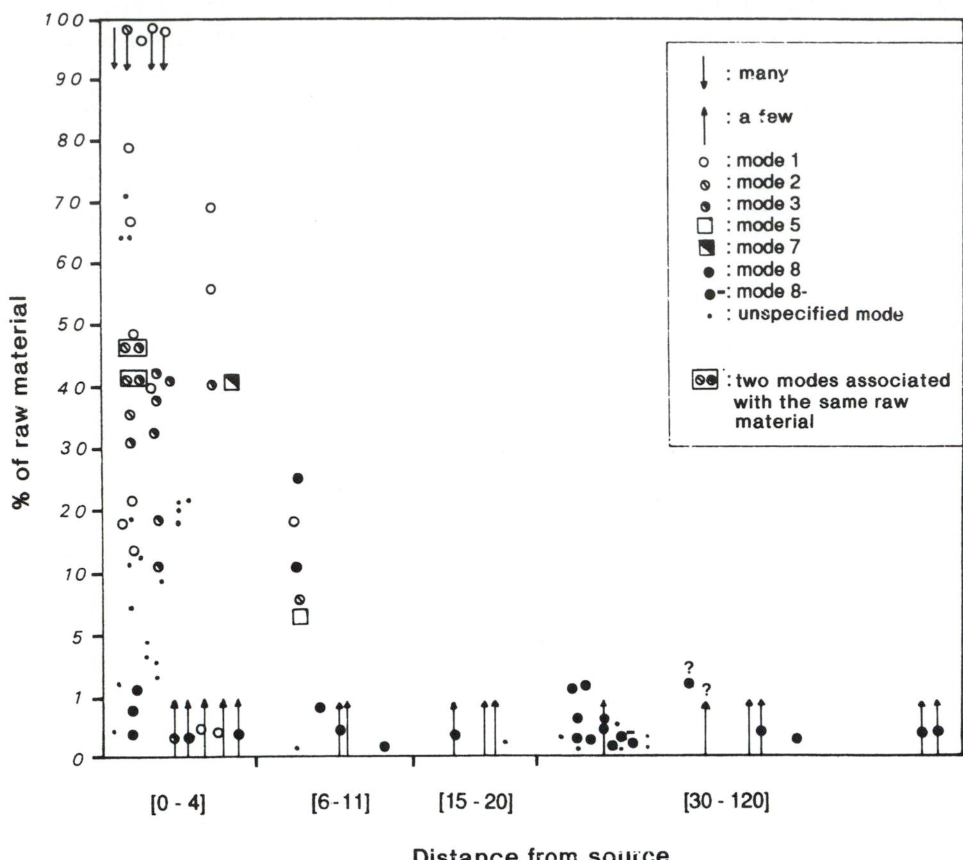


**5.24** Quantity of raw materials and different modes of lithic exploitation in relation to distance in Early Middle Palaeolithic assemblages in Europe; see also Table 5.14 for description of the modes (after Féblot-Augustins 1997:Fig. 37).

## Locales

But what of the details of Neanderthal social life at the level of the locale? How different was it, if at all, from the earlier periods reviewed in the previous chapter when we looked in detail at Bilzingsleben? I will examine this question by describing the evidence from gatherings at carcasses and carnivore caves before examining by contrast the OIS 7 locale of Maastricht-Belvédère (Roebroeks 1988, 1993) and the spatial evidence from the Grotte Vaufrey (Rigaud and Geneste 1988). At this level of detail we have a greater chance of establishing the complex character of Neanderthal social life and addressing our third question – was this based upon spoken language?

### *Gatherings at carcasses*

We encountered the second type of faunal occurrence in the earlier period, for example at Notarchirico (Chapter 4). We have already seen some of the

Neanderthal evidence for such isolated gatherings from Neumark-Nord, as opposed to the repeated visits described in the previous section. Also in eastern Germany are the comparable locales of Lehringen (Thieme and Veil 1985) and Gröbern (Erfurt and Mania 1990, Heussner and Weber 1990). These are dated to OIS 5e and both are lakeside settings. The factual details of the Lehringen find are sketchy. No plans exist from the 1948 salvage dig of the skeleton and the position of the spear which the elephant is said to be lying on.[22] Since wood floats and the elephant lies in lake muds, it is conceivable that the water brought two unrelated items together.

The excavations at Lehringen and Gröbern produced approximately twenty-five and twenty-seven stone tools, respectively. At Lehringen these are mostly levallois flakes although one piece is tentatively reconstructed as the broken butt of a handaxe (Thieme and Veil 1985:Abb. 12). None of these artifacts could be refitted. Two raw materials are differentiated.

At Gröbern, the plan shows artifacts lying in close association with the elephant skeleton (Figure 5.25). There are at least five raw materials present (Heussner and Weber 1990). When plotted against the elephant skeleton, it is apparent that raw material types 1 and 5 have mutually exclusive distributions whereas 2, 3 and 4 overlap with these and with each other. There are no retouched pieces and none of the artifacts is reported as refitting.

At La Cotte very few stones were found among the two bone piles in levels 3 and 6 (Scott 1986a). These were protected by the ravine overhang and buried in loess. Preservation of the bones and their surfaces was extremely poor. In the two heaps (Figure 5.26) the numbers of identifiable bones recovered are shown in Table 5.15.

The five rhinos are young individuals while the mammoths span a greater age range but without any very young or old individuals (Scott 1986b:figure 13.18). Scott (1986a:183) makes the case that the headland at La Cotte (Fig 5.27) was used for two separate gatherings when a small herd of prime mammoths accompanied by a few rhinos was driven over the cliff. Selected bones were then dragged up beneath the overhang.

*Carnivore caves*

Limestone caves and rock shelters also contain evidence for single and repeated gatherings. However, they can also contain evidence for carnivore activity, producing a palimpsest where it is difficult to filter out the human component (Brugal and Jaubert 1991). Even in levels where stone tools are abundant the association between hominids and fauna can be problematic. For example, at Grotte Vaufrey cut marks are absent while gnaw marks are common (Binford 1988).

These problems have been studied by Stiner (1994) for four Middle Palaeolithic caves in Latium in the Mediterranean central region. She employs a suite of evidence to discriminate between assemblages used exclusively by either hominids or carnivores, primarily hyenas and wolves, and situations where the frequency suggests, but cannot prove, which was the major agent

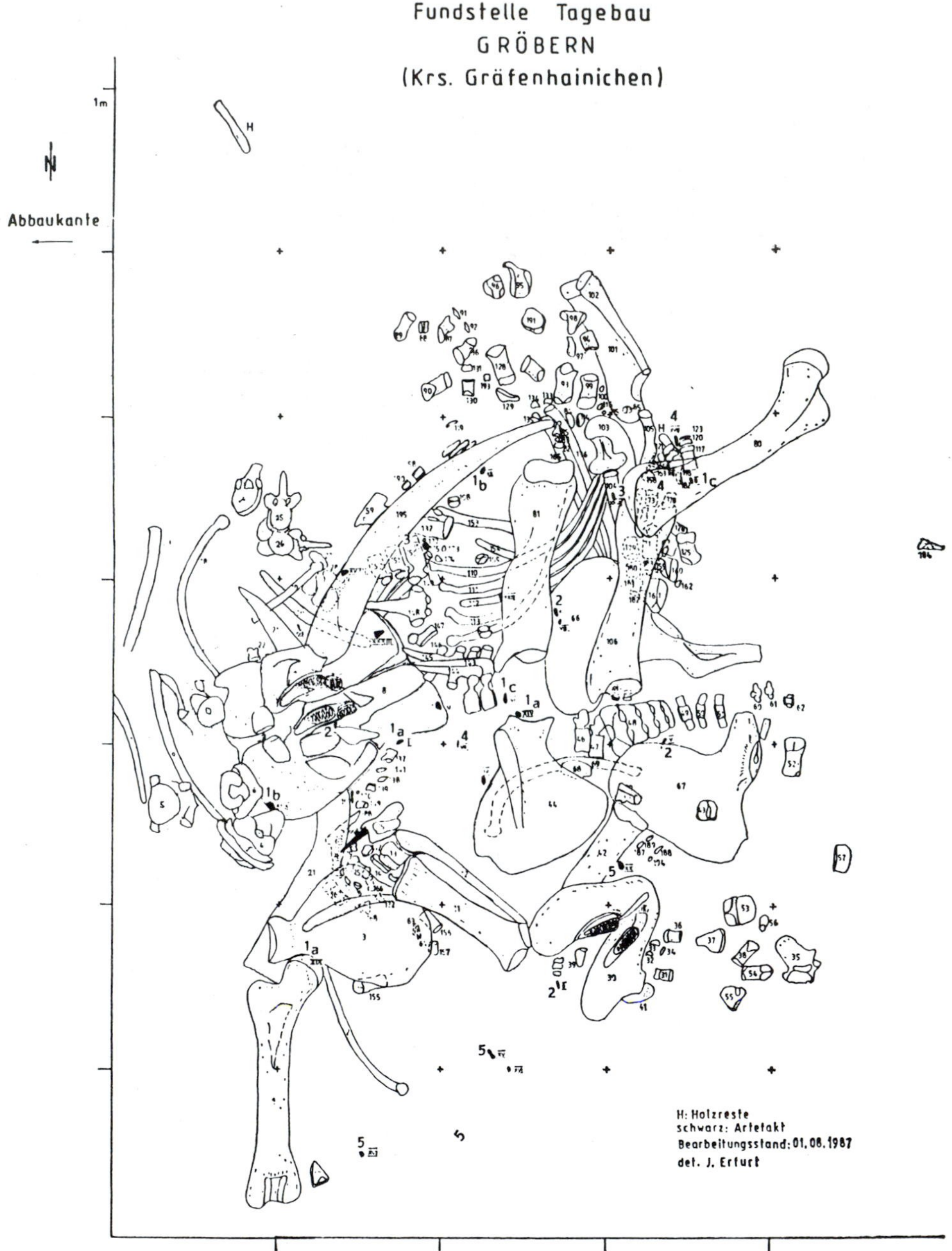


**5.25** The elephant from Gröbern, Germany, NC region. Artifacts are shown in black and the five different raw materials are numbered (after Heussner and Weber 1990:Abb. 1).

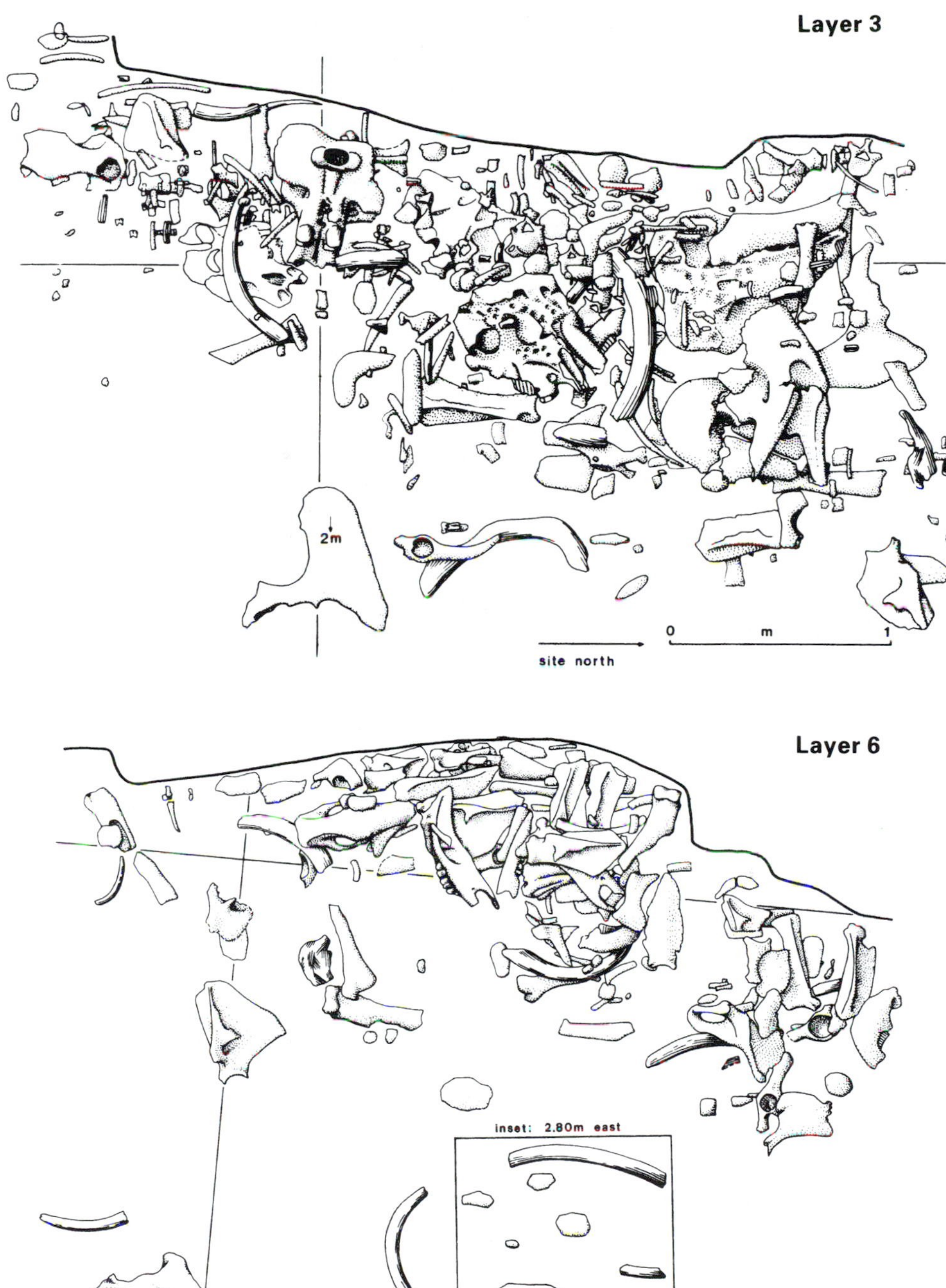


**5.26** The two bone piles excavated beneath the granite walls of La Cotte, Jersey NW region (after Scott 1986a:Figs. 18.2, 18.3). See Table 5.15 for the contents and Figure 5.10 for the position of the layers.

Table 5.15. *The La Cotte bone piles (Scott 1986a, 1986b).*

| | Mammoth | | Woolly rhino | |
|---|---|---|---|---|
| | Identified remains | MNI | Identified remains | MNI |
| Layer 3 | 115 | 7 (skulls) | 18 | 2 (ulna and femur) |
| Layer 6 | 84 | 11 (scapula) | 7 | 3 (skulls) |

**5.27** The granite headland at La Cotte de St Brelade, Jersey, NW region. It is possible that megafauna were stampeded over these cliffs and then subsequently dismembered and dragged into the cave (after Callow and Cornford:Fig. 1.5).

(Stiner 1994: Fig. 5.32). In the sample of nineteen assemblages from the four sites, the exclusive carnivore levels are Moscerini 1, where the only evidence is gnaw marks on herbivore bones, Moscerini 5, Guattari 0 and 1 and Sant'Agostino X. There were four mixed assemblages, where interpretation must rely on frequency data, and the remaining ten were exclusively hominid in character.

One attribute which Stiner uses to establish carnivore occupation is the U-shaped or young-dominated age profile for carnivores (Figure 5.28). The presence of young carnivores is indicative of denning activity. But the number of

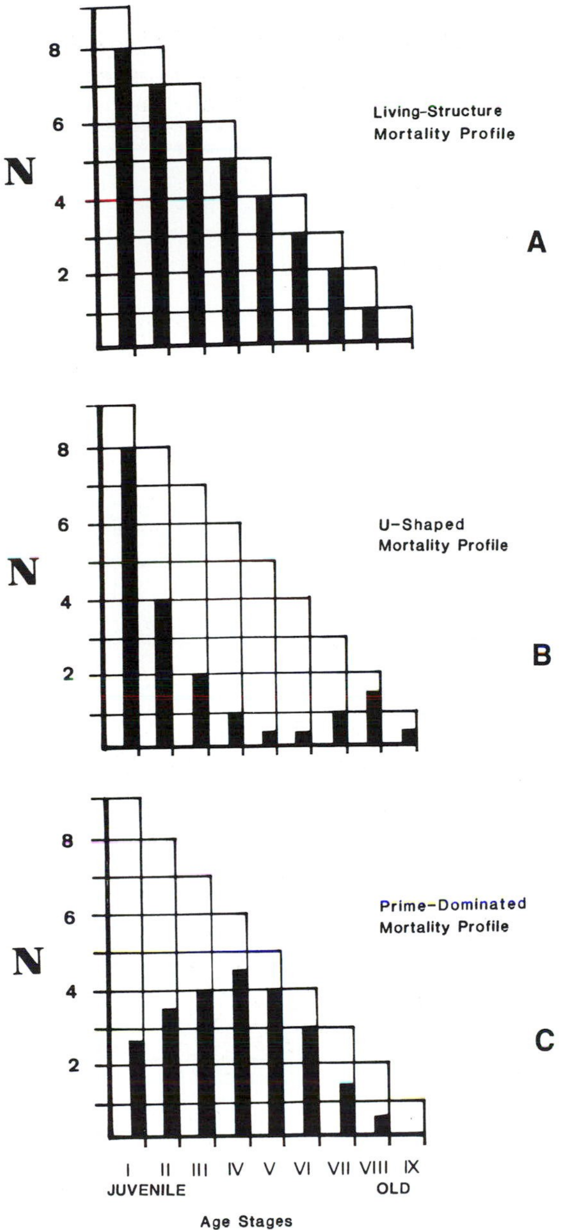


**5.28** Three different age-mortality profiles to interpret assemblages of animal bones. Random mortality for each age group would produce (A) but will only be found when whole herds were killed simultaneously by either natural catastrophes, e.g. volcanic, or human slaughter. Most faunal assemblages have either a U-shaped profile (B), dominated by young and old animals, or an adult-dominated profile (C) which, at a locale such as Wallertheim (Gaudzinski 1992), reflects the evolution of the human niche as a predator of prime animals. The U-shaped profile may indicate winter deaths of the most vulnerable animals and may or may not refer to human involvement (after Stiner 1994:Fig. 10.2).

Table 5.16. *The frequency of carnivores in three Middle Palaeolithic locales in Latium (Stiner 1994:Tables 4.6, 4.7 and 4.8) and one in southern Germany (Gamble 1995d). NISP=number of identified specimens.*

| | NISP total | NISP carnivores | % all carnivores | % bear NISP total |
|---|---|---|---|---|
| Moscerini 5 | 616 | 186 | 30 | 12 |
| Guattari 0 | 957 | 108 | 11 | 1 |
| Guattari 1 | 695 | 80 | 12 | 0.1 |
| Sant'Agostino X | 588 | 115 | 26 | 1 |
| Stadel B Red Mousterian | 4,539 | 3,349 | 74 | 59 |
| Stadel A Black Mousterian | 1,739 | 1,200 | 69 | 52 |

Table 5.17. *A comparison of carnivore age profiles (Gamble 1995d, Stiner 1994). For the Latium caves N is based on MNI, and for Stadel on NISP.*

| % | | Young | Adult | Senile | N |
|---|---|---|---|---|---|
| Sant'Agostino | Wolf | 73 | 27 | | 5.5 |
| Guattari | Hyena | 73 | 27 | | 5.5 |
| | Hyena | 58 | 42 | | 6 |
| Buca della Iena | Hyena | 71 | 29 | | 12 |
| Stadel | Wolf | 3 | 91 | 6 | 70 |
| units V–IX Black & Red Mousterian | Hyena | 11 | 80 | 10 | 290 |

carnivore bones is usually small even in those levels where the combined evidence points to their exclusive use (Table 5.16)

By comparison with the Hohlenstein-Stadel, part of a complex of caves in the small Lone valley, north-central region (Gamble 1979, 1995d), these proportions for carnivores are low. But this is due to the predominance of bear using such caves for hibernation (Gamble 1984, Gargett 1994, Musil 1980–1). Once bear is omitted (Table 5.17), the numbers of the Stadel carnivores are very comparable to those in the Latium caves. But here the similarity ends. The age data for the Stadel material is prime dominated and not U-shaped, strongly suggesting that caves were used for many reasons other than the raising of cubs.

I conclude from this comparison of northern and Mediterranean cave faunas

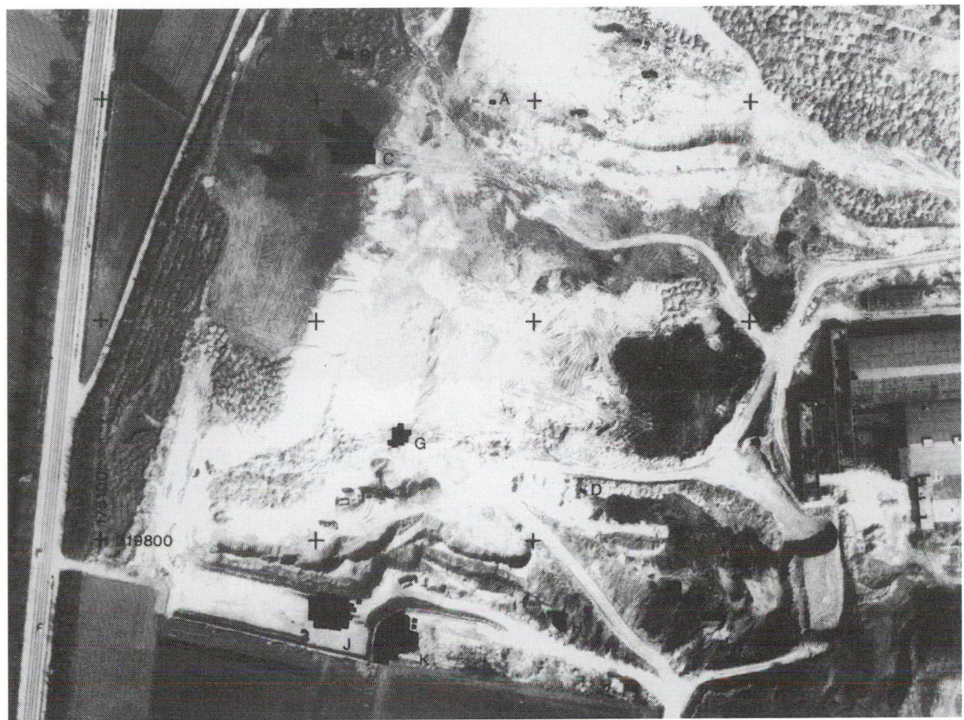


**5.29** The excavated sites, A–K, in the Belvédère gravel pit at Maastricht, Netherlands, NW region (after Roebroeks 1988:Fig. 5).

that, although the co-presence of hominids and carnivores is indicative of community richness (see above), hominids in these two regions are employing some specific skills. In Italy, selection was for locales within the landscape with optimum access to prey density. In Germany competition for the use of locales was based on access to the most productive cohort (prime-aged animals) within the prey species (Gamble 1995d). Viewed against this background we may be justified in identifying specific skills which developed in each region. These involved a variety of rhythms, performed at locales and from which social differentiation was also created.

### Locales: Maastricht-Belvédère, a case study

The extent to which these specific skills shed light on Palaeolithic society can be examined at the open-air locale of Maastricht-Belvédère. Located in the southern part of the Netherlands, the Belvédère sand and gravel pit has been intensively studied since 1980 (De Loecker 1994, Kolfschoten and Roebroeks 1985, Roebroeks 1988, Roebroeks et al. 1992). Seven major areas (sites B, C, F, G, H, K, N) in unit IV of this OIS 7 landscape have been explored (Figure 5.29). I have already reviewed the dating and climatic evidence and on the basis of the molluscs the following local environment is inferred:

> the sites were situated in a wet area which was protected from the mainstream of the river and which had a dense aquatic vegetation. Along its borders this vegetation . . . favour[ed] marshy places with at most 20 cm of water. At a higher level . . . [it] was mixed with, or bordered by, alder forests with ash trees. On even higher grounds the alder woods gave way to deciduous forests of drier habitats; there, the vegetation may have been of an open woodland type with open areas covered with a dense vegetation of grasses and herbs. (Roebroeks et al. 1993:74)

The areas dug and the density of finds recovered from this climatically optimum phase of the interglacial are presented in Table 5.18.

*Structures, spatial patterns and gatherings*

The seven major areas which have been excavated within the Belvédère locale reveal a variety of different patterns across a contemporary landscape.[23] Site G has faunal remains, although their preservation is very poor and only the most resistant elements, usually teeth, have survived. Site K (Table 5.18) is by far the richest in terms of the size of the excavation and the recovery of almost 11,000 lithic artifacts at a density of 29.5 artifacts per m$^2$. This site also produced the largest number of retouched pieces (n=137) at a density of 0.37 per m$^2$ (Roebroeks et al. 1993:figure 5). This is a primary-context locale as shown by the number of refits, which raises the difficult question of determining whether it was produced in one or several visits and by several or one person at each gathering. Roebroeks (et al. 1993) contrast the rich site K with a poor site N, located 100 m to the south. This was the largest area dug (765 m$^2$) and was chosen to establish the 'background noise' to the high-density 'peak'. The artifact density is a very low, 0.6 specimens per m$^2$ (Table 5.18). They conclude from a study of the technology that the rich sites may be recording activities essentially aiming to maintain the technology by producing flakes and tools, while the poor sites are where the technology was used in a variety of tasks (*ibid.*:78). What is interesting in the Belvédère taskscape is just how many subtle activities took place within such a small area (De Loecker 1994:Fig. 6).

The artifact densities from each excavation are presented in Table 5.18. It is interesting to compare these very variable densities over the entire quarry area with Bilzingsleben (Table 4.19), where 355 m$^2$, less than site K alone, has been excavated. The density of all stone artifacts was thirty-two pieces per m$^2$, almost equivalent to Sites K and F at Maastricht-Belvédère, both regarded as rich sites within this locale. Roebroeks et al. (1992) have described these low-density scatters at the locale as a 'veil of stones'. The phrase focuses attention on the context of the denser patches, such as C, F and K, which is supplied by the character of the veil surrounding them as represented by G and N (De Loecker 1994:116, Roebroeks et al. 1993). The phrase also reminds us that the spatial use of these locales was continuous even though occupation was intermittent and stretched over many centuries.

A comparison of density data for open locales in Tables 4.19 and 5.18 reveals that generally the size of excavations in the earlier period is larger. Secondly,

Table 5.18. *Lithic density data for Saalian- and Eemian/Weichsel-age open locales (Conard 1992, 1996, Conard et al. 1995, Gabori-Csank 1968, Jaubert 1994, Masson and Vallin 1996, Pasda 1996a, 1996b, Raposo and Santonja 1995, Roebroeks et al. 1993, Thieme 1990, Tode 1953, Tuffreau 1993, Tuffreau and Sommé 1988).*

| Site | Layer | Region | OIS age | $m^2$ excavated | Total stone | Density per $m^2$ |
|---|---|---|---|---|---|---|
| Wallertheim | E | NC | 5c | 138 | 23 | 0.2 |
| Maastricht-Belvédère | B | NW | 7 | 20 | 5 | 0.3 |
| Erd | Lower | SE | 4 | 214 | 57 | 0.3 |
| Wallertheim | F | NC | 5c | 282 | 101 | 0.4 |
| Maastricht-Belvédère | N | NW | 7 | 765 | 450 | 0.6 |
| Erd | d | SE | 4 | 214 | 201 | 0.9 |
| Maastricht-Belvédère | G | NW | 7 | 50 | 51 | 1.0 |
| Wallertheim | C | NC | 5a | 148 | 190 | 1.3 |
| Wallertheim | O.S | NC | 5 | 375 | 542 | 1.4 |
| Tönchesberg | 2A | NC | 6 | 224 | 423 | 1.9 |
| Wallertheim | B | NC | 5e | 54 | 109 | 2.0 |
| Biache St. Vaast | II base | NW | 7–6 | 340 | 698 | 2.1 |
| Tönchesberg | IB | NC | 4 | 55 | 120 | 2.2 |
| Erd | e | SE | 4 | 214 | 529 | 2.5 |
| Tönchesberg | 2B | NC | 5d | 224 | 557 | 2.5 |
| Erd | c | SE | 4 | 214 | 634 | 3.0 |
| Erd | b | SE | 4 | 214 | 658 | 3.1 |
| Biache St. Vaast | D | NW | 7–6 | 120 | 470 | 3.9 |
| Erd | a | SE | 4 | 214 | 922 | 4.3 |
| Maastricht-Belvédère | H | NW | 7 | 54 | 266 | 4.9 |
| Rheindahlen | Westwand | NW | 6 | 250 | 1,474 | 5.9 |
| Zwochau | III | NC | | 14 | 155 | 11.1 |
| Maastricht-Belvédère | C | NW | 7 | 264 | 3,067 | 11.6 |
| Zwochau | All areas | NC | | 56 | 727 | 13.0 |
| Salzgitter Lebenstedt | | NC | 4 | 150 | c.2,000 | 13.3 |
| Wallertheim | D | NC | 5c | 139 | 2,321 | 16.7 |
| Torre in Pietra | d | MC | 7 | 40 | 744 | 18.6 |
| Zwochau | IV | NC | | 17 | 359 | 21.1 |
| Biache St. Vaast | IIA | NW | 7–6 | 150 | 3,231 | 21.5 |
| Biache St. Vaast | D1 | NW | 7–6 | 115 | 2,842 | 24.7 |
| Maastricht-Belvédère | F | NW | 7 | 42 | 1,215 | 28.9 |
| Maastricht-Belvédère | K | NW | 7 | 370 | 10,912 | 29.5 |
| Riencourt | C | NW | 5a | 600 | 50,000 | 83.3 |
| El Aculadero | | MW | | 100 | 22,000 | 220.0 |
| Hermies, Le Champ Bruquette | Knapping scatter | NW | | 9 | 2,500 | 277.8 |
| Rescoundudou | | SW | | 250 | 100,000 | 400.0 |
| Bérigoule | 1 | MW | | 30 | 30,000 | 1,000.0 |

Table 5.19. *A comparison of density data from open site locales.*

| | Cromer/Holstein (Table 4.19) n=29 | | Saalian–Eemian–Weichsel (Table 5.18) n=37 | |
|---|---|---|---|---|
| | mean | st dev | mean | st dev |
| Area excavated m$^2$ | 216 | 283.4 | 182 | 160.4 |
| Total lithics | 1,940 | 2,855.8 | 6,626 | 18,875.9 |
| Density of lithics per m$^2$ | 30 | 82.7 | 60 | 179.6 |

the total stone recovered appears to increase at a few locales in the later period (Table 5.18), while finally, in both periods most of the density figures are less than ten lithics per m$^2$. However, as Table 5.19 shows, the standard deviations on these selected samples are very large, suggesting that they may be broadly similar.

What unites all the Belvédère sites in this one locale is the very low number of retouched pieces, equivalent to Geneste's stage 3 (Table 5.9). Levallois flakes were produced by both single and recurrent débitage but very few were further retouched into artifacts and only occasionally into scrapers (Table 5.20).

By comparison with Biache St. Vaast (Tuffreau 1988) where the levallois technique dominates, and which is also in primary context, the number of tools at Belvédère is indeed low.[24] The density of retouched pieces is 2.28 per m$^2$, whereas the highest density for this category at Belvédère is 0.37 per m$^2$ at Site K. At Tönchesberg 2B, dated to the last interglacial, retouched pieces occur at densities of 0.06 per m$^2$ (Conard 1992), comparable to Belvédère site G.

*Refitting the gatherings at Belvédère Site C*

A closer look at Site C at Belvédère (Roebroeks 1988) reveals a variety of short-term episodes within the excavated area of 264 m$^2$. Six raw-material units (RMUs) can be identified among the 3,067 artifacts (Figure 5.30, Table 5.21). Twenty-two per cent of all the flint artifacts could be fitted back together, which accounts for 70 per cent by weight of these six RMUs. The reason for such a high proportion by weight is simple. Refitting large, heavy flakes has a much higher success rate than small (<30 mm) pieces.

At Site C the majority of refits were from production sequences (Figure 5.20). The refittings make it possible to see that pieces were either carried away from RMU3 and RMUs 5 and 6 or they represent partially flaked material, rather than untouched nodules, brought into the excavated area (Table 5.21). RMU4, also known as Majorie's core (Figures 5.31 and 5.32), has been described in detail by Schlanger (1996).

Stapert (1992:201–2) has applied his ring and sector model to the southern concentration at Site C in order to test for huts and hearths. The results were

Table 5.20. *Artifact, core and debitage data from Maastricht-Belvédère (Roebroeks et al. 1993:figure 5), Biache IIA, essential count (Tuffreau 1988:171), Tönchesberg 2A (Conard 1992:Table 10) and Vaufrey level VIII (Geneste 1988b:Tableau 19).*

| Site | Tools and fragments | Cores | Flakes and chips | Tools: waste | Cores: waste | % retouched |
|---|---|---|---|---|---|---|
| *Bélvèdere* | | | | | | |
| B | 5 | | | | | |
| C | 3 | 4 | 3,060 | 1:1,020 | 1:765 | 0.1 |
| F | 1 | 1 | 1,213 | 1:1,213 | 1:1,213 | 0.1 |
| G | 3 | 48 | | 1:16 | | 6 |
| H | 12 | 254 | | 1:21 | | 5 |
| K | 137 | 91 | 10,684 | 1:78 | 1:117 | 1.2 |
| N | 26 | 1 | 423 | 1:16 | 1:423 | 6 |
| *Biache St. Vaast* | | | | | | |
| Base IIA | 342 | 336 | 2,553 | 1:7 | 1:8 | 13 |
| *Tönchesberg* | | | | | | |
| 2A | 14 | 16 | 527 | 1:37 | 1:35 | 3 |
| *Grotte Vaufrey* | | | | | | |
| level VIII | 157 | 55 | 1,817 | 1:12 | 1:33 | 8 |

a marked unimodal distribution away from the centre of the patch of burnt artifacts and stones. The density, however, falls off gradually. There are slight indications in the ring and sector patterns that suggest an open-air hearth. No hut signatures were found.

*Refitting the gatherings at Grotte Vaufrey level VIII*

How do these low-density open locales compare with cave occupations? Level VIII at the Grotte Vaufrey is the richest in terms of lithic artifacts from the locale. Refitting in this 50- to 70-cm thick level indicates its stratigraphical integrity (Rigaud and Geneste 1988:Figs. 5 and 6). All chipped stone occurs at a density of 85 per m$^2$, which by comparison with most open locales is very high (Table 5.18), while for retouched artifacts the figure falls to 1.6 per m$^2$. Some of the animal bones can be refitted (Rigaud and Geneste 1988:Fig. 14), as well as four flint nets (*ibid.*:Fig. 17). The two major lithic refittings are production sequences with the largest distance being a 5-m refit. At Site C Belvédère, the distances in RMU 2 extended up to 13 m (Roebroeks 1988:Fig. 51).

*Fire and fireplaces*

Site C at Belvédère was covered by low-energy sands. Apart from a scattering of small ochre pieces (Roebroeks 1988:Fig. 44), the only other materials are faunal remains and several thousand small charcoal fragments concentrated in

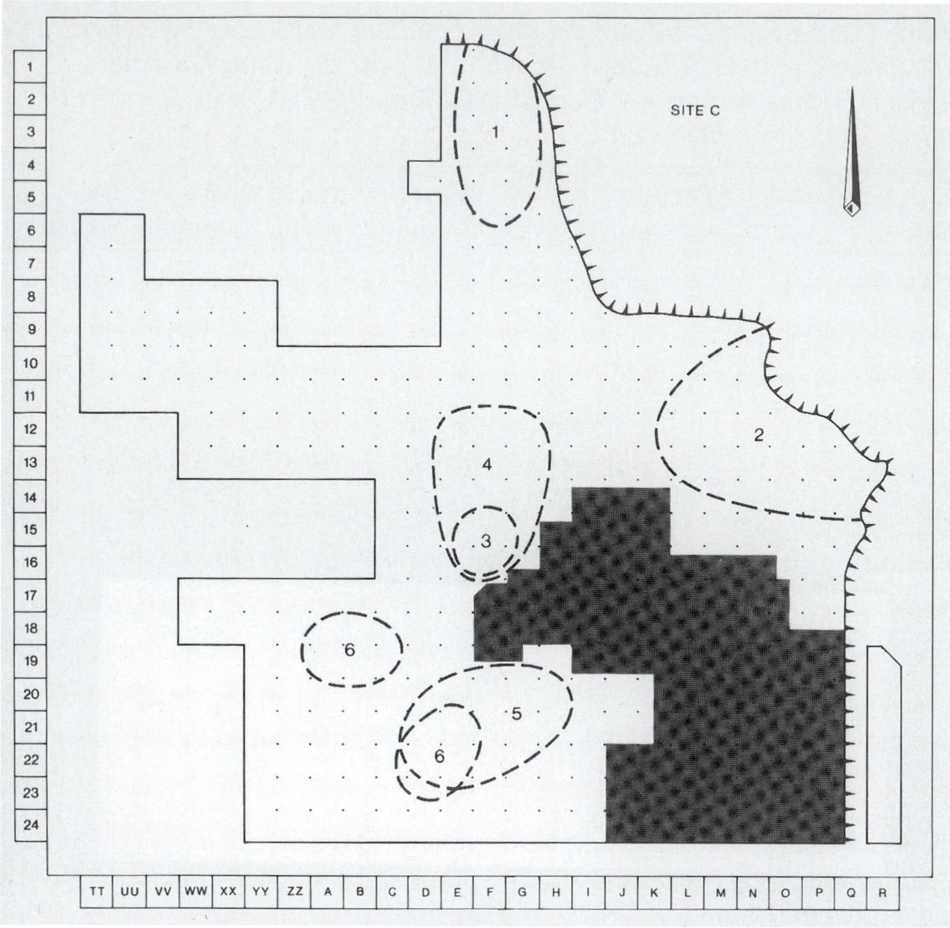


**5.30** The six raw-material units excavated at Site C, Maastricht-Belvédère, Netherlands, NW region (after Roebroeks 1988:Fig. 30). The grid scale is in metres and the shaded area was disturbed by karst.

the northwest corner (*ibid.*:Fig. 27). The latter was excavated with extreme care to establish its origin and even more so when a concentration of stones was found within it (*ibid.*:Fig. 43). However, Roebroeks concludes that the occurrence of the stones, and possibly the charcoal, was not artificial. The only two stones found with the charcoal were burnt, while the size range of the stone concentration was very large, which they interpret as a natural occurrence.

If the charcoal concentration was the result of a fire on the spot, then this fire burned outside the recorded distribution of flint artifacts and bone material. (*ibid.*:37)

Similar evidence for hearths was diligently looked for, but not found, at La Cotte where evidence for burning is commonplace (Callow, Walton and Shell 1986). At Tönchesberg, Conard identifies 'what appears to be' a hearth (Conard

Table 5.21. *Refitting and raw material units at Maastricht-Belvédère (from Roebroeks 1988).*

Site C

| Raw material Unit (RMU) | Estimated weight g | % weight refitted | Type of raw material | Cortex | Supports | Retouched artifacts | Comment |
|---|---|---|---|---|---|---|---|
| 1 | 6,759 | 60 | Fine-grained blueish-white flint | Moderately to severely rolled | Debris, rough flakes | | Only part of the distribution recovered |
| 2 | 3,000 | 83 | Coarse-grained yellow-brown flint | Fresh | Debris, cortex flakes, flakes from a levallois core, core fragments | | Several knapping stages producing a series of flakes |
| 3 | 800 | 75 | Fine-grained blueish-white flint | Slightly abraded | Flakes with cortex | | Prepared core taken away. Spatially overlaps with RMU 4 |
| 4 | 1,300 | 50 | Fine-grained blueish-white flint (finer than RMU 3) | Fresh and thick | Large flakes, cores | | Producing a series of flakes, débitage recurrent levallois, which optimizes the use of a block of flint (Marjorie's core) |
| 5 | 470 | 85 | Very fine-grained dark grey flint | Fresh | Flat discoidal core | 1 scraper ? | RMU introduced to site as an already reduced core with little remaining cortex burnt after knapping |
| 6 | nd | 70 | Fine-grained grey flint | Severely abraded by fluvial action | Cortex flakes | 2 side scrapers | RMU introduced partially flaked |

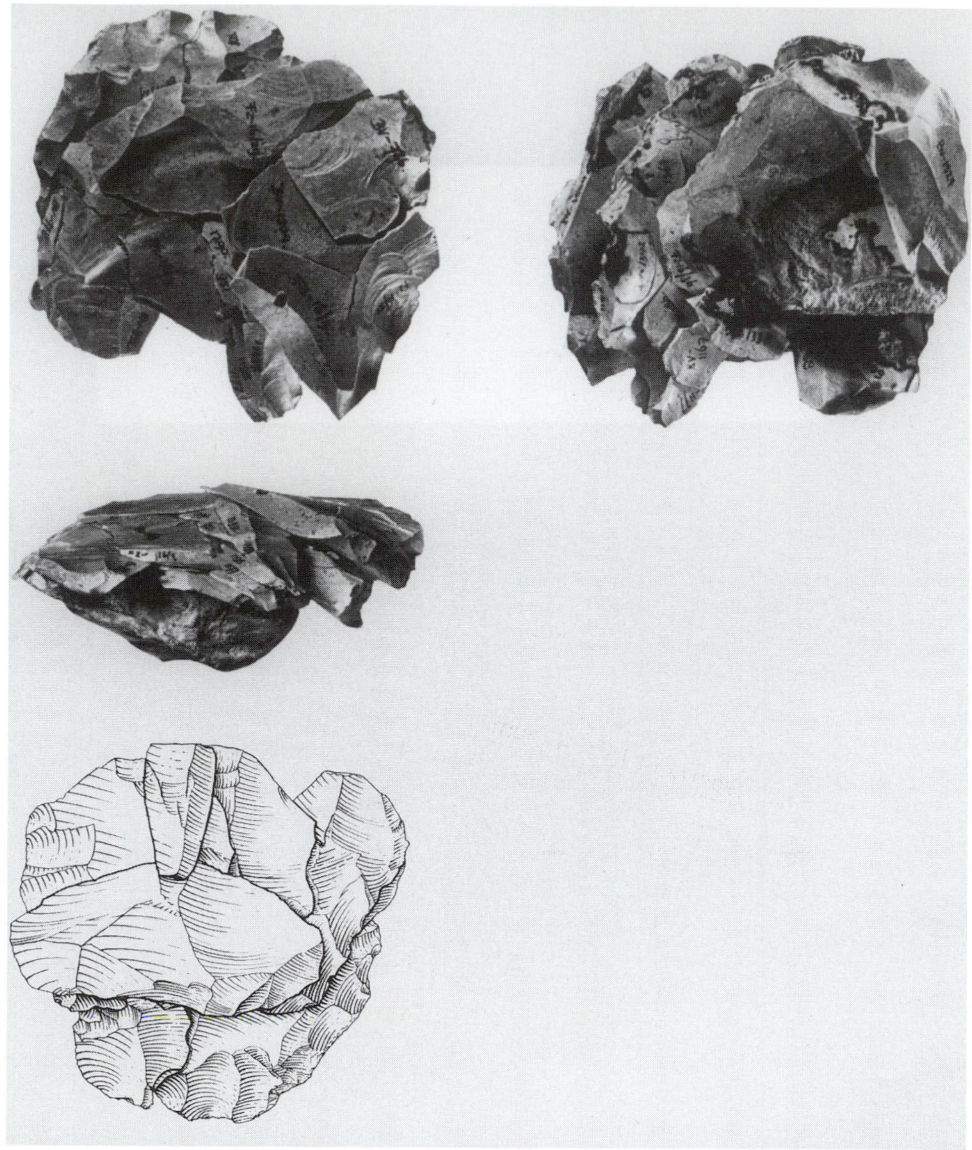

**5.31** Raw material unit 4 (Marjorie's core) from site C at Maastricht-Belvédère, Netherlands, NW region. Two different views are shown of core Bv-1527 with conjoined flakes (after Roebroeks 1988:Fig. 57).

1992:36) from charcoal and burnt flint but without any great degree of conviction. Erd has similar concentrations (Gabori-Csank 1968:figure 6).

The best evidence for hearths occurs in caves and rock shelters. This consists of small scoops with a variety of carefully placed stones in Pech de l'Azé II level 7c dated to the late Saalian (de Sonneville-Bordes 1989:230). Other examples can be found at Hauteroche in the Charente (Debenath 1973, 1976:1074).

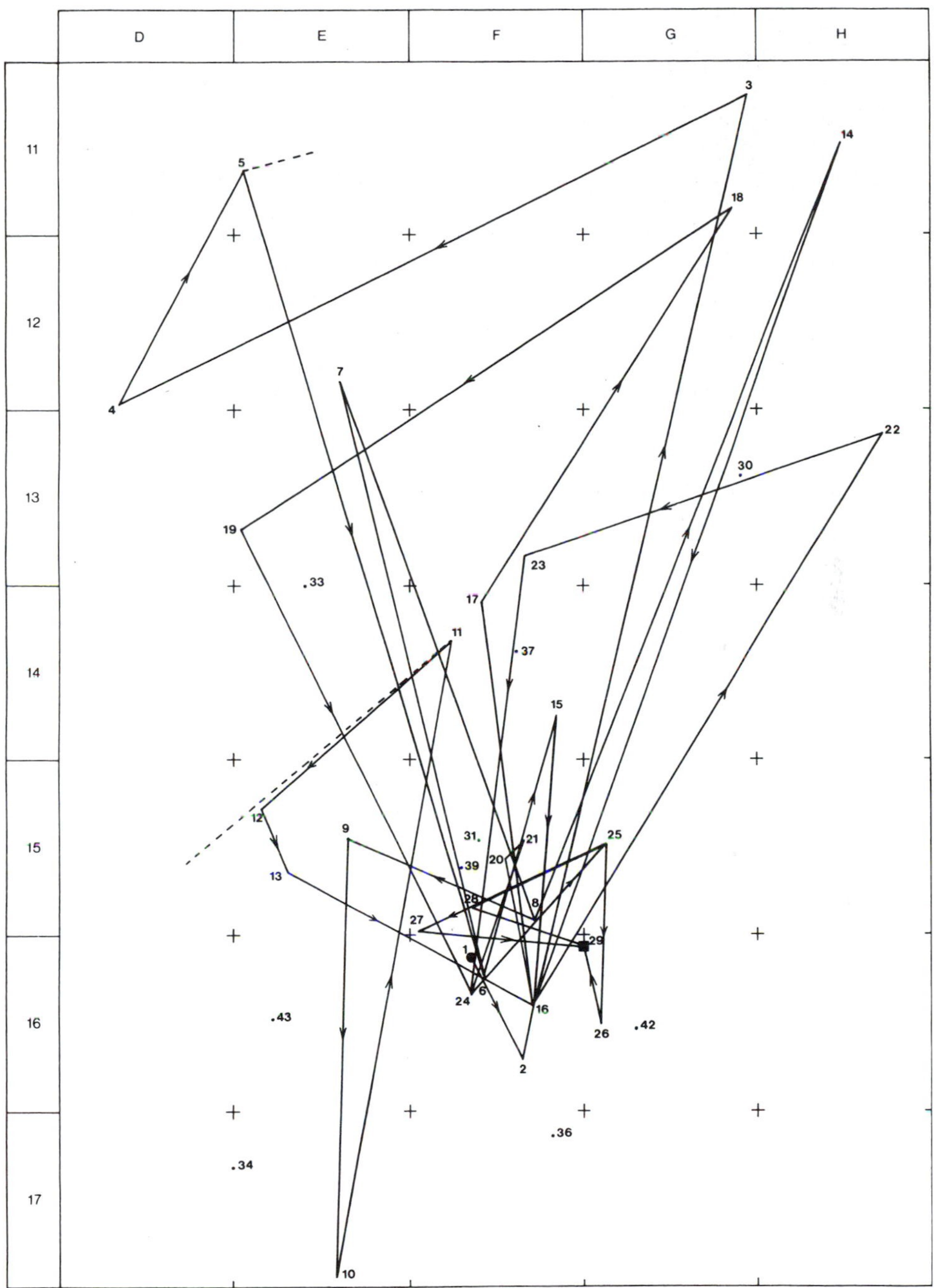


**5.32** The horizontal distribution of flakes refitted to Marjorie's core (Bv-1527) in raw material unit 4 at Site C, Maastricht-Belvédère, Netherlands, NW region (after Roebroeks 1988:Fig. 58). The grid scale is in metres.

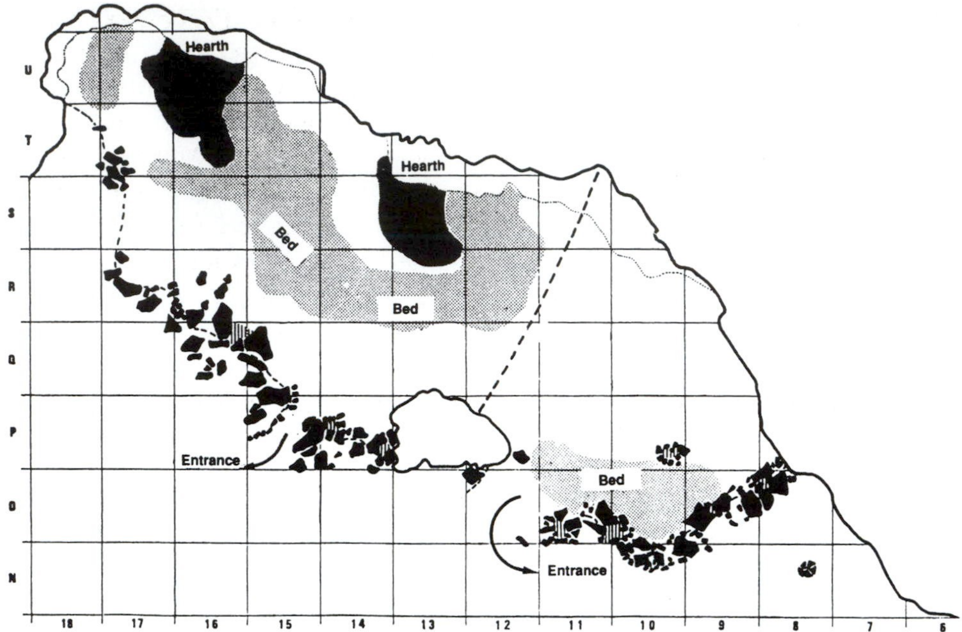


**5.33** The tent reconstructed within the Lazaret cave, France, MW region. Note the semicircular pattern of materials around the two hearths. The line of stones, marked in black, was thought to be weights holding down the edges of the tent. Alternatively, their distance from the hearth lies within the toss zone commonly found around hearths, Figure 3.4 (after de Lumley 1969a, Mellars 1996:Fig. 9.16).

Reviews of the evidence are provided by Perlès (1976:681); see also James (1989), Mellars (1996:295–301), and Olive and Taborin (1989). No hearths have been found at Grotte Vaufrey although the excavators identify the most likely area on the basis of a concentration of charcoals (Rigaud and Geneste 1988:Fig. 13, Binford 1988:Fig. 14), as is also the case at Grotte Lazaret near Nice (Lumley 1969a).

*Space and language*

What, with one possible exception, is currently lacking at any of these locales where either fire or fireplaces are present is spatial evidence corresponding to the hearth seated model discussed in Chapter 3. The distinctive horseshoe-shaped rings of size sorted materials cannot be found in any of the well-preserved plans. The exception is the Grotte Lazaret (Figure 5.33) where there does appear to be such patterning around two charcoal concentrations up against the cave wall (Lumley 1969a).[25] Moreover these appear to be size sorted with the larger blocks lying 3 m from the centre of the two hearths, a distance which would correspond to the inner limit of the toss zone as set out in Stapert's ring and sector model.

The interest in such concentric spatial patterns resides in the context which produces them – conversation around hearths. While it is perfectly possible to hold a conversation without either sitting round a hearth or necessarily leaving any residues behind, the existence of such patterning can be taken as a clear indication that such behaviour was commonplace (Chapter 3). Moreover, since we find no evidence either for built structures or for pits, postholes and other modifications to a locale, I conclude that social occasions and places (Table 3.1) were also lacking. The structure of the gatherings which took place both in open landscapes and in caves and rock shelters depended neither on language nor on the personification of objects and locations. The temporality of these landscapes was instead set by the immediate routines of the taskscapes to which a Neanderthal belonged and the wider landscapes of habit based on the creation of effective-scale networks. Their extended networks were only weakly, if at all, developed.

The lack of good archaeological evidence for fireplaces is also interesting in the light of predictions from Aiello and Dunbar (1993, Dunbar 1996) that by 250 Kyr BP the neocortex of the brain had reached sufficient size to sustain group sizes of 150 people. Such group sizes, they maintain, required a gossip rather than full symbolic language as a means to track people and socially 'groom' them. With this transference from physical to vocal grooming they argue that larger group sizes could be regularly maintained. Foley and Lee (1996) have also pointed to the major shift in life strategies at this time with, in particular, longevity increasing among these bigger-brained hominids who now required a higher quality diet to maintain the energy-expensive big brains (Aiello and Wheeler 1995).

It is of course tempting to see some of the changes outlined in this chapter in these terms. The longer raw-material transfers, more tightly focused food-management strategies and the levallois chaînes point to new patterns of temporality in gesture, material action and mobility. But what we do not see from the spatial evidence is any dramatic change in the record from that seen much earlier at Boxgrove or Bilzingsleben. Nor does this record differ significantly between the nine regions of Europe. Therefore, while it is good to think that Neanderthals had an advanced form of communication, it was only directed towards the negotiation of their intimate and effective networks. These networks would of course be entirely appropriate for the development of Dunbar's gossip language (1996). The selection pressure for such vocal communication came not from group size but from the intensity and limited spatial extension of social interaction. But these networks would not select for a reflexive, symbol-based language using material culture as an external referent to establish meaning (Noble and Davidson 1996).

*Co-operation and the individual*

There is also very little evidence in this period for co-operative behaviour which depended upon the symbolic capacity of language to stretch relations

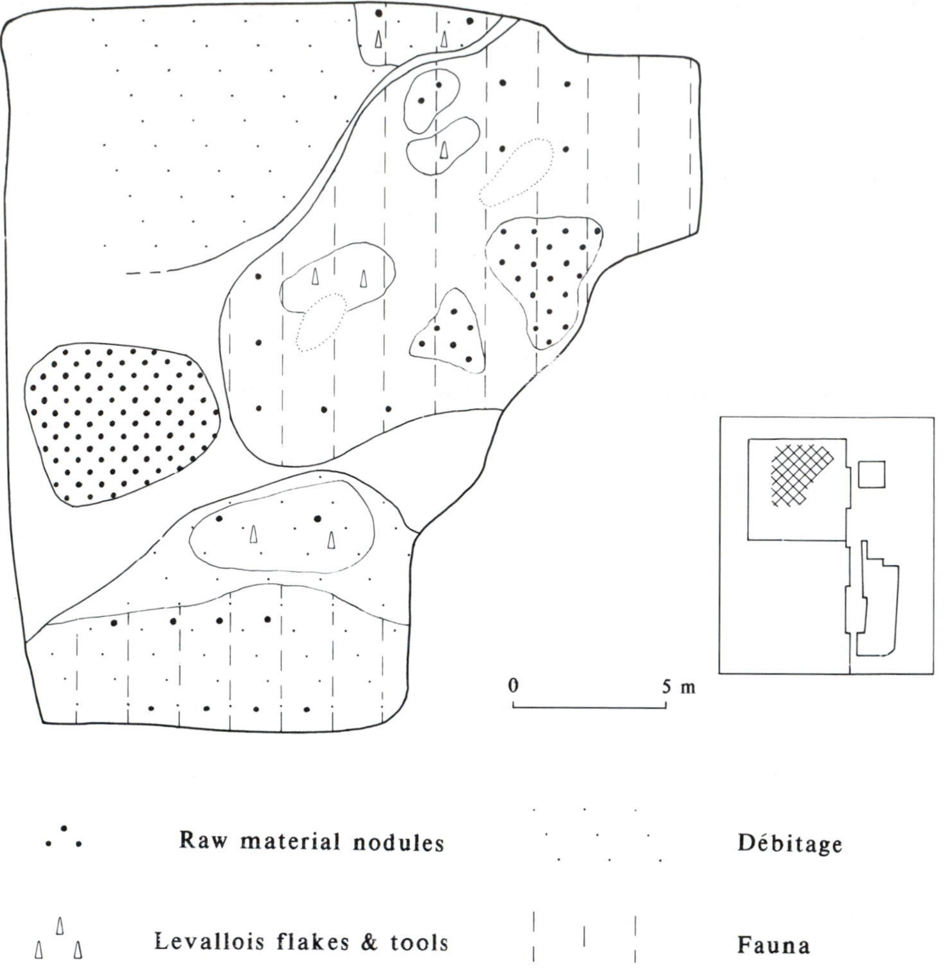


**5.34** The zonation of material resulting from gatherings at the Biache St. Vaast locale, level II base (after Tuffreau 1988:Fig. 20.25).

across time and space. The simple zonation of materials at Biache level II base (Figure 5.34) in an area of 340 m² (Table 5.18) is very similar to that at Tönchesberg 2B, 224 m², (Conard 1992:figure 55) or Erd, 214 m² (Gabori-Csank 1968:figure 6) where fauna and lithics overlap. At Grotte Vaufrey, Rigaud and Geneste (1988:610) conclude that the locale had clearly marked areas for bone cracking, flint knapping and making fire. In his study of the taphonomy, Binford (1988) has more to say about how the carnivores used the cave than about how the hominids did so. He concludes that this shows how different they were from ourselves. Evidence is lacking for co-operation in the form of architecture and the structured use of space. These rich locales (Table 5.18) are difficult to interpret, probably because we use ethnoarchaeological models where sustained co-operation negotiated through symbolic language can be assumed.

Much easier to explain are the brief gatherings as at the Gröbern elephant locale (Figure 5.25) where individuals can be identified by the different raw materials they used as they clustered around the carcass. There is evidence too from La Cotte of some co-operative activity in driving and then stacking parts of the mammoths and woolly rhinos beneath the cliffs.

It might seem too simple to assert that the difference in site structure during this period was determined by a lack of symbolic language alone. Nonetheless, it must be clear by now that locales such as Vaufrey and Belvédère, while rich in material acts, do not contain material evidence for their symbolic externalization. Actions in the Palaeolithic record will always speak louder than words, but in this period there are no conversations to be seen. Co-operation was therefore a routine act, a negotiated outcome between hominids exploring their intimate and effective networks.[26] It was not an external principle which established an overarching principle for the organization of Neanderthal society.

### *The Maastricht-Belvédère taskscape*

The marshy stream banks were the setting for social integration; what people do together. Paths did not cross this landscape with the regularity and intensity seen around some lakesides or within easy reach of selected caves and rockshelters. The frequency of encounters with affordances such as wood, animals, plants, stone and other people was low. The many gatherings which took place never led to assorted residues, although preservation may not have been kind to animal bones and other organic materials.

Materials were carried to the locale but only over short distances. These included blocks of stone. Their further affordance, or use-value, required a pause, the focus of attention on the material in hand and the routine commencement of the attaching ritual.

The ritual of attachment involved making. At Maastricht-Belvédère, I strongly suspect that several of the knapping episodes were solitary performances by individuals acting without the attention and information flow that comes with co-presence. But in an effective sense they were not isolated. As they applied routine gestures to well-understood materials, they tapped into the wider security of regional traditions of action. The longer sequences of rhythms of acquisition and manufacture, as shown by Majorie's refitted core (Schlanger 1996), did come from other times and positions in the individual's taskscape. Worked materials could still be found from further afield but they would have been smaller, already whittled down by many gestures rather than to a pre-determined plan.

The continuous flow of social life was remembered through these routines and reproduced by them. So, by applying learned gestures to stone the individual attached herself or himself to the locale and to the wider effective social network which was defined by rhythmic action applied to material resources.

Social life involves movement and action at different scales. Memories are preserved in the muscles as much as in the brain. Making and walking are two examples of learned rhythms forming the basis for memory and providing a store for future action at both the locale and the regional scale.

What they remembered of locales such as Maastricht-Belvédère was not the enduring artifacts they left behind but instead this memory of the track of individuals travelling alone and together. The locale preserves many individual moments which by themselves were unmemorable: making a scraper, carrying a block a few meters, taking off decortification flakes. But these were more than just practical, unthinking gestures (Chapter 2) because of the effective network which linked them together and gave them wider meaning. These were skills available to the individual to create a specific identity. This was possible because the skills could be recombined into very subtle performances.

When co-presence did occur at Maastricht-Belvédère we see these skills in play. Personal space was respected, as the refittings of these gatherings at Site C demonstrate. If the three main refitted groups were contemporary, as seems likely, then such respect also indicates that the performance space remained small, no more than the rare but longest refit of 10 m (Roebroeks 1988:54). Such a distance emphasizes face-to-face interaction. The attention to others took in the sights and sounds of the taskscape which surrounded either the lone individual or the gathering of people. The phrase, a veil of stone, used by the excavators (Roebroeks et al. 1992) to describe the pattern of archaeology in order to derive a functional explanation could also be used as a metaphor for the continuous (regional), but punctuated (local), social life represented by the locale.

What happened during the social gatherings at Maastricht-Belvédère was not system integration, which deals with how social patterns established in co-presence are extended *in absentia* through symbolic means. Rather it is an example of how the social life of hominids was carried with them rather than just produced at special 'social' occasions. Individuals did not cease to have a social life because they were by themselves. Social activity is not an institutional response defined by set-piece occasions such as marriages or funerals. In Palaeolithic terms these responses would normally be seen as a measure of success in the evolutionary game against the environment. Success or failure in hunting could bring people together or separate them in death. According to this view the ecosystem, not people, selected for behaviour and structured the response in terms of material outcomes. But I have argued here that the ecosystem that has been reconstructed for the Maastricht-Belvédère locale, while important, did not produce the form of social life. This came from the taskscapes, those surrounding environments primed with agency as individuals moved with, in and of the world. They dwelt in the world at Maastricht-Belvédère, they did not adapt to it in the separate sense which is normally implied in Palaeolithic explanation.

**Summary**

Neanderthal society was founded on the intimate and effective networks which individuals routinely constructed as they went about their lives. In answer to the three questions posed at the beginning of this chapter: Yes, they could cope with a greater range, but not with all types of habitat; Yes, there is evidence that Neanderthal social life varied across the continent; No, such social interaction was not necessarily dependent on spoken language but did involve a system of communication dedicated to social relations.

During this period we can see a new temporality to action expressed through longer manufacturing sequences and the larger areas from which raw materials came. A comparison of the circulation of raw material at Arago (Figure 4.10) and Grotte Vaufrey (Figure 5.13), combined with the very different chaînes opératoires at these two caves (Geneste 1988b, Svoboda 1987), provides an important contrast between movement at the scale of landscape and the temporality of gesture at the scale of the locale. Changes at both scales shows how these two facets of behaviour were conjoined, rather than existing as separate realms of action, and that the link is embodied in individual action which is social in origin. Therefore, to talk of Neanderthal technology is also to talk of Neanderthal society.

A contrast with earlier periods (Chapter 4) can be drawn between the manufacture of bifaces using façonnage and the wider use that Neanderthals made of débitage technology where blanks (*supports*) were made by either levallois or prismatic blade techniques. The degree to which these techniques were used both inter- and intra-regionally is testament to an extended temporality of action as Neanderthals constructed their social worlds through elaborated gesture, sequences of action and negotiation. It is also possible that such changes are reflected in larger locales with more densely packed residues (Table 5.18). It is certainly the case that the appearance of prime-age hunting during this period provides a similar opportunity for archaeologists to explore the links in the chaînes opératoires between the gestures and rhythms of the locale and region. The association of the levallois technique with the use of more distant raw materials provides another opportunity to explore the enhanced mobility of individuals.

The focus of their varied social worlds was directed towards the intimate and effective networks that an individual, of any age and either sex, could negotiate. The patterning in material culture can be ascribed to the strength of these networks in Neanderthal social life and the absence of more elaborate time–space distanciation which would have involved the externalization of social life through symbols. These were societies built on co-presence and the reaffirmation of bonds through regular contact instilled in the practices of everyday life. The evidence is for social rather than system integration (Chapter 2); what people did together rather than how they continued to behave to each other once apart.

As a result there is no evidence from the locales I have examined for social occasions in Neanderthal society. No inscribing the landscape to produce places from locales, where the performance of social acts which dealt with techniques of provisioning and production could be disembodied from the routinized gestures and infused with alternative associations. Material objects – including bones, flesh, skin, wood, ochre, ivory, stone, antler and other people – formed a shifting array of external resources whose interrelations became coherent at gatherings but where attention and attenuation constrained such situations of co-presence.

These constraints, and the lack of social occasions as defined in Chapter 3, account for the superficial similarity of Neanderthal society across Europe. Neanderthal society, defined like all societies in this book through the networks which individuals built, was founded on familiar gestures. Some of these were now centred more specifically on the cultural transmission of a social technology literally embodied in rhythms of acquisition and the gestures of manufacture.

I would argue that society at this time saw a shift in emphasis away from the dominance of the intimate network upon the actions of the individual. Negotiation increasingly used the resources of the effective network (Chapter 2) to create new networks. This shift of emphasis can be most clearly seen in Neanderthal mastery as hunters of prime-aged prey. Not only did they take a wide variety of herd animals but they concentrated upon particular taxa, age and sex classes. The inference can be made of larger seasonal gatherings with some co-operation. Overall there is an appreciation of primeness and quality – whether it is animals or stone resources. As we saw in Chapter 2, material resources are used as the primary means of defining the effective network and so this emphasis is expected. Such materials include other people, animals and plants; in sum all the elements in the mutual, surrounding environment of a Neanderthal. Moreover, although not explored by Neanderthals, these same resources can be converted into symbolic resources. A stone is not just a gesture to cut but can also personify a relationship. Carcasses not only meet dietary requirements, they also symbolize social skills and values (Hahn 1986, Mithen 1996).

I have shown in this chapter that the Neanderthals constructed a number of such environments for their social life. Variation can be seen and understood. For example, the dimensions of land use varied between the nine regions in Europe. Raw-material transfers show that the different distances travelled were due to the distribution of resources and the impact of climatic regimes. Neanderthals lived in landscapes of habit rather than a social landscape. The concept adequately summarizes the routinized nature of their activities. As a result life was still local. While there is some evidence for longer raw-material transfers, these still fall comfortably within the dimensions of the landscape of habit, indicating a temporal span of action around individual locales of about two to three days' walking distance. Evidence for the social landscape is lacking. A few pieces of hematite, some enigmatic bone and ivory objects such as the Tata plaque, do not betoken the appearance of negotiated acts that went well beyond the limits of co-presence by using resources unavailable to the intimate and effective Neanderthal networks.

But for all this lack of traditional archaeological social evidence, I can say that the Neanderthals *intensified* social life. They elaborated the non-symbolic use of gesture and material resources. As a result, their intimate network expanded and became a *quasi*-effective one in terms of increased numbers. Hence we now see greater co-operation at gatherings with animals and at workshop locales. But this expansion used the resources more normally associated with supporting the affective relationships of the intimate network. So, while Neanderthals had the capacity for language, it is apparent from the Palaeolithic record that all they used it for was as a means to enhance their use of the emotional resources (Chapter 2) which allowed them to create, by our expectations, a distinctive social reality. Call them the original caring society if you like, but it was only later that language assumed its dominant and self-defining position as a social trait in our equally limited terms.

CHAPTER 6

# THE RHYTHMS OF SOCIAL LIFE 60,000–21,000 YEARS AGO: THE TRANSITION FROM THE MIDDLE TO UPPER PALAEOLITHIC IN EUROPE

There was an old caveman from Spy,
who was very bent at the knee.
When asked, 'Is your gait
an evolutionary trait?'
He replied 'It is when I sneeze!'

Anon.

## The objects of social life

The transition, anatomically from Neanderthals to Crô-Magnon peoples, behaviourally from an ancient to a modern pattern, and culturally from the Middle to the Upper Palaeolithic, represents, in evolutionary terms, the Other becoming Us. The elements in this human revolution have been exhaustively debated using worldwide evidence (Aitken, Stringer and Mellars 1993, Cabrera-Valdés 1993, Mellars 1990, 1996, Mellars and Stringer 1989, Nitecki and Nitecki 1987, Stringer and Gamble 1993, Trinkaus 1989, Trinkaus and Shipman 1993). The debate is by no means over, but a majority view has emerged that on the basis of anatomical and genetic evidence the origin of modern people was in Africa (Stringer and Mackie 1996, Tattersall 1995).[1] The archaeological evidence for behavioural changes which could be regarded as modern is also clear (Mellars 1996). But determining where such behaviour first appeared and under what selective pressures is not (Gamble 1993a).

However, it is apparent that the transition from the Other to Us in Europe was not *the* human revolution. That took place elsewhere. The origins of modern humans lie outside the geographical scope of this book. In this chapter I will review the evidence from Europe which points to the replacement of Neanderthal anatomy, culture and behaviour by their 'modern' counterparts. The European evidence shows that replacement in this continent was a slow process, lasting some 20,000 years. The Palaeolithic record also reveals a specific prehistory to this transition that was probably not repeated in other parts of the Old World and indeed varied between regions in Europe.

The challenge for a social account of the Palaeolithic is to explain such variety in terms of interaction and the development of networks based on the individual. This will be undertaken in Chapter 7 once we have examined the record for the transition. As discussed in Chapter 1, a social approach based on interaction is preferred over accounts of the rise of institutions such as Band Society, male and female collectivities or the family (Gilman 1984, Johnson and Earle 1987, Knight 1991a). The arrival of 'The Moderns', be they anatomically, genetically or culturally defined, is another such institution. The problem with such institutions, while often convenient labels for analysis, is that anyone who apparently lacks them, such as the Neanderthals, is presented as a powerless social agent. It is a short step from there to the environmental determination of all of early prehistory until agrarian-based institutions appear (Chapter 1).

I will therefore argue in these two chapters that the idea of population replacement is a misrepresentation of the social changes that occurred in Europe. It does not matter whether replacement is seen as either a benign accident of mating, or a malign use of technology towards the 'First Nation' Neanderthals. If in either scenario the emphasis is on providing social institutions where previously none existed, then in both cases it is to the detriment of a social Palaeolithic. As Graves has reminded us (1991), the encounters between Crô-Magnons and Neanderthals were not equivalent to the colonial confrontation between Europeans and Indigenous peoples. There was no Upper Palaeolithic empire; there was no shocking disparity in fire power. There were no relevant institutions to frame such a contest.

The perspective I will take is that the transition enshrined in the archaeological units of the Middle and Upper Palaeolithic was about the emergence of individuals as creative agents beyond the limitations set by the rules of co-presence. This could not have happened without the contribution from our evolutionary heritage. In particular those intimate and effective networks still bond and bind us as social actors as they did *Homo heidelbergensis* who first occupied Europe. Such networks use the resources which the rules of interaction and negotiation require. From such interaction emerges a society composed of individuals empowered, through involvement and doing, with agency.

To be human is to have the potential to extend such social integration through system integration (Chapter 2). In that respect to change society is, when considering the Palaeolithic, to extend it as a framework for individual action. I showed in Chapters 4 and 5 that extension did occur in terms of system integration but that this only affected the scale at which hominids used their local networks. Extension *in absentia* could not be maintained by the resources for performance – tactile, olfactory, visual and embodied material gestures – where the stone or wooden implement became, literally, an extension of the hand, a gesture to cut, pound or scrape and where the environment surrounded the hominids as a sea of energy, a source of action which could also be externally inscribed.

The transition, usually described by terms such as the Middle and Upper Palaeolithic, is socially, technically and culturally the separation of the gesture from the body. Objects now took on a social life. They became the rules and

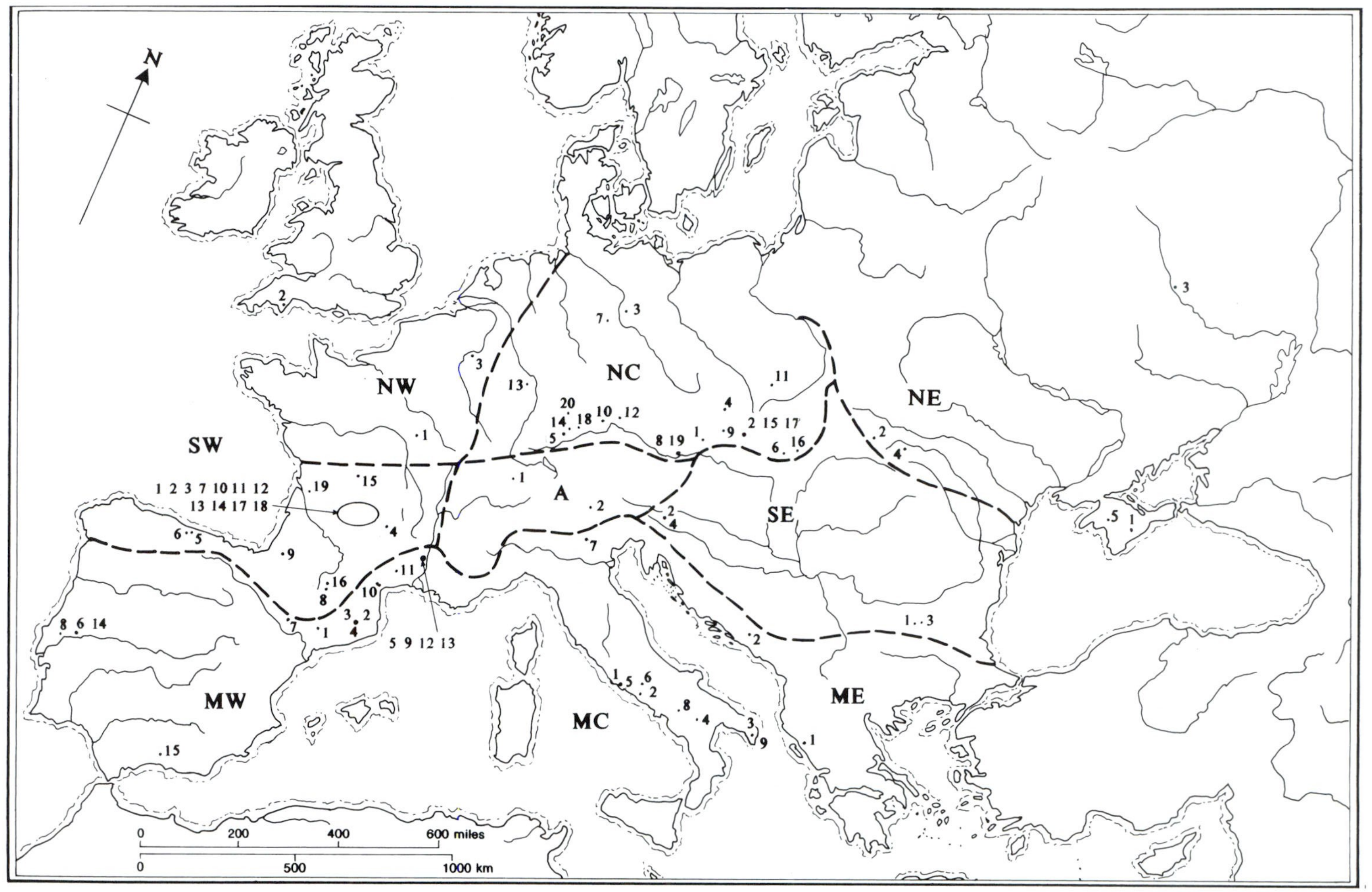

N
SW
NW
NC
NE
A
SE
MW
MC
ME
0 200 400 600 miles
0 500 1000 km

**6.1** Principal locales discussed in this chapter and referred to in Tables 6.1 and 6.27.

KEY: by region

| | NW | NC | NE | SW | ALP | SE |
|---|---|---|---|---|---|---|
| 1 | Arcy-sur-Cure | Alberndorf | Kiik Koba | Abri Pataud | Cotencher | Bacho Kiro |
| 2 | Kents cavern | Bohunice | Korolevo 2 | Castelmerle | Avena | Krapina |
| 3 | Sclayn Cave | Breitenbach | Kostenki | Combe Grenal | | Temnata |
| 4 | | Certova Pec | Ripiceni-Izvor | Coudoulous | | Vindija |
| 5 | | Geißenklösterle | Starosel'e | Cueva Morín | | |
| 6 | | Istállósko | | El Castilló | | |
| 7 | | Königsaue | | Fonseigner | | |
| 8 | | Krems | | Frechet | | |
| 9 | | Kulna | | Isturitz | | |
| 10 | | Mauern | | La Chapelle | | |
| 11 | | Nietoperzowa | | La Ferrassie | | |
| 12 | | Salching | | La Quina | | |
| 13 | | Sprendlingen | | Le Flageolet | | |
| 14 | | Stadel | | Le Moustier | | |
| 15 | | Stránská skála | | Les Cottés | | |
| 16 | | Szeleta | | Mauran | | |
| 17 | | Vedrovice | | Pech de L'Azé | | |
| 18 | | Vogelherd | | Roquette | | |
| 19 | | Willendorf | | St. Césaire | | |
| 20 | | Wittlingen | | | | |

| | MW | MC | ME |
|---|---|---|---|
| 1 | Abric Romani | Canale delle Acque Alte | Asprochaliko |
| 2 | Arbreda | Grotta Breuil | Crvena Stijena |
| 3 | Banyolas | Grotta del Cavallo | |
| 4 | Ermitons | Grotta di Castelcivita | |
| 5 | Esquicho-Grapaou | Grotta di Sant' Agostino | |
| 6 | Foz de Enxarrique | Guattari | |
| 7 | Gabasa | Riparo Fumane | |
| 8 | Gato Preto | Serino | |
| 9 | Grotte Chauvet | Uluzzo | |
| 10 | Grotte Tournal | | |
| 11 | Hortus | | |
| 12 | Ioton | | |
| 13 | Salpêtriere | | |
| 14 | Vilas Ruivas | | |
| 15 | Zafarraya | | |

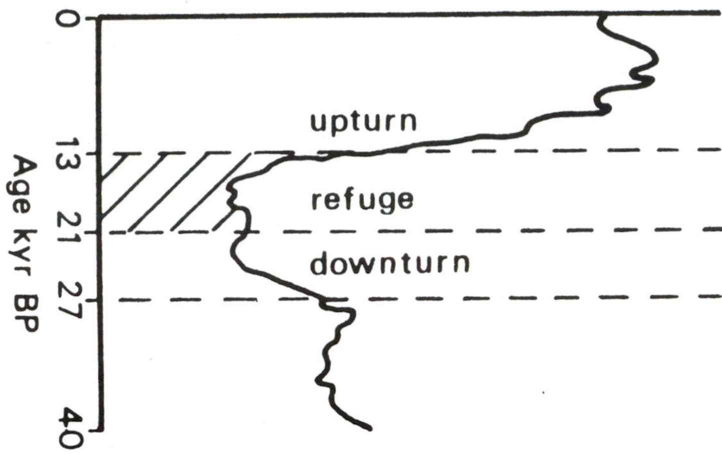


**6.2** A climatic framework for the European Upper Palaeolithic showing a division into three phases as indicated by the deep-sea record from core V-19-30 (after Gamble 1991b:Fig. 2).

resources which still direct us at social occasions and in the rules of performance and production. Language, I will argue, is a further aspect of this separation of the act from the body, the creation, if you like, of society as a severed limb rather than an integral social and technical gesture. Central to this development are the rhythms which linked action and gave it meaning. These form the focus of this chapter.

But first, the chronological, climatic and cultural framework for this varied transition in Europe.

## Chronology, climates and habitats

The period between 58 and 28 Kyr BP is known as the Interpleniglacial. In terms of the marine record this covers OIS 3 and the beginning of OIS 2 (Figure 6.2). This is followed by the climatic downturn to the Last Glacial Maximum (LGM), 28–21 Kyr BP, before the ice sheets achieved their greatest extent between 20–18 Kyr BP.

The period is covered by the following science based dating techniques: conventional C14, radiocarbon dating using accelerator-mass-spectroscopy (AMS) which can date smaller samples and provide greater accuracy (Gowlett and Hedges 1986), TL, U-series and ESR (Aitken 1990). The results of dating from a selected sample in the period 60–32 Kyr BP are shown in Table 6.1. These include for comparative purposes some dates for Neanderthal skeletons and transitional industries from the Middle East.[2]

*How old is old?*

AMS dating obviates the need for bulk samples to provide enough material for conventional C14. The problem with such bulk samples is one of contamination which can cause significant 'younging' of the date. For example, Bischoff (et al. 1989:572) show that a sample with a true age of 67 Kyr will give a date of 37 Kyr on the introduction of only 1 per cent present-day carbon. Moreover, advances in the chemical pre-treatment of samples, especially bone collagen, have allowed samples with evidence for direct human involvement, such as cut-marked, worked or burnt animal bone, to be directly dated. Samples up to 45 Kyr in age can be dated using AMS techniques.

Besides problems of contamination it has long been known that in later prehistory fluctuations in the rate of C14 production in the upper atmosphere require dates obtained by this method to be calibrated against an absolute chronology. This has been done by dendrochronology using long-lived trees such as the bristlecone pine. However, such calibration can only be extended back into the late glacial (Street, Baales and Weninger 1994). Vogel, in an early paper on the problem (1983) suggested that AMS dates at 40 Kyr may be 2.5 Kyr too young. Conventional C14 dates may be much younger still. Just how young is indicated by a calibration curve based on geomagnetic intensity (Laj, Mazaud and Duplessy 1996) where in the interval 20–40 Kyr BP radiocarbon ages may have to be increased by 2 to 3.5 Kyr.

A comparison of two dated cave sequences in Catalonia, Spain, provides a better estimate of the problem. At L'Arbreda cave (Bischoff et al. 1989) there is stratigraphic evidence, confirmed by AMS dating, for an abrupt transition between the Mousterian and Early Upper Palaeolithic (Aurignacian) as set out in Table 6.2.

One hundred kilometers to the southwest at Abric Romani, AMS dates for the basal Aurignacian give an average age of 37 ± 2 Kyr BP whereas the U-series analyses for the same material provide estimates of 43 ± 1 Kyr BP (Bischoff et al. 1994). Using these data Bischoff estimates that in the time range 38–40 Kyr BP 'the difference between radiocarbon and U-series is a startling 5.6 ± 1.5 Ka (66% confidence limit)' (*ibid.*:550). Therefore the Aurignacian, the earliest Upper Palaeolithic in Spain, and dated by AMS at L'Arbreda and at El Castilló in Cantabria (Cabrera-Valdes and Bischoff 1989), may be as old as 43 Kyr BP. It is for these reasons that in this chapter I use the lower case bp to indicate uncalibrated ages.

These dating conundrums do not of course make the discussion of transitions any easier. Radiocarbon, by whichever method, is not giving us a true age but there are as yet very few TL, ESR or U-series dates (Table 6.1). Nor are these techniques without their methodological problems. We are on safer ground when we have a stratigraphic sequence such as L'Arbreda, where the Aurignacian directly overlies the Mousterian, pointing to a rapid transition which is supported by the dates even if they do not indicate the true age. The

Table 6.1. *Absolute dates and archaeology 58–29 Kyr BP. Selected locales from the Middle East have been included for comparative purposes. Caution needs to be used when interpreting these dates since there are many contradictions between bio-stratigraphical evidence and absolute age determinations. For example, the AMS determinations from Königsaue indicate a much later date than a position in the Odderade interstadial (Figure 5.1) which is strongly suggested on bio-stratigraphical evidence. Moreover early attempts at calibration further suggest that major revisions will be necessary (Stringer and Gamble 1993: appendix with additions).*

| Locale | Layer | Region | | Dating method | Hominids | Archaeology | Kyr bp | ± |
|---|---|---|---|---|---|---|---|---|
| **STAGE 2/3 BOUNDARY 24 Kyr BP** | | | | | | | | |
| ***Denekamp*** | | | | | | | | |
| Bacho Kiro | Layer 6a/7 | Europe | SE | 14C | | Early Upper Palaeolithic | 29.1 | |
| Zafarraya | I[3–7] | Europe | MW | 14C | | Mousterian | 29.8 | 0.6 |
| Grotte Chauvet | | Europe | MW | 14C (AMS) | | Cave paintings | 30.3 | 0.5 |
| Grotte Chauvet | | Europe | MW | 14C (AMS) | | Cave paintings | 30.7 | 0.6 |
| Grotte Chauvet | | Europe | MW | 14C (AMS) | | Cave paintings | 30.9 | 0.6 |
| Grotta del Cavallo | Layer E, levels II–I | Europe | MC | 14C | | EUP (Uluzzian) | >31 | |
| Serino | | Europe | MC | 14C | | EUP (Aurignacian) | 31.2 | 0.6 |
| Zafarraya | I [8] | Europe | MW | 14C | | Mousterian | 31.8 | 0.55 |
| Zafarraya | I [8] | Europe | MW | TL | | Mousterian | 31.7 | 3.6 |
| Hohlenstein-Stadel | IV | Europe | NC | 14C | | EUP (Aurignacian) | 31.7 | 1.1 |
| Geißenklösterle Cave | IIb | Europe | NC | 14C | | EUP (Aurignacian) | 31.8 | 1 |
| St. Césaire | Layer 6 | Europe | SW | TL | | Early Upper Palaeolithic | 32.1 | 3 |
| St. Césaire | Layer 6, Ejo | Europe | SW | TL | | EUP (Proto-Aurignacian) | 32.1 | 3 |
| Shanidar | Base C | Middle East | | 14C | | Early Upper Palaeolithic | 32.3 | 3 |
| Grotta di Castelcivita | Level rsa | Europe | MC | 14C | | EUP (Uluzzian) | 32.4 | 0.6 |
| Grotte Chauvet | | Europe | MW | 14C (AMS) | | Cave paintings | 32.4 | 0.7 |
| Geißenklösterle Cave | IIb | Europe | NC | 14C | | EUP (Aurignacian) | 32.6 | 0.4 |
| Bacho Kiro | Layer 6b | Europe | SE | 14C | Modern | Early Upper Palaeolithic | 32.7 | 0.3 |
| Grotta di Castelcivita | Level rsa | Europe | MC | 14C | | EUP (Uluzzian) | 32.9 | 0.7 |

| | | | | | | | | |
|---|---|---|---|---|---|---|---|---|
| Ermitons | IV | Europe | MW | 14C (AMS) | | Mousterian | 33.1 | 0.66 |
| La Ferrassie | K6 | Europe | SW | 14C | | EUP (Aurignacian) | 33.2 | 0.57 |
| Grotta di Castelcivita | Level pie | Europe | MC | 14C | | EUP (Uluzzian) | 33.2 | 0.7 |
| Shanidar | Lower C | Middle East | | 14C | | Early Upper Palaeolithic | 33.3 | 1 |
| Abri Pataud | 14 | Europe | SW | 14C | | EUP (Aurignacian) | 33.3 | 0.4 |
| Abri Pataud | 14 | Europe | SW | 14C | | EUP (Aurignacian) | 33.3 | 0.7 |
| Les Cottés | G | Europe | SW | 14C | | EUP (Châtelperronian) | 33.3 | 0.5 |
| Zafarraya | D | Europe | MW | TL | Neanderthal | Mousterian | 33.4 | 2 |
| Boker A | | Middle East | | 14C | | Early Upper Palaeolithic | >33.4 | |
| Grotte du Renne (Arcy) | VIII | Europe | NW | 14C | | EUP (Châtelperronian) | 33.5 | 0.4 |
| Boker A | | Middle East | | 14C | | Early Upper Palaeolithic | >33.6 | |
| Geißenklösterle Cave | IIb | Europe | NC | 14C | | EUP (Aurignacian) | 33.7 | 0.8 |
| Le Flageolet | Level XI | Europe | SW | 14C (AMS) | | EUP (Aurignacian) | 33.8 | 1.8 |
| Grotte du Renne (Arcy) | VIII | Europe | NW | 14C | | EUP (Châtelperronian) | 33.8 | 0.25 |
| Shanidar | Mid C | Middle East | | 14C | | Early Upper Palaeolithic | 33.9 | 0.9 |
| Shanidar | Mid C | Middle East | | 14C | | Early Upper Palaeolithic | 34 | 0.4 |
| Grotta di Castelcivita | Level rpi | Europe | MC | 14C | | EUP (Uluzzian) | >34 | |
| Foz de Enxarrique | | Europe | MW | U-series | | Middle Palaeolithic | 34.1 | 0.8 |
| Foz de Enxarrique | | Europe | MW | U-series | | Middle Palaeolithic | 34.1 | 0.9 |
| L'Arbreda | E2BE 116-2 | Europe | MW | 14C (AMS) | | Mousterian | 34.1 | 0.75 |
| Geißenklösterle Cave | III | Europe | NC | 14C | | EUP (Aurignacian) | 34.1 | 1 |
| Abri Pataud | 14 | Europe | SW | 14C | | EUP (Aurignacian) | 34.2 | 0.6 |
| Shanidar | Lower C | Middle East | | 14C | | Early Upper Palaeolithic | 34.5 | 0.5 |
| Esquicho-Grapaou | SLC 1b | Europe | MW | 14C | | EUP (Aurignacian) | 34.5 | 2 |
| Boker Tachtit | Level 4 | Middle East | | 14C | | Early Upper Palaeolithic | >35 | |
| Shanidar | Lower C | Middle East | | 14C | | Early Upper Palaeolithic | 35.4 | 0.6 |
| Starosel'e | Vicinity of child 'burial' | Europe | NE | 14C (AMS) | ?Neanderthal | Mousterian | 35.5 | 1.1 |
| ***Hengelo*** | | | | | | | | |
| Geißenklösterle Cave | IIb | Europe | NC | 14C | | EUP (Aurignacian) | 36 | 3.6 |
| St. Césaire | Layer 8, Ejop | Europe | SW | TL | Neanderthal | EUP (Châtelperronian) | 36.3 | 2.7 |
| Kostenki 17 | 2 | Europe | NC | 14C | | EUP (Spitsynian) | 36.4 | 1.7 |
| Starosel'e | Vicinity of child 'burial' | Europe | NE | 14C (AMS) | ?Neanderthal | Mousterian | 36.1 | 1.2 |

Table 6.1 (*cont.*)

| Locale | Layer | Region | | Dating method | Hominids | Archaeology | Kyr bp | ± |
|---|---|---|---|---|---|---|---|---|
| Geißenklösterle Cave | III | Europe | NC | 14C | | EUP (Aurignacian) | 36.5 | 1.5 |
| Vedrovice V | | Europe | NC | 14C | | EUP (Szeletian) | 37.6 | 0.5 |
| El Castilló | 18b2 | Europe | SW | 14C (AMS) | | EUP (Aurignacian) | 37.7 | 1.8 |
| L'Arbreda | E2BE 111-1 | Europe | MW | 14C (AMS) | | EUP (Aurignacian) | 37.7 | 1 |
| L'Arbreda | E2BE 111-2 | Europe | MW | 14C (AMS) | | EUP (Aurignacian) | 37.7 | 1 |
| Boker A | | Middle East | | 14C | | Early Upper Palaeolithic | 37.9 | |
| Gato Preto | Average date | Europe | MW | TL | | EUP (Aurignacian) | 38.1 | 3 |
| St. Césaire | Layer 11, Egp | Europe | SW | TL | | Mousterian (Denticulate) | 38.2 | 3.3 |
| Stránská skála III | 5 | Europe | NC | 14C | | EUP (Bohunician) | 38.2 | 1.1 |
| Kents Cavern | Layer A2 | Europe | NW | 14C | | EUP (Lincombian) | 38.2 | 1.4 |
| Certova Pec | | Europe | NC | 14C | | EUP (Szeletian) | 38.4 | 2.8 |
| Stránská skála III | 5 | Europe | NC | 14C | | EUP (Bohunician) | 38.5 | 1.4 |
| El Castilló | 18b1 | Europe | SW | 14C (AMS) | | EUP (Aurignacian) | 38.5 | 1.8 |
| Korolevo 2 | 2 | Europe | NE | 14C | | Early Upper Palaeolithic | 38.5 | 1 |
| Nietoperzowa | couche 6 | Europe | NC | 14C | | EUP (leaf points) | 38.5 | 1.2 |
| Sclayn Cave | Level 1A | Europe | NW | 14C | | Mousterian | 38.6 | 1.5 |
| Kulna | 7a | Europe | NC | 14C | | Micoquian | 38.6 | 0.95 |
| L'Arbreda | E2BE 111-4 | Europe | MW | 14C (AMS) | | EUP (Aurignacian) | 38.7 | 1.2 |
| Temnata | TDII, layer VI | Europe | SE | 14C | | Early Upper Palaeolithic | >38.7 | |
| Douara | Top IVB | Middle East | | 14C | | Mousterian | 38.9 | 1.7 |
| Combe Grenal | 12 | Europe | SW | 14C | | Mousterian (Denticulate) | 39 | 1.5 |
| L'Arbreda | E2BE 116-1 | Europe | MW | 14C (AMS) | | Mousterian | 39.4 | 1.4 |
| Coudoulous II | Stalagmite floor 2 | Europe | SW | U/Th | | Mousterian | 39.4 | 0.5 |
| Willendorf II | 2 | Europe | NC | 14C | | EUP (Aurignacian) | 39.5 | 1.5 |
| Vedrovice V | | Europe | NC | C14 | | EUP (Szeletian) | 39.5 | 1.1 |
| Istállósko | | Europe | NC | 14C | | EUP (Aurignacian) | 39.7 | 0.9 |
| Cotencher | Couche V | Europe | ALP | 14C | | Mousterian | 39.7 | 1.2 |

| | | | | | | | | |
|---|---|---|---|---|---|---|---|---|
| L'Arbreda | E2BE 111-3 | Europe | MW | 14C (AMS) | | EUP (Aurignacian) | 39.9 | 1.3 |
| Abric Romani | | Europe | MW | U-series | | Mousterian | *39–60* | |
| El Castilló | 18c | Europe | SW | 14C (AMS) | | EUP (Aurignacian) | 40 | 2.1 |
| Riparo Fumane | A2? | Europe | MC | 14C | | EUP (Aurignacian) | 40 | 0.4 |
| Bohunice | 4 | Europe | NC | 14C | | | 40.1 | 1.2 |
| Ripiceni-Izvor | IV/V (minimum age) | Europe | SE | 14C | | Mousterian | 40.2 | 1.1 |
| Le Moustier | J | Europe | SW | TL | Neanderthal | Mousterian (Typical) | 40.3 | 2.6 |
| Cotencher | Couche V | Europe | ALP | 14C | | Mousterian | 40.9 | 1.1 |
| Le Moustier | I | Europe | SW | TL | | None | 40.9 | 5 |
| St. Césaire | Layer 10, Egpf | Europe | SW | TL | | Mousterian (Denticulate) | 40.9 | 2.5 |
| Stránská skála IIIa | 4 | Europe | NC | 14C | | EUP (Bohunician) | 41.3 | 3.1 |
| L'Arbreda | E2BE 116-3 | Europe | MW | 14C (AMS) | | Mousterian | 41.4 | 1.6 |
| Bohunice | 4 | Europe | NC | 14C | | EUP (Bohunician) | 41.4 | 1.4 |
| Amud | Layer B | Middle East | | ESR | Neanderthal | ?Mousterian | 41.5 | 3 |
| Willendorf II | 2 | Europe | NC | 14C | | EUP (Aurignacian) | 41.7 | 3.7 |
| Szeleta | B | Europe | NC | 14C | | EUP (Szeletian) | >41.7 | |
| Frechet Gr de Peyrère I | Upper level | Europe | SW | 14C | | Mousterian | 42 | 3.1 |
| St. Césaire | Layer 12, Egf | Europe | SW | TL | | Mousterian (Denticulate) | 42.4 | 4.8 |
| Ripiceni-Izvor | IV (minimum age) | Europe | SE | 14C | | Mousterian | 42.5 | 1.3 |
| Le Moustier | H2–H9 | Europe | SW | TL | | Mousterian (MTA B) | 42.5 | 2 |
| Le Moustier | K | Europe | SW | TL | | Mousterian | 42.6 | 3.7 |
| Bohunice | 4 | Europe | NC | 14C | | EUP (Bohunician) | 42.9 | 1.7 |
| La Quina | 6a | Europe | SW | TL | | Mousterian (Quina) | 43 | 3.6 |
| Sant'Agostino | Level 1 | Europe | MC | ESR | | Mousterian (Pontinian) | 43 | 9 |
| Bacho Kiro | Layer 11 | Europe | SE | 14C | ?Modern | Early Upper Palaeolithic | >43 | |
| Douara | Mid-IVB | Middle East | | 14C | | Mousterian | >43 | |
| Cotencher | Couche VI | Europe | ALP | 14C | | Mousterian | 43.2 | 1 |
| Douara | Mid-IVB | Middle East | | 14C | | Mousterian | >43.2 | |
| Douara | Lower IVB | Middle East | | 14C | | Mousterian | >43.2 | |
| Ksar Akil | | Middle East | | 14C | | Mousterian | 43.3 | 1.2 |
| Ksar Akil | B? | Middle East | | 14C | | Mousterian | 43.7 | 1.5 |
| Ripiceni-Izvor | IV (minimum age) | Europe | SE | 14C | | Mousterian | 43.8 | 1.1 |
| Königsaue | Ib (minimum age) | Europe | NC | 14C (AMS) | | Micoquian | 43.8 | 2.1 |

Table 6.1 (*cont.*)

| Locale | Layer | Region | | Dating method | Hominids | Archaeology | Kyr bp | ± |
|---|---|---|---|---|---|---|---|---|
| ***Moershoofd*** | | | | | | | | |
| Combe Grenal | 20 | Europe | SW | TL | | Mousterian (Denticulate) | 44 | 4 |
| Sclayn Cave | Level 1A | Europe | NW | TL | | Mousterian | 44 | 5.5 |
| Istállósko | | Europe | NC | 14C | | EUP (Aurignacian) | 44.3 | 1.9 |
| Ripiceni-Izvor | IV (minimum age) | Europe | SE | 14C | | Mousterian | 44.8 | 1.3 |
| Ripiceni-Izvor | III (minimum age) | Europe | SE | 14C | | Mousterian | 45 | 1.4 |
| Banyolas | Matrix | Europe | MW | U-series | Neanderthal | ? | 45 | 4 |
| Temnata | TD1, layer 4 | Europe | SE | TL | | EUP (Aurignacian) | 45 | 7 |
| Boker Tachtit | Level 1 | Middle East | | 14C | | Early Upper Palaeolithic | ≥45.5 | |
| Kulna | 7a | Europe | NC | C14 | | Micoquian | 45.6 | 2.9 |
| Temnata | TD1, layer 4 | Europe | SE | TL | | EUP (Aurignacian) | 46 | 8 |
| Le Moustier | H1 | Europe | SW | TL | | Mousterian (MTA B) | 46.3 | 3 |
| Ripiceni-Izvor | III (minimum age) | Europe | SE | 14C | | Mousterian | 46.4 | 4.7 |
| Gabasa 1 | e | Europe | MW | 14C | | Mousterian (Typical) | 46.5 | 4.4 |
| Boker Tachtit | Level 1 | Middle East | | 14C | | Early Upper Palaeolithic | 46.9 | 2.4 |
| Shanidar | Layer D | Middle East | | 14C | ?Neanderthal | Mousterian | 46.9 | 1.5 |
| Le Moustier | H | Europe | SW | ESR | | Mousterian (MTA B) | *39.7–41* | |
| Guattari | G1 | Europe | MC | ESR | | Mousterian (Pontinian) | *44–54* | |
| Guattari | Surface deposit including cranium | Europe | MC | ESR | Neanderthal | Mousterian (Pontinian) | *44.5–62* | |
| Boker Tachtit | Level 1 | Middle East | | 14C | | Early Upper Palaeolithic | 47.2 | 9 |
| La Chapelle | Bed 1 | Europe | SW | ESR | Neanderthal | Mousterian (Quina) | *47–56* | |
| Bacho Kiro | Layer 13 | Europe | SE | 14C | | Mousterian (Typical) | >47.5 | |

***Glinde***

| | | | | | | | | |
|---|---|---|---|---|---|---|---|---|
| Ioton | | Europe | MW | TL | | Mousterian (Quina) | 48 | 3 |
| Königsaue | Ib (minimum age) | Europe | NC | 14C (AMS) | | Micoquian | 48.4 | 3.7 |
| La Quina | 8 | Europe | SW | TL | | Mousterian (Quina) | 48.7 | 6 |
| Amud | Layer B | Middle East | | ESR | Neanderthal | ?Mousterian | 49.5 | 4 |
| Fonseigner | Level D upper | Europe | SW | TL | | Mousterian (MTA) | 50.2 | 5.3 |
| Le Moustier | G4 | Europe | SW | TL | | Mousterian (MTA A) | 50.3 | 5.5 |
| Le Moustier | G | Europe | SW | ESR | | Mousterian (MTA A) | *43–47* | |
| Shanidar | Layer D | Middle East | | 14C | ?Neanderthal | Mousterian | 50.6 | 3 |
| Guattari | Layer G0 | Europe | MC | U-series | Neanderthal | Mousterian (Pontinian) | 51 | 3 |
| Douara | lower IVB | Middle East | | 14C | | Mousterian | >52 | |
| Ras el Kelb | B | Middle East | | 14C | | Mousterian | >52 | |
| Fonseigner | Level D middle | Europe | SW | TL | | Mousterian (Typical) | 52.8 | 5.5 |
| Sant'Agostino | Level 2 | Europe | MC | ESR | | Mousterian (Pontinian) | 53 | 7 |
| Douara | IIIB | Middle East | | 14C | | Mousterian | >53.8 | |

***Oerel***

| | | | | | | | | |
|---|---|---|---|---|---|---|---|---|
| Sant'Agostino | Level 3 | Europe | MC | ESR | | Mousterian (Pontinian) | 54 | 11 |
| Vilas Ruivas | Averaged date | Europe | MW | TL | | Middle Palaeolithic | 54 | 12 |
| Guattari | Stratum 1 | Europe | MC | ESR | | Mousterian (Pontinian) | 54.2 | 4.1 |
| Pech de L'Azé II | Layer 2 | Europe | SW | ESR | | Mousterian | *54–59* | |
| Le Moustier | G1 | Europe | SW | TL | | Mousterian (MTA A) | 55.8 | 5 |
| Fonseigner | Level E | Europe | SW | TL | | Mousterian (Typical) | 56.4 | 6.8 |
| Guattari | Stratum 1 | Europe | MC | ESR | Neanderthal | Mousterian (Pontinian) | 57 | 8 |
| Roquette II | Levels 2 & 3 | Europe | SW | TL | | Mousterian (Quina) | 57.2 | 4.3 |
| Canale delle Acque Alte | Base of sequence | Europe | MC | 14C | | Mousterian (Pontinian) | 58 | 0.5 |

**STAGE 3/4 BOUNDARY 58 Kyr BP**

Table 6.2. *Accelerator dates using the Arizona facility for L'Arbreda cave in Catalonia (Bischoff et al. 1989).*

| Sample | Lab number | Date Kyr BP |
|---|---|---|
| *Basal Aurignacian between 550–555 cm* | | |
| E2BE 111-1 | AA 3779 | 37.7 ± 1.0 |
| E2BE 111-2 | AA 3780 | 37.7 ± 1.0 |
| E2BE 111-3 | AA 3281 | 39.9 ± 1.3 |
| E2BE 111-4 | AA 3782 | 38.7 ± 1.2 |
| *Uppermost Mousterian between 575–580 cm* | | |
| E2BE 116-1 | AA 3776 | 39.4 ± 1.4 |
| E2BE 116-2 | AA 3777 | 34.1 ± 0.75 |
| E2BE 116-3 | AA 3778 | 41.4 ± 1.6 |

Table 6.3. *The interstadials of the Interpleniglacial, OIS 3 (Behre 1989).*

| Interstadial | Age Kyr BP |
|---|---|
| Oerel | 58–54 |
| Glinde | 51–48 |
| Moershoofd | 46–44 |
| Hengelo | 39–36 |
| Denekamp | 32–28 |

problem lies in comparing the transition between locales and regions and in using such absolute dates to determine rates of change.

*The Interpleniglacial (58–28 Kyr bp)*

The Interpleniglacial is characterized by five interstadials which are widely recorded in pollen profiles from the north of the continent (Table 6.3).

These five major interstadials, which each lasted between 2–4 Kyr, can also be identified in the Summit ice core from central Greenland (Dansgaard et al. 1993:Fig. 1). The appearance and rapid oscillation of these climatic ameliorations stand in stark contrast to the lack of interstadials as recorded in pollen profiles in the preceding Pleniglacial (OIS 4). A reconstruction of conditions at 39 Kyr bp, equivalent to the Hengelo interstadial, is shown in Figure 6.3 (van Andel and Tzedakis 1996:figure 14).

The absolute chronology, based on counting annual laminations, from the Monticchio pollen profile in southern Italy (Watts, Allen and Huntley 1996), makes it possible to correlate the cores from the ocean and ice caps (Figure 5.4).

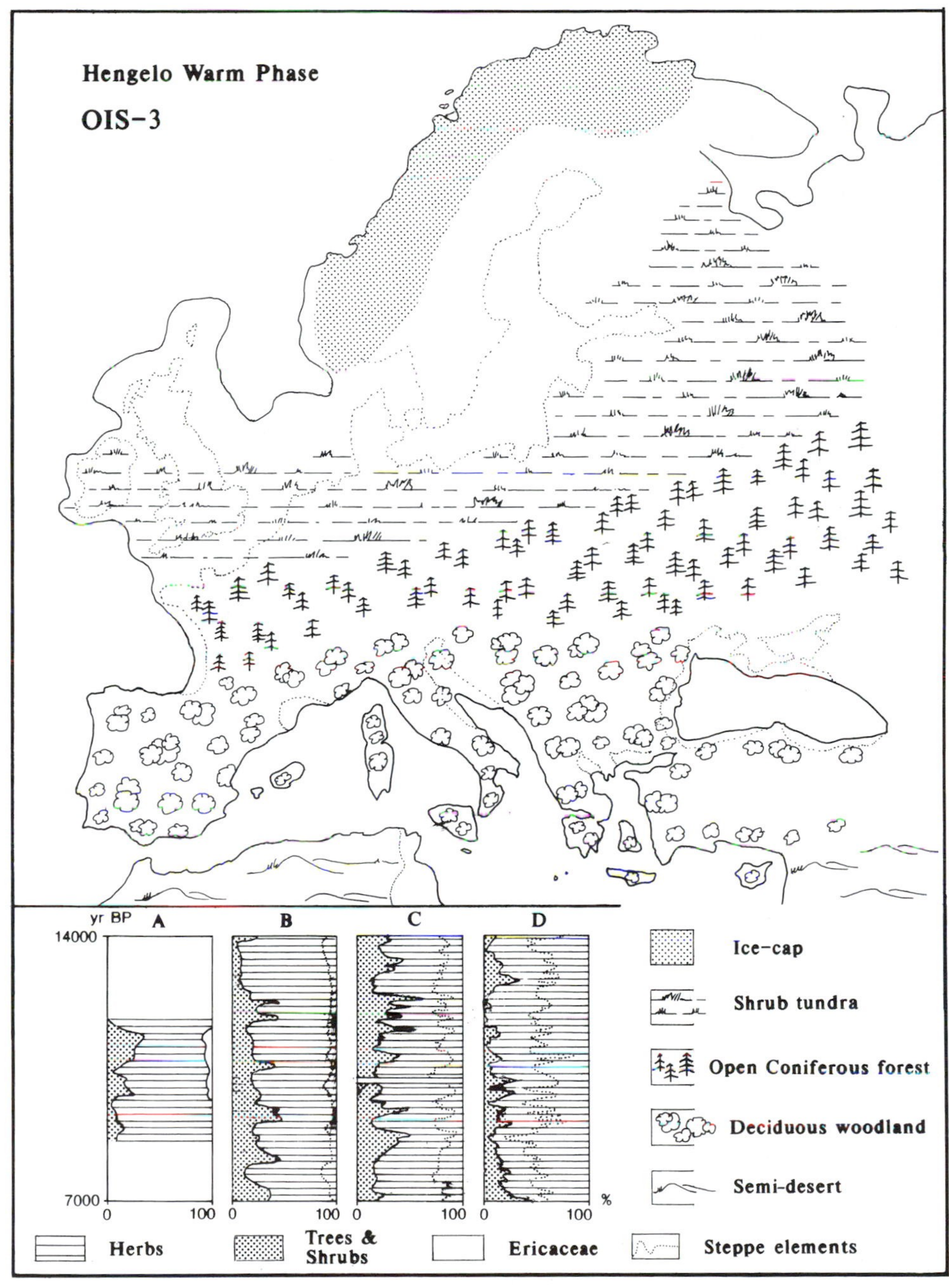


**6.3** European habitats during the Hengelo interstadial in OIS 3, at 39–36 Kyr bp. (after van Andel and Tzedakis 1996:Fig. 6, Zagwijn 1992:Fig. 2).

Key to pollen profiles:

A Hengelo, Netherlands, NW region
B La Grande Pile, France, NC region
C Les Echets, France, SW region
D Philippi, Greece, ME region

In particular Watts et al. (1996:149–51) were able to revise the ages of the so-called six Heinrich events recorded in the ocean cores. These refer to the short-lived but massive discharge of icebergs from the North American Laurentide ice sheet into the North Atlantic. They occurred at 14.5 Kyr (H1), 20.5 Kyr (H2), 23.4 Kyr (H3), 31.8 Kyr (H4), 41.9 Kyr (H5) and 64.2 Kyr (H6). Their significance lies in the sudden changes they brought to the temperature of the oceans and hence the effect this had on the climate of continental areas such as Europe. At Monticchio these events correspond to high herb values indicating more open conditions.

Zagwijn (1992:Fig. 2) has compared the Interpleniglacial interstadials on a north–south transect through Europe (Figure 6.3). He comments that in the Netherlands the vegetation was dominated by moss-tundra, shrub-tundra and tundra meadows. For example, the landscape during the Oerel interstadial, from the type site near Hamburg, is described by Behre (1989:33) as an open treeless shrub-tundra with a rich variety of herbs. The dwarf shrubs which expanded at this time were *Empetrum* and *Calluna* (heathers), while the tree pollen came from the small, shrub-like dwarf birch (*Betula nana*), willows (*Salix*) and juniper (*Juniperus*). Trees were not present in this area of northern Europe during the Oerel interstadial (Behre 1989) and the same conditions characterized the later Glinde interstadial.

The absence of pollen either side of these interstadials is noticeable. This does not mean that such time-periods in the north of the continent were polar deserts, devoid of vegetation like an arctic Sahara. It does however point to generally poorer plant communities. The Interpleniglacial saw an increase in grasses and herbs, and in particular *Artemisia*, which produced the steppe-tundras that supported the mixed communities of large grazing herbivores (Stanley 1980:664). Guthrie (1990) has also argued that snow cover was probably slight and disappeared earlier in the year. The result was a longer growing season while the grazers also benefited from herb diets with higher protein levels (see Bell 1971).

In southern Europe, at the pollen sites of Grande Pile in the Vosges and les Echets in the Rhone valley, steppe elements were more common. Pine and shrubs were present throughout the Pleniglacial, Interpleniglacial and last Glacial maximum. Zagwijn (1992:12) describes the vegetation as generally open and probably meadow-like. At Monticchio woodland was particularly extensive around the lake between 50–42.5 Kyr BP and again between 40.7–37.6 Kyr BP (Watts, Allen and Huntley 1996). Finally, in the western Mediterranean true steppe dominated and the proportion of tree pollen is less than elsewhere in the continent (Suc and Zagwijn 1983).

*Last glacial maximum, downturn phase (28–21 Kyr bp)*

The analysis of the Summit core also points to at least three further interstadials between 28 and 21 Kyr bp (Dansgaard et al. 1993).[3] The $^{18}O$ ratios suggest that these were more ephemeral events.

These weak signals are difficult to match to the continental evidence where there is widespread soil development. At Königsaue in eastern Germany (Mania and Toepfer 1973), peat horizons which formed during more temperate conditions in cycle V are dated to 25.6 Kyr bp (Figure 6.4), equivalent in age to the widespread Briansk soil on the Russian plain dated between 30 and 25 Kyr bp (Desbrosse and Kozlowski 1988:17, Hoffecker 1987:Figure 5).

The Monticchio core (Watts, Allen and Huntley 1996) records rapid fluctuations between tree/vine/shrub and herb pollen between 30–20 Kyr BP. Between 26–14.3 Kyr BP, which broadly corresponds to OIS 2, the local environment was exceptionally treeless with a predominantly seasonally dry, steppe-like vegetation (*ibid.*:145). After Heinrich cycle 4 at 31.8 Kyr BP there is a marked decline in the mean temperature of the coldest month (Figure 5.4) as estimated from pollen data.

The period between 30–20 Kyr bp is generally marked by increased aeolian activity on the northern plains as measured by the deposition of loess. For example, the Briansk soil is overlain by relatively thick loess beds (Hoffecker 1987:269). In her summary of the north European Plain, Kolstrup (1995:figure 2) notes that after 25 Kyr there is increased evidence for frost wedge casts, frost mounds, slope deposits and cold soil surfaces. These all indicate increased erosion and unstable land surfaces which would disrupt vegetation communities. But soils also developed in the loess profiles of Moravia and the Russian plain *between* 25 and 23 Kyr (Hoffecker 1987:269, Kozlowski 1986:Figure 13.2).

In the southwest region the oceanic effect, though reduced, still prevailed. A number of oscillations have been recorded from pollen in cave sediments (Leroi-Gourhan 1980) and of these the Tursac interstadial shows a minor, temperate oscillation between 22–23 Kyr bp.[4]

The temporal and spatial mosaic that existed in continental Europe is well illustrated by Kozlowski's summary of the environmental data (Table 6.4) based mostly on the analysis of major loess profiles in Moravia, the Ukraine and Russia. Vegetation types alternated between steppe, the most productive in terms of herbs and vegetation for grazing species, and tundras. Precipitation and snow cover varied across the region, and in consequence the development of soils within the rapidly accumulating loess deposits is also highly variable by region and period. Kozlowski (1986:136) makes the point that in the central Russian Plain there were greater differences between summer and winter temperatures. This produced a greater depth of annual thaw in the permafrost, which resulted in those productive steppe floras in the northeastern region. In the northcentral region the smaller annual temperature variation, particularly after 23 Kyr bp, would have established a quantitative difference in plant productivity between the two regions.

This complicated mosaic was controlled by ice advance, which accelerated after 25 Kyr bp, and by the changing configurations of the Baltic ocean and the Black and Caspian Seas. The shrinking Adriatic between Croatia and Italy also conditioned the Mediterranean refuges in Greece (Tzedakis 1993), the Balkans generally, and in the Italian peninsula (Mussi 1990).

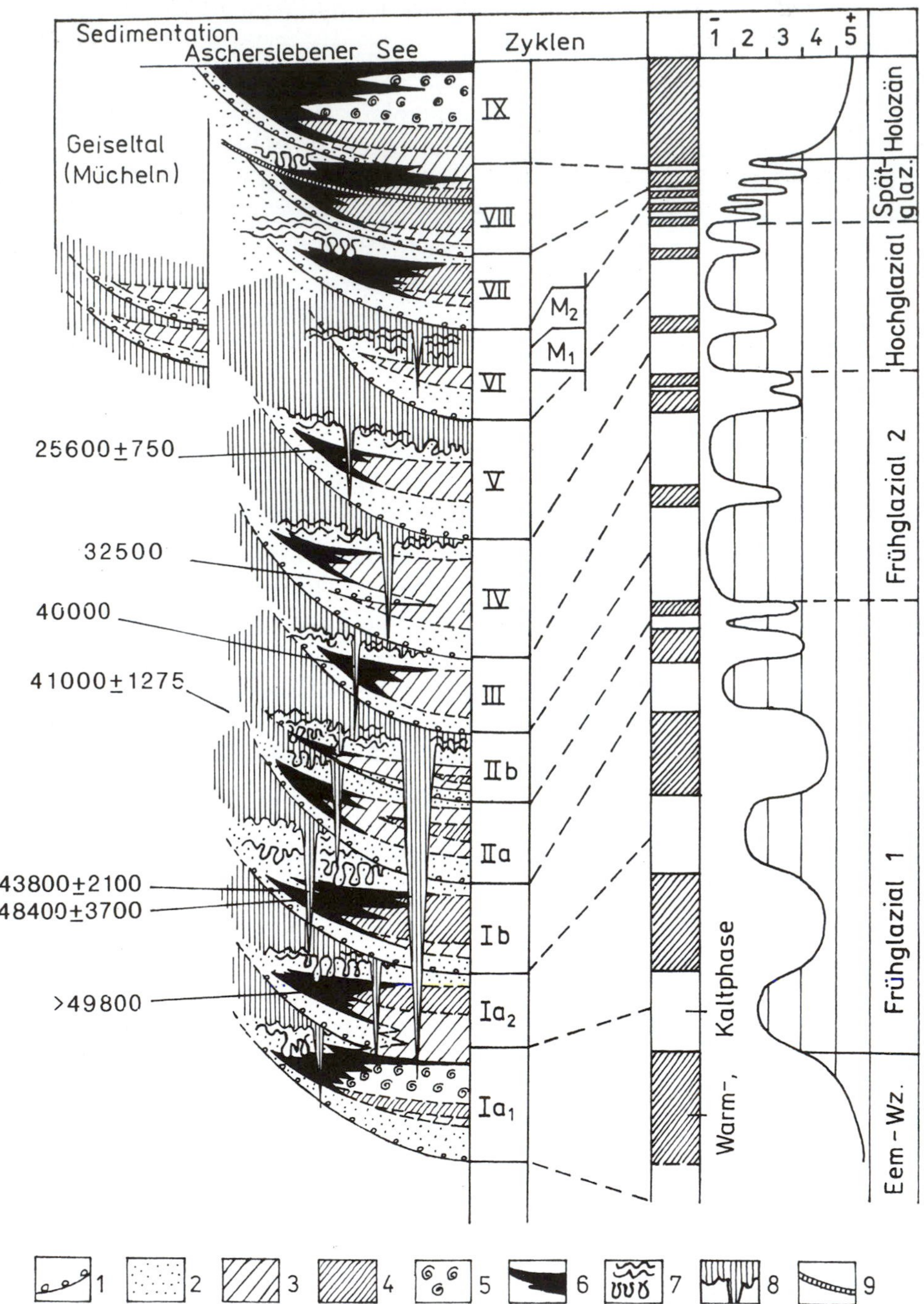

Sedimentation
Aschersiebener See
Geiseltal
(Mücheln)
Zyklen
IX
VIII
VII
VI
V
IV
III
IIb
IIa
Ib
Ia2
Ia1
M2
M1
25600±750
32500
40000
41000±1275
43800±2100
48400±3700
>49800
1 2 3 4 5
Holozän
Spät-glaz.
Hochglazial
Frühglazial 2
Frühglazial 1
Eem-Wz.
Warm-, Kaltphase
1 2 3 4 5 6 7 8 9

*A simplified chronology for the Early Upper Palaeolithic (EUP)*

The transition period is rich in local names for the latest Middle Palaeolithic and the earliest Upper Palaeolithic. In order to simplify what follows I have compiled in Table 6.5 a general chronology for the major archaeological entities which will be discussed later.

A compilation of radiocarbon dates by Davies and Pettitt for the period 44–21 Kyr bp makes it possible to trace the overall pattern of occupation in the continent. In Figure 6.5 I have plotted these dates using the moving sum method (Holdaway and Porch 1995, Housley et al. 1997, Rick 1987) and where the assumption is that the number of dates reflects, in general terms, the density of site and regional occupation. When the dates are plotted in this manner as settlement data we see four main peaks at c. 38, 32, 27 and 21.5 Kyr bp. Van Andel and Tzedakis (1998:figure 6.2) have further calibrated these dates with the geomagnetic curve (Laj, Mazaud and Duplessy 1996). As a result they identify two maxima at c. 40–44 and 31–36 Cal BP coincident with the older ages (see below) for Hengelo and Denekamp interstadials as determined from the GRIP Summit ice core from Greenland (Dansgaard et al. 1993:figure 1). The uncalibrated data (Figure 6.5) only suggest a possible correlation with the Denekamp interstadial.

The sample of radiocarbon dates from which the moving sum curve was calculated has an equal distribution (Table 6.6) between the three main provinces of Europe (Figure 3.1). Only in the period 30–23 Kyr bp does one region, the NC, dominate. The moving sum data can be interpreted as recurrent fluctuations in the numbers of sites, and hence population, across the continent. The peak at 21.5 Kyr bp marks a refuge phase prior to the last glacial maximum (20–18 Kyr bp) with occupation in restricted parts of all three provinces (Table 6.7).

When the number of locales is examined from which these dates were

**6.4** (left) The section of successive lake deposits at the Ascherslebener See, Königsaue, Germany, NC region (after Mania and Toepfer 1973:Abb. 7). Cycles $Ia_1$, $Ia_2$ and Ib are correlated with the Eem, Brørup and Odderade respectively (Figure 5.1). Cycle VI is the last glacial maximum. The AMS dates for level Ib where the three archaeological levels are found must be treated as minimum estimates. The age of the Odderade interstadial lies between 71–85 Kyr BP.

KEY:

1 Erosion surface
2 Sandy sediments
3 Sand and silts
4 Clay silts
5 Organic rich silts
6 Peat
7 Cryoturbation and frozen ground features
8 Solifluction deposits and ice wedge casts
9 Laacher See, east Eifel, volcanic ash in cycle VIII (see Figure 5.8)

Table 6.4. *Environmental data from Central and eastern Europe, 30–17 Kyr BP (Kozlowski 1986 Table 3.1).*

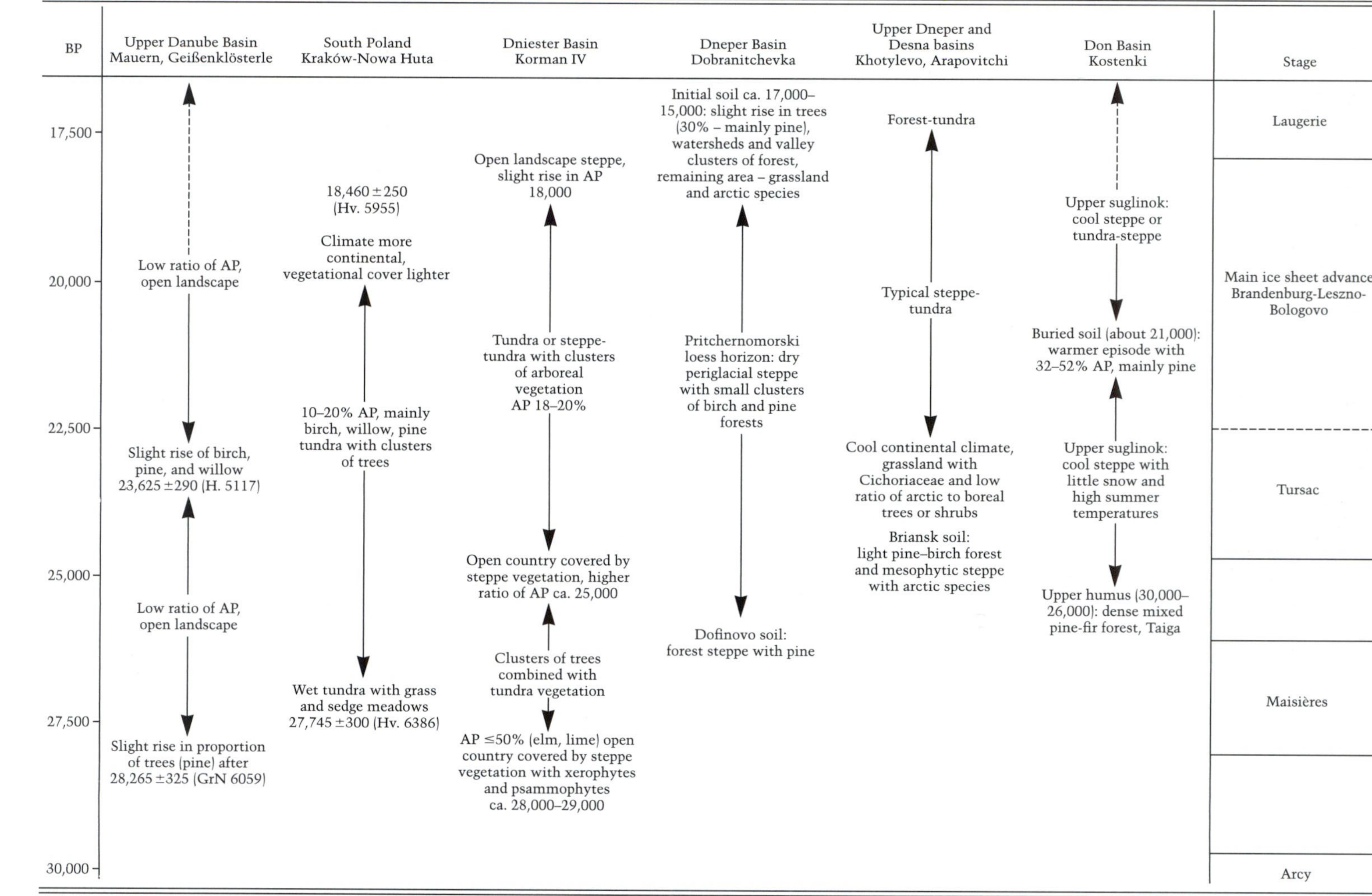

| BP | Upper Danube Basin Mauern, Geißenklösterle | South Poland Kraków-Nowa Huta | Dniester Basin Korman IV | Dneper Basin Dobranitchevka | Upper Dneper and Desna basins Khotylevo, Arapovitchi | Don Basin Kostenki | Stage |
|---|---|---|---|---|---|---|---|
| 17,500 | | | | Initial soil ca. 17,000–15,000: slight rise in trees (30% – mainly pine), watersheds and valley clusters of forest, remaining area – grassland and arctic species | Forest-tundra | | Laugerie |
| | | 18,460 ±250 (Hv. 5955) | Open landscape steppe, slight rise in AP 18,000 | | | Upper suglinok: cool steppe or tundra-steppe | |
| 20,000 | Low ratio of AP, open landscape | Climate more continental, vegetational cover lighter | | | Typical steppe-tundra | | Main ice sheet advance Brandenburg-Leszno-Bologovo |
| | | | Tundra or steppe-tundra with clusters of arboreal vegetation AP 18–20% | Pritchernomorski loess horizon: dry periglacial steppe with small clusters of birch and pine forests | | Buried soil (about 21,000): warmer episode with 32–52% AP, mainly pine | |
| 22,500 | Slight rise of birch, pine, and willow 23,625 ±290 (H. 5117) | 10–20% AP, mainly birch, willow, pine tundra with clusters of trees | | | Cool continental climate, grassland with Cichoriaceae and low ratio of arctic to boreal trees or shrubs | Upper suglinok: cool steppe with little snow and high summer temperatures | Tursac |
| | | | | | Briansk soil: light pine–birch forest and mesophytic steppe with arctic species | | |
| 25,000 | Low ratio of AP, open landscape | | Open country covered by steppe vegetation, higher ratio of AP ca. 25,000 | | | Upper humus (30,000–26,000): dense mixed pine-fir forest, Taiga | |
| | | | Clusters of trees combined with tundra vegetation | Dofinovo soil: forest steppe with pine | | | |
| 27,500 | Slight rise in proportion of trees (pine) after 28,265 ±325 (GrN 6059) | Wet tundra with grass and sedge meadows 27,745 ±300 (Hv. 6386) | AP ≤50% (elm, lime) open country covered by steppe vegetation with xerophytes and psammophytes ca. 28,000–29,000 | | | | Maisières |
| 30,000 | | | | | | | Arcy |

Table 6.5. *An outline chronology for the archaeological cultural groups 60–21 Kyr bp (Allsworth-Jones 1986, 1990, Anikovich 1992, Kozlowski 1986, Oliva 1984, Rigaud 1988b, Svezhentsev 1993, Svoboda 1994c, Svoboda and Simán 1989, Vega Toscano 1993). The division at 33 Kyr bp follows Desbrosse and Kozlowski (1988).*

| | Region | Kyr bp |
|---|---|---|
| *Late Middle Palaeolithic* | | |
| Mousterian of Acheulean Tradition | SW | 60–35 |
| Mousterian | MW | 60–28 |
| *Earliest Upper Palaeolithic 45–33 Kyr bp* | | |
| Bohunician | NC | 44–38 |
| Szeletian | NC, SE | 43–35 |
| Proto-Aurignacian (Bachokirian) | SE | 43 |
| Earliest Aurignacian | MW | 43–33 |
| Uluzzian | MC | >33 |
| Châtelperronian | SW, NW | 37–33 |
| *Leaf point assemblages* | | |
| Altmühlian | NC | 38 |
| Lincombian/Ranis/Jerzmanovician | NW | 39–36 |
| *Early Upper Palaeolithic (EUP) 33–21 Kyr bp* | | |
| Later Aurignacian | All regions | 33–25 |
| Perigordian V–VI (Gravettian) | SW | 27–21 |
| Kostenki-Streletskayan/Sungirian | NE | 33–24 |
| Gravettian (technocomplex) | All except SW & ALP | 30–21 |
| Early Pavlovian | NC, NE | 30–27 |
| Evolved Pavlovian | NC, NE | 27–24 |
| Willendorf/Kostenki | NC, NE | 24–20 |

obtained, the southern regions dominate in all periods except the earliest. This may reflect the interest in dating locales with lithic evidence for the earliest Upper Palaeolithic rather than using the same technique to date Mousterian artifacts.

*Dividing the data at 33 Kyr bp*[5]

There are no convenient matches between the cultural groupings in Table 6.5 and climatic episodes in either the Interpleniglacial or the climatic downturn to the LGM. But one significant chronological hinge does stand out. It is possible to see that the archaeological record changes after 33 Kyr. This involves not only the character of space–time constellations at a regional scale but also corresponding developments in the structure of locales as social occasions (Chapter 3).

The period between 60 and 33 Kyr presents a complicated and longwinded

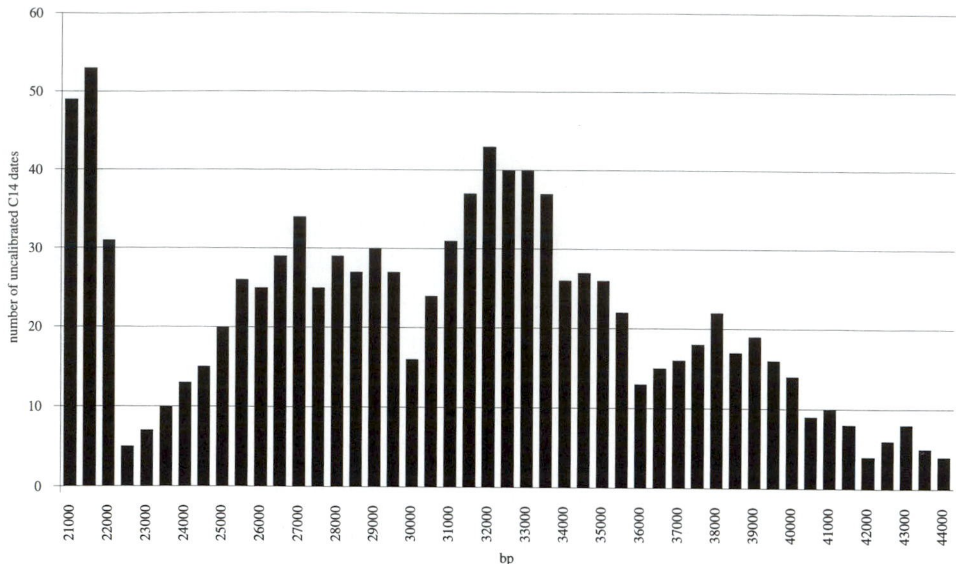


**6.5** The moving sum for uncalibrated C14 dates in the Late Middle and Early Upper Palaeolithic. The method uses a 1000-year moving sum and a 500-year span (data kindly supplied by W. Davies and P. Pettitt with additions).

transition, far removed from the expectations raised by phrases such as 'the human revolution'. But however the transition is characterized, either by replacement or by continuity, the data for technological and typological changes within the nine regions of Europe show it was a polythetic process (Clarke 1968, Stringer and Gamble 1993:Figure 74). Such subtleties have been well summarized by Kozlowski in his multi-aspectual model (1990), shown here in Table 6.8. Under his seven thematic headings there is considerable evidence for continuity and the appearance of new traits during this period. What is most telling in his analysis is that after 30 Kyr bp there is a definite rupture in the record. Only four of his aspects cross this particular timeline:

- Upper Palaeolithic blade technology
- Aurignacian tool kit
- unspecialized use of local raw materials
- figurative art

By contrast nine aspects cross Kozlowski's 40-Kyr bp timeline and at least ten the 35-Kyr bp boundary. These represent the transfer of social skills embodied in technology and subsistence practices. By contrast, the two structural changes which strike me as significant after 33 Kyr are settlement hierarchies and the pronounced inter- and intra-regional variation in material culture. These aspects can be interpreted in terms of new social skills. The conceptual distinction, which I will explore further in the next chapter, is between the

Table 6.6. *The distribution of radiocarbon dates (N=446) between the three provinces of Palaeolithic Europe and within the four main distributions of dates as shown by the moving sum analysis (Figure 6.5).*

| | North % | South % | Mediterranean % | N |
|---|---|---|---|---|
| 40–36 Kyr bp | *36* | *32* | *32* | 60 |
| 36–30 Kyr bp | *32* | *37* | *31* | 174 |
| 30–23 Kyr bp | *43* | *36* | *21* | 157 |
| 22–21 Kyr bp | *36* | *34* | *30* | 55 |

Table 6.7. *The distribution of locales with radiocarbon dates (N=202) in the three provinces of Palaeolithic Europe and within the four main distributions of dates as shown by the moving sum analysis (Figure 6.5).*

| | North % | South % | Mediterranean % | N |
|---|---|---|---|---|
| 40–36 Kyr bp | *43* | *33* | *23* | 30 |
| 36–30 Kyr bp | *25* | *40* | *35* | 67 |
| 30–23 Kyr bp | *32* | *40* | *28* | 68 |
| 22–21 Kyr bp | *30* | *38* | *32* | 37 |

landscape of habit and the social landscape. Let me briefly summarize for this chapter the case for continuity and innovation in social skills.

*Inter- and intra-regional cultural variation*

The regionality of Palaeolithic Europe is very apparent in this period. The late Mousterian is often highly distinctive both within regions and between them. The small leaf point assemblages with their mix of Middle and Upper Palaeolithic techniques are another clear expression of such patterning. Nor does this regionality in the distribution of material culture appear to be an artifact of just better dating and more data.

In Table 6.9 I have used the regional model based on latitude, longitude and relief (Figure 3.1) to provide a geographical summary of some of the differences. While these are simplified snapshots of a complicated cultural geography for the period, they provide a reference point for what follows. In Chapter 7 a series of case studies is presented from each region to emphasize the difference between a cultural and a social approach to the data.

Table 6.8. *A multi-aspectual model of the Middle to Upper Palaeolithic transition (Kozlowski 1990:table 15.1).*

| Date B.P. | Technology | Lithic tools | Bone tools | Raw material economy | Subsistence pattern | Dwelling structures | Art and symbolic system |
|---|---|---|---|---|---|---|---|
| 30,000<br>35,000<br>40,000<br>60,000 | Levallois sensu stricto<br>Mousterian<br>Jankovichian<br>Bohunician<br>Proto-UP blade techn.<br>Upper Palaeolithic Blade Technology<br>Aurignacian and Northern Leaf-point industries<br>Mixed blade and flake technologies (Szeletian, Châtelperronian, Sungirian, etc.)<br>Middle Palaeolithic flake technologies<br>Mousterian | Side-scrapers and denticulate dominated industries/Mousterian<br>Non-specific Upper Palaeolithic tool kit (Bohunician, some EUP industries of Eastern Europe)<br>EUP Eastern industries with backed blades<br>Kostenki 17/1, Early Molodovian<br>Leaf point industries (Szeletian, L-R-J, Sungirian)<br>EUP Western backed blade industries (Châtelperronian, Uluzzian)<br>Aurignacian tool kit | Mousterian unshaped or weakly defined bone tools<br>Aurignacian bone points<br>Large Gravattian bone tool sets | Unspecialized use of local raw materials (Mousterian)<br>Special set of imported raw materials (Early Aurignacian)<br>Unspecialized use of local raw materials (Aurignacian)<br>Systematic extraction of high grade raw materials (Gravettian)<br>Specialized workshops producing leaf points (Balkan Moustero-Levalloisian, Szeletian) | Highly specialized big-game hunting / Post-Acheulian<br>Generalized hunting in the Early Upper Palaeolithic (leaf point industries, Aurignacian)<br>Highly specialized mammoth hunting | Bone used for construction of dwelling structures (Mousterian, Moustero-Levalloisian)<br>(Châtelperronian)<br>Semi-subterranean dwellings with wooden construction (Aurignacian)<br>Bone used for dwellings (Gravettian) | Ornaments and incisions (Mousterian, EUP)<br>Figurative art (Aurignacian, Gravettian) |

Table 6.9. *A simplified cultural geography for the Early Upper Palaeolithic using the nine regional divisions in Figure 3.1.*

| | | |
|---|---|---|
| **60–33 Kyr bp** | | |
| Mousterian<br>Leaf points/<br>Aurignacian<br>Pendants | Mousterian<br>Leaf points/Bohunician<br>Szeletian/Aurignacian<br>Portable art, music<br>(Geißenklösterle) | Mousterian<br>Leaf points/Aurignacian |
| Mousterian<br>Châtelperronian<br>Aurignacian<br>Burial<br>(Le Moustier) | Mousterian<br>Aurignacian | Mousterian<br>Leaf point/Aurignacian<br>Earliest Upper<br>Palaeolithic |
| Mousterian<br>Aurignacian<br>Châtelperronian<br>Cave art (Chauvet) | Mousterian<br>Aurignacian<br>Uluzzian | Mousterian<br>Leaf point/Aurignacian |
| **33–24 Kyr bp** | | |
| Gravettian<br>Font Robert projectiles | Gravettian<br>Burials, places, huts, kilns<br>Mediterranean contacts<br>(Dolní Věstonice, Pavlov) | Gravettian<br>Burials<br>(Sunghir) |
| Perigordian/Gravettian<br>Intensive use of rock<br>shelters and cave art | Abandoned | Gravettian |
| Perigordian/Gravettian<br>Mousterian<br>Late Neanderthal refuge<br>(Zafarraya)<br>Cave art | Perigordian/Gravettian<br>Burials<br>(Balzi Rossi) | Gravettian |
| **24–21 Kyr bp** | | |
| Abandoned | Gravettian<br>Female figurines<br>Shouldered points/knives<br>(Willendorf) | Gravettian<br>Burials, houses, pits<br>Places<br>(Kostenki, Avdeevo) |
| Perigordian/Gravettian<br>Intensive use of rock<br>shelters and cave art | Abandoned | Gravettian |
| Perigordian/Gravettian<br>Cave art | Perigordan/Gravettian | Gravettian |

*Normal environments for recovery*

What we have to determine is whether the complicated archaeological picture prior to 33 Kyr bp (Table 6.5) reflects either the nature of the transition from Middle to Upper Palaeolithic, or a change in the normal environments from which data are recovered. For example, there are two environments which, having preserved a number of flagship sites and many dredgers in earlier periods, do so no longer. These are lakes and shorelines. There are few major lacustrine locales to compare with Hoxne or Neumark-Nord, and there are no shoreline landscapes such as those at Boxgrove, the Brittany raised beaches or Terra Amata in the Mediterranean.

It is difficult to account for the lack of lakeside settlement since many lakes existed due to lower temperatures and reduced evaporation rates. It is perhaps worth noting that such locales in earlier periods are usually associated with interglacial rather than interstadial or Pleniglacial conditions.[6] The rarity of shoreline locales is easier to explain since a lowering of sea level at this time means that most of them are currently submerged. But we have evidence that they were used. Taborin (1993) has identified many shells from the exposed Biscay shelf in Upper Palaeolithic locales from inland southwest France.

*Fluvial settings: loess and colluvial deposition*

Riverside locales are particularly common. There is also a significant depositional change in the north central and northeast regions where the archaeology is covered by either loess or colluvium deposits. While this occurred in earlier periods, it is now uncommon to find archaeological materials incorporated within gravel bodies. This change in emphasis has produced very good preservation conditions.

Around the villages of Kostenki and Borshevo on the west bank of the Don river in Russia, a series of terraces has been cut into the chalk bedrock (Anikovich 1992, Praslov and Rogachev 1982). On these terraces a number of large archaeological locales have been found, as at Kostenki 1/1, Kostenki 4, Kostenki 11 (=Anosovka 2) (Praslov 1981) and Borshevo 2 (Klein 1969). Altogether there are twenty-five major locales spread over 6 km in three main clusters. Most of the locales have evidence for multiple occupation within the colluvial and loess loams which overlie, on the second terrace, a series of humic beds divided by a volcanic ash horizon.

Two locations are important. Firstly, there are locales on the lower terrace very close to the course of the modern Don. These include the four Borshevo locales, as well as Kostenki 4 and Kostenki 3, 19 and 21 to the north of the modern village. The second location is for locales to be hidden within the small but steep-sided chalk ravines that cut through the valley side (Figure 6.6). The ravine where the village of Kostenki shelters contains site 1, the best known in the entire complex, while just to the south the Anosov ravine is the location for Kostenki 11. A further 2 km south is the Aleksandrovka ravine with the Streletskaya and Tel'manskaya locales and Kostenki 4 at its mouth (Figure 6.7).

In both locations, ravine and lower terrace, evidence exists for pits, constructions using mammoth bones, numerous post holes and possibly subterranean dwellings. These have been subsequently covered by calcareous rich colluvium, thus providing ideal conditions for the preservation of bone both on the old surface and in features cut into it.

Similar conditions exist along the Dnestr and Prut rivers in the Ukraine, Moldavia and Roumania. Deeply stratified locales can be found at Ripiceni Izvor (Paunescu 1965), Molodova (Chernysh 1961) and Klimautsy (Anikovich 1992).

Preservation and the history of discovery either through agriculture, as at Kostenki, or through digging loess for brick making, have produced a distinctive settlement pattern. Despite searching, no other Palaeolithic locales, not even a flint scatter, are known in the immediate Kostenki area (Praslov pers. comm.). The nearest locale is Avdeevo, 300 km to the west (Grigor'ev 1993). The concentration of known locales along rivers naturally produces a very linear settlement system. This is also the case in Moravia (Svoboda 1994a:Fig. 59). Here a number of deeply stratified and important locales are located along the rivers leading to the Moravian gate which commands the routes through the Carpathians to southern Poland. One of the most intensively researched is the site of Předmostí, a large brick pit on the Becva river (Absolon and Klíma 1977, Svoboda 1994a, Svoboda et al. 1994). Thick loess deposits accumulated in a depression between two limestone outcrops 300 m apart. These were foci for settlement that began in the Middle Palaeolithic during OIS 5. The main archaeological horizon is an Early Upper Palaeolithic Gravettian occupation which has been radiocarbon dated to 26.3–26.8 Kyr bp (Absolon and Klíma 1977, Svoboda, Lozek and Vlček 1996). It is important to note that while depositional conditions were different between the Middle and Upper Palaeolithic use of this locale (Svoboda et al. 1994) they do not explain the very different character of the archaeological records.

The huge loess sections at this multi-period locale have been investigated since the last century but sadly the records are poor. Many of the finds, including an Upper Palaeolithic mass grave found in 1894 by Maska, and which contained at least twenty individuals (Svoboda et al. 1994:459), were destroyed by fire at the end of World War II.

Both Předmostí and Kostenki were important for the development of area excavations and the realization that horizontal, rather than just stratigraphic, information could be recorded in the Palaeolithic. But at Predmostí the records from the excavations undertaken at the end of the last century are inadequate to reconstruct the activities at such a complex locale.[7] Fortunately this was not the case at Kostenki, where the pioneering excavations during the 1930s by Efimenko (1958), and especially at Kostenki 1 horizon 1, are justly regarded as classics for their time. One of their main effects was to revolutionize the scale at which Palaeolithic settlements were conceived. The plan published by Rogachev (1957:figure 3) shows the main area of excavation to be 760 m$^2$. Subsequent work has doubled this figure (Praslov and Rogachev 1982:figure 10).

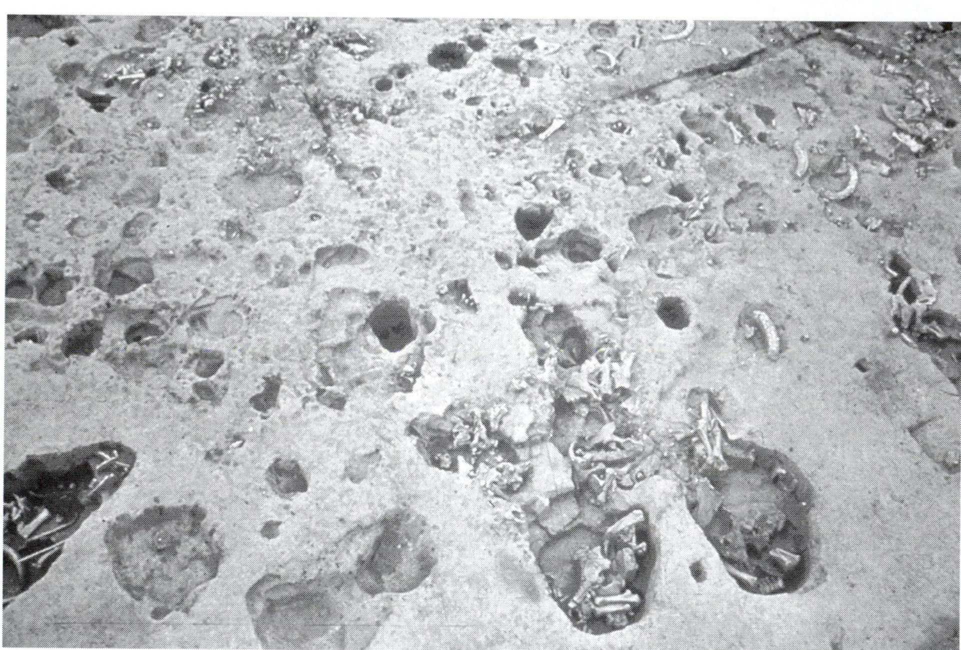

**6.6** (A) The head of the Kostenki ravine within which several locales have been excavated, most notable at Kostenki 1/1 where (B) arrangements of pits and open-air hearths as well as (C) semi-subterranean dwellings have been excavated ((A and C photos by the author; (B) N. D. Praslov).

**6.6** (*cont.*)

*Caves and abris*

There are cave locales occupied during this period in all the European regions, including the Alps. There are sufficient differences between the character of the archaeological record at these locales to warrant inter-regional comparison.

*Northern and Alpine regions* This period sees the first occupation of the Alpine region (Figure 3.1). The cave of Cotencher at an altitude of 660 m near Lake Neuchâtel in Switzerland has a collection of 400 Mousterian artifacts dated to 43.2 Kyr bp (Le Tensorer 1993:138).[8] At the eastern end of the Alpine region, Potocka Zijalka in Slovenia lies at an altitude of 1,700 m and contains Early Upper Palaeolithic artifacts (Allsworth-Jones 1990).

This last locale is one of a number of caves in the northwest and north-central regions which have produced collections considered both stratigraphically and typologically important in the discussion of transitions (Allsworth-Jones 1986, 1990). These include, from southern England, Kents Cavern, in southern Germany the Weinberghöhlen at Mauern in the Altmühl valley, the Ilsenhöhle at Ranis in eastern Germany, the Nietoperzowa cave at Jerzmanovice in southern Poland, in the Hungarian Bükk mountains the Szeleta and Istállósko caves, and Jankovich cave in Transdanubian Hungary in the southeast region.

However, despite their celebrity in the literature of the Middle to Upper Palaeolithic transition, these caves have invariably produced numerically small collections from very extensive excavations (Table 6.10).

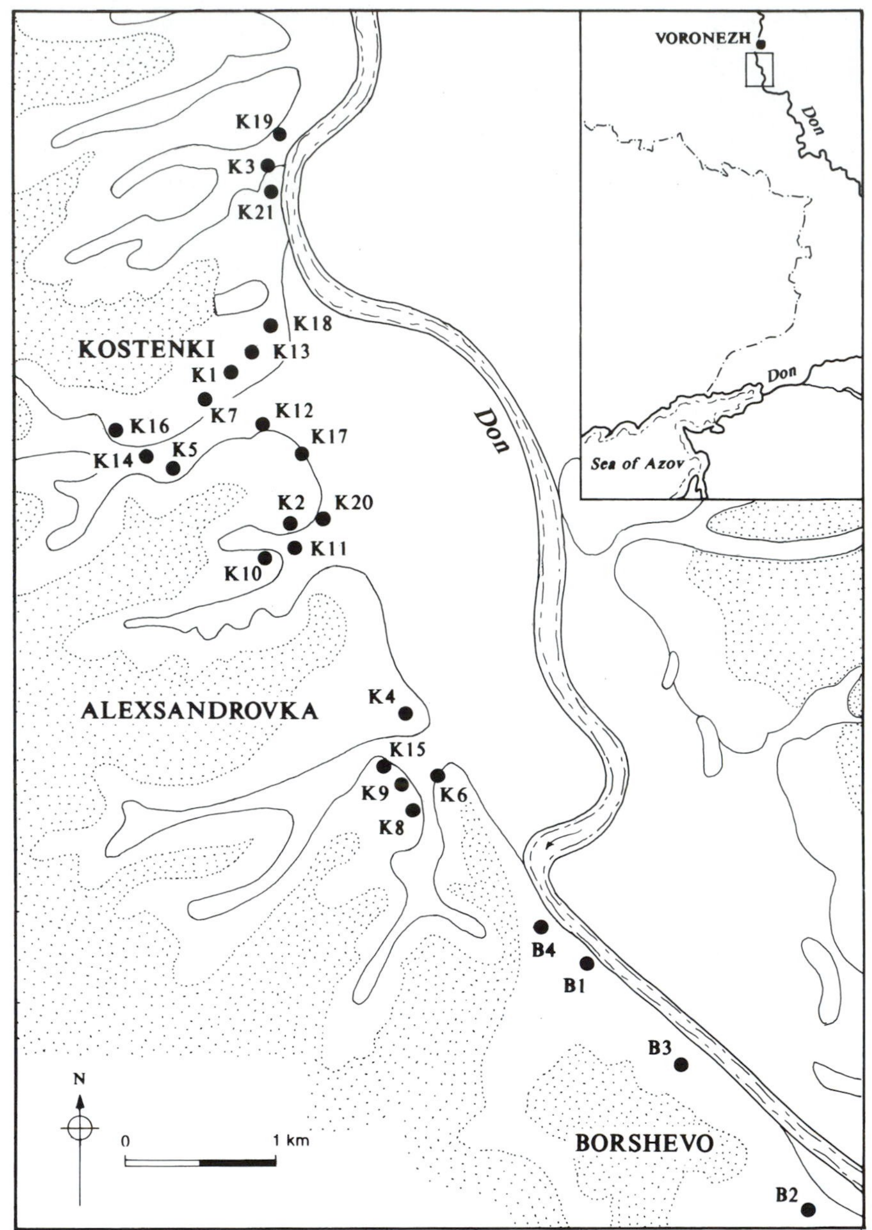


**6.7** The archaeological locales which lie on the west bank of the Don around the modern villages of Kostenki, Alexsandrovka and Borshevo, Russia, NE region (after Valoch 1995:Abb. 3).

Table 6.10. *Artifact totals and calculated indices for nine central European cave sites with important transitional assemblages between the Middle and Upper Palaeolithic (Allsworth-Jones 1990:Table 7.6, with additions from Freund (1987)). Bacho Kiro from the southeast region is included for comparison (Kozlowski 1982).*

| Locale | Stone tools | Cores | Flakes, blades, debris | Total stone artifacts | Bone and ivory artifacts | Cores as % of tools and cores | Tools and cores as % total of stone artifacts |
|---|---|---|---|---|---|---|---|
| *Mousterian* | | | | | | | |
| Mauern G | 94 | 56 | 463 | 613 | | *38* | *25* |
| *Leaf point* | | | | | | | |
| Mauern F | 114 | 17 | 269 | 400 | | *13* | *33* |
| Oberneder 3 gen | 62 | 3 | 143 | 205 | | *5* | *32* |
| Ranis 2 | 60 | | 3 | 63 | | | *95* |
| Ranis 3 | 91 | 9 | 40 | 140 | | *9* | *71* |
| Nietoperzowa, layers 6,5,4 | 132 | 5 | 116 | 253 | ?1 | *4* | *54* |
| Krizova, layers 7,8,9 | 10 | 1 | 19 | 30 | | *9* | *37* |
| *Jankovician* | | | | | | | |
| Jankovich | 102 | | 14 | 116 | 21 | | *88* |
| *Szeletian* | | | | | | | |
| Szeleta | | | | | | | |
| layers 3&4 | 259 | 9 | 635 | 903 | 2 | *3* | *30* |
| layers 5–7 | 216 | 5 | 479 | 700 | | *2* | *32* |
| *Aurignacian* | | | | | | | |
| Istállósko (1950–1) | | | | | | | |
| layer 9 | 17 | 2 | 27 | 46 | 114 | *11* | *41* |
| layers 7&8 | 54 | 2 | 53 | 109 | 31 | *4* | *51* |
| Potocka Zijalka | 70 | 6 | 229 | 305 | 130 | *8* | *25* |
| *Bachokirian/earliest Aurignacian* | | | | | | | |
| Bacho Kiro, level 11 | 667 | 18 | 19,149 | 19,834 | | *2.6* | *3.5* |

This point has been well made by Allsworth-Jones in his comprehensive review of the evidence (1990:192–4). For example, Potocka Zijalka is a 115-m-long cave which has been cleared by excavators. The small number of finds (Table 6.10) come variously from the front and the back and are in places associated with large hearths containing charcoal (Brodar and Brodar 1983).

The tiny collection from the Transdanubian cave of Jankovich has given its name to a local culture. Allsworth-Jones (1990:192) reminds us that not only is this the 'richest' Jankovichian assemblage but it came from excavations in the cave which in places were 5 m in depth![9]

In summary, Allsworth-Jones comments that all nine transitional sites in Table 6.10

> clearly give the impression of having constituted specialised, intermittent, and for the most part strictly temporary settlements. (Allsworth-Jones 1990:196)

This is a conclusion also reached by Freund (1987) in her detailed discussion of the small collections including leaf points from the Oberneder cave in the Altmühl valley.

It is therefore unfortunate that they have been used to form the basis for charting the transition between the Middle and earliest Upper Palaeolithic in the region. Such are the complexities of discovery, reporting and even survival in museums of the material (Allsworth-Jones 1986, 1990) that these sites and their collections have ravelled rather than unravelled the skein of possible connections. It is not that we should ignore the evidence they contain but rather put it into perspective when judged against other, larger and probably more representative collections such as the Bacho Kiro (Table 6.10) and Temnata caves in Bulgaria, southeast region (Kozlowski, Laville and Ginter 1992, Kozlowski 1982).

Two factors keep these caves and their collections under the transitional spotlight. Firstly, some are C14 dated to >40 Kyr bp which, given the problems of contamination discussed above, probably means they are in fact much older. The second factor is that these tiny collections do contain distinctive type-fossils in the form of stone leaf-shaped points and bone tools, often in the form of projectile points which would have been hafted.

While they are by no means the only criteria, the presence of leaf points is often a key element in talking about the transition in central and eastern Europe (Desbrosse and Kozlowski 1988). These highly varied, but always distinctive types occur with Middle Palaeolithic artifacts at Mauern (Müller-Beck 1973), which is the type site for the Altmühlian, and with an Upper Palaeolithic technology and typology at Szeleta, after which the Szeletian is named, and Kents Cavern, type site of the Lincombian (Campbell 1977). Bone and antler points are a trademark of the Aurignacian, which is an undisputed Upper Palaeolithic industry. They outnumber the retouched stone tools at Istállósko level 9. Two occur in Szeletian levels at Szeleta cave although the stratigraphy here is very confused (Svoboda and Simán 1989:299). They are absent in the leaf point assemblages (Table 6.10) and have not been found with the Mousterian. They are also absent in Bacho Kiro level 11 where a rich Upper Palaeolithic assemblage with Aurignacian features has been called the Bachokirian (Kozlowski 1982:141).

It can be seen therefore that the environment of recovery has contributed in no small measure to the debate on transitions from Middle to Upper Palaeolithic technologies and typologies. It is Hahn's opinion (1987), based on his experience of excavating the Geißenklösterle cave in southern Germany, that cryoturbation by moving artifacts through the sediments has produced more levels than truly existed. Refitting is the key to understanding the problem. His observations add to the problem of demonstrating developmental sequences for leaf points based on such small samples. At Szeleta, the effect of cryoturbation on artifacts misled some typologists into regarding them as primitive (Allsworth-Jones 1986). The conclusion must be that on this evidence the transition was at best polythetic in character and at worst cannot be traced with such data. It would be more sensible, as Desbrosse and Kozlowski (1988, Kozlowski 1988) and Svoboda and Simán (1989) have done, to concentrate on the larger collections of material dated to >40 Kyr bp in the open locales of Moravia. These include the Bohunician, an Early Upper Palaeolithic industry confined to Moravia (Oliva 1984, Valoch 1995), and the large surface collections and excavated assemblages of Szeletian and Aurignacian artifacts in the same region (Table 6.11).

The point made by this comparison is that the quantities of material deposited in the caves is very small. This reinforces Allsworth-Jones' conclusion concerning the specialized character of these assemblages.

Elsewhere in the north-central region the situation is different. In southern Germany the Aurignacian is the earliest Upper Palaeolithic and represents the only Palaeolithic presence in the area after the Hengelo interstadial. Two cave locales in the Swabian limestone uplands have significant collections (Table 6.12). The Vogelherd was almost totally excavated by Riek (1934), while the Geißenklösterle (Hahn 1988) still has substantial deposits left.

The contrast between these larger collections, and the open locales of Moravia and the small cave occupations of eastern Europe (Tables 6.11 and 6.12), is that, to date, in southern Germany there are no significant open locales within comparable distances, i.e. less than 200 km. The upper reaches of the Rhine and Danube are both lacking in open settlements from this period and indeed throughout the EUP to 21 Kyr bp. The nearest open locales are Lommersum in the Köln basin, Breitenbach on the middle Elbe, and Krems-Hundssteig in the Austrian Wachau (Hahn 1977). All three are more than 300 km distant from the Vogelherd. A similar pattern between the two areas is found among Gravettian settlements in the period 29–21 Kyr bp.

As a general rule the artifact collections from caves are small during this period in the northern regions. This applies to both Middle and Upper Palaeolithic collections. But, as was noted in Chapter 5, there are exceptions,

Table 6.11. *Collection sizes from surface and excavated locales in Moravia for the earliest Upper Palaeolithic in the region (Allsworth-Jones 1990, Desbrosse and Kozlowski 1988, Svoboda 1994a).*

| | Tools | Total chipped stone |
|---|---|---|
| *Szeletian* | | |
| Jezerany 1 | 737 | 4,527 |
| Jezerany 2 | 524 | 4,139 |
| Neslovice | 507 | 3,913 |
| Orechov 1 | 651 | 4,073 |
| Orechov 2 | 198 | 877 |
| Vedrovice V | 161 | 4,946 |
| *Bohunician* | | |
| Bohunice | 233 | |
| Lisen | 1,391 | |
| Ondratice | 946 | |
| *Aurignacian* | | |
| Vedrovice 2 | 262 | 2,130 |
| Kuparovice 1 | 270 | 5,396 |

Table 6.12. *Collection sizes from two excavated caves in southern Germany for the earliest Upper Palaeolithic in the region and the three largest open locales in the north-central region (Hahn 1977, 1988).*

| | Tools | Total chipped stone | Antler/bone/ivory points |
|---|---|---|---|
| *Aurignacian: cave locales* | | | |
| Vogelherd V | 909 | 2,132 | 40 |
| Vogelherd IV | 1,729 | 3,387 | 13 |
| Geißenklösterle II | 233 | 1,594 | 33 |
| Geißenklösterle III | 96 | 1,413 | 3 |
| *Aurignacian: open locales* | | | |
| Breitenbach | 675 | 5,123 | 0 |
| Krems-Hundssteig | 3,379 | no data | 0 |
| Lommersum | 158 | 1,228 | 0 |

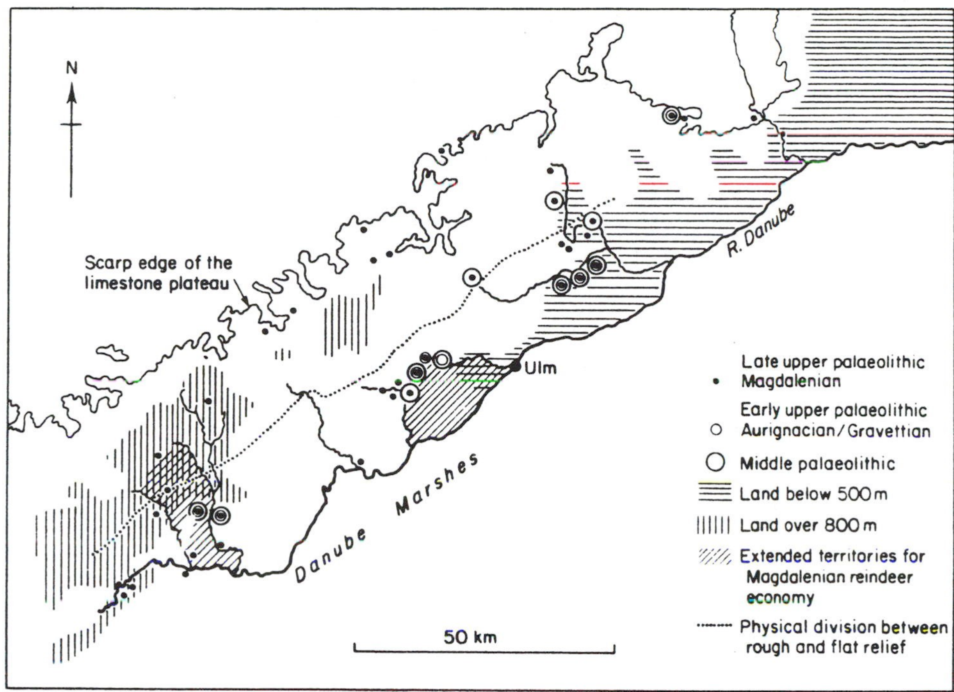


**6.8** The distribution of Palaeolithic sites on the Swabian Alb, southern Germany, NC region. The Ach valley sites (see Figure 6.18) lie to the west of Ulm (after Gamble 1986a:Fig. 5.12).

for example Kulna level 7a with a rich late-Micoquian level (Valoch 1988). More often however the assemblages are small, comparable to those from Mauern level G (Table 6.10).

The comparability of the Palaeolithic cave records, at least in simple quantified terms, can be illustrated with a study from a well-researched area in the north-central region, southern Germany. Here the limestone plateaux of the Swabian and Frankonian Albs lie to the north of the Danube river. The limestone is in places deeply cut by small rivers, among them the Ach/Blau, Lone and Altmühl, some of which now flow in former courses cut by the Danube.

The caves have been intensively studied for more than a century. Even so, recent excavations in the Altmühl valley have shown that the shallow abris close to the river, which for many years were thought to have had their contents eroded, can contain substantial late Middle Palaeolithic deposits, as at Abri Schulerloch (Utz Böhner pers. comm.). Dating such Middle Palaeolithic locales is problematic, but Müller-Beck (1988:Figure 14.1) places several of the larger collections in the period 60–35 Kyr bp.[10]

Taken together, the number of findspots is small (Figure 6.8). In an earlier inventory (Gamble 1986a:Table 6.14) I counted 42 Middle Palaeolithic sites[11] and 21 Early Upper Palaeolithic (Aurignacian and Gravettian) sites from an area of some 15,600 km$^2$, giving densities of 0.0028 and 0.0014 locales per km$^2$ respectively. This figure has not changed dramatically in the meantime. The reason is that open locales, which can be found quickly and so add rapidly to regional site inventories, are uncommon. In 1986 the one major open locale was the Speckberg in the eastern Altmühl valley. It is located on the plateau behind a small river cliff and has produced large quantities of Middle and Upper Palaeolithic artifacts (Hahn 1982, Müller-Beck 1973). But these come from cryoturbated and disturbed contexts making it difficult to assess the significance of the locale. The only other important open locale is Wittlingen (Burkert, et al. 1992) in the northern Swabian Alb. Here fieldwalking has collected a total of 1,322 lithics of which 254 were modified and 62 were cores, several of them levallois. The Middle Palaeolithic artifacts from Wittlingen have been assigned an OIS 4 age.

There is however continuity in the location of Palaeolithic cave occupation within these uplands. Those caves with both Middle and Early Upper Palaeolithic occupation are consistently located in the middle of the flat limestone plateaux close to the Danube, rather than the higher, more rugged relief that runs up to the scarp edge in the north (Gamble 1978, 1979, 1986a:Figure 5.12). Such repeated locations can be explained by the more productive flat landscapes with varied soils, lower altitude and hence increased grazing potential. Caves were selected to position both hominids and carnivores in the middle of this productive zone, thereby optimizing distances as predicted by site catchment analysis (Vita-Finzi and Higgs 1970).

Müller-Beck (1988), however, draws a different conclusion (Figure 6.9). His assessment places the Danube valley, rather than the limestone plateaux, as the most productive area in the landscape. He even draws two hypothetical base camps in the valley, even though no sites of this period have yet been found there. These base camps, if they are ever found, would redefine the relationship of the caves to the north in the Lonetal, such as the Hohlenstein-Stadel, Bockstein and Vogelherd, and in the Achtal with the Geißenklösterle, Sirgenstein and Große Grotte. They would become part of a local settlement system exploiting the different resources in a highly differentiated Danube Valley (Table 6.13).

The flat plateau area which I favour as the main resource area, albeit on a seasonal basis for mixed herds of grazing animals, is in Müller-Beck's assessment the least productive zone. By the same token I would regard the Danube Valley as difficult, marshy country which most grazing species would avoid (Sturdy 1975).

These different interpretations, and the willingness to speculate upon either the contemporaneity of Palaeolithic sites whose ages could be scattered over many millennia, or the existence of as yet undiscovered major home bases, neatly expresses the change in interpretation between this period and those I reviewed in Chapters 4 and 5.

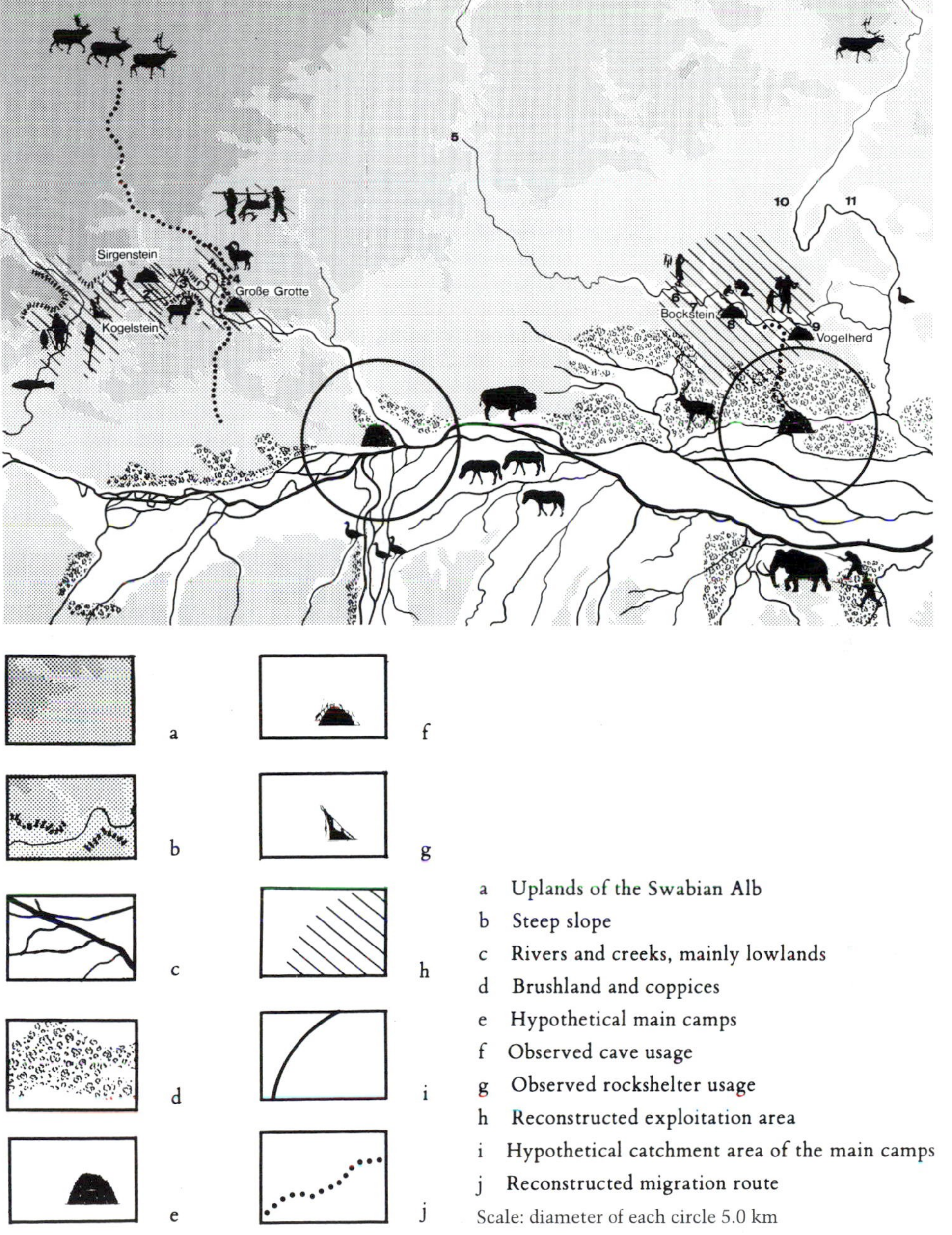


**6.9** Ecology and settlement in the Upper Danube during the Middle Palaeolithic (after Müller-Beck 1988:Fig. 14.10).
KEY to locales:

1 Kogelstein/Schmiechen
2 Sirgenstein
3 Geißenklösterle
4 Große Grotte
5 Urspring/Haldensteinhöhle
6 and 7 Bocksteinschmiede & Bockstein
8 Hohlenstein-Stadel
9 Vogelherd
10 Heidenschmiede
11 Irpfelhöhle

Table 6.13. *Habitats and faunal grazing preferences in the Danube Valley and its tributaries (Müller-Beck 1988:Table 14.1).*

| Taxa | Dry valley bottom | Wet valley bottom | Slope areas | Plateaux |
|---|---|---|---|---|
| Mammoth | Bushes | Grass, sedge | Sedge, copse | Herbs (few) |
| Horse | Grass | Grass, sedge | Sedge | |
| Bison | Grass | Grass, sedge | Sedge | Herbs (few) |
| Red deer | Copse | Grass | Copse | |
| Reindeer | Copse, grass | Grass, sedge | Sedge, copse | Herbs, lichen |

*Southern regions* A feature of all the southern regions, as well as of the Crimean caves in the northeast region (Boriskovsky 1984, Klein 1965), is that open locales are either unknown, or have lower research status when compared to caves and abris.

Straus (1992) notes for Cantabrian Spain, in the southwest region, that open locales have still not been found for this period. In the Périgord and Charente there are late Middle Palaeolithic open locales, for example Barbas and Toutifaut, both of which are Mousterian of Acheulean Tradition (Guichard 1976), as well as Early Upper Palaeolithic open locales such as Tambourets (Bricker and Laville 1977) and Corbiac (Bordes 1968b). However, rock shelters are the normal environment where both late Mousterian (Turq 1992b) and Early Upper Palaeolithic, as at St Césaire (Leveque, Backer and Gilbaud 1993), Abri Pataud (Movius 1975, 1977) and La Ferrassie (Delporte and Maziere 1977), have been investigated. This is also the case in the southeast region with the Bacho Kiro and Temnata caves (Kozlowski, Laville and Ginter 1992, Kozlowski 1982) which have eclipsed in importance, for the discussion of industrial sequences and transitions, the much smaller open locales at Banat in Roumania (Allsworth-Jones 1986, Mogosanu 1976, 1978).

The detailed investigation of cave and abri sediments in Périgord has been undertaken by Laville (1975, Laville, Rigaud and Sackett 1980). This intricate chronostratigraphic scheme using climatic interpretations of the sediments has been revised in the light of C14 and TL dates and correlated with the pollen profiles of Grande Pile and Les Echets (Laville, Raynal and Texier 1986).

One problem with the scheme is that no single site has a complete sequence. This discontinuous record is particularly apparent in the time period 60–21 Kyr bp, which covers in Laville's chronostratigraphy Würm II (OIS 3), Würm III (OIS 2) and the Interpleniglacial interstadials Würm II/III. An abrupt break (Laville, Rigaud and Sackett 1980:135, Fig.6.1) exists in all the cave stratigraphies. Sequences either end at the Würm II/III boundary, as at Combe Grenal and Pech de l'Azé I, or begin after it as at Abri Pataud and Roc de Combe. This is in keeping with Laville's contention that all cave sediments are cold climate in origin and that interstadial periods are only represented by erosion events. But this view of erosion under temperate conditions is not shared by Farrand

(1975:64), also working in the Périgord, or by Brunnacker (1982:128, Brunnacker and Streit 1966) dealing with cave sediments from southern Germany. Neither does Butzer, working on cave sediments from Cantabrian Spain, have any difficulty with assigning sediments either to the last interglacial (OIS 5e) or to the Interpleniglacial interstadials. The chronostratigraphy of the Périgord therefore requires an independent dating framework rather than correlations drawn between cave sequences.

In spite of these methodological uncertainties the chronostratigraphic framework has been widely used. Rolland (1990:Figure 13.2) has adapted Laville's scheme to compare four of the five Mousterian assemblage types against climate. While he acknowledges that the range of climates is broad, Rolland is able to show that the Denticulate Mousterian is commonly associated (70 per cent, n=46) with sediments indicating milder or more temperate climates. On the contrary, both the Quina and Ferrassie variants of the Charentian Mousterian occur predominantly (>80 per cent, n=70) in sediments indicative of more severe conditions. These range from cold/wet to cold/dry and very/cold to very/dry.[12]

The chronological sequence noted by Mellars (1992, 1996, 1969) adds support to Rolland's conclusion. He demonstrated on stratigraphic grounds that Quina assemblages (Table 5.8), dated now by Turq (1992b:77) to be generally OIS 4 and therefore >60 Kyr bp, are always stratified above the Ferrassie variant. Moreover, when present, the Mousterian of Acheulian Tradition (MTA) type A, with triangular bifaces, and type B with none but with naturally backed knives, is always the latest in the stratified sequences, as at Combe Grenal (Figure 6.10). When chronological patterning can be demonstrated as Mellars has done (1996), then the association between climate, resources and assemblage types seems more plausible.

What can be said is that in the southwest region the normal environments for recovery are comparable during the transition from the Middle to the Upper Palaeolithic. Of particular interest are the small number of Châtelperronian assemblages which are found between 37 and 33 Kyr bp`(Harrold 1989:table 33.2). The Neanderthal skeleton at St Césaire layer 8 (Leveque, Backer and Gilbaud 1993) is associated with a Châtelperronian assemblage with its characteristic curved, blunted backed points or knives (Figure 6.11) and dated by TL to 36.3 Kyr bp. Geographically the Châtelperronian is found from the Grotte du Renne (at Arcy sur Cure on the Yonne river in the northwest region) to El Pendo and Cueva Morin in Cantabria (Straus 1992:73).

Apart from its distinctive points it is difficult to characterize the Châtelperronian. As Harrold (1989) demonstrates, one of its main characteristics is small assemblage size (Table 6.14).

Furthermore, while there is continuity in basic flake production between late Mousterian and Châtelperronian, there is also more emphasis on making blades in the latter (*ibid.*:691). The problem, as Harrold notes, is the existence of typological and technological schemes which separate the Middle from the

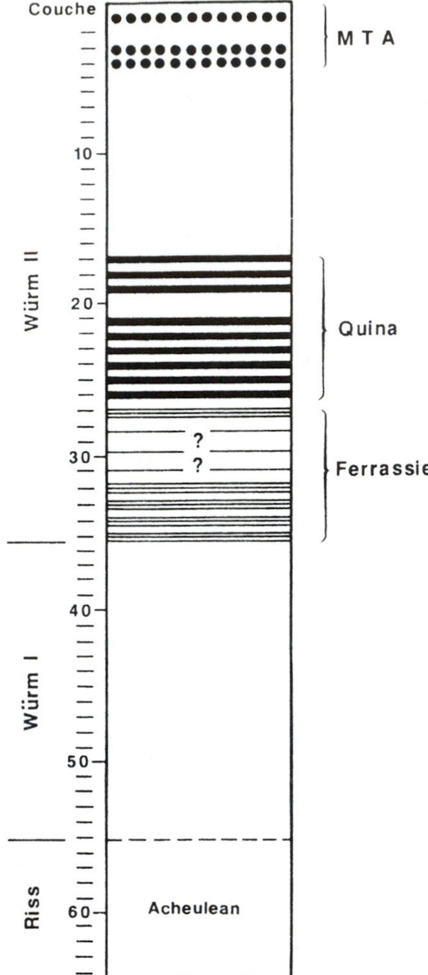


**6.10** The stratigraphic distribution by level (Fr. *couche*) of Ferrassie, Quina and MTA industries within the Mousterian succession at Combe Grenal, France, SW region (after Mellars 1996:Fig. 6.16).

Upper Palaeolithic; for example contrast Bordes' (1961b) approach to the Middle Palaeolithic (Chapter 5) and de Sonneville-Bordes and Perrot's (see also de Sonneville-Bordes 1960, 1954–6) *lexique typologie* for the Upper Palaeolithic. When alternative schemes are applied the transition is much less abrupt. Simek and Price (1990), for example, tested the notion that Upper Palaeolithic assemblages were more diverse than their Mousterian counterparts and so represent a radically different type of techno-economic system.[13] Their statistical analysis showed no fine-scale breaks in assemblage diversity between the Mousterian and the Early Upper Palaeolithic. Interestingly, richness in assemblages, which is often dependent on sample size, does show a break between the Châtelperronian and the Aurignacian, as might be expected

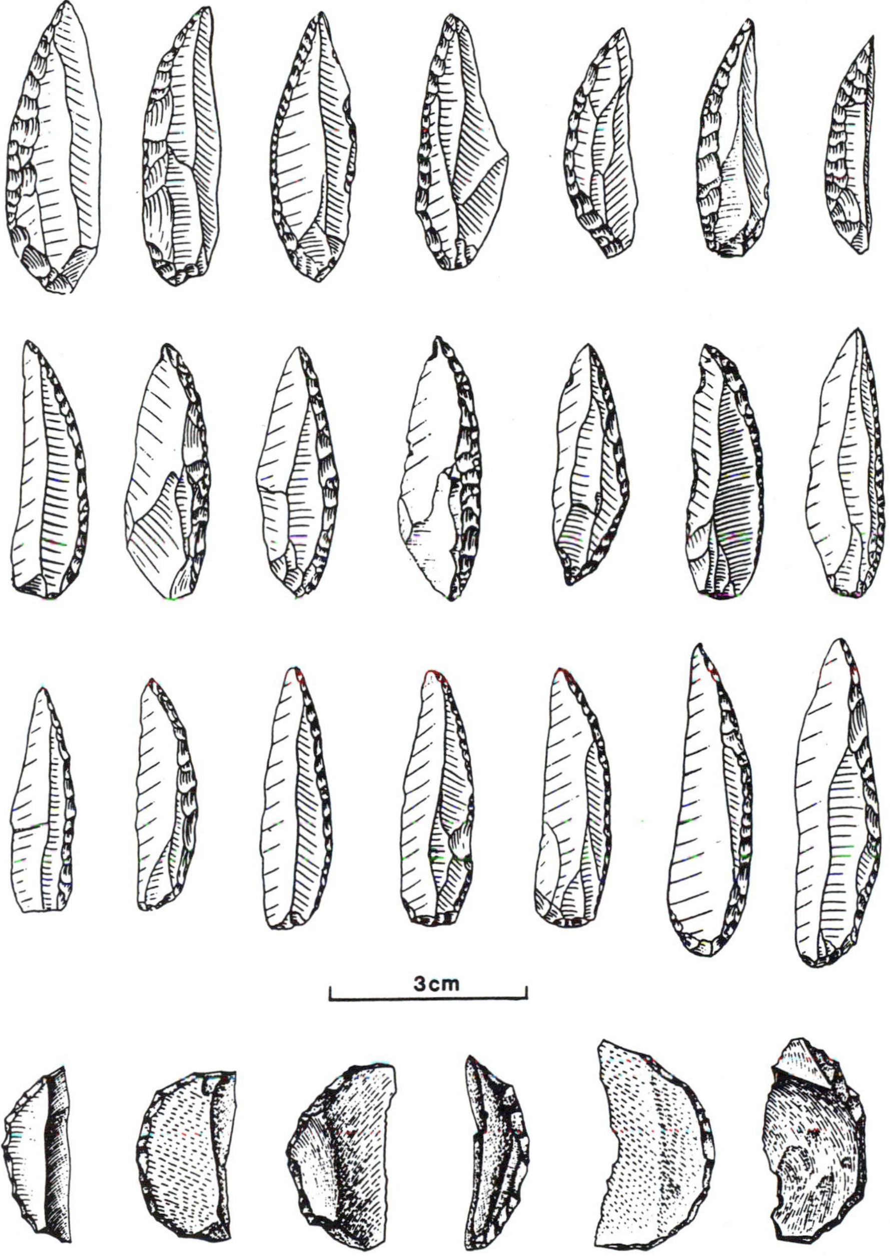


**6.11** Early Upper Palaeolithic points. Upper three rows: Châtelperronian points from EUP locales in France; lower row: Uluzzian crescents from EUP locales in Italy (after Mellars 1989:Fig. 20.3).

Table 6.14. *Assemblage diversity as measured by the number of de Sonneville-Bordes/Perrot types and average numbers of tools (Harrold 1989:Table 33.3). There are ninety-two types in the list.*

| | Mean number of types represented | Range | Mean assemblage size |
|---|---|---|---|
| Châtelperronian n=14 | 33.6 | 23–42 | 281.8 tools |
| Early Aurignacian n=13 | 42.1 | 32–54 | 617.6 tools |

from Table 6.14. But the major change in the evenness of assemblage composition occurs later, in the Upper Perigordian/Gravettian.

These studies of the transition generally use assemblages in rock shelters as a standard environment for recovery. Under freeze-thaw conditions these abris contain rapidly accumulating sediments, which also preserve bone, and which have not been eroded on anything like the scale that deposits from earlier periods have been. Therefore, the rock shelters of the southwest region have provided Palaeolithic archaeologists with an abundant source of samples, packaged in time, and amenable to stratigraphic and environmental analysis. Compared to the generally poor collections from very large cave excavations in the north-central region it is unsurprising that attention has focused on them and not on the quest for open locales.

*Mediterranean regions* The number of significant open locales in the Mediterranean regions is also small. Isolated leaf points occur in the red beds of Epirus, northwestern Greece, as at Morfi and Kokkinopilos. But these are from erosion surfaces and despite many efforts remain poorly dated (Bailey, Papaconstantinou and Sturdy 1992). In the Mediterranean-central region, excavation of a large open Aurignacian locale at Serino, south of Naples, has produced settlement plans and a C14 date of 31.2 Kyr bp (Accorsi et al. 1979). In Iberia significant open locales are lacking, as they were in Cantabria.

In all regions the normal environment for recovery is caves and rock shelters. These include Crvena Stijena (Brodar 1958–9) and Asprochaliko in the eastern region (Bailey, Papaconstantinou and Sturdy 1992) and in the French section of the western region the caves of Hortus, a multi-level Mousterian cave fissure (Lumley 1972), Tournal (Patou-Mathis 1994) and La Salpêtrière in the Gardon valley where a long sequence of Early Upper Palaeolithic industries was excavated (Bazile 1976, Escalon de Fonton 1966).

Comparisons with assemblages from the southern regions are often complicated by analytical approaches. Typologists in Iberia and Italy and Mediterranean France have either used or adapted Laplace's (1961, 1964, 1966)

Table 6.15. *The Middle/Upper Palaeolithic transition at Abric Romani (Carbonell 1992).*

| Kyr bp | Level 2 Aurignacian 39.2–43.8 % | Level 4 Mousterian 43.4–45.6 % |
|---|---|---|
| Negative bases of production BNP (=cores and nodules) | 0 | 1 |
| Positive bases BP (=flakes, blades) | 52 | 68 |
| Fragments of positive bases FBP (=chips and chunks) | 24 | 14 |
| Negative configuration bases BNC (=retouched pieces ) | 17 | 7 |
| Broken positive bases BPF (=broken blades and flakes) | 7 | 10 |
| N | 154 | 846 |

*typologie analytique*, which uses the concept of primary morphological types.[14] It differs from de Sonneville-Bordes' (1960) approach, the *lexique typologie*, in that Laplace recognizes fourteen typological groups which are then compared by a series of indices rather than through a comparison of the entire assemblage. In Laplace's model, leptolithic[15] assemblages form part of an organic whole and so represent different manifestations of a common polymorphic base. Change occurs through catalysts and mutations to the stone tools. The end result is a purposive goal-seeking evolutionary drive where the stone tools are imbued with their own internal dynamism to evolve.

There is one advantage, however, to the Laplacian approach: typological schemes do not need to be changed between the Middle and Upper Palaeolithic. One problem in understanding the transition is therefore potentially avoided. For example, Vaquero's study (1992) of the lithics from Abric Romani, near Capellades in Catalonia, stresses the production sequences involved. The results are set out in Table 6.15 where I have translated their terms into more familiar concepts.[16]

The scheme, which aims to establish cognitive changes through the study of morphology and the concept of volume this reveals (Vaquero 1992:54), does come to the conclusion that in the Aurignacian at Romani there was variety in retouch, but not in production sequences, while in the Mousterian the opposite was the case (*ibid.*:89).[17]

Besides producing long sequences and sometimes rich assemblages, for reasons already discussed (Figure 5.11), the Mediterranean-central region has also produced a distinctive transitional industry, the Uluzzian (Palma di

Cesnola 1976, 1981). This bears some similarity to the Châtelperronian in that it contains crescent-shaped backed points/knives (Figure 6.11). The reduction sequences are however predominantly Middle Palaeolithic, with many flakes and a variable use of levallois technique. Bone tools are present at Grotta di Castelcivita (Mussi 1992:Fig. IV.4).

The Uluzzian is confined to southern Italy (Mussi 1992:Fig. IV.1) and has a more restricted distribution than the Châtelperronian (Harrold 1989:Figs. 33.1 and 33.2). The principal caves are located in Uluzzo bay in the province of Lecce in the heel of the Italian peninsula. The Grotta di Castelcivita (Cioni, Gambassini and Torre 1979) is the only cave to have produced uncontentious C14 dates for the Uluzzian (Table 6.1), while at Cavallo cave (Palma di Cesnola 1976) there are three stages to the Uluzzian marked by a decrease through time in Middle Palaeolithic forms.

The Aurignacian is widespread throughout Italy and Iberia as at Latium with the Barbara and Fosselone caves (Zampetti and Mussi 1988), Riparo Fumane (Cassoli and Tagliacozzo 1991) and at Mollet I and Arbreda, two of the Reclau river caves in Catalonia (Maroto and Soler 1990, Maroto, Soler and Mir 1987, Soler and Maroto 1987). In both areas Gravettian assemblages are present, if not widespread, by 28 Kyr bp (Fullola 1983:342).

One final aspect of the caves of the Mediterranean region deserves mention, the appearance of cave art. Four AMS dates on organic materials contained within the paintings found in Chauvet Cave range in age from 30.3–32.4 Kyr bp, while two pieces of charcoal from a torch gave identical ages of 26.9 Kyr bp (Chauvet, Brunel Deschamps and Hillaire 1995). The cave with its spectacular paintings of animals, in particular lions, horses and rhinos, was discovered in 1995 at Pont d'Arc in the Ardèche Gorge, Mediterranean-west region (Chauvet, Brunel Deschamps and Hillaire 1995). It simultaneously extended the age of European cave paintings by 16,000 years and provided this region with its first major painting locale.[18] The paintings at Cosquer cave near Nice, now partly submerged, have also been directly dated by AMS to 27 Kyr bp. The implication of these two discoveries is that either the Iberian and Périgord paintings are much later in age, perhaps by as much as 20 kyr, or their preservation and dating urgently need to be reconsidered.

*Burials and carnivores*

One final aspect of recovery concerns the distribution of complete and nearly complete skeletons in this period. This is particularly the case with the Neanderthal skeletons which have received a number of recent syntheses (Defleur 1993, Gargett 1989, Smirnov 1991).

The sample is small but does emphasize the concentration of finds of complete skeletons in two restricted areas, southwest France and Israel. The northwest region has one certain burial at Spy cave in Belgium, while the two probable occurrences in the northeast region come from the Crimean locale of Kiik Koba.[19] Elsewhere in Europe Neanderthal remains are highly fragmented

Table 6.16. *The occurrence of Neanderthal burials (after Defleur 1993:tableau 1).*

| | | Burials | | |
|---|---|---|---|---|
| Region | Number of locales | Certain | Probable | Possible |
| Europe | | | | |
| Southwest | 7 | 11 | 3 | 1 |
| Northwest | 2 | 1 | 1 | 1 |
| Northeast | 2 | | 2 | |
| Israel | 5 | 12 | 4 | 2 |
| Western Asia | 2 | 6 | 1 | 3 |

(Oakley, Campbell and Molleson 1971).[20] The dating of these finds is poor. With the exception of Kebara, the Israeli sample dates to the Early Glacial and Pleniglacial. Four locales in the French group are Interpleniglacial in age, as is the disputed child burial from Starosele in the Crimea (Gvozdover et al. 1996, Marks et al. 1997).[21]

Leaving aside the significance of these finds as burials (see below), it is apparent that the French sample occurs at a time and in a region where the remains of carnivores in the rock shelters used by Neanderthals are extremely rare (Gamble 1986a). This is also the case for the Israeli sample (Marshall 1993). Although large carnivores are present in the region they are usually poorly represented in the cave faunas.

This is not the case in other regions such as the southeast, and Mediterranean-east where large numbers of fragmentary Neanderthal remains have been found, as at Vindija and Krapina (Smith 1984, Wolpoff et al. 1980). Here the number of carnivores, particularly bear and hyena, is not only greater in all the caves and rock shelters of the region but on occasion their bones dominate the faunal assemblages in locales which humans also visited (Gargett 1994).

The possibility exists that the complete Neanderthal bodies recovered from France and Israel may be the result of differences in carnivore behaviour. If the carnivores did not use the rock shelters for denning or cub rearing (Chapter 5) then they would not have disturbed the hominid bodies which had been left behind either in a pit or on the surface. We do not have to suggest that carnivores such as lion or hyenas were hunting and bringing back Neanderthals to their lairs but rather that, post mortem, they disturbed the archaeological record of a hominid gathering.

The contrast with the Mediterranean-west and central regions where Neanderthal remains are common, but fragmentary, is instructive. Stiner (1994) has convincingly shown that the skull from the Grotta Guattari forms part of a hyena den assemblage. At Hortus cave the remains of at least twenty

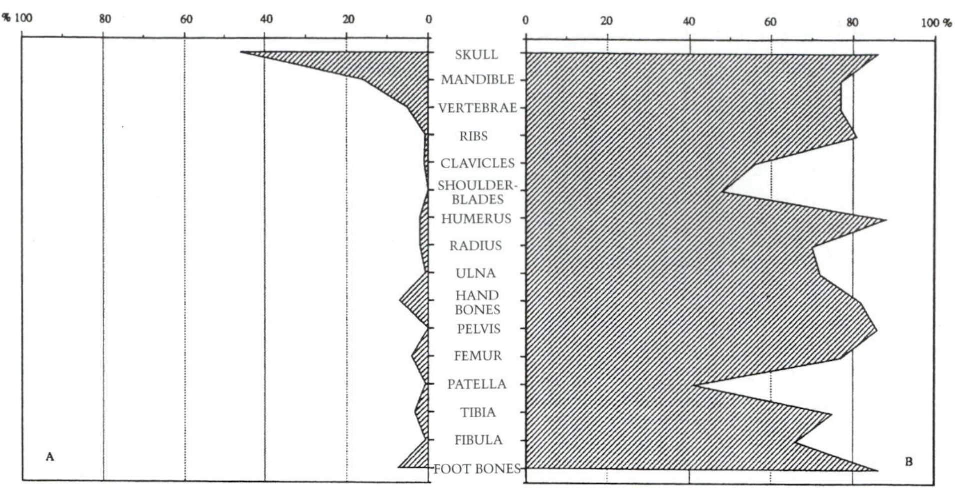


**6.12** The survival of anatomical parts from Neanderthal skeletons (after Defleur 1993:Fig. 69).
A: Isolated finds, which are dominated by hard, resistant teeth and skull elements;
B: articulated finds where, with the exception of the shoulder blades, clavicles and knee caps, preservation and recovery is good.

individuals are dominated by the resistant parts of the skeleton (Lumley 1976: 569). They occur in a cave fissure where leopard and bear are common elements in the fauna (Pillard 1972).

Defleur (1993) has compared the isolated finds with the discoveries of remains in anatomical connection (Figure 6.12). The former comprise parts of 262 individuals and are dominated by teeth, parts of the skull and by the numerically more abundant bones of the hands and feet. By comparison, the twenty-two Neanderthal adults and twelve children known from burials have the softer skeletal elements preserved.

There are many fragmentary human remains from the Upper Palaeolithic as well as burials, for example in the Balzi Rossi caves on the Ligurian coast of the Mediterranean-central region. But the novelty in this period are open air burials as at Sunghir, Kostenki and Dolní Věstonice-Pavlov in the northeast and north-central regions. This seems to be a cultural development rather than a change in preservation and recovery (see Chapter 7 for full discussion).

## Rhythms and social technology

There has been much debate about the importance of lithics in the transition from the Middle to the Upper Palaeolithic. The shift to blades rather than flakes as *supports*, the implications this had for hafted, composite tools and the consequences for hunting practices has been a productive area for discussion (Mellars and Stringer 1989, Nitecki and Nitecki 1987). The issues have included the explanation of Mousterian variability and the concept of culture as applied to stone tools. In his recent overview of variability in Middle Palaeolithic stone tool assemblages Mellars concludes that

> the only plausible explanation for these patterns lies in the notion of separate technological traditions – i.e. separate patterns of technological development, fostered by the variable degrees of social distance maintained between the human populations involved. In this sense, the existence of a real element of 'cultural' patterning in the character of technological variation within the Middle Palaeolithic seems difficult, if not impossible, to deny. (1996:355)

With an emphasis on the social aspects of technology I would expect this and more. In particular I would stress the individual rather than the group or population as the unit where the explanation for such variation resides. My additional perspective is to concentrate on the skills of negotiation and interaction between individuals and their involvement with objects and landscapes as social life was created and reaffirmed. Emphasizing the rhythms of human action (Table 3.1) provides a means to investigate these skills. This question returns us to the mutual, surrounding environments which all hominids have created and which constrain them. The rhythms of a social technology, by now familiar from Chapters 4 and 5 where I examined why archaeological cultures vary, provide a way of approaching in this chapter that other fundamental archaeological question – why do cultures change? This topic is also addressed in Chapter 7.

### *Paths and tracks: raw-material acquisition and transfers*

The paths and tracks indicated by the transfer of raw materials are important aspects of the transition to, and subsequent development of the Early Upper Palaeolithic. In her study Féblot-Augustins (1993:Fig. 9) found that Late Middle Palaeolithic transfers in central Europe during the Interpleniglacial[22] were still predominantly local, i.e. less than 100 km, but that there were six examples, as opposed to only one in the earlier Middle Palaeolithic, of transfers between 100 and 300 km. An example is provided by Wittlingen (Table 6.17), a surface collection, in the Swabian Alb, north central region (Burkert et al. 1992).

We also saw in Chapter 5 that the raw materials of the Middle Palaeolithic Blade Group were invariably obtained close to the locale where this technique was employed. The earliest Upper Palaeolithic in Moravia, north-central region, the Bohunician, is also almost exclusively made on local raw materials. Indeed the distribution of Bohunician industries is limited to the distribution of chert from Stránská skála which has a maximum radius of 40 km along the southeastern slopes of the Bohemian massif (Svoboda and Simán 1989:293). In both cases the different technologies have patterns of raw-material transfer which are very similar to those used in flake based assemblages from the Late Middle Palaeolithic (Féblot-Augustins 1993) of which Wittlingen is a good example.

Table 6.17. *Raw materials at the Middle Palaeolithic surface locale of Wittlingen, north-central region (Burkert et al. 1992:Table 35). An indication of flaking quality, +/−, has been given.*

| Raw material | N | % | Distance km | Raw material quantity | Raw material quality | Cores | Unmodified flakes | Modified flakes |
|---|---|---|---|---|---|---|---|---|
| Brown Jurahornstein | 1,241 | 94 | 0 | + | + | 61 | 977 | 203 |
| Keuper Jurahornstein | 33 | 3 | 1–10 | + | + | 1 | 19 | 13 |
| Hornstein? | 1 | 0.1 | >20 | − | − | | | 1 |
| Radiolarit | 6 | 0.5 | >30 | +/− | +/− | | | 6 |
| Muschelkalkstein | 29 | 2.5 | >40 | + | + | 1 | 6 | 22 |
| Kieselschiefer? | 1 | 0.1 | >120 | +/− | +/− | | | 1 |
| Unknown | 11 | 0.8 | ? | ? | + | | 4 | 7 |
| Totals | 1,322 | | | | | 63 | 1,006 | 253 |

Table 6.18. *A comparison between three regions of the average maximum distance in each locale/level over which lithic material has been transferred. N=the number of locales/levels in each region (data from Féblot-Augustins 1997).*

| Region | SW km | NW km | NC km |
|---|---|---|---|
| Lower Palaeolithic | 32.7<br>n=25 | 17.5<br>n=2 | |
| Early Middle Palaeolithic | 35.0<br>n=18 | 25.3<br>n=3 | 120.0<br>n=2 |
| Late Middle Palaeolithic | 40.0<br>n=61 | 56.2<br>n=16 | 119.1<br>n=23 |
| Early Upper Palaeolithic | 51.6<br>n=66 | 82.2<br>n=20 | 157.3<br>n=112 |
| Late Upper Palaeolithic | 61.0<br>n=46 | 80.6<br>n=9 | 202.6<br>n=50 |

A wider comparison (Table 6.18) does however reveal two major trends. The first is that within each region the maximum distance increases through time. In each case there is almost a doubling between the early Middle Palaeolithic and the Late Upper Palaeolithic. The second trend is geographical. As noted in Chapter 5 distances increase between the oceanic (SW) and continental (NC) regions of the continent. In most cases these maximum distances follow

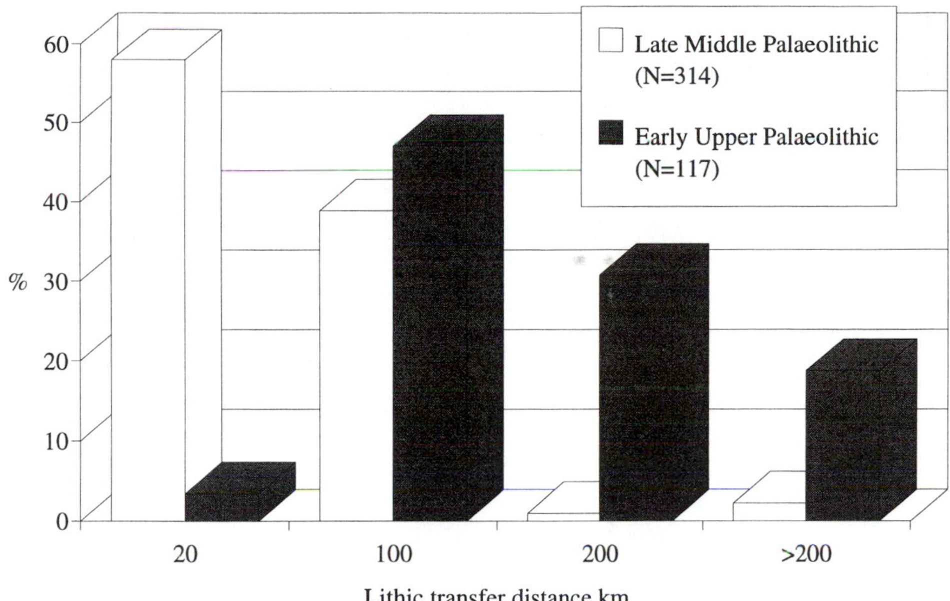


**6.13** Changes in the distances over which raw materials were regularly transferred in the Late Middle and Early Upper Palaeolithic in the SW, SE, NW and NC regions; see also Figure 5.14 (data from Féblot-Augustins 1997; Floss 1994; Roebroeks, Kolen and Rensink 1988).

Geneste's principle (Chapter 3) that the furthest distances are represented by very small amounts of raw material and by tools. While this results in very small quantities we are nonetheless seeing in Table 6.18 a very substantial increase in the scale of mobility that is not expected on purely ecological grounds.

Figure 6.13 compares all transfers in the north-central region for the Late Middle and Early Upper Palaeolithic. Distances of over 300 km are unknown until the Early Upper Palaeolithic (Féblot-Augustins 1993, Floss 1994, Roebroeks, Kolen and Rensink 1988) and these are almost all associated with non-lithic materials. This pattern is confirmed with the addition of data on the movement of shells which first begins in the Early Upper Palaeolithic (see below).

*Quality of raw material*

It is noticeable in several regions that the earliest Upper Palaeolithic is marked by a shift towards finer-grained raw materials, particularly flint, that unlike the Bohunician example often has to be acquired at greater distances from gatherings.

This is the case in Catalonia where Soler (et al. 1990:454) comments that with the appearance of the Upper Palaeolithic there was a dramatic change in raw materials. The sequence at l'Arbreda, where a very early Aurignacian overlies the Mousterian, emphasizes the abruptness of this change. At Arcy sur

Cure in the northwest region, Farizy's analysis (1990:figure 11.10) shows a rise from 10 to 70 per cent in the proportions of flint at Grotte du Renne between the Mousterian, levels XI and XII, and the Châtelperronian, levels Xc and Xb. This is matched by a corresponding increase in the proportions of Upper Palaeolithic tool types and to a lesser extent blade elements.

The Middle Palaeolithic, as we saw in Chapter 5, has workshop locales but it is during the Early Upper Palaeolithic that special raw-material locations are used. One example is Monte Avena in the Dolomite mountains of the Alpine region. Located at 1,450 m, the open locale was first exploited for flint during the Aurignacian. This involved testing the material and knapping pre-cores presumably for transfer elsewhere (Lanziger and Cremaschi 1988).

These special locations are mirrored in the spatial organization of the open locales to which such material was transferred. For example, there are two discrete concentrations of raw materials which have been transferred in from some distance at the Aurignacian locale of Stránská skála III (Svoboda 1994a:Fig. 58). At Salching, a Gravettian open locale in Bavaria (Weißmüller 1987:Abb 2), there are distinct zones within the excavation for the keratophyre imported over 150 km.

*Quantity in transfers*

However, in the southwest region Turq's (1993) study of raw materials reminds us that there are other strategies operating in this change of raw materials than merely simple cultural preference as some have assumed. He found, in a sample of twenty-eight Mousterian and four Châtelperronian assemblages, that there was a very rapid decline in the proportions of raw material with distance from the locale. No raw material transferred from more than 16 km away accounted for more than 6 per cent of the raw material in that locale (*ibid.*:Fig.1). By comparison, people in the earliest Aurignacian in the same small region of northeast Aquitaine were transferring materials in greater proportions from further afield (*ibid.*:Fig.2). Even in those locales, in the sample of twelve Aurignacian locales, which were located in flint-rich areas,[23] material transferred from 20 to 30 km away still accounted for 10 to 20 per cent of the raw materials. In flint-poor areas transfers of between 50 and 80 km accounted for up to 30 per cent of the lithic resources in those locales.

Kozlowski (1990:430) reminds us that the Aurignacian use of raw materials displays a good deal of variation. He regards this as a combination of site function and age. In Moravia and Bulgaria there is considerable variation among the earliest Aurignacian locales. The Vedrovice locales in Moravia used almost exclusively immediate flint from hornstone deposits. By contrast, at Bacho Kiro in the southeast region the raw materials in the Aurignacian levels consist of 53 per cent flint transferred from more than 120 km (Kozlowski 1990:430 and Figure 15.5). By contrast, in the Mousterian level 13 at Bacho Kiro only 13 per cent of the raw materials was flint transferred over the same distance (Gamble 1986a:Table 6.4, Kozlowski 1982). No doubt the greater distances in this region, when compared to the Aquitaine study (Turq 1993), reflect the pattern presented in Table 6.18 where longer transfers are a feature of more continental conditions (see also Figure 5.14).

*Change and regional variety after 33 Kyr bp*

The earliest Upper Palaeolithic and Late Middle Palaeolithic therefore share a variety of transfer strategies as reflected in the distances and use, or non-use, of raw materials within 20 km. The major change occurs after 33 Kyr bp and in particular with the Gravettian and its French counterpart, the Perigordian (Rigaud 1988b). As Kozlowski remarks,

> It is only during the Gravettian technocomplex in the middle phase of the Upper Palaeolithic that another period of raw material specialization sets in, with a stable system of procurement of high grade materials from distant deposits. (Kozlowski 1990:432–3)

This pattern has been documented by Svoboda (1994a:fig. 89) for Moravia. In the period 40–30 Kyr bp no single source dominates and several are utilized. However, between 30 and 20 Kyr bp flints from southern Poland become much more common and the number of sources used in transfers declines. This coincides with the appearance of large settlements along the Moravian rivers as at Předmostí, Dolní Věstonice-Pavlov and Milovice.

In the north central region where such large settlements are lacking it is still possible to see the regular transfer of more distant materials on a bulk scale. At Salching on the south side of the Danube in Bavaria, fieldwalking and excavation (Weißmüller 1987) have uncovered a Gravettian locale. The small stone assemblage from the excavation (n=254) comprised 51 per cent keratophyre. When combined with material collected from the plough zone (n=949) this same stone accounted for 42 per cent of the entire collection (Weißmüller 1987). The closest source of keratophyre to Salching is 150 km to the north in the Fichtelgebirge (Scheer 1993:200). The artifacts from Salching included a tanged Font Robert point made of a fine grained quartzite. At the Maisières canal in Belgium these distinctive points are dated to 28 Kyr bp. This type-fossil is among those used to distinguish the Perigordian V, or Gravettian, in southwest France (Rigaud 1988b). It appears that at Salching raw material was brought into the locale as pre-forms and then knapped.

A similar picture can be found in the southwest region as shown by Larick's study (1984) of the raw materials from couche V in the Le Flageolet I rock shelter. This level is dated by AMS to 25.7 Kyr bp. Most of the artifacts from this level are made on nodular cherts from the Senonian series of Upper Cretaceous limestones. These occur in the immediate vicinity of the rock shelter. All the other raw materials are found within 80 km of the locale (Table 6.19).

However, it is difficult to agree with Larick that these non-local cherts were invariably transferred into the rock shelter in an already processed form (*ibid.*:33). The large quantities of unretouched and small débitage shows that

Table 6.19. *Distance to non-local chert sources from Le Flageolet based on a sample of the number of non-local cherts found within couche V (after Larick 1984).*

| Structure | Form | Area | Distance km | N | % |
|---|---|---|---|---|---|
| Chalcedonic | Blocks | South Périgord | 5–20 | 225 | 53 |
| Fossiliferous | Nodules | Bergerocis | 40–60 | 173 | 40 |
| Lepispheric | Nodules | Fumelois | 30–40 | 24 | 6 |
| Argillitic | Plaquettes | Bassins de l'Est | 50–80 | 6 | 1 |

Table 6.20. *A comparison of lithic products at Le Flageolet I couche V according to Larick (1984:Tables 2 and 3).*

| | Local | % | Non-local | % |
|---|---|---|---|---|
| Unretouched débitage | 11,919 | *48.3* | 1,995 | *47.6* |
| Flakes and fragments | 1,167 | *4.7* | 139 | *3.3* |
| Blades and fragments | 492 | *2.0* | 62 | *1.5* |
| Bladelets and fragments | 318 | *1.3* | 80 | *1.9* |
| Small debris | 9,502 | *38.5* | 1,529 | *36.5* |
| Cortical debris | 172 | *0.7* | 12 | *0.3* |
| Burin spalls | 268 | *1.1* | 173 | *4.1* |
| **Total** | **23,838** | | **3,990** | |
| Retouched pieces | 418 | *1.7* | 99 | *2.4* |
| End-retouched tools | 73 | *0.3* | 12 | *0.3* |
| Burins | 226 | *0.9* | 30 | *0.7* |
| Bassaler burins | 15 | *0.1* | 18 | *0.4* |
| Edge retouched tools | 63 | *0.3* | 24 | *0.6* |
| Microliths | 41 | *0.2* | 15 | *0.4* |
| **Total** | **836** | | **198** | |
| **Totals** | **24,674** | ***100.0*** | **4,188** | ***100.0*** |

non-local materials were systematically reduced at Le Flageolet rather than elsewhere in the landscape (Table 6.20).

When compared to Salching it is noteworthy that the non-local sources at Le Flageolet not only account for less than 15 per cent of the total lithic assemblage but comfortably fall within the spatial dimensions of the landscape of habit. In this instance the operation of Geneste's principle (Chapter 3) concerning transfer distance and retouch appears to be highly selective, for example in the preference for non-local materials to make specific tools, such as Bassaler burins (Table 6.20).

*Inter-mollusca; say it with shells*

The EUP sees the transfer of shells over considerably larger distances than stone (Floss 1994, Roebroeks, Kolen and Rensink 1988, Taborin 1993). At the Gravettian locales of Mainz-Linsenberg and Sprendlingen in the Middle Rhine there are shells from the Mediterranean shore (Floss 1994: 376). The direct distance for such transfers is 700 km. The numbers of shells involved are small: seventeen at Mainz-Linsenberg from three species, and nine at Sprendlingen from two species. These two open locales are 30 km apart and are the only EUP locales in the Middle Rhine (Figure 6.14) to have any transfers of stone or shell to the south (Floss 1994:Abb. 210, 211). The stone transfers in this area are along the axis of the Rhine and towards the Maas basin to the northwest. A comparison of the two locales (Floss 1994:Abb. 108 and 112) emphasizes the local use of raw material with only two pieces of Baltic flint at Mainz-Linsenberg, apart from the molluscs, breaking the 20-km transfer ring.

The overall number of shell transfers is small. Floss (1994:337) records seventy-two for the entire European Upper Palaeolithic. While these include later Magdalenian transfers they do show (Figure 6.15) that the 100-km limit of the landscape of habit was regularly exceeded. These include transfers of 500 km for shells into Aurignacian assemblages at Kostenki from the Black Sea (Hahn 1977:Karte 5).

The transfer of shells in southern France has been exhaustively studied by Taborin (1993). The major locales where shells have been found are in the Périgord, Lot and Gironde. Apart from the cave at Isturitz (de Saint-Périer 1930, 1936, 1952) the Pyrenean locales have few shell transfers until the Magdalenian in the LUP.

Taborin identifies six main sources which include fossil shells from Eocene, Miocene and Pliocene deposits, as well as shells available from the Atlantic and Mediterranean coasts during the last glaciation when sea levels were lower. The distance from a central locale such as the Abri Pataud, a rock shelter on the Vézère river in the Dordogne, to either of these Pleistocene shorelines was of the order of 400 km.

Taborin's study reveals a change in the transfer of shells between the Early and Late Upper Palaeolithic for the three most important sources (Figure 6.16). In the former period the majority of shells which can be provenanced (Table 6.21) come from the Atlantic coast. In the Late Upper Palaeolithic such specificity is not possible and the majority come from all shores with a small increase in fossil Miocene shells. These also come from either an Atlantic or a Mediterranean source.

*Chaîne opératoire: technology and tool production*

A number of approaches to the study of technology exist for the period 60–21 Kyr bp. I have already described the unified approach to the Mousterian and Aurignacian assemblages at the Abric Romani (Carbonell 1992). A similar

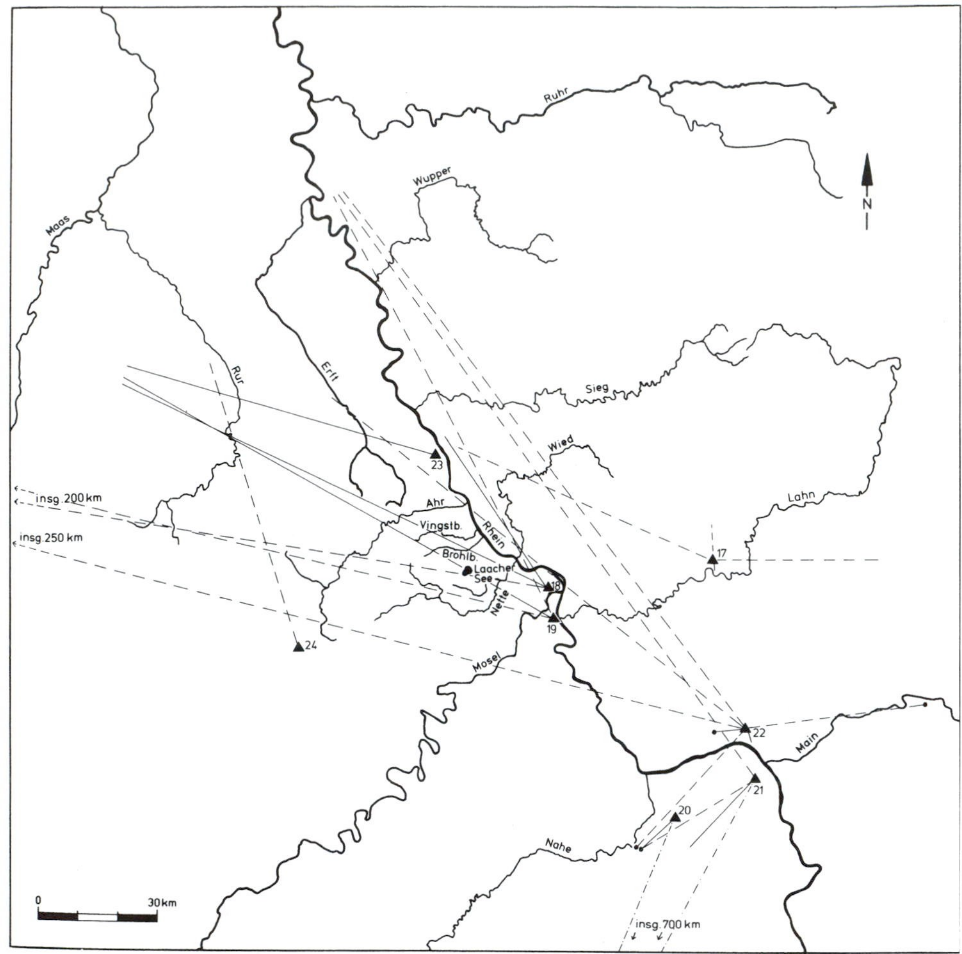


**6.14** The origin of lithic raw material and shell during the Gravettian of the Middle Rhine region of western Germany, NC region (after Floss 1994:Abb. 211).

Key:

| | |
|---|---|
| solid line | origin certain |
| dashed line | possible origin |
| dash/dotted line | origin for the shells |

Key to locales:

17 Wildscheuer
18 Koblenz-Metternich
19 Rhens
20 Sprendlingen
21 Mainz-Linsenberg
22 Wiesbaden-Adlerquelle
23 Bonn-Muffendorf
24 Magdalenahöhle

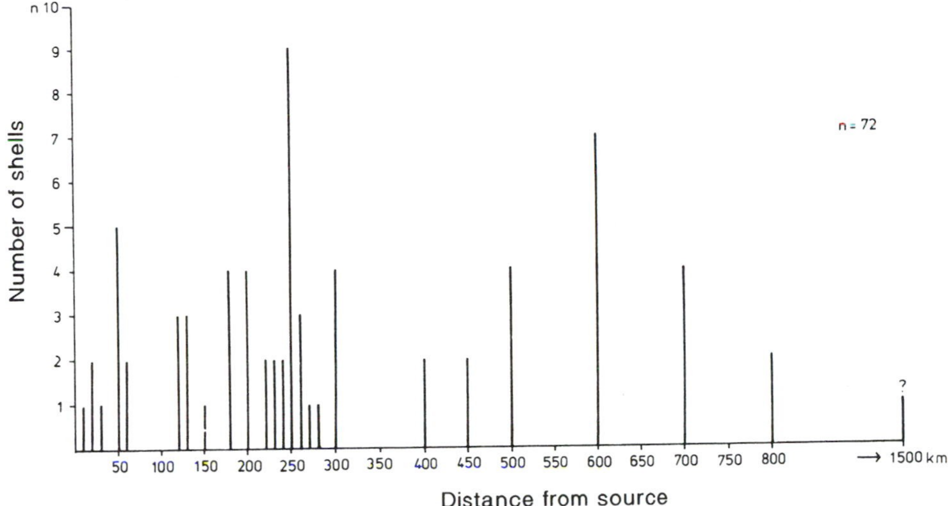


**6.15** The distances over which shells used in the visual culture of the European Upper Palaeolithic were obtained (after Floss 1994:Abb. 207).

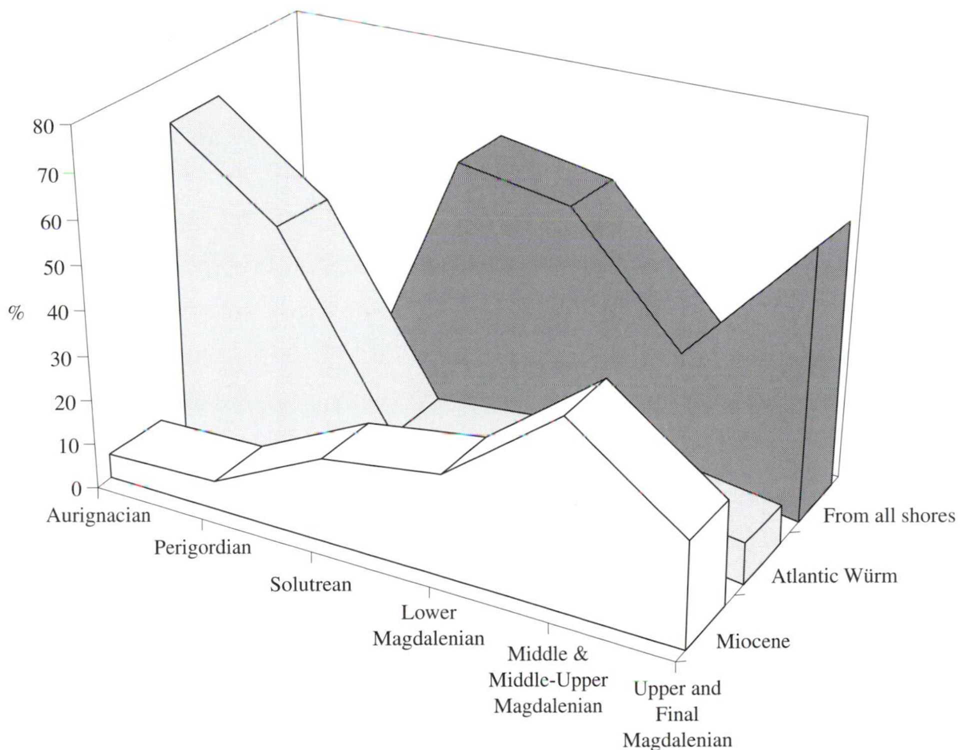


**6.16** The changing sources for shells in the Early Upper Palaeolithic (Aurignacian and Perigordian) and Late Upper Palaeolithic (Solutrean and Magdalenian) in the SW region (data from Taborin 1993).

Table 6.21. *The numbers of shells found in locales in the Périgord, Lot and Gironde regions of southern France (Taborin 1993:Tab. II–IX). The number of* Dentalium *shells is shown but not included in the total. NISP=number of individual specimens.*

| | Aurignacian | Perigordian | Solutrean | Lower Magdalenian | Middle and Middle-Upper Magdalenian | Upper and Final Magdalenian |
|---|---|---|---|---|---|---|
| Sources | | | | | | |
| Eocene | 3 | 4 | 3 | 17 | 67 | 0 |
| Miocene | 37 | 19 | 53 | 185 | 321 | 100 |
| Atlantic Würm | 481 | 166 | 35 | 122 | 92 | 37 |
| Pliocene | 34 | 6 | 5 | 11 | 13 | 18 |
| Mediterranean Würm | 19 | 6 | 11 | 16 | 36 | 22 |
| All shores | 110 | 117 | 178 | 485 | 240 | 259 |
| *Dentalium* | | | *100* | | *900* | *118* |
| Total NISP | 684 | 318 | 285 | 836 | 769 | 436 |

approach using Laplace's theory of the *synthétotype* has been applied by Guilbaud (1993) to the Châtelperronian assemblage associated with a Neanderthal skeleton at St Césaire in the Charente-Maritime of France. This find of the last Neanderthal in France (ApSimon 1980) is dated by TL to 36.3 ± 2.7 Kyr bp (Mercier et al. 1991). The assemblage blends Mousterian and Upper Palaeolithic lithic 'themes' in a model of stone transitions that borrows heavily, but inappropriately, from the vocabulary of genetics (see Guilbaud 1993:51–2). The chaîne opératoire and other models of reduction sequences provide a more understandable route to lithic variation (Jaubert 1993) and will be discussed here for two widespread cultural assemblages from the Early Upper Palaeolithic. These can be compared with a similar approach to Middle Palaeolithic assemblages, such as Quina Mousterian discussed in Chapter 5.

*Aurignacian*

In his study of the Aurignacian assemblage from the Geißenklösterle, Hahn (1988, 1991, Hahn and Owen 1985, Owen 1988) has produced a multi-stage reduction sequence (Figure 6.17). Less formal than the chaînes opératoires applied to the levallois (Chapter 5), the analysis nonetheless systematizes the production of blade supports against a background of local and distant raw materials.

The essence of Upper Palaeolithic prepared cores is to flute the surface of the nodule through débitage (Table 4.9) so as to facilitate the radial detachment of blades of predetermined size. This involves preparing the platform area by topping the nodule, flaking its margins to correct for angles, removing these corrections, which produces a distinctive crested blade, and then detaching blades. These can be removed from one (unipolar) or both (bipolar) ends of what is now a core. They will continue to be removed in a radial fashion until the platform and the edges need further correction. This leads to rejuvenation flakes to establish a new platform area as well as, in the Geißenklösterle example, shaping the foot of the core to correct for convexity in blade shape.

In the Aurignacian levels at Geißenklösterle there were six raw-material types. Only one per cent of all materials used came from more than 20 km from the cave and 95 percent was from local hornstein picked up in the Ach valley. The size of nodules was small which led to an opportunistic reduction strategy (Hahn and Owen 1985:71). Most of them are unipolar and the cores were worked down as far as they could be taken and still produce blades of 30–40 mm in length.

*Gravettian*

Radiolarite transferred from 15 km away is more common in the Gravettian at the Geißenklösterle (Hahn and Owen 1985:72). But although blades made with this raw material are common, the cores from which they were struck are not. In general the treatment of the cores is more standardized and less opportunistic. They are also more elaborately prepared. Individual details, such as the

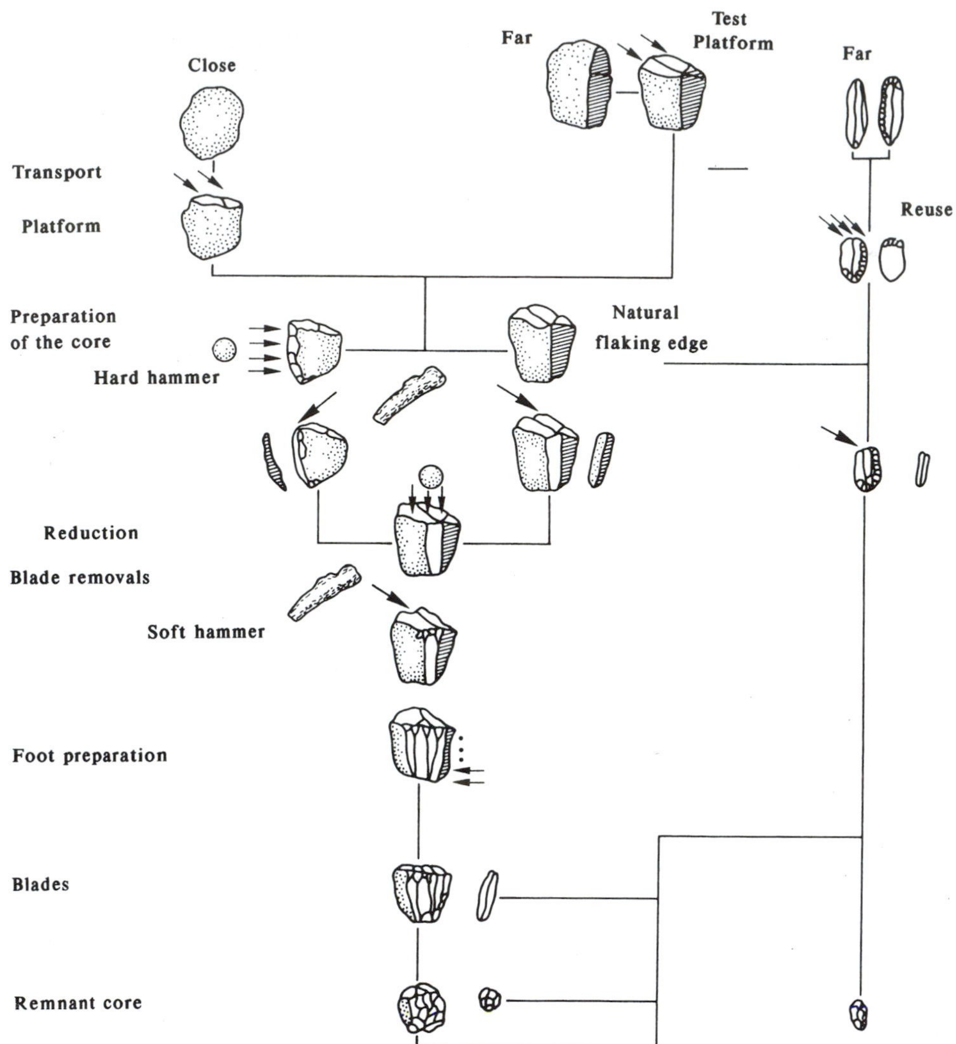


**6.17** An Upper Palaeolithic chaîne opératoire which takes into account the proximity of raw material and the transport to locales of retouched pieces which are subsequently reduced (after Hahn 1991:Fig. 36).

presence or absence of ground platform edges on the cores, suggest they were made by different knappers.

At a more general level, Hahn (1991:119) has summarized the difference between the chaînes opératoires in the Aurignacian and Gravettian as follows:

- a general decrease in blade thickness
- in the Aurignacian the striking platform for the flakes was usually prepared first. Often a natural ridge was used as a guide to begin flaking the nodule. In the Gravettian this ridge was prepared before the striking platform was formed

Table 6.22. *Dimensions of blade* supports *in three periods in the Achtal, southern Germany, north-central region (Owen 1988).*

| | | N | Mean | Range | St Dev |
|---|---|---|---|---|---|
| *Length* | | | | | |
| Geißenklösterle | Aurignacian | 892 | 31.9 | 7.2–121.2 | 15.6 |
| Geißenklösterle | Aurignacian | 356 | 31.8 | 7.4–121.2 | 17.77 |
| Geißenklösterle | Aurignacian | 494 | 32.2 | 7.2–93.5 | 14.13 |
| Geißenklösterle | Gravettian | 1,113 | 27.8 | 4.7–88.9 | 13.89 |
| Hohler Fels | Gravettian | 133 | 30.8 | 7.2–83.4 | 17.74 |
| Hohler Fels | Early Magdalenian | 145 | 28.8 | 6.6–86.5 | 15.1 |
| *Width* | | | | | |
| Geißenklösterle | Aurignacian | 890 | 16.3 | 3.1–37 | 6.18 |
| Geißenklösterle | Aurignacian | 356 | 16.69 | 3.1–37 | 7.07 |
| Geißenklösterle | Aurignacian | 492 | 16.14 | 4.5–34.5 | 5.46 |
| Geißenklösterle | Gravettian | 1,113 | 12.72 | 1.7–40.5 | 5.18 |
| Hohler Fels | Gravettian | 133 | 12.86 | 2.3–36.2 | 6.19 |
| Hohler Fels | Early Magdalenian | 145 | 13.2 | 4.1–29 | 5.85 |
| *Thickness* | | | | | |
| Geißenklösterle | Aurignacian | 886 | 5.3 | 0.7–25.4 | 2.54 |
| Geißenklösterle | Aurignacian | 356 | 5.4 | 0.7–15.3 | 2.64 |
| Geißenklösterle | Aurignacian | 488 | 5.3 | 1.3–25.4 | 2.51 |
| Geißenklösterle | Gravettian | 1,113 | 4.47 | 1.1–23.8 | 2.43 |
| Hohler Fels | Gravettian | 133 | 4.42 | 0.7–24.2 | 3.43 |
| Hohler Fels | Early Magdalenian | 145 | 4.34 | 1.2–9.8 | 2.06 |

- Aurignacian cores generally have one striking platform and one flaking surface. Bipolar cores are common in the Gravettian as well as opposed striking platforms
- the bipolar cores of the Gravettian are particularly suited to the production of blades and micro-blades for steep, blunting retouch on one edge. These supports for backed blades are produced in a serial, painstaking fashion (Owen 1988:186)
- direct percussion was used predominantly in the Aurignacian, while in the Gravettian more use is made of indirect percussion in the form of bone or antler punches (Owen 1988:186).

In Owen's study of the blades produced in the Early Upper Palaeolithic (Table 6.22), it is noticeable how little variation there is in terms of their dimensions. Widths and thicknesses do decline between the Aurignacian and the Gravettian as does the upper range of blade length. However, even with a shift to radiolarite in the Gravettian and with all the changes in preparing and flaking the cores as listed above (see Hahn and Owen 1985 for full description), what we have here is a set of alternatives producing a very standardized product – blade *supports*. Moreover, as Table 6.22 also shows, this standardization continues in

Table 6.23. *The nodule exploitation model (after Scheer 1993:195).*

| Nodule exploitation |
|---|
| • nodules from the immediate vicinity can be brought to the site without testing or preparation. As a result many useless cores will be found |
| • local nodules will be tested and prepared with part of the cortex removed to lower the weight to be transported |
| • distant raw materials will be introduced as blades or tools, either because raw material was imported during extended trips from distant regions, or because it was obtained through exchange with other individuals |
| • some partially reduced nodules may be introduced to the site regardless of origin. Of the nodules flaked at the site, some may have been used for blade production, while other parts may have been exported as blanks, tools or cores. |

this same valley in the Early Magdalenian during the Late Upper Palaeolithic some 10 Kyr after the Gravettian occupation in the Geißenklösterle.

*Moving cores*

The Achtal has been exhaustively studied to examine the links between locales. In particular, Scheer has developed a model of nodule exploitation and tested it with the Gravettian data from the Geißenklösterle (Scheer 1990, 1993). She follows, in essence, the aim of the chaîne opératoire which is to link the various spatial scales of action – locale and landscape – through associated technical gestures (Table 6.23).

Scheer tests the possibilities in the model (Table 6.23) with a detailed study of the Gravettian in the Achtal. Four main caves are involved, the Sirgenstein, Geißenklösterle, Brillenhöhle and Hohler Fels. The pattern of core reduction followed the Aurignacian study at the Geißenklösterle with local materials dominating. However, Scheer was also able to make eight refits between the caves which in the case of the Geißenklösterle and Hohler Fels are almost 3 km apart (Figure 6.18).

Among the eight refittings are examples of all three of Cziesla's categories. Four indicate transport from Geißenklösterle to the Brillenhöhle and one the reverse. There are also refits between the Brillenhöhle, the largest collection, and the Hohle Fels. One refitted burin is a product of artifact modification (see Figure 5.20). It was modified several times at the Brillenhöhle before being carried to Geißenklösterle where it was resharpened a final time (Scheer 1993:203). These assemblages, which are dated at the Geißenklösterle Ia to 23.6 ± 0.3 and at Hohler Fels IIb to 21.1 ± 0.5 and 23.1 ± 0.07 Kyr bp (*ibid.*:197), are also linked by similar ivory pendants (Scheer 1985). This valley study shows very clearly that cores were frequently transferred around the landscape since refitting failed to conjoin large series (Scheer 1993:209). This is a very different result than, for example, that from the Middle Palaeolithic locale of

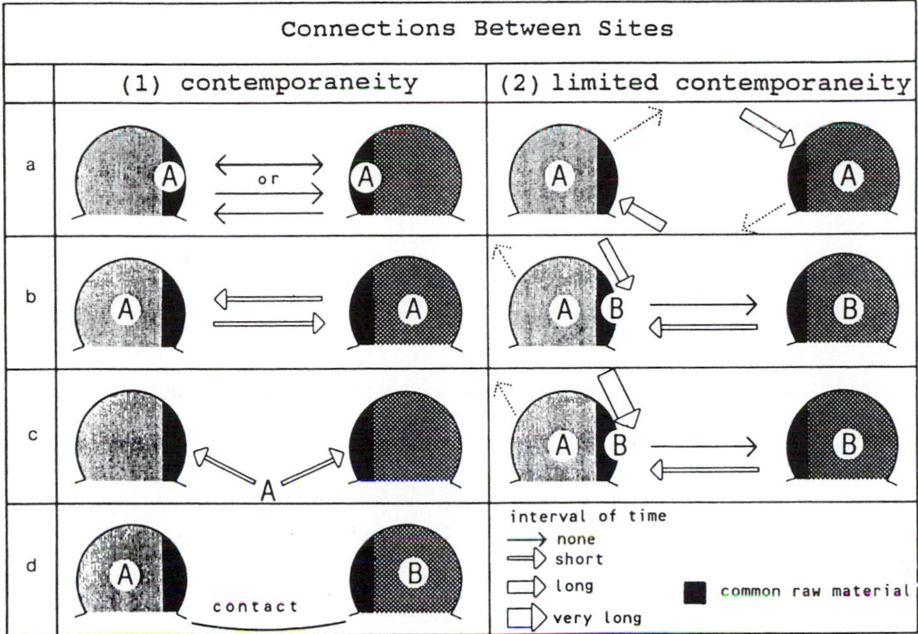


**6.18** The patterns of occupation between three Achtal locales, Germany, NC region: Geißenklösterle, Brillenhöhle and Hohler Fels (see Figures 6.8 and 6.9) based on conjoins. The reduction sequence and the size of objects moving between Geißenklösterle and Brillenhöhle support 1a, b and c. The most probable interpretation is for a camp in the valley, now deeply buried under alluvium, and from which the caves were visited (after Scheer 1993:Fig. 5, 205–6). Key:

1a A small group simultaneously occupies two or more caves
1b A large group separates to occupy different sites
1c A group has a base camp in the valley from which the caves are visited alternately
1d Separate groups have mutual contacts
2a One group alternately occupies two or more caves with a long span of time between occupations
2b After some time, one or more group(s) collect raw material of the first group(s) at one site and use(s) the material in another site
2c After a long span of time, a second group excavates raw material at one site and uses it in another cave

Maastricht-Belvédère which I examined in Chapter 5. In the Achtal there is evidence not only for contemporaneity but also for the local movement of tools and raw material within a local reduction sequence (Figure 6.19).

*Middle and Upper Palaeolithic technological transitions*

Vaquero, in his study of the assemblages at Abric Romani (Carbonell 1992), concluded that in the Aurignacian there was variety in retouch, but not in production sequences, while the opposite characterized the Mousterian. The case

**6.19** The view southwest down the Ach valley from the Sirgenstein cave, southern Germany NC region. In the middle distance is the Hohle Fels where at least two flakes and blades could be refitted with pieces from the Brillenhöhle cave 3 km to the northeast in the same valley (photo by the author).

studies presented here and in Chapter 5 using chaîne opératoire and reduction sequences to examine technological decisions come to the opposite conclusion. The Upper Palaeolithic production sequences in the Achtal locales were highly varied yet produced standardized blade supports (Table 6.22). This was also the finding in Turq's (1992a, 1992b) wider study of Quina Mousterian assemblages where the levallois technique was sparingly used.

The movement of materials between locales does not explain these alternative production sequences. We know that Mousterian tools were regularly introduced into locales (Conard and Adler 1997) so it is probably only a matter of time before refitting between locales is achieved for this period. Instead, the variety of approaches to producing supports through débitage technology (examined in Chapter 4) illustrates how the chaîne opératoire deals with a suite of gestures, learned and transmitted in the social act of making. The emphasis, quite rightly, is therefore on the *gestures* of making rather than the *thoughts* of what the knappers were making, in this instance flake and blade supports. Retouching these blanks into tools is thus an extension of the chaîne opératoire as further, linked action. The analytical emphasis must be on process rather than final form. It is those learned sequences which are the cultural and social products, the ways of doing, rather than the things produced.

*Organic artifacts*

The technology of non-lithic materials provides another opportunity to examine the social, embodied nature of technology. Fibre-based weaving is now known from the study of clay impressions at Pavlov (Adovasio, Soffer and Klíma 1996) and is discussed further in Chapter 7. Here I will examine beads and antler projectile points. In both examples there is the archaeologically invisible thread and wooden haft, essential for such composite artifacts to function. This must also have been the case with many stone tools and I will briefly consider the evidence for their mounting on hafts and claims for wooden artifacts in this period.

*Beads*

The earliest evidence for the deliberate piercing of items either for suspension as pendants or as parts of necklaces, or to allow attachment onto clothing, comes from level 11 at Bacho Kiro (Kozlowski 1982:141). The evidence in this Aurignacian/Bachokirian level consists of two pierced animal teeth and a spindle-shaped bone pendant. These are of course much earlier, as White (1993b:279) has pointed out, than similar pierced items from the Châtelperronian levels of Arcy sur Cure (Farizy 1990, Leroi-Gourhan and Leroi-Gourhan 1964). The range of raw materials used to produce Aurignacian pierced ornaments is impressive. White (1993b: 279–80) lists the following:

- limestone, schist, talc-schist, steatite, mammal teeth, bone, antler, ivory, fossil and contemporary species of marine and freshwater shells, fossil coral, fossil belemnite, jet, lignite, hematite and pyrite.

Two geographical patterns can be discerned in the selection of these raw materials. The first concerns the use of fox canines. These are very common in Aurignacian locales in France, Belgium, Germany and Russia – the southwest, north-central and northeastern regions (Hahn 1977). Deer canines are also common. However in the Cantabrian region of the southwest region (Straus 1992: 80) and throughout the Mediterranean west and central regions (Mussi 1992) fox canines are absent and deer canines dominate.

The second pattern concerns the distribution of shells. These are common in France, as we have seen above (Taborin 1993), but very rare in the Aurignacian elsewhere in Europe (Hahn 1977).

*Brilliance*

White (1997) has stressed the textural qualities of ivory, its surface lustre and smooth texture. However, these properties have to be coaxed from the material by polishing. These actions replicate the tactile qualities of other ornamental media such as the tooth enamel on fox canines, mother of pearl and steatite (*ibid.*:95). According to White (1997), 'the polishing of ivory was itself a *representation* of textures experienced elsewhere in the natural world'.

His argument can be extended. Morphy (1989) has drawn attention to the quality of brilliance in aesthetics (Gamble 1991c, 1995a). He defines aesthetics as *how* something appeals to the senses (*ibid*.:21). Using the art of the Yolngu of Eastern Arnhem Land as an example, he shows how spiritual power is expressed in their art through the quality of *bir'yun* or brilliance. This is caught in the shimmering quality of the art as well as being present in natural objects such as ochre and stones. Blood forms a similar important source of spiritual power (Knight 1983, 1991a). People can be made to shine, *wangaar*, by rubbing them with fat, ochre and blood. Bark paintings shimmer, like a Bridget Riley op-art painting, with their fine hatched lines and basic colours. *Bir'yun* produces effects that humans find stimulating and appealing. Brilliance, Morphy believes, is an effect that operates cross-culturally (1989:36).

Therefore, in Morphy's argument what catches the eye is aesthetic. In his example if that something also expresses spiritual power, such meaning will be context based and the brilliant messages will be related to it. But the power of ritual, as Morphy points out, is not an aesthetic effect (*ibid*.:38). That possibility depends upon a belief by the Yolngu in Ancestral Beings. However, to succeed as a performance, ritual requires the enhancement of aesthetic qualities of natural and artificial objects brimming with brilliance.[24]

Let us briefly consider brilliance in the European Palaeolithic. If we regard it as a relevant attribute, on a par say with good flaking properties of stone, then examples of shining stones such as the rock crystal tools from Mousterian levels at Les Merveilles (McCurdy 1931) or the swirling multicoloured jasper handaxes from Fontmaure-en-Vellèches (Gruet 1976:1092) are easy to find. However, such local examples of Mousterian brilliance do not necessarily reflect Neanderthal aesthetics but rather a particular affordance within the landscape. However, such qualities are available for elaboration, as shown by the later use of ivory and its ability to shine, and represent a wider set of perceptual categories, both visual and tactile.

While these properties are revealed by working ivory, so too are the properties in some of the other materials they represent. Shells have to be washed, steatite has to be dug from the ground and fox teeth have to be bared to be seen. Moreover, the use of fox canines as an ornamental medium corresponds to the distribution of the arctic fox, *Alopex lagopus*, in the *Mammuthus–Coelodonta* fauna (Khalke 1994:Abb. 4). *Alopex* is not found in Cantabria or the Mediterranean regions. In the northern regions its white shining fur must have been a perceived quality while its teeth also provided an edge that revealed, through their cutting and slicing, more brilliance in the form of the blood of prey.

*The production of beads*

The production of beads in the Aurignacian has been studied by White (1989, 1993a, 1993b) and Taborin (1993:169ff) using the concept of the chaîne opératoire (Table 6.24).

The most common raw material used was ivory and the production sequence

Table 6.24. *A schematic outline of a chaîne opératoire for Aurignacian (or any other) system of personal ornamentation (White 1997). The outline, with slight modification, could also apply to the manufacture of stone tools or the construction of shelters.*

1 Cultural assumptions about personhood
2 Beliefs about the relationship between materials, representational acts, representational constructs and social/supernatural efficacy
3 Choice and acquisition (by direct extraction or by social mechanisms of exchange) of raw material based on above
4 Choice of forms, textures, colours or subject matters
5 Organization of production (social, temporal and spatial)
6 Combination of gestures and tools into techniques for ornament production that are coherent with the encompassing, regional technical system
7 These enable the representation of desired signifiers of social identity, age, reproductive status, supernatural associations etc.
8 Use of the ornamental representations in (socially, aesthetically and cosmologically) meaningful acts
9 Purposeful (based on intentions for future retrieval/use or ideas about their residual power and efficacy) or accidental (as a by-product of human activity) disposal of the ornament

can be divided into five stages. These are based on the abundant production debris as well as finished objects at locales such as the three neighbouring abris in the Vallon de Castelmerle (Abri Blanchard, Abri Castanet, la Souquette) and the Pyrenean caves of Isturitz, Saint Jean de Verges and Brassempouy (White 1993c: 336). White's detailed study shows that these beads were not finely drilled but rather laboriously gouged out and then ground and polished. Traces of hematite, red ochre, in the polishing striae establish one use for this material as a polishing abrasive (*ibid.*:338).

The end product, a distinctive basket-shaped bead, is very different from the two-holed beads made in ivory in the Aurignacian occupations at the Geißenklösterle (Scheer 1985). However, the production sequence, starting with a rod and producing a string of beads, is very similar (Figure 6.20). Here is another example, comparable to the chaînes opératoires mentioned above for stone tools, of diverse production techniques with a standardized outcome. With the beads the similar production sequences produce *supports* which are then transformed into different items, but both for suspension of some kind.

Two of White's conclusions are relevant to our understanding of the chaîne opératoire. Firstly there is his suggestion (White 1989:376), still to be verified, that since mammoth remains are rare in the faunal assemblages of the south-west region, the ivory for the Vallon de Castelmerle locales was imported in the form of small rods about 10 cm in length and less than 0.5 cm in diameter from

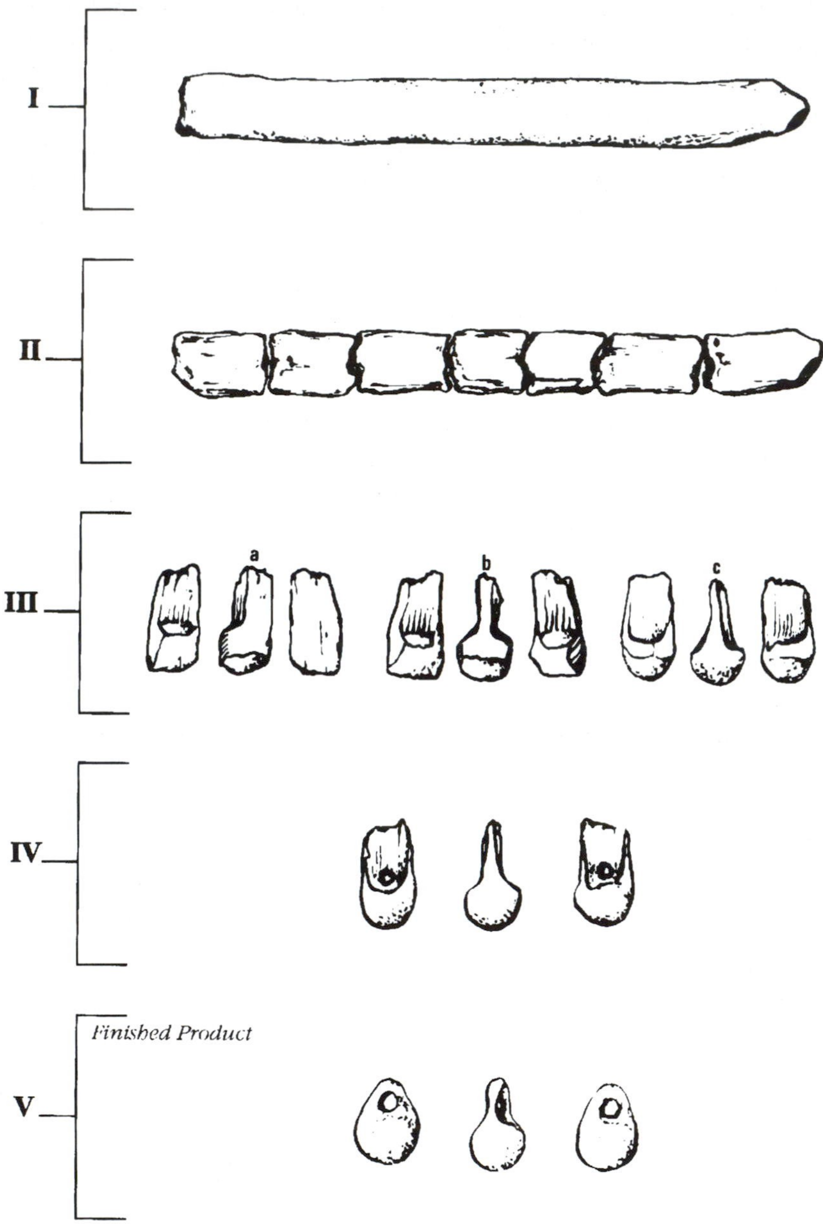


**6.20** The chaîne opératoire for the production of ivory and steatite basket-shaped beads (after White 1993c:Fig. 3).

some unknown distance. By contrast, in the German Aurignacian there are numerous tusk sections as well as bones and molars of mammoth (Hahn 1986) which are either lacking or extremely rare in the French locales. The second point, based on experimentation, is that it takes on average three hours to make a single Aurignacian basket-shaped bead. At La Souquette there are 400 such beads in the basal Aurignacian assemblage, adding up to 1,200 hours of work. The possible connection in this instance between the transfer distance of the raw material and the investment in production is noteworthy. The time involved in the acquisition and production of these small items far exceeds the time invested in the manufacture of stone points where the reduction of a nodule to produce a pocketful of Aurignacian *supports* might have taken a skilled knapper twenty minutes.

Finally, a significant difference emerges between the Aurignacian and Gravettian use of beads and pierced shells. Taborin (1993:304–5) lists the incidence of ornaments and other art objects with Upper Palaeolithic burials in France and elsewhere in Europe. It is very apparent that beads and shells were not part of the very few burials which may be earlier than 30 Kyr bp. The rarity of Aurignacian burials is an interesting pattern which I will examine in Chapter 7. The abundant use of ivory beads and shells in the Gravettian/Perigordian in the north-central (Dolní Věstonice) (Svoboda and Dvorsky 1994), north-eastern (Sunghir) (Bader 1978), and Mediterranean-central (Balzi Rossi) (Mussi 1986a) regions is largely due to the presence of burials.

### *Antler tools*

The addition of artifacts made in bone, ivory and antler is a characteristic of the European Upper Palaeolithic (Albrecht, Hahn and Torke 1972, Camps-Fabrer 1974). A variety of implements were made during the Early Upper Palaeolithic and include hafted points of a variety of shapes, sizes and technical details, borers/piercers, pierced staffs (Ger., *Lochstab*), carvings and engraved pieces. Production of these objects is by façonnage rather than débitage.[25]

The study of Aurignacian antler projectile points by Knecht (1993a, 1993b) serves as an example. Most bone tools in the early Upper Palaeolithic do not show a correspondence with a particular raw material. This is not the case with the distinctive split-based bone points, a feature of the early Aurignacian (de Sonneville-Bordes 1960). In her sample of 381 from France, Belgium and Germany, Knecht found that 97 per cent were made on antler (Table 6.26). Moreover, the other element in the hafting process, the tongued pieces (Figure 6.21), are exclusively made of antler, almost certainly from reindeer.

The production sequence for these split-based antler points is shown in Figure 6.22 (Knecht 1993a:Figure 6). The tongued pieces (Figure 6.21) which were once thought to be the way that the split was obtained in the base of the point are explained by Knecht as wedges to expand the split and so assist hafting. Experiments show that if hafted in this manner (Figure 6.22) separation from the haft, rather than breakage of the point, is more likely (Knecht 1993a: 155). Lashing rather than a resin adhesive is perfectly sufficient.

Wedging techniques were therefore integral to the production and manufacture of these points. Stone wedges were used to exploit the mechanical properties of antler to produce supports for working into points. Wedges were also used to split the base of the point. Finally, antler wedges expanded the split to

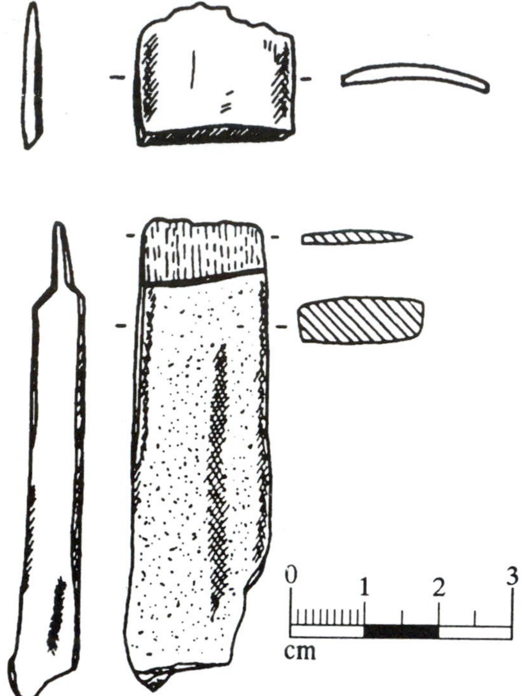


**6.21** A tongued piece, from Abri Cellier, and a wedge, from Abri Castanet, France, SW region, which could have been cut from it to be used in hafting split-based antler points; see Figure 6.22. Both pieces are made from antler (after Knecht 1993b:Fig. 3.4 and 3.5).

form an integral element in the haft. As Knecht (1993a:157) also points out, the techniques of grooving and snapping were used to break apart long segments of antler and ivory to produce those rods for either bead or point manufacture. These transferrable skills from one material to another, and from one production sequence to another, were a suite of habitual gestures, a segment in the chaîne of production.

The repetition is also revealed in two other ways. Albrecht (et al. 1972) studied antler and bone points from sixty-eight, principally EUP assemblages, in the north-central, northeast and southeast regions. They found that all the split-base antler points came from caves and rock shelters whereas three-quarters of the rest also came from such locales. Breakage rates (Table 6.25) were also high in their sample.

However in the southwest region a study of 111 split-base antler points by Leroy-Prost (1974) found that 68 per cent were unbroken. Breakage rates for the lozenge-shaped points were much higher at 64 per cent.

Even allowing for these different patterns of use, discard and replacement (Gamble 1986a:286) we see that the Aurignacian antler points were made in similar ways over large areas (Knecht 1993b:45). Not so with the Gravettian

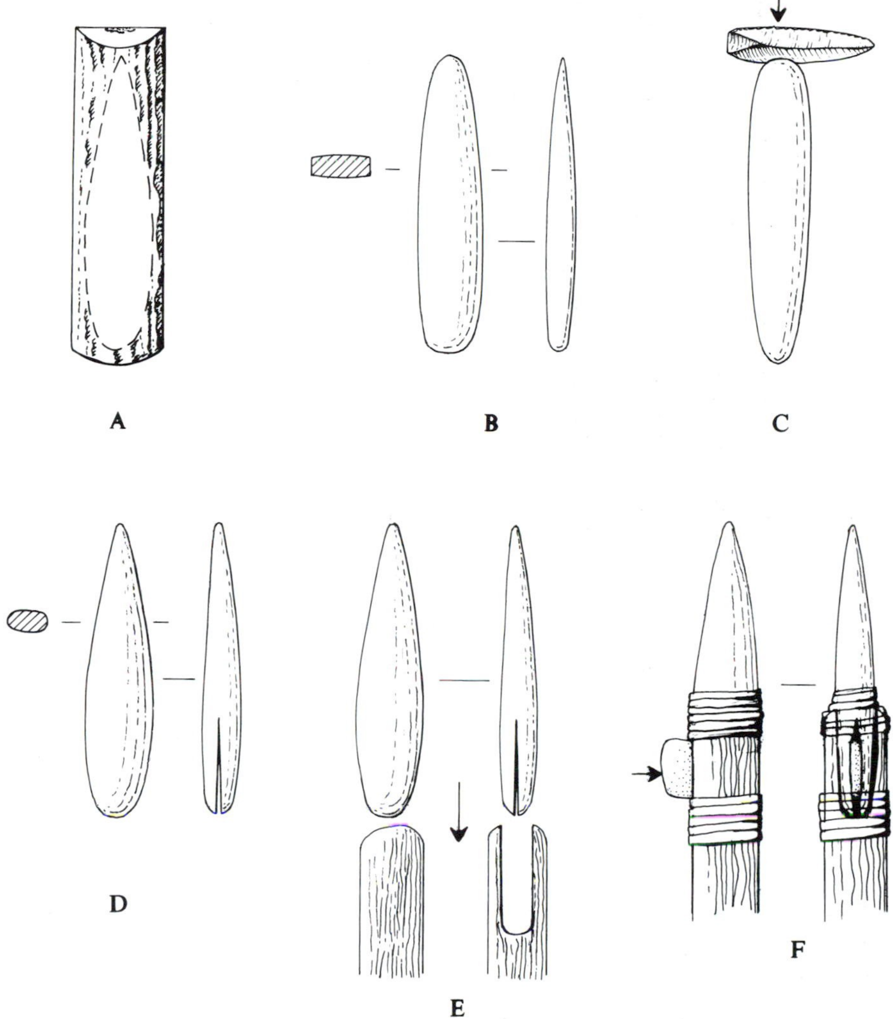


**6.22** The chaîne opératoire for making and hafting split-based antler points (after Knecht 1993b:Figs. 3.3 and 3.7).
KEY:
A&B *Façonnage* of the point from antler
C Wedging the split base
D Finished point
E Fitting to the haft
F Expanding the split with a wedge (see Figure 6.21)

projectiles. The single bevelled points were made on long bones broken into splinters (*ibid.*:40) and bone was the preferred raw material (Table 6.26).

The Gravettian production of organic projectiles resulted in streamlined spears (Knecht 1993b:45) which lacked the bulge at the junction of the haft with the projectile head. The choice of how this smooth outline was produced, by single or double bevelling, varied between regions.

Table 6.25. *The condition of antler and bone boints from sixty-eight predominantly Early Upper Palaeolithic assemblages in central and eastern Europe (Albrecht, Hahn and Torke 1972).*

| | % |
|---|---|
| Complete/unbroken | 17.3 |
| Slight damage | 14.8 |
| Fragmentary/broken | 67.8 |
| **N** | **277** |

Table 6.26. *Raw-material choice and early Upper Palaeolithic projectile technology (Knecht 1993a, 1993b). The single bevel points are from one locale, Laugerie-Haute.*

| | *Aurignacian* | | | |
|---|---|---|---|---|
| | Split-base | Solid base | | *Perigordian/Gravettian* |
| | | Lozenge | Spindle | Single bevel |
| Antler | 371 | 101 | 35 | 2 |
| Antler? | | 2 | 0 | 1 |
| Bone or antler | | 0 | 2 | 1 |
| Ivory | | 1 | 0 | |
| Bone | 1 | | | 57 |
| Bone? | | | | 4 |
| Uncertain | 9 | | | |

*Wooden objects and evidence for hafting stone*

There is evidence from microwear studies that in the French Mousterian of Acheulean Tradition stone tools, usually scrapers, were hafted (Anderson-Gerfaud 1990, Beyries 1988).[26] The evidence takes the form of polishes left by the rubbing of the haft on the surface of the flint. These traces may have occurred precisely because adhesives, such as bitumen which does survive on some tools from the Middle East, have never been found on French material. Such adhesives prevent friction and hence the possibility of wear traces on the surfaces of the tool. Use-wear evidence that stones were hafted as projectile points or on the end of spears is therefore difficult to find, leading Holdaway (1989) to argue that what we call Mousterian points in our typologies should be regarded functionally as scrapers. This interpretation cannot be supported.

Elsewhere in Europe two pieces of resin from Königsaue A and B, NC region, have been AMS dated to 43,800±2100 and 48,400±3700 bp (Hedges et al. 1998:229).[27] One piece bears the negative impression of a backed bifacial tool, the possible imprint of a wooden haft and a fingerprint, presumably of a Neanderthal (Mania and Toepfer 1973:Plate 11).

Use-wear studies involve slow, painstaking analyses that depend upon experimental work for interpretation (Beyries 1987, Keeley 1980, 1982). Much of this work still has to be done and consequently it is not presently possible to say how widespread or frequent such hafting behaviour might have been. Even the proposition that the haft was made of wood remains conjectural although entirely reasonable. The split- and solid-based antler points of the Aurignacian and bevelled bone Gravettian points were certainly hafted, probably without adhesive (Knecht 1993a, 1993b) and the likely material for the haft was wood.

Use-wear studies on stone tools have shown that, in both the Middle and Early Upper Palaeolithic, wood was commonly worked (Anderson-Gerfaud 1990). However, very few pieces have survived from the Interpleniglacial period. One exception is in the Mousterian level H at Abric Romani in the Mediterranean-west region (Carbonell 1992, Carbonell and Castro-Curel 1992). Four poorly preserved wooden objects, none of them hafts, were recovered during excavation. One of the pieces is a slab of juniper wood measuring 22 by 32 cm with a thickness of 3 cm and possibly hollowed out to form a 'dish-like' object. But the close association of all four objects to hearths (Carbonell and Castro-Curel 1992:Figure 7) and their poor preservation makes it difficult to be certain if they were artifacts or fuel.[28]

### *Musical rhythms*

New sounds accompanied the Early Upper Palaeolithic. Two bone flutes have been pieced together from horizon IIab in the Geißenklösterle (Hahn and Münzel 1995). This Aurignacian level is AMS dated to 36.8 Kyr bp so that these are very possibly the oldest musical instruments in Europe. The best preserved is made on a swan's radius (Figure 6.23) and has three remaining sound holes. It is also rhythmically marked with seven surviving transversal cuts on its dorsal surface. It does not occur in a special context, such as a burial or hut structure, but was found in front of a flat rock (Hahn and Münzel 1995:Abb. 2) along with stone tools and animal bones. At the Isturitz cave in the Pyrenees a single flute was found in Aurignacian deposits and a further nine in the later Gravettian and six in the Perigordian V (Buisson 1990).

Music-making is a good example of a chaîne opératoire. There are the gestures involved in making the instrument as well as those to play it. There is the context for its performance, either alone or in company. It is a social and technical act, at once individually creative yet constrained by convention. The rhythmic sounds and phrases negotiate mood by playing on emotional resources which in turn stem from other contexts and performances where

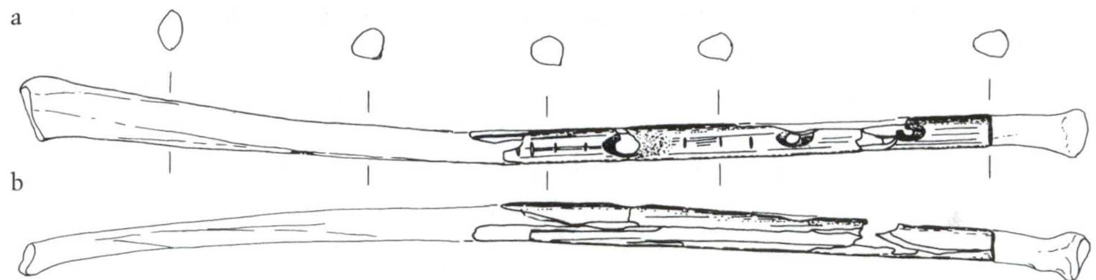


**6.23** Flute 1 made on a swan's radius from the Aurignacian level AH IIab at the Geißenklösterle, southern Germany, NC region (after Hahn and Münzel 1995:Abb. 3 Scale 3:4).

gestures of attention create intimate and effective relationships. The structured sound of music, like the structured view of representational art, is part of the taskscape, the surrounding environment of sounds, rhythms and action, where people attend to each other and experience the process of living.

It could however be argued that something similar would have resulted from the sounds and sights of knapping and using stone tools. Such social and technical activity arrived with the oldest Europeans (Chapter 4) as they created and shaped their social lives based on the variable use of emotional and material resources (Table 2.8). By contrast formal music-making and formal depictions of the world are derived from an additional, symbolic, use of resources so that it comes as no surprise that such social technology appears much later. These forms are created, and they linger, as threads in the chaîne opératoire, through the stretching of social life across time and space. The sounds from these simple flutes, like the swan from which they were fashioned, carries us beyond the immediate construction of society and into a wider world.

### *Taskscape: skills and the surrounding environment*

One way that I examined the taskscape in Chapter 5 was through regional patterns among faunal assemblages. I concluded that increased carnivore presence within regions, as measured both syn- and diachronically, pointed to the positioning of locales in rich areas for prey resources. This assessment of community richness provided the background for assessing the skills of the Neanderthals as they moved about their taskscapes. While there was evidence for the development of some specific skills, the overall impression was that transferrable skills still formed the basis for social and technical organization. This was further reflected in the emphasis on intimate and effective networks when it came to wider, regional behaviour.

Following the demonstration above of changes in the rhythms associated with paths of movement and chaînes of making, the question now must be whether evidence exists for greater emphasis on specific skills. Is it possible in this transition period to talk of specialized skills closely associated with a knowledge of place and particular animals?

I will undertake to answer this question by returning to the issue of specialization (see Chapter 5). The ability to exploit poorer resource environments, as well as areas where animal communities were rich, provides an example. Attention will be paid here to the use of herds as well as two species widely regarded as requiring a specialist approach, mammoth and ibex.

*Specializing in animals: specific skills*

We saw in Chapter 5 that the evidence for prime-aged hunting precedes, by a long time, the Middle-to-Upper transition in Europe (Gaudzinski 1995). Stiner has summarized the position:

> New kinds of data on the Eurasian Palaeolithic indicate that Mousterian resource use was more internally complex and geographically diverse than previously thought. These data also show that hominids' behavioural repertoires could be complex in overall structure without necessarily seeming modern. To the extent that archaics differed from anatomically modern humans, these differences are in the rules of strategy combination and territory use in response to resource availability. (1993: 74)

An appreciation of the diversity she refers to can be gained from Table 6.27 where a sample of specialized faunas predominantly from caves and abris is presented. These are specialized in the sense used in Chapter 5 where one species dominates. The locales/levels are sorted according to the proportion of bones identified to one species.

Mousterian assemblages are found throughout the list, rather than clustered, and a variety of different taxa and carnivores are represented. Some of the assemblages in Table 6.27 can be explained through taphonomy, for example the Mousterian and Aurignacian levels in the Stadel and Geißenklösterle were frequently used by cave bears as hibernation dens (Gamble 1979, Münzel, Morel and Hahn 1994). But it would be difficult from this list to argue for a change in behaviour between the Middle and Upper Palaeolithic.

*Intercepting herds*

How different were the Middle and Upper Palaeolithic responses to Stiner's point about resource availability? Excavations at the aven locale of Mauran (Farizy, David and Jaubert 1994) in Haute Garonne, have produced a midden of bison bone. It is the largest collection in Table 6.27 and consists of 99 per cent bison. Raw materials for the denticulate Mousterian artifacts were obtained within 15 km of the locale and were predominantly quartzite cobbles from the Garonne (Figure 6.24).[29] Heavy tools such as choppers form a significant part of the assemblage where retouched pieces account for 7.5 per cent, N=161 (Jaubert 1993).

Mauran commands the gap through the Petites Pyrénées which is accentuated by cliffs and the local topography. The MNI for bison is 83 from a small excavation of 25 $m^2$ and an estimated area of 1,000 $m^2$ which could be

Table 6.27. *Specialized animal faunas 60–21 Kyr BP (Blasco Sancho 1995, Bouchud 1975, Cassoli and Tagliacozzo 1994, Delpech 1984, Enloe 1993, Estévez 1987, Farizy, David and Jaubert 1994, Fladerer 1996, Gamble 1979, 1995d, Gvozdover et al. 1996, Hahn 1989, Klein and Cruz-Uribe 1994, Münzel, Morel and Hahn 1994, Patou-Mathis 1993, 1994, Pillard 1972, Stiner 1994, Straus 1992).*

| Site | Layer | Archaeology | Region | OIS age | No. of IDs | No. of carnivore species/bones | No. of herbivore species/bones | Dominant species | % of identified bones | MNI |
|---|---|---|---|---|---|---|---|---|---|---|
| Mauran | | Mousterian | SW | 3 | 4,193 | 1/1 | 3/4,192 | Bison | 99 | 83 |
| Abri Pataud | 13 | Aurignacian | SW | 3 | 224 | 0/0 | 2/224 | Reindeer | 99 | |
| Abri Pataud | 14 | Aurignacian | SW | 3 | 1,499 | 1/4 | 5/1,495 | Reindeer | 99 | |
| Abri Flageolet I | Couche V | Perigordian V | SW | 2 | 1,900 | 0/0 | 7/1,900 | Reinder | 95 | |
| Starosel'e | | Mousterian | NE | 3 | 18,363 | 5/74 | 10/18,289 | Steppe ass | 95 | 240 |
| Abri Pataud | 3 | Perigordian VI | SW | 2 | 2,431 | 3/14 | 7/2,417 | Reindeer | 86 | |
| El Castilló | 11–18 | EUP | SW | 3 | 407 | 0/0 | 4/407 | Horse | 86 | 22 |
| Geißenklösterle | IV | Aurignacian | NC | 3 | 189 | 5/168 | 6/21 | Bear | 85 | |
| Lommersum | | Aurignacian | NC | 3 | 3,202 | 4/9 | 3/3,193 | Reindeer | 85 | 36 |
| Geißenklösterle | I | Gravettian | NC | 3 | 1,648 | 5/1,563 | 6/85 | Bear | 81 | |
| Stadel | IV and IVA | Aurignacian | NC | 3 | 2,422 | 6/2,264 | 5/158 | Bear | 80 | |
| La Ferrassie | K4 to base K | Aurignacian I & II | SW | 3 | 225 | 6/221 | 2/4 | Reindeer | 77 | |
| Geißenklösterle | III | Aurignacian | NC | 3 | 995 | 4/820 | 7/175 | Bear | 76 | |
| La Ferrassie | D2&D3, D2–E4 | Perigordian V | SW | 2 | 1,041 | 9/990 | 3/51 | Red deer | 76 | |
| Hortus | All levels | Mousterian | MW | 3 | 2,332 | 6/392 | 7/1,940 | Ibex | 75 | 103 |
| La Ferrassie | F&Go | Aurignacian IV | SW | 3 | 155 | 7/154 | 1/1 | Reindeer | 73 | |
| Abri Pataud | 12 | Aurignacian | SW | 3 | 183 | 2/6 | 4/177 | Reindeer | 70 | |
| Geißenklösterle | II | Aurignacian | NC | 3 | 1,774 | 4/1,252 | 6/522 | Bear | 66 | |
| Stadel | V–VII | Mousterian | NC | 3 | 4,524 | 8/3,349 | 8/1,175 | Bear | 59 | |
| Arbreda (Alpha sector) | E | Aurignacian | MW | 3 | 380 | 4/7 | 7/373 | Horse | 59 | |
| Alberndorf | Open site | Aurignacian | NC | 3 | 191 | 2/12 | 5/179 | Reindeer | 57 | 9 |
| Abri Pataud | 11 | Aurignacian | SW | 3 | 1,036 | 3/70 | 6/966 | Reindeer | 57 | |
| Arbreda (Alpha sector) | F, Ga, Gbc | Mousterian | MW | 3 | 483 | 4/294 | 9/189 | Bear | 54 | |

| | | | | | | | | | | |
|---|---|---|---|---|---|---|---|---|---|---|
| La Ferrassie | J–K1–K3 | Aurignacian I & II | SW | 3 | 156 | 9/155 | 1/1 | Bos | 52 | |
| St Césaire | EJOP | Châtelperronian | SW | 3 | 516 | 4/28 | 9/488 | Reindeer | 48 | 12 |
| Grotta Breuil | B3/4 | Mousterian | MC | 3 | 396 | 5/45 | 8/351 | Ibex | 47 | |
| Gabasa 1 | d | Mousterian | MW | 3 | 702 | 7/71 | 7/631 | Ibex | 47 | 24 |
| Grotte Tournal | IIIFA,FB, F1–F4 | Aurignacian | MW | 3 | 696 | 5/63 | 9/633 | Reindeer | 44 | 25 |
| Cueva Morín | 17 | Mousterian | SW | 3 | 506 | 2/3 | 7/503 | Bos | 43 | |
| Grotte Tournal | IIb | Mousterian | MW | 3 | 1,225 | 5/315 | 8/910 | Horse | 41 | 33 |
| Gabasa 1 | a+c | Mousterian | MW | 3 | 658 | 6/51 | 8/607 | Ibex | 40 | 27 |
| Riparo Fumane | A3 to DI–Ic | Aurignacian | MC | 3 | 1,287 | 8/216 | 7/1,071 | Ibex | 38 | 48 |
| Riparo Fumane | A13-2 to A4 III–II | Mousterian | MC | 3 | 678 | 5/45 | 8/633 | Red deer | 37 | 36 |
| Gabasa 1 | f | Mousterian | MW | 3 | 1,123 | 8/30 | 9/1,094 | Ibex | 36 | 21 |
| Gabasa 1 | g | Mousterian | MW | 3 | 1,814 | 9/176 | 9/1,638 | Ibex | 36 | 46 |
| Gabasa 1 | h | Mousterian | MW | 3 | 806 | 7/83 | 8/723 | Ibex | 34 | 14 |
| Gabasa 1 | e | Mousterian | MW | 3 | 1,405 | 9/120 | 9/1,285 | Ibex | 31 | 29 |
| Grotta di Sant'Agostino | SO–SX | Mousterian | MC | 3 | 3,141 | 7/529 | 9/2,612 | Red deer | 26 | 34 |

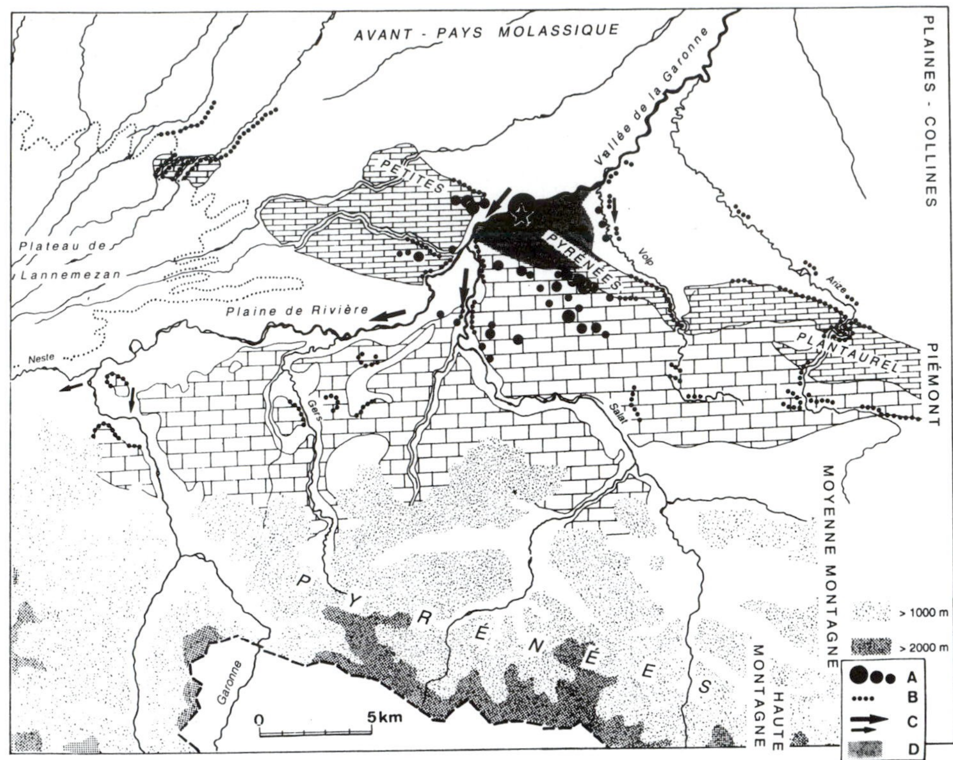


**6.24** The location of Mauran (marked by a star) in the Petites Pyrénées, France, SW region. The bison were probably dispersed in small groups in the hills to the east of the locale. The locale takes advantage of natural features to predict animal movements and facilitate ambush hunting (after Farizy, David and Jaubert 1994:Fig. 128).

Key
A Location of raw materials less than 15 km from the locale
B Main cliffs and rocky outcrops which could be used in hunting
C Main tracks through the area
D Area reached in one hour's walk from the locale

excavated. If bison were recovered at the same density over this entire area then almost 4,000 animals must be present.

Tooth eruption suggests that the bison were killed at the end of summer and into the autumn. Eighty per cent of the individuals were adult females and calves. Adult males made up the remainder of the kill. The age profile is described as catastrophic with a high ratio of young individuals. Elsewhere such a mortality structure profile might be indicative of carnivore acitivity (Stiner 1994:Chapter 5). But at Mauran, only one carnivore bone was found, a bear's scapula, and no gnawing is present.

There is no spatial patterning in the bone midden (see David and Farizy 1994:Figs. 120–123) and poor preservation of bone surfaces has removed most of the evidence for cut marks. Many of the bones were, however, systematically smashed to extract marrow by using a hammer and anvil (Farizy, David and Jaubert 1994:Fig. 129).

Contrast this locale dedicated to killing and processing bison with the Aurignacian level 14 at the Abri Pataud on the Vézère river in the Dordogne (Bouchud 1975, Movius 1977, Spiess 1979). Here, reindeer is the dominant animal as it is in all four Aurignacian levels (Table 6.27) as well as in the Perigordian/Gravettian. In level 14 it accounts for 99 per cent, and the 1,500 identifiable bones come from an occupation area estimated to be 15 $m^2$ (Spiess 1979:table 6.20). This level, the earliest in the locale, produced 101 retouched tools (Movius 1977:140).[30]

There has been considerable discussion over the season when the site was used (Boyle 1990:111–14), with Spiess' (1979) view prevailing that it was occupied during the late autumn and winter as indeed were all the Early Upper Palaeolithic levels in the Abri Pataud. His interpretation is supported by evidence of seasonality from tooth sectioning (*ibid.*:table 6.6). On the basis of these findings he concludes that the Vézère provided a winter refuge.

Ageing information is sparse, but Spiess (1979:197–203) argues that the hunters culled small mixed herds. His data (*ibid.*:table 6.10) suggest a prime-aged profile with an emphasis, 53 per cent, on animals between three and nine years old (n=93).[31] Mass driving was not taking place.

At the rock shelter of Le Flageolet I level V, also in southwest France, the Perigordian V lithic assemblage has an accompanying fauna dominated by reindeer (Enloe 1993:Table 6.27). The seasonality data point to winter while the age profile is dominated by prime-aged animals of between two and six years (*ibid.*:Figure 1). Interestingly, only 3 per cent of all the identified specimens carry cutmarks (*ibid.*:109), even though bones which are both surrounded by large amounts of meat and which contain substantial marrow reserves, tibia, femur and metatarsal, are well represented. Enloe (1993: 109) interprets these findings as evidence for single hunters transporting food over a considerable distance. This conclusion requires that the bones associated with high utility parts of the skeleton (Binford 1978b, 1981a, Binford and Bertram 1977) are filleted out to reduce weight for the bearers.[32] Binford has referred to these as gourmet and bulk strategies as indicated by the bones left behind. Absence of the bones associated with the highest food values, in terms of meat, fat, marrow and grease, for carcass segments would indicate a gourmet strategy which is also associated with hunting prime-aged prey (Binford 1978b:81). Bulk strategies occur when supply is reduced and as a result older and younger animals are also taken and processed.

Table 6.28. *Locales with more than ten mammoths (after Soffer 1993). All are open locales and associated with Gravettian assemblages from the period 29–21 Kyr bp.*

| Locale | Region | MNI Mammoth |
|---|---|---|
| Dolní Věstonice I & II | NC | >150 |
| Pavlov | NC | >30 |
| Milovice | NC | >30 |
| Předmostí | NC | >1,000 |
| Spadzista | NC | 60 |
| Voronovitsa | NE | 12 |
| Kostenki 1/1 | NE | >10 (minimum estimate) |

The faunal evidence does not therefore suggest very different strategies or organizational capabilities between the hominids at Mauran and Abri Pataud. A similar conclusion has been reached by Patou-Mathis (1994) for the Grotte Tournal, Mediterranean-west region. Mousterian and Aurignacian levels in the cave are respectively dominated by horse and reindeer (Table 6.27). However, a careful taphonomic study of the faunas showed little difference in the treatment of these two species. The cave provides an example of a palimpsest fauna where many short visits were paid by people in both periods (*ibid.*:25). The sporadic use of the locale in the Mousterian is underscored by the strong presence of bear and hyena in the assemblage.

*Mammoths*

It is noticeable that during the period 60–21 Kyr bp there is a lack of gatherings associated with single carcasses. The rarity of lakeside sites noted above may explain this finding. In the earlier Saalian period (Chapter 5) there were several examples which included aurochs, rhinos and elephants, for example at Neumark Nord. By contrast, locales such as Mauran are associated with many hundreds of bison accumulated over time at the same locale. These are comparable to earlier locales such as Wallertheim (Gaudzinski 1992), La Borde (Jaubert et al. 1990) or Il'skaya (Hoffecker, Baryshnikov and Potapova 1991).

The major difference in this period occurs after 33 Kyr bp and more particularly with the downturn in climate to the LGM after 28 Kyr bp. The new aspect is locales with many mammoth remains. These are restricted to some regions in the continent. As Kozlowski (1990:Table 15.1) points out in his multi-aspectual study of the Early Upper Palaeolithic, several Gravettian locales in the north-central and northeastern regions were associated with large mammoth middens. On occasion the mammoth bones were used to build windbreaks and structures as at Ripiceni-Izvor complex I (Gamble 1986a:Figure 6.4, Paunescu 1965) and Spadzista Street (Kozlowski 1974). Soffer (1993) provides an overview of the distribution of mammoths (Table 6.28).

Table 6.29. *The distribution of 152 faunal assemblages with* Capra ibex *by region and period. The proportions refer to the total sample of 588 assemblages. MP=Middle Palaeolithic, EUP=Early Upper Palaeolithic, LUP=Late Upper Palaeolithic.*

| Region | Faunas with *Capra ibex* | % of archaeological faunas |
|---|---|---|
| NC | 78 | 21 |
| SE | 27 | 31 |
| ME | 47 | 34 |
| Period | | |
| LUP | 33 | 20 |
| EUP | 65 | 38 |
| MP | 54 | 22 |

Soffer emphasizes that these mammoth remains resulted not only from hominid kills but also from natural accumulations, the so-called mammoth graveyards that accumulate along rivers in permafrost landscapes. Generally the bones lack cut marks but are carnivore gnawed, which strongly suggests they were as much collected as obtained from hunted carcasses (Soffer 1993:37). The mammoth bones are usually dominated by sub-adult animals although all ages are present. In an interesting suggestion Soffer notes the association between the Moravian locales and the presence of mineral licks in their immediate vicinity (1993:40). This may have been an attractor around which seasonal deaths occurred (see Conybeare and Haynes 1984). It is noticeable at the Moravian locales that mammoth bone was not burnt as fuel, nor was it stored in pits. Both of these features are found at Kostenki 1/1 and on the Central Russian Plain after the LGM (Soffer 1985b).

*Ibex hunters*

The ability to cope with resource-poor areas may be a fairer test of Stiner's suggestion that different strategy combinations mark the transition from the Middle to the Upper Palaeolithic. In order to examine this proposition I have concentrated here upon faunas with *Capra ibex*, a medium-sized bovid forming small herds and associated today with steep terrain at high altitudes (Gamble 1995e:Table IV). As Straus (1987) has argued, if these animals were being exploited then it indicates a hunter using the landscape with specialist skills and, in Stiner's terms, in complex ways.

Among a sample of 588 faunal assemblages from three regions within Europe,

Table 6.30. *Four communities in Upper Pleistocene Europe (Gamble 1995e:Table VI). For key see Table 6.29. Large carnivores include bear, lion, hyena and wolf, all members of the carnivore guild most closely in competition with hominids. Small carnivores include foxes, wolverines, lynx, wild cat, badger, otter and* Cuon.

| Community | Hominids | Large carnivores | Small carnivores | Inferred conditions |
|---|---|---|---|---|
| 1. MP, EUP, LUP | X | X | X | Resource rich |
| 2. PNT | | X | X | │ |
| 3. LUP | X | | X | │ |
| 4. PNT | | | X | Resource poor |

152 contained *Capra ibex* (Table 6.29). This taxon was most abundant by period in the early Upper Palaeolithic and by region in the Mediterranean east.

When ibex occurs in a faunal assemblage it is noticeable that the number of large carnivore species is also much greater than in those assemblages where it is absent (Gamble 1995e:Tables I and V).[33] This is true for all three regions but not all periods. The LUP has ibex assemblages, such as Klithi in northwest Greece (Bailey 1997, Gamble 1997), where large carnivores are very rare or absent and small carnivores predominate. Palaeontological assemblages cover both types.

This pattern of carnivore occurrence is interpreted as a measure of resource richness represented by four different animal communities (Table 6.30).

*Capra ibex* would therefore be found in community 1, where evidence for both large and small carnivores as well as hominids is present and the indications are for rich resources in areas of differentiated but not extreme topography (see Chapter 5). This taxon would also be found in restricted areas, such as the high Pindhos mountains of Greece, in community 3 where its presence and the absence of large carnivores are indicative of poorer resources.

Examples of community 1 would be Early Upper Palaeolithic locales such as Bacho Kiro in the SE region (Kozlowski 1982) and Subalyuk (Mottl 1941) in the NC region. Ibex are common in these assemblages but so too is evidence for carnivore activity, in the form of their bones, the number of species, or evidence for gnawing which characteristically produces bone assemblages where the toughest elements only, teeth and foot bones, survive. The Middle Palaeolithic cave of Hortus (Pillard 1972) in the Mediterranean-west region with its *Capra ibex* and fragmentary Neanderthals is also a community-1 assemblage (Table 6.27). Taphonomic studies are needed to discover to what extent leopards were bringing this species back to the cave.[34]

A further example comes from the cave of Gabasa 1 in Huesca province, northeast Spain (Blasco Sancho 1995). The locale has six levels of typical Mous-

Table 6.31. *Population structure at Gabasa 1 (Blasco Sancho 1995:Table 36).*

| | Neonate % | Juvenile % | Adult % | Old % | N |
|---|---|---|---|---|---|
| Red Deer | 60.4 | 9.4 | 29.2 | 1.0 | 96 |
| Horse | 61.7 | 7.5 | 28.0 | 2.8 | 107 |
| Ibex | 13.7 | 5.6 | 72.0 | 8.7 | 161 |
| Chamois | 18.9 | 10.8 | 62.2 | 8.1 | 37 |

terian where *Capra ibex* is the most common species.[35] Carnivores account for 9 per cent of the fauna and gnawing is present. The bones of the main species are from the high food value parts of the carcass.

In her study of the large herbivores at Gabasa 1, Blasco Sancho (1995) uses four age categories based on tooth eruption and wear (Table 6.31). Ibex and chamois are dominated by the adult class and are very different in terms of population structure than the major herd animals, horse and red deer.

The differences in age data would normally be assessed in terms of prey selection. However, it is also possible to interpret them in terms of the importance of the structure of the local animal community in governing decisions over the short-haul transportation of parts to the cave. The decisions are less to do with what to kill (selection) but rather with what to do with it once it has been killed (transport).

This model supposes that heads (low utility parts) were only brought back to the site for processing and consumption when either smaller (young) or poorer-condition (old) animals were killed and hence the food value of the carcass was low. If a prime (adult) animal was killed, the head, a lower food value element, was left behind. This decision about what parts of the carcass to transport can therefore be modelled as a demand/supply curve analogous to the bulk and gourmet strategies proposed by Binford (1978b:81). When prime adult animals were killed the body parts selected for transport resembled a gourmet curve. Here the emphasis was on parts with high and medium food utility. A bulk curve, which included low food utility parts such as heads, resulted when either younger or older animals were killed. If this is the case then we should expect transport decisions to produce very different age profiles for teeth and bodies for the same species. The teeth data would indicate an attritional, U-shaped profile (Stiner 1990:Fig. 2) and the pattern of bone fusion a prime-dominated profile (Figure 5.28). The long-term success of the Gabasa 1 hunters in generally acquiring prime-aged prey reflects their good fortune in predating a more diverse community (Gamble 1995e).

Resource richness therefore accounts for the patterning in faunal assemblages and suggests some continuity in behaviour rather than a shift to novel behaviour patterns. Ibex hunting within a resource rich community was a set of skills transferred across the Middle-to-Upper Palaeolithic transition. These skills have a specific content in that the antiquity of using this species is comparatively recent and seems to date to after the last interglacial, 118 Kyr bp.

Novel skills are however found after the last glacial maximum at *Capra ibex*-dominated locales, high in the mountains and with very few other species (Gamble 1995e, 1997, Straus 1987). The skills of the Late Upper Palaeolithic hunters lay in exploiting resource poor communities (Table 6.30). These skills were more than periodic adjustments to the availability of prey (Stiner 1992:447) since they involved novel patterns of landscape use with specific knowledge applied to acquiring selected resources (Bailey 1997). Specific skills created within the context of an individual's taskscape could therefore occur at any time. They are not species specific but instead dependent upon the routines and habitual rhythms which create social life at the spatial level of the taskscape.

A similar conclusion can be placed on the study by Simek and Snyder (1988) of the diversity in faunal assemblages in southwest France. They find a decline in measures of evenness and diversity after 28 Kyr bp and a trend toward specialized, i.e. non-diverse faunas (ibid.:329). Faunal changes are therefore greater within the Upper Palaeolithic than between the Middle and Upper Palaeolithic. Simek and Price (1990:258) also argue that the change which they observed in lithic assemblage richness and evenness at the same time, c. 28 Kyr bp, with the Perigordian can be partly explained by declining animal diversity providing increased selection pressure for technological change.

### *Summary*

There is an essential requirement in the study of the transition from the Middle to Upper Palaeolithic; we must be satisfied that a level playingfield exists so that differences can be understood as social change rather than variation due to factors such as ecology or preservation.

The evidence in this chapter has demonstrated that the playingfield on which the transition was enacted was more or less level during the period 60–21 Kyr bp. Its level character is measured by climate and the survival and recovery of the evidence. In three respects – artifact assemblage size, the intensity with which regions were occupied and prime-aged hunting – there is evidence for continuity from the Middle Palaeolithic through the earliest Upper Palaeolithic. This has been presented previously by Kozlowski (1990) in his multi-aspectual model (Table 6.8).

But these continuities are also matched by innovative rhythms and social technology during this transition period. The most significant are the distance of raw material transfers, the transfer of shells and the fashioning of material representations be they ornament, sculpture or musical phrases.

However, despite these innovations the major structural changes occur in the Palaeolithic record *after* 33 Kyr bp as revealed by the multi-aspectual model.

This does not mean for a moment that we are ready to relocate the Upper Palaeolithic boundary in Europe from its traditional place, which is a moveable feast somewhere between 45–35 Kyr bp. But when we come to consider how the rhythms, discussed in this chapter, linked the regions and locales that we will examine in Chapter 7, we must be aware of this temporal patterning. This will be of particular importance when we come to examine quantitative and qualitative changes in the structure of locales.

The pattern of archaeological cultures can be summarized as follows:

- Late Middle Palaeolithic locales are no more complex in terms of architecture, contents and the numerical size of collections than the Early Middle Palaeolithic. There are no appreciable changes in raw-material transfers either in distance or for the types of material transferred.
- Leaf point and so-called transitional industries such as the Szeletian and Châtelperronian are numerically small in size. Some changes in the distances of transfers are apparent.
- Aurignacian assemblages are numerically small and the evidence for complex base camps limited. However, there is more evidence for changes in both the distance and variety of materials transferred. Investment of time in manufacturing display items and altering the taskscape through cave painting and music occurs for the first time.
- Gravettian assemblages are on occasion very large, but these are restricted to the north-central and northeastern regions. There are changes in the movement of raw materials with larger proportions of far-distant materials being moved. Burial data assume a new dimension in the centre and west of the continent, as well as along the Ligurian coast, while contacts now exist through the transfer of shells between central Europe and the Mediterranean.

The interpretation I place on this patterning emphasizes how the innovative rhythms resulted in system integration, as defined in Chapter 2. This was achieved through the use of symbolic resources and went beyond the limitations set by co-presence. Such system integration which, as we shall see in the next chapter, resulted in the extension of society, occurred selectively prior to 33 Kyr bp. The existence of two different social systems, Neanderthal and Crô-Magnon, based on the distinct use of resources – emotional, material and symbolic – both confirms the level playingfield and focuses attention on what needs explaining in terms of Middle Palaeolithic replacement. This approach emphasizes that we will indeed misrepresent the subtlety of the transition if it is portrayed purely as one of population replacement.

In this chapter I have concentrated on rhythms and social technology and continued to emphasise the skills of social life as they applied to individuals. From this perspective the skills of a Neanderthal hunter at Grotte Tournal or Mauran only seem to differ from his or her Crô-Magnon counterpart at the scale of the locale. We shall explore these hearths and structures in more detail in the next chapter when we consider locales as social occasions and places. But this is a rather different conclusion to Stiner's view that 'differences [were] in the rules of strategy combination and territory use in response to resource availability' (1993:74). I have proposed that the taskscapes of Neanderthals involved specific skills which brought people together and created gatherings involving resources. If there were differences between individual Neanderthals and Crô-Magnons then these resided not at the level of strategy combinations – human decisions determined primarily by an external environment – but as a result of living within that environment. Human agency, irrespective of any fossil name-tag, created the immediate taskscape which surrounded the individual irrespective of what hominid species he or she happened to be.

This suggests that we will never adequately understand changes in the Palaeolithic record of this or any period by simply trying to relate aspects of organization to the design and organization of technology. Neither will a satisfactory result come from investigating spatial patterning in terms of functionally distinct areas based on the distribution of animal bones. I therefore concur with Farizy and David's conclusion that

> this does not mean that Middle Palaeolithic groups were not able to plan short- or even long-term foraging strategies. Their behaviour seems to be highly dependent on social constraints, and this could explain why behavioural patterns appear to change so slowly. (1992:93)

We need to integrate the evidence for these behavioural patterns within a framework of social action. Such an approach, explored in the next chapter, focuses on the individual rather than just the organizational system which provided adaptive responses to the external environment. If we concentrate on the system we learn only that our position within the carnivore guild remained the same. If we change focus to the individual we learn instead, as we have in this and the previous chapter, that many social skills were transferred between the Middle and the Upper Palaeolithic but that new ones emerged. It is now time to examine how the common rhythms such as acquiring, making, walking, performing and attending now linked the different scales of regions and locales in the Upper Palaeolithic to form new and specific skills for living.

CHAPTER 7

# THE EXTENSION OF SOCIAL LIFE 60,000–21,000 YEARS AGO: REGIONS AND LOCALES, NETWORKS AND LANDSCAPES

Social life . . . is not the performance of a
programme but the very process of composition

Peter Wilson, 1980

## Power and the Palaeolithic

I will argue in this chapter that there can be no significant transition between Palaeolithic societies which did not involve the transformation of power. These changes involved more than new ways to kill a reindeer or technical solutions to keeping warm. They entailed more than planning further ahead to meet resource shortage by organizing the distribution of personnel and the timing of movements. Most importantly, these changes extended the ambit of individual action and hence radically altered the structure of power.

The problem of investigating power lies in our conception of it. This is particularly acute in the Palaeolithic, which has usually been presented as a power-less period with the actions of Men guided by the forces of Nature, rather than arising from the interactions between people and their surrounding environments (Chapter 1). Instead, as I discussed in Chapter 2, power should be conceived as rules and resources which both enable and constrain the individual.

The resources I have discussed in this book are those available to mediate the interactions between people. The three networks, intimate, effective and extended, are principally defined by the resources – emotional, material and symbolic (Table 2.8) – which are appropriate to their maintenance. They create the fully-rounded social being with whom we can engage. The rules which enable and constrain such networks lie in the character of those resources. They are both inherent as well as revealed through the performance of society by individuals, through the structure of action by involvement with life and living.

For example, it is not possible to base an extended network of any significant size on emotional resources because they involve time, attention and co-presence. Nor are symbolic resources appropriate to maintain the intimate network, since they disembody action. They are therefore largely unnecessary in the network where embodiment is a defining characteristic for interaction.

In Chapter 6 I showed that the transition between the Middle and Upper Palaeolithic is marked by significant differences in the rhythms which structure action. The aim in this chapter is to account for these changes in terms of the rules and resources available for the construction of social life through such action. To achieve this we need to examine the process of social integration, what people did together, as routinely acted out at the level of the locale and region. I will argue that the transition marks the appearance of extended networks (Table 2.8) with the social occasion and the creation of place within social landscapes (Table 3.1). Individuals now used the rules and resources of interaction with people and objects to create fresh social knowledge. We now encounter the individual's personal network – with its intimate, effective and extended domains – as well as his/her global network of social opportunity and constraint (Table 2.8). Individual agency is not constraint free but those rhythms which result from living in, of and with the world (Chapter 3) are now readily available for multiplication and transference. The result is system integration which deals with action *in absentia* (Chapter 2). Personal as well as institutional power is extended across time and space. The 'release from proximity' (Rodseth et al. 1991), building on our primate and hominid social heritage, now occurred.

But let me be clear on one point: power had no recent origin. These transformations were not negative in the sense that women 'lost' their power at a particular environmental moment (Knight 1991a, 1991b) or that power could be 'seized' as a consequence of organizational changes to do with big-game, large-herd hunting (Gilman 1984). To consider such asymmetries of power between persons, genders and peoples as universal in history and prehistory is to prejudge the issue. Ernest Gellner once remarked that he found it quaint that political historians felt it necessary to account for the origins of exploitation.[1] I am sure he was correct and exploitation, as an instance of negative power, never needed inventing by any hominid. But the corollary must also be admitted: neither did they have to devise at some moment the invitation to others to become involved in creative action negotiated through networks with rules and resources.

I will now examine these changes for the period 60–21 Kyr bp using the framework of regions and locales as in previous chapters. The emphasis in this chapter is on the social landscape and the social occasion/place, concepts which until now have been little discussed. The social landscape is explored through a series of regional case studies, while the locale of Dolní Věstonice-Pavlov in the Czech Republic is studied as a social occasion.

## Regions

### *Landscapes of habit*

The landscape of habit is centred on the individual and the decisions she/he must make. It is the wider spatial network for the negotiation and reproduction of social life that occurs during encounters, gatherings and social occasions

(Chapter 3). It applies to all hominids and encompasses the skills associated with mobility, environmental knowledge and survival that have been transferred and modified in the course of human evolution. It is an environment for learning, not only about the proximate skills of interaction but also how to explore their spatial limits.

To that extent the landscape of habit contains the rules and resources for social integration, as we saw in Chapters 4 and 5. However, it does not imply system integration beyond the limits imposed by the intimate and effective networks which characterize landscapes of habit until the late Pleistocene.

The dimensions of the landscape of habit can be traced through the transfer of raw materials between locales (Chapters 4, 5 and 6). Distances of 80–100 km invariably represent the furthest transfers, although the majority of materials are moved over much shorter distances, normally less than 20 km. These distances remain the same in the Late Middle Palaeolithic and characterize many Early Upper Palaeolithic locales. However, I noted in Chapter 6 that in the EUP there were significant increases both in furthest distance and, at some locales, in the quantities of raw material being transferred. This was combined with novel items for transfer – shell and possibly ivory.

*Mobility*

These changes do not imply that the landscape of habit expanded in size during the Aurignacian and Gravettian as opposed to the Mousterian. The bulk of transfers are still well within the limits of the model (Féblot-Augustins 1997). But the existence of regular transfers beyond the 80–100-km threshold, and the discovery that simple fall-off curves no longer describe the transfer of materials either into a locale or from a source (Turq 1993:Figs. 1 and 2), carry implications for the patterns of individual mobility.

It appears from studies in Aquitaine in the southwest region (Geneste 1988a, 1988b, Turq 1992a, 1993) that the transfer of raw materials in the Mousterian was embedded in other routines. The predominant distances point to a temporality of social action that lasts about one or two days, the time needed to travel between 5 and 20 km. Geneste's principle (1988a) maintains that even with these distances the material from further away will be transferred into the locale as a retouched tool rather than as a pre-core or lump of raw material. We saw in Chapter 5 how the levallois chaîne opératoire, which appears after 300 Kyr BP, fits this pattern (Geneste 1989).

In terms of refitting we might expect all three types of refit (Figure 5.20), as described by Cziesla (1987, 1990), among raw materials transferred from less than 20 km. However, the so-called 'exotic' category, 30–80 km (Table 3.4), would normally only have subsequent modifications to artifacts such as resharpenings. The implication is that the production sequences for such pieces will be found in locales closer to where the raw material was obtained.

This model characterizes Neanderthals as constantly renewing their lithic technology. Carrying stone was a habitual activity, probably more so than

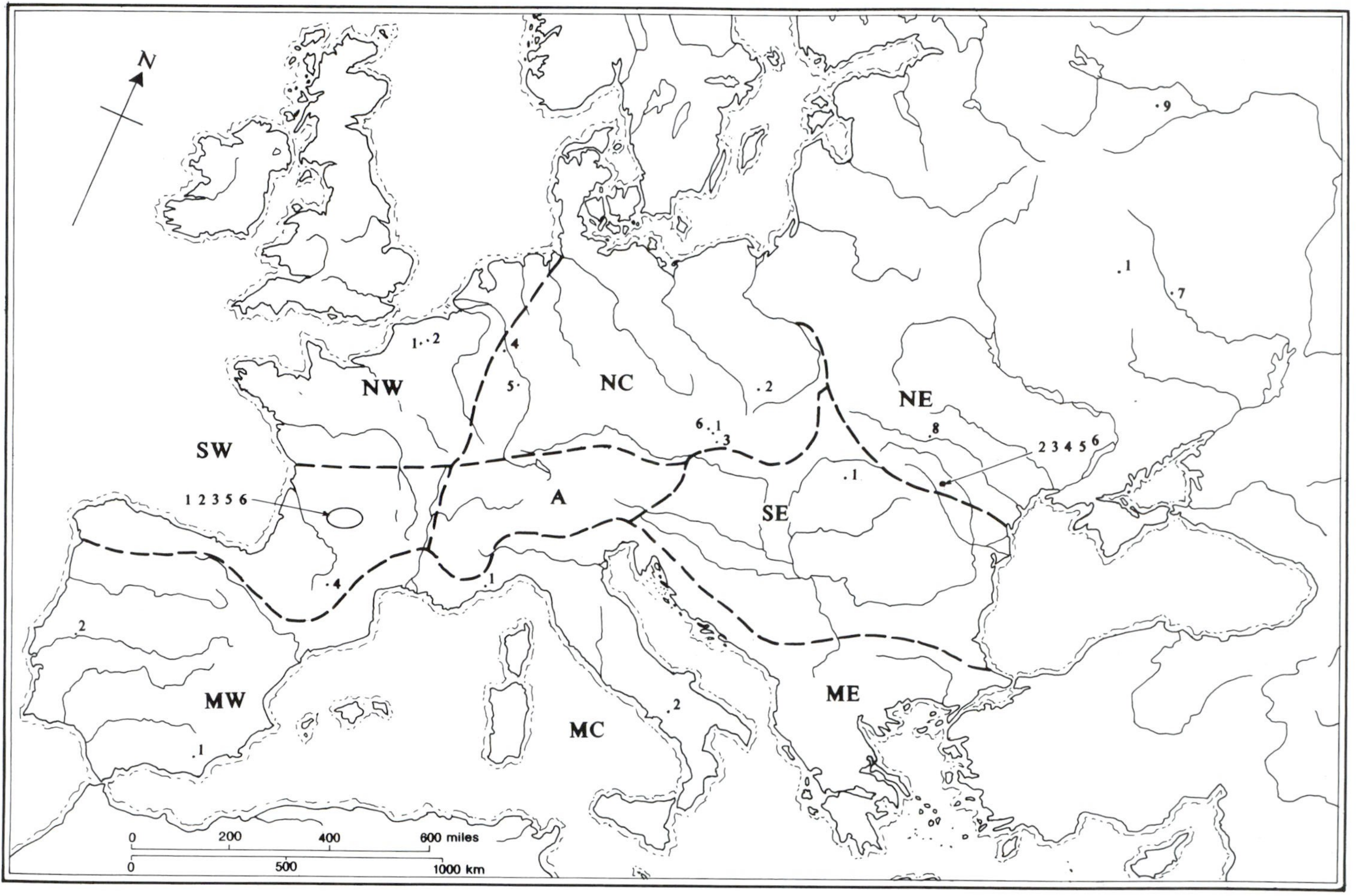
N
NW
NC
NE
SW
A
SE
MW
MC
ME
1 2 3 5 6
2 3 4 5 6
0 200 400 600 miles
0 500 1000 km

**7.1** Principal locales discussed in this chapter and referred to in Table 7.11.

KEY: by region

| | NW | NC | NE | SW | SE | MW | MC |
|---|---|---|---|---|---|---|---|
| 1 | Chabiague | Brno | Avdeevo | Corbiac | Remetea-Somos | Carihuela | Grimaldi |
| 2 | Hénin | Cracow Spadzista | Bistricioara-lutarie | Gohoud | | Vilas Ruivas | Serino |
| 3 | | Dolní Věstonice-Pavlov | Ceahlau-Bofu Mic | Le Côte | | | |
| 4 | | Lommersum | Ceahlau-Cetatica | Mauran | | | |
| 5 | | Sprendlingen | Ceahlau-Dîrtu | Tambourets | | | |
| 6 | | Vedrovice | Ceahlau-Podis | Vaufrey | | | |
| 7 | | | Kostenki | | | | |
| 8 | | | Molodova | | | | |
| 9 | | | Sunghir | | | | |

visiting rock outcrops to pick up higher quality materials. They no doubt carried other items made of wood, and also animals, as well as children and items of food. In other words they transferred their environment with them. They remained surrounded by what was familiar and useful rather than moving from one place, as defined in Chapter 3, to another and letting the associations of that environment encompass them.

Nor does this have to be a unique property of the anatomical type known as Neanderthal. It applied to *Homo heidelbergensis* as well as to anatomically modern humans such as those from the Middle East who have been found with Mousterian implements (Stringer and Gamble 1993). Turn out your own pockets and you will see that it is a property of anatomically modern humans who could have made either the Levallois-Mousterian or the Aurignacian, it doesn't matter which.

The big difference is that we move from social occasion to social occasion while Neanderthals moved at most from gathering to gathering. I referred earlier (Chapter 5) to Kuhn's conclusion that they regularly carried tools but did not stock locales with caches of material. Once such provisioning occurs the social implications are immense. The temporality of action changes as places for future action are created. Instead of a continuous process of acquisition, reduction, use, resharpening and discard, there are now interruptions to such a sequence with refashioning of the material as it moves (Scheer 1993).

I would therefore rephrase Kuhn's conclusion that Neanderthals carried tools as 'a hedge against unforeseen, generalized needs' (1992:206). They were not constantly thinking about being in the world any more than we spend much of our time locked in such discursive consciousness (Chapter 3). What they carried was a sequence of embodied gestures (artifacts) which were an extension of their hands. In the same way the form and shape of the clothes which they most certainly wore were conditioned by the bodies they concealed.

Carrying artifacts, be it a hat or a handaxe, is part and parcel of being a hominid. They are part of our sequence of gestures. The associated actions of learning, acquisition, manufacture and use formed the mutual Neanderthal environment. The objects being carried were significant because of their association with the person who carried these material representations of habitual gestures.[2]

### *Middle Palaeolithic transfers at the Grotte Vaufrey*

If Neanderthals routinely moved short distances, was there a predictable sequence preceding and then following their arrival at a locale, further evidence, perhaps, of attaching rituals (Chapter 5)?

The raw materials in the Aquitaine locales show that lithics arrived from all directions of the compass. For example, the Grotte Vaufrey (Figure 5.13), which has a long Middle Palaeolithic sequence (Geneste 1988b, Rigaud 1988a), has a star-shaped pattern of transfers into the locale (Féblot-Augustins 1993:239).

These patterns can be interpreted in two ways. Firstly, the cave was just a

Table 7.1. *Grotte Vaufrey raw materials (Geneste 1988b:tables 2–14 with revisions).*

| Raw material types | | Couches | | | | | | | | | | | |
|---|---|---|---|---|---|---|---|---|---|---|---|---|---|
| | km | XII | XI | X | IX | VIII | VII | VI | V | IV | III | II | I |
| 1 | <5 | 11 | 41 | 57 | 26 | 966 | 209 | 82 | 28 | 153 | 21 | 194 | 66 |
| 2 | <5 | | 34 | 10 | 5 | 864 | 178 | 86 | 59 | 191 | 71 | 254 | 23 |
| 3 | <5 | | 1 | 5 | 1 | 151 | 141 | 24 | 24 | 34 | 6 | 56 | 20 |
| 4 | <5 | | | | | 16 | 1 | 2 | 2 | 2 | | 2 | |
| 5 | 40 | | | | | 7 | 1 | | | 2 | | | |
| 6 | 30 | | | | | 12 | 6 | 3 | 2 | 2 | 2 | | |
| 7 | 25 | | | | | 4 | | | | | | | |
| Various | | | | | | | 1 | | 1 | 10 | | 2 | |
| Indeterminate | | | | 3 | | 9 | 6 | | | 23 | | | |
| Quartz | <5 | 3 | 21 | 9 | 4 | 46 | 15 | 6 | 5 | 46 | | 20 | 3 |
| Total | | 14 | 97 | 84 | 36 | 2,075 | 558 | 203 | 121 | 463 | 100 | 528 | 112 |

node on a network of tracks so that the star pattern indicates that it was approached from all directions. This implies that visits were always short. What was carried in was sufficient for that stay. Secondly, materials from less than 10 km away were brought into the locale for as long as people stayed there. In this, more plausible, scenario, couches III, V and VI were all approached, at least once, from the northwest, the source of raw material type 6 (Figure 5.13). Couches IV and VII–VIII were approached from at least three and possibly as many as five directions.[3]

These differences appear to be a function of sample size (Tables 5.5 and 7.1). The larger the artifact sample the larger the number of raw material sources and the number of transfers exceeding 5 km. This is not however the case with couche II, which has a large sample suggesting that here it was the length of occupation that accumulated such numbers of local flint. This study also suggests that the amount of stone being carried to the Grotte Vaufrey, rather than being picked up from around the cave, was in fact very small.

*Transfers as networks*

Now let us look at the transfer patterns another way. We can conceive of the routes into and out of the Grotte Vaufrey in terms of two extremes: either as part of a circular round where the locale was visited in strict rotation, perhaps once a year, or as the hub of a wheel where it was constantly visited as people criss-crossed the landscape. These model networks have already been investigated in Table 2.4 for measures of ties and connectivity between individuals in a network. They represent, respectively, examples of high- and low-density networks.

Extreme seasonality in the distribution of food might lead to individuals following a circular pattern around the landscape. As a result locales would be used in strict rotation. This pattern would produce a predictable fall-off curve in terms of raw material collected from a single source in the course of that round (Figure 7.2a). The two closest locales to the raw-material source would have the highest and lowest values for that raw-material type and, of course, very different proportions of retouched tools.

The circular round can be considered as high density in a network sense (Chapter 2) because it could involve people either moving as a group or staying put and expecting to be provisioned by more mobile individuals tracking the circuit. If they moved together, ties and connectivity would be maintained through close contact, if not continual co-presence, as people went in search of food. In the latter instance the circle rapidly becomes an all-channel network (Figure 2.1), with criss-crossing links and correspondingly more complex results for raw-material transfers into the central location.

It would be tempting to cast the Middle Palaeolithic as an example of a circular system. Here networked individuals would travel together in a seasonally dictated sequence of moves and disperse at other times of the year when food resources allowed individual action (Gamble 1987). However, this environmentally driven view does not accommodate the raw-material data for social action.

Within a single locale such as the Grotte Vaufrey, the distance fall-off curves are predictable and standard, as they are from a much larger sample of locales in the same area (Turq 1992a). None of these data suggests a sequence of moves based on strict rotation. Nor does the seasonal distribution of resources anywhere in the southwest region (Auguste 1993:table 1) appear to have been pronounced enough to produce a single path to follow and then force people to travel together along it for appreciable times and distances.

Instead, the pattern which is found in the Middle Palaeolithic is closer to the low density wheel network (Figure 7.2b). If the raw-material source was a central hub, and paths were only up and down each spoke, all locales would have high values for that raw-material type. But if we change the position of the source (Figure 7.2c) to the end of a spoke, then the hub becomes a high-value node/locale and all the other nodes become medium value.

We can expand the wheel network into a star-burst model (Figure 7.2d). The number of nodes has been increased, but ties and connectivity are still very low. The simple fall-off rule, that the number of links changes the proportion of raw materials found in that locale, produces low values in all the nodes radiating from each subsidiary hub.

The Middle Palaeolithic transfers show that these links were conditioned by distance and the temporality of action. Individuals did not carry amounts of raw materials further than 20 km. If they had they would have changed the shape of the simple fall-off curves. Nor were materials passed in bulk from hand to hand since that mechanism would also alter the fall-off curves.

If that is the case then each link between the nodes, or locales, in the wheel

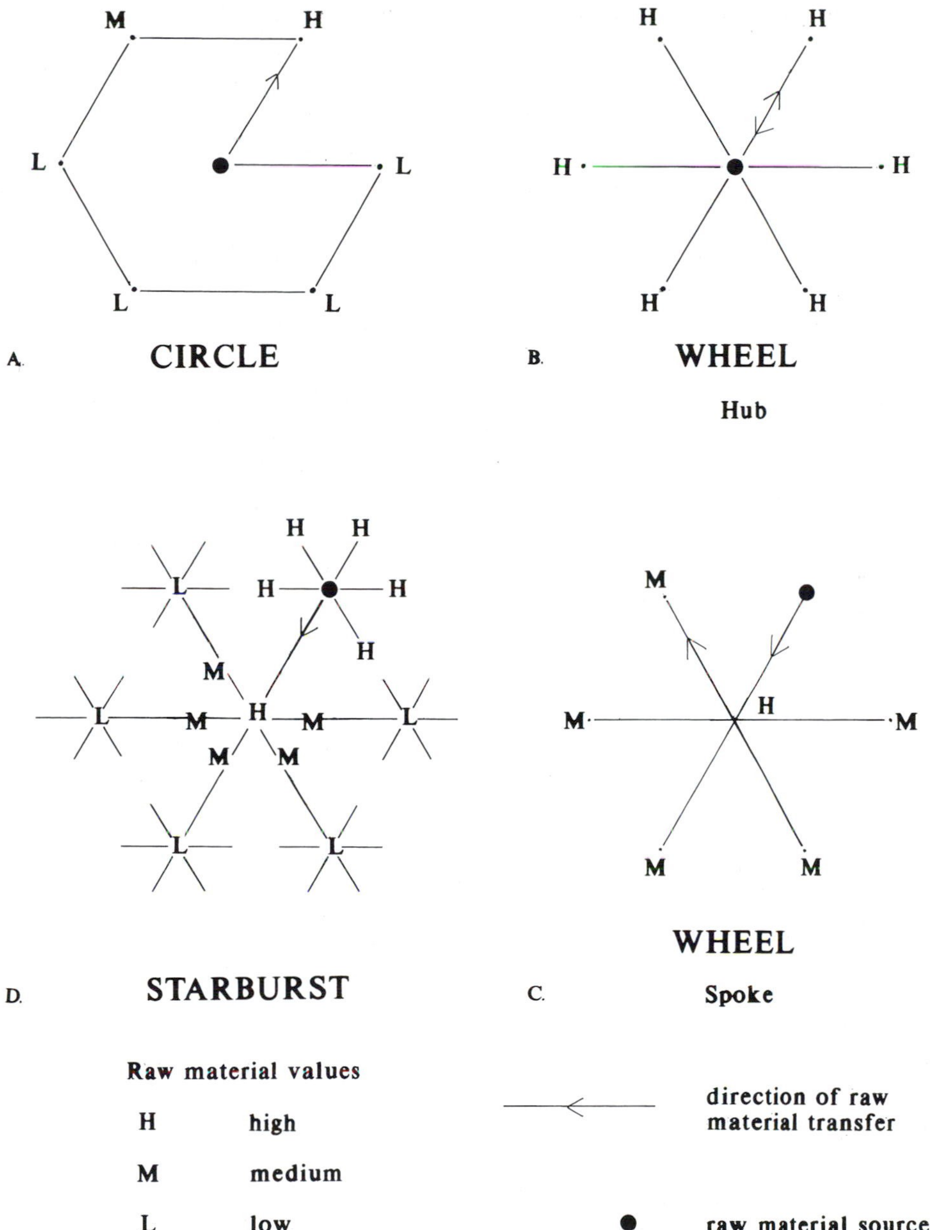


**7.2** Raw-material transfer networks (see Table 7.2).

network must be some 5–10 km in length. Otherwise there would be a greater incidence of raw materials from further afield in each of the locales. This conclusion also frees up the movement of individuals either by themselves or with others. They can roam the star-burst network (Figure 7.2d) in any direction they wish. And, by keeping distances between locales short, and their residence once

Table 7.2. *Predicted values for raw materials found at locales in different networks (Figure 7.2). Each network has seven nodes, one of which is a raw-material source. The star-burst network consists of seven wheel networks connected by one central tie (Figure 7.2d). High values are represented by one link, medium by two and low by more than two links.*

| | Raw-material values at nodes/locales | | |
|---|---|---|---|
| Network | High | Medium | Low |
| Circle | 1 | 1 | 4 |
| Wheel (hub) | 6 | | |
| Wheel (spoke) | 1 | 5 | |
| Star burst | 6 | 5 | 25 |

arrived brief, then interaction is accomplished with all members of an effective network. Moreover this interaction is achieved in the normal course of travel and the encounters that brings.

The Middle Palaeolithic settlement data point to the transfer of raw materials to locales where gatherings rather than social occasions took place (Chapter 3). No doubt survival and recovery of the evidence have reduced the number of such locales. Furthermore, there would have been many more encounters which are 'unrecorded' archaeologically. So, the implication is that Middle Palaeolithic hominids regularly encountered one another within the lattices of a small spatial framework where the distances between gatherings were a maximum of between 5 and 10 km.

This conclusion does not support a case for random or even opportunistic movement by individuals across the landscape. Mobility was patterned, as might be expected. It does however emphasize the local character of the Middle Palaeolithic networks which both constrained the use of resources and enabled the rules of interaction to operate.

The indications from the Upper Palaeolithic transfers for the structure of networks are rather different. The Aurignacian, for example, points to a high-density all-channel structure as shown by Turq's fall-off curves for Aquitaine (Turq 1993:Fig. 2). These no longer present a simple fall-off in quantity related to distance, but instead a directed pattern of transfers which were either provisioning places or focusing on particular individuals in an exchange system. This conclusion that Upper Palaeolithic networks were organized differently is

Table 7.3. *The frequency of technological modes found on raw materials which have been transferred more than 20 km from source (Féblot-Augustins 1997:figures 43, 47, 58, 65 and 66). The one Late Middle Palaeolithic locale with mode 1 is Zwolen in Poland. For key to modes see Table 5.14.*

| >20 km distance | Modes 1 | 2 | 3 | 4 | 5 | 6 | 7 | 8 |
|---|---|---|---|---|---|---|---|---|
| **Late Middle Palaeolithic** | | | | | | | | |
| Western Europe | | | | | | | | + |
| Central Europe | + | | | | | | | + |
| **Upper Palaeolithic** | | | | | | | | |
| Western Europe | + | + | + | | + | + | + | + |
| Central Europe | + | | | + | + | | + | + |

based upon the increased distances as well as the differences between locales in terms of transfers (Table 6.18). There were larger distances between locales, fewer of them and hence a reduction in the number of those archaeologically invisible encounters. The case of the Aurignacian caves and open sites separated by 300 km in the north-central region is a case in point (Chapter 6). Finally, the number of technological modes (Table 5.14) other than blanks and tools (mode 8) which are found on materials transferred beyond 20 km increases markedly (Table 7.3). None of these changes was environmentally forced upon the individuals concerned, although regional constraints continued to determine some aspects of the scale of the system as indicated by greatest distance (Gamble 1986a:chapter 2, table 6.18).

*Network densities*

The mobility of individuals during the Middle Palaeolithic, as reconstructed through raw-material transfers, is pointing to a fairly low density pattern for personal networks. But one objection to this conclusion might be that distance does not necessarily measure ties or connectivity between individuals. As we saw in Chapter 2, we have other ways to maintain dense networks *in absentia*, the obvious examples today being the letter and the telephone.

The absence of such mechanisms makes the point that in these Middle Palaeolithic systems distance is relevant for the negotiation of society through the resources available to the individual. As individuals criss-crossed through nodes and along the paths of a wheel or star-burst network, their effective and intimate networks were frequently affirmed. People were available for negotiation without assigning a special temporality to such action. These paths led to opportunities of seasonal abundance and involved choices about movement and the frequency of sojourns once gatherings were initiated. Such a network is low density but represents a very satisfactory solution to problem solving because information is readily pooled (Chapter 2:Tables 2.6 and 2.7).

By comparison, the circle is a less efficient arrangement for disseminating information since it requires more messages and there is the opportunity for copying errors as they are transmitted down the line. The information is only as good as the last person you heard it from. It may also be out of date before you can act upon it since time and distance appear to have been greater between such encounters and gatherings.

However, this circular, all-channel network seems to characterize the pattern of movement in the EUP. This is seen, in particular, in the very linear movements of raw materials along the Rhine and Danube (Hahn 1987) and across the Carpathians from southern Poland into Moravia (Djindjian 1994, Féblot-Augustins 1997:Figures 107, 111, 121, 122 and 123, Kozlowski 1994, Svoboda 1994a). These 'tramlines' are accentuated by the continental conditions in the north-central and northeastern regions during the downturn to the last glacial maximum. However the 'tramlines' are also there in southwest France, as shown by the preponderance of shells in those locales which came from the Atlantic coast during the EUP.

But we have also seen (Chapter 6) that the transition from the Middle to Upper Palaeolithic takes on a different character between the various regions. In the Périgord, southwest region, there appears to be an increase in the number of known locales during the EUP (Mellars 1973, White 1982), while in Cantabria, and still within the same region, the opposite occurs (Straus 1992). While it is difficult to control for different timescales in other regions, there are strong indications (Chapter 6) that the EUP has fewer site inventories in the north-central region. In parts of the northeast region, and in particular along the major rivers of the central Russian and Ukrainian plains, the first major occupation appears in the EUP and is markedly linear in character.

No doubt climate played a part. As we saw in Chapter 6, a much clearer archaeological picture emerges after 33 Kyr bp, a time of climatic downturn as ice sheets began to build. As Kuhn (1995) has pointed out, this environmental trend imposes a linearity on the transition which may be more apparent than real.

These differences suggest that one reason we have a more complicated archaeological picture in the period before 33 Kyr bp (Table 6.5) is due to a degree of structural incoherence in the regional networks. This incoherence stemmed from alternative uses of the same resources to negotiate landscapes of habit. It was *not* the case that wheel and circular networks represented two different types of society, Neanderthal and Crô-Magnon, in competition with each other, but rather that individuals from both anatomical populations were defining such systems through different means (compare with Table 2.7). Increasingly after 33 Kyr bp the high-density circular systems predominate and the incoherence, from our perspective, in the archaeological regional patterns is reduced.

*Social landscape*

But is this evidence for the appearance of my second regional concept, the social landscape? So far in this book I have maintained that the social landscape was not found before the Upper Palaeolithic. This may seem nothing more than a convenient adherence to a long-established division in the data. But I hope to have shown by concentrating upon aspects of scale, distance and temporality in the archaeological record that the division is justified. The rest of this chapter explores the concept through regional case studies and the investigation of a social occasion, itself a property of the social landscape.

The construction of social landscapes is also based on negotiation. This involves the splicing together of landscapes of habit with the result that agency, what individuals do, is further extended across time and space. I noted in Chapter 3 that the social landscape has no spatial boundaries since wherever people can go, there, potentially, lies the opportunity to construct a global network.

As a consequence, increased inter-regional variability in human creativity is a hallmark of the social landscape. Such patterning is expected for the reason that while the construction of these landscapes is potentially unlimited, in practice the paths which connect and transcend the landscape of habit are finite. The opportunity for cultural variety might be increased but attenuation, where the meaning of such variety fades, is an important constraint on the outcome. Therefore, while the system has enormous opportunities for expansion it also has boundaries based on the resources available to individuals to build networks. I will therefore examine aspects of the social landscape that address intra- and inter-regional variety and examine, where possible, the scale at which it occurs.

*Complex and complicated society*

It may seem paradoxical that the transition between the Middle and Upper Palaeolithic resulted in a loss of rather than an improvement in information processing. This assessment would be based on the radial patterns of movement. After all, the selective advantage of art and artifact style has been interpreted as an enhancement of information exchange (Gamble 1982).

But the critical point concerns the information itself. Knowing more about the world is not necessarily a route to evolutionary success. It may be a better strategy just to produce more offspring, rather than to invest in fewer by using expensively acquired information to minimize risk and so ensure their future.[4] So, as we saw in Chapter 2, it is not bits of information but rather the chunks into which they can be assembled that is significant. To become information these chunks require signs and symbols to provide a code for action. In perceptual terms these can be visual and verbal as well as tactile and olfactory. In evolutionary terms it is the externalization of information which such codes permit and which allow it to serve as a representation of action irrespective of whether it is communicated by language or through material culture.

The categories created by chunking allow us to explore the possibilities of an infinitely rich world of information based on movement and interaction. Instead of dealing with each information source on a one-by-one basis, the individual now groups and categorizes such sources into a variety of patterns. Through the multiplication of such a process a social fabric is created, one that is constrained by what went before but always open to novel interpretation.

More information can therefore generate more ambiguity about appropriate action which might be seen as the apparent loss in processing power. But this is not a problem, if we recall the distinction, examined in Chapter 2, between complex and complicated societies. In a complicated society the individual aims to reduce ambiguity by performing sequences of simple operations. Making beads (White 1993b, 1993c) is one such example. These are usually referred to an external, symbolic code. Categories exist in a complicated society. We act through them since we perceive them as information sources, externalized as symbols. On the contrary complex society is performed by the individual through the resources of the body alone. In the complex society the process of perceiving information is slower. The individual alone is the information source because individuals deal with each other, usually one at a time, through interaction and the embodiment of gesture and technique.

*Artifacts as people*

There is a further aspect to this simple characterization between complex and complicated hominid society. While both societies have intimate and effective networks, only complicated societies have significant extended networks. It is in this network that the chunking of information sources is most prevalent.

In the intimate networks in both types of society the individual, as an information source, is dealt with in a similar manner, as a function of affective resources. The interaction time this entails is the defining characteristic of that network and is part of our primate heritage.

However, it is also possible to see a difference between the intimate networks in complex and complicated societies which reiterates the point about power as both enabling and constraining. In complex societies the constraints are obvious and the opportunities for individuals to negotiate their own power rely entirely upon embodied, affective resources. These factors still operate in complicated societies. But here it must also be acknowledged that the intimate network is touched by the categorization and externalization of action that characterizes the extended network. Hence power is of a potentially different order. It is no longer based solely on the rules and resources of the intimate network alone, but is open to reinterpretation and the introduction of ambiguity as it is affected by experience in a wider social world. It then becomes important either to deny or to resolve such ambiguity and the contradictions it can produce about these external signs. In this ambiguity lies the germ of what we often understand by ritual.

I have argued that in the Middle Palaeolithic artifacts were embodied as a sequence of gestures and were, quite literally, extensions of the body. Therefore such materials were also resources of the body for the performance of society. Power in these societies was therefore an expression of these material relations as they related seamlessly with the body and its actions and gestures. The difference with the Upper Palaeolithic is that here power was expressed through a conscious play on ambiguity created by the material representation of the body. Artifacts were no longer adjuncts to persons, meaningful only when attached in acquisition, manufacture or use and linked in action by rhythms. Artifacts now became personified since they represented either that person or the existence of an extended network *in absentia*. When associated with social occasions and the transformation of locale into place (Table 3.1), they formed a substitute for co-presence that can be understood because they belonged to a complicated, sequenced set of routines.

*Use of regional space*

It is therefore unsurprising that the archaeological entities of the Upper Palaeolithic are both more understandable in terms of space and time and yet more diverse. This leads us to a different appreciation of the entities in the transition.

> There is both a level of affinity in the composition of [Upper Palaeolithic] assemblages and a predictable character to the appearance of type fossils that is lacking in the earlier Palaeolithic traditions. The type fossils in the Upper Palaeolithic do define some sort of chronological position. They can act as a reference point for building culture historical groupings. For example if you pick up a handaxe during fieldwalking the best you can say is that it is earlier than 35 Kyr bp . . . However if you picked up a Font Robert point it would be possible both to define its chronological position with some precision, just by looking at it, and furthermore to infer the general characteristics of the assemblage from which it came. (Gamble 1986a:248)

The appreciation lies in deciding when such characteristics appear. Bosinski (1982) regards this as a feature of the Middle Palaeolithic, while Mellars (1992:39) places the appearance of such regionalization in the Late Middle Palaeolithic, possibly after 60 Kyr bp. Idiosyncratic tools, such as triangular bifaces in the Mousterian of Acheulean Tradition and, of course, leaf points with Mousterian reduction sequences, as in the Altmühlian, provide examples. Valoch presents a detailed review of such intra-regional patterning among EUP assemblages and cultures in the Czech Republic (1995, 1996). This regionalization coincides with an increase in the distances over which raw materials were transferred (Féblot-Augustins 1993:table 2, Svoboda, Lozek and Vlček 1996).

When compared to the Upper Palaeolithic we see that the chains of connection were now forged over much longer distances (Table 6.18). They involved a greater diversity of items and were expressed in a number of ways as ornament, raw material and stone tools as well as by technological modes (Table 7.3). In the time–space patterning of the Upper Palaeolithic the information in these representations undoubtedly became blurred and attenuated but still existed as a basis for negotiation at some unspecified point in the future. But these chains of connection were also diverse since the material and symbolic resources which they used can be exapted to form an almost infinite variety. We are still exploring this variety in our own social experiments.

### *Social landscape: case studies*

The best way to examine the concept of social landscape is through case studies of the extended networks which help define it. Furthermore, the Middle-to-Upper Palaeolithic transition is an opportunity to examine variation in these networks within the regions of Europe.

It is therefore important to be clear about the entities which archaeologists commonly use when studying this transition. Some of the definitions which I have been using in previous chapters now need to be tightened up and compared (Table 7.4).

*Assemblage* – a collection of artifacts from a specific segment of an archaeological site (Laville, Rigaud and Sackett 1980:13–14).

*Industry* – a distinctive complex or configuration of artifact types and type frequencies that recurs among two or more assemblages (Laville, Rigaud and Sackett 1980:14).

*Tradition* – a group of industries whose artifactual similarities are sufficient that they belong to some broader culture-historical block of technological ideas and practices (Laville, Rigaud and Sackett 1980:14).

*Culture* – a polythetic set of specific and comprehensive artifact types which consistently recur together in assemblages within a limited geographic area (Clarke 1978:490).

*Technocomplex* – a group of cultures characterized by assemblages sharing a polythetic range but differing specific types of the same general families of artifact types, shared as a widely diffused and interlinked response to common factors in environment, economy and technology. A negligible level of affinity, perhaps 5 per cent or less, uniting the group in terms of shared specific types, but a residual medium-level affinity, perhaps 30–60 per cent, uniting the group in terms of type families (Clarke 1978:495).

Of particular interest here is Clarke's comment that cultures are associated with a limited geographical area, since this is relevant to my argument for the extension of networks through the use of symbolling. I will attempt to put some figures to his definitions. His term technocomplex, which seems to know no spatial boundaries (Gamble 1986a:10), has been widely used to describe aspects of the Upper Palaeolithic (e.g. Hahn 1977). I would however subsume the common factors of environment, economy and technology which Clarke

Table 7.4. *The use and correspondence of Palaeolithic terms (see Table 3.1).*

| Middle Palaeolithic | Upper Palaeolithic | Scale | Networks |
|---|---|---|---|
| Assemblage | Assemblage | Locale | Intimate |
| Industry | Industry | Inter-locale | |
| Landscape of habit | Landscape of habit | Regional | Effective |
| Tradition | Culture | Regional | |
| | Technocomplex | Inter-regional | Extended |
| | Social landscape | Regional/inter-regional | Global |

puts in his definition as part of the social. Therefore a technocomplex should not be perceived as purely adaptive in a survival sense.

While Clarke's levels of affinity are difficult to measure, the use of technocomplex obviously fills a need in the archaeological vocabulary for a term to express broad similarity. Where the term is problematic is in its application to both Middle and Upper Palaeolithic entities. Hence the Typical Mousterian and the Gravettian could both be regarded as technocomplexes in the sense that they are both 'weak' cultures. Significant differences then become submerged in the desire to see common cultural responses at all times and places. The landscape of habit avoids this problem and provides a way to assess differences between archaeological entities while recognizing the roots of a common core of evolutionary behaviour.

*The size of regions*

In order to support the claim that it is social extension which marks the transition to the Upper Palaeolithic, I need to be able to measure the entities listed above. Moreover, I also need a baseline to assess the changes and analyse the scale at which individuals regularly interacted. This can be supplied by estimating the size of the nine regions (Figure 3.1). These give a range of regional sizes (Figure 7.3), from 150,000 km$^2$ to more than 1,000,000 km$^2$.

*Demography*

The other aspect of network size is the extent to which demographic patterns varied across the continent. These have been investigated by Simán (1990, 1990–1). Using C14 and TL dates she has produced a cumulative curve for settlement in three broad zones – the Mediterranean, periglacial and northern.[5] She makes the assumption that the number of C14 dates acts as a proxy measure of population numbers and continuity in regional settlement.

| | WEST | CENTRAL | EAST |
|---|---|---|---|
| NORTH | 400 | 800 | 1,000 |
| SOUTH | 550 | 150 | 550 |
| MEDITERRANEAN | 550 | 300 | 300 |

**7.3** The approximate sizes in thousand km$^2$ for each of the nine regions. Due to the changes in regional size because of sea level change and ice sheet advance, these should be taken as guidelines only.

When plotted, these data show reasonable agreement with the interstadial data, leading Simán to conclude that population movements were controlled by climatic changes (see also van Andel and Tzedakis 1996). In her analysis the Mediterranean stands out as the most densely populated area of Europe in the period after 40 Kyr bp when the number of dates becomes more reliable. This conclusion can be supported by the artifact density and multiple horizon observations in many Mediterranean locales (Chapter 6). This can also be found in the southwest region, which emphasizes the southward shifts of population, either by migration or by extinction during the period after 33 Kyr bp.

*Mousterian groupings: cultures or traditions?*

It is difficult to plot the geographical extent of the major Mousterian traditions. The problems are well illustrated by Beyries (1987:Carte 1), who has indicated the distribution of the five variants widely recognized in France. The dominant traditions are plotted for each of the major administrative districts, which are roughly similar in area. Périgord and Bourgogne have four variants while exactly half of all the twenty-two districts have two. Table 7.5 lists the number of districts in which each variant is dominant.

Ashton's pioneering analysis (1983) also noted the widespread character of the MTA in northern and central France and the southerly and Mediterranean distribution for the Charentian. The MTA has the widest distribution. It is found within France in both the northwest and southwest regions (Ashton 1983:Figure 1). It extends into Belgium (Ulrix-Closset 1975) and England (Roe 1981) and has a slight presence in Cantabria (Straus 1992). This suggests an inter-regional distribution of c. 800,000 km$^2$ over a minimum 'life-span' of 20 Kyr during the Interpleniglacial. I would be the first to admit that such estimates are probably wildly inaccurate and no doubt mask a range of processes, such as the ebb and flow of people in such a large area over such a long time span. They are offered here to make the contrast with the Upper Palaeolithic distributions.

Table 7.5. *The occurrence of Mousterian assemblages as a dominant element in the twenty-two administrative subdivisions of France (Beyries 1987:Carte 1).*

| Mousterian assemblages | Number of districts |
|---|---|
| Typical | 12 |
| Charentian | 8 |
| Ferrassie | 1 |
| Quina | 2 |
| Denticulate | 6 |
| MTA | 19 |

If the extent of the MTA is difficult to determine, then the geographical distribution of the other variants is even more problematic for the simple reason that they lack the single diagnostic artifact. Straus (1992:60) charts the changing views of Mousterian assemblage variation in northern Spain over the past thirty years. Work by Freeman (1973) has shown that the numerically small assemblages in Cantabria grade from those dominated by denticulate forms to those where sidescrapers form up to two-thirds of the retouched tool category. I reviewed earlier a similar conclusion reached by Dibble and Rolland (1992, Rolland and Dibble 1990) for the Périgord assemblages. Tradition rather than culture (Turq 1989, 1992b) is indeed the appropriate description.

A similar conclusion can be drawn with the Middle Palaeolithic assemblages from central (Bosinski 1967) and eastern (Gabori 1976) Europe. We have already seen (Chapters 5 and 6) that assemblages are numerically small. There may be distinctive artifact types such as the Micoquian bifaces, and Bosinski has used these to define four regional variants.[6] These may be distinguished from other groupings such as the Upper Acheulean (Jungacheuleen) on the northern Plains (Bosinski 1967). But the degree of affinity between assemblages in these groupings is low, judging by citations in the literature which discuss them. The only variant which Bosinski recognizes which can be defined through distinctive artifact types over anything like a defined area is the Altmühlian with its characteristic leaf points. This is centred on southern Germany and dated to the Hengelo interstadial. But even this entity would have a very weak claim to the title of culture as defined above, partly because the collections are so small (Freund 1987).

*Classifying the Middle Palaeolithic*

A social taxonomy, employing terms such as tradition, can be claimed for the Middle Palaeolithic, but a social typology cannot. The taxonomy exists because technology then, as now, was integral to social action. Style and function were united in the gestures of making and using, repairing and throwing away. We should not be surprised to find patterns of similarity or aspects of symmetry when making artifacts. These attributes of making are why the Middle Palaeolithic can be subdivided. Similarities in technique and typology can be traced over large distances (Gabori 1976:fig. 62). There were local ways of making and there was stability in such behaviour for long periods of time and across large areas. The Middle Palaeolithic was replete with social action and we can examine the structure of Mousterian society, as we did above, through the evidence for its component networks.

But within the Middle Palaeolithic there were no cultures or technocomplexes as the terms have been defined above. Hence there was no material or cultural typology of society as there has been with all societies in Europe since the Upper Palaeolithic. From this time the process of making society has been malleable and changeable across space and time rather than regionally restricted. The finding that life was local, and where the principle of exclusion predominated, is now transformed by the possibility of inclusion through negotiation (Table 1.2 and Chapter 3). As a result social life has been driven in unexpected directions by alternative rhythms linking different scales of individual agency and group action.

By contrast what we call the Middle Palaeolithic, with its subdivisions such as Mousterian or Micoquian, was a rolling tradition supported by the characteristics of the landscape of habit which deals with local decisions. Variation in the rhythms of social technology (compare Chapters 5 and 6) can be accounted for by contingent factors such as regionality (Figure 3.1) and the mechanics of cultural transmission. For example, the gestures routinely employed in making artifacts were closely associated with individuals in local regions. These were learned in the context of face-to-face gatherings defined primarily by the rules and resources of the intimate and effective networks.

A social typology depends instead on the extension of such traditions to form cultures and technocomplexes. While the solutions to many problems such as subsistence were similar, the effect of enhanced system integration through the extended network produced a radical difference. In particular, style was now divorced from actions integral to making and performing.

Let me put it another way. The difference is an illustration, as is much of hominid action, of what you *do* rather than what you *think* you should do. It is the distinction, examined in Chapter 3, between a practical consciousness which leads to routinized action in landscapes of habit and a discursive consciousness which can make relational links between the domains of intelligence (Mithen 1996).

I see some similarity here with the distribution and form of Acheulean bifaces from the Lower Palaeolithic. These could be regarded as elements in a technocomplex which would link northern Europe to southern Africa along a transect discussed in Chapter 4. The limited range of shapes is often put forward as evidence for deliberate, conscious choice, while the symmetry in manufacture is also regarded as an expression of mental skills indistinguishable

Table 7.6. *Three divisions for the Early Upper Palaeolithic with median C14 age (Hahn 1993).*

| | N | Median Kyr bp |
|---|---|---|
| Transitional technocomplexes including Bohunician, leaf points, Bachokirian, Uluzzian and Châtelperronian | 18 | 39 |
| Earliest Aurignacian including Geißenklösterle, Krems-Hundssteig, l'Arbreda and El Castilló | 13 | 35 |
| Aurignacian I | 24 | 31.1 |

from our own. However, these attributes and their distribution do not to my mind demonstrate a technocomplex. Instead it is a tradition of techniques which are limited in the length of their chaînes opératoires by the context of cultural transmission and the social acts they represent. As discussed in Chapter 4, the model of transferrable skills, mediated by local resources and by the network of rules governing gatherings, is sufficient to account for either the lack of variation or the amount of variability that we perceive, and whose significance varies between archaeologists (Gowlett 1984, 1996, Noble and Davidson 1996, 1993, Wynn 1988, 1989, 1993a, 1993b).

However, between the Early Middle Palaeolithic (Chapter 5) and the Late Middle Palaeolithic (Chapter 6) we do see regionalization in this pattern. This seems unsurprising to me given the larger samples and better chronological resolution when compared to the Lower Palaeolithic (Chapter 4). In particular the long stratified sequences in caves provide ideal material for a changing narrative of assemblages and techniques.[7] What is still striking, as I discussed at length in the previous chapter, is that without such obvious sampling discrepancies between the Late Middle and Early Upper Palaeolithic, the differences in the archaeological record are significant in terms of the rhythms and social technology they represent for both periods.

*Arrival of the Aurignacian*

This significance can be seen in the chronology of the transition between the Middle and Upper Palaeolithic. Hahn (1993) has analysed the C14 dates for the Early Upper Palaeolithic and late Mousterian. These fall in the time range 43–30 Kyr bp. Three major divisions are recognized in the EUP (Table 7.6).

When plotted as isochrons (Hahn 1993:Figs. 3–6) for the entire continent two patterns emerge.[8] The Late Mousterian, the transitional technocomplexes and Early Aurignacian all have a meridional (north–south) pattern of isochrons (Figure 7.4). In the first two cases the dates in the east are considerably older

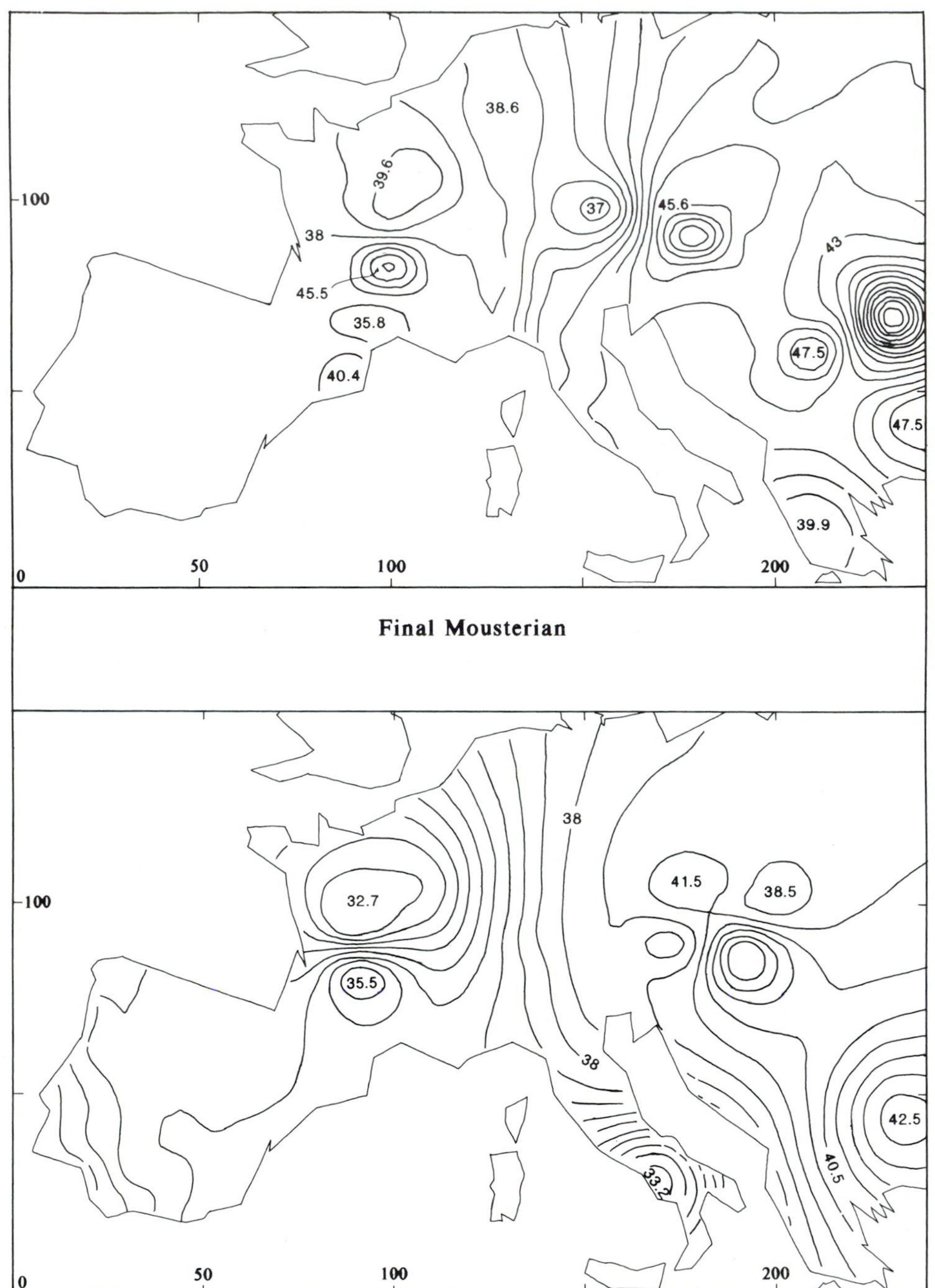


**Transitional Technocomplexes**

**7.4** Spatial patterning of C14 dates in four technocomplexes at the Middle-to-Upper Palaeolithic boundary (after Hahn 1993:Figs. 3–6).

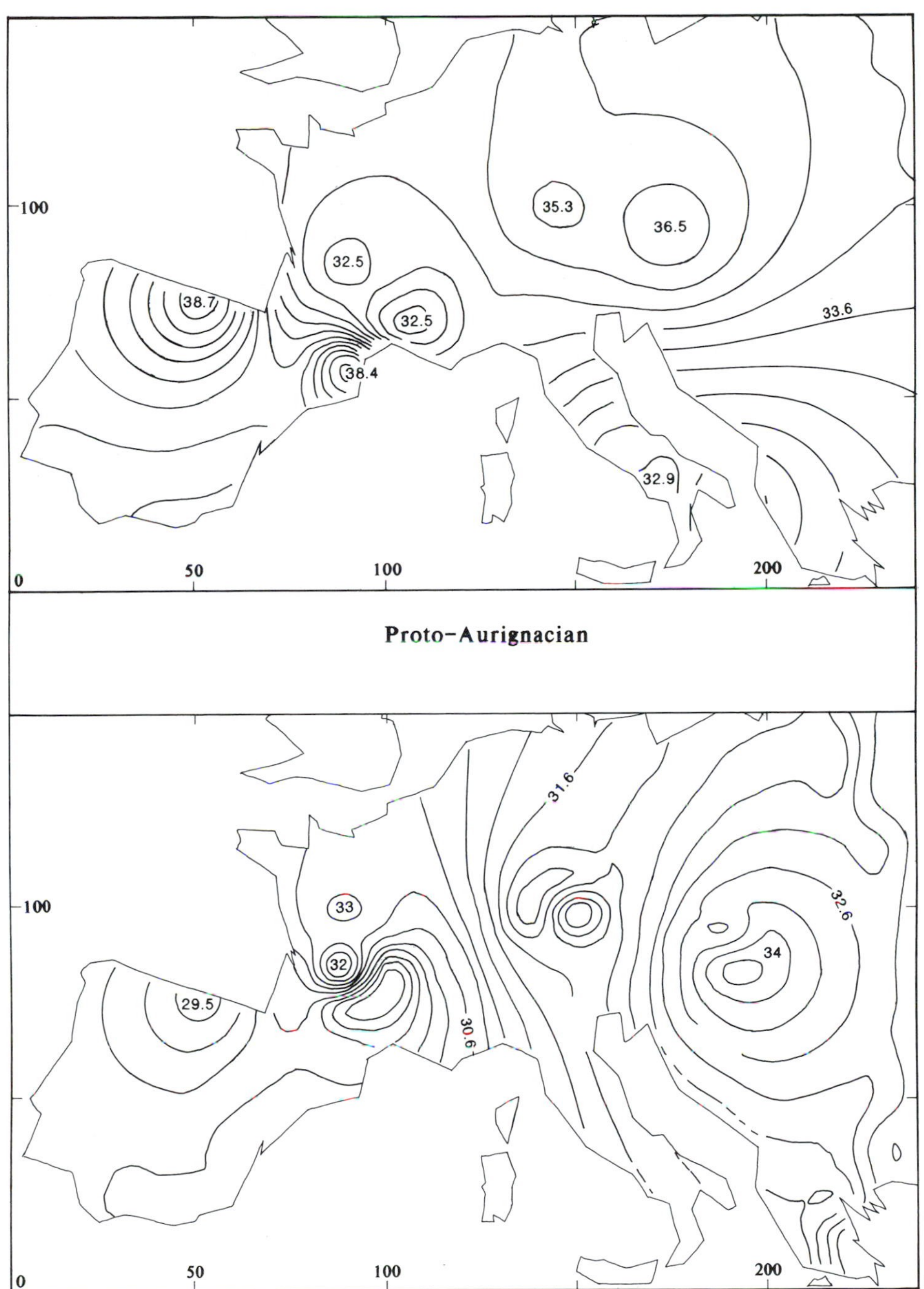


**Early Aurignacian**

**7.4** *(cont.)*

than in the west. The isochron fingerprints are remarkably similar, which implies a very close in-situ association between the two groupings. In particular the 38-Kyr isochron is in a very similar position running from north to south, from Denmark to northern Italy.[9]

If viewed as evidence for in-situ change and the movement of peoples with new technologies and culture, then the close-packed vertical lines in the centre of Europe indicates that nothing was happening. Movement, if it happened at all, would be in a north–south direction and hence against the ecological grain of the Interpleniglacial continent (Figure 6.3). If taken as evidence for contemporaneity between late Mousterian and the small-sized transitional cultures, such as the Châtelperronian or the Szeletian, then these maps support the case that this did indeed occur in two areas centred on the southwest and southeast regions. If regarded as evidence for Interpleniglacial technocomplexes, then the isochron maps point to two such entities. One has a possible extent of 230,000 km$^2$ over a 2,000-year duration between 42 and 40 Kyr bp. The other extends over possibly 850,000 km$^2$ and 5,000 years as measured from 43 to 38 Kyr bp (Figure 7.4). These figures treat the distance from the locale with the earliest date to the later isochron as the radius of a circle which, when calculated, produced the figures given above. They are of course very rough and ready, and must be regarded as maximum figures. The former is of sub-regional scale while the latter is larger than all but the northeast region whose limits are the least defined (Figure 7.3). It is important to remember that much of these areas would have been empty space, rarely if ever visited, as people moved about their habitual business along established paths and tracks at the scale of the landscape of habit.

The contrast with the Proto-Aurignacian is dramatic (Figure 7.4). Instead of a meridional pattern of isochrons there is a zonal distribution indicating very rapid movement. The inclusion of locales such as El Castilló and l'Arbreda in this group puts the oldest dates for the Aurignacian in the west of the continent. The sample has a median of 35 Kyr bp and a degree of dispersion in the inter-quartile range (Hahn 1993:Fig. 7) which indicates that the differences are not significant. Hence, Straus (1989, 1993) reminds us that the east–west migration of the Aurignacian is not yet proved. Not even, according to Straus, if the locales in Hahn's Protoaurignacian and transitional industries are shuffled so that, for example, the TL dates of 46 and 45 Kyr bp for Aurignacian levels in Temnata cave in Bulgaria (Kozlowski, Laville and Ginter 1992) are added to the Protoaurignacian.[10]

As Hahn (1993:78) reminds us, these C14 dates are estimates rather than real values. The patterns produced do however allow us to identify which archaeological entities are more likely to be related to the movement of people. The case could be made from the shape of these maps that the transitional technocomplexes and the late Mousterian are in fact the same thing. What we are seeing is the maintenance of networks and their elaboration through additional items. The recent suggestion by Hublin (et al. 1996) that artifacts were exchanged between Neanderthals and anatomically modern humans at Arcy-sur-Cure provides further evidence.

Having identified movement we can discuss its network implications. The slow movement can be described by Steele's (1994) Tribal network (Figure 2.2). Here there is resistance, due to network structure, to cultural innovation. By contrast, in his Poisson network there is high transitivity of ties and leapfrogging. The difference can be illustrated by comparing cutting your way through a forest, where progress is slow (meridional), to swimming quickly with the current (zonal).

*Abandoning the northern plains and northern Italy*

Considering all the advantages that the EUP, and in particular the Aurignacian, is often supposed to bring, it is perhaps surprising that this does not include occupation of large parts of the North European plain or indeed some areas within the Mediterranean.

There is occupation in the western part of the northwestern region during the Aurignacian, for example at Paviland where a burial was associated with possible Aurignacian objects (Jacobi 1980) and dated to 28 Kyr bp. At the same time a number of distinctive stemmed points, collectively known as Font Robert and belonging to the Perigordian V/Gravettian tradition, have been found in England and at the Maisières canal in Belgium and eastwards into Germany at Bilzingsleben (Otte 1981) and Salching (Weißmüller 1987). Figure 7.5 shows them clustered in southwest France.

However these occurrences are not on the North European Plain proper. This lies in front of the central German uplands, where Bilzingsleben is located, and continues into Poland and western Russia. Across this large area no EUP has been found. Instead, settlement kept to the hills and to the oceanically tempered climates of the west such as Britain. This is in contrast to the central European loess locales of Moravia, southern Poland and Austria (Svoboda 1996). The closest that occupation came to the plains is in the indentations into the central uplands, such as the Köln basin where the Aurignacian locale of Lommersum (Hahn 1974) is found, or Breitenbach in the Thuringian basin (Hahn 1977). Further east, settlement in the EUP was common along the Dnestr and Desna rivers which form the western boundary of the Plain (Chapter 6).

It is tempting to explain this absence by environmental factors. The worsening climate simplified the vegetation into zones. In so doing the ecological mosaics which produced a diversified landscape with reliable resources were removed. While this is an attractive scenario, the earliest Aurignacian (Hahn 1993) occurs during the OIS 3 Interpleniglacial with its suite of interstadials (Chapter 6, Table 6.3) which, it might be expected, would encourage settlement. After all, the Upper Acheulean locale of Salzgitter-Lebenstedt (Busch and Schwabedissen 1991) apparently dates to the climatically severe Pleniglacial in OIS 4 and is located near Hamburg on the German section of the North European Plain.

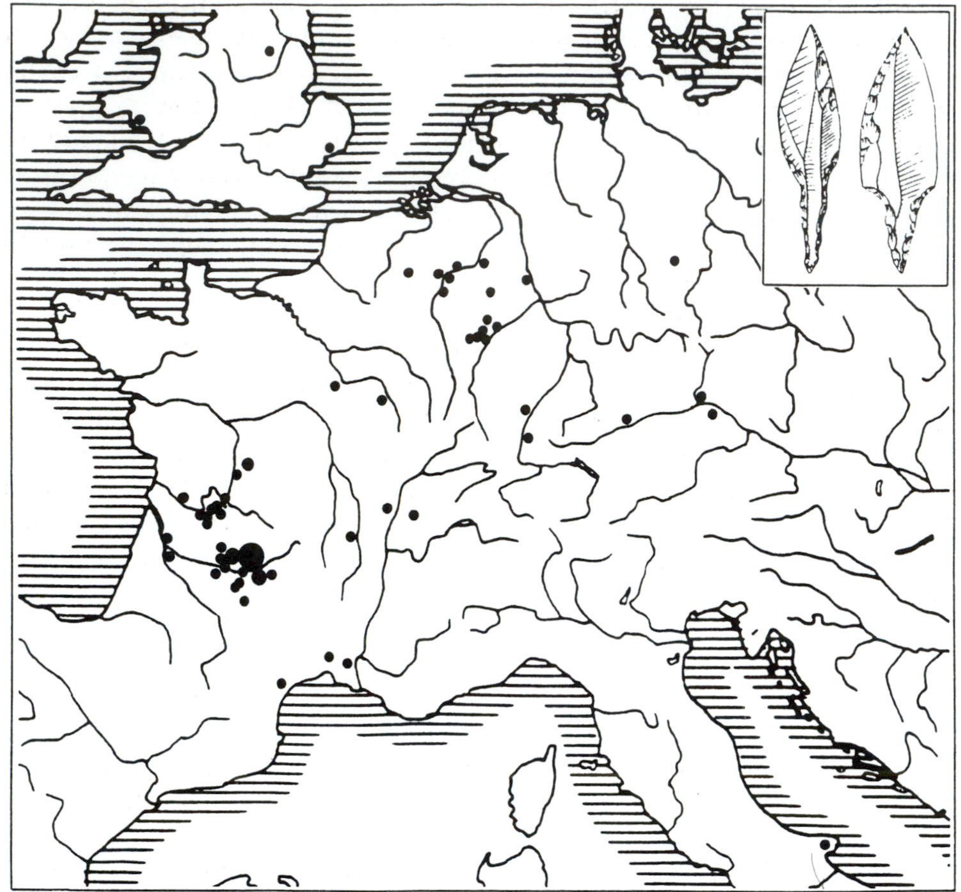

**7.5** The distribution of Font Robert points (after Jöris in Bosinski 1995b).

The Aurignacian is also very rare throughout Italy in the period 30–25 Kyr bp. Mussi (1990:139) does not believe this represents a total abandonment but rather that presence had dropped to such a level that archaeological visibility is extremely low.

*Moving into empty territory*

The closely spaced, meridional trending isochrons (Figure 7.4) are a clear indication of empty or infrequently used space in the centre of the continent. We saw in Chapter 6 that the numbers of Mousterian and EUP locales along the Rhine and Danube of Germany were, during the Interpleniglacial, small in number and generally small in assemblage size. Moreover the largest collections invariably come from caves and rock shelters.

Just how sparse this occupation might be is demonstrated by Hahn (1988) and Scheer's (1993) work on the Achtal locales in southern Germany. Refitting artifacts reveals that cryoturbation was responsible for producing some of these multi-level sites. Once refitting has been carried out, the evidence points to a single major occupation in the same caves. While such occupation may still result from several visits, the numbers of artifacts deposited are small. Furthermore, the refitting of stone artifacts between locales shows that in the Gravettian one visit to the Achtal accounts for deposition in at least three of its caves. It might be that in the period 29–21 Kyr bp the valley was visited by a few individuals for a few months. While this says much for the ability of the archaeological record to preserve ephemeral events, it nonetheless points to minimal use of the area.

This rarely visited, low population density area in the middle of the north-central region may explain the early appearance of the Aurignacian at locales such as the Geißenklösterle. People were moving into empty hominid space, or at least into a landscape which was rarely visited, as the rare leaf points of Hengelo interstadial age in the Altmühl valley and along the Swabian Alb testify (Freund 1987, Koenigswald, Müller-Beck and Pressmar 1974). The lack of any late C14 dates for either the Micoquian or Mousterian in this area supports the conclusion that this part of Europe was vacated during the Late Middle Palaeolithic.

*Co-residence in France*

A very different situation can be found in the southwest region. Here the Châtelperronian, found predominantly in this region, is sufficiently well dated and has large enough lithic collections to be examined as a transitional industry. Bordes (1968a), following Peyrony (1933), maintained that the Châtelperronian developed directly out of the Mousterian of Acheulean Tradition B. The distinctive curved, blunted backed points, or knives, in Châtelperronian assemblages were, in his opinion, derived from the naturally backed knives so common in the MTA B. The Châtelperronian in this scheme was, at the key rock shelter of La Ferrassie in the heart of the Dordogne, the representative of the first two stages of the Perigordian tradition. In Bordes' scheme these early Perigordians were later displaced by the Aurignacians, as evidenced by the upper levels at La Ferrassie. They then returned at a later date to the Dordogne, depositing Perigordian industries III–VI (see Bordes 1973, Laville, Rigaud and Sackett 1980 for full discussion).

This view of a long but interrupted Perigordian tradition in the Dordogne has generally been discarded. The link between the early and later Perigordian is hard to substantiate. However, while this link has faded, the Châtelperronian has become a well-recognized archaeological entity (Farizy 1990, Harrold 1989). It is found interstratified with Aurignacian levels at Roc de Combe (Bordes and Labrot 1967) and Piage (Champagne and Espitalie 1981). Geographically the Châtelperronian extends only from Northern France to Cantabria (Chapter 6). At St Césaire it is associated in level Ejop with an adult Neanderthal skeleton (Leveque, Backer and Gilbaud 1993) and at Arcy-sur-Cure, layer Xb, with the very distinctive bony labyrinth from a Neanderthal ear (Hublin et al. 1996).

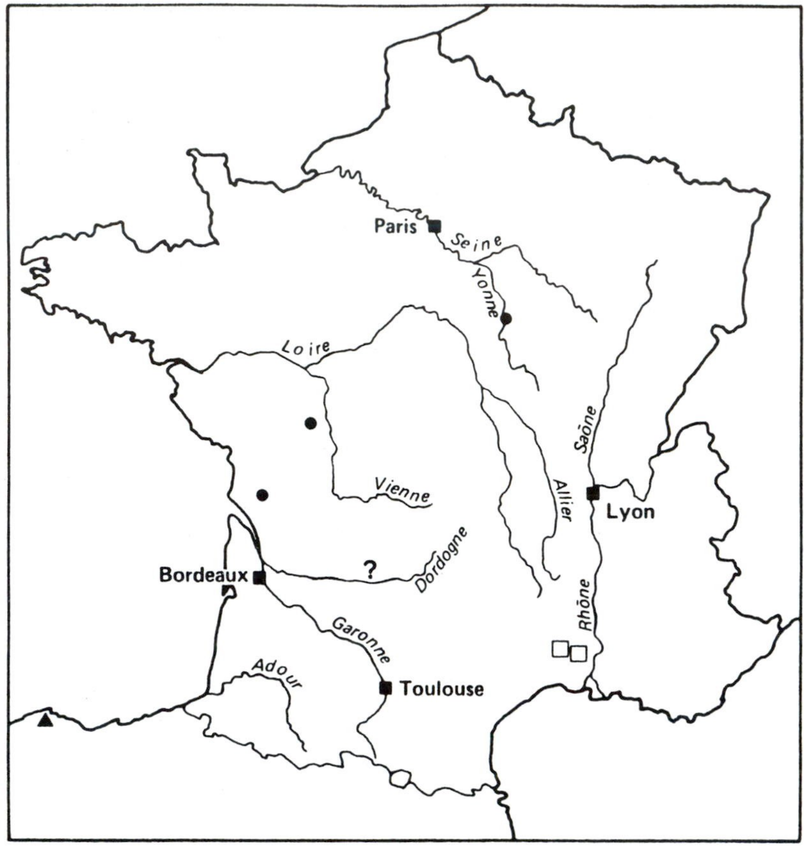


**7.6** The Neanderthal 'pocket' during the interpleniglacial in France (after Harrold 1989:Fig. 33.1–3).
(a) Hengelo interstadial 38–34.5 Kyr bp

Harrold (1989) has provided a detailed review of the composition of Châtelperronian assemblages and compared them with the Mousterian and Aurignacian. In his opinion these assemblages were the handiwork of Neanderthals and developed rapidly from the local Mousterian in the Périgord area (*ibid.*:705).

What is quite clear is that the Châtelperronian co-existed with Aurignacian assemblages. Figures 7.6a–c plot the distributions in the period 38–31.5 Kyr bp.[11] The absolute dates for the Aurignacian at Castilló cave in Cantabria (Cabrera-Valdes and Bischoff 1989) and l'Arbreda in Catalonia (Bischoff et al. 1989) are of course much earlier (Table 6.2). If added to the maps produced by Harrold, they suggest that the Neanderthals were left alone in their Dordogne pocket by incoming people who initially skirted around them. Although the

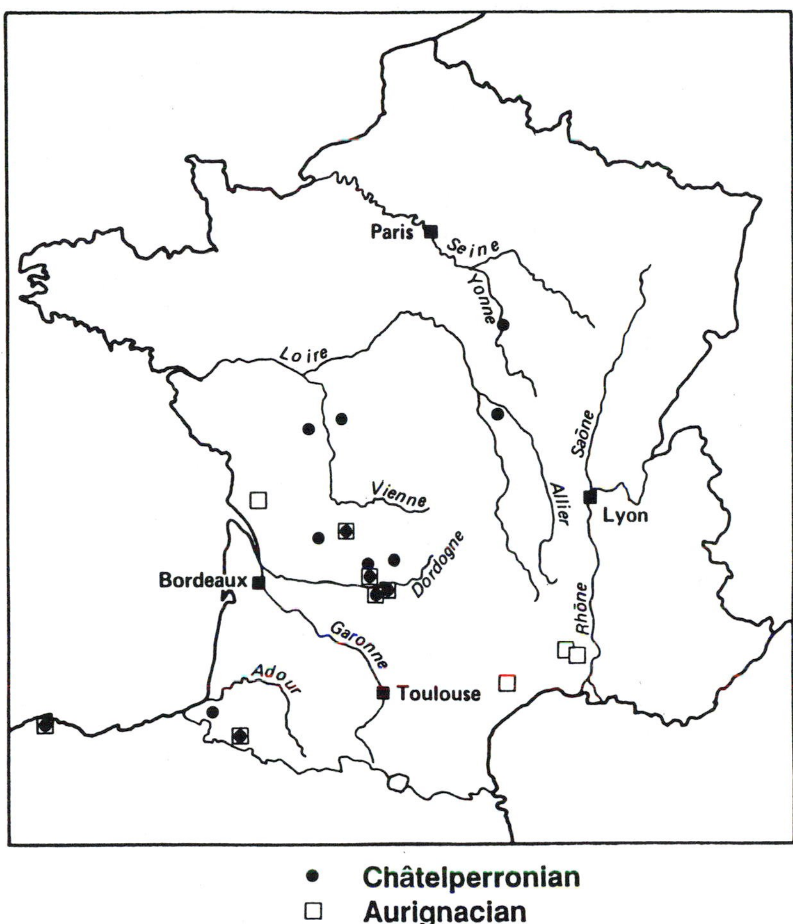


**7.6** (*cont.*)
(b) 34.5–33 Kyr bp early Würm III

true ages (Chapter 6) are still somewhat in doubt, it is very possible that if the Aurignacian is present in Cantabria and Catalonia by 43 Kyr bp it did indeed provide a long-term selective context that produced the Châtelperronian (Harrold 1989:705). As Farizy has remarked,

> It is possible that as a result of external pressures, Neanderthal groups were able to adopt or develop many features of distinctively Upper Palaeolithic culture. (Farizy 1990:325)

The Châtelperronian is of course not all about curved knives with blunted backs. It has evidence for bone and antler working (Leroi-Gourhan and Leroi-Gourhan 1964) as well as a few pierced animal teeth and pendants at Les Cottés and Grotte du Renne, Arcy-sur-Cure levels 9 and 10 (Farizy 1990:320, Harrold 1989:Table 33.8).

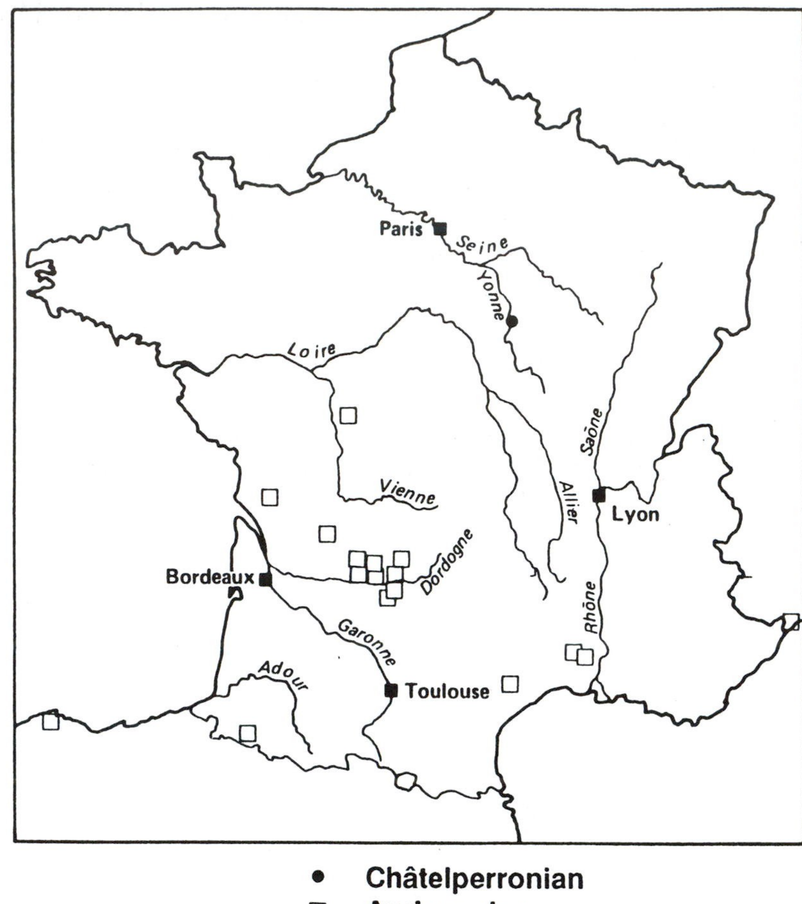


**7.6** (*cont.*)
(c) 33–31.5 Kyr bp later Würm III

The C14 dates now suggest, even though the Aurignacian 'push' into the central Périgord may have been late (Figure 7.6c), that the conditions existed within southwest France and northern Spain for imitation and emulation to occur, as Farizy and Harrold both suggest. For example, there is abundant red ochre in Châtelperronian deposits which may be associated with manufacturing ornaments, as suggested by White (1993b, 1993c) for the Aurignacian (Chapter 6). Hublin (et al. 1996) go further and tentatively suggest exchange of artifacts between individuals from the two species.

It is difficult to be precise about how long this co-existence lasted, but it could minimally have been between 43–36 Kyr bp as indicated by the dates from Castilló and St Césaire. This imitation and exchange could extend to the bone points, pierced teeth and pendants. Interestingly it does not seem to extend to burials, as the evidence is inconclusive that the St Césaire remains, while representing most of a skeleton, were deliberately buried (Defleur 1993, Vandermeersch 1993).

At Arcy-sur-Cure, Grotte du Renne level X and dating to the Hengelo interstadial (Table 6.3), there is a structure with mammoth tusks, post holes and hearths. The plan is circular with limestone plaques that formed a bench (Farizy 1990:308). Leroi-Gourhan proposed that it was a roofed structure covering 12 m² of the terrace at the entrance to the cave.

It is difficult to interpret this and successive structures at Arcy, since full details are not available. However, Farizy has noted a major change in the use of space between the rich Mousterian levels in the Arcy caves and the Châtelperronian levels.[12]

> The changes seem to relate rather to a different quality of life, in which the immediate surroundings of the human groups – the habitation zone – was perceived in a totally different way. Analogous changes can be seen in the character of the lithic industries, in which the forms of the tools appear to have a new, exclusive significance. (Farizy 1990:325)

The structure to locales which is now evident, if not easily interpretable, has also been found at St Césaire (Backer 1993). There were no post holes, benches or mammoth tusks in the upper level Ejop but Backer's spatial analysis (*ibid.*:Figure 9.1) was able to identify two different disposal zones, as measured by artifact composition, in an excavated area of c. 33 m². These distributions fall either side of the rock shelter's dripline.

*The Châtelperronian as a culture and a network*

Straus (1993:xii) has sounded a sensible note of caution concerning the link between Neanderthals and the Châtelperronian. Since St Césaire is the only significant fossil we have,

> we do not even know 'who' made the early Aurignacian of France, or, for that matter, Cantabrian Spain, where in fact the distinctions among Mousterian, Châtelperronian, and Aurignacian are somewhat blurred (*ibid.*)

Given the minimum of seven thousand years of co-residence before the Aurignacian 'push', his conclusion is correct. However, we can look at the problem differently by considering it as a system of networks rather than an association between a fossil hominid and a way of making stone tools.

From this perspective the Châtelperronian identifies an area of resources in the Périgord which in terms of biomass and seasonality were undoubtedly denser and more predictable than in other areas. Such a structure of resources was well suited to the wheel-shaped Neanderthal networks with high mobility, short residential stays and limited carrying of materials. As individuals criss-crossed the terrain along known tracks and between preferred locales they were assured of regular contact. As a result the intimate network could sustain some separation while an individual's effective network could be rapidly called upon. These people had language, which enhanced the transmission of information about other individuals in the landscape. This model of individual movement would suggest that if males and females dispersed then both sexes would have similar low-density networks as measured by transitivity and ties (Chapter 2). However, if the females did not disperse away from their natal territories then we would expect them to have much denser and stronger networks and the males correspondingly weaker ones. High-density female networks will produce a situation where an effective network of females will be co-opted to the task of protecting and parenting offspring. However if both sexes have low-density networks the result should be shared parenting responsibilities so that the intimate rather than the effective network has a more important role for that essential activity.

Can we therefore consider the Châtelperronian as a culture in Clarke's sense given above? Its elements are certainly polythetic in occurrence (Harrold 1989:Tables 33.7, 33.8). Ornaments are absent in most locales as are several features of lithic production. However, what is available satisfies the criteria of recurrence within a definable geographical area (Ashton 1983:Figure 2). Using Harrold's distribution maps as a guide (Figure 7.6a–c) I estimate the following maximum areas:

| Time range | Maximum area | Number of locales |
|---|---|---|
| 37–34.5 Kyr | 200,000 $km^2$ | 3–4 |
| 34.5–33 Kyr | 500,000 $km^2$ | 14 |

When compared with the size of regions (Figure 7.3), we see that the larger corresponds to the size of the southwest region, a fact easily deduced from the distribution map alone. This covers a minimum time span of 1,500 years. It must be remembered that these estimates are only intended to contrast the scale of these widely recognized archaeological units. They are not to be read as Châtelperronian territories, only as an estimate of their potential range. What we are examining is the ability to maintain a similar presence *in absentia* through the use of common technological and stylistic gestures.

By contrast, the Aurignacian appears to excel at extension, that ability to go beyond the confines of face-to-face society and achieve wider system integration performed across a social landscape. How could this be? Let us suppose that the rapid spread resulted from individual males constructing global networks while females had adopted the major task of parenting. As a result we have a situation where an asymmetry existed in network structure which, as we saw in Chapter 2, is commonly found among non-human primates. Moreover, this asymmetry has repercussions for cultural transmission (Steele 1994), as it does for gene flow.

Here then is a possible distinction between Neanderthal and Aurignacian societies. It may also have involved different demographic parameters including mortality and fertility rates (Zubrow 1989) but essentially the difference lay in two ways for individuals to create networks within similar Pleistocene landscapes. This passes no judgement on which was better or worse. There were

Table 7.7. *A comparison of networks for the early Upper Palaeolithic in southwest Europe. No judgements are made about the physical type responsible. Network model from Steele (1994), see Chapter 2.*

| | Residence | Network density | Parenting | Cultural transmission | Network type |
|---|---|---|---|---|---|
| **Châtelperronian** | | | | | |
| Males | Disperse | Low | Shared | Common | Low density |
| Females | Disperse | Low | Shared | Common | Low density |
| **Aurignacian** | | | | | |
| Males | Disperse | Low/high | Minor | Preferential | Poisson |
| Females | Remain | High | Major | Preferential | Tribal |

however important consequences for the construction of power which, in the case of the Aurignacian, now occurred at a wider scale than hitherto had been the case. Power had a particular context since its source lay in the differential use of the three networks by which individuals sustained themselves. The expressions of power were no doubt as varied as they are in any social system. But we can now see how actions were differently empowered through the interactions and the networks which stemmed from them (Table 2.1). As a result individuals were both constrained and enabled in the scale and effects of their actions over others.

If the Châtelperronian really is a transition industry, a Neanderthal social technology, then, as I stated at the outset of this chapter, it must be understood in terms of the transformation of power. The implication here is that cultural transmission in those extended networks will produce an advantage in terms of sourcing the social landscape with opportunity for individual agency. The model is summarized in Table 7.7.

We would expect from this table that the items which are either imitated or exchanged and subsequently adopted are those which were available at encounters and involved in the process of extension. Hence the pierced teeth and the ochre used to make ornaments (White 1993b, 1993c). These were the gestures exchanged. They were imitated by both males and females because there was no network barrier since the limits were set by the rules and resources of the intimate and effective networks. The ornaments which were produced were, however, distinctively Châtelperronian and not pale imitations of Aurignacian forms.

What was transmitted in return acted preferentially on the males since they were constructing fundamentally different networks from the females. Perhaps, as Soffer (1994:Figure 1) has argued, the latter were even being provisioned by the males. Therefore the network and the rules of encounter predicated a change in actions and gestures and a transition to new forms of power based on variety in the networks. Any asymmetry of power flowed from the different networks now constructed by males and females.

*A divided Iberia*

The early arrival of the Aurignacian in Spain (Cabrera-Valdés 1993) has also thrown open the question of the survival of the Mousterian in Iberia. The possibility has always been hinted at with C14 and TL dates consistently dating Mousterian assemblages from southern Spain to between 20 and 30 Kyr bp. These were usually dismissed as too young. But now the evidence is convincing that in southern Iberia the Mousterian persisted long after it had been replaced in southern and northern Europe.

Zilhao (1988, 1993) reviews the evidence from Portugal. Caldeirao cave is important as it has a sequence spanning the Middle and Upper Palaeolithic. An AMS date of 27.6±0.6 Kyr bp came from the top of level K which marks the end of the Mousterian and the beginning of the Upper Palaeolithic. The artifact collections are small but elsewhere at Columbeira similar dates for the Mousterian have been obtained. Also at this time horizon is a possible Aurignacian level at Pego do Diabo and a Gravettian assemblage from Vale Comprido (Zilhao 1993:tableau 1).[13]

There are clearly complexities here which a small sample may be masking. However, when the evidence from southern Spain is also included the pattern becomes clearer. Here at Gorham's cave, Gibraltar (Vega Toscano 1993), the Aurignacian is dated by C14 to 28 Kyr bp. Following a study of the faunal and sedimentological evidence from a number of locales, Vega Toscano (1993) puts Carihuela V, Cueva Hora and Zafarraya, all three caves from southeastern Spain, in the time bracket 26–30 Kyr bp (Figure 7.7). At Carihuela and Zafarraya there are Neanderthal remains associated with typical Mousterian industries (Garralda 1993). It is also possible that some of the Neanderthal remains associated with Mousterian industries from the Gibraltar caves may also be late in age.

Zilhao (1993) provides a geographical assessment of these data. He proposes that the Ebro formed a boundary up against which the rapid spread of the Aurignacian stopped at 38 Kyr bp (Figure 7.8). He then tentatively suggests that the Neanderthals continued in southern Iberia until being finally replaced between 28–30 Kyr bp. Zilhao (1993:143) favours a rapid replacement at this time rather than a slow transition during a long period of co-existence.

How does a network approach add to this challenging scenario? If we compare this situation with that for the Châtelperronian discussed above, two factors emerge. Firstly, Iberia lacks a transitional industry comparable to the Châtelperronian, the Uluzzian or the leaf points discussed in Chapter 6 (Cabrera-Valdés 1993, 1979, Fullola 1983, Zilhao 1988). Secondly, Iberia lacks assemblages which imitate gestures within a chaîne opératoire, in the way revealed by the Châtelperronian ornaments.

This observation suggests that we are dealing with different networks than those in the southwest region north of the Pyrenees. Moreover, there appear to be some limits to the scale of the extended systems in the Upper Palaeolithic. In this respect it is noticeable that while Middle Palaeolithic locales are known

7.7 Below the Ebro frontier. The landscape around Carihuela cave, Spain, MW region, which formed a late Neanderthal refugium (photo by the author).

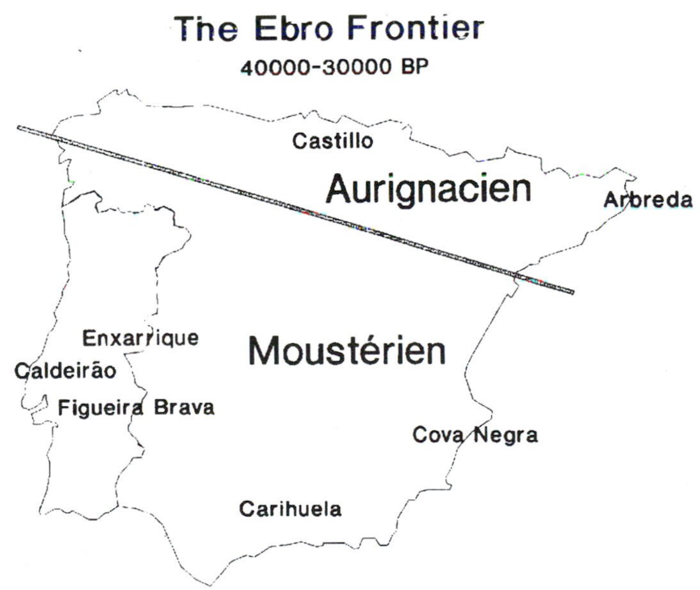


7.8 A divided Spain. The Aurignacian zone lies in both the MW and SW regions (after Zilhao 1993:Fig. 7).

from the Meseta in central Spain (Vega Toscano, Raposo and Santonja 1994), this area does not have any EUP evidence (Cabrera-Valdés 1993, Fullola 1979, 1983).

We have already seen that the Mediterranean was possibly more densely populated than other regions in Europe. The nature of the networks in Middle Palaeolithic Spain, and especially those which flanked the Meseta in Portugal and Andalucia, would have taken these larger numbers into account. The result would have been smaller, more tightly knit networks with high densities. Since there was no point of contact and no empty space for the EUP to move into, the result was continuity. It is possible as climatic changes after 28 Kyr bp thinned out resources in this region that the interstices in the networks opened up and Upper Palaeolithic populations could now enter. The lack of imitation and of so-called transitional industries supports Zilhao's conclusion that replacement was rapid.

But let me put the question another way. Did the Neanderthals at Carihuela cave in a divided Iberia (see above) have a social landscape? And if not, did their Aurignacian and Perigordian contemporaries in Cueva Morin on the other side of the 'frontier' have such a different social framework? At first glance the evidence, as reviewed by Straus (1992), is not overwhelming for a vastly different EUP in Cantabria. The transfers of raw materials are slight, portable art and ornaments are very rare. Only the burials at Cueva Morin (Freeman and González-Echegaray 1970, González-Echegaray and Freeman 1971, 1973) point to something different. Straus sums it up:

> The whole EUP in Cantabrian Spain constituted a long, irregular, and, in many domains, gradual transition from Middle Palaeolithic adaptations to the 'classic Upper Palaeolithic' adaptations . . . Underway since at least 40,000 years ago, the changes in the EUP were a mosaic. (Straus 1992:89)

However, the links established through stone artifact styles key this area into that wider Upper Palaeolithic world north of the Pyrenees rather than to the Neanderthals south of the Ebro. The fact that this notional 'frontier' was not marked by any increase in signalling such as burials, architecture or painted caves strongly suggests that two very different systems were indeed juxtaposed. Because they were so different there was no need for a demonstration of the limits of the extended networks using symbolic resources within a social landscape. By the same token the Neanderthals had no need to draw a line to their systems which operated regionally as landscapes of habit. Both systems were exclusive, unlike those in the southwestern region discussed above. Here, exclusion was complemented by the principle of inclusion, represented by the use of symbolic resources to extend the ambit of social technology.

And this is my point. Recognizing the social landscape does not depend upon a glaringly obvious archaeological record of huts, hearths and art. The opportunity to stretch those space–time bands still remains just that, an opportunity, and not an inevitable outcome. In the same way, the ability to represent the perceived world by carving ivory into the shape of the animal from which the raw material came does not mean that wherever ivory is found mammoths will be sculpted. Following the so-called creative explosion of the Upper Palaeolithic (Pfeiffer 1982) there are as many art- and ornament-poor regions in the world as there are those which command our attention as art rich. Power, in the negative sense of domination and replacement, is everywhere an option but not always an outcome. The Spanish case study provides a Palaeolithic example.

## Locales

The social occasion (Chapter 3) is distinguished from the gathering by the materials and associations it contains for the performance of social life. It is an externalized environment to the extent that locales now become places through association and rhythms as creators of forms (Leroi-Gourhan 1993:309). The gathering, in my terminology, depends on nothing more than the attention that occurs in co-presence between social actors and their embodied artifacts. The social occasion has any number of artifacts but with the distinction that many of them are now disembodied gestures. Although separated in this sense from the performance of social life, they nonetheless have power and significance in shaping and creating it. Thus artifacts structure attention based on the symbolic extension of people across time and space. The past is now used to organize the future by making references between place, person and object not only when they are together but also when they are apart.

## Locales: Dolní Věstonice-Pavlov – a case study

The well-known locale of Dolní Věstonice-Pavlov in southern Moravia, north-central region, provides an opportunity to examine the archaeological components of the social occasion/place. In particular these concern the attaching and detaching rituals which assist in the constitution of the locale as a place (Chapter 3). These rituals epitomize the symbolic resources used to create an extended network (Table 4.1). They invest locales with physical structures and associated temporal rhythms for cultural performance and future action.

### *Setting and excavations*

The landscape of Dolní Věstonice-Pavlov is dominated by the Dyje river and the Pavlovské limestone hills which reach a height of 550m (Figure 7.9). The various locales, which have been investigated over almost eighty years, lie south of the river in the sharply rising terraces on the flanks of the hills. The limestone provides a calcareous environment which has assisted the preservation of bone and other organic materials in the colluvial and loessic deposits.

In its wider setting the Pavlovské hills are centrally located to important routeways. One hundred kilometres to the southwest is the narrow Wachau

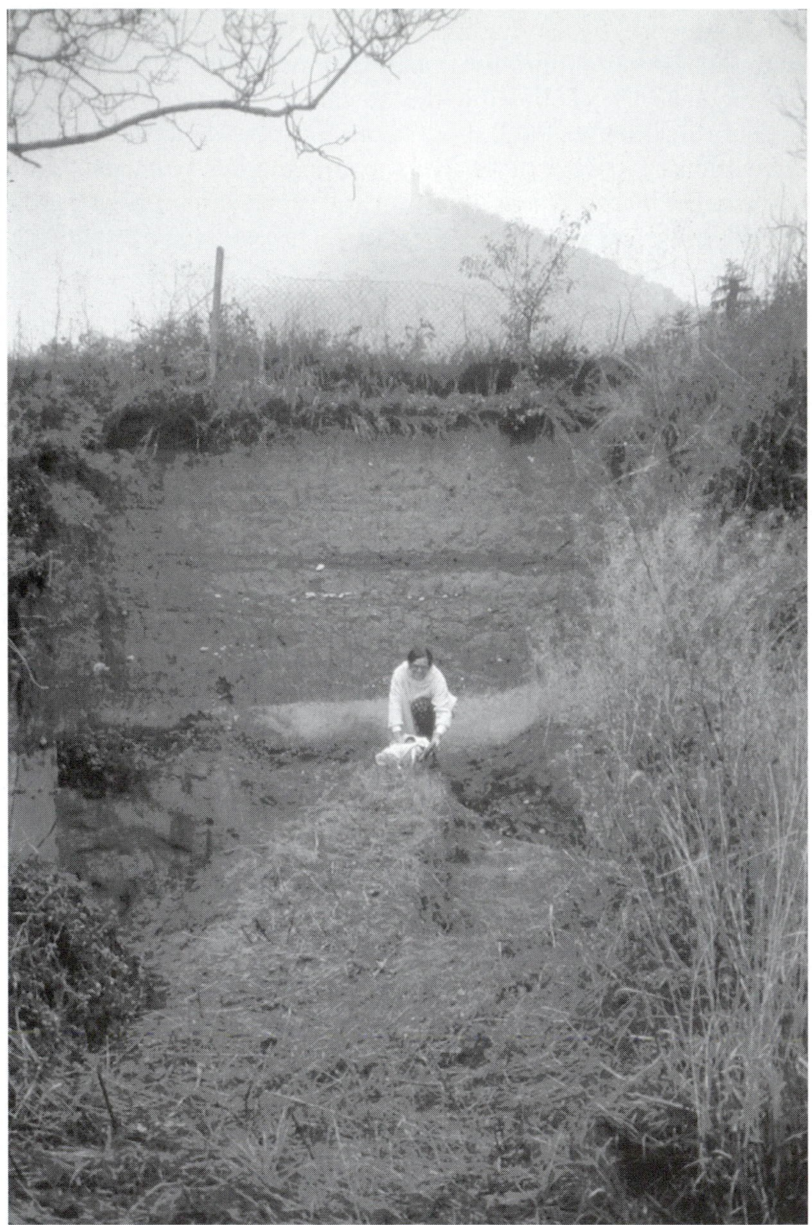

**7.9** (A) The surviving section of Dolní Věstonice I in the vineyards beneath the Pavlovské hills.

gorge, best known for the stratified Willendorf II site, providing access along the Danube to Austria and southern Germany, while 150 km to the northeast lie the Moravian gates with easy access to southern Poland (Djindjian 1994:Figure 3).

Systematic excavations began at Dolní Věstonice with Absolon. Between 1924 and 1938, he made major discoveries at site I of mammoth bones, lithics,

**7.9** (*cont.*) (B) Dolní Věstonice II, foreground, the western slope excavations and mammoth midden in the middleground and behind the modern village and artificial lake (photos by the author).

sub-surface features, hearths and fragments of clay and ivory figurines. Among these are two very well-known pieces (Figure 7.10), the internationally recognized icons of the site. A female figurine modelled in clay was found in 1925. Instead of a face she has a 'hood' with slanting cuts representing the eyes. In 1936 a small 'portrait' head carved in ivory, also interpreted as female, was excavated. Besides these were many clay fragments of small animal figurines modelled in the local loess. Regrettably most of Absolon's finds were destroyed in 1945 when the castle where they were stored was set on fire (Klíma 1954:5).

Absolon started a tradition of plotting the horizontal distribution of material in order to discover the size of the settlement. During the Nazi occupation of the region, 1939–45, the emphasis changed. The excavations by Bohmers were designed primarily to establish the stratigraphy and age of the sites. The artwork was also much discussed as examples of Indo-German origins. During the early years of the Cold War, 1949–56, archaeological investigations stuck with politically neutral aspects of the site, primarily the soils and their relevance to local stratigraphies (Tomásková 1995:310). However, the work of Klíma during the 1950s, at Dolní Věstonice (Klíma 1963, 1983) and at Pavlov (Svoboda 1994c, 1994d, Svoboda, Lozek and Vlček 1996), re-established Absolon's settlement approach. This had the effect of confirming the international status of the site as well as providing the opportunity to comment on its prehistoric social organization through a study of the means of production (Tomásková 1995:312).

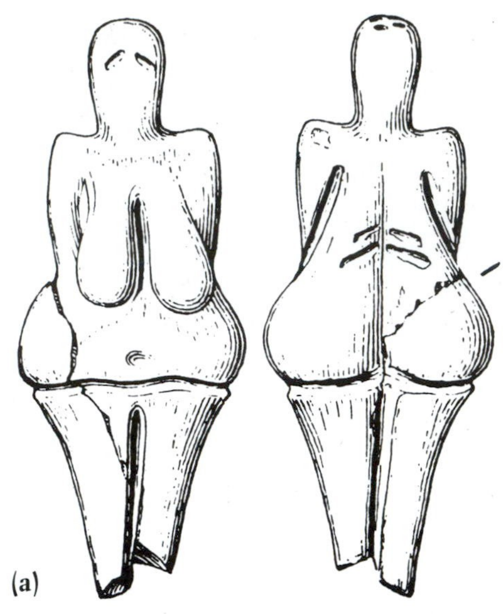


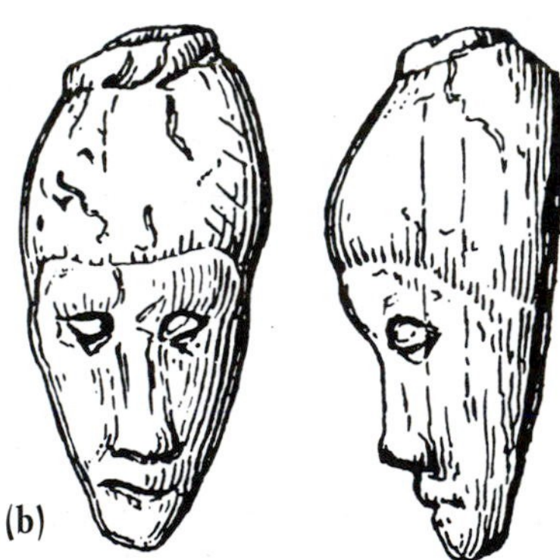


**7.10** Two icons of Dolní Věstonice. The clay figurine (a) was found in 1925 and is shown three-quarters life size. The ivory head (b), shown full size, was excavated in 1936 (after Klíma 1983:Figs. 3 and 37).

Czechoslovak archaeologists are beginning to show that the great Palaeolithic loess sites were more than temporary encampments: considerable settlements with the oldest known buildings of man, inhabited by a numerous society over long periods. Such works could only be undertaken by a society which had progressed towards organized community life (according to certain evidence of a matriarchal cast), and which was guided day by day by definite customs and unwritten laws. (Klíma 1954:14)

Table 7.8. *The chronological ordering of the Pavlovian/Gravettian (Svoboda 1994e:Fig. 2).*

| | |
|---|---|
| **Early Pavlovian** | **30–27 Kyr bp** |
| Lower part of Dolní Věstonice I and II | |
| Willendorf II level 6 | |
| Molodova V level 9 | |
| **Evolved Pavlovian** | **27–24 Kyr bp** |
| Middle and upper part of Dolní Věstonice I and II | |
| Pavlov I | |
| Milovice? | |
| Předmostí | |
| Willendorf II levels 7 and 8 | |
| **Willendorf/Kostenki** | **24–20 Kyr bp** |
| Milovice | |
| Petrkovice | |
| Willendorf II level 9 | |
| Spadzista street C2 | |
| Molodova V level 7 | |
| Kostenki I/1 | |

Since 1985 rescue work in the loess brick pits around Dolní Věstonice, site II and excavations on its western slope and at site III have produced further important settlement and burial evidence (Klíma 1995, Skrdla, Cílek and Prichystal 1996, Svoboda 1991). In 1986, 3 km to the southeast of Pavlov village, mammoth-bone structures and a rich flint industry were found at Milovice (Oliva 1988a, 1988b).

## Chronology

Svoboda provides a chronological summary (1994e:224) of the Gravettian cultures in Moravia, lower Austria, Poland, the Ukraine and Russia (Table 7.8). These are known as Pavlovian after the type site at the village of Pavlov, and consist of assemblages where burins generally outnumber all other classes of retouched tools. The later Willendorf/Kostenki culture is represented by shouldered knives/points that are found across an area stretching from the Don river to Moravia, the Austrian Wachau and southern Poland (Desbrosse and Kozlowski 1988, Praslov and Rogachev 1982, Soffer and Praslov 1993). This culture also contains evidence for houses constructed from mammoth bone, numerous storage pits, several of which were large enough to act as subterranean dwellings, as well as abundant female and animal carvings (Svoboda 1994e:216).

The excavations at Dolní Věstonice-Pavlov can be divided into these three chronological phases.[14] However, the major use of the locale occurred during

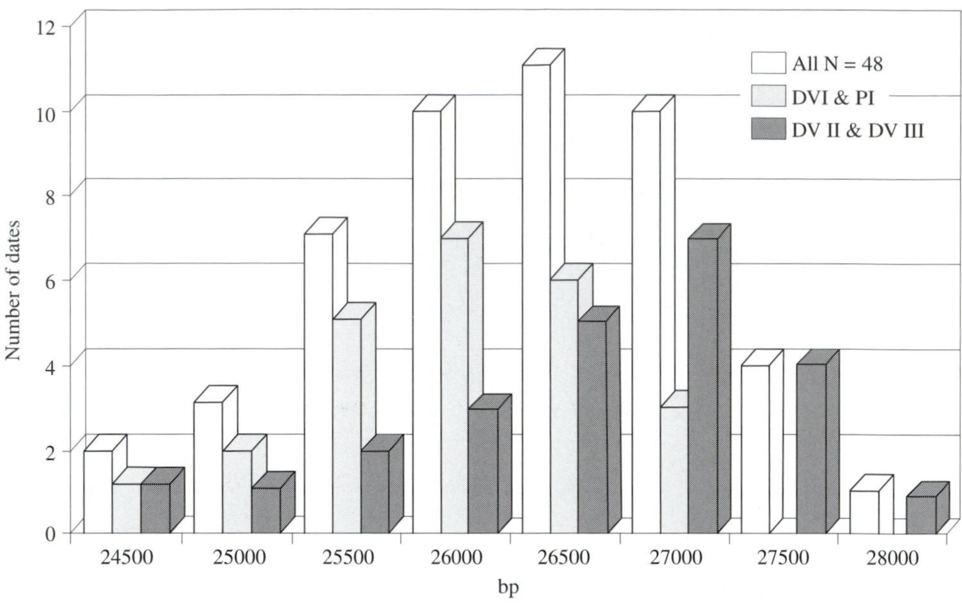


**7.11** Uncalibrated radiocarbon dates for various locales at Dolní Věstonice-Pavlov, Czech Republic, NC region. The histograms use a moving sum of 500 years with a span of 250 years.

the three thousand years of the Evolved Pavlovian. When the Gröningen C14 dates for this period are plotted as a moving sum (Figure 7.11) they show that the excavations in the west of the locale, Dolní Věstonice II and III, are consistently older than the classic double site of Dolní Věstonice I and Pavlov I.[15]

*Internal structure of the locale*

During these three millennia settlement extended for almost 3 km between the modern villages of Pavlov in the east and Dolní Věstonice in the west (Figure 7.12). Within the locale the excavated areas consistently lie between 200 and 300 m ASL (Svoboda, Klíma and Skrdla 1995:283) and form two main clusters.

The archaeological evidence differs between these two areas (Table 7.9). Dolní Věstonice II and its western slope (Klíma 1995, Svoboda 1991) have hearths, burials, abundant lithics and bone tools as well as evidence for refitting (Svoboda, Skrdla and Jarosova 1993:Abb. 3).[16] By contrast, Dolní Věstonice I and Pavlov I, which lie less than 500 m apart and probably represent part of the same phase of occupation, have all of these aspects as well as thousands of clay figurine fragments and a series of excavated features. These have been described by Klíma as semi-subterranean huts built on specially levelled platforms terraced into the slope (Klíma 1954, 1963, 1983, Svoboda 1994c, Valoch 1996). At Dolní Věstonice I, II and II western slope there are large concentrations of mammoth bones. The origin of these as human or natural collections

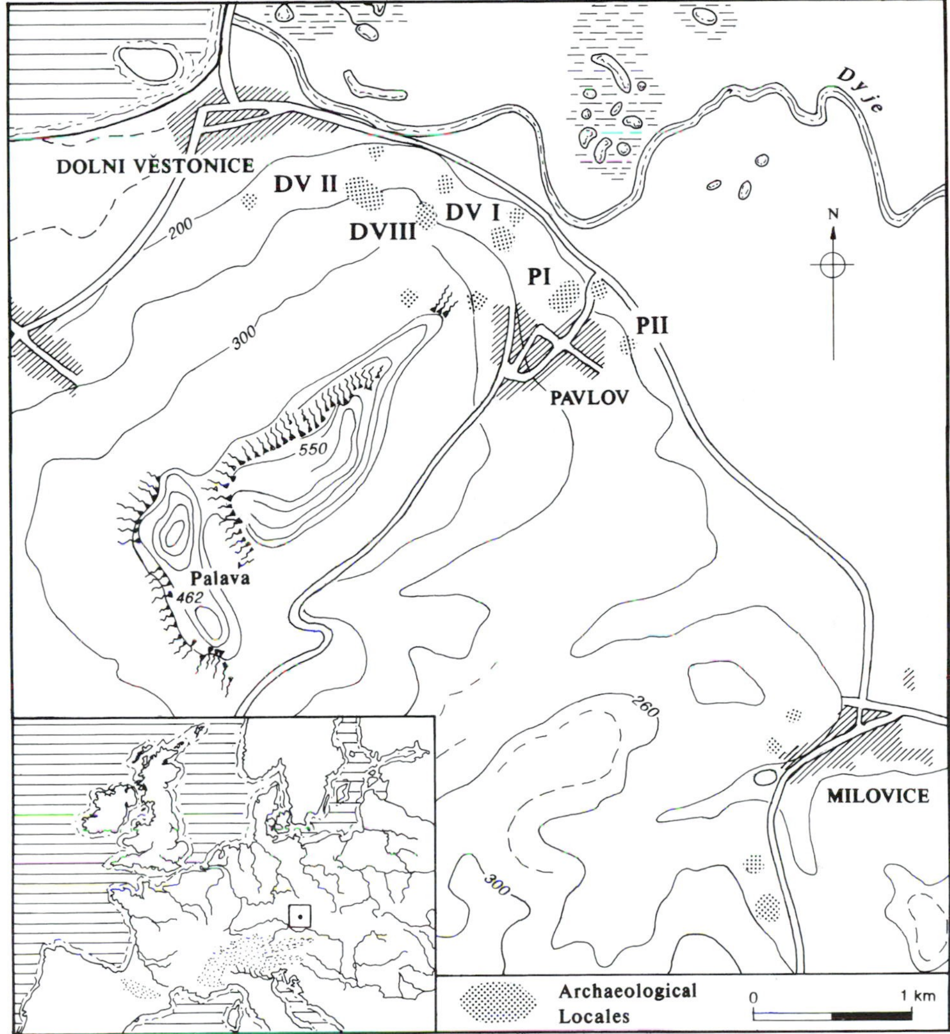


**7.12** The location of archaeological locales around the modern villages of Dolní Věstonice, Pavlov and Milovice which lie beneath the Pavlovské hills, Czech Republic, NC region (after Valoch 1995:Abb. 1).

is still debated but the excavations did find artifacts and charcoal among these densely packed bones.

*Hearth skills*

The fireplaces and kilns at Dolní Věstonice-Pavlov are a very noticeable feature of the locale (Table 7.9). Bodies, artifacts, clay figurines, plant food and dwellings are linked to them and, as we shall see, they provide a focus for performance and social life. They are common at this locale as they are at most Early

Table 7.9. *The components of the Evolved Gravettian occupations, 27–24 Kyr BP, in the Dolní Věstonice-Pavlov locale (Klíma 1983, Svoboda 1991, 1994e, 1996, Valoch 1996).*

| | Dolní Věstonice I | Pavlov I | Dolní Věstonice II |
|---|---|---|---|
| Flexed burials | DV III | P I | DV XVI |
| Triple burial | | | DV XIII–XV |
| Isolated human remains | + | + | + |
| Semi-subterranean huts | 2 | 4–5? | |
| Surface huts | + | + | 3? |
| Storage pits | 0 | 1 | 0 |
| Mammoth bone midden | + | | + |
| Thick ashy deposits | + | + | |
| Outside hearths | + | + | + |
| Kilns | + | + | |
| Fired clay objects | +++ | +++ | + |
| Pierced shell and teeth ornaments | +++ | +++ | + |
| Representational art | +++ | +++ | |
| Lunar calendar | | | + |
| Ochre lumps | + | + | + |
| Predominance of raw materials from >100 km | 60–90% | 60–90% | 60–90% |
| Fibre technology | | + | |
| Settlement duration | Long | Long | Short |
| Season of use | ? | Winter | Winter |
| Fur-bearing animals | + | + | + |
| Reindeer as dominant herbivore | + | + | ? |
| Plant food evidence | | | + |

Upper Palaeolithic locales, both in caves and in the open air. It is therefore surprising that at earlier Middle Palaeolithic locales such as Mauran (Chapter 6) even the simplest hearth is usually lacking.

Mauran is dated to between 35 and 45 Kyr bp on the basis of ESR while level 14 at Abri Pataud, also in the southwest region, is dated by conventional C14 to 33.3–34.2 Kyr bp (Movius 1977). A major difference between these nearly contemporary locales is the hearths. At Mauran, the absence of spatial patterning is matched by the lack of hearths. There are burnt bones and a few charcoal fragments which may be the traces of small ephemeral hearths (Farizy 1994:Fig. 127).

Elsewhere well-built hearths have been found with Mousterian artifacts. At Vilas Ruivas, an open Middle Palaeolithic locale in Portugal, a stone constructed hearth has been dated by TL to 54±12 Kyr bp (Vega Toscano, Raposo and Santonja 1994). At the Grotte de Peyrère, Frechet, located at 825 m in the Aure Valley (Jaubert et al. 1992), the upper level dated by C14 to 42 Kyr bp has a fireplace with charcoal, burnt bone and fire cracked stones.

These are generally single hearths. At the Abri Pataud the Aurignacian hearths are common, very substantial and clearly defined. In level 14 there are five and, for comparison, in level 11 seven with two shallow 'pits'. These hearths are large, sometimes over a metre long and up to 70 cm wide (Movius 1977). They lack the burnt river cobbles that appear in the later Perigordian VI of level 3 dated to 23 Kyr bp. This assemblage is the main occupation level in the rock shelter. Its five large hearths packed with cobbles run parallel to the back wall of the shelter and lie equidistant between it and a line of roof-fall boulders. The spacing between the centres of these hearths is consistently 2 m. In level 11 five hearths also run along the shelter wall and the distances between the hearth centres are smaller, ranging from 1 to 1.5 m (Spiess 1979:231).

Here are two very different techniques of hearth construction but in both instances the hearths are aligned in a linear fashion. Binford has shown (1983a:Fig. 98) that the spacings in level 3 could accommodate sleeping people. Further variety is shown by the hearths in level 14 which Spiess describes as a central focus occupation belonging to a different social configuration. What this might be exactly is unclear. However his estimates of the length of time these features were used suggests that those associated with linear rather than central focus hearths may have lasted longer or involved more people (Spiess 1979:231).[17]

In his study of Le Flageolet level 5, Simek (1987) has emphasized how hearth centred behaviour transforms the archaeological record. His analysis of this EUP rock shelter in the Périgord points to a small-scale occupation, in both time and personnel, with a single intensive activity area and a series of activity spaces containing a variety of evidence (*ibid*.:31).[18] By comparison no such defined patterning emerged from a similar spatial analysis of the Saalian-age locale of Grotte Vaufrey (see Chapter 5).

*Comparison by density*

Excavations were extensive. Absolon dug an estimated 4,500 m$^2$ in three main areas at Dolní Věstonice I. The later excavations, 1947–52, added a further 350 m$^2$, most of which lay next to Absolon's 1924–8 excavation but with an important new trench 70 m to the west (Klíma 1963:Fig. 4). At Pavlov I an estimated 2,000 m$^2$ was excavated, of which only some 300 m$^2$ from the 1952–3 excavations has been published (Svoboda 1994c).[19] The rescue excavations at Dolní Věstonice II and its western slope add up to a further 1,500 m$^2$ (Klíma 1995, Svoboda 1991) divided into two main areas (Klíma 1995:Abb. 33).

In order to gain a further quantitative impression of the locale Table 7.10 presents the density data within the various archaeological complexes.

The density figures (Table 7.11) are particularly high when compared with those for other, earlier open locales (Tables 4.19, 5.18). When the density per m$^2$ of all recorded stone, which includes tools as well as chips and debris, is plotted (Figure 7.13), we see that only four locales from a sample of eighty in the earlier

Table 7.10. *A comparison of the Evolved Gravettian locales, 27–24 Kyr BP, at Dolní Věstonice-Pavlov. + indicates the items were present but not quantified (Klíma 1963, 1995, Svoboda 1991, 1994c).*

| | Dolní Věstonice I | | | | Pavlov I | | Dolní Věstonice II | | | Dolní Věstonice II Western slope Settlement units | | | Pavlov I |
|---|---|---|---|---|---|---|---|---|---|---|---|---|---|
| | Object 1 | Object 2 | Mammoth bone deposit | Lower part of the deposit | 1952 | 1953 Object ? | 1986–7 Area A upper area | 1987 Area B upper part | A–B–C lower part | 1 | 2 | 3 | 4 |
| $m^2$ excavated | 151 | 78 | 105 | | 60 | 217 | 671 | 370 | | 8 | 16 | 24 | 98 |
| Total stone | 35,232 | 6,889 | 1,354 | 3,803 | 13,530 | 39,144 | 14,770 | 14,352 | 2,657 | 2,102 | 2,186 | 2,865 | 4,079 |
| Retouched blades/tools | 1,259 | 385 | 73 | 199 | 593 | 1,494 | 497 | 467 | 163 | 66 | 39 | 59 | 163 |
| Cores | 148 | 29 | 4 | 35 | 47 | | 310 | 149 | 19 | 13 | 14 | 25 | |
| Unretouched blades/flakes | 870 | 471 | 120 | 186 | 3,153 | | 3,439 | 2,565 | 374 | 489 | 832 | 1,118 | |
| Chips and debris | 32,955 | 6,004 | 1,157 | 3,383 | 9,737 | | 10,524 | 11,171 | 2,101 | 1,534 | 1,301 | 1,663 | |
| $m^2$: tools | 8.3 | 4.9 | 0.7 | | 9.9 | 6.9 | 0.7 | 1.3 | | 8.3 | 2.4 | 2.5 | 1.7 |
| $m^2$: cores | 1.0 | 0.4 | 0.04 | | 0.8 | | 0.5 | 0.4 | | 1.6 | 0.9 | 1.0 | |
| $m^2$: all stone | 233.3 | 88.3 | 12.9 | | 225.5 | 180.4 | 22.0 | 38.8 | | 262.8 | 136.6 | 119.4 | 41.6 |
| Bone tools | + | + | + | + | + | + | 204 | 93 | 5 | 2 | 4 | 10 | |
| Shell | + | + | + | + | + | + | 184 | 116 | | 12 | 14 | 15 | |
| Pierced teeth | + | + | + | + | + | + | 31 | 10 | | 5 | | | |
| Fired clay | all areas >5,761 | | | | all areas 1,332 | | 196 | 245 | | 7 | | | |
| Ochre lumps | + | + | + | + | + | + | 246 | 234 | | 18 | 7 | 45 | |
| Stone slabs | + | + | + | + | + | + | + | + | | 4 | 4 | 9 | |

Table 7.11. *Lithic density data for Late Middle Palaeolithic- and Early Upper Palaeolithic-age open locales (Allsworth-Jones 1990, Bitiri 1972, Bordes 1968b, Bricker and Laville 1977, Chernysh 1961, Cziesla 1984, Hahn 1977, Jaubert 1993, Kind 1985, Klíma 1963, 1995, Kozlowski 1974, Marcy et al. 1993, Nicolaescu-Plopsor, Paunescu and Mogosanu 1966, Svoboda 1991, 1994c, 1994d).*

| Site | Layer | Archaeology | Region | $m^2$ excavated | Total stone | Density per $m^2$ |
|---|---|---|---|---|---|---|
| Ceahlau-Cetatica I | | EUP | NE | 220 | 152 | 0.7 |
| Molodova V | X | EUP | NE | 774 | 617 | 0.8 |
| Ceahlau-Bofu Mic | | EUP | NE | 688 | 810 | 1.2 |
| Molodova V | IX | EUP | NE | 774 | 1,282 | 1.7 |
| Molodova V | VIII | EUP | NE | 774 | 1,655 | 2.1 |
| Ceahlau-Dîrtu | | EUP | NE | 461 | 1,405 | 3.0 |
| Bistricioara-lutarie | | EUP | NE | 210 | 1,379 | 6.6 |
| Remetea-Somos I | | EUP | SE | 302 | 2,056 | 6.8 |
| Ceahlau-Podis | | EUP | NE | 505 | 3,535 | 7.0 |
| Chabiague | | EUP | NW | 42 | 405 | 9.6 |
| Dolní Věstonice II | Midden | EUP | NC | 105 | 1,354 | 12.9 |
| Cracow Spadzista B | | EUP | NC | 91 | 1,379 | 15.2 |
| Kostenki 1 | I | EUP | NE | 612 | 12,000 | 19.6 |
| Lommersum | | EUP | NC | 62 | 1,228 | 19.8 |
| Hénin | G | MP | NW | 175 | 3,500 | 20.0 |
| Dolní Věstonice II Area A | | EUP | NC | 671 | 14,770 | 22.0 |
| Kostenki 1 | V | EUP | NE | 46 | 1,300 | 28.3 |
| Sprendlingen | | EUP | NC | 40 | 1,259 | 31.5 |
| Gohoud | | EUP | SW | 39 | 1,350 | 34.6 |
| Dolní Věstonice Area B | | EUP | NC | 370 | 14,352 | 38.8 |
| Vedrovice V | | EUP | NC | 120 | 4,946 | 41.2 |
| Pavlov I | | EUP | NC | 98 | 4,079 | 41.6 |
| Serino South | | EUP | MC | 60 | 2,619 | 43.7 |
| Molodova V | VII | EUP | NE | 774 | 44,947 | 58.1 |
| Le Côte | | EUP | SW | 18 | 1,070 | 59.4 |
| Corbiac | | EUP | SW | 150 | 9,809 | 65.4 |
| Tambourets | | EUP | SW | 8 | 542 | 67.8 |
| Mauran | | MP | SW | 25 | 2,142 | 85.7 |
| Dolní Věstonice Object 1 | | EUP | NC | 78 | 6,889 | 88.3 |
| Dolní Věstonice II Western Slope | | EUP | NC | 24 | 2,865 | 119.4 |
| Dolní Věstonice II Western Slope | | EUP | NC | 16 | 2,186 | 136.6 |
| Pavlov 1 Object? | | EUP | NC | 217 | 39,144 | 180.4 |
| Pavlov 1 | | EUP | NC | 60 | 13,530 | 225.5 |
| Dolní Věstonice I Object 1 | | EUP | NC | 151 | 35,232 | 233.3 |
| Dolní Věstonice II Western Slope | | EUP | NC | 8 | 2,102 | 262.8 |

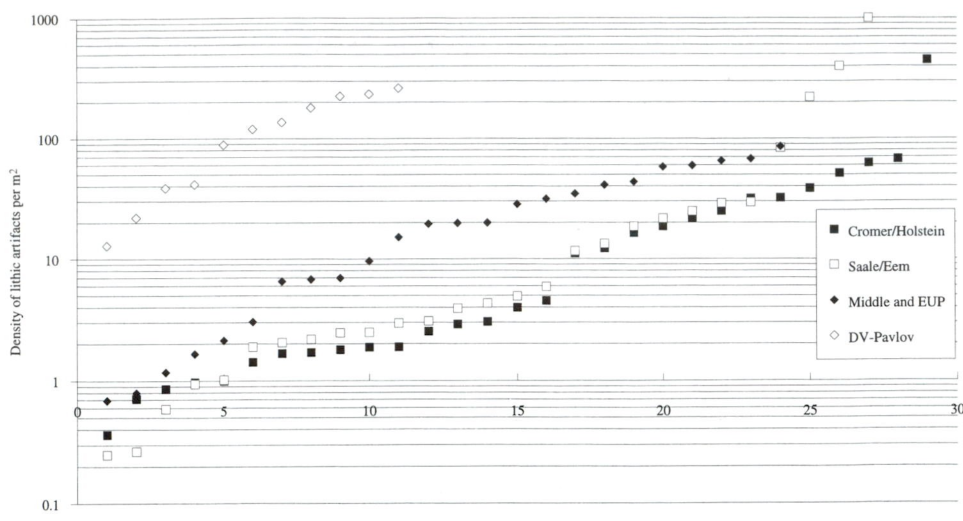


**7.13** A log density plot of lithic density per m$^2$ from open locales (data from Tables 4.19, 5.18, 7.10 and 7.11). A quantifiable increase can be seen through time as the largest locales in each period change from being gatherings to social occasions.

periods, and which included Early Upper Palaeolithic examples, produce densities greater than one hundred pieces per m$^2$.

Of the eleven samples from Dolní Věstonice-Pavlov, six register more than one hundred pieces per m$^2$ and none has a density of less than ten pieces per m$^2$ (Table 7.12).

Comparable densities are found in other Gravettian locales in the north-central region (Table 7.12). These emphasize quantifiable changes in the scale of open locales after 33 Kyr bp.

It is interesting to compare these locales with the major Gravettian assemblages in Germany, north-central region (Table 7.13), which mostly fall in Montet-White's ephemeral/medium group. As we saw with the Achtal data (Chapter 6), these small assemblages, often from caves, emphasize the infrequent use of a region which, during the Gravettian, became increasingly marginal as a corridor between the Scandinavian and Alpine ice sheets.

*Comparison by context: ritual and performance*

But lots of stones do not necessarily make a social occasion, a conclusion I reached for the Lower Palaeolithic (Chapter 4). Can the evidence from Dolní Věstonice-Pavlov be interpreted as anything other than repeated gatherings beside the Dyje river, comparable, say, to the late Middle Palaeolithic locale of Mauran (Chapter 6)?

I propose to examine this difference through two sets of rituals which are

Table 7.12. *Settlement hierarchy in Gravettian open locales from the north-central region (Montet-White 1988:362). These include settlements dating to both the Evolved Pavlovian and the Willendorf/Kostenki culture.*

| Character of settlement | Number of tools | Total stone | Locales |
|---|---|---|---|
| Ephemeral | 10–30 | 100–300 | |
| Medium | 200–1,000 | 1,000–10,000 | Spadzista, Pushkari, Kadar, Lubna, Petrkovice, Willendorf II 5–7 |
| Extensive | >1,000 | >10,000 | Předmostí, Willendorf II 9, Dolní Věstonice-Pavlov, Milovice |

Table 7.13. *Assemblage size for selected Gravettian locales in Germany (Bosinski et al. 1985:Abb. 56, Cziesla 1984).*

| Locale | Type | Number of tools | Total stone |
|---|---|---|---|
| Magdalena-Höhle | Cave | 10 | 115 |
| Wildscheuer IV | Cave | 40 | 180 |
| Bockstein-Törle VI | Cave | 71 | |
| Geißenklösterle 1a/b | Cave | 91 | |
| Brillenhöhle VI | Cave | 103 | |
| Sprendlingen | Open | 110 | 1,259 |
| Mainz-Linsenberg | Open | 114 | 775 |
| Weinberghöhlen | Cave | 331 | |
| Brillenhöhle VII | Cave | 409 | |

integral to the extension of action beyond the here and now. These are the rituals of attaching *to* and detaching *from* social gatherings. Such greetings and farewells would always have played a part in the creation of intimate and effective networks among hominids. They involved performances with gestures and routine sequences. The distinction for the Upper Palaeolithic is that now they involved other performances beyond the immediate attention of individuals. In other words people did not have to be present to participate and to influence action.

The reason for concentrating on the performances associated with these rituals is that they can be both mundane as well as special. They are part of those landscapes of habit where we experience our lives in a largely unthinking fashion. But they also involve punctuated events that mark those transitions which establish the patterns of social reproduction and resolve the ambiguities of much larger social cycles.

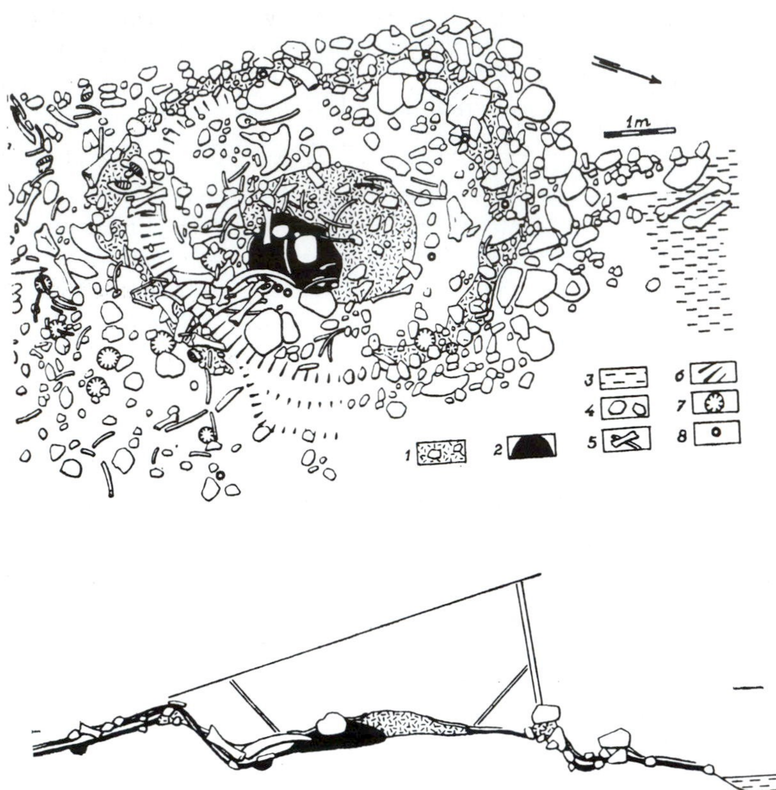


**7.14** A reconstruction of settlement object 2 found in 1951 at Dolní Věstonice I. This is sometimes known as the magician's hut and lies some way from the larger winter huts (after Klíma 1983:Fig. 30).
KEY:
1 Kiln
2 Charcoal
3 Ash
4 Limestone blocks
5 Bone
6 Edge of artificial depression
7 Post holes
8 Stake holes

The three performances I will discuss here relate to setting up home, playing with fire and saying goodbye to the dead.

*Setting up home*

The locale was marked by clearing the ground. Platforms 4–5 m in diameter were cut into the loess sediments producing a shallow semi-subterranean base. Post holes at Dolní Věstonice I suggest a covering (Figure 7.14). A hearth lies in the centre while large stones and bones mark the edge of the circular construction (Svoboda 1991:Fig. 26). Alternatively, a ring of selected mammoth bones was placed, as at Milovice, directly on the ground surface (Oliva 1988a:109) to form a space. Elsewhere at Dolní Věstonice II the size of the hearth in the third settlement unit, 3 m × 2 m with a thickness of 40 cm, points to several reoccupations. It was surrounded by scoops and holes, some of which probably carried posts for a small tent-like structure. The central '8'-shaped feature at Pavlov I, with four internal hearths, may in fact represent two small huts with two hearths apiece (Tomáskova 1994). The semi-subterranean feature is also well defined by the distribution of lithic and bone remains which are found outside rather than inside it.[20]

Setting up home therefore took a number of different forms. Firstly, there was the return to existing dwellings such as Milovice and Dolní Věstonice I where local materials had been used. These were either mammoth bones or wood from the pockets of spruce, pine and even some deciduous trees such as oak, lime, hornbeam and beech (Opravil 1994, Svobodova 1991) scattered in sheltered locations within the dominant forest-steppe vegetation.[21] These structures had permanence. They survived beyond the lifetime of a seasonal gathering either as permanently occupied dwellings for some years or, as seems most probable, as facilities to be reused on repeated visits to the Pavlovské hills. The small size of the various dwellings (Figure 7.14) suggests small households which repeatedly used this location. Occupation varied from several months to several days (Svoboda 1994d:75). The discovery of what has been tentatively identified as a plant food 'mush' for infants at Dolní Věstonice II (Mason, Hather and Hillman 1994:53) provides some pointer to the range of ages present.[22] Mixed age and sex is also indicated by the human remains scattered throughout the locale. A second style of homecoming involved the reuse of camping places. Poles for tents were carried to the locale with that purpose in mind.

In both examples there would have been repairs and reconstruction; making things function and performing the rituals of attaching to the place with its memories and people. This performance involved the use of local and distant materials; mammoth bones washed together by the Dyje and flint transferred from southern Poland to make stone tools. It included materials already fashioned into artifacts, such as tent poles and varied elements of a fibre technology as revealed by textile/basketry impressions and possibly nets preserved in burnt clay (Adovasio, Soffer and Klíma 1996, Soffer, Adovasio and Hyland 1997).[23] There were also other raw materials which were transformed at the locale. These included the local animals used for fur, food, tents and clothing (Musil 1994) as well as the Slovakian and Austrian radiolarites which were made into burins.

### *Style and cultural contexts*

These performances of renewal were part of the attaching ritual to the locale. They provided it with that sense of place as the gestures which were used both created and recreated its history and continuing significance for the people.

Style, the process which merges the locale with the region and which extends people beyond the landscape of habit and into the domain of the social landscape, was present in many forms. Part of the style of the attaching ritual lay in building and transforming. Another part had an older ancestry in hominid society since it involved artifacts and objects. Making and display, in the context of either killing or processing reindeer and fur-bearing animals such as arctic fox, wolf and glutton, were part of the process of reaffirming the social context of the locale. Negotiated style can be found in the shape of familiar, highly charged objects such as the ventrally retouched pointed blade which is found at Pavlov I, Predmostí and Willendorf II layers 5 and 8, but not in the Dolní Věstonice assemblages (Svoboda 1994d:75). Style can be traced in the similarity of more mundane-looking bone tools between Moravian sites such as Předmostí and Dolní Věstonice-Pavlov (Klíma 1994, Valoch 1982). It is therefore unsurprising that evidence for the long-distance transport of flint from southern Poland and radiolarite stone from Slovakia and Austria is very common (Svoboda 1994e:217, 1994d:71–2). These were more than just good raw materials. They were social objects in their own right. They derived meaning from the cultural context built up from many individual networks.

The style of objects at these social activities of building, greeting, killing animals and making things also presented an opportunity to pass on information (Gamble 1982). But it was what the objects symbolized rather than what they communicated visually that was important. They symbolized distant hunting grounds, future encounters and other social occasions both in the lifetime of an individual and in the history that had shaped them. The context which invested such objects with the force of individual agency resided in the social landscape where the act of doing was stretched and extended across time and space.

*Playing with fire*

People were now structured by what they did, what they brought to a locale and how they performed. There was attention to the role of objects as independent agents structuring action, while in previous eras it had been attention only to other people. This change allowed attachment to social occasions and gatherings through the resources of the extended network. Previously, attaching to gatherings had been negotiated solely through the resources of the intimate and effective networks (Table 2.8) as at Bilzingsleben (Chapter 4) and Maastricht-Belvédère (Chapter 5).

But underlying all these networks is the notion that technical acts are also social acts. Making a stone tool is not just about meeting a functional requirement. It is also about the involvement of the knapper in a wider world of negotiation and creation and where the body acts as a reference for power and meaning.

In previous chapters I have elaborated upon a model of transferable skills where the landscape of habit provides a framework to examine them. At Dolní

Věstonice-Pavlov the case can be made for these same skills as well as for place-specific skills – knowledge that is only relevant to that locale through a combination of physical resources and the social context for its production. The chaîne opératoire associated with the use of loess in pyrotechnic displays provides an example.

The many thousands of clay pellets and figurine fragments (Table 7.9) have already been mentioned as one of the hallmarks of Dolní Věstonice I and Pavlov I (Klíma 1983). Elsewhere at the locale they are very rare, while fewer than ten pieces are known from other evolved Pavlovian locales in Moravia. Vandiver (et al. 1989:1007) describe it as a 'precocious Upper Palaeolithic soft stone technology'. But it is noteworthy that the vast majority of the figurines are fragmentary (Soffer and Vandiver 1994:172).

This observation led Vandiver (Soffer et al. 1993, Vandiver et al. 1989) to reconsider the entire process by examining the technological skills which were involved. They analysed the ceramic properties of the local loess from which the figures were roughly modelled. Their most important finding was that the loess at the two locales was suitable for firing in kilns. But unexpectedly they found evidence on many pieces of thermal shock – an explosive reaction which shatters clay when it is being fired. This could not be achieved with the local loesses unless the normal process of firing was changed (Vandiver et al. 1989:1007). Thermal shocking was therefore intentional – something a modern potter would not contemplate. We can conclude that it was a recognized skill where the process of making and firing was the most important activity rather than achieving a durable final product.[24] It was the way the clay models exploded in the two kilns excavated at Dolní Věstonice I that mattered and not their future as long-lasting images (Figure 7.15). Perhaps the analogy is with a firework which may look very impressive as a rocket but its significance is as an exploding, temporary star-burst in the night sky.

Therefore these were not Pavlovian Leonardo da Vincis, stumbling across pottery manufacture many millennia before it was required. Rather they were utilizing the properties of the loess as an active agent in a performance (Soffer et al. 1993:272). Soffer and Vandiver (1994) also note that the suitability of the loess differs between Dolní Věstonice I and Pavlov I, 500 m apart, which suggests very place-specific skills. This was reflected in the location of the pyrotechnic displays. At Dolní Věstonice I the kiln was 70 m away from the main concentration, while at Pavlov I it lay within the settlement area.

We may not be able to reconstruct who among the population of infants, children and adults was most involved, but we can point to the skills level and its association with a place. The act of making and firing these clay pellets and figurines could be for entertainment of young and old alike or, as Klíma originally suggested (1963), indicative of a religious purpose. What it involved was building a special feature (Figure 7.15), fuelling it and watching its contents explode. The dominant animal imagery in the shattered figurines may not be an expression of hunting magic but equally an affirmation of the renewability of

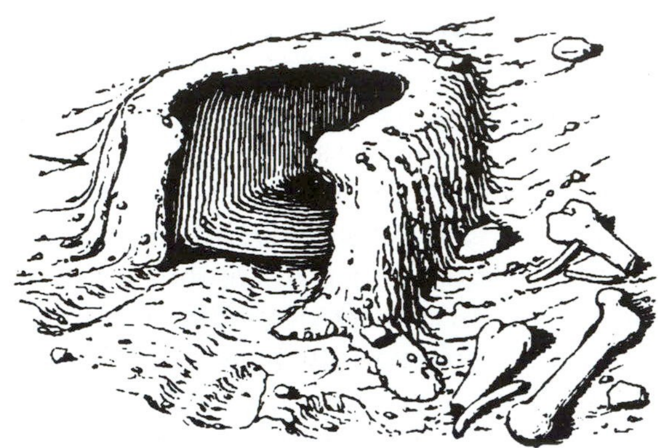

**7.15** Two kilns from Dolní Věstonice I. The upper was found within object 2 (Figure 7.14) and more than 2,300 fired clay pieces were found within it. The lower was found in 1978, 40 m to the west. It is one metre in diameter, dug to a depth of 60 cm and surrounded by a horeshoe-shaped clay wall. It also contained fired clay figurine fragments (after Valoch 1996:Fig. 64; Soffer et al. 1993).

resources which were as unlimited as the loess in that place. It seems unlikely that people went to the locale just to watch clay explode. But it is very possible that it formed one of the memories of that place when they were far away from the other people who also watched the pyrotechnics.

*Goodbye to the dead*

Burial provides an extreme case of a detaching ritual. We saw in Chapter 6 that the evidence for Neanderthal burial had the sense of an *adieu* rather than an *au revoir*. The latter might be expected with a true detaching ritual since it implies meeting again in some other context. Such detaching, while admittedly extreme, nonetheless allows us to examine a major difference in the use of locales, with Dolní Věstonice-Pavlov providing a further example of the place as social occasion.

The Gravettian is the key period for the study of Upper Palaeolithic burials in Europe. Apart from the pseudo-morph at Cueva Morín in Cantabria (Freeman and González-Echegaray 1970) there is a lack of burials with early Aurignacian artifacts.[25] In Europe complete skeletons older than 30 Kyr are, with the possible exception of Combe-Capelle in France, exclusively

Neanderthal (Quéchon 1976). After this date the picture changes dramatically. Burials in open sites are found for the first time. Multiple burials are known of which the largest is the 'mass grave' at Předmostí (Svoboda 1994a, Svoboda et al. 1994) where up to twenty individuals, eight adults and twelve children, were found by Maska in 1894 (Absolon and Klíma 1977, Valoch 1996:Fig. 121).[26] The Pavlovian at this very rich multi-period site was later C14 dated to 26.8 and 26.3 Kyr BP.

Another Pavlovian-age burial was found in 1891 in the Moravian city of Brno.[27] It consisted of a male skeleton with a complex array of grave goods (Jelínek, Pelísek and Valoch 1959, Valoch 1996:144–5). These included a mammoth scapula, tusks, horse teeth and the ribs and skull of a woolly rhino. There were also more than 600 Dentalium shells as well as two large perforated stone discs and fourteen smaller discs carved in a variety of raw materials (Jelínek, Pelísek and Valoch 1959:Taf. II and III). In amongst these items were three carved ivory pieces, the head, body and left arm of a marionette (Figure 7.16). The head and body together measure 20.3 cm in length and the thread holes for the strings to attach the legs to the body are visible (Jelínek, Pelísek and Valoch 1959:Taf. IV).

Double burials from this period have been found more widely and include the two children laid head to head in a grave among settlement debris at Sunghir, northeast of Moscow (Bader 1967, Bader 1978). These are associated with ivory beads sewn onto caps and clothing as well as with figurines and ivory spears. Similar decorated clothing is common in the burials from the Grimaldi caves situated on the border between France and Italy on the Ligurian coast (Figure 7.17).

The documentation and dating of the Ligurian burials is not good but even so they point to a recognizable tradition of Gravettian burial albeit in a cave rather than an open context (Mussi 1986a, 1986b, 1988, 1992, Zampetti and Mussi 1991). This applies to single and double burials (Table 7.14) as well as to the triple burial at Barma Grande. Mussi (1986b:548–9) summarizes a typical Gravettian burial in these caves as an adult male or adolescent, lying in an extended position on their back or side and placed in an inner part of the cave, close to the wall. The internment followed the axis of the cave with the skull lying on the left and oriented mostly to the east. Graves were always dug and sometimes stones were used to protect the corpse. Ochre, personal ornaments and selected bone and flint implements were placed as grave goods.

The Dolní Věstonice-Pavlov material forms a comparable local tradition of open-air burials which are characterized by

- repeated use of a locale for burial
- multiple burials
- extensive use of ochre, ornament and clothing

Up to 1995 some thirty-four individuals ranging from isolated finds to complete bodies have been found at Dolní Věstonice (Klíma 1995). A further three

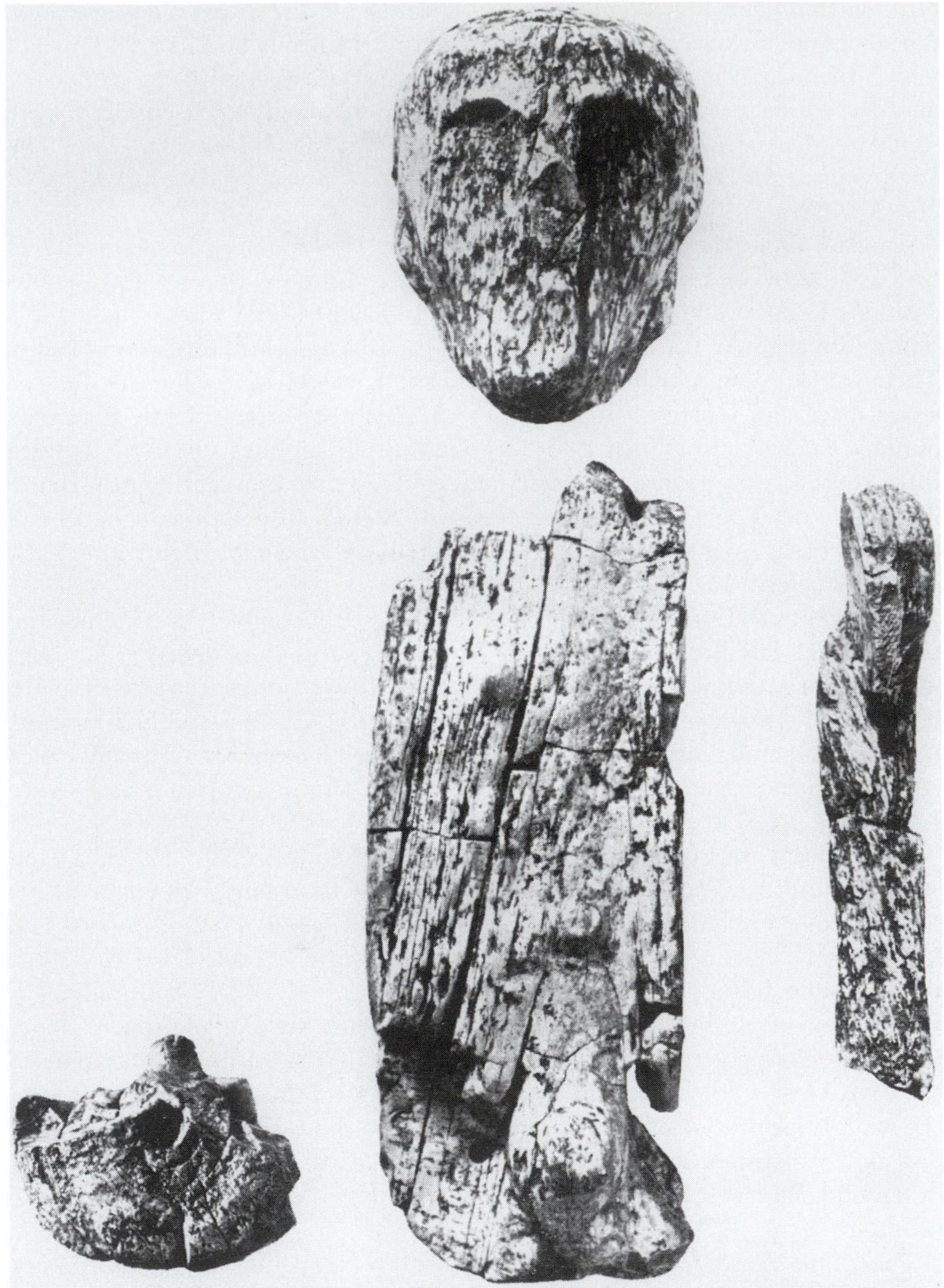

**7.16** The three pieces of the ivory marionette from Brno, Czech Republic, NC region. The string hole drilled into the base of the trunk is shown at the bottom left (after Jelínek et al. 1959:Tafel IV).

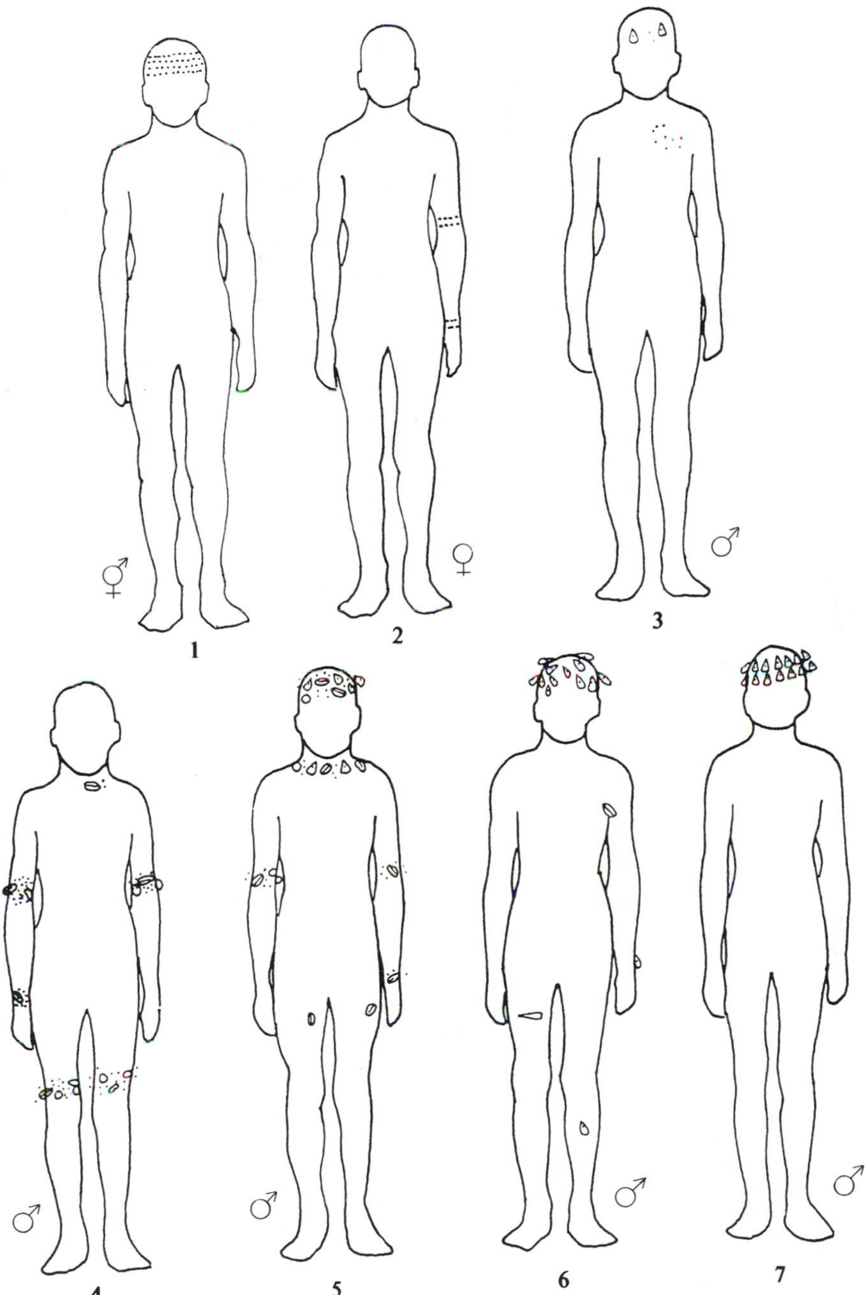


**7.17** The positioning of ornaments and worked bone found in selected Gravettian burials from Grimaldi and elsewhere in Italy, MC region (after Zampetti and Mussi 1991:Fig. 2).
Key:
1–2 Grotte des Enfants, double burial 6 & 5
3 Grotte des Enfants 4
4 Baousso da Torre 1
5 Baousso da Torre 2
6 Grotta Paglicci
7 Grotta delle Veneri

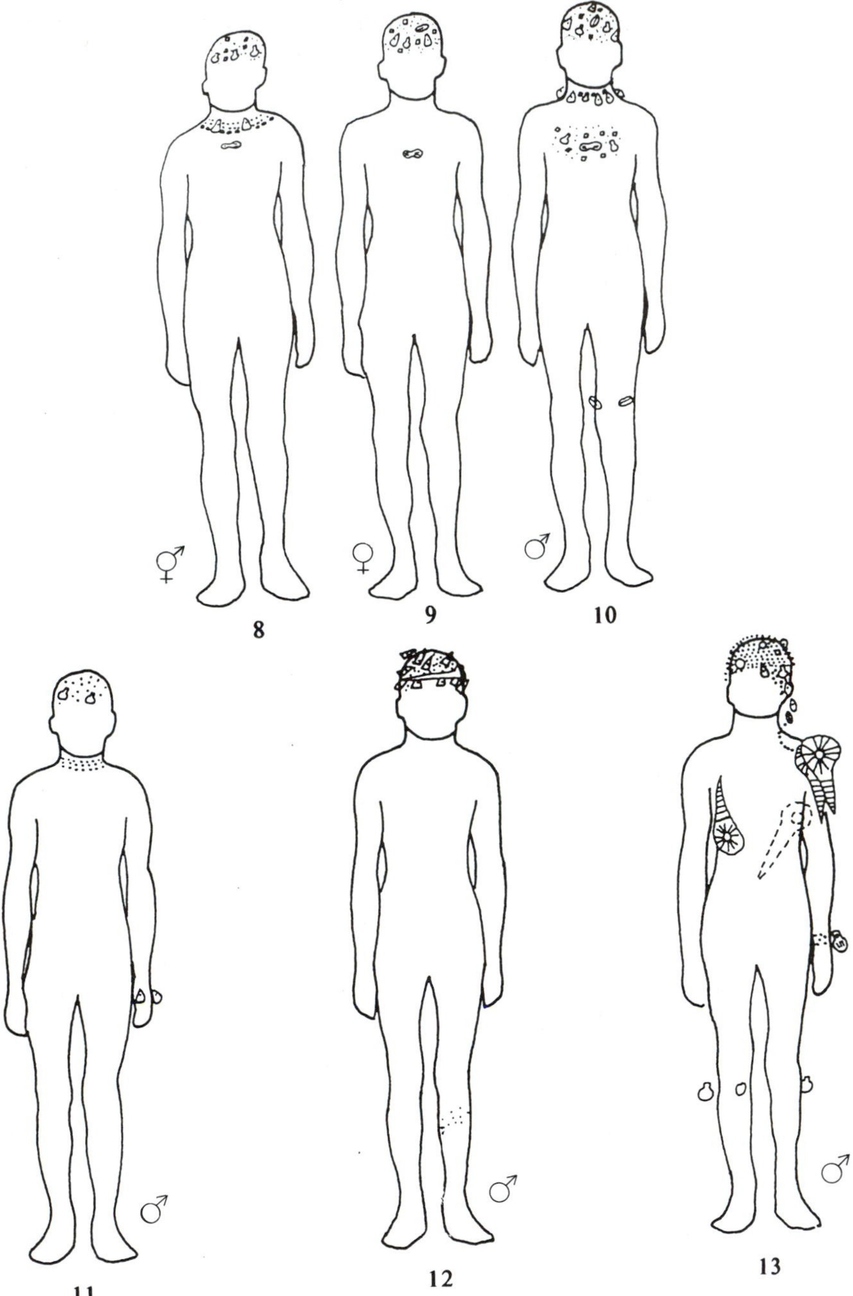


**7.17** (*cont.*) The positioning of ornaments and worked bone found in selected Gravettian burials from Grimaldi and elsewhere in Italy, MC region (after Zampetti and Mussi 1991:Fig. 2).

8–10 Barma Grande, triple burial 4, 3 & 2

11 Barma Grande 5

12 Grotta del Caviglione 1

13 Grotta delle Arene Candide 1

Table 7.14. *The Gravettian–early Epi-Gravettian-age burials (25–18 Kyr bp) at the Grimaldi caves, Balzi Rossi, in Liguria (Mussi 1986a, 1986b, Oakley, Campbell and Molleson 1971). The double child burial in Grotte des Enfants is dated to after 14 Kyr bp (Mussi 1986a:95–6).*

| | | |
|---|---|---|
| Grotte des Enfants=Grotta dei Fanciulli | | |
| 4 | Single burial | Adult male |
| 5, 6 | Double burial | Old female, adolescent male/female |
| Grotte du Cavillon=Grotta del Caviglione | | |
| 1 | Single burial | Adult male |
| Barma Grande | | |
| 1 | Single burial | Adult male |
| 2,3,4 | Triple burial | Adult male, adolescent female, adolescent male/female |
| 5 | Single burial | Adult male |
| 6 | Single burial | Adult male (partially cremated) |
| Baousso da Torre | | |
| 1 | Single burial | Adult male |
| 2 | Single burial | Adult male |
| 3 | Single burial | Adolescent male |

major finds are known from Pavlov (Oakley, Campbell and Molleson 1971, Valoch 1996). Six of these finds are complete bodies (Table 7.9). The three single burials are all adults. The small gracile female, Dolní Věstonice III, is very tightly flexed and was probably bound (Klíma 1963, Trinkaus and Jelínek 1997).[28] The legs of Dolní Věstonice XVI are less firmly flexed but still appear to have been bound (Figure 7.18). The female, DV III, lay under several mammoth scapulae, one with cut marks (Klíma 1963:Fig. 60), as did the poorly reported male burial, Pavlov I (Valoch 1996:Fig. 126). The male, DV XVI, faced the hearth, the same one which preserved the infant's acorn mush, with his knees 20cm from its edge. The skeletons are described as robust individuals with healed traumas on their skulls and well-worn dentition.

The triple burial lay, like Dolní Věstonice XVI, in a very shallow depression rather than a grave. It is reasonably certain that the two outside individuals are adolescent males. The sex of the central person, DV XV, is less clear due to a number of pathologies (Klíma 1988:834). These included scoliosis of the spine with marked left curvature and a deformed right femur. She/he would have limped on their right leg. The outside individuals have ivory and carnivore canine pendants. The bodies lay in different positions: face up (Dolní Věstonice XV), face down (Dolní Věstonice XIV), and with both arms extended (Dolní Věstonice XIII) to touch the central person, Dolní Věstonice XV (Figure 7.19). All three heads were covered in ochre as was the pelvic area of the central body. Plenty of charcoal was found in the grave pit suggesting that the bodies had been covered by branches, set alight and then quickly covered by earth to extinguish the fire since the bones were not burnt (Figure 7.20).

**7.18** Burial DV XVI excavated at Dolní Věstonice II western slope. The hearth lies at the centre of a small depression interpreted as a hut platform (after Svoboda 1991:Fig. 6).
Key:
A Shallow artificial depression with charcoal, small animal bones and artifactual debris including ochre and two *Dentalia* shells
B & C Clusters of lithics and bones
D Hearth, with bowl-shaped base, consisting of charcoal, burnt loess and many limestone blocks. Lying across it is a large animal rib and carbonized plant food was found in it.
E Hollowed pit containing bones of large and small animals, a pierced tooth, six *Dentalia* shells, ochre, bone and stone tools

In the immediate area of the grave pit two fragments of a small limestone rod with notational markings were found (Emmerling, Geer and Klíma 1993, Klíma 1995). The reconstruction proposes twenty-nine marks which are interpreted as the notations for a lunar calendar month.[29] These are grouped in units of 5, 7, 7, 5 and 5 which, if correct, would reflect changes in the moon's brightness as it goes through its waxing and waning cycle (Marshack 1972), a tangible example of measured performance.

The isolated human remains at Dolní Věstonice II show a strong linear patterning (Klíma 1995:Abb. 91). Seven finds, including two partial crania, extend north from the triple burial in the western part of the excavation. A line of small hearths and pits also follows the same orientation (Klíma 1995:Abb. 33). At Předmostí, where cut-marked mammoth scapulae covered the bodies in the 'mass grave', Maska remarked that

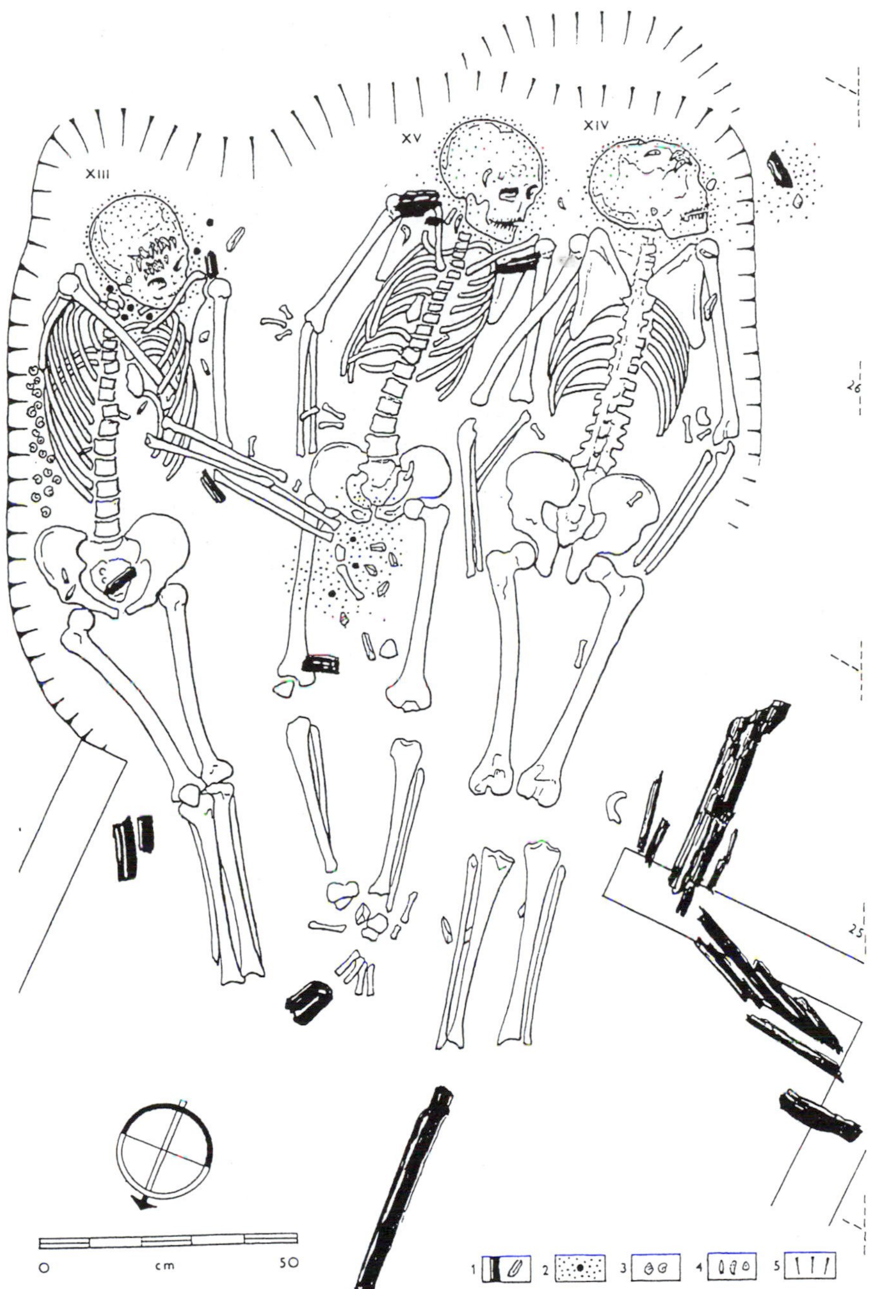


**7.19** The triple burial from Dolní Věstonice II containing skeletons DV XIII, XV and XIV (after Klíma 1995:Abb. 76).
KEY:
1 Burnt wood and stone tools
2 Spreads and small pieces of red ochre
3 Shell ornaments
4 Human and pierced animal teeth, ivory beads
5 Edge of depression

**7.20** The triple burial from Dolní Věstonice II. In the foreground is skeleton DV XIII (Photo J. Svoboda).

an important circumstance should be mentioned: single human bones continued quite frequently to the south and SE, outside the grave, together with mammoth, reindeer and fox bones. (quoted in Svoboda et al. 1994:459)

At Dolní Věstonice II similar deposits of animal bones including paws and lower legs of wolf and large slabs of mammoth bones were also found leading away from the triple burial (Klíma 1995:65).

### *Dolní Věstonice-Pavlov: the social occasion and the place*

These examples of attaching and detaching rituals helped create the Dolní Věstonice-Pavlov locale as a place. This was achieved through people's varied involvement and experiences with that locale as a social occasion rather than simply as a gathering or encounter (Table 3.1).

But what, you may ask, allows us to identify this archaeological evidence as a social occasion? The answer is straightforward. Social occasions can only be investigated within the wider context of regional behaviour, here presented as a social landscape for organizing action and providing meaning to life by involvement with the world (Ingold 1993:155). The social occasion would not exist as a context for action if networks never extended beyond the intimate (Table 2.8). Neither would they have much impact if only the effective level was reached. At both these levels the attention and interaction supported by gatherings and encounters would be entirely sufficient for social life. It is the extension of social life through system integration (Chapter 2) and in particular its externalization in objects that marks the difference. It is therefore no surprise that the elaboration of evidence, which I have reviewed here for regional interaction, is matched at locales such as Dolní Věstonice-Pavlov by specific evidence for attaching and detaching rituals. Moreover, the stay at the locale involved at least one further heightened experience – the performance of exploding life – which fixed the place in the memories and minds of those who created and lived in it.

Let me continue this line of argument by returning to one of the central ideas in this book – that social life is negotiated and varies according to the resources – affective, material and symbolic – which individuals can mobilize to create their surrounding environment (Chapter 2). The activities of attending and attention are essential to such an interaction model and in the earlier periods these aspects were both weakly developed and poorly preserved. The evidence mostly amounts to knapping stone and making wooden artifacts. Skills were transferable and non-specific from locale to locale within a regional framework of landscapes of habit.

Now consider the evidence for attention and attending, those rhythms of the taskscape, at Dolní Věstonice-Pavlov. Not only do we have a vivid example with the hissing, spitting, exploding clay creatures, but we also have in fireplaces and ochre two further sources of evidence for attention during interaction.[30] These two elements are linked at Dolní Věstonice-Pavlov. The flexed male burial DV XVI lies facing a hearth, while the triple burial contains charcoal, probably from a burnt covering of branches. The heads of all four individuals in these two burials are heavily ochred. Attention is being drawn to the face, the focus for interaction, greeting and recognition and with spoken language the prime source of negotiation. Moreover, the association with fire draws the social occasion into the domestic setting of the household, one social/spatial context for the negotiation and performance of bonds in the intimate and effective networks.

It is assumed that the bodies of DV XVI and DV XV were clothed and these corpses had ochre plastered over their pelvic areas (Svoboda and Dvorsky 1994:74–5). Drawing attention to the head and the groin of the dead with blood red pigment in this detaching ritual echoed the archaeologically invisible attaching ritual of birth and blood. Arrival and departure, attaching and detaching to social life, had a shared symbolism. These rituals partitioned the temporal continuum. Cultural significance was drawn from the context and from the temporality of action devoted to attention. People were attending to each other and thereby making the activity social (Ingold 1993:159–60).

With this perspective we can see that ochreing the groin area was not a simple signal about sex or gender. By deliberately setting the bodies in fixed positions and selectively daubing them, the living were instead emphasizing temporal continuity but acknowledging its inevitable partitions. These disruptions were seen in terms of arrivals and departures from social life. The Dolní Věstonice-Pavlov burials were rituals of detachment from an enduring social occasion. As such they indeed had the character of an *au revoir* rather than an *adieu* because they affirmed the seamless continuity of the place as lived experience. The dead, as ancestors, now formed part of the extended network of the living.

The repeated act of digging at Dolní Věstonice-Pavlov is further evidence for the character of the rituals of attaching and detaching associated with this place. Ochre had to be dug from the ground. Digging was also the primary rhythm, the sequence of gestures in a chaîne opératoire (Leroi-Gourhan 1993:309), which created the forms of the hut platforms and the shallow graves, as well as obtaining the loess for the pyrotechnic performances.

The earth was permanently frozen below a certain depth which, judging by the hut floor, might have been around 80 cm.[31] Here was a physical, cold limit to their world. The boundary contrasted with the surface where action occurred as people attended to each other, where fire transformed materials and built structures kept out the elements. Fire released the properties in materials and transformed them, through manufacture, into social objects. The isolated bones, testament to the power of the body as a culturally significant object, lie scattered across the spaces of daily life. Individuals, alive or dead, may have been remote in time and place but they were not forgotten.

Corpses were also materials to be turned into objects. In life the attention to the face and the transformation of the body into a cultural object occurred by decking it with pendants, clothes and tools. We can also trace the attention to all these social objects by studying recurrent details. For example, the constricting belt that cuts into the hips of the clay figurines from Dolní Věstonice is echoed in the bindings of the bodies, male and female, in the single burials.

Finally, the archaeological evidence for the social occasion at this locale deals with values of protection and preservation. The mammoth scapulae placed over the bodies of P I and DV III, as well as the brushwood covering on the triple burial, are examples of protection. DV XVI has the protection of the hearth and DV XV the gesture of the extended arms of DV XIII. The preservation of the person as an object created by gestures and rhythms is assured. The temporality of this place was expressed in the rituals of continuity, with the resources of the locale and with the 'looking beyond' to the landscape and the region. The elision between absence and distance and the expression of the extended network that has no practical limits is well demonstrated beneath the shelter of the enduring Pavlovské hills.

## Summary

The regions and locales of Upper Palaeolithic Europe were constructed differently to those which went before. The rhythms which linked action from the micro to the macro scale now drew on symbolic as well as material and emotional resources to create and channel agency. In this chapter I have examined the evidence for the existence of a personal network incorporating intimate, effective and extended networks (Table 2.8). The locale and region have been examined through the concepts of the social occasion and social landscape. In practice these terms are inseparable and form an unbroken stream of human action that results in the definition of locales as places (Table 3.1).

But while the framework of social occasion/social landscape is new, the linking rhythms between the micro and macro scales remain the same. These are the chaîne opératoire with its sequences of gestures and routinized habits, the paths and tracks which link individuals to each other and to locales, and the taskscape where attention by individuals to one another makes interaction culturally meaningful.

What has changed with the Upper Palaeolithic are the societies which these rhythms produce. The objects and artifacts used in the performance of social life now have an existence independent from the bodies of the people who made and used them. These same artifacts now represent gestures which continue to live even though they are no longer animated by use or direct association with an individual. In the Lower and Middle Palaeolithic they contributed to the social integration of performance and people through face-to-face contact. For the first time they now serve the more complicated role of system integration beyond face-to-face interaction. Those moments which the objects define, those social occasions and places where the performance of life takes place, now influence individual agency. They emphasize a different order of temporality in the creative power of individuals and the constraints imposed by wider structures.

I have argued in this chapter that such symbolic involvement between the locale and region occurred, for the first time, in the Upper Palaeolithic. The extended network became a source of power and, through the global counterpart to this novel personal network, such categories as the 'other' were defined. Previously the scale of hominid society was limited by the effective network, with its scale predicated on the use of material resources. Life in such societies was local and based on the principle of social exclusion. The emphasis on material and emotional resources meant that individuals created their social lives from immediate resources. They traversed their landscapes of habit, which had well-known temporal rhythms of renewal.

What we have seen in this chapter is the evidence for both social and system integration which goes well beyond the social universe that can be defined by an effective network with its emphasis on gatherings and landscapes of habit. I have examined in a series of regional case studies the difference which emerges between Neanderthals and Crô-Magnons when we look at the evidence for their co-existence. One consequence of these differences was the varied regional histories and the structure of power which these imply.

In this sense power means nothing more than the greater involvement between people and the ever-present resources of their surrounding environment. Once such involvement was current then the opportunities for cultural diversity as those social landscapes and places are reinterpreted and recreated were immense. Power in this sense was the opportunity for exploring the potential of such diversity and harnessing it to individual social projects. Life was no longer simply local but could now be both exclusive and inclusive in terms of access to and closure of new and existing relationships (Table 1.2).

At the level of the locale, the social occasion of Dolní Věstonice-Pavlov displays very different skills to those seen previously in such gatherings as Bilzingsleben (Chapter 4) and Maastricht-Belvédère (Chapter 5). In particular, at Dolní Věstonice-Pavlov place-specific skills are manifest in the creation of structures, not only for the rituals of attaching and detaching from the locale but also, in the case of the kilns, for the rituals which made the performance of living there memorable. Like all skills, generic or specific, these were social. However, in accordance with the extended network and the system integration this allowed, these skills now drew on symbolic as well as material and emotional resources to achieve that release from proximity (Chapter 2).

Social life, as a result, was now truly complicated rather than simply complex as discussed in Chapter 2. This does not mean that earlier periods lacked power in their social networks. It is instead the case that the structure from which power was derived differed in significant respects. Among these the ability to externalize memory through the ascription of power to objects remains the most telling. Since power resides in acts of association and in attending to other individuals, this ability to transfer such contexts symbolically created a personal network which now included people and objects. The surrounding environment in the Upper Palaeolithic was now richly layered with meaning and symbolically linked. Social occasions with rituals and resources now structured the seemingly unfettered life of the Palaeolithic person.

CHAPTER 8

# THE PALAEOLITHIC SOCIETIES OF EUROPE

Human history is created by intentional activities
but is not an intended project

Anthony Giddens
*The Constitution of Society*

Under the paving stones – the beach

Student slogan
*Paris, May 1968*

I have now reviewed the evidence for social life during the Palaeolithic period in Europe. I am conscious that the continent I have drawn the data from, and the time frame of 500,000 to 21,000 years ago, are to some extent the filling in the sandwich of human evolution. I have omitted early social evolution in Africa and stopped at the last glacial maximum after which the data increase geometrically in quantity. Moreover, on a Palaeolithic timescale it is a short step from there to plant and animal domestication and further exponential changes in human affairs.

It has not however been my intention to present an overview of social evolution. My main concern has been to demonstrate how Childe's judgement, still widely followed, that the reconstruction of Palaeolithic social life is doomed by the data was incorrect (1951:85). While Palaeolithic data have never been helpful in the way that pyramids, palaces, ball-courts and granaries most definitely have been to the social archaeologist working in later periods, it is not the evidence which is at fault. We have always had, relative to the knowledge of the times, high-quality and often well-dated evidence for all periods of the Palaeolithic and particularly from Europe. These data have always been available to examine intra- and inter-regional variation, which has been a rewarding framework for writing social narratives about the Minoans or the Romans. We now have more Palaeolithic data than fifty years ago but so, by comparison, does every other period. If we blame the data for the difficulties of investigating Palaeolithic society then we will always be running to catch up.

It has been my aim in the preceding chapters to show that it has been the way we approach the investigation of Palaeolithic society that has doomed such projects to failure. I deliberately stopped the analysis at 21,000 bp because at that point it does get easier in a pyramids and ball-courts sort of way. For a start there are many more data from all regions of Europe. The timescales are short and we can examine in detail questions of recolonization (Housley et al. 1997) and compare it, for example, to the wave of advance among later farmers (van Andel and Runnels 1995). There is, apparently, abundant cave and mobiliary art as well as more burials leading to the later cemeteries of the early Mesolithic (Whittle 1996). The transition from studying ecological adaptations to reconstructing social relations is smooth. Several global overviews bear out this point (Gamble and Soffer 1990, Soffer and Gamble 1990, Straus et al. 1996, Zvelebil 1986). But none of these Late Glacial advantages must deflect us from the possibility of investigating much earlier Palaeolithic societies. We should not judge the exercise as doomed because of the expectations of a social archaeology worked out with later, more varied materials.

My point, however, is more fundamental for the pursuit of a social archaeology. If, as I have argued here, we need to recast the way we approach the reconstruction and understanding of society in the Palaeolithic, then we must necessarily rethink many of the assumptions and approaches to social archaeology in the more recent periods. This has already been done in a number of post-processual critiques (Hodder 1990, Thomas 1991, Tilley 1996). By adding the Palaeolithic to such agendas there can be no turning back to the days of social typologies and evolutionist accounts (e.g. Johnson and Earle 1987). I hope that by bringing the Palaeolithic into such discussions we will now find many new things to do with our painstakingly collected data than just talking about calories and tool maintenance. I also hope that we will move beyond social reconstruction as merely an assertion of what must have gone on during rituals around open graves, against cave walls and in our ancestors' heads. In other words, we will move beyond the idea that their social life only resided in the space between meals.

What follows is intended as my personal summary of the issues which can now be investigated. Here is a framework for new research with data that, while theory laden, are still the assets for writing more interesting stories. The task which faces us will not just be composing those narratives but also verifying them.

### *The starting point*

Wilson stated one of the ground rules for studying Palaeolithic society:

> we must imagine *H. erectus* or early *sapiens* not so much as a blank upon which any and all impressions can fall, but as a creature of immense but inchoate promise and potential, whose problem is to devise from his capacities the instruments and means to create specific modes of organisation that will enable survival. (Wilson 1980:41)

The individual is presented to us as a creative but constrained agent rather than a hominid cipher pre-programmed to produce *Homo heidelbergensis* society. Wilson goes on to argue that the challenge which faces us is not the detailed reconstruction of social forms. It is instead deciding upon the general principle that made it possible for our ancestors to construct the varieties of social life comparable to our individual experience of the complex business of living (*ibid.*:54).

The generalized principle I have pursued came from studies of both primate and modern societies. I returned to the individual rather than the group as the object of society and based social life upon the opportunities and rules which stem from interaction. I have stressed how it is involvement with the world and with others, summed up by the concept of agency, which marks this distinction. This removes the goal of searching for the material remains of social institutions such as rank, religion, economies or bureaucracy. Instead we must examine the acts which arise from co-presence, the varied performances which are possible when the body is the prime form of social communication and power. We can also examine the changing role of artifacts and culture in such performances, especially when objects and other animals take on the traits of people. This extension of social behaviour results in the 'release from proximity' (Giddens 1984:35, Rodseth et al. 1991:240) which is identified as the hallmark of human social evolution.

Rules and resources can be measured and predicted. Patterned outcomes result from interaction. These concern the use of different resources – emotional, material and symbolic – to create bonds of distinct intensity and importance in an individual's varied networks. The outcomes from such a bottom-up approach to social structure can be seen in the recurrent demographic patterns that emerge.

### *The methods*

But the individual has always been regarded as a shadowy creature lost in the long corridors of Palaeolithic time. This view, expressed to me on many occasions, still strikes me as strange since it runs counter to our Palaeolithic data. There is more contact with the micro-scale world of individual action in the Palaeolithic than there is with the invisible face in the crowd at the Roman Colosseum. Why do we bother to piece-plot thousands of artifacts at Lower Palaeolithic excavations such as Boxgrove if we do not think we can get closer to individual action? Roe was right when he described such events as precious moments in time (1981:197). If we want to investigate Palaeolithic society through individual and group action we can devise methodologies which tack repeatedly between such fine-grained scales to the wider contexts of space and time where the data are often coarser (Figure 3.2). But even without such well preserved, freeze-frame moments, 'the fact that prehistorians cannot identify individuals is no reason why they should ignore their existence' (Clark 1957:248).

The methods need to bridge the micro and macro scales of human social life and social history. The middle-range theory advocated here has adopted the insights of Leroi-Gourhan (1993), who was particularly concerned to apply ethnological approaches to archaeological contexts. The body as a source of action and a reference for power lies at the heart of his analysis. The body produces patterns through movement and gestures applied to materials. It creates, but it is also limited by physical constraints. The link between the locale and the region, the micro and macro scale of social activity, is based on rhythms involving performance and gesture. The key point which I have emphasized continually is that technical acts are at the same time social acts. It is involvement with the world rather than analysis of the world which marks this out.

Hence I have preferred a phenomenological definition of culture in this book. The emphasis has been on the active engagement of people with their environment rather than the enhanced linkages between mental modules that a cognitive, or classificatory, view of culture requires (Mithen 1996, Parker and Milbrath 1993). In deciding on this emphasis I followed Dennett's view that 'the trouble with brains is that when you look in them, you discover that there's nobody home' (1991:29). Brains need to be put into a context of action if we are to understand the changes and selection they underwent. They cannot be the main object of study by themselves if we are to avoid falling into a circular argument to explain social and cultural change. That context can only be supplied by the creation of social life where brains are a part of the whole organism and its surrounding environment. They are not in the driving seat plotting their own destiny. It is for these reasons that I have distinguished culture from society. Culture is an expression of that active engagement. It structures the social processing of information through activities that involve rhythms and gestures which encompass other people and materials. This processing is not necessarily linguistic. Nor is it solely recorded in the style of artifacts. Instead it is an outcome of attention, perception and movement without which social life does not exist.

This approach identifies two areas where we have hardly begun to investigate Palaeolithic culture, learning and memory. These involve the cultural transmission of information about how to act and how to control the body during the performance of social life. Currently a strong tradition exists which accounts analytically for change in the Palaeolithic. Here the emphasis is more on training the mind to anticipate problems and to use culture as a means to solve problems in a game against the environment.

For example, the important discussions over planning depth by Binford (1989:19) focused attention on the differences in organization between Neanderthals and Crô-Magnons. This concept deals with variation in the amount of time and technological investment between anticipatory behaviour and the actions it facilitates. The outcome points to greater planning depth among Crô-Magnons who had more complex and varied tools 'designed for use in directly coping with the environment' (*ibid.*:21).

I now see this transition differently (Gamble 1995b). Planning depth and anticipation are concepts which depend upon detachment from the world. Life becomes compartmentalized for understandable analytical purposes. Specific behaviours emerge and the individual starts to fade into the murk of an imposed institutional-like framework.

Clark was well aware of this danger when he reminded us that human foresight does not imply that every time we engage in activities directed to our future well-being we display this valuable quality. Instead 'our planning is as social as our sharing of memories' (1989:431). Using the vocabulary of this book, we are engaged with the world and evolve within its social networks rather than outside them. Thus, Clark's view about learning and memory as applied to anticipation and planning sits more comfortably with the perspective from a less analytical tradition, here described by Brody living among Athabaskan hunters:

> To make a good, wise sensible hunting choice is to accept the interconnection of all possible factors, and avoids the mistake of seeking rationally to focus on any one consideration that is held as primary. What is more, the decision is taken in the doing: there is no step or pause between theory and practice . . . Planning as other cultures understand the notion, is at odds with this kind of sensitivity and would confound such flexibility. The hunter, alive to constant movements of nature, spirits, and human moods, maintains a way of doing things that repudiates a firm plan and any precise or specified understanding with others of what he is going to do. (1981:37)

The course of action cannot therefore be predetermined since activity itself undermines any so-called plans. It is for these reasons that, as well as using the rhythms of the chaîne opératoire and paths and tracks, I have also developed Ingold's notion of the taskscape. This concept of a mutual environment which surrounds individuals as they go about the business of living allows us to break out of the way of thinking that in the Palaeolithic all people did was adapt to the environment. These games against the environment, as McGlade (1995:115–16) has commented, place nature out there and so relegate the role of the social to specialists other than archaeologists. The taskscape with its emphasis on continual action and attention to others removes this unhelpful dichotomy. It still allows for selection on action but it also allows for that creature of immense but inchoate promise and potential.

### *The earliest Palaeolithic societies in Europe: 500,000± to 300,000 years ago*

Europe was colonized late. The exact date is disputed but at some time between one and half a million years ago hominids are found in regions along the north Mediterranean and throughout all but the northeastern parts of the continent. The archaeological record changes very significantly after 500,000 years ago. This suggests that there is still a great deal to be discovered about the process of early colonization and that we should cease to treat it as an event with a fixed date.

I attribute the process of colonization, the late date and the earlier evidence from the Mediterranean rather than southern and northern Europe to social factors. The first Europeans had purpose in that they undertook intentional acts within socially constituted contexts. However, it was never their intention to colonize Europe. That was a consequence of changes and organization within their social lives. What we can be clearer about are the skills which they brought to the negotiation of these social lives – the face-to-face interaction in a complex society. These skills were generic to hominids throughout those parts of the Old World then occupied. These skills dealt with rituals of attachment to locales and attention to other people. The body was the prime resource for individuals to perform their version of society and to engage others in their projects. The resources which they used depended upon the conversion of patterns of attention, grooming, caring and parenting into emotional ties. Such a basis for society required frequent reaffirmation, close contact and affective responses. Learning was vertically transmitted from one generation to another in contexts supported by these emotional ties. The result was the faithful copying of gestures and responses structured by these affective bonds negotiated face to face. Repetition and redundancy are therefore expected in their technical acts. The memory of the relationships was long lasting because the performance of the bonds was contained in the muscle-memories of gesture and action enacted between individuals and learnt by successive generations.

The intimate bonds in such complex societies were elaborated through the use of material resources to build effective networks. At this level co-operation existed as the outcome of practical action. It was not a planned activity or a new piece of behaviour. We do not need to look for the origins of such behaviour since it must have been part of the social legacy from the last common ancestor five million years ago. But while we do not have to be surprised by evidence for co-operative behaviour, we do need to recognize that the form it took was constrained by the networks which supported it. Therefore, co-operation at this time depended on co-presence and the negotiation of social relationships using embodied resources.

The archaeological evidence has well-preserved locales which show very little formal structure. There are patterns as people came and went, and these can now be examined as sets of gestures which followed the attaching and detaching of individuals to and from gatherings. Searching for explanation solely in terms of functional or practical survival misses the information contained in the data. A very great variety of individual action resides here precisely because the taskscapes of these individuals did not involve the regular movement of materials. Individuals usually built the next gathering from materials *at* hand rather than *in* hand. They must have carried babies, clothing, food and raw materials but only if these confirmed, through movement over distance, those intimate and effective bonds performed in locales.

The scale of movement is consistently small, as studies of raw materials show. The landscape of habit rather than the social landscape contained these people. As a result life was local and the principle of exclusion dominated relations beyond those negotiated in intimate and effective networks.

These micro and macro scales and the rhythms which supported them conditioned the patterns of cultural transmission. While these people no doubt added verbal accompaniments to their social performances, such utterances acted as an attention device rather than as an organizing principle. In the same way making objects was an important social act, defining individuals by what they did, rather than necessarily by what they made. But the outcomes are sufficiently standard to show that learning gestures and rhythms of action with, and away from, others produced a vertical pattern of cultural transmission that was heavily determined by the rules of face-to-face interaction. I cannot say whether males and females had different networks and even if they did there would have been great individual variation. But this is a question for further investigation. To sum up: they had lives of great variety within a small social neighbourhood of possibilities.

### *Neanderthal complex society: 300,000 to 27,000 years ago*

Individual variation provides the basis for change in biological as well as cultural systems. The locus for any selective developments resided in the effective network since here was the opportunity for negotiating more varied ties based upon a wide range of resources. This network differs from the intimate in the strength of the bonds which an individual forges. Thus ambiguity and alternative interpretations of performances are introduced into social relationships. An individual's intimate network is limited by time and numbers. But the quality of the ties which bind its members is such that relationships are more often than not unquestioned, unanalysed and hence unambiguous. The effective component of an individual's personal network has far more possibilities for competition, negotiation, creativity and hence ambiguity. The most obvious archaeological example of this occurs within the landscape of habit where raw materials start to be transferred over greater distances and in more altered states. After 300,000 BP chains of connection were extended in all regions of Europe. It was no longer necessary to see a gesture for its outcome, the artifact, to have significance. Therefore, the objects individuals produced now carried the potential to represent the act. The difference lies in making these away-from-body performances simpler, if not in execution then at least in meaning. They had a system of communication dedicated to social relations but it did still not act as one means of stretching relationships across time and space.

The skills they employed were generic to being a hominid rather than specific to place and the construction of a social landscape. But in some instances we can see a move in the direction of such specific skills. For example, a greater degree of inter-regional variation can be found as well as more complex routines and longer chaînes opératoires.

Greater co-operation in hunting has been suggested by some for this period but is not surprising, reflecting only the larger scale of effective networks which individual Neanderthals achieved. Much is made at this time of pre-determined flint working, the levallois technique, and further planning to secure prime-aged animals. But as we saw above, such anticipation was only possible due to the networks that individuals lived in and which extend their ambit of action. These changes in the acquisition, manufacture and use of resources, be they stone or animal, do not measure changes in complexity. Instead they reflect the latent properties of social relationships to change the necessity for resources.

This assessment of novelty in the archaeological record of the Neanderthals stems directly from the social approach I have taken in this book. Moreover, it has an important repercussion for evolutionary models. It is often stated that our bodies are under darwinian selection whereas our culture is open to Lamarckian development (Gould 1996:219–22). This is true to the extent that culture represents ideas which are transmitted and accumulated outside the body. We can therefore speed up and direct the course of cultural change in ways which we cannot where biological evolution under natural selection is concerned. Nowhere does this seem more so than with the manufacture and design of artifacts.

However, this may not always be the case and for a simple conceptual reason. The lamarckian view of cultural change proposes a separation of object and person to justify a progressive view of cultural development. Thought is applied to objects in a very rational way so that spears become more accurate, huts warmer, nets tougher, and technology lighter and more portable. Directed problem solving, similar to anticipation and planning depth discussed above, is essential to the structure of learning and memory that leads to cultural evolution in a material sense.

I would contend that in this period there was no separation between object and person. Such detachment remained a latent possibility rather than an acknowledged act integral to social performance. Objects still needed to be animated by gestures to have significance. When they were used in the performance of social life they formed part of the mutual environment which surrounded the individual, the taskscape. What was being learnt and remembered were the gestures and rhythms of individuals rather than the accumulated products of history and the innovations which marked breakthroughs in survival. These were not bright ideas to be worked on or adapted to changing circumstances. The pace of change in the Palaeolithic was not slow because the number of people and minds were so few (Clark 1957:249) and hence the likelihood of new ideas limited. Instead it was because of the use made of resources to define social life in the intimate and effective components of an individual's personal network. The vertical transmission of knowledge, concerning chaînes opératoires, tracks and taskscapes, and which occurred as individuals moved between locales within regions of varying sizes, greatly reduced the options for new solutions to be selected.

These Neanderthal societies, the product of large-brained hominids, equipped with language to talk about themselves, alive with gestures and incorporating objects, were, for all that variety and creativity, still exclusive, local and complex. Theirs was a most successful hominid society. Well matched to the longer rhythms of the ice ages and interglacials, they drew on renewable resources to perform social lives of subtle differentiation.

### *Transition and complicated Crô-Magnon society: 60,000–21,000 years ago*

The stretching of social relations across time and space, the release from our primate heritage of proximity, marks the development of complicated social life (Strum and Latour 1987). Paradoxically for any progressive view of change in the Palaeolithic, the archaeological record becomes simpler, more understandable, at this point. It is possible, for example, to describe consistently the time–space dimensions of archaeological cultures. This is partly due to an increase in the variety of material culture to include ornament and display. Furthermore, locales were now invested with association and meaning. They not only hosted gatherings but also became social occasions and places. At the macro scale these locales were structured within a social landscape, whereas previously it was the landscape of habit alone which described action at this scale. Objects became people and the externalization of memory and action was possible due to the extended component of the personal network and the global network this immediately defines.

However, we should not assume that such understanding results from the fact that we are now investigating people-like-us, modern humans in both limb length and network skills. We must reject the impulse to raise the curtain at this moment on the first act of civilization. Human society did not start at this time, associated with new objects and the colonization of new lands (Gamble 1993a). We have not reached the first rung on the evolutionist ladder of bands, tribes, chiefs and states.

The European evidence indicates a gradual transition to the replacement of Neanderthal people. This is emphasized by over 15,000 years of contact and co-existence between Neanderthals and Crô-Magnons in some parts of the continent.

But rather than seeing this replacement as an absolute change – a new type of society to match a new type of hominid – we see instead that its roots lie deep in the effective and intimate networks, our hominid heritage. The use of materials as symbolic resources in an individual's extended network of negotiated ties was foreshadowed in the gestures which made handaxes. The eventual use of artifacts as symbols, be they handaxes or carved horses, is an exaptation, available for use by reason of their form rather than designed by natural selection for that purpose (Gould and Vrba 1982). What makes them symbols is their contribution to integrating and structuring what people do when they are separated. In the same way the gestures involved with attaching and detaching from gatherings and locales formed an existing rhythm for the elaboration of ritual based on symbolic performance rather than material and emotional resources alone.

Away from the structure that flows from co-presence, attention and perception new resources are required if, on the one hand, ambiguity and incoherence are to be avoided and yet, on the other, the richness and creativity of social life are to be preserved. Here is another example of the two sides of power. Extension comes at a price; social life must become complicated, reduced to simpler sequences of actions. The selective pressure for such change works on the variety which each individual possesses biologically, historically and culturally. The context for selection lies in the overlapping networks within which individuals find themselves; those constraints and possibilities which are inherent in a full personal and global network. These forces place demands on time, attention and the decisions about allocating resources. Instead of learning and memory being transmitted vertically there is now the possibility of horizontal transmission. The effect was dramatic. Rather than the familiar gestures, which empower an individual as an active social agent, being passed between parent and child and within intimate, or at most effective networks, they can now skip horizontally between networks (Cullen 1996:425). In a vertical system faithful reproduction of sequences and rhythms is expected. Culture and the individual are in the same evolutionary boat, so neither rocks it. Stasis and gradualism are expected. But in a horizontal system such a benign relationship need not exist. That curious alchemy takes over where culture begins to negotiate us as much as we use it to moderate our lives. Extended networks can be used by individuals to negotiate their social position as well as those of others who are bound into their intimate and effective spheres. Faithful transmission gives way to asymmetrical power relations that now fall along the lines of age, sex and genealogy. In particular, the principle that life was local and access exclusive to the overlapping personal network of a small demographic unit has changed. Now life can be both exclusive and inclusive through the extension of social life and the creation of an individual's global network. Power, in the sense of harnessing and enhancing the lives of others to a particular symbolic performance, now takes on a simpler but more familiar aspect. It replaced that same enhancing and harnessing based on the affective and material resources used by Neanderthals.

The Palaeolithic societies of Europe provide an opportunity to observe, in some detail, the variable outcomes of social interaction over a period of some 500,000 years. I have not attempted a full explanation of why the extended networks developed late in human evolution. But I hope that by examining a model for Palaeolithic society and a method for applying it to Palaeolithic data we can now move in that direction. To attempt such a big question without considering the societies either of the late glacial in Europe or from further afield would run into accusations of parochial answers to a world inquiry. However, what I hope to have shown is that with a social perspective we can begin to move beyond reconstructions of Palaeolithic people as either stomach-led or brain-dead. We can raise the curtain on a much more interesting past.

# NOTES

### Chapter 1: Pulling aside the Palaeolithic curtain

1 No anthropologists contributed although Raymond Firth had been involved in planning the conference.

2 I will not review here the so-called revisionist debate in hunter-gatherer studies (Barnard 1992, Schrire 1984, Wilmsen 1989). While I agree completely that contemporary foragers are not and never can be analogues of prehistoric societies, I nonetheless concur with Wilmsen's comment (1989:352) that accepting the revisionist critique does not mean 'that nothing useful to the study of human evolution can come from investigating certain aspects of San culture, *but only those aspects of knowledge and technique employed in foraging itself are relevant to a study of foragers*. Furthermore, unless one insists that there is, after all, a Palaeolithic residue in San-speaking populations, there is no reason to single out these peoples for such investigations' (1989:352, my emphasis).

3 Following Birdsell (1958), the amount of rainfall is used to measure this gradient.

4 Richards (1987:306–31) provides a very useful survey of the literature on social evolution and reminds us that 'Historically, [social evolution] has been one of those issues which perennially attract discussion from widely differing directions, while being the clear province of no particular discipline at all. The upshot is that until the last decade or so, for all the spilt ink, it is hard to identify a coherent body of cumulatively developing scientific or academic literature on the subject. Too often what we have is a final chapter in which the author of a text unwinds, following the hard scientific slog, and waxes philosophical about the human condition' (*ibid.*:207).

5 What is striking is the way these arguments, derived from so many strands of evidence, are often presented. Several authors provide imaginative accounts of what it was like on those East African savannahs (see in particular Fox 1967:175–80, Gamble 1993a:108–12, Humphrey 1983:48–55, Isaac 1976:483–5, Reynolds 1966:446–50) in order to reconstruct social relationships. These stories bear many points of similarity as they search for a fresh twist to the evolutionary tale. The form they take is partly determined by the fact that they are dealing with descriptions in ecological, or immediate time (Gamble 1993a:36–7) to describe a great conflation of data from many hundreds of thousands of years and often widely separated in space.

6 The other works were Freud (1913) *Totem and taboo*, Dawkins (1976) *The selfish gene*, and Trivers (1978) *The evolution of reciprocal altruism*.

7 Another British social anthropologist, Radcliffe-Brown (1952) did give limited support to the study of social evolution although he was more inclined to consider it as conjectural history. This view has been followed by most of his British students (see Ingold 1986a).

8 Similarities can be seen with Gardner's (1966:406) division of hunting societies into refugee societies under intercultural pressure (e.g. the !Kung and Paliyans) from powerful neighbours, and insular, unpressurized societies (e.g. the Tlingit and Walbiri).

9 Constandse-Westermann and Newell (1991, Newell 1984, Newell and Constandse-Westermann 1986) have reassessed population numbers among North American hunters and gatherers. They propose two types of society, labelled Band level and Tribal level but which, confusingly, both contain bands and dialect tribes. Their argument is that population densities which would support endogamy and group closure (i.e. Band Society) are only found in Tribal-level societies (1991:Table 1). These are the Tribes discussed in Service (1971) and which are normally associated with food producing.

10 Constandse-Westermann and Newell claim that these Band Society models have failed to appreciate the existence of two levels of social organization among hunters and gatherers (1991:110); the Band and the Tribe. Steward and Service considered a division into composite and patrilocal bands, which has been the starting point for much of the previous discussion. Tribes were generally equated with food producers. However, Newell and Constandse-Westermann (1986) maintain that during the European Mesolithic there was a gradual development from Band to Tribal level, that is from open to closed mating networks associated with tribes within the Tribal level which are distinguished by dialects. A population density of 0.1 person per $km^2$ is, according to their ethnographic survey of 256 North American populations at or near first contact, an important but not sufficient threshold for this transition. The problem with their model is that it advances us no further towards an understanding of what a prehistoric hunter-gatherer society might be. Social structure for them is nothing more than a table of demographic and linguistic units (*ibid.*:259–60).

11 The traditional anthropological approach to this distinction was succinctly expressed by Gellner, 'the idea was that a tribal society has a certain structure or organisation, each part of which imposed such pressures and sanctions on the individuals within it as to ensure that they behaved in a way that in turn sustained that structure, and so on for ever, or at any rate for quite a long time' (Gellner 1985:135). The anthropologist's task was to investigate these structures. The varied cultural expressions that these structures took were regarded as unimportant. Culture was a distraction and regarded as trivial. As Gellner put it, 'structure was whom one could marry; culture was what the bride wore' (*ibid.*:136).

**Chapter 2: The individual, society and networks**

1 An earlier, and shorter version of the models presented in Chapters 2 and 3 can be found in Gamble (1998).

2 I would also agree with Mithen (1993a:394) that just because we cannot always observe individuals in the Palaeolithic record we should not reject them as an analytical device. Scientists have used such concepts as the unconscious, the gene, the atom or the molecule long before they had the opportunity to observe them directly rather than some proxy effect of their actions.

3 This view is supported by Damas (1972:50) who sees kinship among the Copper Eskimo as a charter for potential alliances.

4 See Kuper (1988:241–3) for further examples of how kinship models determined what anthropologists saw and what they chose to ignore.

5 I can highly recommend J. Turner's (1991) discussion of Giddens and many other social theorists.
6 Unfortunately Strum and Latour (1987:Figure 1) go on to develop their model of complicated social life by rather uncritically using the concept of primitive society which Kuper has warned against (1988:243). They regard hunter-gatherers, agriculturalists and industrial societies as differentiated by an increasing level of material and symbolic means to construct society. This finds expression in the ability to organize others on ever vaster scales. However, I do not see such implications for subsequent social evolution within their concept of complication. A similar view to Strum and Latour's can be found in Maryanski and Turner (1992), where the elaboration of social structure by horticultural societies puts people into a 'social cage' that violated our ancestral (i.e. hunter-gatherer) genetic tendencies.
7 Kephart (1950) calculated the possible number of relationships which can exist within a group. When 5 are in the group then 90 potential relationships exist. This figure rises to 7,133,616 with 15 group members.
8 They conclude that the modern socially mobile, middle-class family is analogous to the monogamous gibbon – a lack of strong ties and reduced role segregation, a conclusion supported by Milroy's (1987) study where social mobility was found to correlate with low-density personal networks.
9 As Miller's title *The magical number seven plus or minus two* declared, seven was his original figure although he was careful not to make exaggerated claims for it. Simon (1974:487, fn.2) recast the magic number as five chunks which could be stored in the short-term memory.

**Chapter 3: A Palaeolithic framework: locales, rhythms and regions**

1 This aspect of embodiment has been studied by Chance and Larsen (1976) where different primate social organizations are supported by varied attention structures.These are primarily hedonic (rewards and approval in return for display), agonistic (bound with threats), centric (individual surrounded by others) and acentric (individuals in a group continually divide their attention between themselves and the objects of the environment). See Wilson (1988:20) for discussion.
2 Binford's specific point is that increasing dependence on hunting, which is inescapable with increasing latitude, will result in kinship playing less of an organizing role in spatial patterning. Security, rather than risk, selects for the social relationships and camping patterns that ensure hunting success. The contrast is between youth (endurance) and age (knowledge). When combined they provide the best strategy against failure. Since the old men have already passed their knowledge on to close kin, the camping arrangements do not follow the kinship pattern and camp mates during the winter are chosen for other reasons.
3 Gilbert Ryle referred to this as knowing-how (Heidegger's position) and distinguished it from knowing-that which represents the cartesian tradition of philosophy (Magee 1987:258).
4 White (1993a:xxi) points out that Derrida refers to him in his *Grammatology*.
5 For Europe these include Bíró (1981), Féblot-Augustins (1993, 1997), Féblot-Augustins and Perlès (1992), Floss (1994), Geneste (1991, 1988a, 1988b), Kuhn (1995, 1992), Lebel (1992), Pasda (1994, 1996a, 1996b), Perlès (1992), Rensink (1993), Roebroeks, Kolen and Rensink (1988), Svoboda (1994a), Turq (1988, 1990, 1992a, 1993), White and Pettitt (1995). For South America, Africa and

Australia see Bar-Yosef (1991), Féblot-Augustins (1990), Franco (1990, 1991, 1994), Hiscock (1984), McNiven (1990), Potts (1988, 1993).

6 None of these distances relates to migration distances (Rowley 1985) but instead to the expected movement of individuals through their social systems.

7 However, this is possibly not a hominid feature alone. Rowell (1991) has discussed the difficulties which face primatologists when studying a small part of an open social system whose extent is largely undetermined. She reviews the evidence, such as it is, for a population-wide element in animal social structure and concludes that 'sociality at and above the group level among animals is concerned with and determined by place' (Rowell 1991:267). The difficulty of detecting such an element is put down to Hinde's (1976) observation that each level of social organization among primates has emergent properties which are not deducible from the lower level.

8 The importance of larger-scale social units, such as the social landscape, has been discussed by Hill (1978) in terms of area-level adaptations. These regional adaptations, revealed through a study of linguistic exogamy, 'are highly significant clues to the existence of systematically maintained long-distance contact networks in which we must see phenomena like refugee movements and trespass *as systematic rather than as accidents or failures of the local level of adaptation*' (Hill 1978:9, emphasis added).

**Chapter 4: The first European societies 500,000–300,000 years ago**

1 This corresponds to the end of the Olduvai magnetic reversal event at 1.66 Myr BP (Aitken 1990).

2 A distinction is made between the Lower and Middle Pleistocene, which are recognized internationally at particular geological sections, and the early and middle Pleistocene where correlation to these type sections is not possible but which through extrapolation can be assumed. Hence in this book Lower and Middle Pleistocene refer to the Brunhes/Matuyama boundary, an absolute marker, while archaeological sites dated to the early and middle Pleistocene are assigned a relative position within this standard chronology.

3 Fifty years after the classic Alpine synthesis of Penck and Brückner (1909), Zeuner (1959:80) summarized the situation that locally the Mindel glaciation was often, though sometimes not by much, more extensive than the Riss. Their classic scheme of four glaciations, Günz, Mindel, Riss and Würm, separated by three interglacials, has now been abandoned as the ice-age framework in favour of the continuous record from the deep-sea cores which indicates many more glacial episodes during the Pleistocene.

4 Roebroeks and Kolfschoten point out, however (1994:492), that locally the maximum advance can contradict this pattern. In parts of the Netherlands the Saale moraines are more extensive while in Russia those belonging to the Dnepr glaciation can exceed the Oka. This supports Zeuner's earlier comment on the often comparable extent of the Riss and Mindel glaciations and reminds us that ice extent is controlled by many factors.

5 In the Alpine scheme of Penck and Brückner this would be part of the Mindel gravels (Sibrava 1986:chart 1). Shackleton (1987:187) describes OIS 12 as 'an exceptionally large glaciation' whose oxygen isotope values are only matched by OIS 16.

6 Cromer IV is put by Zagwijn in OIS 11 (1992:figure 9), although this is too late if the succeeding Elsterian is to be correlated, as most believe, with OIS 12. I therefore prefer correlating Cromer IV with OIS 13 as seems to be the case at Boxgrove.

7 *Abies* cannot tolerate very low winter temperatures and prefers cool summers with high rainfall (Zagwijn 1992:590).
8 Shackleton, using isotopic evidence, characterizes OIS 11 as the warmest interglacial in the last 1 Myr and notes that it follows a major faunal extinction event (1987:187).
9 The evolutionary transition from *Mimomys* to *Arvicola* marks the boundary between the Biharian and Toringian faunas. The oldest example of *Arvicola* is found in the Cromer IV deposits from Kärlich G in Germany (Roebroeks and Kolfschoten 1994:494).
10 These are assigned to the early arvicolid form, *Arvicola terrestris cantiana*. Species with rootless molars are believed to have an evolutionary advantage in that the accelerated tooth eruption permits intensive wear so that more abrasive plant material can be included in the diet (Koenigswald and Kolfschoten 1996:214).
11 In broad terms Cordy's division reflects the transition from Late Biharian to Toringian faunas. In the former *Arvicola terrestris cantiana* is found with species such as *Talpa minor* (a mole) and *Trogontherium cuvieri* (a giant beaver). This would include the faunas from Miesenheim I, Kärlich G, Mauer, Boxgrove, Westbury sub Mendip and Sprimont. The Toringian faunas with an advanced arvicolid (*Arvicola* ssp A and B) are found with a more modern mammal fauna at Swanscombe and Bilzingsleben (Koenigswald and Kolfschoten 1996).
12 The geographical origin of the woolly mammoth/woolly rhino fauna of the Upper Pleistocene has been traced by R-D. Khalke (1994:tab. 1) to Asian taxa with some elements from the Nearctic (horses and wolves) and Aethiopian (elephants and hyena) faunal provinces.
13 For example musk ox and leopard, beaver and reindeer in Mediterranean France at the site of Caune de l'Arago, sol G (Lumley 1979:39).
14 This is level CXCA in unit 6 of the Cagny section (Antoine and Tuffreau 1993:figure 3).
15 Assuming preservation to be in a band 300 m wide in front of the cliff, then potentially some 9 $km^2$ of in-situ middle Pleistocene landscape may be preserved.
16 At an even wider scale further absolute dates have recently suggested that the age of the Java fossils is in the order of 1.8 Myr (Swisher et al. 1994). This would of course make them comparable in age to the earliest *Homo erectus* finds in East Africa. As a result serious consideration is now being given by those who accept these dates to the suggestions from Groves (1989) and Clarke (1990) that *Homo habilis* rather than *Homo erectus* was the hominid which first left Africa.
17 This material was also critically examined and the various claims debated at a European Science Foundation workshop held in Tautavel in November 1993 (Roebroeks and Kolfschoten 1995).
18 Genuine artifacts have been accepted by Raynal, Magoga and Bindon (1995:141) from Soleihac-Centre (MW region). The tephrostratigraphy, which is to be preferred to the palaeomagnetic dates from the site, indicates an age of 0.5–0.6 Myr BP.
19 I have a copy of Hazzledine Warren's elegant paper (1914) which he annotated, as follows, in 1948 when sending it to F. E. Zeuner, 'This paper needs revision of wording, but criticism has found no error of fact, and I confirm the conclusions.'
20 Often quoted in textbooks.
21 Not everyone agrees with the OIS 13 age for Boxgrove preferring a later age based upon isoleucine epimerization in non-marine molluscs which provides a relative chronology (Bowen et al. 1989).

22 I was able to inspect these items thanks to the invitation of Dr J. Gibert and Professor M. Walker. In my opinion there is no reason to regard them as hominid artifacts (see Roe 1995).
23 A guild is defined by the resources it uses and not by the methods by which they are procured. Hence, human hunters and hyenas belong to the same guild as long as their main subsistence focus is on ungulates (see Stiner 1994).
24 Supporters of the long chronology still need to address the question of why the threshold of archaeological visibility is so low for finds which they accept as older than 500 Kyr BP (see Gamble 1995a).
25 There is no evidence for a further alternative, namely storage and/or increasing procurement rates through technological improvements.
26 One of the urgent tasks which now faces environmental approaches to the Middle Pleistocene is the quantification of the spatial structure of these landscapes – locally, regionally and for the entire continent. Furthermore, we need to agree from which end of this spatial framework we will begin the investigation of hominids as colonizing animals.
27 This terminological house-cleaning can also be seen in northern France with the rejection of the term Abbevillian as a chronological indicator (Tuffreau and Antoine 1995) and the rejection of collections of geofacts among the archaeological material from the Iberian peninsula (Raposo and Santonja 1995).
28 Ohel (1979) claimed that the Clactonian was merely an early stage in the knapping process of the Acheulean, although at the time his view gained little credence, as the commentaries on his article reveal.
29 Earlier disagreements between geologists and archaeologists over the age of High Lodge delayed its publication for several years. The artifacts were seen as simply too advanced for the geological age which was being proposed.
30 *Débitage* is often translated as waste but this is misleading. Much better to retain the French term 'cutting from' with its close association to the technique of knapping rather than passing judgement on the value of one flake (a tool) over another (a waste flake). Kuhn (1995:81) appropriately calls it 'stone butchery'.
31 Geneste (1991:Fig. 1) elaborates these differences further by drawing a distinction between ramifying and scalariform reduction sequences.
32 Neither is recurrence restricted to levallois sequences. For example, Kuhn (1995:169) has commented on the existence of recurrent sequences in Italian Pontinian assemblages where the local raw materials are small pebbles and where classic levallois is rare (*ibid.*:47).
33 White's study of the Hoxne flake material (pers. comm.) shows that in the Lower (ovate) industry 67 per cent of all flakes were made on fresh nodules. In the Upper (pointed) industry 69 per cent of all flakes were made on derived flint pebbles.
34 The elephant skull was found in level A1. Above this in the topmost, Alpha, level at the site some 2,000 stone artifacts and 800 bones of elephants, fallow deer and bovids were found. The shaft of a human femur was found in the in-situ sediments which cover the alpha level (Belli et al. 1991).
35 Applying the Hadza site-size:carcass-size regression, rhino and mammoth, to Bilzingsleben, would result in larger areas still since both weigh >1,000 kg.
36 Gaudzinski (et al. 1996) comment that at Kärlich Seeufer the evidence for a connection between the numerous wooden and faunal remains and the stone artifacts cannot be demonstrated. The eight elephants were accumulated over a long period of time.
37 There are claims that some of the wood at Torralba is burnt (see James 1989).
38 The date of La Polledrara is still preliminary but is broadly Holsteinian in age,

including OIS 12 (478–303 Kyr BP), and therefore comparable to other Italian fluvial sites such as Notarchirico, Fontana Ranuccio and Torre in Pietra (Mussi 1995).

39 The association of wild cat and leopard with musk ox and reindeer in Mediterranean France (Table 4.13) makes this an extraordinary and very interesting faunal community.

40 Schwarcz (et al. 1988) have published dates of 185 Kyr and 210 Kyr BP for the cultural layer.

41 Nests of pebbles possibly rafted in with seaweed are common at Boxgrove (Roberts pers. comm.).

42 A fourth, adult, individual has recently been reported (Mania 1995:92).

43 *Homo heidelbergensis*, previously referred to as archaic *Homo sapiens* (Stringer 1981), forms a variable but distinct regional group. It includes the Atapuerca, Steinheim, Swanscombe, Bilzingsleben, Arago and Petralona remains. Stringer (1981:12, 1984) sees no evidence for *Homo erectus*-grade fossils in Europe.

44 More recently, Mania (1995:92) describes zone V as follows: 'an oval paved area with a diameter of 9 m. It consists of pebbles and bone fragments of nut to fist size. There were no objects found lying on top of this paved area.' Excavations since 1986 have extended the area.

45 Svoboda (1987) has compared the small-sized, non-biface stone industries from Bilzingsleben, Arago and Vértesszöllös.

46 Recent reviews by James (1989) and Rigaud (et al. 1995) have concluded that while fire was present on many of these sites it was not controlled. Recent claims for a stone-lined hearth and fire-altered rock from Menez-Drégan in Brittany (Monnier 1994), dated by ESR to between 350–500 Kyr BP, need to be treated with caution until the full results are published.

47 I chose this shelter since it has, at least by eye, the most convincing shape.

**Chapter 5: Neanderthal societies 300,000 to 60,000 years ago**

1 The local, i.e. European, evolution from 'archaic' *Homo sapiens* (=*Homo heidelbergensis*) to *Homo neanderthalensis* is supported by the recent finds of complete crania from Atapuerca, Sima de los Huesos (Arsuaga et al. 1993:536).

2 The dates help dispense with interpretations that two, or even three, climatic cycles are represented in the Swanscombe sequence (Conway, McNabb and Ashton 1996).

3 Similarly 'young' dates obtained for Bilzingsleben (Harmon, Glazek and Nowak 1980) and Vértesszöllös (Schwarcz et al. 1988) should also be rejected. On a more positive note, for many years the age of the travertine site of Ehringsdorf, in eastern Germany, was bitterly contested with ages ranging through what would now be OIS 5e, 7 and 9. U-series dates have now sorted the dating out to most people's satisfaction. The lower travertine at the site is OIS 7 in age (Blackwell and Schwarcz 1986).

4 Dansgaard (et al. 1993:Fig. 1) identify twenty-four interstadials between the last glacial maximum in OIS 2 and the end of OIS 5e. The seven interstadials referred to by Behre (1989) are those of longest duration which can be reconciled with pollen horizons.

5 Interstadials are distinguished from interglacials by the comparatively weak response of arboreal taxa, especially deciduous species, to ameliorations in climate.

6 It seems clear that the Amersfoort interstadial should now be seen as part of the Brørup (OIS 5c) interstadial.

7 Guiot (et al. 1989:313) also make the case that ice formation was initiated during these forested sub-stages OIS 5a and OIS 5c, indicative of a cold but humid continent.
8 Quaternary scientists are now wondering why the present interglacial seems apparently so stable by comparison with OIS 5e.
9 The site of Mikhajlovskoe on the lower northern Donets river is cautiously regarded by Hoffecker (1987:277) as last interglacial in age.
10 Hoffecker (et al. 1991:117) report that absolute dates from the site are inconsistent and so cannot resolve this problem.
11 Locht (et al. 1994) have not ruled out an OIS 6 age until absolute age estimates can be obtained. Roebroeks and Tuffreau (1994) place it in OIS 6.
12 Two other early European sites have produced ochre, Becov in Czechoslovakia and Ambrona in Spain (Roebroeks 1988:40).
13 A blade is defined as a flake which is at least twice as long as it is wide.
14 Named after the Paris suburb where it was first recognized as a knapping technique.
15 The thickness of level VIII varied between 20 and 80cm.
16 'With two intersecting surfaces of lateral and distal convexity, one serving for the preparation of the striking platform, the other for the flaking of the éclat préférentiel' (Tuffreau and Antoine 1995).
17 See Arts and Cziesla (1990) for a comprehensive bibliography 1880–1988 of refitting studies.
18 The exaggerated claims for the great age of Korylevo, a site claimed to be of Cromerian age, are widely regarded as unreliable (Ranov 1991).
19 This intensification is a feature of the archaeological record of the Mesolithic where populations of northern Europe coped with a much reduced animal biomass and a succession of forest environments (Gamble 1986c). This model has also been applied to questions of global colonization (Gamble 1993a).
20 These are red deer, horse, steppe ass and wolf.
21 Wallertheim is dated to OIS 5d and equivalent to level C in the current excavations (Conard et al. 1995a). Gaudzinski's (1992) analysis of Wallertheim B1 is based on the 1928 excavations at the site by Schmidtgen. Recent work by Conard (et al. 1995a, et al. 1995b) has uncovered further levels and a correspondingly varied taphonomic and faunal history for the site.
22 The photograph of the spear resting under an elephant rib is the only published record (Thieme and Veil 1985:Abb. 3) to support the killing scenario favoured by most archaeologists. I would encourage them to undertake some experimental work on the efficacy of a 281-cm-long stick, which has an average thickness of only 2.5 cm, in killing a 4-tonne elephant with a clean hit as is often implied (M. Roberts pers. comm.). Experiments by Frison (1989) using spears tipped with Clovis projectile points to penetrate elephant hide showed how important it was to have a stone projectile point as part of the weapon system if you are going to behave like a 'big-game' hunter. Of course hunters can be sneaky and wait for the animal to bleed to death!
23 Contemporary does not necessarily mean same day or even same year but that the artifacts were deposited during the same climatic conditions that would have affected all visits to this locale.
24 The dating of Biache to a very late OIS 7/early OIS 6 age is based on TL dating and environmental indicators (Tuffreau and Sommé 1988:118–19)
25 The dating of the Lazaret level is far from secure. Level III of stratigraphic unit c lies above the beaches which are dated absolutely to 200–300 Kyr BP and beneath the stalagmite floor with dates of 114–66 Kyr BP. This suggests an OIS 6 or late Saalian-age date (Valensi 1991).

26 Co-operative behaviour is found to a varying degree among all social mammals where, as with chimpanzee or lion hunting, it is normally tied to their equivalent of the intimate network.

### Chapter 6: The rhythms of social life, 60,000–21,000 years ago: the transition from the Middle to Upper Palaeolithic in Europe

1 The recent extraction of ancient DNA from the Neander Valley skeleton, possibly 50 Kyr old, and its interpretation as similar to but significantly distinct from the DNA of modern people is powerful evidence for the supporters of population replacement (Ward and Stringer 1997).
2 See Stringer and Gamble (1993:Appendix 1) for fuller listing.
3 Dansgaard et al. (1993) place Denekamp at c. 35 Kyr BP which is not in agreement with C14 dated pollen profiles (Behre 1989). The interstadial stages 5, 6 and 7 in the Greenland core should instead be correlated with Denekamp while stages 8–11 are equivalent to Hengelo. These discrepancies point to the need for a fully calibrated system.
4 The problems of pollen profiles in cave sediments have been discussed by Turner and Hannon (1988). Percolation of pollen through the limestone joint structure and then through the sediments makes interpretation extremely hazardous.
5 This division follows Desbrosse and Kozlowski (1988).
6 The presence of mosquitos around open-landscape glacial lakes might have been a disincentive to go near them.
7 This was not due to failings on the part of the excavators. Svoboda (et al. 1994:457) remarks that later archaeological work was conducted under a climate of intense commercial pressure for loess extraction, with the result that they concentrated their attention on recording standing sections in the pit rather than making plans of the archaeology.
8 A maxilla of a female, attributed to a Neanderthal, was found in 1964 (Le Tensorer 1993:260).
9 It is not just the caves which produce tiny collections. Molodova V level 10 has thirty-seven tools of which one is a leaf point (Kozlowski 1986:table 3.4) yet this has sometimes been called the Molodovian.
10 His scheme is based on a chronostratigraphic approach and includes the upper level at Schambach, Große Grotte II and the leaf point (Blattspitzen) levels at Mauern and the Haldenstein cave at Urspring.
11 This number includes all Middle Palaeolithic occupations and not just those from the period 60–40 Kyr bp.
12 This may not however be an adaptation to different conditions but rather a reflection of different rates of sediment accumulation combined with the frequency of visits to the abris. If this was the case then it might be possible that Denticulate artifacts, which have little retouch, were buried more quickly, while Charentian pieces lay on the surface longer and were therefore successively retouched as Dibble (1987) has argued.
13 Diversity has two components: taxonomic richness and assemblage evenness. They stress the importance of the latter since it is less dependent upon sample size (Simek and Price 1990:245).
14 When discussing these schemes with lithic specialists working in the regions of northern and southern Europe I have often found them mystified by the Laplacian scheme and some of its more recent elaborations.
15 *Lit.* light stone, which refers to the use of blades and the general weight reduction that is obvious in the Upper Palaeolithic.

16 I doubt that I have been successful in this translation. Discrepancies exist in terminology and usage in the same volume. Contrast Vaquero (1992:55) with Carbonell (1992:205) for an appreciation of the problem.
17 The *typologie analytique* and its offshoot the *sistema lògico-analític* divide the Palaeolithic into three great periods: the bio-functional 2.5–1.5 Myr, the biomorphotechnical 1.5 Myr–30 Kyr and the bio-potential 30–6 Kyr bp (Vaquero 1992:51). These are not divisions I would support.
18 The dating of Chauvet is powerful evidence against Clark and Lindly's claims (Clark 1992b, Clark and Lindly 1989, Lindly and Clark 1990) for cultural and behavioural continuity between Neanderthals and anatomically modern humans. Their main evidence is the creative explosion in art after 20 Kyr bp. As a result they downplay the innovations in the 20,000 years before this date. The Chauvet and Cosquer dates indicate that such a creative explosion happened much earlier than traditionally believed.
19 The child burial at Starosel'e which is widely accepted (Gvozdover et al. 1996, Smirnov 1991) has recently been questioned as an intrusive late-medieval burial, fully consistent with Muslim burial practices (Marks et al. 1997:122).
20 The discovery in 1993 of a skull and heavily encrusted skeleton at Grotta Lamalunga near Altamura in southern Italy will provide further evidence of this burial pattern (Ventura 1993).
21 Le Moustier, la Quina and St Césaire have absolute dates (Table 6.1) while La Chapelle aux Saints is considered by Defleur to be Interpleniglacial in age (1993:Fig. 68).
22 Timeblocks 2 and 3 in her scheme (Féblot-Augustins 1993:table 2).
23 The preferred flint was that from Bergeracois, a silex grand crû if ever there was one!
24 Clark's cross-cultural discussion of symbols of excellence also stresses brilliant qualities. 'Ivory attracts by reason of its smoothness and creamy colour, jade by its translucence, hues and touch, gold by its untarnishable gleam, pearls by their orient and the most precious stones by their fire' (Clark 1986:6).
25 Alice Kehoe (pers. comm.) has made the challenging suggestion that many of the objects interpreted as spear points and arrow straighteners were in fact to do with weaving. This interpretation certainly needs further investigation but here I concentrate on the techniques of manufacture rather than the use of the object.
26 The hafting notch in one of the Schöningen spears (Thieme and Maier 1995) from the Saalian complex reminds us of the antiquity of this technology.
27 These must be regarded as minimum ages. Bio-stratigraphical evidence points to an Odderade age between 81–85 Kyr BP (Chapter 5).
28 Two of the pieces were charred and one had been heated to an estimated temperature of 290–300°C (Carbonell and Castro-Curel 1992:714) suggesting that they were fuel irrespective of whether they had previously been worked or not.
29 There were seventeen raw materials used in the main sector of the excavations (Farizy, David and Jaubert 1994:Fig. 32). Quartzites and flint account for over 70 per cent in a lithic collection of 2,142 pieces.
30 These are referred to as catalogued pieces (Spiess 1979) and I am assuming that manufacturing waste would not be catalogued. A figure of 289 catalogued pieces including flint, bone and stone objects is given by Movius for level 14 (1977:140).
31 Numbers are low at the Abri Pataud but there is little variation between levels with regard to reindeer ages. Pike-Tay and Bricker (1993:Figures 9.8 and 9.9) present combined data for a number of Perigordian/Gravettian locales in southwest France. All of these have prime-aged profiles for red deer as well as reindeer.

32 However, rather confusingly, Enloe says that 'only high utility parts have been transported' but refers to the bones rather than the invisible meat which surrounded them.

33 Because of unevenness in the sample the measure is based on presence and absence in assemblages, not on the number of bones, which would be preferable. Obviously a detailed taphonomic study of each assemblage would be desirable to discover, as Gaudzinski did at Wallertheim (1992, 1995), which species were present because of human activity. In the absence of such a general assessment, species diversity is used as a measure of local and regional resource richness.

34 Hortus also produced, like Mauran, a denticulate Mousterian assemblage. It will be interesting to compare results with the locale of Fréchet in the Pyrenees (Jaubert 1994) where a preliminary analysis shows that from a small sample (NISP=241) ibex and chamois comprise 59 per cent of the identified remains.

35 Level e, third from the top, is dated to 46,500+4,400–2,800 BP (GrN 12.809).

### Chapter 7: The extension of social life 60,000–21,000 years ago: regions and locales, networks and landscapes

1 Machiavellian behaviour among the great apes and monkeys supports his view (Waal 1982).

2 The notion of different degrees of planning depth and anticipation (Binford 1989b), which have been profitably explored as a significant difference between the mobility in the Middle and Upper Palaeolithic (Chapter 5), can also be recast in these terms.

3 There is some inconsistency in the number of sources plotted by Geneste (1988b:Fig. 2), recorded in his text figures for each level and listed in his Tables 2–14. Hence the differences between my Tables 5.5 and 7.1, and Fig. 5.13.

4 The difference between an r and a K strategy (Gamble 1993a:Table 3.1).

5 These regions are drawn as follows; Northern – Carpathians, Alps and northern part of the Russian Plain; Periglacial – central France, Carpathian basin and the Ukraine; Mediterranean – combined with the Atlantic coastline (Simán 1990–1:13). They are not comparable to the regions used in the analysis of moving sum data in Chapter 6.

6 Based on the sites of Rörshain, Bockstein, Klausennische and Schambach. The last three have overlapping distributions in southern Germany.

7 It is this structure to the archaeological record which unites the approach of Bordes and Bosinski however much they may disagree with each other's interpretations.

8 Hahn reviewed 281 C14 dates and used 74 in plotting the isochrons (Hahn 1993:65 and Fig. 2).

9 The 30 Kyr bp isochron for Hahn's Aurignacian I map is in an almost identical position (*ibid.*:Fig. 6).

10 However, Straus (et al. 1993:14) does acknowledge a 5-Kyr difference between the oldest Aurignacian dates in Central and Eastern Europe and those from northern Spain. But they think this is too short a time for people or ideas to spread over 2,000 km from southeast to southwest Europe. A rate of 400 m per annum does not seem excessive to me given ethno-historic data on the distance arctic peoples moved in less than a generation (Rowley 1985).

11 This begins with the Hengelo interstadial equivalent to the Würm II/III interstadial in the French sequence and ends with the Würm II Phase II (Laville, Rigaud and Sackett 1980).

12 There are Mousterian occupations in the deep gallery at Grotte du Renne where people lived in cramped conditions (Farizy 1990:307).
13 This may not be the full story. TL dates on burnt flint for an Aurignacian level at Gato Preto have given an age of 38.1±3 Kyr bp (Zilhao 1993:Tableau 1). Zilhao comments that such an age probably corresponds to an uncalibrated C14 date of 38–30 Kyr bp.
14 One problem which Svoboda (1994c) comments on is the lack of precise chronological resolution. There are wide discrepancies between C14 determinations on bone and wood charcoal from different laboratories. This has made it difficult, except in broad outline as shown in Table 7.8, to place the various excavations at Dolní Věstonice-Pavlov in their respective chronological positions. Current preference is to rely on the determinations from the Gröningen laboratory since these show both internal and stratigraphic consistency. However, it should be noted that the variable ages may be pointing to problems of contamination and a consequently more complex settlement history than is currently appreciated.
15 Dolní Věstonice III, located between Dolní Věstonice I and II, has been dated to 24.5 Kyr, which makes it the latest occupation in the locale, excluding Milovice to the southeast (Svoboda, Klíma and Skrdla 1995, Valoch 1995). To the east of the village of Pavlov is the Pavlov II site about which little has been published (Klíma 1995:Abb. 12).
16 Small but continuing excavations at DV III (Skrdla, Cílek and Prichystal 1996) may help in linking the various parts of the locale together. So far one radiocarbon date exists for these excavations of 24,560 + 660–610 bp (GrN 20342).
17 Person days of occupation are calculated by the meat weights derived from the MNI and divided by calorific requirements.
18 Level 5 has a Perigordian V assemblage comparable in age to level 3 at Abri Pataud (Laville, Rigaud and Sackett 1980:Figure 8.2).
19 The Gravettian project (Svoboda, Klíma and Skrdla 1995) has as one of its goals the publication of the later excavations.
20 Sklenár (1976) provides an overview of the variety of dwellings which have been claimed at the site.
21 Wood charcoals of elm and fir (*Abies*) have also been identified (Mason, Hather and Hillman 1994).
22 The very small sample of charred remains from hearth D (26,390±270 bp) consisted of four elements: wood charcoal, tissues from roots and tubers, one seed and a possible acorn mush. Elsewhere similar mush has been identified as an important component in infant foodstuffs and is preserved as charred faeces (Mason, Hather and Hillman 1994). Owen provides a full discussion of the plant foods which might have been available in the Late Glacial (1996).
23 The textile/basketry impressions came from the 1954 excavations at Pavlov I (Adovasio, Soffer and Klíma 1996).
24 A similar argument might be made for the property of brilliance in raw materials rather than their flaking qualities (Gamble 1995a); see Chapter 6.
25 The early excavations at the Crô-Magnon rock shelter found five skeletons. Their dating is unsure but the associated artifacts are an evolved rather than early Aurignacian (de Sonneville-Bordes 1960:73).
26 The original specimens were destroyed when Mikulov castle was burnt down in 1945.
27 This is the Brno II hominid.
28 One of the best examples of corpse binding comes from Kostenki 14 (Praslov and Rogachev 1982).

29 One section of seven notations is missing and of course there is no indication of the length of this section. Neither is it known which way the rod should be 'read'. This could be either 5,5,7,7,5 or 5,7,7,5,5 which would alter its accuracy as a tally of the lunar month. There is also a thirtieth mark, which is only half the length of the other twenty-nine marks.

30 Ochre and fire would be comparable to the brilliant qualities of stone, discussed in Chapter 6 (Morphy 1989), to focus attention on action.

31 At Kostenki the pits and houses have a maximum depth of 1.10 m below which permafrost was found (Praslov pers. comm.).

# BIBLIOGRAPHY

Absolon, K., and B. Klíma. 1977. *Předmostí, ein Mammutjägerplatz in Mähren.* Prague: Fontes Archaeologiae Moraviae 8.

Accorsi, C. A., E. Aiello, C. Bartolini, L. Castelletti, G. Rodolfi, and A. Ronchitelli. 1979. Il giacimento paleolitico di Serino (Avellino): stratigrafia, ambiente e paletnologia. *Atti Società Toscano Scienze Naturali* 86:435–87.

Adovasio, J. M., O. Soffer, and B. Klíma. 1996. Upper Palaeolithic fibre technology: interlaced woven finds from Pavlov I, Czech Republic, c.26,000 BP. Paper presented at The Society for American Archaeology, St Louis, 1996.

Aguirre, E., and G. Pasini. 1985. The Pliocene–Pleistocene boundary. *Episodes* 8:116–20.

Aiello, L., and R. Dunbar. 1993. Neocortex size, group size and the evolution of language. *Current Anthropology* 34:184–93.

Aiello, L., and P. Wheeler. 1995. The expensive-tissue hypothesis: the brain and the digestive system in human and primate evolution. *Current Anthropology* 36:199–221.

Aitken, M. 1990. *Science based dating in archaeology.* London: Longman.

Aitken, M. J., C. B. Stringer, and P. A. Mellars (editors). 1993. *The origin of modern humans and the impact of chronometric dating.* Princeton: Princeton University Press.

Albrecht, G., J. Hahn, and W. G. Torke. 1972. *Merkmalsanalyse von Geschoßspitzen des mittleren Jungpleistozäns in Mittel- und Osteuropa.* Tübingen: Archaeologica Ventoria 2.

Aldhouse-Green, S. 1995. Pontnewydd Cave, Wales, a later Middle Pleistocene hominid and archaeological site: a review of stratigraphy, dating, taphonomy and interpretation, in *Evolución humana en Europa y los yacimientos de la Sierra de Atapuerca.* Edited by J. M. Bérmudez de Castro, J. L. Arsuaga, and E. Carbonell, pp. 37–55. Valladolid: Junta de Castilla y León.

Allsworth-Jones, P. 1986. *The Szeletian and the transition from Middle to Upper Palaeolithic in Central Europe.* Oxford: Clarendon Press.

1990. The Szeletian and the stratigraphic succession in Central Europe and adjacent areas: main trends, recent results, and problems for resolution, in *The emergence of modern humans: an archaeological perspective.* Edited by P. Mellars, pp. 160–243. Edinburgh: Edinburgh University Press.

Ameloot-van der Heijden, N. 1994. L'ensemble lithique du niveau CA du gisement de Riencourt-les-Bapaume (Pas-de-Calais), in *Les industries laminaires au Paléolithique moyen.* Edited by S. Révillion and A. Tuffreau, pp. 63–75. Paris: Centre National de la Recherche Scientifique 18.

Ames, K. M. 1985. Hierarchies, stress, and logistical strategies among hunter-gatherers in northwestern North America, in *Prehistoric hunter-gatherers: the emergence of cultural complexity.* Edited by T. D. Price and J. A. Brown, pp. 155–80. Orlando: Academic Press.

Anconetani, P., L. Evangelista, U. Thun, and C. Peretto. 1995. The Lower Palaeolithic site Isernia la Pineta. Conference on *The role of early humans in the accumulation of European Lower and Middle Palaeolithic bone assemblages*, Schloss Monrepos, Neuwied, 1995.

Anderson-Gerfaud, P. 1990. Aspects of behaviour in the Middle Palaeolithic: functional analysis of stone tools from southwest France, in *The emergence of modern humans: an archaeological perspective*. Edited by P. Mellars, pp. 389–418. Edinburgh: Edinburgh University Press.

Andrews, J. T. 1983. Short ice age 230,000 years ago? *Nature* 303:21–2.

Andrews, P., and Y. Fernandez Jalvo. 1997. Surface modifications of the Sima de los Huesos fossil humans. *Journal of Human Evolution* 33:191–218.

Anikovich, M. 1992. Early Upper Paleolithic industries of Eastern Europe. *Journal of World Prehistory* 6:205–45.

Antoine, P. 1990. *Chronostratigraphie et environnement du Paléolithique du bassin de la Somme*. Lille: Université des Sciences et Technologies Publications de CERP 2.

Antoine, P., and A. Tuffreau. 1993. Contexte stratigraphique, climatique et paléotopographique des occupations Acheuléennes de la moyenne terrasse de la Somme. *Bulletin de la Société Préhistorique Française* 90:243–50.

Anzidei, A. P., and P. Gioia. 1992. The lithic industry at Rebibba – Casal de'Pazzi, in *New developments in Italian archaeology*, Part 1. Edited by E. Herring, R. Whitehouse and J. Wilkins, pp. 155–79. University of London: Accordia Research Centre, The Fourth Conference of Italian Archaeology.

Anzidei, A. P., and A. A. Huyzendveld. 1992. The Lower Palaeolithic site of La Polledrara di Cecanibbio (Rome, Italy), in *New developments in Italian archaeology*, Part 1. Edited by E. Herring, R. Whitehouse and J. Wilkins, pp. 141–53. University of London: Accordia Research Centre, The Fourth Conference of Italian Archaeology.

ApSimon, A. M. 1980. The last Neanderthal in France? *Nature* 287:271–2.

ApSimon, A. M., C. S. Gamble, and M. L. Shackley. 1977. Pleistocene raised beaches on Portsdown, Hampshire. *Proceedings of the Hampshire Field Club* 33:17–32.

Argyle, M. 1969. *Social interaction*. London: Tavistock.

Arsuaga, J. L., J. M. Bermúdez de Castro, and E. Carbonell (editors).1997. The Sima de los Huesos hominid site. *Journal of Human Evolution* 33:105–421.

Arsuaga, J. L., I. Martinez, A. Gracia, J. M. Carratero, and E. Carbonell. 1993. Three new human skulls from the Sima de los Huesos Middle Pleistocene site (Atapuerca, Spain). *Nature* 362:534–7.

Arts, N., and E. Cziesla. 1990. Bibliography (1880–1988) on the subject of refitting stone artefacts, in *The big puzzle*. Edited by E. Cziesla, S. Eickhoff, N. Arts, and D. Winter, pp. 677–90. Bonn: Holos, Studies in Modern Archaeology 1.

Ashton, N. M. 1983. Spatial patterning in the Middle–Upper Palaeolithic transition. *World Archaeology* 15:224–35.

Ashton, N. M., D. Q. Bowen, J. A. Holman, C. O. Hunt, B. G. Irving, R. A. Kemp, S. G. Lewis, J. McNabb, S. A. Parfitt, and M. B. Seddon. 1994. Excavation at the Lower Palaeolithic site at East Farm Barnham, Suffolk: 1989–1992. *Journal of the Geological Society* 151:599–605.

Ashton, N. M., J. Cook, S. G. Lewis, and J. Rose. 1992. *High Lodge: excavations by G. de G. Sieveking 1962–68 and J. Cook 1988*. London: British Museum Press.

Ashton, N. M., and J. McNabb. 1992. The interpretation and context of the High Lodge industries, in *High Lodge: excavations by G. de G. Sieveking 1962–68 and J. Cook 1988*. Edited by N. M. Ashton, J. Cook, S. G. Lewis, and J. Rose, pp. 164–8. London: British Museum Press.

Asquith, P. J. 1996. Japanese science and western hegemonies: primatology and the limits set to questions, in *Naked science: anthropological enquiry into boundaries, power, and knowledge*. Edited by L. Nader, pp. 239–56. New York: Routledge.

Auguste, P. 1988. Etude des restes osseux des grands mammifères des niveaux D, D1, II Base, in *Le gisement Paléolithique moyen de Biache-Saint-Vaast (Pas de Calais)*. Edited by A. Tuffreau and J. Sommé, pp. 133–69. Paris: Mémoires de la Société Préhistorique Française 21.

1992. Etude archéozoologique des grands mammifères du site pleistocène moyen de Biache-Saint-Vaast (Pas-de-Calais, France). *L'Anthropologie* 96:49–70.

1993. Acquisition et exploitation du gibier au Paléolithique moyen dans le nord de la France. Perspectives paléoécologiques et paleoethnographiques, in *Exploitation des animaux sauvages à travers le temps*, pp. 49–61. Antibes, Juan les Pins.

1995. Adaptations biologique et culturelle des Prénéandertaliens et des Néandertaliens aux modifications paléoécologiques et fauniques en France septentrionale, in *Nature et culture*. Edited by M. Otte, pp. 99–117. Liège: ERAUL 68.

Axelrod, A., and W. D. Hamilton. 1981. The evolution of cooperation. *Science* 211:1390.

Backer, A. M. 1993. Spatial distributions at La Roche à Pierrot, Saint-Césaire: changing uses of a rockshelter, in *Context of a late Neanderthal: implications of multidisciplinary research to Upper Palaeolithic adaptations at Saint-Césaire, Charente-Maritime, France*. Monographs in World Archaeology 16. Edited by F. Lévêque, A. M. Backer, and M. Guilbaud, pp. 103–27. Madison, Wisconsin: Prehistory Press.

Bader, O. N. 1967. Eine ungewöhnliche paläolithische Bestattung in Mittelrussland. *Quartär* 18:191–4.

1978. *Sunghir*. Moscow: Nauka.

Bahuchet, S. 1992. Spatial mobility and access to resources among the African Pygmies, in *Mobility and territoriality: social and spatial boundaries among foragers, fishers, pastoralists and peripatetics*. Edited by M. J. Casimir and A. Rao, pp. 205–57. Oxford: Berg.

Bailey, G. (editor). 1997. *Klithi: Archaeology of a Late Glacial landscape in Epirus (Northwest Greece)*. Cambridge: McDonald Institute for Archaeological Research.

Bailey, G., V. Papaconstantinou, and D. Sturdy. 1992. Asprochaliko and Kokkinopilos: TL dating and reinterpretation of Middle Palaeolithic sites in Epirus, north-west Greece. *Cambridge Archaeological Journal* 2:136–44.

Bar-Yosef, O. 1980. Prehistory of the Levant. *Annual Review of Anthropology* 9:101–33.

1991. Raw material exploitation in the Levantine Epi-Paleolithic, in *Raw material economies among prehistoric hunter-gatherers*. Edited by A. Montet-White and S. Holen, pp. 235–50. University of Kansas, Publications in Anthropology 19.

Barker, G., and C. S. Gamble (editors).1985. *Beyond domestication in prehistoric Europe*. London: Academic Press.

Barnard, A. 1992. *Hunters and herders of southern Africa: a comparative ethnography of the Khoisan peoples*. Cambridge: Cambridge University Press.

Barnes, J. A. 1972. *Social networks*. Addison-Wesley Module in Anthropology 26.

Barrett, J. 1994. *Fragments from antiquity*. Oxford: Blackwell.

Barrett, J., R. Bradley, and M. Green. 1991. *Landscape, monuments and society: the prehistory of Cranborne Chase*. Cambridge: Cambridge University Press.

Barth, F. 1978. Scale and network in urban western society, in *Scale and social organization*. Edited by F. Barth, pp. 163–83. Oslo: Universitets Forlaget.

Barton, C. M. 1988. *Lithic variability and Middle Palaeolithic behaviour*. Oxford: British Archaeological Reports, International Series 408.

Baryshnikov, G., and J. F. Hoffecker. 1994. Mousterian hunters of the NW Caucasus: preliminary results of recent investigations. *Journal of Field Archaeology* 21:1–14.

Baryshnikov, G., and J. F. Hoffecker. in press. Neanderthal ecology: a regional view from the Northwestern Caucasus. *Research and Exploration* :1–28.

Bassinot, F. C., L. D. Labeyrie, E. Vincent, X. Quidelleur, N. J. Shackleton, and Y. Lancelot. 1994. The astronomical theory of climate and the age of the Brunhes–Matuyama magnetic reversal. *Earth and Planetary Science Letters* 126:91–108.

Baumann, W., D. Mania, V. Toepfer, and L. Eissmann. 1983. *Die paläolithischen Neufunde von Markkleeberg bei Leipzig*. Berlin: Deutscher Verlag der Wissenschaften.

Bazile, F. 1976. Datations absolues sur les niveaux Paléolithiques supérieurs anciens de la grotte de l'Esquicho-Grapaou (Ste. Anastasie, Gard). *Bulletin de la Société Préhistorique Française* 73:207–17.

Beck, D. in preparation. The Stadel. PhD dissertation, University of Köln.

Behre, K. 1989. Biostratigraphy of the last glacial period in Europe. *Quaternary Science Reviews* 8:25–44.

Bell, R. H. V. 1971. A grazing system in the Serengeti. *Scientific American* 225:86–93.

Belli, G., G. Belluomini, P. F. Cassoli, S. Cecchi, M. Cuarzi, L. Delitala, G. Fornaciari, F. Mallegni, M. Piperno, A. G. Segre, and E. Segre-Naldini. 1991. Découverte d'un fémur humain acheuléen à Notarchirico (Venosa, Basilicate). *L'Anthropologie* 95:47–88.

Bender, B. 1978. Gatherer-hunter to farmer: a social perspective. *World Archaeology* 10:204–22.

1981. Gatherer-hunter, intensification, in *Economic Archaeology*. Edited by A. Sheridan and G. Bailey, pp. 149–57. Oxford: British Archaeological Reports, International Series 96.

1985. Prehistoric developments in the American Midcontinent and in Brittany, Northwest France, in *Prehistoric hunter-gatherers: the emergence of cultural complexity*. Edited by T. D. Price and J. A. Brown, pp. 21–57. Orlando: Academic Press.

Bergman, C. A., M. B. Roberts, S. Collcutt, and P. Barlow. 1990. Refitting and spatial analysis of artefacts from quarry 2 at the Middle Pleistocene Acheulean site of Boxgrove, West Sussex, England, in *The big puzzle*. Edited by E. Cziesla, S. Eickhoff, N. Arts, and D. Winter, pp. 265–81. Bonn: Holos, Studies in Modern Archaeology 1.

Bermúdez de Castro, J. M. 1995. Los homínidos de la Sima de los Huesos del karst de la Sierra de Atapuerca: número minimo de individuos, edad de muerte y sexo, in *Evolución humana en Europa y los yacimientos de la Sierra de*

*Atapuerca*. Edited by J. M. Bérmudez, J. L. Arsuaga, and E. Carbonell, pp. 263–81. Valladolid: Junta de Castilla y León.

Bermúdez de Castro, J. M., J. L. Arsuaga, E. Carbonell, A. Rosas, I. Martinez, and M. Mosquera. 1997. A hominid from the Lower Pleistocene of Atapuerca, Spain: possible ancestor to Neandertals and modern humans. *Science* 276:1392–5.

Bermúdez de Castro, J. M., and M. E. Nicolás. 1997. Palaeodemography of the Atapuerca-SH Middle Pleistocene hominid sample. *Journal of Human Evolution* 33:333–55.

Bernard, H. R., and P. D. Killworth. 1973. On the social structure of an ocean-going research vessel and other important things. *Social Science Research* 2:145–84.

Bettinger, R. 1991. *Hunter-gatherers: archaeological and evolutionary theory*. New York: Plenum.

Beyries, S. 1987. *Variabilité de l'industrie lithique au Moustérien: approche fonctionelle sur quelques gisements françaises*. Oxford: British Archaeological Reports, International Series 328.

1988. Functional variability of lithic sets in the Middle Palaeolithic, in *Upper Pleistocene prehistory of Western Eurasia*. Edited by H. Dibble and A. Montet-White, pp. 213–24. Philadelphia: University of Pennsylvania, University Museum Monograph 54.

Bicchieri, M. G. (editor) 1972. *Hunters and gatherers today*. New York: Holt, Rinehart and Winston.

Binford, L. R. 1972. Contemporary model building: paradigms and the current state of Palaeolithic research, in *Models in archaeology*. Edited by D. L. Clarke, pp. 109–66. London: Methuen.

1973. Interassemblage variability – the Mousterian and the 'functional' argument, in *The explanation of culture change*. Edited by C. Renfrew, pp. 227–54. London: Duckworth.

1977. Forty seven trips, in *Stone tools as cultural markers*. Edited by R. V. S. Wright, pp. 24–36. Canberra: Australian Institute of Aboriginal Studies.

1978a. Dimensional analysis of behaviour and site structure: learning from an Eskimo hunting stand. *American Antiquity* 43:330–61.

1978b. *Nunamiut ethnoarchaeology*. New York: Academic Press.

1979. Organization and formation processes: looking at curated technologies. *Journal of Anthropological Research* 35:172–97.

1980. Willow smoke and dogs' tails: hunter-gatherer settlement systems and archaeological site formation. *American Antiquity* 45:4–20.

1981a. Behavioral archaeology and the Pompeii premise. *Journal of Anthropological Research* 37:195–208.

1981b. *Bones: ancient men and modern myths*. New York: Academic Press.

1983a. *In pursuit of the past*. London: Thames and Hudson.

1983b. *Working at archaeology*. New York: Academic Press.

1988. Etude taphonomique des restes fauniques de la Grotte Vaufrey, couche VIII, in *La Grotte Vaufrey à Cenac et Saint-Julien (Dordogne), paléoenvironments, chronologie et activités humaines*. Edited by J.-P. Rigaud, pp. 535–64. Paris: Mémoires de la Société Préhistorique Française 19.

1989a. *Debating archaeology*. New York: Academic Press.

1989b. Isolating the transition to cultural adaptations: an organizational approach, in *The emergence of modern humans. Biocultural adaptations in the later Pleistocene*. Edited by E. Trinkaus, pp. 18–41. Cambridge: Cambridge University Press.

1991. When the going gets tough, the tough get going: Nunamiut local groups, camping patterns and economic organisation, in *Ethnoarchaeological approaches to mobile campsites: hunter-gatherer and pastoralist case studies*. Edited by C. S. Gamble and W. A. Boismier, pp. 25–138. Ann Arbor: International Monographs in Prehistory, Ethnoarchaeological Series 1.

Binford, L. R., and J. Bertram. 1977. Bone frequencies and attritional processes, in *For theory building in archaeology*. Edited by L. R. Binford, pp. 77–153. New York: Academic Press.

Binford, L. R., and S. R. Binford. 1966. A preliminary analysis of functional variability in the Mousterian of Levallois facies. *American Anthropologist* 68:238–95.

Binford, S. R., and L. R. Binford. 1969. Stone tools and human behaviour. *Scientific American* 220:70–84.

Birdsell, J. B. 1953. Some environmental and cultural factors influencing the structuring of Australian Aboriginal populations. *American Naturalist* 87:171–207.

1958. On population structure in generalized hunting and collecting populations. *Evolution* 12:189–205.

1968. Some predictions for the Pleistocene based on equilibrium systems among recent hunter-gatherers, in *Man the hunter*. Edited by R. Lee and I. DeVore, pp. 229–40. Chicago: Aldine.

1976. Realities and transformations: the tribes of the Western Desert of Australia, in *Tribes and boundaries in Australia*. Edited by N. Peterson, pp. 95–120. Canberra: Australian Institute of Aboriginal Studies.

Bíró, T. K. 1981. A Kárpát-Medencei obszidiánok Vizsgálata. *Különlenyomat az Archeologiai Ertesito* 108:194–205.

Bischoff, J. L., J.-F. Garcia, and L. G. Straus. 1992. Uranium-series isochron dating at El Castilló Cave (Cantabria, Spain): the 'Acheulean'/'Mousterian' question. *Journal of Archaeological Science* 19:49–62.

Bischoff, J. L., K. R. Ludwig, J. F. Garcia, E. Carbonell, M. Vaquero, T. W. Stafford, and A. J. T. Jull. 1994. Dating of the basal Aurignacian sandwich at Abric Romani (Catalunya, Spain) by radiocarbon and uranium series. *Journal of Archaeological Science* 21:541–51.

Bischoff, J. L., N. Soler, J. Maroto, and R. Julia. 1989. Abrupt Mousterian/Aurignacian boundary at c.40 ka bp: accelerator 14C dates from L'Arbreda cave (Catalunya, Spain). *Journal of Archaeological Science* 16:563–76.

Bitiri, M. 1972. *Paleoliticul in Tara Oasului*. Bucuresti: Institul de Archeologie.

Blackwell, B., and H. P. Schwarcz. 1986. U-series analyses of the lower travertine at Ehringsdorf, DDR. *Quaternary Research* 25:215–22.

Blasco Sancho, M. F. 1995. *Hombres, fieras y presas: estudio arqueozoológico y tafonómico del yacimiento del paleolitico medio de la Cueva de Gabasa 1 (Huesca)*. Zaragoza: Monografías Arqueológicas 38.

Bleed, P. 1986. The optimal design of hunting weapons. *American Antiquity* 51:737–47.

Boëda, E. 1988. Analyse technologique du débitage du niveau 2A, in *Le gisement Paléolithique moyen de Biache-Saint-Vaast (Pas de Calais)*. Edited by A. Tuffreau and J. Sommé, pp. 185–214. Paris: Mémoires de la Société Préhistorique Française 21.

1994. *Le concept Levallois: variabilité des méthodes*. Paris: CNRS Editions, Centre Récherche Archéologique 9.

Boëda, E., J.-M. Geneste, and L. Meignen. 1990. Identification de chaînes opératoires lithiques du Paléolithique ancien et moyen. *Paléo* 2:43–80.

Boëda, E., and B. Kervazo. 1991. Une vieille industrie du Sud-Ouest de la France: le niveau inférieur de Barbas (Dordogne), in *Les premiers Européens*. Edited by E. Bonifay and B. Vandermeersch, pp. 27–38. Paris: CTHS.

Boissevain, J. 1968. The place of non-groups in the social sciences. *Man* 3:542–56.

1974. *Friends of friends: networks, manipulators and coalitions*. Oxford: Blackwells.

1979. Network analysis: a reappraisal. *Current Anthropology* 20:392–4.

Bonifay, E., and P. Vandermeersch. 1991. Vue d'ensemble sur le très ancien Paléolithique de l'Europe, in *Les premiers Européens*. Edited by E. Bonifay and B. Vandermeersch, pp. 309–19. Paris: CTHS.

Bonsall, C. (editor). 1991. *The Mesolithic in Europe*. Edinburgh: Edinburgh University Press.

Bordes, F. 1950. L'évolution buissonnante des industries en Europe occidentale. Considérations theorétiques sur le Paléolithique ancien et moyen. *L'Anthropologie* 54:393–420.

1953. Essai de classification des industries 'Mousteriénnes'. *Bulletin de la Société Préhistorique Française* 50:457–66.

1961a. *Typologie du Paléolithique ancien et moyen*. Bordeaux: Publications de l'Institut de Préhistoire de l'Université de Bordeaux, Mémoire No. 1.

1961b. Mousterian cultures in France. *Science* 134:803–10.

1968a. *The old stone age*. London: Weidenfeld and Nicholson.

1968b. Emplacements de tentes du Périgordien supérieur évolué à Corbiac (prés Bergerac, Dordogne). *Quartär* 19:251–62.

1972. *A tale of two caves*. New York: Harper and Row.

1973. On the chronology and contemporaneity of different Palaeolithic cultures in France, in *The explanation of cultural change: models in prehistory*. Edited by C. Renfrew, pp. 217–26. London: Duckworth.

1980. Le débitage Levallois et ses variants. *Bulletin de la Société Préhistorique Française* 77:45–9.

1981. Vingt-cinq ans après: le complexe Moustérien revisité. *Bulletin de la Société Préhistorique Française* 78:77–87.

Bordes, F., and M. Bourgon. 1951. Le complexe Moustérien: Moustérien, Levalloisien, et Tayacien. *L'Anthropologie* 57:1–44.

Bordes, F., and J. Labrot. 1967. La stratigraphie du gisement de Roc de Combe (Lot) et ses implications. *Bulletin de la Société Préhistorique Française* 64:15–28.

Bordes, F., and F. Prat. 1965. Observations sur les faunes de Riss et du Würm I en Dordogne. *L'Anthropologie* 69:31–45.

Bordes, F., and D. de Sonneville-Bordes. 1970. The significance of variability in Palaeolithic assemblages. *World Archaeology* 2:61–73.

Boriskovsky, P. I. (editor). 1984. *Palaeolithic of the USSR*. Moscow: Nauka.

Bosinski, G. 1966. Der paläolithische Fundplatz Rheindahlen, Stadtkreis Mönchengladbach. *Prähistorische Zeitschrift* 43:312–16.

1967. *Die Mittelpaläolithischen Funde im Westlichen Mitteleuropa*. Köln: Fundamenta Reihe A/4.

1982. The transition from Lower/Middle Palaeolithic in Northwestern Germany, in *The transition from Lower to Middle Palaeolithic and the origin of modern man*. Edited by A. Ronen, pp. 165–75. Oxford: British Archaeological Reports, International Series 151.

1983. Die Ausgrabungen in Kärlich/Neuwieder Becken, in *Beilage zum Jahresbericht 1982 der Gerda Henkel-Stiftung*, pp. 9–20. Düsseldorf.

1992a. *Eiszeitjäger im Neuwieder Becken: Archäologie des Eiszeitalters am Mittelrhein*. Koblenz: Gesellschaft für Archäologie an Mittelrhein und Mosel 1.

1992b. Die ersten Menschen in Eurasien. *Jahrbuch des Römisch-Germanischen Zentralmuseums Mainz* 39:131–81.

1994. Settlement patterns Central Europe. Paper presented at the *ESF Workshop on the European Middle Palaeolithic*. Arras.

1995a. The earliest occupation of Europe: western central Europe, in *The earliest occupation of Europe*. Edited by W. Roebroeks and T. van Kolfschoten, pp. 103–28. Leiden: University of Leiden and European Science Foundation.

1995b. The period 30,000–20,000 14C BP in the Rheinland. Paper presented at the *ESF Workshop on the European Upper Palaeolithic*. Pavlov.

Bosinski, G., H. Bosinski, K. Brunnacker, E. Cziesla, K. P. Lanser, F. O. Neuffer, J. Preuss, H. Spoerer, W. Tillmanns, and B. Urban. 1985. Sprendlingen: ein Fundplatz des mittleren Jungpaläolithikums in Rheinhessen. *Jahrbuch des Römisch-Germanischen Zentralmuseums* 32:3–91.

Bosinski, G., T. van Kolfschoten, and E. Turner. 1988. *Miesenheim 1 Die Zeit des Homo erectus*. Andernach: Andernach Stadtmuseum.

Bosinski, G., K. Kröger, J. Schäfer, and E. Turner. 1986. Altsteinzeitliche Siedlungsplätze auf den Osteifel-Vulkanen. *Jahrbuch des Römisch-Germanischen Zentralmuseums* 33:97–130.

Botella, M., J. Vera, and J. Porta. 1976. El yacimiento achelense de la 'Solana del Zamborino', Fonelas (Granada). Primera campana de excavaciones. *Cuadernos de Prehistoria* 1:1–45.

Bott, E. 1957. *Family and social network*. London: Tavistock.

Bouchud, J. 1975. Etude de la faune de l'Abri Pataud, in *Excavation of the Abri Pataud, Les Eyzies (Dordogne)*. Edited by H. L. Movius, pp. 69–153. Cambridge, Mass.: Peabody Museum Press, American School of Prehistoric Research Bulletin 30.

Bowen, D. Q., S. Hughes, G. A. Sykes, and G. H. Miller. 1989. Land–sea correlations in the Pleistocene based on isoleucine epimerization in non-marine molluscs. *Nature* 340:49–51.

Boyle, K. V. 1990. *Upper Palaeolithic faunas from South-West France: a zoogeographic perspective*. Oxford: British Archaeological Reports, International Series 557.

Bradley, B. 1977. Experimental lithic technology with special reference to the Middle Palaeolithic. Ph.D. dissertation, University of Cambridge.

Bradley, R. J. 1984. *The social foundations of prehistoric Britain*. London: Longmans.

Breuil, H. 1912. Les subdivisions du Paléolithique supérieur et leur signification, in *Comptes rendus du 14e Congrès International d'Anthropologie et d'Archéologie Préhistorique, Genève, 1912*, pp. 165–238.

Brézillon, M. 1968. Le dénomination des objects de pierre taillée. *Gallia Préhistoire* Supplement 4.

Bricker, H. M., and H. Laville. 1977. Le gisement Châtelperronien de plein air des Tambourets (Commune de Coulardere, Haute-Garonne). *Bulletin de la Société Préhistorique Française* 74:505–17.

Bridgland, D. R. 1985. New information and results from recent excavations at Barnfield Pit, Swanscombe. *Quaternary Newsletter* 46:1–10.

1994. *Quaternary of the Thames*. London: Chapman and Hall.

Brodar, M. 1958–9. Crvena Stijena, eine neue Paläolithstation aus dem Balkan in Jugoslavien. *Quartär* 10/11:227–36.

Brodar, S., and M. Brodar. 1983. *Potocka Zijalka*. Ljubljana: Slovenska Akademija Znanosti in Umetnosti.

Brody, H. 1981. *Maps and dreams*. Vancouver: Douglas and McIntyre.

Brown, J. A., and T. D. Price. 1985. Complex hunter-gatherers: retrospect and prospect, in *Prehistoric hunter-gatherers: the emergence of cultural complexity*. Edited by T. D. Price and J. A. Brown, pp. 435–42. Orlando: Academic Press.

Brugal, J., and J. Jaubert. 1991. Les gisements paléontologiques pléistocènes à indices de fréquentation humaine: un nouveau type de comportement de prédateur? *Paléo* 3:15–41.

Brunnacker, K. 1982. Environmental conditions in Middle Europe during the Lower/Middle Palaeolithic transition, in *The transition from Lower to Middle Palaeolithic and the origin of modern man*. Edited by A. Ronen, pp. 123–9. Oxford: British Archaeological Reports, International series S151.

Brunnacker, K., and R. Streit. 1966. Neuere Gesichtspunkte zur Untersuchung von Höhlensedimenten. *Jahresheft für Karst und Höhlenkunde* 7:29–44.

Buisson, D. 1990. Les flûtes Paléolithiques d'Isturitz (Pyrénées Atlantiques). *Bulletin de la Société Préhistorique Française* 87:420–33.

Burch, E. S. 1975. *Eskimo kinsmen: changing family relationships in Northwest Alaska*. New York: West Publishing, American Ethnological Society Monograph 59.

Burch, E. S., and L. J. Ellanna (editors). 1994. *Key issues in hunter-gatherer research*. Oxford: Berg.

Burkert, W., B. Cep, Ç.-J. Kind, C. Pasda, M. Schrantz, and U. Simon. 1992. Wittlingen: Eine mittelpaläolithische Freilandfundstelle bei Bad Urach. *Fundberichte aus Baden-Württemberg* 17:1–110.

Busch, R., and H. Schwabedissen. 1991. *Salzgitter-Lebenstedt II*. Köln: Fundamenta Reihe A, Band 11/II.

Byrne, R. 1995. *The thinking ape: evolutionary origins of intelligence*. Oxford: Oxford University Press.

Byrne, R. W., and A. Whiten (editors). 1988. *Machiavellian intelligence: social expertise and the evolution of intellect in monkeys, apes and humans*. Oxford: Clarendon Press.

Cabaj, V., and V. Sitlivyl. 1994. The blade component in the Middle Palaeolithic of Ukraine: origin and evolution, in *Les industries laminaires au Paléolithique moyen*. Edited by S. Révillion and A. Tuffreau, pp. 161–77. Paris: CNRS.

Cabrera-Valdés, V. 1984. *El yacimento de la cueva de 'el Castilló' (Puente Viesgo, Santander)*. Madrid: CSIC, Bibliotheca Praehistorica Hispana XXII.

Cabrera-Valdés, V. (editor). 1993. *El origen del hombre moderno en el suroeste de Europa*. Madrid: Universidad de Educación a Distancia.

Cabrera-Valdés, V., and J. L. Bischoff. 1989. Accelerator 14C dates for Early Upper Palaeolithic (Basal Aurignacian) at El Castilló Cave (Spain). *Journal of Archaeological Science* 16:577–84.

Callow, P. 1986a. Raw materials and sources, in *La Cotte de St. Brelade 1961–1978. Excavations by C.B.M. McBurney*. Edited by P. Callow and J. M. Cornford, pp. 203–11. Norwich: Geo Books.

1986b. An overview of the industrial succession, in *La Cotte de St. Brelade 1961–1978. Excavations by C.B.M. McBurney*. Edited by P. Callow and J. M. Cornford, pp. 219–30. Norwich: Geo Books.

1986c. The stratigraphic sequence: description and problems, in *La Cotte de St. Brelade 1961–1978. Excavations by C.B.M. McBurney*. Edited by P. Callow and J. M. Cornford, pp. 55–71. Norwich: Geo Books.

Callow, P., and J. M. Cornford (editors). 1986. *La Cotte de St. Brelade 1961–1978. Excavations by C.B.M. McBurney*. Norwich: Geo Books.

Callow, P., D. Walton, and C. A. Shell. 1986. The use of fire at La Cotte de St. Brelade, in *La Cotte de St. Brelade 1961–1978. Excavations by C.B.M. McBurney*. Edited by P. Callow and J. M. Cornford, pp. 193–5. Norwich: Geo Books.

Caloi, L., G. B. L. Coccolini, M. Mussi, M. R. Palombo, S. Vitagliano, and D. Zampetti. 1988. Le Moustérien du Latium (Italie centrale): archéologie, milieu natural, chronologie. *L'Anthropologie* 92:73–98.

Campbell, J. B. 1977. *The Upper Palaeolithic of Britain*. Oxford: Oxford University Press.

Campbell, J. B., and G. Sampson. 1971. A new analysis of Kent's Cavern, Devonshire, England. *University of Oregon Anthropological Papers* 3.

Camps-Fabrer, H. (editor). 1974. *L'industrie de l'os dans la préhistoire*. University of Provence: CNRS.

Carbonell, E. 1992. Abric Romani nivell H: un model d'estraregia ocupacional al plistoce superior mediterrani. *ESTRAT: Revista d'arquelogia, prehistoria i historia antiga* 5:157–308.

Carbonell, E., J. M. Bérmudez de Castro, J. L. Arsuaga, J. C. Diez, A. Rosas, G. Cuenca-Bescos, R. Sala, M. Mosquera, and X. P. Rodriguez. 1995. Lower Pleistocene hominids and artifacts from Atapuerca-TDS (Spain). *Science* 269:826–30.

Carbonell, E., and Z. Castro-Curel. 1992. Palaeolithic wooden artefacts from the Abric Romani (Capellades, Barcelona, Spain). *Journal of Archaeological Science* 19:707–19.

Carbonell, E., S. Giralt, B. Marquez, A. Martin, M. Mosquera, A. Ollé, X. P. Rodriguez, R. Sala, M. Vaquero, J. M. Vergès, and J. Zaragoza. 1995. El conjunto Lito-Técnico de la Sierra de Atapuerca en el marco del Pleistoceno Medio europeo, in *Evolución humana en Europa y los yacimientos de la Sierra de Atapuerca*, vol. II. Edited by J. M. Bérmudez de Castro, J. L. Arsuaga, and E. Carbonell, pp. 445–555. Valladolid: Junta de Castilla y León.

Carbonell, E., M. Mosquera, X. P. Rodriguez, and R. Sala. 1996. The first human settlement of Europe. *Journal of Anthropological Research* 51:107–14.

Carbonell, E., and X. P. Rodriguez. 1994. Early middle Pleistocene deposits and artefacts in the Gran Dolina site (TD4) of the 'Sierra de Atapuerca' (Burgos, Spain). *Journal of Human Evolution* 26:291–311.

Carls, N., J. Groiss, B. Kaulich, and L. Reisch. 1988. Neue Beobachtungen in der mittelpleistozänen Fundstelle von Hunas im LDKR. Nürnberger Land, Vorbericht zu den Grabungskampagnen 1983–1986. *Archäologisches Korrespondenzblatt* 18:109–19.

Carlstein, T. 1982. *Time resources, society and ecology: preindustrial societies*. London: George Allen and Unwin.

Carrithers, M. 1990. Why humans have cultures. *Man* 25:189–206.

Cassoli, P. F., D. Lefevre, M. Piperno, J. P. Raynal, and A. Tagliacozzo. 1993. Una paleosuperficie con resti di *Elephas* (*Palaeoloxodon*) *antiquus* e industria acheuleana nel sito di Notarchirico (Venosa, Basilicata), in *Paleosuperfici del pleistocene e del primo olocene in Italia processi di formazione e interpretazione, Firenze, 1993*, pp. 101–16.

Cassoli, P. F., and A. Tagliacozzo. 1994. Considerazioni paleontologiche, paleoecologiche e archeozoologiche sui macromammiferi e gli uccelli dei livelli del pleistocene superiore del Riparo di Fumane (VR) (Scavi 1988–91). *Bolletino Museo Civilita Statale Naturale Verona* 18:349–445.

Champagne, F., and R. Espitalié. 1981. *Le Piage, site préhistorique du Lot*. Paris: Société Préhistorique Française.

Chance, M. R. A., and R. R. Larsen (editors). 1976. *Social structure of attention*. London: John Wiley.

Chase, P. G. 1989. How different was Middle Palaeolithic subsistence? A zooarchaeological perspective on the Middle to Upper Palaeolithic transition, in *The human revolution: behavioural and biological perspectives on the origins of modern humans*. Edited by P. Mellars and C. Stringer, pp. 321–37. Edinburgh: Edinburgh University Press.

Chase, P. G., and H. L. Dibble. 1987. Middle Palaeolithic symbolism: a review of current evidence and interpretations. *Journal of Anthropological Archaeology* 6:263–96.

Chauvet, J.-M., E. Brunel Deschamps, and C. Hillaire. 1995. *Chauvet Cave: the discovery of the world's oldest paintings*. London: Thames and Hudson.

Cheney, D., and R. Seyfarth. 1990. *How monkeys see the world: inside the mind of another species*. Chicago: University of Chicago Press.

Chernysh, A. P. 1961. *Palaeolitiginia Stoanka Molodova 5*. Kiev: An. Ukr. SSR.

Childe, V. G. 1951. *Social evolution*. London: Watts.

Chmielewski, W. 1961. *Civilisation de Jerzmanovice*. Wroclaw-Warzawa-Krakow: Institut Historicae Kultury Materialnej Polskiej Akademii Nauka.

Cioni, O., P. Gambassini, and D. Torre. 1979. Grotta di Castelcivita: risultati delle ricerche negli anni 1975–77. *Atti Toscana di Scienze Naturali Memorie, Serie A* 86:275–96.

Clark, G. A. 1992a. A comment on Mithen's ecological interpretation of Palaeolithic art. *Proceedings of the Prehistoric Society* 58:107–9.

1992b. Continuity or replacement? Putting modern human origins in an evolutionary context, in *The Middle Palaeolithic: adaptation, behaviour, and variability*. Edited by H. L. Dibble and P. Mellars, pp. 183–207. Philadelphia: University of Pennsylvania, University Museum 72.

1993. Paradigms in science and archaeology. *Journal of Anthropological Research* 1:203–33.

Clark, G. A., and J. M. Lindly. 1989. The case for continuity: observations on the biocultural transition in Europe and western Asia, in *The human revolution: behavioural and biological perspectives in the origins of modern humans*. Edited by P. Mellars and C. Stringer, pp. 626–76. Edinburgh: Edinburgh University Press.

1991. On paradigmatic biases and Palaeolithic research traditions. *Current Anthropology* 32:577–87.

Clark, J. D. 1976. *The prehistory of Africa*. London: Thames and Hudson.

Clark, J. G. D. 1957. *Archaeology and society*, 3rd edition. London: Methuen.

1986. *Symbols of excellence*. Cambridge: Cambridge University Press.

1989. *Economic prehistory*. Cambridge: Cambridge University Press.

Clarke, D. L. 1968. *Analytical archaeology*. London: Methuen.

Clarke, R. J. 1990. The Ndutu cranium and the origin of *Homo sapiens*. *Journal of Human Evolution* 19:699–736.

Colson, E. 1978. A redundancy of actors, in *Scale and social organization*. Edited by F. Barth, pp. 150–62. Oslo: Universitets Forlaget.

Coltorti, M., M. Cremaschi, M. C. Delitala, D. Esu, M. Fornaseri, A. McPherron, M. Nicoletti, R. van Otterloo, C. Peretto, B. Sala, V. Schmidt, and J. Sevink. 1982. Reversed magnetic polarity at an early lower Palaeolithic site in Central Italy. *Nature* 300:173–6.

Combier, J. 1967. *Le Paléolithique de l'Ardèche, dans son cadre paléoclimatique*. Bordeaux: Delmars.

Conard, N. J. 1992. *Tönchesberg and its position in the Palaeolithic prehistory of northern Europe*. Bonn: Habelt, Römisch-Germanisches Zentralmuseum Mainz, Monograph 20.

1994. On the prospects for an ethnography of extinct hominids. *Current Anthropology* 35:281–2.

1995. The Middle Palaeolithic faunal assemblages from the 1991–1994 excavations in Wallertheim, Rheinhessen. Paper presented at *The role of early humans in the accumulation of European Lower and Middle Palaeolithic bone assemblages, Schloss Monrepos*. Neuwied.

1996. Middle Palaeolithic settlement in the Rhineland. Paper presented at Workshop 5, *Middle Palaeolithic and Middle Stone Age settlement systems*. UISPP, Forli.

Conard, N. J., and D. S. Adler. 1997. Lithic reduction and hominid behaviour in the Middle Palaeolithic of the Rhineland. *Journal of Anthropological Research* 53:147–76.

Conard, N. J., D. S. Adler, D. T. Forrest, and P. J. Kaszas. 1995. Preliminary archaeological results from the 1991–1993 excavations in Wallertheim. *Archäologisches Korrespondenzblatt* 25:13–27.

Conard, N. J., J. Preuss, R. Langohr, P. Haesaerts, T. van Kolfschoten, J. Becze-Deak, and A. Rebholz. 1995. New geological research at the Middle Palaeolithic locality of Wallertheim in Rheinhessen. *Archäologisches Korrespondenzblatt* 25:1–11.

Conkey, M. W. 1978. Style and information in cultural evolution: toward a predictive model for the Palaeolithic, in *Social archaeology*. Edited by C. L. Redman, M. J. Berman, E. V. Curtin, W. T. Langhorne, N. M. Versaggi, and J. C. Wanser, pp. 61–85. New York: Academic Press.

1985. Ritual communication, social elaboration, and the variable trajectories of Palaeolithic material culture, in *Prehistoric hunter-gatherers: the emergence of cultural complexity*. Edited by T. D. Price and J. A. Brown, pp. 299–323. Orlando: Academic Press.

Conkey, M. W., and S. H. Williams. 1991. The political economy of gender in archaeology, in *Gender at the crossroads of knowledge: feminist anthropology in a post modern era* . Edited by M. di Leonardo, pp. 102–39. Berkeley: University of California Press.

Connerton, P. 1989. *How societies remember*. Cambridge: Cambridge University Press.

Constandse-Westermann, T. S., and R. R. Newell. 1991. Social and biological aspects of the western European Mesolithic population structure: a comparison with the demography of North American Indians, in *The Mesolithic in Europe*. Edited by C. Bonsall, pp. 106–15. Edinburgh: Edinburgh University Press.

Conway, B., J. McNabb, and N. Ashton (editors). 1996. *Excavations at Barnfield Pit, Swanscombe, 1968–1972*. London: British Museum Press, British Museum Occasional Paper 94.

Conybeare, A., and G. Haynes. 1984. Observations on elephant mortality and bones in water holes. *Quaternary Research* 22:189–200.

Cook, J. 1986. A blade industry from Stoneham's pit, Crayford, in *The Palaeolithic of Britain and its nearest neighbours: recent trends*. Edited by S. N. Collcut, pp. 16–20. Sheffield: University of Sheffield, Department of Archaeology and Prehistory.

Cook, J., C. B. Stringer, A. P. Currant, H. P. Schwarcz, and A. G. Wintle. 1982. A review of the chronology of the European Middle Pleistocene hominid record. *Yearbook of Physical Anthropology* 25:19–65.

Cordy, J.-M. 1992. Apport de la paléomammologie à la paléoanthropologie en Europe, in *Cinq millions d'années, l'aventure humaine*. Edited by M. Toussaint, pp. 77–94. Liège: ERAUL 56.

Cornford, J. M. 1986. Specialised resharpening techniques and evidence of handedness, in *La Cotte de St. Brelade 1961–1978: excavations by C.B.M. McBurney*. Edited by P. Callow and J. M. Cornford, pp. 337–53. Norwich: Geo Books.

Coudret, P., M. Larriere-Cabiran, M. Olive, N. Pigeot, and Y. Taborin. 1994. Etiolles, in *Environments et habitats Magdaléniens dans le centre du Bassin parisien*. Edited by Y. Taborin, pp. 132–46. Paris: Documents d'Archéologie Française 43.

Cremaschi, M., and C. Peretto. 1988. Les sols d'habitat du site Paléolithique d'Isernia La Pineta (Molise, Italie centrale). *L'Anthropologie* 92:1017–40.

Cubitt, T. 1973. Network density among urban families, in *Network analysis: studies in human interaction*. Edited by J. Boissevain and J. C. Mitchell, pp. 67–82. The Hague: Mouton.

Cullen, B. 1996. Social interaction and viral phenomena, in *The archaeology of human ancestry: power, sex and tradition*. Edited by J. Steele and S. Shennan, pp. 420–33. London: Routledge.

Currant, A. 1989. The Quaternary origins of the modern British mammal fauna. *Biological Journal of the Linnaean Society* 38:23–30.

Cziesla, E. 1984. Das mittlere Jungpaläolithikum im westlichen Deutschland. *Archäologische Informationen* 7:28–39.

1987. L'analyse des raccords ou le concept du dynamisme en préhistoire. *Bulletin de la Société Préhistorique Luxembourgeoise* 10:77–111.

1990. On refitting of stone artifacts, in *The big puzzle*. Edited by E. Cziesla, S. Eickhoff, N. Arts, and D. Winter, pp. 21–56. Bonn: Holos, Studies in Modern Archaeology 1.

Cziesla, E., S. Eickhoff, N. Arts, and D. Winter (editors). 1990. *The big puzzle*. Bonn: Holos, Studies in Modern Archaeology 1.

D'Errico, F., and P. Villa. 1997. Holes and grooves: the contribution of microscopy and taphonomy to the problem of art origins. *Journal of Human Evolution* 33:1–31.

Damas, D. 1972a. The Copper Eskimo, in *Hunters and gatherers today*. Edited by M. G. Bicchieri, pp. 3–50. New York: Holt, Rinehart and Winston.

1972b. The structure of Central Eskimo associations, in *Alliance in Eskimo society*. Edited by L. Guemple pp. 40–55. Seattle: Proceedings of the American Ethnological Society 1971, Supplement.

Damas, D. (editor). 1969. *Contributions to anthropology: band societies*. National Museum of Canada Bulletin 228.

Dansgaard, W., S. J. Johnsen, H. B. Clausen, D. Dahl-Jensen, N. S. Gundestrup, C. U. Hammer, C. S. Hvidberg, J. P. Steffensen, A. E. Sveinbjörnsdottir, J. Jouzel, and G. Bond. 1993. Evidence for general instability of past climate from a 250-kyr ice-core record. *Nature* 364:218–20.

David, F., and C. Farizy. 1994. Les vestiges ossueux: étude archéozoologique, in *Hommes et bisons du Paléolithique Moyen à Mauran*. Edited by C. Farizy, F. David, and J. Jaubert, pp. 177–303. Paris: CNRS.

Davidson, I., and W. Noble. 1989. The archaeology of perception: traces of depiction and language. *Current Anthropology* 30:125–55.

1993. Tools and language in human evolution, in *Tools, language and cognition in human evolution*. Edited by K. R. Gibson and T. Ingold, pp. 363–88. Cambridge: Cambridge University Press.

de Jong, J. 1988. Climatic variability during the past three million years, as indicated by vegetational evolution in northwest Europe and with emphasis on data from the Netherlands. *Philosophical Transactions of the Royal Society of London B* 318:603–17.

De Loecker, D. 1994. On the refitting analysis of Site K: a Middle Palaeolithic findspot at Maastricht-Belvédère (The Netherlands). *Ethnographisch Archäologische Zeitschrift* 35:107–17.

Débenath, A. 1973. Un foyer aménagé dans le Moustérien de Hauteroche à Chateauneuf-sur-Charente (Charente). *L'Anthropologie* 77:329–38.

1976. Les civilisations du Paléolithique inférieur en Charente, in *La Préhistoire française*, vol. I. Edited by H. de Lumley, pp. 929–35. Paris: CNRS.

1992. The place of the Mousterian of the Charente in the Middle Palaeolithic of Southwest France, in *The Middle Palaeolithic: adaptation, behaviour, and variability*. Edited by H. L. Dibble and P. Mellars, pp. 53–9. Philadelphia: University of Pennsylvania, University Museum 72.

Debénath, A., and H. L. Dibble. 1994. *Handbook of Palaeolithic typology*. Vol. I. *Lower and Middle Palaeolithic of Europe*. Philadelphia: University Museum, University of Pennsylvania.

Defleur, A. 1993. *Les sépultures moustériennes*. Paris: CNRS.

Delpech, F. 1976. Les faunes du Paléolithique supérieur dans le sud-ouest de la France. Thèse, Doctorat d'Etat, Université de Bordeaux.

1984. La Ferrassie: carnivores, artiodactyles et périssodactyles, in *Le Grand Abri de la Ferrassie: fouilles 1968–1973*. Edited by H. Delporte, pp. 61–90. Paris: Etudes Quaternaires Mémoire 7.

1988. Les grands mammifères de la Grotte Vaufrey à l'exception des ursidés, in *La Grotte Vaufrey à Cenac et Saint-Julien (Dordogne), paléoenvironments, chronologie et activités humaines*. Edited by J.-P. Rigaud, pp. 213–90. Paris: Mémoires de la Société Préhistorique Française 19.

Delporte, H., and G. Mazière. 1977. L'aurignacien de la Ferrassie: observations préliminaires à la suite des fouilles récentes. *Bulletin de la Société Préhistorique Française* 74:343–61.

Dennell, R. W. 1983. A new chronology for the Mousterian. *Nature* 301:199–200.

1997. The world's oldest spears. *Nature* 385:767–8.

Dennell, R. W., H. M. Rendell, L. Hurcombe, and E. A. Hailwood. 1994. Archaeological evidence for hominids in Northern Pakistan before one million years ago. *Courier Forschungs-Institut Senckenberg* 171:151–5.

Dennell, R. W., and W. Roebroeks. 1996. The earliest colonization of Europe: the short chronology revisited. *Antiquity* 70:535–42.

Dennett, D. 1991. *Consciousness explained*. Harmondsworth: Penguin.

Desbrosse, R., and J. Kozlowski. 1988. *Hommes et climats à l'âge du mammouth: le Paléolithique supérieur d'Eurasie centrale*. Paris: Masson.

Dibble, H. L. 1987. The interpretation of Middle Palaeolithic scraper morphology. *American Antiquity* 52:109–17.

Dibble, H. L., and N. Rolland. 1992. On assemblage variability in the Middle Palaeolithic of Western Europe: history, perspectives, and a new synthesis, in *The Middle Palaeolithic: adaptation, behaviour, and variability*. Edited by H. L. Dibble and P. Mellars, pp. 1–29. Philadelphia: University of Pennsylvania, University Museum 72.

Dixon, R. M. W. 1976. Tribes, languages and other boundaries in northeast Queensland, in *Tribes and boundaries in Australia*. Edited by N. Peterson, pp. 207–38. Canberra: Australian Institute of Aboriginal Studies.

Djindjian, F. 1994. L'influence des frontières naturelles dans les déplacements des chasseurs-cueilleurs au Würm récent. *Preistoria Alpina* 28:7–28.

Dobres, M.-A., and C. R. Hoffman. 1994. Social agency and the dynamics of prehistoric technology. *Journal of Archaeological Method and Theory* 1:211–58.

Douglas, M. 1973. *Natural symbols*. Harmondsworth: Pelican Books.

Dunbar, R. I. M. 1992a. Time: a hidden constraint on the behavioural ecology of baboons. *Behavioural Ecology and Sociobiology* 31:35–49.

1992b. Neocortex size as a constraint on group size in primates. *Journal of Human Evolution* 20:469–93.

1993. Coevolution of neocortical size, group size and language in humans. *Behavioural and Brain Sciences* 16:681–735.

1996. *Grooming, gossip and the evolution of language*. London: Faber and Faber.

Dzaparidze, V., G. Bosinski, T. Bugianisvili, L. Gabunia, A. Justus, N. Klopotovskaja, E. Kvavadze, D. Lordkipanidze, G. Majsuradze, N. Mgeladze, M. Nioradze, E. Pavelenisvili, H-U. Schmincke, D. Sologasvili, D. Tusabramisvili, M. Tvalcrelidze, and A. Vekua. 1989. Der altpaläolithische Fundplatz Dmanisi in Georgien (Kaukasus). *Jahrbuch des Römisch-Germanischen Zentralmuseums Mainz* 36:67–116.

Edmonds, M. 1990. Descriptions, understanding and the chaîne opératoire. *Archaeological Review from Cambridge* 9:55–70.

Efimenko, P. P. 1958. *Kostenki I*. Moscow–Leningrad: Nauka.

Emmerling, E., H. Geer, and B. Klíma. 1993. Eine Mondkalenderstab aus Dolní Věstonice. *Quartär* 43/44:151–62.

Enloe, J. G. 1993. Subsistence organisation in the Early Upper Paleolithic: reindeer hunters of the Abri du Flageolet, Couche V, in *Before Lascaux: the complex record of the Early Upper Paleolithic*. Edited by H. Knecht, A. Pike-Tay, and R. White, pp. 101–15. Boca Raton: CRC Press.

Erfurt, J., and D. Mania. 1990. Zur Paläontologie des jungpleistozänen Waldelefanten von Gröbern, Kreis Grafenhainichen, in *Neumark-Gröbern: Beiträge zur Jagd des mittelpaläolithischen Menschen*. Edited by D. Mania, pp. 215–44. Berlin: Deutscher Verlag der Wissenschaften.

Escalon de Fonton, M. 1966. Du Paléolithique supérieur au Mesolithique dans le midi méditerranéen. *Bulletin de la Société Préhistorique Française* 63:66–180.

Estévez, J. 1987. La fauna de l'Arbreda (sector Alfa) en el conjunt de faunes del Plistocè Superior. *Cypsela* 6:73–87.

Evans-Pritchard, E. E. 1965. *Theories of primitive religion*. Oxford: Clarendon.

Farizy, C. 1990. The transition from Middle to Upper Palaeolithic at Arcy-sur-Cure (Yonne, France): technological, economic and social aspects, in *The emergence of modern humans: an archaeological perspective*. Edited by P. Mellars, pp. 303–27. Edinburgh: Edinburgh University Press.

1993. Les prémiers européens venaient-ils d'Afrique? *L'Histoire* 165:42–5.

1994. Spatial patterning of Middle Palaeolithic sites. *Journal of Anthropological Archaeology* 13:153–60.

Farizy, C., and F. David. 1992. Subsistence and behavioural patterns of some Middle Palaeolithic local groups, in *The Middle Palaeolithic: adaptation, behaviour, and variability*. Edited by H. L. Dibble and P. Mellars, pp. 87–97. Philadelphia: University of Pennsylvania, University Museum 72.

Farizy, C., J. David, and J. Jaubert. 1994. *Hommes et bisons du Paléolithique moyen à Mauran (Haute-Garonne)*. Paris: CNRS, Gallia-Préhistoire Supplement 30.

Farrand, W. 1975. Analysis of the Abri Pataud sediments, in *Excavation of the Abri Pataud, Les Eyzies (Dordogne)*. Edited by H. L. Movius, pp. 27–68.

Cambridge, Mass.: American School of Prehistoric Research vol. 30: Peabody Museum Press.

Féblot-Augustins, J. 1990. Exploitation des matières premières dans l'Acheuléen d'Afrique: perspectives comportementales. *Paléo* 2:27–42.

1993. Mobility strategies in the late Middle Palaeolithic of central Europe and western Europe: elements of stability and variability. *Journal of Anthropological Archaeology* 12:211–65.

1997. *La circulation des matières premières au Paléolithique*. Liège: ERAUL 75.

Féblot-Augustins, J., and C. Perlès. 1992. Perspectives ethno-archéologiques sur les échanges à longue distance. *Ethnoarchéologie. Justification, problèmes, limites, Juan-les-Pins, 1992*, pp. 195–209. XIIe Rencontres Internationales d'Archéologie et d'Histoire d'Antibes.

Fedigan, L. M. 1986. The changing role of women in models of human evolution. *Annual Review of Anthropology* 15:25–66.

Firth, R. 1951. *Elements of social organization*. London: Watts.

Fischer, K., E. W. Guenther, W. D. Heinrich, D. Mania, R. Musil, and T. Nötzold. 1991. *Bilzingsleben IV Homo erectus – seine Kultur und seine Umwelt*. Berlin: Veröffentlichungen Landesmuseum für Vorgeschichte Halle 44.

Fisher, J. W., and H. C. Strickland. 1991. Dwellings and fireplaces: keys to Efe Pygmy campsite structure, in *Ethnoarchaeological approaches to mobile campsites: hunter-gatherer and pastoralist case studies*. Edited by C. Gamble and W. A. Boismier, pp. 215–36. Ann Arbor: International Monographs in Prehistory Ethnoarchaeological Series 1.

Fladerer, F. A. 1996. Die Tierreste von Alberndorf in Niederösterreich, in *Palaeolithic in the Middle Danube region: Anniversary volume to Bohuslav Klíma*. Edited by J. Svoboda, pp. 247–72. Brno: Archeologicky Ustav AV CR, Svazek 5.

Flannery, K. V. (editor). 1976. *The Early Mesoamerican village*. New York: Academic Press.

Flannery, K. V., and J. Marcus. 1994. On the perils of 'politically correct' archaeology. *Current Anthropology* 35:441–2.

Floss, H. 1994. *Rohmaterialversorgung im Paläolithikum des Mittelrheingebietes*. Bonn: Habelt, Römisch-Germanisches Zentralmuseum, Forschungsinstitut für Vor- und Frühgeschichte 21.

Foley, R. A. 1989. The evolution of hominid social behaviour, in *Comparative socioecology*. Edited by V. Standen and R. A. Foley, pp. 473–94. Oxford: Blackwell Scientific Publications.

Foley, R. A., and P. C. Lee. 1989. Finite social space, evolutionary pathways, and reconstructing hominid behaviour. *Science* 243:901–6.

1996. Finite social space and the evolution of human social behaviour, in *The archaeology of human ancestry: power, sex and tradition*. Edited by J. Steele and S. Shennan, pp. 47–66. London: Routledge.

Fox, R. 1967. *Kinship and marriage*. Harmondsworth: Penguin Books.

Franco, N. 1990. El aprovisionamiento de los recursos liticos por parte de los grupos del area interserrana Bonaerense, in *Estudios liticos en Argentina vias de analisis y desarrollo actual*. Edited by H. Nami, pp. 39–51. S. F. del V. de Catamarca.

1991. Algunas tendencias distribucionales en el material litico recuperado en el area interserrana Bonaerense. *Boletín de Centro* 1:72–9.

1994. Maximizacion en el aprovechamiento de los recursos liticos: un caso analizado en el area interserrana Bonaerense, in *Arqueología de cazadores-*

*recolectores: limites, casos y aperturas*, Edited by L. A. Borrero and J. L. Lanata, pp. 75–88. Buenos Aires: Arqueología Contemporánea 5.

Freeman, L. G. 1973. The significance of mammalian faunas from Palaeolithic occupations in Cantabrian Spain. *American Antiquity* 38:3–44.

1975. Acheulean sites and stratigraphy in Iberia and the Magreb, in *After the Australopithecines*. Edited by K. W. Butzer and G. Isaac, pp. 661–743. The Hague: Mouton.

Freeman, L. G., and K. W. Butzer. 1966. The Acheulean station of Torralba (Spain). A progress report. *Quaternaria* 8:9–21.

Freeman, L. G., and J. González-Echegaray. 1970. Aurignacian structural features and burials at Cueva Morín (Santander, Spain). *Nature* 226:722–6.

Frenzel, B. 1973. *Climatic fluctuations of the Ice Age*. Cleveland: Case Western Reserve University.

Freund, G. 1987. *Das Paläolithikum der Oberneder-Höhle (Landkreis Kelheim/Donau)*. Quartär Bibliothek 5. Bonn: Ludwig Rohrscheid Verlag.

Fridrich, J. 1989. *Prezletice: a lower Palaeolithic site in Central Bohemia (excavations 1969–1985)*. Prague: Museum Nationale Prague.

Friedman, J., and M. Rowlands (editors). 1977. *The evolution of social systems*. London: Duckworth.

Frison, G. 1989. Experimental use of Clovis weaponry and tools on African elephants. *American Antiquity* 54:766–84.

Fullola, J. M. 1979. Las induztrias líticas de paleolitico superior Ibérico. *Trabajo Vario del servico de Investigación Prehistórica* 60.

1983. Le Paléolithique supérieur dans la zone méditerranéenne ibérique. *L'Anthropologie* 87:339–52.

Gábori, M. 1976. *Les civilisations du Paléolithique moyen entre les Alpes et l'Oural*. Budapest: Akadémiai Kiadó.

Gábori-Csank, V. 1968. *La station du Paléolithique moyen d'Erd, Hongrie*. Budapest: Akadémiai Kiadó.

Gabunia, L. and A. Vekua. 1995. A Plio-Pleistocene hominid from Dmanisi, East Georgia, Caucasus. *Nature* 373:509–12.

Gamble, C. S. 1978. Resource exploitation and the spatial patterning of hunter-gatherers: a case study, in *Social organisation and settlement*. Edited by D. Green, C. Haselgrove, and M. Spriggs, pp. 153–85. Oxford: British Archaeological Reports, International Series 47(i).

1979. Hunting strategies in the central European Palaeolithic. *Proceedings of the Prehistoric Society* 45:35–52.

1982. Interaction and alliance in Palaeolithic society. *Man* 17:92–107.

1983a. Culture and society in the upper Palaeolithic of Europe, in *Hunter-gatherer economy in prehistory*. Edited by G. N. Bailey, pp. 201–11. Cambridge: Cambridge University Press.

1983b. Caves and faunas from last glacial Europe, in *Animals and archaeology: 1. Hunters and their prey*. Edited by J. Clutton-Brock and C. Grigson, pp. 163–72. Oxford: British Archaeological Reports, International Series 163.

1984. Regional variation in hunter-gatherer strategy in the Upper Pleistocene of Europe, in *Hominid evolution and community ecology*. Edited by R. Foley, pp. 237–60. London: Academic Press.

1986a. *The Palaeolithic settlement of Europe*. Cambridge: Cambridge University Press.

1986b. Hunter-gatherers and the origin of states, in *States in history*. Edited by J. A. Hall, pp. 22–47. Oxford: Basil Blackwell.

1986c. The Mesolithic sandwich: ecological approaches and the archaeological record of the early post-glacial, in *Hunters in transition; postglacial adaptations in the temperate regions of the Old World*. Edited by M. Zvelebil, pp. 33–42. Cambridge: Cambridge University Press.

1987. Man the shoveller: alternative models for middle Pleistocene colonization and occupation in northern latitudes, in *The Pleistocene Old World: regional perspectives*. Edited by O. Soffer, pp. 81–98. New York: Plenum.

1991a. Raising the curtain on human origins. *Antiquity* 65:412–17.

1991b. The social context for European Palaeolithic art. *Proceedings of the Prehistoric Society* 57:3–15.

1991c. Brilliant – rock art and art rock in Australia. *Nature* 351:608.

1992a. Reflexions from a darkened room. *Antiquity* 66:426–31.

1992b. Archaeology, history and the uttermost ends of the earth – Tasmania, Tierra del Fuego and the Cape. *Antiquity* 66:712–20.

1992c. Comment on Roebroeks, Conard and van Kolfschoten. *Current Anthropology* 33:569–71.

1993a. *Timewalkers: the prehistory of global colonization*. Harmondsworth: Penguin.

1993b. The center at the edge, in *From Kostenki to Clovis: Upper Paleolithic–Paleo-Indian adaptations*. Edited by O. Soffer and N. D. Praslov, pp. 313–21. New York: Plenum.

1993c. Ancestors and agendas, in *Archaeological theory – who sets the agenda?* Edited by N. Yoffee and A. Sherratt, pp. 39–52. Cambridge: Cambridge University Press.

1993d. Exchange, foraging and local hominid networks, in *Trade and exchange in prehistoric Europe*. Edited by C. Scarre and F. Healy, pp. 35–44. Oxford: Oxbow Monograph 33.

1993e. People on the move: interpretations of regional variation in Palaeolithic Europe, in *Cultural transformations and interactions in eastern Europe*. Edited by J. Chapman and P. Dolukhanov, pp. 37–55. Aldershot: Avebury.

1995a. Interpretation in the Palaeolithic, in *Interpreting archaeology; finding meaning in the past*. Edited by I. Hodder, M. Shanks, A. Alexandri, V. Buchli, J. Carman, J. Last, and G. Lucas, pp. 87–91. London: Routledge.

1995b. Lithics and social evolution, in *Lithics in context: suggestions for the future direction of lithic studies, Lithic Studies Society Occasional Paper 5*. Edited by J. Schofield, pp. 19–26. Oxford: Oxbow Books.

1995c. The earliest occupation of Europe: the environmental background, in *The earliest occupation of Europe*. Edited by W. Roebroeks and T. van Kolfschoten, pp. 279–95. Leiden: European Science Foundation & University of Leiden.

1995d. Revisiting the Middle Palaeolithic faunas of the Hohlenstein-Stadel. Paper presented at *The role of early humans in the accumulation of European Lower and Middle Palaeolithic bone assemblages.* Neuwied, Schloß Monrepos.

1995e. Large mammals, climate and resource richness in Upper Pleistocene Europe. *Acta Zoologica Cracovensis* 38:155–75.

1996a. Making tracks: hominid networks and the evolution of the social landscape, in *The archaeology of human ancestry: power, sex and tradition*. Edited by J. Steele and S. J. Shennan, pp. 253–77. London: Routledge.

1996b. Hominid behaviour in the Middle Pleistocene; an English perspective, in *The English Palaeolithic reviewed*. Edited by C. S. Gamble and A. J. Lawson, pp. 63–71. Salisbury: Trust for Wessex Archaeology.

1997. The animal bones from Klithi, in *Klithi: archaeology of a Late Glacial landscape in Epirus (Northwest Greece)*. Edited by G. Bailey, pp. 225–68. Cambridge: McDonald Institute for Archaeological Research.

1998. Palaeolithic society and the release from proximity: a network approach to intimate relations. *World Archaeology* 29:426–49.

Gamble, C. S., and O. Soffer (editors). 1990. *The world at 18 000 BP. Volume II. Low latitudes*. London: Unwin Hyman.

Gamble, C. S., and J. Steele. 1998. Hominid ranging patterns and dietary strategies. Paper presented at the Palaeoanthropology Society Meetings. Seattle.

Gardin, J. C. 1980. *Archaeological constructs*. Cambridge: Cambridge University Press.

Gardner, P. M. 1966. Symmetric respect and memorate knowledge: the structure and ecology of individualistic culture. *Southwestern Journal of Anthropology* 22:389–415.

Gargett, R. H. 1989. Grave shortcomings: the evidence for Neanderthal burial. *Current Anthropology* 30:157–90.

1994. Taphonomy and spatial analysis of a cave bear (*Ursus spelaeus*) fauna from Pod Hradem Cave, Czech Republic: implications for the archaeology of modern human origins. Ph.D. dissertation, Berkeley: University of California.

Garralda, M. D. 1993. La transición del Paleolítico Medio al Superior en la Península Ibérica: perspectivas antropológicas, in *El origen del hombre moderno en el suroeste de europa*. Edited by V. Cabrera-Valdés, pp. 373–90. Madrid: Universidad de Educación a Distancia.

Gascoyne, M., A. P. Currant, and T. C. Lord. 1981. Ipswichian fauna of Victoria Cave and the marine palaeoclimatic record. *Nature* 294:652–4.

Gaudzinski, S. 1992. Wisentjäger in Wallertheim: zur Taphonomie einer mittelpaläolithischen Freilandfundstelle in Rheinhessen. *Jahrbuch des Römisch-Germanischen Zentralmuseums Mainz* 39:245–423.

1995. Wallertheim revisited: a reanalysis of the fauna from the Middle Palaeolithic site of the Wallertheim (Rheinhessen/Germany). *Journal of Archaeological Science* 22:51–66.

Gaudzinski, S., F. Bittmann, W. Boenig, M. Frechen, and T. van Kolfschoten. 1996. Palaeoecology and archaeology of the Kärlich-Seeufer open-air site (Middle Pleistocene) in the central Rhineland, Germany. *Quaternary Research* 46:319–34.

Geist, V. 1978. *Life strategies, human evolution, environmental design*. New York: Springer Verlag.

Gellner, E. 1985. *Relativism and the social sciences*. Cambridge: Cambridge University Press.

Geneste, J.-M. 1985. Analyse lithique d'industries Moustériennes du Périgord: une approche technologique du comportement des groupes humains au Paléolithique moyen. Ph.D. dissertation: University of Bordeaux I.

1988a. Systèmes d'approvisionnement en matières premières au Paléolithique moyen et au Paléolithique supérieur en Aquitaine, in *L'Homme de Néandertal*. Edited by M. Otte. Vol. VIII, *La Mutation*, edited by J. K. Kozlowski, pp. 61–70. Liège: ERAUL 35.

1988b. Les industries de la Grotte Vaufrey: technologie du débitage, économie et circulation de la matière première lithique, in *La Grotte Vaufrey à Cenac et Saint-Julien (Dordogne), Paléoenvironments, chronologie et activités humaines*. Edited by J.-P. Rigaud, pp. 441–518. Paris: Mémoires de la Société Préhistorique Française 19.

1989. Economie des ressources lithiques dans le Moustérien du sud-ouest de la France, in *L'Homme de Néandertal.* Edited by M. Otte. Vol. VI, *La Subsistance,* edited by L. G. Freeman and M. Patou, pp. 75–97. Liège: ERAUL 33.

1990. Développement des systèmes de production lithique au cours du Paléolithique moyen en Aquitaine septentrionale, in *Paléolithique moyen récent et Paléolithique supérieur ancien.* Edited by C. Farizy, pp. 203–13. Nemours: Mémoires du Musée de Préhistoire d'Ile-de-France 3.

1991. Systèmes techniques de production lithique: variations techno-économiques dans les processus de réalisation des outillages Paléolithiques. *Techniques et culture* 17–18:1–35.

Geneste, J.-M., J. Texier, and J. Rigaud. 1991. Les plus anciens vestiges de la présence humaine en Aquitaine, in *Les premiers Européens.* Edited by E. Bonifay and B. Vandermeersch, pp. 11–26. Paris: CTHS.

Gibbard, P. L. 1988. The history of the great northwest European rivers during the past three million years. *Philosophical Transactions of the Royal Society of London B* 318:559–602.

Gibert, J. 1992. *Proyecto Orce-Cueva Victoria (1988–1992): Presencia humana en el Pleistoceno inferior de Granada y Murcia.* Orce: Museo de Prehistoria.

Gibson, J. J. 1979. *The ecological approach to visual perception.* Hillsdale: Erlbaum Associates.

Giddens, A. 1984. *The constitution of society.* Berkeley: University of California Press.

Gifford-Gonzalez, D. 1993. You can hide, but you can't run: representation of women's work in illustrations of Palaeolithic life. *Visual Anthropology Review* 9:23–41.

Gilman, A. 1984. Explaining the Upper Palaeolithic revolution, in *Marxist perspectives in archaeology.* Edited by M. Spriggs, pp. 115–26. Cambridge: Cambridge University Press.

Giusberti, G., M. Ferrari, and C. Peretto. 1991. Tipologia, frequenza e distribuzione dei reperti paleontologici e paletnologici della paleosuperficie T.3a del I settore di scavo di Isernia la Pineta (Isernia, Molise), in *Isernia la Pineta, nuovi contributi scientifici.* Edited by C. Peretto, pp. 5–42. Isernia: Istituto regionale per gli studi storici del Molise 'V. Cuoco'.

Goffman, E. 1959. *The presentation of self in everyday life.* Garden City NY: Anchor Books.

1963. *Behaviour in public places: notes on the social organisation of gatherings.* New York: Free Press.

1967. *Interaction ritual: essays on face to face behaviour.* London: Allen Lane.

González-Echegaray, J., and L. G. Freeman. 1971. *Cueva Morín, Excavaciones 1966–8.* Santander: Publicaciones del patronato de las cuevas prehistóricas de la provincia de Santander VI.

1973. *Cueva Morín, Excavaciones 1969.* Santander: Publicaciones del patronato de las cuevas prehistóricas de la provincia de Santander X.

Goodall, J. 1986. *The chimpanzees of Gombe: patterns of behaviour.* Cambridge, Mass.: Belknap Press.

Gorecki, P. P. 1991. Horticulturalists as hunter-gatherers: rock shelter usage in Papua New Guinea, in *Ethnoarchaeological approaches to mobile campsites: hunter-gatherer and pastoralist case studies.* Edited by C. S. Gamble and W. A. Boismier, pp. 237–62. Ann Arbor: International Monographs in Prehistory, Ethnoarchaeological Series 1.

Goretsky, G. I., and I. K. Ivanova. 1982. *Molodova I: unique mousterian settlement in the middle Dniestr.* Moscow: Nauka.

Goretsky, G. I., and S. M. Tseitlin (editors). 1977. *The multilayer Palaeolithic site Korman IV on the middle Dniestr*. Moscow: Nauka.

Gosden, C. 1989. Prehistoric social landscapes of the Arawe Islands, West New Britain Province, Papua New Guinea. *Archaeology in Oceania* 24:45–58.

1994. *Social being and time*. Oxford: Blackwell.

Goudie, A. 1977. *Environmental change*. Oxford: Clarendon Press.

Gouédo, J. M. 1994. Remontage d'un nucléus à lames du gisement Micoquien de Vinneuf (Yonne), in *Les industries laminaires au Paléolithique moyen*. Edited by S. Révillion and A. Tuffreau, pp. 77–102. Paris: Centre National de la Recherche Scientifique 18.

Gould, R. A. 1980. *Living archaeology*. Cambridge: Cambridge University Press.

Gould, S. J. 1991. Exaptation: a crucial tool for an evolutionary psychology. *Journal of Social Issues* 47:43–65.

1994. So near and yet so far. *New York Review of Books*, October 20:24–8.

1996. *Life's grandeur: the spread of excellence from Plato to Darwin*. London: Jonathan Cape.

Gould, S. J., and E. S. Vrba. 1982. Exaptation – a missing term in the science of form. *Palaeobiology* 8:4–15.

Gowlett, J. A. J. 1984. Mental abilities of early man: a look at some hard evidence, in *Hominid evolution and community ecology*. Edited by R. A. Foley, pp. 167–92. London: Academic Press.

1996. The frameworks of early hominid social systems: how many useful parameters of archaeological evidence can we isolate? in *The archaeology of human ancestry: power, sex and tradition*. Edited by J. Steele and S. Shennan, pp. 135–83. London: Routledge.

Gowlett, J. A. J., and R. E. M. Hedges (editors). 1986. *Archaeological results from accelerator dating*. Oxford: Alden Press.

Grahmann, R. 1955. The Lower Palaeolithic site of Markkleeberg and other comparable localities near Leipzig. *Transactions of the American Philosophical Society* 45:509–687.

Grant, J. W. A., C. A. Chapman, and K. S. Richardson. 1992. Defended versus undefended home range size of carnivores, ungulates and primates. *Behavioural Ecology and Sociobiology* 31:149–61.

Graves, P. M. 1991. New models and metaphors for the Neanderthal debate. *Current Anthropology* 32:513–41.

1994. My strange quest for Leroi-Gourhan: structuralism's unwitting hero. *Antiquity* 68:438–41.

Graves-Brown, P. M., S. Jones, and C. S. Gamble (editors). 1995. *Cultural identity and archaeology: the construction of European communities*. London: Routledge.

Green, H. S. (editor). 1984. *Pontnewydd Cave*. Cardiff: National Museum of Wales.

Gregory, C. A. 1982. *Gifts and commodities*. London: Academic Press.

Grigor'ev, G. P. 1993. The Kostenki-Avdeevo archaeological culture and the Willendorf-Pavlov-Kostenki-Avdeevo cultural unity, in *From Kostenki to Clovis: Upper Paleolithic–Paleo-Indian Adaptations*. Edited by O. Soffer and N. D. Praslov, pp. 51–65. New York: Plenum Press.

GRIP (Greenland Ice-core Project Members). 1993. Climate instability during the last interglacial period recorded in the GRIP ice core. *Nature* 364:203–7.

Groiß, J. Th., B. Kaulich, and L. Reisch. 1995. *Hunas: Menschen und ihre Umwelt im Eiszeitalter*. Institut für Paläontologie und Lehrstuhl für Ur- und Frühgeschichte der Friedrich-Alexander-Universität Erlangen-Nürnberg.

Grönhaug, R. 1978. Scale as a variable in analysis: fields in social organisation in Herat, northwest Afghanistan, in *Scale and social organisation*. Edited by F. Barth, pp. 78–121. Oslo: Universitets Forlaget.

Groves, C. P. 1989. *A theory of human and primate evolution*. Oxford: Oxford University Press.

Gruet. 1976. Les civilisations du Paléolithique moyen dans les Pays de la Loire, in *La Préhistoire française*, vol. II. Edited by H. de Lumley, pp. 1089–93. Paris: CNRS.

Guemple, L. 1972. Kinship and alliance in Belcher Island Eskimo society, in *Alliance in Eskimo society*. Edited by L. Guemple, pp. 56–78, Seattle: Proceedings of the American Ethnological Society 1971, Supplement.

Guenther, E. W. 1991. Die Gebisse der Waldelefanten von Bilzingsleben, in *Bilzingsleben IV Homo erectus – seine Kultur und seine Umwelt*. Edited by K. Fischer, E. W. Guenther, W. D. Heinrich, D. Mania, R. Musil, and T. Nötzold, pp. 149–74. Berlin: Veröffentlichungen des Landesmuseum für Vorgeschichte Halle 44.

Guichard, J. 1976. Les civilisations du Paléolithique moyen en Périgord, in *La Préhistoire française*, vol. II. Edited by H. de Lumley, pp. 1053–69. Paris: CNRS.

Guilbaud, M. 1993. Débitage from the Upper Castelperronian level at Saint-Césaire: methodological approach and implications for the transition from Middle to Upper Palaeolithic, in *Context of a late Neanderthal: implications of multidisciplinary research to Upper Palaeolithic adaptations at Saint-Césaire, Charente-Maritime, France*, Edited by F. Lévêque, A. M. Backer, and M. Guilbaud, pp. 37–58. Madison, Wisconsin: Prehistory Press, Monographs in World Archaeology 16.

Guiot, J., A. Pons, L. de Beaulieu, and M. Reille. 1989. A 140,000-year continental climate reconstruction from two European pollen records. *Nature* 338:309–13.

Guthrie, R. D. 1982. Mammals of the mammoth steppe as palaeoenvironmental indicators, in *Palaeoecology of Beringia*. Edited by D. M. Hopkins, J. V. Matthews, C. E. Schweger, and S. B. Young, pp. 307–26. New York: Academic Press.

1984. Mosaics, allelochemics and nutrients: an ecological theory of Late Pleistocene megafaunal extinctions, in *Quaternary extinctions: a prehistoric revolution*. Edited by P. Martin and R. Klein, pp. 259–98. Tucson: University of Arizona Press.

1990. *Frozen fauna of the mammoth steppe*. Chicago: Chicago University Press.

Gvozdover, M. D., V. M. Kharitonov, P. Allsworth-Jones, and R. A. Housley. 1996. AMS dates from Formozov's excavations at Starosel'e in the Crimea. *Cambridge Archaeological Journal* 6:139–49.

Hahn, J. 1974. Die jungpaläolithische Station Lommersum, Gemeinde Weilerswist, Kreis Euskirchen. *Rheinische Ausgrabungen* 15:1–49.

1977. *Aurignacien: das ältere Jungpaläolithikum in Mittel und Osteuropa*. Köln: Fundamenta Reihe A 9.

1982. *Archäologie des Jungpaläolithikums des Speckberg bei Meilenhofen*. München: Katalog Prähistorische Staatsammlung 20.

1986. *Kraft und Aggression: Die Botschaft der Eiszeitkunst im Aurignacien Süddeutschlands*? Tübingen: Archaeologica Venatoria 7.

1987. Aurignacian and Gravettian settlement patterns in Central Europe, in *The Pleistocene Old World: regional perspectives*. Edited by O. Soffer, pp. 251–61. New York: Plenum.

1988. *Die Geißenklösterle-Höhle im Achtal bei Blaubeuren I*. Stuttgart: Theiss, Landesdenkmalamt Baden-Württemberg Band 26.
1989. *Genese und Funktion einer jungpaläolithischen Freilandstation: Lommersum im Rheinland*. Köln: Rheinische Ausgrabungen 29.
1991. *Erkennen und Bestimmen von Stein- und Knochenartefakten: Einführung in die Artefaktmorphologie*. Tübingen: Archaeologica Venatoria 10.
1993. L'origine du Paléolithique supérieur en Europe Centrale: les datations C14, in *El origen del hombre moderno en el suroeste de Europa*. Edited by V. Cabrera-Valdés, pp. 61–80. Madrid: Universidad de Educación a Distancia.
Hahn, J., and S. Münzel. 1995. Knochenflöten aus dem Aurignacien des Geißenklösterle bei Blaubeuren, Alb-Donau-Kreis. *Fundberichte aus Baden-Württemberg* 20:1–12.
Hahn, J., and L. R. Owen. 1985. Blade technology in the Aurignacian and Gravettian of Geißenklösterle Cave, southwest Germany. *World Archaeology* 17:61–75.
Hallowell, A. I. 1961. The protocultural foundations of human adaptation, in *Social life of early man*. Edited by S. L. Washburn, pp. 236–55. New York: Wenner-Gren.
Haraway, D. 1989. *Primate visions: gender, race, and nature in the world of modern science*. New York: Routledge, Chapman & Hall.
Hare, A. P. 1976. *Handbook of small group research*. New York: The Free Press.
Harmon, R. S., J. Glazek, and K. Nowak. 1980. $^{230}$Th/$^{234}$U dating of travertine from the Bilzingsleben archaeological site. *Nature* 284:132–5.
Harrold, F. J. 1989. Mousterian, Châtelperronian and early Aurignacian in western Europe: continuity or discontinuity? in *The human revolution: behavioural and biological perspectives on the origins of modern humans*. Edited by P. Mellars and C. Stringer, pp. 677–713. Edinburgh: Edinburgh University Press.
Hayden, B., M. Eldridge, A. Eldridge, and A. Cannon. 1985. Complex hunter-gatherers in interior British Columbia, in *Prehistoric hunter-gatherers: the emergence of cultural complexity*. Edited by T. D. Price and J. A. Brown, pp. 181–200. Orlando: Academic Press.
Head, L., C. Gosden, and J. P. White (editors). 1994. Social landscapes. *Archaeology in Oceania* 29.
Hedges, R. E. M., P. B. Pettitt, C. Bronk Ramsey, and G. J. Van Klinken. 1998. Radiocarbon dates from the Oxford AMS system: *Archaeometry* datelist 25. *Archaeometry* 40:227–39.
Helms, M. W. 1988. *Ulysses' sail: an ethnographic odyssey of power, knowledge, and geographical distance*. Princeton: Princeton University Press.
Heussner, K. U., and T. Weber. 1990. Das archäologische Inventar-Spezielle Untersuchungen zu den Feuersteinartefakten, in *Neumark-Gröbern: Beiträge zur Jagd des mittelpaläolithischen Menschen*. Edited by D. Mania, M. Thomae, T. Litt, and T. Weber, pp. 225–36. Berlin: Deutscher Verlag der Wissenschaften.
Hewlett, B. S., J. M. H. van de Koppel, and L. L. Cavalli-Sforza. 1986. Exploration and mating range of Aka pygmies of the Central African Republic, in *African pygmies*. Edited by L. L. Cavalli-Sforza, pp. 65–79. New York: Academic Press.
Hiatt, L. R. 1962. Local organisation among the Australian Aborigines. *Oceania* 32:267–86.
Hidjrati, N. I. 1995. Palaeolithic archaeology in north-central Caucasus: Weasel

Cave. Paper presented at the Conference of the Society for American Archaeology, Minneapolis.
Hill, J. H. 1978. Language contact systems and human adaptations. *Journal of Anthropological Research* 34:1–26.
Hinde, R. A. 1976. Interactions, relationships and social structure. *Man* 11:1–17.
1987. *Individuals, relationships and culture*. Cambridge: Cambridge University Press.
Hiscock, P. 1984. Raw material rationing as an explanation of assemblage differences: a case study of Lawn Hill, Northwest Queensland, in *Archaeology at Anzaas 1984*. Edited by G. Ward, pp. 178–90. Canberra: AIAS.
Hivernel, F. 1986. Artefacts made of quartz, in *La Cotte de St. Brelade 1961–1978: excavations by C.B.M. McBurney*. Edited by P. Callow and J. M. Cornford, pp. 315–25. Norwich: Geo Books.
Hodder, I. 1990a. *The domestication of Europe*. Oxford: Blackwell.
1990b. Commentary. *Archaeological Review from Cambridge* 9:154–7.
Hoffecker, J. F. 1987. Upper Pleistocene loess stratigraphy and Palaeolithic site chronology on the Russian Plain. *Geoarchaeology* 2:259–84.
Hoffecker, J. F., G. Baryshnikov, and O. Potapova. 1991. Vertebrate remains from the Mousterian site of Il'skaya 1 (Northern Caucasus, U.S.S.R): new analysis and interpretation. *Journal of Archaeological Science* 18:113–47.
Holdaway, S. 1989. Were there hafted projectile points in the Mousterian? *Journal of Field Archaeology* 16:79–85.
Holdaway, S., and N. Porch. 1995. Cyclical patterns in the Pleistocene human occupation of Southwest Tasmania. *Archaeology in Oceania* 30:74–82.
Hosfield, R. T. 1996. Quantifying the English Palaeolithic: GIS as an approach, in *The English Palaeolithic reviewed*. Edited by C. Gamble and A. Lawson, pp. 40–51. Salisbury: Trust for Wessex Archaeology.
Housley, R. A., C. S. Gamble, M. Street, and P. Pettitt. 1997. Radiocarbon evidence for the Late glacial human recolonisation of Northern Europe. *Proceedings of the Prehistoric Society* 63: 25–54.
Howell, F. C. 1965. *Early man*. London: Time Life Books.
1966. Observations of the earlier phases of the European Lower Palaeolithic. *American Anthropologist* 68 (2):88–201.
Howell, N. 1988. Understanding simple social structure: kinship units and ties, in *Social structures: a network approach*. Edited by B. Wellman and S. D. Berkowitz, pp. 62–82. Cambridge: Cambridge University Press.
Howell, N., and V. A. Lehotay. 1978. Ambush: a computer program for stochastic microsimulation of small human populations. *American Anthropologist* 80:905–22.
Hublin, J.-J., F. Spoor, M. Braun, F. Zonneveld, and S. Condemi. 1996. A late Neanderthal associated with Upper Palaeolithic artefacts. *Nature* 381:224–6.
Humphrey, N. K. 1976. The social function of intellect, in *Growing points in ethology*. Edited by P. Bateson and R. A. Hinde, pp. 303–17. Cambridge: Cambridge University Press.
1983. *Consciousness regained*. Oxford: Oxford University Press.
Hunn, E., and N. Williams (editors). 1982. *Resource managers: North American and Australian hunter-gatherers*. Boulder, Colorado: Westview.
Huxtable, J. 1993. Further thermoluminescence dates for burnt flints from Maastricht-Belvédère and a finalised thermoluminescence age for the Unit IV Middle Palaeolithic sites. *Mededelingen Rijks Geologische Dienst* 47:41–4.
Imbrie, J., and K. P. Imbrie. 1979. *Ice Ages: solving the mystery*. London: Macmillan.

Ingold, T. 1981. The hunter and his spear: notes on the cultural mediation of social and ecological systems, in *Economic Archaeology*. Edited by A. Sheridan and G. Bailey, pp. 119–30. Oxford: British Archaeological Reports, International Series 96.

1986a. *Evolution and social life*. Cambridge: Cambridge University Press.

1986b. *The appropriation of nature: essays on human ecology and social relations*. Manchester: Manchester University Press.

1993. The temporality of the landscape. *World Archaeology* 25:152–73.

1994. Introduction to culture, in *Companion encyclopedia of anthropology*. Edited by T. Ingold, pp. 329–49. London: Routledge.

Ingold, T., D. Riches, and J. Woodburn (editors). 1991. *Hunters and gatherers*. Volume I, *History, evolution and social change*; Volume II, *Property, power and ideology*. Oxford: Berg.

Isaac, G. 1972. Early phases of human behaviour: models in Lower Palaeolithic archaeology, in *Models in archaeology*. Edited by D. L. Clarke, pp. 167–99. London: Methuen.

1976. The activities of early African hominids: a review of archaeological evidence from the time span two and a half to one million years ago, in *Human origins: Louis Leakey and the East African evidence*. Edited by G. Isaac and E. McCown, pp. 483–514. Menlo Park: Benjamin.

1978. The food sharing behaviour of proto-human hominids. *Scientific American* 238:90–108.

1989. *The archaeology of human origins; papers by Glynn Isaac edited by Barbara Isaac*. Cambridge: Cambridge University Press.

Ivanova, I. K., and A. P. Chernysh. 1965. The Palaeolithic site of Molodova V on the middle Dniestr (USSR). *Quaternaria* 7:197–217.

Ivanova, I. K., and S. M. Tseitlin (editors). 1987. *The multilayered Palaeolithic site of Molodova V. Stone Age men and environment*. Moscow: Nauka.

Jacobi, R. M. 1980. The Upper Palaeolithic in Britain, with special reference to Wales, in *Culture and environment in prehistoric Wales*. Edited by J. A. Taylor, pp. 15–99. Oxford: British Archaeological Reports 76.

Jacobson, D. 1978. Scale and social control, in *Scale and social organization*. Edited by F. Barth, pp. 184–93. Oslo: Universitets Forlaget.

James, S. R. 1989. Hominid use of fire in the Lower and Middle Pleistocene. *Current Anthropology* 30:1–26.

Jaubert, J. 1993. Le gisement Paléolithique moyen du Mauran (Haute-Garonne): techno-économie des industries lithiques. *Bulletin de la Société Préhistorique Française* 90:328–35.

1994. Environmental background of Middle Palaeolithic occupation and Middle Palaeolithic settlement systems: Bassin de la Garonne: Region Midi-Pyrénées. Paper presented at the ESF Workshop on the European Middle Palaeolithic. Arras.

Jaubert, J., J.-P. Brugal, and Y. Quinif. 1993. Tour de Faure: Coudoulous I et II. *Bilan Scientifique 1993: Direction Régionale des Affaires Culturelles Midi-Pyrénées, Service régional de l'Archéologie*: 144–6.

Jaubert, J., B. Kervazo, Y. Quinif, J.-P. Brugal, and O. Y. Wilford. 1992. Le site Paléolithique moyen du Rescoundudou (Aveyron, France): datations U/Th et interpretation chronostratigraphique. *L'Anthropologie* 96:103–12.

Jaubert, J., M. Lorblanchet, H. Laville, R. Slott-Moller, A. Turq, and J. Brugal. 1990. *Les Chasseurs d'Aurochs de La Borde*. Paris: Documents d'Archéologie Française 27.

Jelínek, J., J. Pelísek, and K. Valoch. 1959. Der fossile Mensch Brno II. *Anthropos* 9:5–30.

Johnson, A. W., and T. Earle. 1987. *The evolution of human societies*. Stanford: Stanford University Press.

Johnson, G. A. 1978. Information sources and the development of decision-making organizations, in *Social archaeology: beyond subsistence and dating*. Edited by C. Redman, M. J. Berman, E. V. Curtin, W. T. Langhorne, N. M. Versaggi, and J. C. Wanser, pp. 87–111. New York: Academic Press.

1982. Organizational structure and scalar stress, in *Theory and explanation in archaeology: the Southampton Conference*. Edited by C. Renfrew, M. Rowlands, and B. Segraves, pp. 389–422. New York: Academic Press.

Jourdan, L., and A.-M. Moigne. 1981. Les faunes de la Caune de l'Arago à Tautavel. Significations stratigraphique, paléoclimatique, paléoecologique et paléthnographique, in *Datations absolues et analyses isotopiques en préhistoire, méthodes et limites: datation du remplissage de la Caune de l'Arago à Tautavel*. Edited by H. de Lumley and J. Labeyrie, pp. 133–62. Tautavel: Colloque International du Centre National de la Recherche Scientifique.

Jouzel, J., N. I. Barkov, J. M. Barnola, M. Bender, J. Chappellaz, C. Genthon, V. M. Kotlyakov, V. Lipenkov, C. Lorius, J. R. Petit, D. Raynaud, G. Raisbeck, C. Ritz, T. Sowers, M. Stievenard, F. Yiou, and P. Yiou. 1993. Extending the Vostok ice-core record of paleoclimate to the penultimate glacial period. *Nature* 364:407–12.

Julien, M. 1992. Du fossile directeur à la chaîne opératoire, in *La préhistoire dans le monde: nouvelle édition de La Préhistoire d'André Leroi-Gourhan*. Edited by J. Garanger, pp. 163–93. Paris: Nouvelle Clio.

Kapferer, B. 1973. Social network and conjugal role in urban Zambia: towards a reformulation of the Bott hypothesis, in *Network analysis in human interaction*. Edited by J. Boissevain and J. C. Mitchell, pp. 83–110. The Hague: Mouton.

Karlin, C., and M. Julien. 1994. Prehistoric technology: a cognitive science? in *The ancient mind: elements of cognitive archaeology*. Edited by C. Renfrew and E. Zubrow, pp. 152–64. Cambridge: Cambridge University Press.

Keeley, L. H. 1980. *Experimental determination of stone tool use: a microwear analysis*. Chicago: University of Chicago Press.

1982. Hafting and retooling: effects on the archaeological record. *American Antiquity* 47:798–809.

1988. Hunter-gatherer economic complexity and 'population pressure': a cross-cultural analysis. *Journal of Anthropological Archaeology* 7:373–411.

Kelly, R. 1983. Hunter-gatherer mobility strategies. *Journal of Anthropological Research* 39:277–306.

1995. *The foraging spectrum: diversity in hunter-gatherer lifeways*. Washington and London: Smithsonian Institution Press.

Kephart, W. M. 1950. A quantitative analysis of intragroup relationships. *American Journal of Sociology* 60:544–9.

Khalke, R.-D. 1994. Die Entstehungs-, Entwicklungs- und Verbreitungsgeschichte des oberpleistozänen *Mammuthus–Coelodonta* Faunenkomplexes in Eurasien (Großsäuger). *Abhandlungen der Senckenbergischen Naturforschenden Gesellschaft* 546:1–164.

Killworth, P. D., H. R. Bernard, and C. McCarty. 1984. Measuring patterns of acquaintanceship. *Current Anthropology* 25:381–96.

Killworth, P. D., E. C. Johnson, H. R. Bernard, G. A. Shelley, and C. McCarty. 1990. Estimating the size of personal networks. *Social Networks* 12:289–312.

Kind, C.-J. 1985. *Die Verteilung von Steinartefakten in Grabungsflächen: ein Modell zur Organisation Alt- und Mittelsteinzeitlicher Siedlungsplätze*. Tübingen: Urgeschichtliche Materialhefte 7.

King, T. F. 1978. Don't that beat the band? Nonegalitarian political organisation in prehistoric central California, in *Social archaeology: beyond subsistence and dating*. Edited by C. L. Redman, M. J. Berman, E. V. Curtin, W. T. Langhorne, N. M. Versaggi, and J. C. Wanser, pp. 225–48. New York: Academic Press.

Klein, R. G. 1965. The Middle Palaeolithic of the Crimea. *Arctic Anthropology* 3:34–68.

1969. *Man and culture in the Late Pleistocene: a case study*. San Francisco: Chandler.

Klein, R. G., and K. Cruz-Uribe. 1994. The Palaeolithic mammalian fauna from the 1910–14 excavations at El Castilló cave (Cantabria). *Museo y Centro de Investigación de Altamira* 17:141–58.

Kleinschmidt, A. 1953. Die zoologischen Funde der Grabung Salzgitter-Lebenstedt, 1952. *Eiszeitalter und Gegenwart* 3:166–88.

Klíma, B. 1954. Palaeolithic huts at Dolní Věstonice, Czechoslovakia. *Antiquity* 28:4–14.

1963. *Dolní Věstonice. Vyzkum táboriste lovcù mamutù v letech 1947–1952*. Prague: Academia.

1983. *Dolní Věstonice: táboriste lovcù mamutù*. Prague: Akademia nakladatelstvi Ceskoslovenske akademie ved.

1988. A triple burial from the Upper Palaeolithic of Dolní Věstonice, Czechoslovakia. *Journal of Human Evolution* 16:831–5.

1994. Die Knochenindustrie, Zier- und Kunstgegenstände, in *Pavlov I: excavations 1952–3*. Edited by J. Svoboda, pp. 97–159. Liège: ERAUL 66.

1995. *Dolní Věstonice II*. Liège: ERAUL 73.

Knecht, H. 1993a. Splits and wedges: the techniques and technology of early Aurignacian antler working, in *Before Lascaux: the complex record of the Early Upper Palaeolithic*. Edited by H. Knecht, A. Pike-Tay, and R. White, pp. 137–62. Boca Raton: CRC Press.

1993b. Early Upper Palaeolithic approaches to bone and antler technology, in *Hunting and animal exploitation in the later Palaeolithic and Mesolithic of Eurasia*. Edited by G. L. Peterkin, H. Bricker, and P. A. Mellars, pp. 33–47. Archaeological Papers of the American Anthropological Association 4.

Knight, C. 1983. Lévi-Strauss and the dragon: *Mythologiques* reconsidered in the light of an Australian Aboriginal myth. *Man* 18:21–50.

1991a. *Blood relations: menstruation and the origins of culture*. New Haven: Yale University Press.

1991b. *The origins of human society*, 4th edition. London: Radical Anthropology Group.

Koenigswald, W. von. 1992. Various aspects of migrations in terrestrial mammals in relation to Pleistocene faunas of central Europe, in *Mammalian migration and dispersal events in the European Quaternary*. Edited by W. von Koenigswald and L. Werdelin, pp. 39–47. *Courier Forschungsinstitut Senckenberg* 153.

Koenigswald, W. von, and T. van Kolfschoten. 1996. The *Mimomys–Arvicola* boundary and the enamel thickness quotient (SDQ) of *Arvicola* as stratigraphic markers in the Middle Pleistocene, in *The early Middle Pleistocene in Europe*. Edited by C. Turner, pp. 211–26. Rotterdam: Balkema.

Koenigswald, W. von, H.-J. Müller-Beck, and E. Pressmar. 1974. *Die Archäologie und Paläontologie der Weinberghöhlen bei Mauern (Bayern)*. Tübingen: Archaeologica Venatoria 3.

Kolfschoten, T. van. 1992. Aspects of the migration of mammals to northwestern

Europe during the Pleistocene, in particular the re-immigration of *Arvicola terrestris*, in *Mammalian migration and dispersal events in the European Quaternary*. Edited by W. von Koenigswald and L. Werdelin, pp. 213–20. *Courier Forschungsinstitut Senckenberg* 153.

Kolfschoten, T. van, W. Roebroeks, and J. Vandenberghe. 1993. The middle and late Pleistocene sedimentary and climatic sequence at Maastricht-Belvédère Interglacial. *Mededelingen Rijks Geologische Dienst* 47:81–91.

Kolfschoten, T. van, and W. Roebroeks (editors). 1985. Maastricht-Belvédère: Stratigraphy, palaeoenvironment and archaeology of the Middle and Late Pleistocene deposits. *Mededelingen Rijks Geologische Dienst* 39:1–121.

Kolfschoten, T. van, and E. Turner. 1996. Early Middle Pleistocene mammalian faunas from Kärlich and Miesenheim I and their biostratigraphical implications, in *The early Middle Pleistocene in Europe*. Edited by C. Turner, pp. 227–53. Rotterdam: Balkema.

Kolstrup, E. 1995. Palaeoenvironments in the north European lowlands between 50 and 10 ka BP. *Acta Zoologica Cracovensis* 38:35–44.

Kosse, K. 1990. Group size and societal complexity: thresholds in the long-term memory. *Journal of Anthropological Archaeology* 9:275–303.

Koyama, S., and D. H. Thomas (editors). 1982. *Affluent foragers*. Osaka: National Museum of Ethnology, Senri Ethnological Studies 9.

Kozlowski, J. K. 1974. Upper Palaeolithic site with dwellings of mammoth bone – Cracow, Spadzista Street B. *Quaternaria* 44:1–110.

Kozlowski, J. K. (editor). 1982. *Excavation in the Bacho Kiro cave, Bulgaria*. Warsaw: Paristwowe Wydarunictwo, Naukowe.

1986. The Gravettian in Central and Eastern Europe. *Advances in World Archaeology* 5:131–200.

1988. Problems of continuity and discontinuity between the Middle and Upper Palaeolithic of Central Europe, in *Upper Pleistocene Prehistory of Western Eurasia*. Edited by H. Dibble and A. Montet-White, pp. 349–60. Philadelphia: University of Pennsylvania, University Museum Monograph 54.

1990. A multiaspectual approach to the origins of the Upper Palaeolithic in Europe in *The emergence of modern humans: an archaeological perspective*. Edited by P. Mellars, pp. 419–38. Edinburgh: Edinburgh University Press.

1994. Le Paléolithique des Carpathes occidentales. *Preistoria Alpina* 28:113–26.

Kozlowski, J. K., H. Laville, and B. Ginter. 1992. *Temnata cave: excavations in Karlukovo Karst area, Bulgaria*. Crakow: Jagellonian University Press.

Kretzoi, M., and V. T. Dobosi (editors). 1990. *Vértesszöllös: man, site and culture*. Budapest: Akadémiai Kiadó.

Kretzoi, N., and L. Vértes. 1965. Upper Biharian (intermindel) pebble-industry site in western Hungary. *Current Anthropology* 6:74–87.

Kuhn, S. L. 1989. Hunter-gatherer foraging organisation and strategies of artefact replacement and discard, in *Experiments in lithic technology*. Edited by D. Amick and R. Mauldin, pp. 33–47. Oxford: British Archaeological Reports, International Series 528.

1991. "Unpacking" reduction: lithic raw material economy in the Mousterian of West-Central Italy. *Journal of Anthropological Archaeology* 10:76–106.

1992. On planning and curated technologies in the Middle Palaeolithic. *Journal of Anthropological Research* 48:185–214.

1995. *Mousterian lithic technology: an ecological perspective*. Princeton: Princeton University Press.

Kummer, H. 1968. *Social organisation of Hamadryas baboons*. Chicago: Chicago University Press.

Kuper, A. 1988. *The invention of primitive society*. London: Routledge.

Laj, C., A. Mazaud, and J. C. Duplessy. 1996. Geomagnetic intensity and $^{14}C$ abundance in the atmosphere and ocean during the past 50 kyr. *Geophysical Research Letters* 23:2045–8.

Landau, M. 1991. *Narratives of human evolution*. New Haven: Yale University Press.

Lanziger, M., and M. Cremaschi. 1988. Flint exploitation and production at Monte Avena in the Dolomite Region of the Italian East Alps: lithic industry, site pattern, and paleoenvironmental context, in *Upper Pleistocene prehistory of Western Eurasia*. Edited by H. Dibble and A. Montet-White, pp. 125–39. Philadelphia: University of Pennsylvania, University Museum Monograph 54.

Laplace, G. 1961. Recherches sur l'origine et l'évolution des complexes leptolithiques. *Quaternaria* 5:153–240.

1964. Les subdivisions du leptolithique italien (étude de typologie analytique). *Bulletino di Paletnologia Italiana* 15:25–63.

1966. Recherches sur l'origine et l'évolution des complexes leptolithiques. *Ecole Française de Rome, Mélanges d'Archéologie et d'Histoire* 4.

Larick, R. 1984. Palaeolithic occupations of Périgord rock shelters viewed from the cherts found within Le Flageolet I, couche V, in *Jungpaläolithische Siedlungsstrukturen in Europa*. Edited by H. Berke, J. Hahn, and C.-J. Kind, pp. 29–38. Tübingen: Urgeschichtliche Materialhefte 6.

Latour, B., and S. C. Strum. 1986. Human social origins: oh please, tell us another story. *Journal of Social and Biological Structure* 9:169–87.

Laville, H. 1975. *Climatologie et chronologie du Paléolithique en Périgord: étude sédimentologique de dépots en grottes et sous abris*. Université de Provence: Mémoire No. 4, Etudes Quaternaires.

Laville, H., J.-P. Raynal, and J.-P. Texier. 1986. Le dernier interglaciaire et le cycle climatique würmien dans le sud-ouest et le Massif Central française. *Bulletin de l'Association Française pour l'Etude du Quaternaire* 1–2:35–46.

Laville, H., J.-P. Rigaud, and J. R. Sackett. 1980. *Rock shelters of the Périgord*. New York: Academic Press.

Layton, R. 1986. Political and territorial structures among hunter-gatherers. *Man* 21:18–33.

Leacock, E., and R. B. Lee (editors). 1982. *Politics and history in band societies*. Cambridge: Cambridge University Press.

Leakey, L. 1951. *Olduvai Gorge*. Cambridge: Cambridge University Press.

Leakey, M. D., 1971. *Olduvai Gorge Volume 3: excavations in Beds I and II 1960–1963*. Cambridge: Cambridge University Press.

Leakey, M. D. and D. A. Roe. 1994. *Olduvai Gorge Volume 5: excavations in Beds III, IV and the Masek Beds, 1968–71*. Cambridge: Cambridge University Press.

Leakey, R., and R. Lewin. 1977. *Origins*. New York: Dutton.

Lebel, S. 1992. Mobilité des hominides et systèmes d'exploitation des ressources lithiques au Paléolithique ancien: La Caune de l'Arago (France). *Canadian Journal of Archaeology* 16:48–69.

Lee, R. B. 1976. !Kung spatial organisation: an ecological and historical perspective, in *Kalahari hunter-gatherers*. Edited by R. B. Lee and I. DeVore, pp. 73–97. Cambridge, Mass.: Harvard University Press.

1979. *The !Kung San: men, women, and work in a foraging society*. Cambridge: Cambridge University Press.

Lee, R. B., and I. DeVore (editors). 1968. *Man the hunter*. Chicago: Aldine.

(editors). 1976. *Kalahari hunter-gatherers: studies of the !Kung San and their neighbours*. Cambridge, Mass.: Harvard University Press.

Lemmonier, P. 1980. *Les Salines de l'ouest – logique technique, logique sociale*. Paris: Maison des Sciences de l'Homme.

1986. The study of material culture today: towards an anthropology of technical systems. *Journal of Anthropological Archaeology* 5:147–86.

1990. Topsy turvy techniques. Remarks on the social representation of techniques. *Archaeological Review from Cambridge* 9:27–37.

1993. Introduction, in *Technological choices: transformations in material cultures since the Neolithic*. Edited by P. Lemmonier, pp. 1–35. London: Routledge.

Leroi-Gourhan, A. 1961. Les fouilles d'Arcy-sur-Cure (Yonne). *Gallia Préhistoire* 4:1–16.

1968. *The art of prehistoric man in western Europe*. London: Thames and Hudson.

1993. *Gesture and speech*. Cambridge, Mass.: MIT Press.

Leroi-Gourhan, A., and M. Brézillon. 1966. L'habitation magdalénienne no. 1 de Pincevent près Montereau (Seine-et-Marne). *Gallia Préhistoire* 9:263–365.

1972. Fouilles de Pincevent: essai d'analyse ethnographique d'un habitat magdalénien (la section 36). *Gallia Préhistoire* supplément 7.

Leroi-Gourhan, A., and Arlette Leroi-Gourhan. 1964. Chronologie des grottes d'Arcy-sur-Cure (Yonne). *Gallia Préhistoire* 7:1–64.

Leroi-Gourhan, Arlette 1980. Les interstades du Würm supérieur, in *Problèmes de stratigraphie Quaternaire en France et dans les Pays Limitrophes*. Edited by J. Chaline, pp. 192–4. Dijon: Association Française pour l'Etude du Quaternaire.

Leroy-Prost, C. 1974. Les pointes en matière osseuse de l'Aurignacien. *Bulletin de la Société Préhistorique Française* 77:449–58.

Lesser, A. 1961. Social fields and the evolution of society. *Southwestern Journal of Anthropology* 17:40–7.

Lévêque, F., A. M. Backer, and M. Guilbaud (editors). 1993. *Context of a Late Neanderthal: implications of multidisciplinary research for the transition to Upper Paleolithic adaptations at Saint-Césaire, Charente-Maritime, France*. Monographs in World Archaeology 16. Madison, Wisconsin: Prehistory Press.

Lévi-Strauss, C. 1969. *The elementary structures of kinship*. Boston: Beacon Press.

Lhomme, J.-P., and S. Maury. 1990. *Tailler le silex*. Périgueux: Conseil Général de la Dordogne, Service de l'Archéologie.

Lindly, J., and G. A. Clark. 1990. Symbolism and modern human origins. *Current Anthropology* 31:233–40.

Liubin, V. P. 1989. Palaeolithic of Caucasus, in *The old stone age of the world: the Palaeolithic of Caucasus and Northern Asia*. Edited by P. I. Boriskovsky, pp. 9–142. Leningrad: Nauka.

Liubin, V. P., and G. Bosinski. 1995. The earliest occupation of the Caucasus region, in *The earliest occupation of Europe*. Edited by W. Roebroeks and T. van Kolfschoten, pp. 207–55. Leiden: University of Leiden and European Science Foundation.

Locht, J. L., C. Swinnen, P. Antoine, M. Patou-Mathis, and P. Auguste. 1994. Le gisement de Beauvais: deux occupations du Paléolithique moyen durant une phase pléniglaciaire. *Notae praehistoricae* 13:15–20.

Lockwood, J. G. 1974. *World climatology*. London: Edward Arnold.

Lourandos, H. 1977. Aboriginal spatial organization and population: southwestern Victoria reconsidered. *Archaeology and Physical Anthropology in Oceania* 12:202–25.

1985. Intensification and Australian prehistory, in *Prehistoric hunters and gatherers: the emergence of cultural complexity*. Edited by T. D. Price and J. A. Brown, pp. 385–423. New York: Academic Press.

Lovejoy, C. O. 1981. The origin of man. *Science* 211:341–50.

Lumley, H. de. 1969a. *Une cabane acheuléenne dans la Grotte du Lazaret*. Paris: Mémoires de la Société Préhistorique Française 7.

1969b. A Palaeolithic camp site at Nice. *Scientific American* 220:42–50.

1969c. Le Paléolithique inférieur et moyen du Midi méditerranéen dans son cadre géologique, 1. Ligurie-Provence. *Gallia Préhistoire* supplément 5.

1975. Cultural evolution in France in its palaeoecological setting during the middle Pleistocene, in *After the Australopithecines*. Edited by K. W. Butzer and G. Isaac, pp. 745–808. The Hague: Mouton.

1979. L'homme de Tautavel; le prémier homme en Europe. *Dossiers de l'archéologie* 36:5–111.

(editor). 1972. *La grotte Moustérienne de l'Hortus*. Marseille: Etudes Quaternaires 1.

Lumley, H. de, and M.-A. de Lumley. 1979. L'homme de Tautavel. *Dossiers de l'archéologie* 36:54–9.

Lumley, M. A. de. 1976. Les anténéandertaliens dans le Sud, in *La Préhistoire Française*, vol. I. Edited by H. de Lumley, pp. 547–60. Paris: CNRS.

Luttropp, A., and G. Bosinski. 1971. *Der altsteinzeitliche Fundplatz Reutersruh bei Ziegenhain in Hessen*. Köln: Fundamente Reihe A/6.

MacRae, R. J. 1988. The Palaeolithic of the upper Thames and its quartzite implements, in *Non-flint stone tools and the Palaeolithic occupation of Britain*. Edited by R. J. MacRae and N. Moloney, pp. 123–54. Oxford: British Archaeological Reports 189.

Magee, B. 1987. *The great philosophers*. London: BBC Books.

Mai, D. H., D. Mania, T. Nötzold, V. Toepfer, E. Vlcek, and W. D. Heinrich. 1983. *Bilzingsleben II*. Berlin: Veröffentlichungen des Landesmuseums für Vorgeschichte Halle 36.

Mandryk, C. A. S. 1993. Hunter-gatherer social costs and the nonviability of submarginal environments. *Journal of Anthropological Research* 49:39–71.

Mania, D. 1978. *Homo erectus* von Bilzingsleben, Kreis Arten, und seine Kultur. *Jahresschrift Mitteldeutsche Vorgeschichte* 62:51–86.

1986. Die Siedlungsspuren des *Homo erectus* von Bilzingsleben, in *Bilzingsleben III*. Edited by D. Mania and T. Weber, pp. 9–64. Berlin: Veröffentlichungen des Landesmuseums für Vorgeschichte Halle 39.

1990. *Auf den Spuren des Urmenschen: Die Funde von Bilzingsleben*. Berlin: Theiss.

1991a. The zonal division of the Lower Palaeolithic open-air site Bilzingsleben. *Anthropologie* 29:17–24.

1991b. Eiszeitarchäologische Forschungsarbeiten in den Tagebauen des Saale – Elbe-Gebietes. *Veröffentlichungen des Museums für Ur- und Frühgeschichte Potsdam* 25:78–100.

1995. The earliest occupation of Europe: the Elbe-Saale region (Germany), in *The earliest occupation of Europe*. Edited by W. Roebroeks and T. van Kolfschoten, pp. 85–102. Leiden: University of Leiden and European Science Foundation.

Mania, D., and A. Dietzel. 1980. *Begegnung mit dem Urmensch*. Leipzig: Theiss.

Mania, D., M. Thomae, T. Litt, and T. Weber. 1990. *Neumark-Gröbern. Beiträge zur Jagd des mittelpaläolithischen Menschen*. Berlin: Veröffentlichungen des

Landesmuseums für Vorgeschichte Halle 43.
Mania, D., and V. Toepfer. 1973. *Königsaue*. Berlin: Veröffentlichungen des Landesmuseums für Vorgeschichte Halle 26.
Mania, D., V. Toepfer, and E. Vlcek. 1980. *Bilzingsleben I*. Berlin: Veröffentlichungen des Landesmuseums für Vorgeschichte Halle 32.
Mania, D., and T. Weber (editors). 1986. *Bilzingsleben III*. Berlin: Veröffentlichungen des Landesmuseums für Vorgeschichte Halle 39.
Marcy, J.-L., P. Auguste, M. Fontugne, A.-V. Munaut, and B. Van Vliet-Lanoé. 1993. Le gisement Moustérien d'Hénin-sur-Cojeul (Pas-de-Calais). *Bulletin de la Société Préhistorique Française* 90:251–6.
Marks, A. E. 1983. The Middle to Upper Palaeolithic transition in the Levant. *Advances in World Archaeology* 2:51–98.
Marks, A. E., Y. E. Demidenko, K. Monigal, V. I. Usik, C. R. Ferring, A. Burke, J. Rink, and C. McKinney. 1997. Starosel'e and the Starosel'e child: new excavations, new results. *Current Anthropology* 38:112–23.
Maroto, J., and N. Soler. 1990. La rupture entre le Paléolithique moyen et le Paléolithique supérieur en Catalogne: Paléolithique moyen récent et Paléolithique supérieur ancien en Europe. Ruptures et transitions: examen critique des documents archéologiques. *Actes du Colloque international de Nemours, Nemours, 1990*, pp. 263–5. Mémoires du Musée de Préhistoire d'Ile de France 3.
Maroto, J., N. Soler, and A. Mir. 1987. La cueva de Mollet I (Serinya, Gerona). *Cypsela* 6:101–10.
Marquardt, W. H. 1985. Complexity and scale in the study of fisher-gatherer-hunters: an example from the eastern United States, in *Prehistoric hunter-gatherers: the emergence of cultural complexity*. Edited by T. D. Price and J. A. Brown, pp. 59–98. Orlando: Academic Press.
Marshack, A. 1972. *The roots of civilization*. New York: McGraw-Hill.
1990. Early hominid symbol and the evolution of the human capacity, in *The emergence of modern humans: an archaeological perspective*. Edited by P. Mellars, pp. 457–99. Edinburgh: Edinburgh University Press.
Marshall, G. 1993. Carnivores and Neanderthals: structured interaction, a critique of the evidence for the burial hypothesis. Unpublished Undergraduate Dissertation, University of Southampton.
Maryanski, A. R. 1993. The elementary forms of the first protohuman society: an ecological/social network approach. *Advances in Human Ecology* 2:215–41.
1996. African ape social networks: a blueprint for reconstructing early hominid social structure, in *The archaeology of human ancestry: power, sex and tradition*. Edited by J. Steele and S. J. Shennan, pp. 67–90. London: Routledge.
Maryanski, A., and M. Ishii-Kuntz. 1991. A cross-species application of Bott's hypothesis on role segregation and social networks. *Sociological Perspectives* 34:403–25.
Maryanski, A., and J. H. Turner. 1992. *The social cage: human nature and the evolution of society*. Stanford: Stanford University Press.
Mason, S., J. Hather, and G. Hillman. 1994. Preliminary investigation of the plant macro-remains from Dolní Věstonice II and its implications for the role of plant foods in Palaeolithic and Mesolithic Europe. *Antiquity* 68:48–57.
Masson, B., and L. Vallin. 1996. Ein unverlagerter Schlagplatz für Levalloisabschläge im Weichselzeitlichen Löss bei Hermies (Pas-de-Calais, Frankreich). *Archäologisches Korrespondenzblatt* 26:225–31.
Mauss, M. 1906. Essai sur les variations saisonnières des sociétés Eskimos: étude de morphologie sociale. *L'Année Sociologique* 9:39–132.

1936. Les techniques du corps. *Journal de Psychologie* 32.
1967. *The gift.* New York: W. W. Norton.
McBryde, I. 1978. Wil-im-ee Moor-ring: or, where do axes come from? *Mankind* 11:354–82.
1988. Goods from another country: exchange networks and the people of the Lake Eyre basin, in *Archaeology to 1788.* Edited by J. Mulvaney and P. White, pp. 253–73. Sydney: Waddon Associates.
in press. 'The landscape is a series of stories.' Grindstones, quarries and exchange in aboriginal Australia: a case study from the Cooper/Lake Eyre Basin, Australia, in *Siliceous rocks and culture: Proceedings of the VI International Flint Symposium.* Edited by A. Ramos-Millán. Granada: Madrid University.
McCurdy, G. G. 1931. The use of rock crystal by Palaeolithic man. *Proceedings of the National Academy of Sciences* 17:633–7.
McGlade, J. 1995. Archaeology and the ecodynamics of human-modified landscapes. *Antiquity* 69:113–32.
McNabb, J., and N. M. Ashton. 1993. The cutting edge: bifaces in the Clactonian. *Lithics* 13:4–10.
McNiven, I. J. 1990. Prehistoric aboriginal settlement and subsistence in the Cooloola region, coastal southeast Queensland. Unpublished Ph.D. Thesis, The University of Queensland.
Meillassoux, C. 1973. On the mode of production of the hunting band, in *French perspectives in African studies.* Edited by P. Alexandre, pp. 187–203. London: Oxford University Press.
Mellars, P. A. 1969. The chronology of Mousterian industries in the Périgord region of south-west France. *Proceedings of the Prehistoric Society* 35:134–71.
1970. Some comments on the notion of 'functional variability' in stone tool assemblages. *World Archaeology* 2:74–89.
1973. The character of the Middle–Upper Palaeolithic transition in south-west France, in *The explanation of culture change: models in prehistory.* Edited by C. Renfrew, pp. 255–76. London: Duckworth.
1985. The ecological basis of social complexity in the Upper Palaeolithic of southwestern France, in *Prehistoric hunter-gatherers: the emergence of cultural complexity.* Edited by T. D. Price and J. A. Brown, pp. 271–97. Orlando: Academic Press.
(editor). 1990. *The emergence of modern humans.* Edinburgh: Edinburgh University Press.
1992. Technological change in the Mousterian of southwest France, in *The Middle Palaeolithic: adaptation, behaviour, and variability.* Edited by H. L. Dibble and P. Mellars, pp. 39–45. Philadelphia: University of Pennsylvania, University Museum 72.
1996. *The Neanderthal legacy: an archaeological perspective from Western Europe.* Princeton: Princeton University Press.
Mellars, P. A., and C. Stringer (editors). 1989. *The human revolution: behavioural and biological perspectives on the origins of modern humans.* Edinburgh: Edinburgh University Press.
Mercier, N., H. Valladas, J.-L. Joron, J.-L. Reyss, F. Lévêque, and B. Vandermeersch. 1991. Thermoluminescence dating of the late Neanderthal remains from Saint Césaire. *Nature* 351:737–9.
Milardo, R. M. 1992. Comparative methods for delineating social networks. *Journal of Social and Personal Relationships* 9:447–61.

Miller, G. A. 1956. The magical number seven plus or minus two: some limits on our capacity for processing information. *Psychological Review* 63:81–97.
Milroy, L. 1987. *Language and social networks*, 2nd edition. Oxford: Blackwell.
Milton, K. 1988. Foraging behaviour and the evolution of primate intelligence, in *Machiavellian intelligence*. Edited by R. Byrne and A. Whiten, pp. 285–305. Oxford: Clarendon Press.
Miracle, P. T., L. E. Fisher, and J. Brown (editors). 1991. *Foragers in context: long-term, regional, and historical perspectives in hunter-gatherer studies*. Ann Arbor: Michigan Discussions in Anthropology 10.
Mitchell, J. C. 1974. Social networks. *Annual Review of Anthropology* 3:279–99.
Mithen, S. 1990. *Thoughtful foragers*. Cambridge: Cambridge University Press.
1993a. Individuals, groups and the Palaeolithic record: a reply to Clark. *Proceedings of the Prehistoric Society* 59:393–8.
1993b. Language, technology, and intelligence: a holy trinity for cognitive archaeology. *Cambridge Archaeological Journal* 3:285–300.
1994. Technology and society during the Middle Pleistocene: hominid group size, social learning and industrial variability. *Cambridge Archaeological Journal* 4:3–32.
1996. *The prehistory of the mind: a search for the origins of art, religion and science*. London: Thames and Hudson.
Mogosanu, F. 1976. L'Aurignacien du Banat, in *L'Aurignacien en Europe*. Congrès IX, Colloque XVI. Edited by J. K. Kozlowski, pp. 75–97. Nice: UISPP.
1978. *Paleoliticul din Banat*. Bucuresti: Academi Republicae Socialae Romanici.
Moncel, M. H. 1994. L'industrie lithique des trois niveaux supérieurs de l'abri du Maras (Ardèche), in *Les industries laminaires au Paléolithique moyen*. Edited by S. Révillion and A. Tuffreau, pp. 117–23. Paris: Centre National de la Recherche Scientifique 18.
Monnier, J.-L. 1994. A new regional group of the Lower Palaeolithic in Brittany (France), recently dated by electron spin resonance. *Centre Recherche Academie Science Paris* 319:155–60.
Montet-White, A. 1988. Raw-material economy among medium-sized Late Palaeolithic campsites of Central Europe, in *Upper Pleistocene prehistory of Western Eurasia*. Edited by H. Dibble and A. Montet-White, pp. 361–74. Philadelphia: University of Pennsylvania, University Museum Monograph 54.
Moore, H. 1986. *Space, text and gender*. Cambridge: Cambridge University Press.
Morphy, H. 1989. From dull to brilliant: the aesthetics of spiritual power among the Yolngu. *Man* 24:21–40.
Morris, B. 1982. *Forest traders: a socio-economic study of the Hill Pandaram*. New Jersey: Humanities Press.
Moser, S. 1989. A history of reconstructions. Unpublished BA thesis, LaTrobe University.
1992. The visual language of archaeology: a case study of the Neanderthals. *Antiquity* 66:831–44.
1998. *Ancestral images*. Stroud: Sutton Publishing.
Moser, S., and C. S. Gamble. 1997. Revolutionary images: the iconic vocabulary for representing human antiquity, in *The cultural life of images: visual representation in archaeology*. Edited by B. L. Molyneaux, pp. 184–212. London: Routledge.
Moss, C. 1988. *Elephant memories*. London: Montana.
Mottl, M. 1941. Die Interglazial-und Iinterstadial-Zeiten im Lichte der

Ungarischen Säugetierfauna. *Mitteilungen aus dem Jahrbuche der Königlich-Ungarischen Geologischen Anstalt* 35:1–33.

Movius, H. L. (editor). 1975. *Excavation of the Abri Pataud, Les Eyzies (Dordogne)*. American School of Prehistoric Research, Bulletin 30. Cambridge, Mass.: Peabody Museum Press.

Movius, H. L. (editor). 1977. *Excavation of the Abri Pataud, Les Eyzies (Dordogne): Stratigraphy*. American School of Prehistoric Research, Bulletin 31. Cambridge, Mass.: Peabody Museum Press.

Moyà-Solà, S., and M. Köhler. 1997. The Orce skull: anatomy of a mistake. *Journal of Human Evolution* 33:91–7.

Mueller-Wille, S., and D. B. Dickson. 1991. An examination of some models of late Pleistocene society in southwestern Europe, in *Perspectives of the past: theoretical biases on Mediterranean hunter gatherer research*. Edited by G. A. Clark, pp. 25–55. Philadelphia: University of Pennsylvania Press.

Müller-Beck, H. 1973. Weinberghöhlen (Mauern) und Speckberg (Meilenhofen) 1964–1972, in *Neue paläolithische und mesolithische Ausgrabungen in der Bundesrepublik Deutschland*. Edited by H.-J. Müller-Beck, pp. 29–36. Tübingen, zum 9. INQUA-Kongress.

1988. The ecosystem of the 'Middle Paleolithic' (Late Lower Paleolithic) in the Upper Danube region: a stepping-stone to the Upper Paleolithic, in *Upper Pleistocene prehistory of Western Eurasia*. Edited by H. Dibble and A. Montet-White, pp. 233–54. Philadelphia: University of Pennsylvania, University Museum Monograph 54.

Münzel, S., P. Morel, and J. Hahn. 1994. Jungpleistozäne Tierreste aus der Geißenklösterle-Höhle bei Blaubeuren. *Fundberichte aus Baden-Württemberg* 19:63–93.

Murray, T. 1987. Remembrances of things present: appeals to authority in the history and philosophy of archaeology. Unpublished Ph.D. dissertation, University of Sydney.

Musil, R. 1980–1. *Ursus spelaeus. Der Höhlenbar*. Weimar: Museum für Ur und Frühgeschichte Thüringens.

1994. The fauna, in *Pavlov I: excavations 1952–3*. Edited by J. Svoboda, pp. 181–209. Liège: ERAUL 66.

Mussi, M. 1986a. On the chronology of the burials found in the Grimaldi caves. *Human evolution* 1:95–104.

1986b. Italian Palaeolithic and Mesolithic burials. *Human evolution* 1:545–56.

1988. Continuité et discontinuité dans les practiques funéraires au Paléolithique: le cas de l'Italie, in *L'Homme de Néandertal*. Edited by M. Otte, vol. V, *La Pensée*, pp. 93–107. Liège: ERAUL 32.

1990. Continuity and change in Italy at the last glacial maximum, in *The world at 18 000 BP, Volume 1: High latitudes*. Edited by O. Soffer and C. Gamble, pp. 126–47. London: Unwin Hyman.

1992. *Il Paleolitico e il Mesolitico in Italia*. Bologna: Stilus, Popoli e civiltà dell' Italia 10.

1995. The earliest occupation of Europe: Italy, in *The earliest occupation of Europe*. Edited by W. Roebroeks and T. van Kolfschoten, pp. 27–49. Leiden: University of Leiden and European Science Foundation.

Nelson, R. K. 1973. *Hunters of the northern forest*. Chicago: University of Chicago Press.

Newell, R. R. 1984. On the Mesolithic contribution to the social evolution of western European society, in *European social evolution: archaeological perspectives*. Edited by J. L. Bintliff, pp. 69–82. Bradford: University of Bradford.

Newell, R. R., and T. S. Constandse-Westermann. 1986. Testing an ethnographic analogue of Mesolithic social structure and the archaeological resolution of Mesolithic ethnic groups and breeding populations. *Proceedings of the Koninklijke Nederlandse Akademie van Wetenschappen* 89:243–310.

Nicholson, A., and S. Cane. 1991. Desert camps: analysis of Australian Aboriginal proto-historic campsites, in *Ethnoarchaeological approaches to mobile campsites: hunter-gatherer and pastoralist case studies*. Edited by C. S. Gamble and W. A. Boismier, pp. 263–354. Ann Arbor: International Monographs in Prehistory, Ethnoarchaeological Series 1.

Nicolaescu-Plopsor, C. S., A. L. Paunescu, and F. Mogosanu. 1966. Paléolithique du Ceahlau. *Dacia* 10:5–116.

Ninkovitch, D., and N. J. Shackleton. 1975. Distribution, stratigraphic position and age of ash layer 'L' in the Panama basin. *Earth and Planetary Science Letters* 27:20–34.

Nitecki, M. H., and D. V. Nitecki (editors). 1987. *The evolution of human hunting*. New York: Plenum.

Noble, W., and I. Davidson. 1996. *Human evolution, language and mind*. Cambridge: Cambridge University Press.

O'Connell, J. F., K. Hawkes, and N. G. Blurton-Jones. 1992. Patterns in the distribution, site structure and assemblage composition of Hadza kill-butchering sites. *Journal of Archaeological Science* 19:319–45.

Oakley, K. P. 1949. *Man the tool maker*. London: Natural History Museum.

Oakley, K. P., P. Andrews, L. H. Keeley, and J. D. Clark. 1977. A re-appraisal of the Clacton spearpoint. *Proceedings of the Prehistoric Society* 43:13–30.

Oakley, K. P., B. G. Campbell, and T. I. Molleson. 1971. *Catalogue of fossil hominids. Part II: Europe*. London: British Museum (Natural History).

Oakley, K. P., and M. D. Leakey. 1937. Report on excavations at Jaywick Sands, Essex (1934); with some observations on the Clactonian Industry, and on the fauna and geological significance of the Clacton Channel. *Proceedings of the Prehistoric Society* 3:217–60.

Ohel, M. 1979. The Clactonian: an independent complex or an integral part of the Acheulian? *Current Anthropology* 20:685–726.

Oliva, M. 1984. Le Bohunicien, un nouveau groupe culturel en Moravie; quelques aspects psycho-technologiques du développement des industries Paléolithiques. *L'Anthropologie* 88:209–20.

1988a. A Gravettian site with mammoth-bone dwelling in Milovice (Southern Moravia). *Anthropologie* 26:105–12.

1988b. Discovery of a Gravettian mammoth bone hut at Milovice (Moravia, Czechoslovakia). *Journal of Human Evolution* 17:787–90.

Olive, M., and Y. Taborin (editors). 1989. *Nature et fonction des foyers préhistoriques*. Nemours: Mémoires du Musée de Préhistoire d'Ile de France 2.

Opravil, E. 1994. The vegetation, in *Pavlov I: excavations 1952–3*. Edited by J. Svoboda, pp. 175–80. Liège: ERAUL 66.

Otte, M. 1981. *Le Gravettien en Europe*. Brugge: Dissertationes Archaeologicae Gandenses, de Tempel 20.

1994. Rocourt (Liège, Belgique): Industrie laminaire ancienne, in *Les industries laminaires au Paléolithique moyen*. Edited by S. Révillion and A. Tuffreau, pp. 179–86. Paris: Centre National de la Recherche Scientifique 18.

Owen, L. R. 1988. *Blade and microblade technology. Selected assemblages from the North American Arctic and the Upper Paleolithic of Southwest Germany*. Oxford: British Archaeological Reports, International Series 441.

1996. Der Gebrauch von Pflanzen im Jungpaläolithikum Mitteleuropas. *Ethnographisch-Archäologische Zeitschrift* 37:119–46.

Paine, R. 1967. What is gossip about? An alternative hypothesis. *Man* 2:278–85.

Palma di Cesnola, A. 1976. Le leptolithique archaïque en Italie, in *Périgordien et Gravettien en Europe*. Congrès IX, Colloque XV. Edited by B. Klíma, pp. 66–99. Nice: UISPP.

1981. Italie, in *Resumen de las Investigaciones de 1976 a 1981*, vol. X Congresso, Comision X. Edited by R. Desbrosse and J. K. Kozlowski, pp. 31–5. Mexico City: UISPP.

1996. *Le Paléolithique inférieur et moyen en Italie*. Grenoble: Millon, Préhistoire d'Europe.

Palmqvist, P. 1997. A critical re-evaluation of the evidence for the presence of hominids in Lower Pleistocene times at Venta Micena, Southern Spain. *Journal of Human Evolution* 33:83–9.

Parés, J. M., and A. Pérez-González. 1995. Paleomagnetic age for hominid fossils at Atapuerca archaeological site, Spain. *Science* 269:830–2.

Parish, A. R. 1996. Female relationships in Bonobos (*Pan paniscus*): evidence for bonding, cooperation, and female dominance in a male-philopatric species. *Human Nature* 7:61–96.

Parker, S. T. 1987. A sexual selection model for hominid evolution. *Human Evolution* 2:235–53.

Parker, S. T., and C. Milbrath. 1993. Higher intelligence, propositional language, and culture as adaptations for planning, in *Tools, language and cognition in human evolution*. Edited by K. Gibson and T. Ingold, pp. 314–33. Cambridge: Cambridge University Press.

Parkington, J., and G. Mills. 1991. From space to place: the architecture and social organisation of Southern African mobile communities, in *Ethnoarchaeological approaches to mobile campsites: hunter-gatherer and pastoralist case studies*. Edited by C. S. Gamble and W. A. Boismier, pp. 355–70. Ann Arbor: International Monographs in Prehistory, Ethnoarchaeological Series 1.

Pasda, C. 1994. *Das Magdalenian in der Freiburger Bucht*. Stuttgart: Materialhefte zur Archäologie in Baden-Württemberg 24.

1996a. Rohknolle, Vollkern oder Abschlag? Strategien der Rohmaterialnutzung im Mittelpaläolithikum von Zwochau (Leipziger Tieflandsbucht). *Archäologisches Korrespondenzblatt* 26:1–12.

1996b. Silexverarbeitung am Rohmaterialvorkommen im Mittelpleistozän. *Arbeits- und Forschungsberichte zur Sächsischen Bodendenkmalpflege* 38:13–55.

Patou-Mathis, M. 1993. Etude taphonomique et paléthnographique de la faune de l'abri des Canalettes, in *L'Abri des Canalettes. Un habitat Moustérien sur les grands Causses (Nant, Aveyron)*. Edited by L. Meignen, pp. 199–237. Paris: CNRS, Monographies du Centre de Recherches Archéologiques, Monograph 10.

1994. Archéozoologie des niveaux Moustériens et Aurignaciens de la grotte Tournal à Bize (Aude). *Gallia Préhistoire* 36:1–64.

Paunescu, A. L. 1965. Sur la succession des habitats Paléolithiques et postpaléolithiques de Ripiceni-Izvor. *Dacia* 9:1–32.

Penck, A., and E. Brückner. 1909. *Die Alpen in Eiszeitalter*. Leipzig.

Peretto, C. 1991. Les gisements d'Isernia la Pineta (Molise, Italie), in *Les Premiers Européens*. Edited by E. Bonifay and B. Vandermeersch, pp. 153–68. Paris: Editions du C.T.H.S.

(editor). 1992. *I primi abitanti della Valle Padana: Monte Poggiolo nel quadro delle conoscenze Europée*. Milano: Jaca Book.

Peretto, C., C. Terzani, and M. Cremaschi (editors). 1983. *Isernia La Pineta, un accampamento più antico di 700,000 anni*. Bologna: Calderini.

Peris, J. F., P. M. G. Calatayud, and R. M. Valle. 1994. Cova del Bolomor (Tavernes de la Valldigna, Valencia) primeros datos de una secuencia del Pleistoceno medio. *Sagvntvm* 27:9–35.

1997. *Cova del Bolomor: los primeros habitantes de las tierras Valencianas*. Valencia: Diputació de València.

Perlès, C. 1976. Le feu, in *La Préhistoire française*, vol. I. Edited by H. de Lumley, pp. 679–83. Paris: CNRS.

1992. In search of lithic strategies: a cognitive approach to prehistoric chipped stone assemblages, in *Representations in archaeology*. Edited by J. Gardin and C. Peebles, pp. 223–47. Bloomington and Indianapolis: Indiana University Press.

Peterson, N. 1986. *Australian territorial organisation*. Sydney: Oceania Monograph 30.

Peyrony, D. 1933. Les industries aurignaciennes dans le bassin de la Vézère. Aurignacien et Périgordien. *Bulletin de la Société Préhistorique Française* 30:543–59.

Pfeiffer, J. E. 1982. *The creative explosion*. New York: Harper and Row.

Pickering, M. 1994. The physical landscape as a social landscape. *Archaeology in Oceania* 29:149–61.

Pigeot, N. 1990. Technical and social actors: flint knapping specialists at Magdalenian Etiolles. *Archaeological Review from Cambridge* 9:126–41.

Pillard, B. 1972. La faune des grands mammifères du Würmien II, in *La Grotte de Hortus*, Edited by H. de Lumley, pp. 163–205. Marseille: Etudes Quaternaires 1.

Piperno, M., and I. Biddittu. 1978. Studio tipologico ed interpretazione dell'industria acheulena e pre-musteriana dei livelli *m* e *d* di Torre in Pietra (Roma). *Quaternaria* 20:441–536.

Pitts, M., and M. Roberts. 1997. *Fairweather Eden: life in Britain half a million years ago as revealed by the excavations at Boxgrove*. London: Century.

Politis, G. G. 1996. Moving to produce: Nukak mobility and settlement patterns in Amazonia. *World Archaeology* 27:492–511.

Potts, R. 1988. *Early hominid activities at Olduvai*. New York: Aldine.

1993. The hominid way of life, in *The Cambridge Encyclopedia of Human Evolution*. Edited by S. Jones, R. Martin, and D. Pilbeam, pp. 325–34. Cambridge: Cambridge University Press.

Praslov, N. D. (editor). 1981. *Ketrosy. A Mousterian Site on the middle Dniestr region*. Moscow: Nauka.

Praslov, N. D., and A. N. Rogachev (editors). 1982. *Palaeolithic of the Kostenki-Borshevo area on the Don river, 1879–1979*. Leningrad: NAUKA.

Price, T. D., and J. A. Brown (editors). 1985a. *Prehistoric hunters and gatherers: the emergence of cultural complexity*. Orlando: Academic Press.

Price, T. D., and J. A. Brown. 1985b. Aspects of hunter-gatherer complexity, in *Prehistoric hunter-gatherers: the emergence of cultural complexity*. Edited by T. D. Price and J. A. Brown, pp. 3–20. Orlando: Academic Press.

1985c. Preface, in *Prehistoric hunter-gatherers: the emergence of cultural complexity*. Edited by T. D. Price and J. A. Brown, pp. xiii–xv. Orlando: Academic Press.

Quéchon, G. 1976. Les sépultures des hommes du Palaéolithique supérieur, in *La Préhistoire Française*, vol. I. Edited by H. de Lumley, pp. 728–33. Paris: CNRS.

Quiatt, D., and V. Reynolds. 1993. *Primate behaviour: information, social knowledge, and the evolution of culture*. Cambridge: Cambridge University Press.

Radcliffe-Brown, A. R. 1952. *Structure and function in primitive society*. London: Cohen and West.

Ramaswamy, V. 1992. Explosive start to the last ice age. *Nature* 359:14.

Ranov, V. A. 1991. Les sites très anciens de l'âge de la pierre en U.R.S.S, in *Les premiers Européens*. Edited by E. Bonifay and B. Vandermeersch, pp. 209–16. Paris: CTHS.

Raposo, L., and M. Santonja. 1995. The earliest occupation of Europe: the Iberian peninsula, in *The earliest occupation of Europe*. Edited by W. Roebroeks and T. van Kolfschoten, pp. 7–26. Leiden: University of Leiden and European Science Foundation.

Raynal, J.-P., L. Magoga, and P. Bindon. 1995. Tephrofacts and the first human occupation of the French massif, in *The earliest occupation of Europe*. Edited by W. Roebroeks and T. van Kolfschoten, pp. 129–46. Leiden: University of Leiden and European Science Foundation.

Raynal, J.-P., L. Magoga, F.-Z. Sbihi-Alaoui, and D. Geraads. 1995. The earliest occupation of Atlantic Morocco: the Casablanca evidence, in *The earliest occupation of Europe*. Edited by W. Roebroeks and T. van Kolfschoten, pp. 255–62. Leiden: University of Leiden and European Science Foundation.

Redman, C., M. J. Berman, E. V. Curtin, W. T. Langhorne, N. M. Versaggi, and J. C. Wanser (editors). 1978. *Social archaeology*. New York: Academic Press.

Reiff, W. 1986. Die Sauerwasserkalke von Stuttgart. *Fundberichte aus Baden-Württemberg* 11:2–25.

Renfrew, C. 1973. *Before civilization*. London: Jonathan Cape.

Renfrew, C., and S. J. Shennan (editors). 1982. *Ranking, resource and exchange*. Cambridge: Cambridge University Press.

Rensink, E. 1993. *Moving into the north: Magdalenian occupation and exploitation of the loess landscapes of northwestern Europe*. Proefschrift: Leiden University.

Révillion, S., and A. Tuffreau (editors). 1994a. *Les industries laminaires au Paléolithique moyen*. Paris: Centre National de la Recherche Scientifique 18.

Révillion, S., and A. Tuffreau. 1994b. Introduction, in *Les industries laminaires au Paléolithique moyen*. Edited by S. Révillion and A. Tuffreau, pp. 11–17. Paris: Centre National de la Recherche Scientifique 18.

1994c. Valeur et signification du débitage laminaire du gisement Paléolithique moyen de Seclin (Nord), in *Les industries laminaires au Paléolithique moyen*. Edited by S. Révillion and A. Tuffreau, pp. 19–43. Paris: Centre National de la Recherche Scientifique 18.

Reynolds, V. 1966. Open groups in hominid evolution. *Man* 1:441–52.

Richards, G. 1987. *Human evolution: an introduction for the behavioural sciences*. London: Routledge.

Rick, J. 1987. Dates as data: an examination of the Peruvian preceramic radiocarbon record. *American Antiquity* 52:55–73.

Riek, G. 1934. *Die Eiszeitjägerstation am Vogelherd, Band 1: Die Kulturen*. Tübingen: Heine.

Rigaud, J.-P. (editor). 1988a. *La Grotte Vaufrey à Cenac et Saint-Julien*

*(Dordogne): Paléoenvironments, chronologie et activités humaines.* Paris: Mémoires de la Société Préhistorique Française 19.

Rigaud, J.-P. 1988b. The Gravettian peopling of Southwestern France: taxonomic problems, in *Upper Pleistocene prehistory of western Eurasia.* Edited by H. Dibble and A. Montet-White, pp. 387–96. Philadelphia: University of Pennsylvania, University Museum Monograph 54.

Rigaud, J.-P., and J.-M. Geneste. 1988. L'utilisation de l'espace dans la Grotte Vaufrey, in *La Grotte Vaufrey à Cenac et Saint-Julien (Dordogne), Paléoenvironments, chronologie et activités humaines.* Edited by J.-P. Rigaud, pp. 593–611. Paris: Mémoires de la Société Préhistorique Française 19.

Rigaud, J.-P., J. F. Simek, and G. Thierry. 1995. Mousterian fires from Grotte XVI (Dordogne, France). *Antiquity* 69:902–12.

Roberts, M. B. 1986. Excavation of the Lower Palaeolithic site at Amey's Eartham Pit, Boxgrove, West Sussex: a preliminary report. *Proceedings of the Prehistoric Society* 52:215–46.

Roberts, M. B., C. S. Gamble, and D. R. Bridgland. 1995. The earliest occupation of Europe: the British Isles, in *The earliest occupation of Europe.* Edited by W. Roebroeks and T. van Kolfschoten, pp. 165–91. Leiden: University of Leiden and European Science Foundation.

Roberts, M. B., C. B. Stringer, and S. A. Parfitt. 1994. A hominid tibia from Middle Pleistocene sediments at Boxgrove, U.K. *Nature* 369:311–13.

Rodseth, L., R. W. Wrangham, A. Harrigan, and B. B. Smuts. 1991. The human community as a primate society. *Current Anthropology* 32:221–54.

Roe, D. A. 1964. The British Lower and Middle Palaeolithic: some problems, methods of study and preliminary results. *Proceedings of the Prehistoric Society* 30:245–67.

1981. *The Lower and Middle Palaeolithic periods in Britain.* London: Routledge and Kegan Paul.

1995. The Orce basin (Andalucia, Spain) and the initial Palaeolithic of Europe. *Oxford Journal of Archaeology* 14:1–12.

Roebroeks, W. 1988. *From find scatters to early hominid behaviour: a study of Middle Palaeolithic riverside settlements at Maastricht-Belvédère (The Netherlands).* University of Leiden: Analecta Praehistorica Leidensia 21.

1996. The English Palaeolithic record: absence of evidence, evidence of absence and the first occupation of Europe, in *The English Palaeolithic reviewed.* Edited by C. S. Gamble and A. J. Lawson, pp. 57–62. Salisbury: Trust for Wessex Archaeology.

Roebroeks, W., N. J. Conard, and T. van Kolfschoten. 1992. Dense forests, cold steppes, and the Palaeolithic settlement of northern Europe. *Current Anthropology* 33:551–86.

Roebroeks, W., D. De Loecker, P. Hennekens, and M. van Ieperen. 1992. 'A veil of stones': on the interpretation of an early Middle Palaeolithic low density scatter at Maastricht Belvédère (The Netherlands). *Analecta Praehistorica Leidensia* 25:1–16.

1993. On the archaeology of the Maastricht-Belvédère pit. *Mededelingen Rijks Geologische Dienst* 47:69–80.

Roebroeks, W., J. Kolen, and E. Rensink. 1988. Planning depth, anticipation and the organization of Middle Palaeolithic technology: the 'archaic natives' meet Eve's descendants. *Helinium* 28:17–34.

Roebroeks, W., and T. van Kolfschoten. 1994. The earliest occupation of Europe: a short chronology. *Antiquity* 68:489–503.

(editors). 1995. *The earliest occupation of Europe.* Leiden: University of Leiden and European Science Foundation.

Roebroeks, W., and A. Tuffreau. 1994. The Middle Palaeolithic of continental northwestern Europe. Paper presented at the ESF Workshop on the European Middle Palaeolithic. Arras.

Rogachev, A. N. 1957. The multilevel sites of the Kostenki-Borshevo region on the Don and the problem of the development of culture in the Upper Paleolithic epoch on the Russian Plain. *Materials and Researches on the Archaeology of the USSR* 59:9–134.

Rolland, N. 1981. The interpretation of Middle Palaeolithic variability. *Man* 16:15–42.

1990. Middle Palaeolithic socio-economic formations in Western Eurasia: an exploratory survey, in *The emergence of modern humans: an archaeological perspective*. Edited by P. Mellars, pp. 347–89. Edinburgh: Edinburgh University Press.

Rolland, N., and H. Dibble. 1990. A new synthesis of Middle Palaeolithic variability. *American Antiquity* 55:480–99.

Ronen, A. 1991. The Yiron-Gravel lithic assemblage; artifacts older than 2.4 my in Israel. *Archäologisches Korrespondenzblatt* 21:159–64.

Rowell, T. E. 1991. What can we say about social structure? in *The development and integration of behaviour*. Edited by P. Bateson, pp. 255–69. Cambridge: Cambridge University Press.

Rowley, S. 1985. Population movements in the arctic. *Etudes/Inuit/Studies* 9:3–21.

Ruddiman, W. F., and M. E. Raymo. 1988. Northern hemisphere climate régimes during the past 3Ma: possible tectonic connections. *Philosophical Transactions of the Royal Society of London B* 318:1–20.

Ruddiman, W. F., M. Raymo, and A. McIntyre. 1986. Matuyama 41,000–year cycles: North Atlantic Ocean and northern hemisphere ice sheets. *Earth and Planetary Science Letters* 80:117–29.

Rudwick, M. 1976. The emergence of a visual language for geological science 1760–1840. *History of Science* 14:149–95.

Sackett, J. R. 1982. Approaches to style in lithic archaeology. *Journal of Anthropological Archaeology* 1:59–112.

Sahlins, M. 1972. *Stone age economics*. London: Tavistock.

Saint-Périer, R. de. 1930. *La Grotte d'Isturitz I: Le Magdalénien de la Salle de St Martin*. Archives d l'Institut de Paléontologie Humaine 7. Paris: Masson.

1936. *La Grotte d'Isturitz II: Le Magdalénien de la Grande Salle*. Archives de l'Institut de Paléontologie Humaine 17. Paris: Masson.

Saint-Périer, R. de and S. de Saint-Périer. 1952. *La Grotte d'Isturitz III: Les Solutréens, les Aurignaciens et les Moustériens*. Archives de l'Institut de Paléontologie Humaine 25. Paris: Masson.

Santonja, M. 1991–2. Los últimos diez anos en la investigación del Paléolítico inferior de la cuenca del Duero. *Veleia* 8–9:7–41.

1992. La adaptación al medio en el Paleolítico inferior de la Peninsula ibérica. Elementos para una reflexión, Elephantes, ciervos y ovicaprinos, in *La Economia de la prehistoria de la peninsula iberica*. Edited by A. Moure Romanillo, pp. 37–76. Santander: Universidad de Cantabria.

Santonja, M., N. Lopez-Martinez, and A. Perez-Gonzalez. 1980. Ocupaciones Achelenses en el Valle del Jarama. *Arqueologia y Paleoecologia* 1:1–352.

Santonja, M., and P. Villa. 1990. The Lower Paleolithic of Spain and Portugal. *Journal of World Prehistory* 4:45–94.

Schafer, D. 1981. Taubach. *Ethnographisch-Archäologische Zeitschrift* 22:369–96.

Scheer, A. 1985. Elfenbeinanhänger des Gravettien in Süddeutschland. *Archäologisches Korrespondenzblatt* 15:269–85.

1990. Von der Schichtinterpretation bis zum Besiedlungsmuster – Zusammensetzungen als absoluter Nachweis, in *The big puzzle*. Edited by E. Cziesla, S. Eickhoff, N. Arts, and D. Winter, pp. 623–50. Bonn: Holos, Studies in Modern Archaeology 1.
1993. The organization of lithic resource use during the Gravettian in Germany, in *Before Lascaux: the complex record of the Early Upper Palaeolithic*. Edited by H. Knecht, A. Pike-Tay, and R. White, pp. 193–210. Boca Raton: CRC Press.
Schlanger, N. 1990. Technique as human action: two perspectives. *Archaeological Review from Cambridge* 9:18–26.
1994. Mindful technology: unleashing the chaîne opératoire for an archaeology of mind, in *The ancient mind: elements of cognitive archaeology*. Edited by C. Renfrew and E. Zubrow, pp. 143–51. Cambridge: Cambridge University Press.
1996. Understanding Levallois: lithic technology and cognitive archaeology. *Cambridge Archaeological Journal* 6:231–54.
Schmidt, R. R. 1936. *The dawn of the human mind: a study of Palaeolithic man*. London: Sidgwick and Jackson.
Schrire, C. (editor). 1984. *Past and present in hunter-gatherer studies*. London: Academic Press.
Schwarcz, H. P., R. Grun, A. G. Latham, D. Mania, and K. Brunnacker. 1988. The Bilzingsleben archaeological site: new dating evidence. *Archaeometry* 30:5–17.
Schwarcz, H. P., and I. Skoflek. 1982. New dates for the Tata, Hungary, archaeological site. *Nature* 295:590–1.
Scott, K. 1986a. The bone assemblage from layers 3 and 6, in *La Cotte de St. Brelade 1961–1978. Excavations by C.B.M. McBurney*. Edited by P. Callow and J. M. Cornford, pp. 159–83. Norwich: Geo Books.
1986b. The large mammal fauna, in *La Cotte de St. Brelade 1961–1978: excavations by C.B.M. McBurney*. Edited by P. Callow and J. M. Cornford, pp. 109–37. Norwich: Geo Books.
Segre, A., and A. Ascenzi. 1984. Fontana Ranuccio: Italy's earliest Middle Pleistocene hominid site. *Current Anthropology* 25:230–3.
Service, E. R. 1966. *The hunters*. Englewood Cliffs, NJ: Prentice-Hall.
1971. *Primitive social organization: an evolutionary perspective*, 2nd edition. New York: Random House.
Shackleton, N. J. 1987. Oxygen isotopes, ice volume and sea level. *Quaternary Science Review* 6:183–90.
Shackleton, N. J., and N. D. Opdyke. 1973. Oxygen isotope and palaeomagnetic stratigraphy of Equatorial Pacific core V28–238. *Quaternary Research* 3:39–55.
Shanks, M., and C. Tilley. 1987a. *Social theory and archaeology*. London: Polity.
1987b. *Reconstructing archaeology*. Cambridge: Cambridge University Press.
Shennan, S. J. 1996. Social inequality and the transmission of cultural traditions in forager societies, in *The archaeology of human ancestry: power sex and tradition*. Edited by J. Steele and S. J. Shennan, pp. 365–79. London: Routledge.
Shipman, P., and J. Rose. 1983. Evidence of butchery and hominid activities at Torralba and Ambrona: an evaluation using microscopic techniques. *Journal of Archaeological Science* 10:465–74.
Shnirelman, V. A. 1992. Complex hunter-gatherers: exception or common phenomenon? *Dialectical Anthropology* 17:183–96.
Sibrava, V. 1986. Correlation of European glaciations and their relation to the deep-sea record. *Quaternary Science Reviews* 5: 433–42.

Silberbauer, G. 1981. *Hunter and habitat in the central Kalahari desert*. Cambridge: Cambridge University Press.

Simán, K. 1990. Population fluctuation in the Carpathian basin from 50 to 15 thousand years BP. *Acta Archaeologica Academiae Scientiarum Hungaricae* 42:13–19.

1990–1. Some features of populational fluctuations in Europe between 50 to 15 thousand BP. *Antaeus* 19–20:11–16.

Simek, J. 1987. Spatial order and behavioural change in the French Palaeolithic. *Antiquity* 61:25–40.

Simek, J. F., and H. A. Price. 1990. Chronological change in Périgord lithic assemblage diversity, in *The emergence of modern humans: an archaeological perspective*. Edited by P. Mellars, pp. 243–62. Edinburgh: Edinburgh University Press.

Simek, J. F., and L. M. Snyder. 1988. Changing assemblage diversity in Périgord archaeofaunas, in *Upper Pleistocene prehistory of Western Eurasia*. Edited by H. Dibble and A. Montet-White, pp. 321–32. Philadelphia: University of Pennsylvania, University Museum Monograph 54.

Simon, H. A. 1974. How big is a chunk? *Science* 183:482–8.

1981. *Sciences of the artificial*. Cambridge, Mass.: MIT Press.

Singer, R., B. G. Gladfelter, and J. J. Wymer. 1993. *The Lower Palaeolithic site at Hoxne, England*. London: The University of Chicago Press.

Singer, R., J. J. Wymer, B. G. Gladfelter, and R. G. Wolff. 1973. Excavation of the Clactonian industry at the golf course, Clacton-on-Sea, Essex. *Proceedings of the Prehistoric Society* 39:6–74.

Sklenář, K. 1976. Palaeolithic and Mesolithic dwellings: problems of interpretation. *Památky Archeologické* 68:249–340.

Skrdla, P., V. Cílek, and A. Prichystal. 1996. Dolní Věstonice III, excavations 1993–1995, in *Palaeolithic in the Middle Danube region*. Edited by J. Svoboda, pp. 173–206. Brno: Archeologicky ústav AV CR.

Smiley, F. E., C. M. Sinopoli, H. Jackson, W. H. Wills, and S. A. Gregg (editors).1980. *The archaeological correlates of hunter-gatherer societies: studies from the ethnographic record*. Ann Arbor: Michigan Discussions in Anthropology 5.

Smirnov, Y. A. 1989. Intentional human burial: Middle Palaeolithic (Last Glaciation) beginning. *Journal of World Prehistory* 3:199–233.

1991. *Middle Palaeolithic burials*. Moscow: Nauka.

Smith, F. H. 1984. Fossil hominids from the Upper Pleistocene of Central Europe and the origin of modern Europeans, in *The origins of modern humans: a world survey of the fossil evidence*. Edited by F. H. Smith and F. Spencer, pp. 137–209. New York: Alan Liss.

Soffer, O. 1985a. Patterns of intensification as seen from the Upper Palaeolithic of the central Russian plain, in *Prehistoric hunter-gatherers:the emergence of cultural complexity*. Edited by T. D. Price and J. A. Brown, pp. 235–70. Orlando: Academic Press.

1985b. *The Upper Palaeolithic of the Central Russian Plain*. New York: Academic Press.

(editor). 1987. *The Pleistocene Old World: regional perspectives*. New York: Plenum.

1989. The Middle to Upper Palaeolithic transition on the Russian Plain, in *The Human Revolution: behavioural and biological perspectives on the origins of modern humans*. Edited by P. Mellars and C. Stringer, pp. 714–42. Edinburgh: Edinburgh University Press.

1993. Upper Palaeolithic adaptations in Central and Eastern Europe and man–mammoth interactions, in *From Kostenki to Clovis: Upper Paleolithic–Paleo-Indian adaptations*. Edited by O. Soffer and N. D. Praslov, pp. 31–49. New York: Plenum.

1994. Ancestral lifeways in Eurasia – the Middle and Upper Palaeolithic records, in *Origins of anatomically modern humans*. Edited by M. H. Nitecki and D. V. Nitecki, pp. 101–19. New York: Plenum.

Soffer, O., J. M. Adovasio, D. C. Hyland, B. Klíma and J. Svoboda. 1998. Perishable technologies and the genesis of the Eastern Gravettian. *Anthropologie* 36:43–68.

Soffer, O., and C. S. Gamble (editors). 1990. *The world at 18 000BP. Volume 1: High latitudes*. London: Unwin Hyman.

Soffer, O., and N. D. Praslov (editors). 1993. *From Kostenki to Clovis: Upper Paleolithic–Paleo-Indian adaptations*. New York: Plenum.

Soffer, O., and P. Vandiver. 1994. The ceramics, in *Pavlov I: excavations 1952–3*. Edited by J. Svoboda, pp. 161–73. Liège: ERAUL 66.

Soffer, O., P. Vandiver, B. Klíma, and J. Svoboda. 1993. The pyrotechnology of performance art: Moravian venuses and wolverines, in *Before Lascaux: the complex record of the Early Upper Paleolithic*. Edited by H. Knecht, A. Pike-Tay, and R. White, pp. 259–75. Boca Raton: CRC Press.

Soler, N., and J. Maroto. 1987. L'estratigrafia de la cova de l'Arbreda (Serinya, Girona). *Cypsela* 6:53–66.

Soler, N., X. Terradas, J. Maroto, and C. Plana. 1990. Le silex et les autres matières premières au Paléolithique moyen et supérieur, au nord-est de la Catalogne, in Le silex de sa genèse à l'outil: Actes du V Colloque international sur le Silex. *Cahiers du Quaternaire* 17:453–60.

de Sonneville-Bordes, D. 1960. *Le Paléolithique supérieur en Périgord*. Bordeaux: Delmas.

1974–5. Les listes types. Observations de méthode. *Quaternaria* 18:9–43.

1989. Foyers Paléolithiques en Périgord. *Mémoires du Musée de Préhistoire d'Ile de France* 2:225–37.

de Sonneville-Bordes, D., and J. Perrot. 1954–6. Lexique typologique du Paléolithique supérieur. Outillage lithique. *Bulletin de la Société Préhistorique Française* 51:327–35, 52:76–9, 53:408–12, 547–59.

Sperling, S. 1991. Baboons with briefcases: feminism, functionalism, and sociobiology in the evolution of primate gender. *Journal of Women in Culture and Society* 17.

Spiess, A. E. 1979. *Reindeer and caribou hunters: an archaeological study*. New York: Academic Press.

Stanley, V. 1980. Palaeoecology of the arctic-steppe mammoth biome. *Current Anthropology* 21:663–6.

Stanner, W. E. H. 1965. Aboriginal territorial organisation: estate, range, domain and regime. *Oceania* 36:1–26.

Stapert, D. 1992. Rings and sectors: intrasite spatial analysis of stone age sites. Doctoraat in de Letteren, Rijksuniversiteit Groningen.

Steele, J. 1994. Communication networks and dispersal patterns in human evolution: a simple simulation model. *World Archaeology* 26:126–43.

1996. On predicting hominid group sizes, in *The archaeology of human ancestry: power, sex and tradition*. Edited by J. Steele and S. Shennan, pp. 230–52. London: Routledge.

Steele, J., A. Quinlan, and F. Wenban-Smith. 1995. Stone tools and the linguistic capabilities of earlier hominids. *Cambridge Archaeological Journal* 5:245–56.

Steiner, W., and O. Wagenbreth. 1971. Zur geologischen Situation der altsteinzeitlichen Rastplätze in unteren Travertin von Ehringsdorf bei Weimar. *Alt-Thüringen* 11:47–75.

Stern, N. 1993. The structure of the Lower Pleistocene archaeological record. *Current Anthropology* 34:201–25.

Steward, J. H. 1936. The economic and social basis of primitive bands, in *Essays in anthropology presented to A. L. Kroeber*. Edited by R. H. Lowie, pp. 331–50. Berkeley: University of California Press.

1955. *Theory of culture change*. Urbana: University of Illinois Press.

Stiner, M. C. 1990. The use of mortality patterns in archaeological studies of hominid predatory adaptations. *Journal of Anthropological Archaeology* 9:305–51.

1992. Overlapping species 'choice' by Italian Upper Pleistocene predators. *Current Anthropology* 33:433–51.

1993. Modern human origins – faunal perspectives. *Annual Review of Anthropology* 22: 55–82.

1994. *Honor among thieves: a zooarchaeological study of Neandertal ecology*. Princeton: Princeton University Press.

Stiner, M. C., and S. L. Kuhn. 1992. Subsistence, technology, and adaptive variation in Middle Paleolithic Italy. *American Anthropologist* 94:306–39.

Straus, L. G. 1987. Upper Palaeolithic ibex hunting in SW Europe. *Journal of Archaeological Science* 14:163–78.

1989. Age of the modern Europeans. *Nature* 342:476–7.

1992. *Iberia before the Iberians: The Stone Age Prehistory of Cantabrian Spain*. Albuquerque: University of New Mexico Press.

1993. Preface, in *Context of a late Neanderthal: implications of multidisciplinary research for the transition to Upper Palaeolithic adaptations at Saint-Césaire, Charente-Maritime, France*. Edited by F. Lévêque, A. M. Backer, and M. Guilbaud, pp. xi–xii. Madison, Wisconsin: Prehistory Press, Monographs in World Archaeology 16.

Straus, L. G., J. L. Bischoff, and E. Carbonell. 1993. A review of the Middle to Upper Palaeolithic transition in Iberia. *Préhistoire Européenne* 3:11–27.

Straus, L. G., B. V. Eriksen, J. M. Erlandson, and D. R. Yesner (editors). 1996. *Humans at the end of the ice age: the archaeology of the Pleistocene–Holocene transition*. New York: Plenum.

Street, M., M. Baales, and B. Weninger. 1994. Absolute Chronologie des späten Paläolithikums und des Frühmesolithikums im Nördlichen Rheinland. *Archäologisches Korrespondenzblatt* 24:1–28.

Stringer, C. B. 1981. The dating of European Middle Pleistocene hominids and the existence of *Homo erectus* in Europe. *Anthropologie* 19:3–13.

1984. The definition of *Homo erectus* and the existence of the species in Africa and Europe. *Courier Forschungsinstitut Senckenberg* 69:131–43.

Stringer, C. B., and C. S. Gamble. 1993. *In search of the Neanderthals: solving the puzzle of human origins*. London: Thames and Hudson.

Stringer, C. B., and E. Mackie. 1996. *African exodus*. London: Cape.

Strum, S. C., and B. Latour. 1987. Redefining the social link: from baboons to humans. *Social Science Information* 26:783–802.

Stuart, A. J. 1982. *Pleistocene vertebrates in the British Isles*. London: Longman.

1996. Vertebrate faunas from the early Middle Pleistocene of East Anglia, in *The early Middle Pleistocene in Europe*. Edited by C. Turner, pp. 9–24. Rotterdam: Balkema.

Sturdy, D. A. 1975. Some reindeer economies in Palaeolithic Europe, in

*Palaeoeconomy*. Edited by E. S. Higgs, pp. 55–95. Cambridge: Cambridge University Press.

Suc, J.-P., and W. H. Zagwijn. 1983. Plio-Pleistocene correlations between the northwestern Mediterranean region and northwestern Europe according to recent biostratigraphic and palaeoclimatic data. *Boreas* 12:153–66.

Sutcliffe, A. J., and K. Kowalski. 1976. Pleistocene rodents of the British Isles. *Bulletin of the British Museum (Natural History), Geology* 27:37–137.

Svezhentsev, Y. S. 1993. Radiocarbon chronology for the Upper Paleolithic sites on the East European plain, in *From Kostenki to Clovis: Upper Paleolithic–Paleo-Indian Adaptations*. Edited by O. Soffer and N. D. Praslov, pp. 23–49. New York: Plenum Press.

Svoboda, J. 1987. Lithic industries of the Arago, Vértesszöllös, and Bilzingsleben hominids: comparison and evolutionary interpretation. *Current Anthropology* 28:219–27.

1989. Middle Pleistocene adaptation in Central Europe. *Journal of World Prehistory* 3:33–70.

(editor). 1991. *Dolní Věstonice II: western slope*. Liège: ERAUL 54.

1994a. *Paleolit Moravy a Slezska*. Brno: Dolnovesonické studies 1.

1994b. Environment and Middle Palaeolithic adaptations in eastern Central Europe. Paper presented at the ESF Workshop on the European Middle Palaeolithic. Arras.

(editor). 1994c. *Pavlov I: excavations 1952–53*. Liège: ERAUL 66.

1994d. The Pavlov site: lithic evidence from the Upper Palaeolithic. *Journal of Field Archaeology* 21:69–81.

1994e. Afterword, in *Pavlov I: excavations 1952–53*. Edited by J. Svoboda, pp. 213–25. Liège: ERAUL 66.

(editor). 1996. *Palaeolithic in the Middle Danube region: anniversary volume to Bohuslav Klíma*. Svazek 5. Brno: Archeologicky Ustav AV CR 5.

Svoboda, J., and P. Dvorsky. 1994. *Archeologové na loveckych stezkách*. Brno: Albatros.

Svoboda, J., B. Klíma, and P. Skrdla. 1995. The Gravettian project: activities during the 1991–1994 period. *Archeologické Rozhledy* 47:279–300.

Svoboda, J., J. Lozek, H. Svobodová, and P. Skrdla. 1994. Předmostí after 110 years. *Journal of Field Archaeology* 21:457–71.

Svoboda, J., V. Lozek, and E. Vlček. 1996. *Hunters between east and west: the Palaeolithic of Moravia*. New York: Plenum.

Svoboda, J., and K. Simán. 1989. The Middle–Upper Paleolithic transition in Southeastern Central Europe (Czechoslovakia and Hungary). *Journal of World Prehistory* 3:283–322.

Svoboda, J., P. Skrdla, and L. Jarosova. 1993. Analyse einer Siedlungsfläche von Dolní Věstonice. *Archäologisches Korrespondenzblatt* 23:393–404.

Svobodova, H. 1991. The pollen analysis of Dolní Věstonice II, section No.1, in *Dolní Věstonice II Western Slope*. Edited by J. Svoboda, pp. 75–88. Liège: ERAUL 54.

Swisher, C. C., G. H. Curtis, T. Jacob, A. G. Getty, A. Suprijo, and Widiasmoro. 1994. Age of the earliest known hominids in Java, Indonesia. *Science* 263:1118–21.

Taborin, Y. 1993. *La parure en coquillage au Paléolithique*. Paris: CNRS, Gallia Préhistoire supplement 29.

Tanner, N. 1981. *On becoming human*. Cambridge: Cambridge University Press.

Tattersall, I. 1995. *The last Neanderthal: the rise, success, and mysterious extinction of our closest human relatives*. New York: Macmillan.

Tavoso, A. 1984. Reflexion sur l'économie des matières premières au Moustérien. *Bulletin de la Société Préhistorique Française* 81:79–82.

Thieme, H. 1983. Der paläolithische Fundplatz Rheindahlen. Dissertation, Köln.

1990. Wohnplatzstrukturen und Fundplatzanalysen durch das Zusammensetzen von Steinartefakten: Ergebnisse vom mittelpaläolithischen Fundplatz Rheindahlen B 1 (Westwand-Komplex), in *The big puzzle*. Edited by E. Cziesla, S. Eickhoff, N. Arts, and D. Winter, pp. 543–68. Bonn: Holos, Studies in Modern Archaeology 1.

1997. Lower Palaeolithic hunting spears from Germany. *Nature* 385:807–10.

Thieme, H., and R. Maier. 1995. *Archäologische Ausgrabungen im Brauaohletagebau Schöningen, Landkreis Helmstadt*. Hannover: Verlag Habüsche Buchhandlung.

Thieme, H., and S. Veil. 1985. Neue Untersuchungen zum eemzeitlichen Elefanten-Jagdplatz Lehringen, Landkreis Verden. *Die Kunde* 36:11–58.

Thomas, J. 1991. *Rethinking the Neolithic*. Cambridge: Cambridge University Press.

Thrasher, F. M. 1927. *The gang*. Chicago: Chicago University Press.

Tilley, C. 1996. *An ethnography of the Neolithic*. Cambridge: Cambridge University Press.

Tindale, N. B. 1974. *Aboriginal tribes of Australia*. Los Angeles: University of California Press.

Tode, A. (editor). 1953. Die Untersuchung der paläolithischen Freilandstation von Salzgitter-Lebenstedt. *Eiszeitalter und Gegenwart* 3:144–220.

1982. *Der Altsteinzeitliche Fundplatz Salzgitter-Lebenstedt*. Köln: Bohlau Verlag.

Tomásková, S. 1994. Use-wear analysis and its spatial interpretation, in *Pavlov I: excavations 1952–3*. Edited by J. Svoboda, pp. 35–47. Liège: ERAUL 66.

1995. A site in history: archaeology at Dolní Věstonice/Unterwisternitz. *Antiquity* 69:301–16.

Torrence, R. 1983. Time budgeting and hunter-gatherer technology, in *Hunter-gatherer economy in prehistory*. Edited by G. Bailey, pp. 11–22. Cambridge: Cambridge University Press.

(editor). 1989. *Time, energy and stone tools*. Cambridge: Cambridge University Press.

Trinkaus, E. (editor). 1989. *The emergence of modern humans: biocultural adaptations in the later Pleistocene*. Cambridge: Cambridge University Press.

Trinkaus, E., and J. Jelínek. 1997. Human remains from the Moravian Gravettian: the Dolní Věstonice 3 postcrania. *Journal of Human Evolution* 33:33–82.

Trinkaus, E., and P. Shipman. 1993. *The Neandertals*. New York: Alfred A. Knopf.

Tuffreau, A. 1982. The Transition lower/middle Palaeolithic in northern France. in *The transition from Lower to Middle Palaeolithic and the origin of modern man*. Edited by A. Ronen, pp. 137–49. Oxford: British Archaeological Reports, International Series 151.

1988. L'industrie lithique du niveau 2A, in *Le gisement Paléolithique moyen de Biache-Saint-Vaast (Pas de Calais)*. Edited by A. Tuffreau and J. Sommé, pp. 171–85. Paris: Mémoires de la Société Préhistorique Française 21.

(editor). 1993. *Riencourt-les-Bapaume (Pas-de-Calais)*. Paris: Documents d'Archéologie Française.

Tuffreau, A., and P. Antoine. 1995. The earliest occupation of Europe: continental northwestern Europe, in *The earliest occupation of Europe*. Edited by W. Roebroeks and T. van Kolfschoten, pp. 147–63. Leiden: University of Leiden and European Science Foundation.

Tuffreau, A., J. P. Bouchet, A. V. Moigne, and A. V. Munaut. 1986. Les niveaux acheuléens de la moyenne terrasse de la vallée de la Somme à Cagny-l'Epinette (Somme). *L'Anthropologie* 90:9–27.

Tuffreau, A., S. Révillion, J. Sommé, and B. Van-Vliet-Lanoe. 1994. Le gisement Paléolithique moyen de Seclin ( Nord). *Bulletin de la Société Préhistorique Française* 91:23–45.

Tuffreau, A., and J. Sommé (editors). 1988. *Le gisement Paléolithique moyen de Biache-Saint-Vaast (Pas-de-Calais).* Paris: Mémoirs de la Société Préhistorique Française 21.

Turner, A. 1990. The evolution of the guild of larger terrestrial carnivores during the Plio-Pleistocene in Africa. *Geobios* 23:349–68.

1992. Large carnivores and earliest European hominids: changing determinants of resource availability during the Lower and Middle Pleistocene. *Journal of Human Evolution* 22:109–26.

Turner, C. 1996. A brief survey of the early Middle Pleistocene in Europe, in *The early Middle Pleistocene in Europe.* Edited by C. Turner, pp. 295–317. Rotterdam: Balkema.

Turner, C., and G. E. Hannon. 1988. Vegetational evidence for late Quaternary climatic changes in southwest Europe in relation to the influence of the North Atlantic Ocean. *Philosophical Transactions of the Royal Society of London B* 318:451–85.

Turner, E. 1989. Miesenheim I: A lower Palaeolithic site in the Middle Rheineland (Neuwied Basin), FRG. *Ethnographisch Archäologische Zeitschrift* 30:521–31.

1990. Middle and Late Pleistocene macrofaunas of the Neuwied Basin region (Rhineland-Palatinate) of West Germany. *Jahrbuch des Römisch-Germanischen Zentralmuseums Mainz* 37:133–403.

1991. Pleistocene stratigraphy and vertebrate faunas from the Neuwied basin region of western Germany. *Cranium* 8:21–34.

Turner, J. H. 1991. *The structure of sociological theory,* fifth edition. Belmont: Wadsworth.

Turner, J. H., and A. Maryanski. 1991. Network analysis, in *The structure of sociological theory.* Edited by J. H. Turner, pp. 540–72. Belmont: Wadsworth.

Turq, A. 1988. L'approvisionnement en matières premières lithiques du Magdalénien du Quercy et du Haut-Agenais: étude préliminaire. *Colloque de Chancelade,* October 1988, pp. 301–8.

1989. Approche technologique et économique du faciès Moustérien de type Quina: étude preliminaire. *Bulletin de la Société Préhistorique Française* 86:244–55.

1990. Exploitation des matières premières lithiques dans le Moustérien entre Dordogne et Lot. *Cahiers du Quaternaire* 17:415–27.

1992a. Le Paléolithique inférieur et moyen entre les vallées de la Dordogne et du Lot. Thèse, L'Université de Bordeaux I.

1992b. Raw material and technological studies of the Quina Mousterian in Périgord, in *The Middle Palaeolithic: adaptation, behaviour, and variability.* Edited by H. L. Dibble and P. Mellars, pp. 75–87. Philadelphia: University of Pennsylvania, University Museum 72.

1993. L'approvisionnement en matières premières lithiques au Moustérien et au début du Paléolithique supérieur dans le nord-est du bassin Aquitain (France), in *El origen del hombre moderno en el suroeste de Europa.* Edited by V. Cabrera-Valdés, pp. 315–25. Madrid: Universidad de Educación a Distancia.

Tylor, E. B. 1881. *Anthropology: an introduction to the study of man and civilisation*. London: Macmillan.

Tzedakis, P. C. 1993. Long-term tree populations in northwest Greece through multiple Quaternary climatic cycles. *Nature* 364:437–40.

Tzedakis, P. C., and K. D. Bennett. 1995. Interglacial vegetation succession: a view from southern Europe. *Quaternary Science Reviews* 14:967–82.

Ulrix-Closset, M. 1975. *Le Paléolithique moyen dans le bassin Mosan en Belgique*. Wetteren, Bibliothèque de la Faculté de Philosophie et Lettres de l'Université de Liège, Publications Exceptionélles No. 3, Editions Universa.

Valensi, P. 1991. Etude des stries de boucherie sur les ossements de cerf élaphe des niveaux supérieurs de la grotte du Lazaret (Nice, Alpes Maritimes). *L'Anthropologie* 95:797–830.

Valeri, V. 1992. Buying women but not selling them: gift and commodity exchange in Huaulu alliance. *Man* 29:1–26.

Valladas, H., J. L. Reyss, J. L. Joron, G. Valladas, O. Bar-Yosef, and B. Vandermeersch. 1988. Thermoluminescence dating of Mousterian 'Proto-Cro-Magnon' remains from Israel and the origin of modern man. *Nature* 331:614–16.

Vallois, H. V. 1961. The social life of early man: the evidence of skeletons, in *Social life of early man*. Edited by S. L. Washburn, pp. 214–35. New York: Wenner-Gren.

Valoch, K. 1982. Die Beingeräte von Předmostí in Mähren (Tschechoslowakei). *Anthropologie* 20:57–69.

1988. *Die Erforschung der Kulna Höhle 1961–1976*. Brno: Moravske Muzeum, Anthropos 24.

1995a. Einige Aspekte der Besiedlungsstabilität im Paläolithikum, in *Man and environment in the Palaeolithic*. Edited by H. Ullrich, pp. 283–9. Liège: ERAUL 62.

1995b. Territoires d'implantation, contacts et diffusion des sociétés du Paléolithique supérieur dans l'ancienne Tchécoslovaquie. *L'Anthropologie* 99:593–608.

1996. *Le Paléolithique en Tchéquie et en Slovaquie*. Grenoble: Millon.

Van Andel, T. H. 1996. European Palaeolithic landscapes 140,000–30,000 years ago – a summary. *XIII Congress UISPP, Forli, 1996*, pp. 1–17.

Van Andel, T. H., and C. Runnels, N. 1995. The earliest farmers in Europe. *Antiquity* 69:481–500.

Van Andel, T. H., and P. C. Tzedakis. 1996. Palaeolithic landscapes of Europe and environs, 150,000–25,000 years ago: an overview. *Quaternary Science Reviews* 15:481–500.

1998. Priority and opportunity: reconstructing the European Middle Palaeolithic climate and landscape, in *Science in Archaeology*. Edited by J. Bayley, pp. 37–45. London: English Heritage.

Van den Boggard, P., C. M. Hall, H.-U. Schmincke, and D. York. 1989. Precise single grain dating of a cold to warm climate in central Europe. *Nature* 342:523–5.

Vandenberghe, J., W. Roebroeks, and T. van Kolfschoten. 1993. Maastricht-Belvédère: stratigraphy, palaeoenvironment and archaeology of the Middle and Late Pleistocene deposits: part II. *Medelingen Rijks Geologische Dienst* 47:1–91.

Vandermeersch, B. 1993. Was the Saint-Césaire discovery a burial?, in *Context of a late Neanderthal: implications of multidisciplinary research for the transition to Upper Palaeolithic adaptations at Saint-Césaire, Charente-Maritime, France*. Edited by F. Lévêque, A. M. Backer, and M. Guilbaud, pp. 129–31. Madison, Wisconsin: Prehistory Press, Monographs in World Archaeology 16.

Vandiver, P. B., O. Soffer, B. Klíma, and J. Svoboda. 1989. The origins of ceramic technology at Dolní Věstonice, Czechoslovakia. *Science* 246:1002–8.

Vaquero, M. 1992. Processos de canvi technologic al voltant del 40,000 BP. Continuitat o rutura. *ESTRAT: Revista d'arquelogia, prehistoria i historia antiga* 5:1–156.

Vega Toscano, L. G. 1989. Ocupaciones humanas en el Pleistoceno de la depresion de Guadix-Baza: elementos de discusion, in *Geologia y paleontologia de la cuenca de Guadix-Baza*. Edited by M. T. Alberdi and F. P. Bonadonna, pp. 327–45. Madrid: E.T.S. 11.

1993. El transito del Paleolitico Medio al Paleolitico Superior en el sur de la Peninsula Iberica, in *El origen del hombre moderno en el suroeste de europa*. Edited by V. Cabrera Valdés, pp. 147–70. Madrid: Universidad de Educación a Distancia.

Vega Toscano, L. G., L. Raposo, and M. Santonja. 1994. Environments and settlements in the Middle Palaeolithic of the Iberian peninsula. Paper presented at the ESF Workshop on the European Middle Palaeolithic. Arras.

Ventura, D. 1993. La Grotta di Lamalunga. *Atti della I conferenza cittadina Altamura*.

Vértes, L. 1964. *Tata – eine mittelpaläolithische Travertinsiedlung in Ungarn*. Budapest: Akadémiai Kiado.

Villa, P. 1976–7. Sols et niveaux d'habitat du Paléolithique inférieur en Europe et du Proche Orient. *Quaternaria* 19:107–34.

1982. Conjoinable pieces and site formation processes. *American Antiquity* 47:276–90.

1991. Middle Pleistocene prehistory in southwestern Europe: the state of our knowledge and ignorance. *Journal of Anthropological Research* 47:193–217.

Vita-Finzi, C., and E. S. Higgs. 1970. Prehistoric economy in the Mount Carmel area of Palestine, site catchment analysis. *Proceedings of the Prehistoric Society* 36:1–37.

Vlček, E. 1978. A new discovery of *Homo erectus* in Central Europe. *Journal of Human Evolution* 7:239–51.

Vogel, J. 1983. C14 variations during the Upper Pleistocene. *Radiocarbon* 25:213–18.

Von den Driesch, A., and J. Boessneck. 1975. Schnittspuren an neolithischen Tierknochen. *Germania* 53:1–23.

Waal, F. de 1982. *Chimpanzee politics*. London: Jonathan Cape.

Waechter, J. d'A., M. H. Newcomer, and B. W. Conway. 1970. Swanscombe 1970. *Proceedings of the Royal Anthropological Institute of Great Britain and Ireland for 1970*: 43–64.

Ward, R., and C. Stringer. 1997. A molecular handle on the Neanderthals. *Nature* 388:225–6.

Warren, S. H. 1914. The experimental investigation of flint fracture and its application to problems of human implements. *Journal of the Royal Anthropological Institute* 44:412–50.

1920. A natural 'eolith' factory beneath the Thanet Sand. *Quarterly Journal of the Geological Society* 76:238–53.

Washburn, S. L. (editor). 1961. *Social life of early man*. New York: Wenner-Gren.

Washburn, S. L., and I. DeVore. 1961. Social behaviour of baboons and early man, in *Social life of early man*. Edited by S. L. Washburn, pp. 91–105. New York: Wenner-Gren.

Watts, W. A., J. R. M. Allen, and B. Huntley. 1996. Vegetation history and palaeoclimate of the last glacial period at Lago Grande di Monticchio, southern Italy. *Quaternary Science Reviews* 15:133–53.

Weber, T. 1986. Die Steinartefakte des *Homo erectus* von Bilzingsleben, in *Bilzingsleben III*. Edited by D. Mania and T. Weber, pp. 65–231. Berlin: Veröffentlichungen des Landesmuseums für Vorgeschichte Halle 39.

Weißmüller, W. 1987. Eine Freilandfundstelle des mittleren Jungpaläolithikums (Périgordien-Gravettien) am Südrand der Straubinger Senke bei Salching. Ldkr. Straubing-Bogen. *Quartär* 37–38:109–34.

1995. *Sesselfelsgrotte II: Die Silexartefakte der unteren Schichten der Sesselfelsgrotte, ein beitrag zum Problem des Moustérien*. Saarbrücken: Saarbrücker Druckerei und Verlag, Quartär-Bibliothek 6.

Wellman, B., and S. D. Berkowitz (editors). 1988. *Social structures: a network approach*. Cambridge: Cambridge University Press.

Wellman, B., P. J. Carrington, and A. Hall. 1988. Networks as personal communities, in *Social structures: a network approach*. Edited by B. Wellman and S. D. Berkowitz, pp. 130–84. Cambridge: Cambridge University Press.

Wetzel, R. 1958. *Die Bocksteinschmiede mit dem Bocksteinloch der Brandplatte und dem Abhang sowie der Bocksteingrotte*. Stuttgart: Müller und Gräff.

Wetzel, R., and G. Bosinski. 1969. *Die Bocksteinschmiede im Lonetal (Markung Rammingen, Kreis Ulm)*. Stuttgart: Veröffentlichungen der Staatliche Amtes für Denkmalpflege A.15.

Whallon, R. 1984. Unconstrained clustering for the analysis of spatial distributions in archaeology, in *Intrasite spatial analysis in archaeology*. Edited by H. Hietala, pp. 242–77. Cambridge: Cambridge University Press.

1989. Elements of cultural change in the later Palaeolithic, in *The human revolution: behavioural and biological perspectives on the origins of modern humans*. Edited by P. Mellars and C. Stringer, pp. 433–54. Edinburgh: Edinburgh University Press.

White, J. W. C. 1993. Climate change: don't touch that dial. *Nature* 364:186–220.

White, L. A. 1959. *The evolution of culture*. New York: McGraw-Hill.

White, M. J. 1995. Raw materials and biface variability in southern Britain: a preliminary examination. *Lithics* 15:1–20.

White, M. J., and P. P. Pettitt. 1995. Technology of early Palaeolithic western Europe: innovation, variability and a unified framework. *Lithics* 16:27–40.

White, R. 1982. Rethinking the Middle/Upper Palaeolithic transition. *Current Anthropology* 23:169–92.

1989. Production complexity and standardization in early Aurignacian bead and pendant manufacture: evolutionary implications, in *The human revolution: behavioural and biological perspectives on the origins of modern humans*. Edited by P. Mellars and C. Stringer, pp. 366–90. Edinburgh: Edinburgh University Press.

1993a. Introduction: Gesture and speech, in *Gesture and speech*, by A. Leroi-Gourhan, pp. xiii–xxii. Cambridge, Mass.: MIT Press.

1993b. Technological and social dimensions of 'Aurignacian-age' body ornaments across Europe, in *Before Lascaux: the complex record of the Early Upper Paleolithic*. Edited by H. Knecht, A. Pike-Tay, and R. White, pp. 277–99. Boca-Raton: CRC Press.

1993c. A social and technological view of Aurignacian and Castelperronian personal ornaments in SW Europe, in *El origen del hombre moderno en el suroeste de Europa*. Edited by V. Cabrera-Valdés, pp. 327–57. Madrid: Universidad de Educación a Distancia.

1997. Substantial acts: from materials to meaning in Upper Palaeolithic representation, in *Beyond art: Pleistocene image and symbol*. Edited by M. W. Conkey, O. Soffer, D. Stratmann, and N. G. Jablonski, pp. 93–121. San Francisco: Wattis Symposium Series in Anthropology, Memoirs of the California Academy of Sciences 23.

Whitelaw, T. M. 1989. The social organisation of space in hunter-gatherer communities: some implications for social inference in archaeology. Unpublished Ph.D. thesis, Cambridge University.

1991. Some dimensions of variability in the social organisation of community space among foragers, in *Ethnoarchaeological approaches to mobile campsites: hunter-gatherer and pastoralist case studies*. Edited by C. S. Gamble and W. A. Boismier, pp. 139–88. Ann Arbor: International Monographs in Prehistory, Ethnoarchaeological Series 1.

1994. Order without architecture: functional, social and symbolic dimensions in hunter-gatherer settlement organisation, in *Architecture and order: approaches to social space*. Edited by M. Parker-Pearson and C. Richards, pp. 217–43. London: Routledge.

Whittle, A. 1996. *Europe in the Neolithic: the creation of new worlds*. Cambridge: Cambridge University Press.

Wiessner, P. 1982. Risk, reciprocity and social influences on !Kung San economics, in *Politics and history in band societies*. Edited by E. Leacock and R. Lee, pp. 61–84. Cambridge: Cambridge University Press.

Williams, B. J. 1974. A model of Band Society. *Memoir of the Society for American Archaeology* 29.

1981. Hunters: the structure of bands and the structure of the brain. *Anthropology UCLA* 7:239–53.

Wilmsen, E. N. 1989. *Land filled with flies: a political economy of the Kalahari*. Chicago: University of Chicago Press.

Wilson, L. 1988. Petrography of the Lower Palaeolithic tool assemblage of the Caune de l'Arago (France). *World Archaeology* 19:376–87.

Wilson, P. J. 1980. *Man the promising primate: the conditions of human evolution*. New Haven: Yale University Press.

1988. *The domestication of the human species*. New Haven: Yale University Press.

Wobst, H. M. 1974a. Boundary conditions for Palaeolithic social systems: a simulation approach. *American Antiquity* 39:147–78.

1974b. The archaeology of Band Society: some unanswered questions. *Memoir of the Society for American Archaeology* 29:v–xiii.

1976. Locational relationships in Palaeolithic society. *Journal of Human Evolution* 5:49–58.

1977. Stylistic behaviour and information exchange, in *Papers for the Director: research essays in honor of James B. Griffin*. Edited by C. E. Cleland, pp. 317–42. Museum of Anthropology, University of Michigan, Anthropological Papers 61.

1978. The archaeo-ethnology of hunter gatherers or the tyranny of the ethnographic record in archaeology. *American Antiquity* 43:303–9.

Woillard, G. M. 1978. Grande Pile peat bog: a continuous pollen record for the last 140,000 years. *Quaternary Research* 9:1–21.

Wolf, E. R. 1988. Inventing society. *American Ethnologist* 15:752–61.

Wolpoff, M. H., F. H. Smith, M. Malez, J. Radovcic, and D. Rukavina. 1980. Upper Pleistocene human remains from Vindija Cave. *American Journal of Physical Anthropology* 54:499–545.

Woodburn, J. 1980. Hunters and gatherers today and reconstruction of the past, in *Soviet and Western Anthropology*. Edited by E. Gellner, pp. 95–117. London: Duckworth.

1982. Egalitarian societies. *Man* 17:431–51.

1991. African hunter-gatherer social organization: is it best understood as a product of encapsulation? in *Hunters and gatherers*. Volume I: *History, evolution and social change*. Edited by T. Ingold, D. Riches, and J. Woodburn, pp. 31–64. New York: Berg.

Woodcock, A. 1981. *The Lower and Middle Palaeolithic periods in Sussex*. Oxford: British Archaeological Reports 94.

Wrangham, R. W. 1980. An ecological model of female-bonded primate groups. *Behaviour* 75:262–99.

Wylie, A. 1993. A proliferation of new archaeologies: 'beyond objectivism and relativism', in *Archaeological theory: who sets the agenda?* Edited by N. Yoffee and A. Sherratt, pp. 20–6. Cambridge: Cambridge University Press.

Wymer, J. J. 1968. *Lower Palaeolithic archaeology in Britain, as represented by the Thames valley*. London: John Baker.

1985. *Lower Palaeolithic sites in East Anglia*. Norwich: Geo Books.

1996. The English rivers Palaeolithic survey, in *The English Palaeolithic reviewed*. Edited by C. S. Gamble and A. J. Lawson, pp. 7–22. Salisbury: Trust for Wessex Archaeology.

Wynn, T. 1988. Tools and the evolution of human intelligence, in *Machiavellian intelligence*. Edited by R. Byrne and A. Whiten, pp. 271–84. Oxford: Clarendon Press.

1989. *The evolution of spatial competence*. Urbana: University of Illinois Press.

1993a. Two developments in the mind of early *Homo*. *Journal of Anthropological Archaeology* 12:299–322.

1993b. Layers of thinking in tool behaviour, in *Tools, language and cognition in human evolution*. Edited by K. Gibson and T. Ingold, pp. 389–406. Cambridge: Cambridge University Press.

Yellen, J. E. 1977. *Archaeological approaches to the present. Models for reconstructing the past*. New York: Academic Press.

Yellen, J. E., and H. Harpending. 1972. Hunter-gatherer populations and archaeological inference. *World Archaeology* 3:244–52.

Yoffee, N., and A. Sherratt (editors). 1993. *Archaeological theory: who sets the agenda?* Cambridge: Cambridge University Press.

Zagwijn, W. H. 1992a. Migration of vegetation during the Quaternary in Europe, in *Mammalian migration and dispersal events in the European Quaternary*. Edited by W. von Koenigswald and L. Werdelin, pp. 9–20. *Courier Forschungsinstitut Senckenberg* 153.

1992b. The beginning of the ice age in Europe and its major subdivisions. *Quaternary Science Reviews* 11:583–91.

Zampetti, D., and M. Mussi. 1988. Du Paléolithique moyen au Paléolithique supérieur dans le Latium (Italie centrale), in *L'Homme de Néandertal*. Edited by M. Otte. vol. VIII, *La Mutation*, edited by J. K. Kozlowski, pp. 273–88. Liège: ERAUL 35.

1991. Segni del potere, simboli del potere: la problematica del Paleolitico Superiore italiano, in *The archaeology of power*, Part 2. Edited by E. Herring, R. Whitehouse, and J. Wilkins, pp. 149–60. London: Accordia Research Centre, Papers of the Fourth Conference of Italian Archaeology.

Zavernyaev, T. M. 1978. *Xhotylevo*. Leningrad: Nauka.

Zeuner, F. E. 1959. *The Pleistocene period*. London: Hutchinson.

Zihlman, A. 1978. Women in evolution, part II: subsistence and social organisation in early hominids. *Signs. Journal of Women in Culture and Society* 4:4–20.

Zilhao, J. 1988. The early Upper Palaeolithic of Portugal, in *The early Upper Paleolithic: evidence from Europe and the Near East*. Edited by J. F. Hoffecker and C. A. Wolf, pp. 135–55. Oxford: British Archaeological Reports, International Series 437.

1993. Le passage du Paléolithique moyen au Paléolithique supérieur dans le Portugal, in *El origen del hombre moderno en el suroeste de Europa*. Edited by V. Cabrera-Valdés, pp. 127–46. Madrid: Universidad de Educación a Distancia.

Zubrow, E. 1989. The demographic modelling of Neanderthal extinction, in *The human revolution: behavioural and biological perspectives on the origins of modern humans*. Edited by P. Mellars and C. Stringer, pp. 212–32. Edinburgh: Edinburgh University Press.

Zvelebil, M. (editor). 1986. *Hunters in transition; Postglacial adaptations in the temperate regions of the Old World*. Cambridge: Cambridge University Press.

# SITE INDEX

# GENERAL INDEX